W0232174

WORKSHOPS IN COMPUTING
Series edited by C. J. van Rijsbergen

John Rosenberg and David Koch

Persistent Object Systems

Proceedings of the Third International
Workshop
10–13 January 1989, Newcastle, Australia

Published in collaboration with the
British Computer Society

Springer-Verlag
London Berlin Heidelberg New York
Paris Tokyo Hong Kong

John Rosenberg, BSc, PhD
Department of Electrical Engineering and Computer Science,
University of Newcastle,
NSW 2308, Australia

David Koch, BTech
Department of Electrical Engineering and Computer Science,
University of Newcastle,
NSW 2308, Australia

ISBN-13:978-3-540-19626-6   e-ISBN-13:978-1-4471-3173-1
DOI: 10.1007/978-1-4471-3173-1

British Library Cataloguing in Publication Data
International Workshop on Persistent Object Systems, (1989; Newcastle, N.S.W.). –
(Workshops in computing)
Third International Workshop on Persistent Object Systems: Newcastle, Australia
10–13 January 1989
    1. Computer systems. Programming
    I. Rosenberg, John *1953–*   II. Koch, David *1955–*   III. Series
005.1

Library of Congress Cataloging-in-Publication Data
International Workshop on Persistent Object Systems (3rd:1989: Newcastle, N.S.W.)
Third International Workshop on Persistent Object Systems, Newcastle, Australia,
10–13 January, 1989/compiled by John Rosenberg and David Koch
    p. cm. – (Workshops in computing)
Includes index.
ISBN 3–540–19626–9. – ISBN 0–387–19626–9
1. Object-oriented programming (Computer science) – Congresses.
I. Rosenberg, John, 1953–   .   II. Koch, David, 1955–   .   III. Title.   IV.Series.
QA76.64.I57 1989
005.1–dc20   90–9964
                                                                           CIP

Printed and bound by Alden Press Ltd, Osney Mead, Oxford
2128/3916–543210   Printed on acid-free paper

Preface

This book presents the proceedings of a workshop held in Newcastle, Australia in January 1989. The central theme of the workshop was *persistent object systems*. Persistent object systems are systems which support the creation and manipulation of objects in a uniform manner, regardless of how long they persist. This is in direct contrast with conventional systems where temporary objects are created and manipulated using one mechanism (typically programming language data structures) and permanent objects are maintained using a different mechanism (usually a filestore). The unification of temporary and permanent objects yields systems which are both smaller and more efficient than conventional systems, whilst providing a powerful and flexible platform for the development of large, data intensive applications.

The workshop held in Newcastle was the third in a series of such workshops. The first was held in Appin, Scotland in 1985 and concentrated mainly on language issues, particularly the relationship between data types and persistence. The second workshop, also held in Appin in 1987, saw a natural progression to a discussion of design and implementation issues. This theme continued at the Newcastle workshop. The papers presented in these proceedings have been organised into seven groups, roughly reflecting the sessions held at the workshop. These are:

- Type systems and persistence
- Persistent programming languages
- Implementing persistence
- Object stores
- Measurement of persistent systems
- Transactions and persistence
- Persistent machines

The workshop was deliberately kept small to encourage technical discussion amongst the attendees and the papers presented in this volume reflect these discussions. The total number of people attending the workshop was 43 and 26 papers were presented over four days, allowing some time for enjoyment of the excellent Australian summer and wines.

We would like to acknowledge the support and assistance provided by many people during organisation of the workshop. In particular we must mention Malcom Atkinson and Ron Morrison who started this workshop series and have been involved in the organisation of all three, and Frans Henskens and Mrs Diana Edwards without whose tireless efforts the Newcastle workshop would not have taken place. We must also thank Mrs Helen Bremner of the University of St Andrews for her help during the preparation of these Proceedings.

April, 1990   John Rosenberg
                                                               David Koch

Workshop Chairman

John Rosenberg
Department of Electrical Engineering & Computer Science,
University of Newcastle, Australia

Organising Committee

Frans Henskens
Department of Electrical Engineering & Computer Science,
University of Newcastle, Australia

David Koch
Department of Electrical Engineering & Computer Science,
University of Newcastle, Australia

Ron Morrison
Department of Computational Science,
University of St Andrews, Scotland

John Rosenberg
Department of Electrical Engineering & Computer Science,
University of Newcastle, Australia

Programme Committee

Malcom Atkinson
Department of Computer Science,
University of Glasgow, Scotland

Ron Morrison
Department of Computational Science,
University of St Andrews, Scotland

John Rosenberg
Department of Electrical Engineering & Computer Science,
University of Newcastle, Australia

Stan Zdonik
Department of Computer Science,
Brown University, U.S.A.

Contents

Part III: Implementing Persistence

Part IV: Object Stores

Part V: Measurement of Persistent Systems

Part VI: Transactions and Persistence

Part VII: Persistent Machines

List of Authors

Allard, D. G.
USC Information Sciences Institute, 4676 Admiralty Way,
Marina del Rey, California 90292, U.S.A.

allard@vax.isi.edu

Atkinson, M. P.
Department of Computing Science, University of Glasgow,
17 Lilybank Gardens, Glasgow, G12 8QQ, Scotland.

mpa@cs.glasgow.ac.uk

Bailey, P. J.
Department of Computing Science, University of Glasgow,
17 Lilybank Gardens, Glasgow, G12 8QQ, Scotland.

pete@cs.glasgow.ac.uk

Blaustein, B.
Xerox Advanced Information Technology, 4 Cambridge Center,
Cambridge, MA 02139, U.S.A.

Brössler, P.
Fachbereich 3 (Informatik), Universitat Bremen, Bibliothekstrasse,
Postfach 33 04 40, D-2800 Bremen 33, West Germany.

pb@informatik.uni-Bremen.de

Brown, A. L.
Department of Computational Science, University of St. Andrews,
North Haugh, St. Andrews, KY16 9SS, Scotland.

ab@uk.ac.st-and.cs

Buhr, P.
Department of Computer Science, University of Waterloo, Waterloo,
Ontario, N2L 3G1, Canada.

pabuhr@uwaterloo.edu

Carey, M.
Computer Sciences Department, University of Wisconsin-Madison,
Madison, WI 53706, U.S.A.

carey@cs.wisc.edu

Carrick, R.
Computer Centre, University of Glasgow, Glasgow, G12 8QQ,
Scotland.

ray@uk.ac.gla.eng.sun1

Cockshott, W. P.
Department of Computer Science, University of Strathclyde,
Livingstone Tower, 26 Richmond Street, Glasgow, G1 1XH,
Scotland.

wpc@cd.strath.ac.uk

Colomb, R. M.
CSIRO Division of Information Technology, Box 1599, North Ryde,
New South Wales 2113, Australia.

colomb@ditsyda.oz.au

Connor, R. C. H.
Department of Computational Science, University of St. Andrews,
North Haugh, St. Andrews, KY16 9SS, Scotland.

richard@uk.ac.st-and.cs

Cooper, R. L.
Department of Computing Science, University of Glasgow,
17 Lilybank Gardens, Glasgow, G12 8QQ, Scotland.

rich@cs.glasgow.ac.uk

Cutts, Q.
Department of Computational Science, University of St. Andrews,
North Haugh, St. Andrews, KY16 9SS, Scotland.

quintin@uk.ac.st-and.cs

Dearle, A.
Department of Computational Science, University of St. Andrews,
North Haugh, St. Andrews, KY16 9SS, Scotland.

al@uk.ac.st-and.cs

Fekete, A.
Department of Computer Science, University of Sydney, New South
Wales 2006, Australia.

fekete@cluster.cs.su.oz.au

Fernandez, M. F.
Princeton University, Princeton, New Jersey 08544, U.S.A.
mff@princeton.edu

Freisleben, B.
Technische Hochschule Darmstadt, Fachbereich Informatik,
Alexanderstrasse 24, D-6100 Darmstadt, West Germany.
X1B1BFRE@DDATHD21.BITNET

Gehringer, E. F.
Department of Electrical Engineering, Department of Computer
Science, North Carolina State University, Raleigh, NC 27695-7911,
U.S.A.
efg@csl.ncsu.edu

Heiler, S.
Xerox Advanced Information Technology, 4 Cambridge Center,
Cambridge, MA 02139, U.S.A.

Hurst, A. J.
Department of Computer Science, Monash University, Clayton,
Victoria 3168, Australia.
ajh@bruce.cs.monash.oz.au

Keedy, J. L.
Fachbereich 3 (Informatik), Universitat Bremen, Bibliothekstrasse,
Postfach 33 04 40, D-2800 Bremen 33, West Germany.
keedy@informatik.uni-Bremen.de

Kirby, G.
Department of Computational Science, University of St. Andrews,
North Haugh, St. Andrews, KY16 9SS, Scotland.
graham@uk.ac.st-and.cs

Koch, D. M.
Department of Electrical Engineering & Computer Science, University
of Newcastle, New South Wales 2308, Australia.
dmk@nucs.cs.nu.oz.au

Loboz, C. Z.
Department of Computer Science, Australian National University,
GPO Box 4, Canberra, ACT 2601, Australia.

Lynch, N.
Laboratory for Computer Science, Massachusetts Institute of
Technology, 545 Technology Square, Cambridge, MA 02139, U.S.A.
lynch@tds.lcs.mit.edu

Merritt, M.
AT&T Bell Laboratories, 3D-458, 600 Mountain Avenue, Murray Hill,
NJ 07974, U.S.A.

mischu@research.att.com

Michaelson, G. J.
Department of Computer Science, Heriot-Watt University,
79 Grassmarket, Edinburgh, EH1 2HJ, Scotland.

greg@cs.hw.ac.uk

Morrison, R.
Department of Computational Science, University of St. Andrews,
North Haugh, St. Andrews, KY16 9SS, Scotland.

ron@uk.ac.st-and.cs

Mosseri, L.
INRIA, BP 105, 78153 Rocquencourt Cedex, France.

mosseri@sor.inria.fr

Porter, H.
Department of Computer Science, Portland State University,
P.O. Box 751, Portland, OR 97207-0751, U.S.A.

harry@cs.pdx.edu

Powell, M. S.
Department of Computation, University of Manchester Institute of
Science and Technology, P.O. Box 88, Sackville Street, Manchester,
M60 1QD, U.K.

Richardson, J.
K55/801, IBM Almaden Research Center, 650 Harry Road, San
Jose, CA 95120, U.S.A.

joelr@ibm.com

Rosenberg, J.
Department of Electrical Engineering & Computer Science, University
of Newcastle, New South Wales 2308, Australia.

johnr@nucs.cs.nu.oz.au

Sajeev, A. S. M.
Department of Computer Science, Massey University, Palmerston
North, New Zealand.

S.Sajeev@massey.ac.nz

Shapiro, M.
INRIA, BP 105, 78153 Rocquencourt Cedex, France.

shapiro@sor.inria.fr

Stemple, D.
Department of Computer & Information Science, University of
Massachusetts, Amherst, MA 01003, U.S.A.

stemple%cs.umass.edu

Wai, F.
Department of Computing Science, University of Glasgow,
17 Lilybank Gardens, Glasgow, G12 8QQ, Scotland.

fw@cs.glasgow.ac.uk

Weihl, W.
Laboratory for Computer Science, Massachusetts Institute of
Technology, 545 Technology Square, Cambridge, MA 02139, U.S.A.

weihl@tds.lcs.mit.edu

Wile, D. S.
USC Information Sciences Institute, 4676 Admiralty Way,
Marina del Rey, California 90292, U.S.A.

wile@vax.isi.edu

Wright, S. L.
Computer Science Program, School of MPS, Murdoch University,
Murdoch, WA 6150, Australia.

Zarnke, C. R.
Waterloo Microsystems Inc., 175 Columbia Street West, Waterloo,
Ontario, N2L 5Z5, Canada.

Zdonik, S.
Department of Computer Science, Brown University, Box 1910,
Providence, Rhode Island 02912, U.S.A.

sbz@cs.brown.edu

Part I

Type Systems and Persistence

The Napier Type System

R.Morrison, A.Brown, R.Carrick, R.Connor & A.Dearle
University of St Andrews

M.P. Atkinson
University of Glasgow

ABSTRACT

Persistent programming is concerned with the construction of large and long lived systems of data. In designing and building persistent object systems, we are attempting to regularise the activities that are performed on data by programming languages, operating systems, database management systems and file systems. We have identified the following areas of research which we are investigating in the context of persistent systems. They are: controlling complexity, protection of data, orthogonal persistence, controlled system evolution and concurrent computation.

In this paper, we describe the data modelling facilities of the Napier type system. We also demonstrate the flexible and incremental nature of the type checking mechanism that is required for persistent programming. The type system is central to the nature of the Napier language and we will demonstrate how it has been designed to solve problems in the five areas identified above.

1. INTRODUCTION

In our attempts to design and build a persistent information space architecture (PISA) [2], we have identified a number of problem areas. These require solutions before we can achieve our goal of less complex systems in which all programs are integrated with their environments. They are:

a. Controlling complexity: The complexity of the system must be kept under control, so that developers and users can concentrate on the application. This depends on establishing consistent rules which apply throughout the design of the underlying system and being parsimonious in the introduction of new concepts into the design.

b. Protection of data: Large bodies of data are inherently valuable. It is necessary to protect them from misuse and from hardware and software failure. This implies sophisticated type, protection and recovery mechanisms to limit the losses due to component failure.

c. Orthogonal persistence: The discontinuity between the use of short term data, manipulated by program, and long term data, manipulated by the file system or

DBMS, causes unnecessary complexity. We have defined the persistence of data to be the length of time for which the data exists and is usable[1]. We aspire to systems where the use of data is independent of its persistence.

d.   Controlled system evolution: The uses of data (including program) are neither limited nor predictable. It is therefore necessary to support the construction of unanticipated software systems or databases which make use of existing data (or program) even when the data and program were defined independently of one another. For large scale, widely used or continuously used systems any alteration to part of the system should not require total rebuilding. We require a mechanism which will allow the programmer to control the units of reconstruction.

e.   Concurrent computation: A large body of data requires a community effort for its construction and maintenance. Any useful body of data is likely to be of concurrent interest to many users, probably in dispersed geographic locations. Different models of concurrency and transactions may have to be accommodated by the underlying mechanism.

Based on our experience with PS-algol [31], we have designed and built the language Napier [27] to provide solutions in the above areas. The central design theme in Napier is that of the type system and the type checking mechanism which allows flexible and incremental typing and binding within the persistent environment. It is through the type system that the solutions to the above problem areas are resolved. We will discuss each in turn.

2. CONTROLLING COMPLEXITY

Type systems provide two separate facilities that often interact. They are the ability to structure data in a regular form and the ability to protect data from accidental or deliberate misuse. Historically, the domination of the protection aspects of type over the modelling aspects has led developers of large systems to regard type systems as too inflexible for their needs. We believe that it is now appropriate to alter this balance in order to demonstrate the modelling benefits of strong type systems. This we will do in the following sections.

Ideally, we would like a set of types and a type algebra, so that by a succession of operations of the algebra and the provision of parameters, we could define a data type equivalent to any data model or conceptual data model [2]. This we call *the type alchemist's dream* and, as yet, has not been fully achieved.

The complexity of any language or system is determined by the number of defining rules. When applied to type systems this means the model of type, and the rules used to ensure its consistency. There are many models of type and sets of rules which may be applied to ensure consistency. Here we present our initial preferences.

The Napier type system is based on the notion of types as sets of objects from the value space [7]. These sets may be built in, like integer, or they may be formed by using one of the built in type constructors, like **structure**. The constructors obey the Principle of Data Type Completeness [23,24] which states that all data objects have first class citizenship in the language. That is, where a type may be used in a constructor, any type is legal without exception. This has two benefits. Firstly, since all the rules are general, it allows a very rich type system to be described using a small number of defining rules. This reduces the complexity of the defining rules. The second benefit is that the type constructors are as powerful as they can be since there is no restriction to their domain. This increases the power of the language.

The choice of base types and constructors determines the universe of discourse of a language.

This choice is constrained by the data modelling capabilities that are required for the application domain. Below we present the Napier choices that we contend are desirable for persistent programming. It should be remembered that other sets of constructors are possible. The ability to control complexity depends on the method of definition in the first place and on the suitability of the constructors to the application domain in the second.

There are an infinite number of data types in Napier defined recursively by the following rules:

1.   The scalar data types are integer, real, boolean, string, pixel, picture, file and null.

2.   The type image is the type of an object consisting of a rectangular matrix of pixels.

3.   For any data type t, *t is the type of a vector with elements of type t.

4.   For identifiers $I_1,...,I_n$ and types $t_1,...,t_n$, structure($I_1:t_1,...,I_n:t_n$) is the type of a structure with fields I_i and corresponding types t_i, for i = 1..n.

5.   For identifiers $I_1,...,I_n$ and types $t_1,...,t_n$, variant($I_1: t_1,...,I_n: t_n$) is the type of a variant with identifiers I_i and corresponding types t_i, for i = 1..n.

6.   For any data types $t_1,...,t_n$ and t, proc($t_1,...,t_n$ -> t) is the type of a procedure with parameter types t_i, for i = 1..n and result type t. The type of a resultless procedure is proc($t_1,...,t_n$).

7.   For any procedure type, proc($t_1,...,t_n$ -> t) and type identifiers $T_1,...,T_m$, proc[$T_1,...,T_m$] ($t_1,...,t_n$ -> t) is the type proc($t_1,...,t_n$ -> t) universally quantified by types $T_1,...,T_m$. These are polymorphic procedures.

8.   For identifiers $I_1,...,I_n$ and types $t_1,...,t_n$, env is the type of an environment with bindings of the identifiers I_i to the corresponding types t_i, for i = 1..n.

9.   For any type identifiers $W_1,...,W_m$, identifiers $I_1,...,I_n$ and types $t_1,...,t_n$, abstype [$W_1,...,W_m$] ($I_1: t_1,...,I_n: t_n$), is the type of an existentially quantified data type. These are abstract data types.

10. The type any is the infinite union of all types.

11. For any user-constructed data type t and type identifiers, $T_1,...,T_n$, t[$T_1,...,T_n$] is the type t parameterised by $T_1,...,T_n$.

12. For identifiers $I_1,...,I_n$ and procedure types $t_1,..t_n$, process($I_1: t_1,...,I_n: t_n$) is the type of a process with entries I_i and corresponding types t_i, for i = 1..n.

The world of Napier data objects, its universe of discourse, is defined by the closure of rules 1 and 2, under the recursive application of rules 3 to 12.

An essential element for controlling complexity is that there should be a high degree of abstraction. Thus, in the above type rules, vectors and structures are regarded as store abstractions over all data types, procedures as abstractions over expressions and statements, processes as abstractions over flow control, abstract data types as abstractions over declarations, and polymorphism and type parameterisation as abstractions over type. The infinite unions **env** and **any** are used to support persistence, as well as being a general modelling technique; they are dynamically checked.

In the above, there are two elements in the type system for controlling complexity. The first is in the manner in which the type constructors are defined together with the application of the Principle of Data Type Completeness. With these we get less complex, more powerful systems. The second element in controlling complexity is in the abstraction mechanisms provided by the type constructors. The abstract forms increase the power of the system allowing the complexity of the application to be more readily captured.

3. PROTECTION OF DATA

In determining an appropriate type system for persistent programming, the language designer is faced with a balance between flexibility and safety. The safety in the system is derived from being able to express (or even prove) something about the program before it runs (i.e. statically), in order to improve confidence in its correctness. This explains the wish by most language designers to employ static typing as one of the devices for static checking.

A second aspect of static checking is that the programs so checked are more efficient. By performing the checking statically, the need for dynamic checking is removed, making the run-time representation of the program execute faster and in less space.

Taken to the extreme, totally static systems are not very useful for programming in the large since they cannot accommodate change, the very aspect we frequently wish to model. The mechanism is, however, very safe.

The flexibility in a type system is determined by how late the checking can be delayed before it is performed. In some systems, the type checking is performed dynamically [18]. Reasoning about such systems is more difficult than statically checked systems but they are more flexible. We have already established elsewhere [5,26] that dynamic checking is necessary in providing the persistence abstraction over separately prepared program and data.

Type systems can be devised that offer a mixture of static and dynamic typing more suitable to the requirements of persistent programming applications. Where appropriate, static checking may be used for safety and dynamic checking for flexibility. The mixture of static and dynamic checking is determined by the nature of the particular persistent programming application.

The Napier type system allows the user, by choosing the appropriate constructor, to determine whether the type checking is static or dynamic. The system employs eager type checking where types will be checked as early as possible in the life cycle. This can mean from compile time to run time. The type constructors **env** and **any** are dynamically checked as are projections out of variants; all other type checking is static. We will illustrate this mixture of static and dynamic type checking by examples of the type abstractions for polymorphism and abstract data types along with type **any**.

Polymorphism is a mechanism whereby we can abstract over type. In Napier,

```
let int_id = proc (x : int -> int) ; x
```

defines the identity procedure for integers. We may also define one for reals, such as

```
let real_id = proc (x : real -> real) ; x
```

Polymorphism allows us to combine the two definitions by abstracting over the type, and creating a generic identity procedure. This may be performed by writing

>   **let** id = **proc** [t] (x : t -> t) ; x

which is the identity procedure for all types; in fact, it has the type ∀t.t -> t . To call the procedure, we may write,

>   id [**int**] (3)

which will return the value 3. The important point about this form of type polymorphism is that it is all statically checkable. Objects of these types may be kept in the persistent store and then used to generate specialised procedures. This is an important method of software reuse [25].

Abstract data types may be used where we wish the data object to display some abstract behaviour independent of representation type. Thus it is a second mechanism for abstracting over type.

In Napier,

>   **type** TEST **is abstype** [I] (value : I ; operation : **proc** (I -> I))

declares the type *TEST* as abstract. The type identifiers that are enclosed in the square brackets are called the witness type identifiers and are the types that are abstracted over.

The abstract data type interface is declared between the round brackets. In the above case, the type has two elements, a field *value* with type *I* and a procedure *operation* with type proc (*I* -> *I*). It should be obvious that an infinite number of instances of objects of type *TEST*, each with a different concrete type, may be constructed in Napier.

A comparison can be made with polymorphic procedures which have universally quantified types. These abstract types are existentially quantified and constitute infinite unions over types [22]. Thus *TEST* has type ∃I.abstype (value : I ; operation : proc (I -> I)).

To create an abstract data object we may write,

>   **let** inc_int = **proc** (a : **int** -> **int**) ; a + 1
>   **let** inc_real = **proc** (b : **real** -> **real**) ; b + 1.0
>   **let** this = TEST [**int**] (3, inc_int)

which declares the abstract data object *this* from the type definition *TEST*, the concrete (as opposed to abstract) witness type **int**, the integer 3 and procedure *inc_int*.

Once we have created the abstract data object, we can never again tell how it was constructed. Thus *this* has type,

>   **abstype** [I] (value : I ; operation : **proc** (I -> I))

and we can never discover that the witness type is integer.

>   **let** that = TEST [**int**] (-42, inc_int)

creates another abstract data object. Although it is constructed using the same real witness type, this information is abstracted over. *this* and *that* have the same type, namely, abstype [I] (value : I ; operation : **proc** (I -> I))

as does *also* below

    let also = TEST [real] (-41.99999, inc_real)

We can form a vector of the objects by writing,

    let abs_TEST_vec = **vector** @1 **of** [this, that, also]

since they have the same type.

Two abstract types are equivalent if they have the same number of witness types and the same set of identifier type pairs where the witness types may be substituted consistently.

Since we do not know anything about the internal representation of an abstract data object, it is inappropriate to mix operations from one with another. That is, the abstract data object is totally enclosed and may only be used with its own operations.

A second requirement in our system is that we wish the type checking on the use of these objects to be static.

To achieve the above aims we introduce the **use** clause which defines a constant binding for the abstract data object. This constant binding can then be indexed to refer to the values in a manner that is statically checkable.

For example,

    use abs_TEST_vec (1) **as** X **in**
    begin
            X (value) := X (operation) (X (value))
    end

will apply the procedure *operation* to the value *value*, storing the result in *value*, for the abstract data object refered to by *abs_TEST_vec (1)*. X is declared as a constant initialised to *abs_TEST_vec (1)*. Only fields of X may be indexed or combined. The scope of the identifiers in the interface is restricted to the brackets following the constant binding identifier.

This could be generalised to a procedure to act on any of the elements of the vector. For example

    let increment = **proc** (this_one : TEST)
                            use this_one **as** X **in**
                            begin
                                    X (value) := X (operation) (X (value))
                            end

    let lower = lwb [TEST] (abs_TEST_vec)
    let upper = upb [TEST] (abs_TEST_vec)

    for i = lower **to** upper **do** increment (abs_TEST_vec (i))

In the **use** clause the witness types may be named. We may, for example, wish to write procedures over these witness types. This may be written as,

```
        use this as X [B] in
        begin
              let id = proc [t] (x : t -> t) ; x
              let one := X (value)
              one := id [B] (one)
        end
```

which renames the witness type as *B* and allows it to be used as a type identifier within the use clause.

Both of the above methods of type quantification can be checked statically. Universal quantification yields a very powerful tool for software reuse whereas existential quantification is a powerful tool in data protection in that the user may not interfere with the representation of the objects of these abstract types.

A second form of type polymorphism employing dynamic checking occurs with the type any, which is the union of all types. Values may be injected into and projected from the type dynamically. An example of the polymorphic identity procedure for type any is

```
        let id = proc( x : any -> any) ; x
```

the type of which is **proc (any -> any)**. To call this procedure, the parameter must be of type any. This may be performed by injection, as in the following case:

```
        let this_three = id (any (3) )
```

To retrieve the integer value from the object, we must project. An example of projection is the following:

```
        project this_three as Y onto
        int   : Y + Y    .    .
        default : ...
```

The constant binding, to *Y* in the above, is introduced to ensure that no side effect can occur to the projected object within the **project** clause.

This style of polymorphism is no less secure than the universal quantification. The difference is that it is dynamically checked.

The Napier persistent object store is type secure. However, even though Napier provides a rich set of binding mechanisms, there are some activities that are forbidden to ensure the integrity of the type-secure store.

One forbidden activity is type coercion. That is, the system does not allow the types of objects to be arbitrarily changed. Thus, for example, if a string representing the definition of a procedure is to be converted into a procedure, some special mechanism must be made available to check the validity of the conversion. Such a mechanism is called a compiler, which must be available at run-time within the persistent environment if the above objective is to be met.

The Lisp eval function [18] provides such a facility and we believe that some of the attraction of Lisp is that it allows programs to be constructed, compiled and executed dynamically. This is necessary for handling adaptive data, such as programs that produce programs.

The Napier system provides a callable compiler. It is specified by the declaration let compiler = **proc** (Source : source -> **any**)

Thus, given a textual representation of the source it returns a compiled procedure injected into the type any. To obtain the actual procedure, we must project out of the union. The compiler guarantees the type integrity of the system and is the only program allowed to perform these coercions. We say that it contains the *type magic* for the system [4]. By utilizing the callable compiler, we can produce compiled code for new activities. This compiled code gives us the efficiency that we require and avoids having to have intermediate levels of interpretation on the data to achieve the same functionality.

A final aspect for data security, in Napier, is that all locations in the system may be designated as constant. Since the initial value of the constant may be calculated at run time we call such objects dynamic constants [14]. The constancy applies to all locations and so it is possible to set up complex data structures with constant fields. As applicative programmers know, only a few locations in the store require to be updated in most applications. This can be reflected in Napier by using the dynamic constants.

Thus, for data protection, the Napier type system supports both static and dynamic checking, a type secure object store with a callable compiler and a mechanism for making locations constant.

4. ORTHOGONAL PERSISTENCE

In accordance with the concept of orthogonal persistence, all data objects in Napier may persist. For each incarnation of the Napier object store there is a root of persistence which can be obtained by calling the only predefined procedure in the system, *PS*. Objects that persist beyond the activation of the unit that created them are those which the user has arranged to be reachable from the root of persistence. To determine this the system computes the transitive closure of all objects starting from this root.

The distinguished root of the persistent store graph *PS* is of type environment [9]. Objects of type environment are collections of bindings, that is name-value pairs. They belong to the infinite union of all labelled cross products of typed name-value pairs. They differ from structures by the fact that we can dynamically add bindings to objects . This is perhaps best shown by example. We will create an environment that contains a counter and two procedures, one to increment the counter and one to decrement it. This may be done by

```
let e = environment ()        !standard procedure to creat an environment
in e let count := 0
!We have now placed the binding count : int := 0 in the environment e.
use e with count : int in
begin
    in e let add = proc (n : int -> int) ; {count := count + n ; count}
    in e let subtract = proc (n : int -> int) ; {count := count - n ; count}
end
!The environment now has three bindings, count, add and subtract.
```

The use clause binds an environment and its field names to the clause following the **in**. In the above the name *count* is available in the block as if it had been declared in the immediate enclosing block. The binding occurs at run time since in general the environment value, *e*, may be any expression evaluating to an environment. The binding is therefore dynamic and is similar to projection out of a union. The difference is that here we only require a partial match on the fields and other fields not mentioned in the use clause are invisible in the qualified clause and may not be used.

The environment mechanism provides a contextual naming scheme that can be composed dynamically. The use clauses can be nested and the environments involved calculated dynamically and therefore the name bindings can be constructed dynamically. This does not yield full dynamic scoping in the Lisp sense since all the objects in the individual environments are statically bound.

5. EVOLUTION OF DATA

Since the uses of data cannot be predicted, it is necessary to provide mechanisms that will support the evolution of data.

We can utilize the callable compiler to implement adaptive data [29]. That is, data that adapts to the needs of the application. This is done by a technique that we call *browser technology* [8]. A browser, in this sense, contains a knowledge base of actions that are selected by certain conditions.

When a browser encounters an object, it interrogates its rule base to see if it has an action for that object. In the most primitive case, the interrogation of the rule base can be a matter of matching on structural type and the action would be the application of the known browser procedure to that object.

If, however, the browser does not find a rule for the object, it must produce one. This can be done by automatically generating the source of a browsing procedure for that type of object. The source is then compiled by the callable compiler and the resultant procedure, keyed by the type, is added to the rule base. The browsing can now continue. Since the browser program itself is data, by virtue of the provision of first class procedures, we have outlined a programming paradigm for adaptive data.

This technique of adaptive data is especially powerful when combined with environments. Since all environments have the same type one may be evolved to another, with more or less bindings, by assignment. Thus, using the above technique, data may be evolved *in situ* in the persistent store.

6. CONCURRENT COMPUTATION

One of the major motivations for concurrent activity, be it user or machine, is execution speed. The need for concurrency increases as machines approach their theoretical speed limit at the same time as the complexity of the applications increases to require even greater power.

There is, however, a second major motivation for concurrency. Many of the activities that we wish to model are inherently parallel and if we wish to capture the essential nature of these real world activities then language primitives powerful enough to model them are required. One of the major breakthroughs in the design and understanding of operating systems was gained by modelling the system as a set of co-operating sequential processes[10,11]. Since most of the early operating systems modelled in this manner ran on uni-processor machines this modelling was not done to increase speed. It was performed to simplify the complexity of the system being built in order to gain greater insight into its operation. This process-oriented method of modelling, first applied to operating systems, has now been applied to database systems, graphics systems and general problems in computer science[15].

The model of concurrency in Napier is based on CSP [15] and Ada [16]. Process is a type in the language. The type defines the process interface that the process presents to the world. The interface consists of a set of named procedures called entries. External to the process, the entries act like first class procedures. Inside the process the entries do not act like procedures but are used to establish rendezvous with calling processes.

Within a process, the entry name is used to establish a rendezvous. The **receive** clause uses the entry name, its formal parameter list and a clause to be executed during the rendezvous. When a rendezvous is established the body of the particular entry is executed. The caller is suspended from the time the call is made until the completion of the rendezvous. If, however, a **receive** clause is executed before its entry has been called then the callee is suspended until the entry is called. Each **receive** clause defines a body for the entry allowing entry names to have many bodies in a process.

Processes are created and activated by associating a process body (a void clause) with a process type. To implement the rendezvous there is a separate queue of waiting processes for every entry. These queues are serviced in a first come first served basis.

Non-determinism in the system is provided by the **select** clause. This allows one of a number of clauses to be executed. Each clause may be protected by a boolean clause called a guard. To execute the **select** clause all the boolean guards are evaluated in order. An option is open if it does not contain a boolean guard or the boolean guard is **true**, otherwise it is closed. One of the open options is chosen for execution non-deterministically subject to the constraint that if the clause to be executed is an entry clause it will only be chosen if the entry can be received immediately. If none of the options can be immediately executed, e.g. if there is no entry pending, the process waits until one can be.

An example of a generalised index from any ordered type to any type, modelled as a process is given in Appendix I. For the present, we will use on the problem of the 5 dining philosophers [11] and model it using process objects. Before that, however, we must introduce a form of vector initialisation in Napier.

    let square = **proc** (i : **int** -> **int**) ; i * i

defines a procedure that will return the square of its parameter value. A vector initialised by

    let squares = **vector** 1 **to** 10 **using** square

would consist of ten elements indexed from 1 to 10. The elements themselves are initialised by calling the procedure with the index value and using the result as the element value. In this case each element will have a value that is the square of its index.

The solution to the dining philosophers problem is similar to the one proposed by Hoare [15]. In the system there are three types of objects, forks, philosophers and a room in which they dine. Each philosopher sits at a particular unique seat.

Forks have a very simple existence, being picked up and put down in order by one of two philosophers. The five forks modelled as a vector of processes can be defined by

    type fork **is process** (pickup, putdown : **proc** ( ))

    let fork_generator = **proc** (i : **int** -> fork)
        fork **with**
            while true do
            begin
                receive pickup ( ) **do** { }
                receive putdown ( ) **do** { }
            end

```
let forks = vector 0 to 4 using fork_generator
```

Thus, we now have five processes, *forks (0)* .. *forks (4)* executing in parallel. Notice that the forks will receive messages from anyone and it is therefore up to the philosophers not to abuse this.

The room has an equally simple existence. Philosophers may enter the room to eat and leave after eating. To avoid deadlock, but not starvation, at most four philosophers are allowed in the room at any one time. The room may be modelled by

```
type Room is process (enter, exit : proc () )

let room = Room with
    begin
        let occupancy := 0
        while true do
        begin
            select
            occupancy < 4   : receive enter () do occupancy := occupancy + 1
                            : receive exit () do occupancy := occupancy - 1
            selected
        end
    end
```

Philosophers enter the room, pick up the left hand and then the right hand fork, eat, put down the forks and leave the room. We must model each philosopher so that the philosopher picks up and puts down the correct forks only. The following will do this

```
type philosopher is process ()

let philosopher_generator = proc (i : int -> philosopher)
    philosopher with
        while true do
        begin
            ! Think
            room (enter) ()
            forks (i, pickup) () ; forks ((i + 1) rem 5, pickup) ()
            ! Eat
            forks (i, putdown) () ; forks ((i + 1) rem 5, putdown) ()
            room (exit) ()
        end

    let philosophers = vector 0 to 4 using philosopher_generator
```

Notice that within the closure of each philosopher there is the integer i which is in effect the identity of the process and ensures that the correct forks are selected. Putting the fragments together yields the total solution.

It is possible to store data in the form of a process object in the persistent store. This gives a form of object-oriented database where the objects are processes that receive and send messages [28]. More traditional databases are concerned with the stability of data, for integrity, and transaction mechanisms for safe concurrent use.

For stability we provide a low level primitive *stabilise* that ensures that data is copied onto a stable medium. However, we subscribe to the view that it is premature to build mechanisms for atomic transactions into the low level stable store [1,12,13,17]. The stable store provides a very primitive form of transaction that allows the system to recover from unexpected errors, be they hardware or software. Thus it provides primitive (one level) recovery but not atomicity or general (multi process) reversability. There is little agreement on an appropriate generalised transaction mechanism and for the present we deem it safer to build sophisticated mechanisms for atomic transactions, at a higher level of abstraction, using the concurrency and stability primitives.

Users of the persistent information space access data via concurrency and transaction protocols. This is done by encapsulating the data in concurrency and/or transaction abstractions.

7. FUTURE PLANS

There are three major areas in which we would like to develop the Napier type system. They are:

1. Inheritance,
2. Bulk Data Types, and,
3. Type inference.

There are many models of inheritence for database systems. Our particular preference is the multiple inheritance scheme of Cardelli [6]. We do not regard fully blown, unfettered inheritance as desirable but intend to experiment with bounded universal quantification to achieve our desired aims.

One particularly interesting combination is with processes. The entry list for a process specifies its type and can be considered as the protocol through which it may be accessed. By utilising the multiple inheritance scheme of Cardelli, we can place process types in the type lattice and define a partial ordering of processes. Thus it is possible to define procedures that will operate on processes with at least a given defined protocol. If the process has a more specialised type then that may also be used. For example

    type shared_int_object is process (write : proc (int), read : proc (-> int))
    type read_shared_int_object is process (read : proc (-> int))

    let Read_object = proc [t ≤ read_shared_int_object] (A : t -> int)
                A (read) (value)

    let ron = read_shared_int_object with ...
        ! create a process of type read_shared_int_object

    let this = Read_object [read_shared_int_object] (ron)
        ! pass it to the procedure Read_object

    let fred = shared_int_object with ... ; Write_object [shared_int_object] (fred)

The procedure *Read_object* takes as a parameter an object of type *t* which is a process with at least the entry *read*. In the example, the procedure is called twice with a process parameter. The first *ron* has exactly the entry *read* whereas the second *fred* has more. Inside the procedure, only the entry *read* may be used. By using this bounded universal quantification we can abstract over entry protocols that are common to processes.

Such a mechanism is important in object-oriented programming. Although the mechanism is available for all data types in Napier it is particularly important for processes since they are the environments may be used to provide adapative data within the type secure store.

For concurrent computation, we have provided the data type process together with a non-deterministic **select** clause. We have also speculated on how bounded universal quantification may be used to control the inter-process communication protocols in a type secure object store.

ACKNOWLEDGEMENTS

This work was carried out despite the attempts of the funding bodies to turn us into full time authors of grant applications.

REFERENCES

1. Atkinson, M.P., Bailey, P.J., Chisholm, K.J., Cockshott, W.P. & Morrison, R. "An approach to persistent programming". *The Computer Journal* 26,4, November 1983, pp. 360-365.

2. Atkinson, M.P., Morrison, R. & Pratten, G.D.
    "Designing a persistent information space architecture". *Proc. of the 10th IFIP World Congress*, Dublin, September 1986, pp. 115-120, North-Holland, Amsterdam.

3. Atkinson, M.P. & Morrison, R.
    "Types, bindings and parameters in a persistent environment". *Proc. of the Appin Workshop on Data Types and Persistence*, Universities of Glasgow and St Andrews, PPRR-16, August 1985, pp. 1-25. In *Data Types and Persistence* (Eds Atkinson, Buneman & Morrison), Springer-Verlag, 1988, pp. 3-20.

4. Atkinson, M.P. & Morrison, R.
    "Polymorphic Names, Types, Constancy and Magic in a Type Secure Persistent Object Store". *Proc. of the 2nd International Workshop on Persistent Object Systems*, Universities of Glasgow and St Andrews PPRR-44, Appin, August 1987, pp. 1-12.

5. Atkinson, M.P., Buneman, O.P. & Morrison, R.
    "Binding and Type Checking in Database Programming Languages", *The Computer Journal*. 31, 2, 1988, pp. 99-109.

6. Cardelli, L.
    "A semantics of multiple inheritance". In *Lecture Notes in Computer Science*. 173, Springer-Verlag (1984), pp. 51-67.

7. Cardelli, L. & Wegner, P.
    "On understanding types, data abstraction and polymorphism". ACM *Computing Surveys* 17, 4, December 1985, pp. 471-523.

8. Dearle, A. & Brown, A.L.
    "Safe browsing in a strongly typed persistent environment". *The Computer Journal*, 31, 2 (1988), pp. 540-545.

9. Dearle, A.
    "Environments: a flexible binding mechanism to support system evolution". *Proc. HICSS-22*, Hawaii, January 1989, pp. 46-55.

10. Dijkstra, E.W.
    "The structure of THE multiprogramming system". *Comm.ACM* 11, 5, May 1968, pp.

341-346.

11. Dijkstra, E.W.
"Cooperating sequential processes". In *Programming Languages* (editor F. Genuys), Academic Press, London, 1968, pp. 43-112.

12. Fredrich, M. & Older, W.
"HELIX : the architecture of a distributed file system". *Proc. 4th Conf. on Distributed Computer Systems,.* May 1984, pp. 422-431.

13. Gammage, N.D., Kamel, R.F. & Casey, L.M.
"Remote Rendezvous". *Software, Practice & Experience* 17, 10, 1987, pp. 741-755.

14. Gunn, H.I.E. & Morrison, R.
"On the implementation of constants". *Information Processing Letters* 9, 1, 1979, pp. 1-4.

15. Hoare, C.A.R.
"Communicating sequential processes". *Comm.ACM* 21, 8, August 1978, pp. 666-677.

16. Ichbiah et al.,
"The Programming Language Ada Reference Manual". In *Lecture Notes in Computer Science.* 155. Springer-Verlag, 1983.

17. Krablin, G.L.
"Building flexible multilevel transactions in a distributed persistent environment". *Proc. of Data Types and Persistence Workshop*, Appin, August 1985, pp. 86-117. In *Data Types and Persistence* (Eds Atkinson, Buneman & Morrison) Springer-Verlag, 1988, pp. 213-234.

18. McCarthy, J., Abrahams, P.W., Edwards, D.J., Hart, T.P. & Levin, M.I.
"The Lisp Programmers Manual". MIT Press, Cambridge, Massachusetts, 1962.

19. Matthews, D.C.J.
"Poly manual". Technical Report 65, 1985, University of Cambridge, U.K.

20. Milner, R.
"A theory of type polymorphism in programming". *JACM* 26, 4, pp. 792-818.

21. Milner, R.
"A proposal for standard ML". *Technical Report CSR-157-83.* University of Edinburgh.

22. Mitchell, J.C. & Plotkin, G.D
"Abstract types have existential type". *Proc POPL* 1985.

23. Morrison, R.
"S-algol Reference Manual". *CS 79/1* University of St Andrews, 1979.

24. Morrison, R.
"On the development of algol". Ph.D. thesis, University of St Andrews, 1979.

25. Morrison, R., Brown, A.L., Carrick, R., Connor, R.C., Dearle, A. & Atkinson, M.P.
"Polymorphism, persistence and software reuse in a strongly typed object-oriented environment". *Software Engineering Journal*, December 1987, pp. 199-204.

26.   Morrison, R., Brown, A.L., Dearle, A. & Atkinson, M.P.
       "Flexible Incremental Binding in a Persistent Object Store". *ACM.Sigplan Notices*, 23,
       4, April 1988, pp. 27-34.

27.   Morrison, R., Brown, A.L., Carrick, R., Connor, R. & Dearle, A.
       "Napier88 Reference Manual". *PPRR-77-89*. Universities of St Andrews and Glasgow.
       (1989).

28.   Morrison, R., Brown, A.L., Carrick, R., Connor, R.C. & Dearle, A.
       "On the Integration of Object-Oriented and Process-Oriented Computation in Persistent
       Environments". *Proc. 2nd International Workshop on Object-Oriented Database
       Systems*, West Germany, 1988. In *Lecture Notes in Computer Science*, 334.
       Springer-Verlag, September 1988, pp. 334-339.

29.   Morrison, R., Dearle, A. & Marlin, C.D.
       "Adaptive Data Stores". *Proc. AI'88 Conference*, Adelaide, November 1988, pp.
       135-145.

30.   Schmidt, J.W.
       "Some high level language constructs for data of type relation".*ACM.TODS* 2, 3, 1977,
       pp. 247-261.

31.   PS-algol reference manual. 4th Edition. Universities of Glasgow and St Andrews
       PPRR-12, July 1987.

Appendix I

```
type general_index [KEY, VALUE] is process (
                        Enter       : proc (KEY, VALUE),
                        Lookup      : proc (KEY -> VALUE) )

let generate_general_index = proc [Key, Value] (less_than : proc (Key, Key -> bool) ;
                        fail_value : Value -> general_index [Key, Value])
general_index [Key, Value] with
begin
        rec type index is variant (node : Node ; tip : null)
        & Node is structure (key : Key ; value : Value ; left, right : index)

        let null_index = index (tip : nil)
            !Compute the empty index by injecting the nil value into the variant

        let i := null_index
            !This is the internal index structure initialisation

        rec let enter = proc (k : Key ; v : Value ; i : index -> index)
        !Enter the value into the binary tree indexed by key k
        if i is tip then index (node : Node (k, v, null_index, null_index)) else
        case true of
        less_than (k,i'node (key) )   : { i'node (left) := enter (k, v, i'node (left)) ; i }
        k = i'node (key)              : { i'node (value) := v ; i }
        default                       : { i'node (right) := enter (k, v, i'node (right)) ; i }

        let lookup = proc (k : Key ; i : index -> Value)
        !lookup the value in the binary tree
        begin
              let head := i
              while head is node and k ≠ head'node (key) do
                      head := if less_than (k, head'node (key) ) then head'node (left)
                                                          else head'node (right)
              if head is node then head'node (value) else fail_value
        end

        while true do
              select
                  : receive Enter (key : Key ; value : Value) do i := enter (key, value, i)
                  : receive Lookup (key : Key -> Value) do lookup (key, i)
              selected
end
```

Grammars and implementation independent structure representation

Greg Michaelson
Heriot-Watt University

ABSTRACT

It is well known that every context free grammar has an equivalent structure type. However, every structure type also has an equivalent context free grammar. Thus, the context free grammar corresponding to a structure type in one language may be converted into equivalent structure types in different languages: a grammar forms a language independent structure type representation. Furthermore, a non-cyclic structure instantiation may be represented by a canonical character sequence formed by inorder structure traversal. That instantiation may then be recreated by parsing the character sequence using the grammar corresponding to the structure type. Thus, a grammar and canonical character sequence form an implementation independent structure instantiation representation.

The equivalence of structure types and context free grammars is illustrated. The exploitation of this equivalence for implementation independent structure representation and to extend the orthogonality of programming language I/O and type coercion is discussed.

1. INTRODUCTION

A persistent problem for computing in general lies in the representation of structured data when it is not being manipulated by a program. For languages which provide canonical representations of structured data, for example FORTRAN, Prolog and LISP, language I/O may be used directly to copy such representations to and from files. However, most programming languages lack such canonical representation. Thus, a typical approach is to devise an explicit special representation for each structure type and write sub-programs to copy the representation to and from files. Where the structured data is manipulated by programs written in the same language, these copying sub-programs need only be constructed once and language specific file facilities can be used. However, if the structured data is manipulated by programs written in different languages then the copying programs must be constructed for each language with attendant problems of ensuring inter-language consistency. Furthermore, a lowest common denominator such as sequential character files must be used as a transport medium.

In principle, this is not a problem for persistent programming systems as they maintain transparent representations of persistent objects independently of the programs that manipulate them. In practise, however, standards for implementation independent schemas for persistent objects are still being discussed[2]. Thus, sequential character files of explicit object specific representations with associated language specific copying programs still form a lowest common denominator between different persistent systems, as well as between persistent and non-persistent systems.

One solution is to devise a canonical sequential character based representation for structured data which is language independent and easily transformable to and from structure types in different languages. This paper discusses an approach based on the equivalence between structure types and context free grammars.

2. CONTEXT FREE GRAMMARS AND STRUCTURE TYPES

It is well known that every context free grammar has an equivalent structure type representation for parse trees[1]. Let us illustrate this using Pascal record structures.

A context free grammar is a 4-tuple:

```
{N,T,S,P}

where

N = non-terminal symbols - {N(1), N(2) ... }
T = terminal symbols
S = sentence symbol - member of N
P = productions - N(i) ::= R(i,1) R(i,2) ...

      where R(i,j) is the jth symbol on right hand side
            of N(i) and is a member of (N U T)
```

The terminal symbols T are atomic entities, often characters or character sequences. Within the context of Pascal we might allow T to be the set of valid atomic I/O values, that is valid CHARs, INTEGERs and REALs.

There may be several productions with the same left hand side non-terminal:

```
N(i) ::= R(i,1,1) R(i,1,2) ...
N(i) ::= R(i,2,1) R(i,2,2) ...
...

where R(i,j,k) = kth right hand side symbol of
                 jth alternative for N(i)
```

These may be grouped together as options on the right hand side of a single production:

```
N(i) ::= R(i,1,1) R(i,1,2) ...  |
         R(i,2,1) R(i,2,2) ...  |
         ...
```

Corresponding to this production is the Pascal variant record structure:

```
TYPE
    N(i)TAGTYPE = 1..?
    N(i)PTYPE = ^N(i)TYPE;
    N(i)TYPE =
    RECORD
          CASE N(i)TAG : N(i)TAGTYPE OF
          1: (V(i,1,1) : R(i,1,1)TYPE;
              V(i,1,2) : R(i,1,2)TYPE ... );
          2: (V(i,2,1) : R(i,2,1)TYPE;
              V(i,2,2) : R(i,2,2)TYPE ... );
          ...
    END

where R(i,j,k)TYPE = N(n)PTYPE if R(i,j,k) = N(n)
      R(i,j,k)TYPE = CHAR/INTEGER/REAL
```

$$\text{if } R(i,j,k) = CHAR/INTEGER/REAL$$

where N(i) TAGTYPE, N(i) PTYPE, N(i) TYPE, N(i) TAG are
    appropriate distinct names

where V(i,j,k) is an appropriate distinct name to
    identify the variant record field for R(i,j,k)

Note that the field type for a non-terminal is a pointer to the appropriate type rather than the type itself. This will be considered further in the next section.

For example, consider the grammar to recognise simple stock control records:

```
<identification> ::= INTEGER
<stock level> ::= INTEGER
<reorder level> ::= INTEGER
<item> ::= <id> <stock level> <reorder level>
<items> ::= <item> |
            <item> <items>
```

An equivalent record type is:

```
TYPE
    ITEMP = ^ITEM;
    ITEM =
     RECORD
            ID, STOCK, REORDER : INTEGER
     END;

    ITEMTAG = 1..2;
    ITEMSP = ^ITEMS;
    ITEMS =
     RECORD
            CASE I : ITEMTAG OF
            1: (FIRSTITEM : ITEMP);
            2: (FIRSTITEM : ITEMP; NEXTITEM : ITEMSP)
     END;
```

after substituting for the redundant terminal productions.

There is an apparent difficulty with constant terminal symbols. For example, consider the grammar to recognise binary numbers:

```
<digit> ::= '1' |
            '0'
<binary> ::= <digit> |
             <digit> <binary>
```

Pascal record types do not allow for constant fields so the constants '1' and '0' must be generalised to CHARs:

```
TYPE
    BINARYTAG = 1..2;
    BINARYP = ^BINARY;
    BINARY =
     RECORD
```

```
                    CASE B : BINARYTAG OF
                    1: (DIGIT : CHAR);
                    2: (DIGIT : CHAR; NEXTBINARY : BINARYP);
        END
```

after substituting for the redundant terminal production.

This lack of constant record fields will be considered again in a later section.

3. STRUCTURE TYPES AND CONTEXT FREE GRAMMARS

Just as every context free grammar has an equivalent structure type, every structure type has an equivalent context free grammar.

To illustrate this, consider the generalised Pascal record structure, with field types restricted to CHAR, INTEGER, REAL and pointer types:

```
    TYPE
        N(i)TAGTYPE = 1..?
        N(i)PTYPE = ^N(i)TYPE;
        N(i)TYPE =
        RECORD
                F(i,1) : F(i,1)TYPE;
                F(i,2) : F(i,2)TYPE;

                ...
                CASE N(i)TAG : N(i)TAGTYPE OF
                1: (V(i,1,1) : V(i,1,1)TYPE;
                    V(i,1,2) : V(i,1,2)TYPE; ... )
                2: (V(i,2,1) : V(i,2,1)TYPE;
                    V(i,2,2) : V(i,2,2)TYPE; ... )
                ...
        END

    where F(i,j)TYPE & V(i,j,k)TYPE = CHAR, INTEGER, REAL
                                      or pointer type

    where N(i)TAGTYPE, N(i)PTYPE, N(i)TYPE, N(i)TAG
          F(i,j), V(i,j,k) are appropriate distinct names
```

An equivalent definition may be constructed by preceding each variant part with the common fixed part:

```
        N(i)TYPE =
        RECORD
                CASE N(i)TAG : N(i)TAGTYPE OF
                1: (F(i,1) : F(i,1)TYPE;
                    F(i,2) : F(i,2)TYPE;
                    ...
                    V(i,1,1) : V(i,1,1)TYPE;
                    V(i,1,2) : V(i,1,2)TYPE; ... );
                2: (F(i,1) : F(i,1)TYPE;
                    F(i,2) : F(i,2)TYPE;

                    ...
                    V(i,2,1) : V(i,2,1)TYPE;
                    V(i,2,2) : V(i,2,2)TYPE; ... );
                ...
```

```
            END
```

This record structure may be used to represent the parse tree node for the context free production:

```
    N(i)  ::= F(i,1) F(i,2) ... V(i,1,1) V(i,1,2) ... |
              F(i,1) F(i,2) ... V(i,2,1) V(i,2,2) ... |
              ...

    where F(i,j), V(i,j,k) = N(n)
                                if F(i,j)TYPE, V(i,j,k)TYPE =
                                N(n)PTYPE

          F(i,j), V(i,j,k) = CHAR/INTEGER/REAL
                                if F(i,j)TYPE, V(i,j,k)TYPE =
                                CHAR/INTEGER/REAL
```

For example, the INTEGER list structure:

```
    TYPE
        LISTTAG = (ATOM, CONS);
        LISTP = ^LIST;
        LIST =
         RECORD
                CASE L : LISTTAG OF
                ATOM: (VALUE : INTEGER);
                CONS: (LBRA : CHAR;
                        CAR, CDR : LISTP;
                        RBRA : CHAR)
            END
```

may be used to represent parse trees for the production:

```
    <list> ::= INTEGER |
               CHAR <list> <list> CHAR
```

This correspondence may be extended to allow ARRAY and RECORD fields in the data structure. An ARRAY field:

```
    A : ARRAY [1..N] OF TYPE
```

holds N values of type TYPE and so has the equivalent the production right hand side symbol sequence:

```
    R(1) R(2) ... R(N)

    where R(i) is the ith occurrence of the production right
           hand side symbol sequence corresponding to TYPE.
```

Similarly, a RECORD field:

```
    R =
     RECORD
            F(1) : F(1)TYPE;
            F(2) : F(2)TYPE;
            ...
            F(R) : F(R)TYPE
```

END

holds R values with types F(1)TYPE, F(2)TYPE ... F(R)TYPE and so has the equivalent production right hand side symbol sequence:

```
RF(1)  RF(2)  ...  RF(N)

where RF(i) is the production right hand side symbol
      sequence corresponding to F(i)TYPE
```

Note that in the above scheme, non-terminals will be produced for both record fields and for pointer fields. This will result in pointer fields being used to represent parse tree nodes in both cases if the structure type is reconstructed subsequently from the grammar using the scheme in section 2 above. One alternative is to replace record fields by their sub-fields though, arguably, this loses the original structure. Another alternative is to generate non-terminals for all record fields and to use some naming convention to distinguish pointer field non-terminals from record field non-terminals, though this involves introducing additional grammar notations.

4. IMPLEMENTATION INDEPENDENT STRUCTURE REPRESENTATION

As noted above, representing an object when it is not being manipulated by a program involves defining an explicit object representation and constructing sub-programs to transfer the object too and from that representation. Now, grammars and canonical character sequences might be used for such representation and to act as an object bridge between different languages and systems.

First of all, if every structure type has an equivalent context free grammar and every context free grammar has an equivalent structure type then a context free grammar forms an implementation independent structure type representation which may be used to construct equivalent structure types in different languages:

```
S(1)  <= G => S(2)

where S(i) = structure type in language L(i)
      G = grammar
```

Furthermore, a canonical character representation of a non-cyclic structure type instantiation may be produced by inorder traversal and that instantiation may then be reconstructed from the character representation by parsing:

```
P(T(V))  ==  V

where V = value of type S
      T = inorder traverser for S
      P = parser for grammar for S
```

This equivalence might be used to communicate structure types and instantiations between different languages and systems which only share a sequential character file store.

Note that there is an assumption that some lowest common denominator semantic equivalence may be found between different languages' structure type provisions.

Consider a program written in language L(1) which defines a new external type S(1) with full structure details and a new external variable V(1) of type S(1). The compiler recognises that S(1) is new and external, produces a character representation of the corresponding grammar in file S, generates an appropriate inorder traverser T(1) and plants termination code to call T(1) to generate a canonical character representation of V(1)'s value in file V.

Suppose that another program written in language L(2) is to access object V(1). First of all the programmer needs to know V(1)'s type definition within L(2) in order to access it. Within an interactive environment, the programmer might define S(2) as old and external, and the system might then locate file S, extract the grammar and produce the equivalent structure definition, generating field names or prompting the programmer to supply appropriate ones. The programmer then uses S(2) in other definitions, in particular to define the old, external variable V(2) to hold V(1)'s value. Subsequently, when the program is compiled, the compiler recognises that S(2) is old and external, and generates an appropriate parser P(2) and traverser T(2). The compiler also recognises that V(2) is old and external, and plants initialisation code to locate file V and call P(2) to parse its contents to construct V(2). It also plants termination code to call T(2) to generate a canonical character representation of V(2) in V.

Note that this is a generalisation of a textual flattening approach[3] to a system independent object address space using character sequences as a lowest common denominator.

5. LANGUAGE EXTENSIONS

The data structure/context free grammar equivalence demonstrated above may be used to extend programming language orthogonality, in some cases at no extra syntactic cost.

5.1. I/O extensions

Most imperative languages restrict I/O to the recognition of atomic objects from character sequences[1]. Some "declarative" languages like LISP & Prolog will allow the I/O of character sequence representations of structured objects though the structure must correspond exactly to the language's syntactic rules. The above approach may be used to extend I/O orthogonality. In particular, for input, character sequence recognition, validation and data structure construction may be automated.

For example, Pascal I/O might be extended to pointer, ARRAY and RECORD types. For input, with:

    READ (V)

where V is a pointer, ARRAY or RECORD variable, a Pascal compiler normally detects V's type as non-atomic and generates an error. Now, it might generate a parser for the grammar corresponding to V's structure and replace the READ with a call to that parser. For output, with:

    WRITE (V)

where V is a pointer, ARRAY or RECORD variable, a Pascal compiler normally detects V's type as non-atomic and generates an error. Now, it might generate an inorder traverser corresponding to V's structure and replace the WRITE with a call to that traverser.

For input with discriminated union types some means must be found to indicate which option has been recognised. For languages like Algol68 and PSAlgol information enabling the

---

[1] FORTRAN is an exception . COBOL8X might have been had CODASYL been brave enough to accept the VALIDATE clause proposal.

identification of union types must already be present at run time. For Pascal the programmer must always provide explicit tags to identify different variant record options so these may be planted by the parser to indicate which option has been recognised. For C, however, conventions would have to be introduced for tagging union types.

A disadvantage of the above approach is the inability to recognise constants during the input of character sequences. Generalised fields must be still be checked after input for specific values. This might be alleviated by allowing constant fields in structure types which would correspond to constant terminal symbols in the equivalent grammars. For example, Pascal might be extended to allow character and string constant record fields. Thus, the Pascal record structure:

```
TYPE
     EXPTAG = (ADD, SUB, ETERM);
     EXPP = ^EXP;
     EXP =
     RECORD
            CASE E : EXPTAG OF
            ADD: (ET : TERMP; '+'; EE : EXPP);
            SUB: (ET : TERMP; '-'; EE : EXPP);
            ETERM: (ET : TERMP)
     END;

     TERMTAG = (MULT, DIV, TBASE);
     TERMP = ^TERM;
     TERM =
     RECORD
            CASE T : TERMTAG OF
            MULT: (BB : BASEP; '*'; TT : TERMP);
            DIV: (BB : BASEP; '/'; TT: TERMP);
            TBASE: ( BB : BASEP)
     END;

     BASETAG = (BRA, NUMB);
     BASEP = ^BASE;
     BASE =
     RECORD
            CASE B : BASETAG OF
            BRA: ('('; BE : EXPP; ')');
            NUMB: (BN : INTEGER)
     END
```

has equivalent grammar:

```
<exp> ::= <term> '+' <exp> | <term> '-' <exp> | <term>
<term> ::= <base> '*' <term> | <base> '/' <term> | base>
<base> ::= '(' <exp> ')' | INTEGER
```

The parser for a grammar corresponding to a structure type with constant fields may be used to validate constants in character sequences on input. However, this extension involves introducing new syntactic constructs into extant languages.

5.2. Type coercion extensions

This approach might also be used to extend the orthogonality of type coercions. For example, C allows objects to be 'cast' from one type to another though this only enables the inter-conversion of atomic types and the use of structured objects in different type contexts, usually for addressing purposes, without physical conversion. Now casting might be extended to inter-conversion of structured types.

Consider for example, string/structure coercion. Note that a C string is an array of characters. First of all, a C string might be cast to a structure type and be physically converted from a character sequence to a nested structure. The compiler might recognise the cast, generate the parser corresponding to the structure which accepts a character sequence as an array of characters, and replace the cast with a call to the parser with the string as argument.

Similarly, a C structure might be cast to a string and physically converted from a nested structure to an array of characters. The compiler might recognise the cast, generate an inorder traverser corresponding to the structure which generates a character sequence as an array of characters, and replace the cast with a call to the traverser.

To generalise, all structure/structure coercion may be extended to physical conversion. In principle, the compiler might construct an inorder traverser for the first structure and a parser for the second, and replace the cast with a call to the parser with input from the traverser. Thus, given the declarations:

```
...
... <type1> ...;
... <type2> ...;
...
<type1> <variable1>;
```

then the cast:

```
... (<type2>) <variable1>
```

would be replaced by:

```
... <type2 parser>(<type1 traverser>(<variable1>)) ...
```

In practise, it would be more efficient to fold traversers and parsers together so they do not communicate through an intermediate form. Thus, the compiler should generate cast specific traverser functions which produce new instantiations directly from old ones.

6. Further work

The above discussion is primarily anecdotal. Further work is required to demonstrate the approach's practicality and to firm up the theoretical background.

In the short term the practicality might be demonstrated through a language specific I/O extension driven by appropriate pre-processors.

In the longer term, the structure/grammar equivalence might be formalised for a variety of languages using, for example, re-write rules. It should also be possible to prove intra and inter-language structure/grammar/structure transformation consistency given formal semantics for the languages.

The formalisations might be used to construct tools to automate the generation of:

a) grammars from structure types
b) structure types from grammars
c) structure type specific parsers from grammars
d) traversers from structure types

These tools might then be used to investigate bolting different systems and languages together.

The above approach will only work with non-cyclic structure instantiations but, in many languages with structure types, cyclic instantiations are permitted through direct and indirect recursive references to pointer fields in structure type definitions. In principle, a cyclic instantiation is the parse tree for a context sensitive or general recursive grammar but it is not yet clear how to make practical use of this. An alternative is to still characterise structures by context free grammars but to devise a labeling notation to make an instantiation's structure explicit within its character representation. However, this raises the question of establishing a standard labeling notation.

ACKNOWLEDGEMENTS

This work was carried out at the Commonwealth Scientific and Industrial Research Organisation Division of Information Technology, in North Ryde, New South Wales, Australia, during 1988.

I would like to thank Paul Cockshott, Bob Colomb and Andrew Parle for reading earlier drafts of this paper.

REFERENCES

1.   Aho, A.V. & Ullman, J.D., *Principles of Compiler Design*, Addison-Wesley, 1977

2.   Balch, P., Cockshott, W.P. & Foulk, P., "A layered implementation of persistent store",*Software Engineering Journal*, pp 123-131, March 1989

3.   Cockshott, W.P., "Addressing mechanisms and persistent programming", In *Proc. of the Appin Workshop on Data Types and Persistence,* M.P. Atkinson, O.P. Buneman, and R. Morrison, Eds., PPRR-16, Universities of Glasgow & St Andrews, Scotland, pp 369-389, 1985

A Program Development Environment Based on Persistence
and
Abstract Data Types

Malcolm S Powell
University of Manchester Institute of Science & Technology

ABSTRACT

This paper describes the design of a program development system used for teaching undergraduate students. The system started life as an experiment with ideas associated with a type domain designed as part of a persistent [1] programming environment [11]. The aim of the experiment was to apply these ideas to the description of facilities usually associated with file-based operating systems, and to find out how well ideas designed to cope with "fine grain" persistent objects, would cope with the kind of "coarse grain" persistent objects usually represented by "files".

In this paper, objects of type *program* are defined by an abstract data type supporting the operations, *edit, parse, make executable* and *run*. The program development process is controlled through the notion of abstract states which constrain the order of application of the available operations. In addition, the type *program* may be parametrised by objects of type *language*.

A more complex type called *system* is provided. *Systems* support the same operations as simple *programs*, but are represented by hierarchies of *programs* and *modules*. A set of navigation operations are supported and the abstract state of a system or subsystem is a composition of the abstract states of its components. Users interact with systems as if they were using an interactive, incremental version of the UNIX *make* command [3].
In addition to the predefined object types described above, the environment supports user defined object types through a mechanism which formalises the concept of a *suite of programs*, e.g. the new type *document* might be installed and described by an appropriate set of operations and abstract states.

The system is described in terms of the type domain supported by the Paradox persistent machine [11]. A version of the programming environment has been used by classes of 100 or more students at UMIST since October 1987.

1. INTRODUCTION

Many applications involve data objects which have some inherent concept of state associated with them. A common class of such applications includes those which support the direct manipulation of complex information structures. In such applications, the set of applicable operations, made available via the user interface, must often be constrained according to the history of operations previously applied to an object, e.g. once a highly structured composite object has been constructed, it may not be desirable to allow *dispose* operations to be applied to it until some or all of its substructure is disposed of.

At the design stage, the notion of state associated with an object is often described by a state transition diagram which relates operations on the object to state names which abstract away from the details of the associated object values. This is particularly true of the design of user interfaces. At the implementation stage, the information from the state transition diagram is either encoded into into the user interface components or into precondition checks associated with individual operations.

A number of language notations provide direct or indirect facilities of specifying constraints on the order of application of operations. Path expressions [5] are a good example of this and similar structures have been represented less directly in such diverse notations as Distributed Processes[4], CCS[8] and even Ada[2]. This paper demonstrates how object states may be incorporated into the notion of object type by a simple extension to the concept of Abstract Data Type. The type domain of the Paradox environment [11] has been extended to incorporate objects which represent such extended abstract data types. It will be demonstrated that this extension and the persistent nature of Paradox objects led to an elegant design for a programming environment for an undergraduate programming laboratory. In particular, it provided a flexible way of integrating the design of the user interface with the design of the overall functionality of the system.

The following sections will describe the programming environment which represents the example application, and the need to associate states with objects of type *program*. A brief description of the Paradox type domain will then be given, followed by details of the extensions introduced above. A more complete description the design of the programming environment will then be presented in terms of the new construct.

2. THE ENVIRONMENT

Towards the end of 1986 the decision was taken to replace the laboratory facilities which had been used for teaching initial programming skills to undergraduate students in the Computation department at UMIST since 1978. There was a general feeling amongst the people involved that teaching software engineering techniques is a special application which requires the use of facilities designed for the purpose. The existing facilities had been based on an extended version of the UCSD Pascal system running on DEC LSI-11s. This had provided an environment which was simple to use for students with no previous computing experience, yet provided language facilities which enabled modular programming techniques to be exploited long before the general availability of languages such as Modula-2. It was originally designed for teaching, but had also provided extensive support for research within the Computation department.

It was decided that a new environment would be constructed and that it should have the following properties.

Δ It should be easy for the novice to use but, as being a novice is a transient state, should be flexible enough to support more advanced users.

Δ It should emphasise a general model of the software development process, and the tools which support it. Students should be able to relate this to the more complex, or less well organised facilities, to which they will be exposed later their careers.

Δ It should allow high level monitoring of the way in which students use the environment so that progress reports can be generated for the benefit of tutors.

Δ The facilities provided should be independent of the language or languages being employed.

Δ Any facilities which apply to simple programs should apply uniformly to systems composed of many individual modules.

3. THE DESIGN STRATEGY

The approach taken to producing a system with the required properties was to consider first the organisation of an environment which supported simple programs, written in a single language, but not complex systems. An overall structure was developed in this way and then generalised to include multiple languages and multi-module systems.

If programs are treated as objects which support a fixed set of operations, it is not too difficult to populate the operation set so that the general steps in the program development process can be described. Most of the operations are dictated by considering programs to possess a number of representational attributes which have to be manipulated directly by a developer.

In a completely general environment, a program would have a specification attribute, one or more implementation descriptions and one or more executable representations. A collection of operations on programs would assist in deriving implementation descriptions from the specification and a further set of operations would assist in deriving executable representations from implementation descriptions. With the current state of development of software engineering tools, the latter operations would exhibit a greater degree of automation than the former.

For the purposes of this paper, a single implementation description and a single executable representation will be assumed and the specification will be external to the environment[1]. Programs will therefore be described by the abstract type supporting the following operations (the underlying representation type will not be defined in this section).

```
TYPE program = CLASS
                edit
                parse
                make executable
                run
             END
```

This description of the type program is designed to provide students with a view of programs which is consistent with a wide range of "real world" program development environments. In particular, it is assumed that the implementation description is represented in some *source language*, strings from which are constructed by applications of the *edit* operation. It is further assumed that applications of the edit operation can result in strings which are not members of the source language. The *parse* operation is used to check that the current implementation description associated with a program is consistent with the source language.

The function of the *make executable* operation is to translate the implementation description into an executable representation for the program which can be executed by applications of the *run* operation. It is assumed that only syntactically correct implementation descriptions can be translated into executable representations and that only the executable representation can be *run*. It should be fairly clear how this view of program manipulation maps onto the use of source text files, object code files and compilers in many conventional development environments.

1. This reflects the approach taken to initial teaching in the Computation department. It is assumed that students must first acquire an intuitive understanding of the possibilities and problems associated with the use of computers and programming languages up to some reasonable level of complexity before they can understand the role of formal specification techniques.

Once such a set of primitive operations on programs has been proposed it is natural to consider what constraints ought to be placed on their application order. The following diagram illustrates one possible set of constraints.

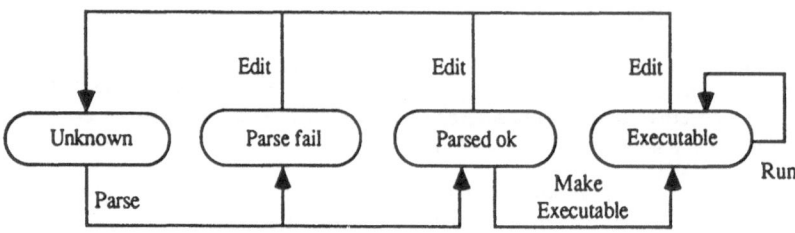

The diagram uses the concept of *abstract states* to organise the total set of operations on programs into applicable sub-sets. Each abstract state is denoted by a box labelled with the name of the state and has a set of operations associated with it, i.e. the operations named on the arcs leading *out of* the box. Each abstract state encapsulates a potentially infinite set of values which objects of type program may take as a result of the application of the operations associated with the type. If the internal representation of programs is text and the language used is Pascal, the following are examples of strings which might be components of the states *Parsed ok* and *Unknown*.

Parsed ok

```
PROGRAM null;     PROGRAM test(output);    PROGRAM divide(input, output);
BEGIN             BEGIN                         VAR a, b: 0..10;
END.                 write(1 DIV 0)         BEGIN
                  END.                         read(a, b); write(a DIV b)
                                             END.
```

Unknown

```
PROGRAM null;     LET    A=0               PROGRAM divide(input, output);
BEGIN             LET    B=0                   VAR a, b;
END.              READ   A,B               BEGIN
                  PRINT  A+B                   read(a, b); write(a DIV b)
                  STOP                      END.
```

It should be noted that, from the users point of view, the outcome of a *parse* operation is non-deterministic. This is consistent with the limited ability of human users to find mistakes in complex formal descriptions.

The relationship between operations and states may be used to structure the manipulation of programs so that the program development process must proceed in an orderly fashion. For example, the state diagram shown above indicates that programs may not be run until they have been parsed and made executable. In addition, if an executable program is changed, it must be re-parsed and made executable before it can be run again, i.e. the executable representation cannot get out of step with the implementation description. Teachers and demonstrators in undergraduate programming laboratories will realise the importance of the last point and the problems caused by many file based system in this respect.

If the operations associated with each state are assembled into classes, then each class is a sub-type of the original type program. Therefore the states associated with programs can be described as follows.

```
TYPE unknown    = CLASS edit, parse              END

     parse fail = CLASS edit                     END

     parsed ok  = CLASS edit, make executable END

     executable = CLASS edit, run                END
```

Given this representation of the major phases of the program development process, a more appropriate way of defining the type program would be as the union of the abstract states which it supports.

```
TYPE program = UNION
               unknown, parse fail, parsed ok, executable
           END
```

The advantage of this representation of programs is that it abstracts away from all of the details of program representation and implementation, including details of the language in which programs are constructed. If the operations on programs, from the standpoint of program development, are to be specified with sufficient completeness [7], it is vital to abstract away from linguistic detail. The alternative is to have the complex axioms associated with parsing and translating languages interleaved with the axioms which specify the required behaviour of the program development operations.

There is also a potential efficiency advantage to be gained in implementations based on this design strategy due to the relationships it is possible to construct between the post-conditions of the operations which comprise a state and the preconditions of the operations in their successor states. For example, the implementation of the translation required of the *make executable* operation need only consider syntactically correct programs. This is further illustrated by the following example which describes a simple *stack* object supporting the usual *push*, *pop* and *top* operations.

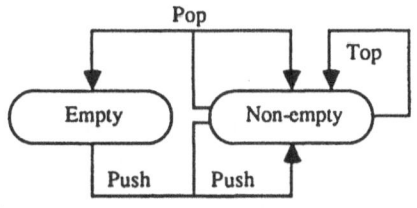

```
TYPE stack    = UNION empty, non-empty END

     empty    = CLASS push END

     non_empty = CLASS push, pop, top END
```

According to this description of a stack, any attempt to perform a *pop* operation on an *empty* stack is a type violation. The *pop* operation does not need to perform any precondition checking in order to cope with this case. In addition, the role of the traditional empty predicate on stacks is taken over by a type enquiry directed at the union type which defines the stack. From the user's point of view, the *pop* operation is non-deterministic (unless they keep an independent tally of the number of pushes and pops which have been performed), as is the *parse* operation in the program type.

The examples given in this section have illustrated parts of the design process for the program development environment. They have also shown how a simple state model of the program development process can be translated into a type description for program objects which will enforce the behaviour required by the model. *Abstract states* are characterised by abstract data types which are sub-types of the object type described by a state diagram. The implementation of the operations of the individual *abstract states* share a common object representation.

4. THE PARADOX SYSTEM

The following sections will give a brief overview of the Paradox environment and its type domain and show how the design ideas described in the previous section are supported. The organisation of the Paradox machine is described more fully in [11] and the organisation of the strongly typed input-output system is described in detail in [9, 10].

The Paradox system is a persistent programming environment in which all objects, including types, are represented by abstract syntax trees. Associated with every *type* object is a set of *views*. Objects of type *view* define projection functions from the *type* with which they are associated to the hierarchically structured *images,* through which the user communicates with the system. An *image* may contain one component for each component of the object of which it is a projection. Thus, in the Paradox environment, objects of type *type* define the *abstract syntax* of objects and objects of type *view* define their *concrete syntax*.

Input is achieved by the user, or some other external device, *pointing* at the components of images. With every component of an image, the system associates a reference to the object of which it is a projection. When an image component is pointed at, the corresponding object reference is added to the queue which supports the implementation of read operations. In this way objects of arbitrary complexity, including procedures and types, may be read as easily as integers or strings in more conventional programming environments.

4.1. The Type Domain

The basis of the Paradox type domain is the notion of *primitive type*. Primitive types are used to represent unique objects such as *nil*, the Boolean values *false* and *true* and the integers values 0, 1, 2 etc. They are also used to provide the unique identifications usually associated with textual names. An object of some primitive type can take only one value, which is the type itself.

The usual scaler types are constructed types based on the use of an ordered union type constructor. This has the advantage that objects may be members of more than one union but still have a single unique type. For example, the primitive type 0 might be a member of the union types called *integer*, *natural* and *decimal*. However, 0 has only one type and that is the primitive type 0. Finite versions of the types integer and natural are provided as standard objects supported by the Paradox machine. As far as the user is concerned, they are union types. However, the machine provides them with an implementation which may exploit the efficient implementation provided by most processors. SmallTalk's integers are defined in a similar fashion [6].

In addition to primitive and union types, Paradox supports *list, array, function* and *procedure* types and an object reference constructor called *shared*. Each of these types supports a unique set of operations defined by objects of type *function* or *procedure*. Thus each of the type constructors is considered to be a shorthand for an equivalent abstract data type definition.

Example

```
LIST OF element ≡ list of(element)
        WHERE FUNCTION list of(element: type): type = list
          WHERE list = CLASS
                        INTERFACE
                          FUNCTION nil(): list
                          FUNCTION head(list): element
                          FUNCTION tail(list): list
                          FUNCTION is nil(list): Boolean
                          FUNCTION cons(element, list): list
                        REPRESENTATION ...
                      END
```

In Paradox terms, the two concrete representations shown above, i.e. "LIST OF element" and "list of(element)", are merely different *views* of the same object. As types are first class objects, new abstract data type descriptions are created by applying the operations associated with the type *type*. For example, the description of the list class in the previous example might be constructed as follows.

```
TYPE list = t
      WHERE t         = list rep ← (nil, head, tail, is nil, cons)
            list rep = ...
            nil      = FUNCTION (): t = ...
            head     = FUNCTION (t): element = ...
            tail     = FUNCTION (t): t = ...
            is nil   = FUNCTION (t): Boolean = ...
            cons     = FUNCTION (element, t): t = ...
```

The "←" operator is pronounced "hidden by" and constructs a class type description from a representation type and a list of *operations* (function or procedure objects), i.e. r ← i is an isomorphic copy of the type graph represented by the Cartesian product of r and i. Types which describe objects defined by sets of abstract states may also be constructed by using the "←" operator. The use of the operator for this purpose can be illustrated by considering the stack objects described previously. The example has been simplified by considering stacks of integers rather than completely general stacks.

```
TYPE stack         = UNION (empty, non empty)
     empty         = empty rep     ← (push)
     non empty     = non empty rep ← (push, pop, top)
     stack rep     = UNION (empty rep, non empty rep)

     empty rep     = nil
     non empty rep = LIST OF integer

     push          = FUNCTION (s: stack rep, x: integer): non empty rep =
                       CASE type of(s) OF
                           empty rep    : cons(x, non empty rep(nil))
                           non empty rep: cons(x, s)
                       END

     top           = FUNCTION (s: non empty rep): integer = head(s)

     pop           = FUNCTION (s: non empty rep): stack rep =
                       IF is nil(tail(s)) THEN empty rep(nil) ELSE tail(s)
```

This definition is rather cumbersome. However, its general structure (abstract syntax) may be captured by a relatively simple type description. A suitable view may be associated with the type so that instances of the it may be manipulated via a less cumbersome concrete representation which hides unnecessary detail. The user constructs instances of such types by direct manipulation of the projected image. If all of the components of the image are specified, then all of the information required to construct a complete type object will be available to the system.

The following example illustrates the concrete syntax which will be used for this purpose in the rest of this paper. It reinforces the connection between abstract states and abstract data types by augmenting the usual class syntax by with an extra section to specify which operations are associated with each abstract state. If the operations available through the interface are not partitioned into abstract states, the STATES section may be omitted. What remains is then a conventional abstract data type specification.

```
TYPE stack = CLASS

        INTERFACE

            FUNCTION push(stack, int): non empty

            FUNCTION pop(non empty): stack

            FUNCTION top(non empty): integer

        STATES

            empty     = (push)

            non empty = (push, pop, top)

        REPRESENTATION

            empty     = nil

            non empty = LIST OF integer

            ...

        END
```

One question which has not yet been answered, is how is the initial state of an object established? In order to answer this question, the Paradox object creation rules must be described.

All objects are created with a well defined value according to their type. All objects described by a union type are created with a value which is an instance of the first type in the union (remember that union types are ordered). Thus, all new Booleans are false and all new naturals are 0.

All new objects which represent shared references [12] are created with the value *nil*. These rules are applied recursively to the components of objects described using the other type constructors. Objects which are instances of types described by classes are created with values which correspond to the initial values of their representation types. However, in this case, explicit initialisation operations may be specified which modify these initial values.

Classes specified by the union of a set of abstract states will therefore be created in the first state in the union. In the concrete representation used here, this will be the first state specified in the interface of the class. Thus, *programs* as described earlier would be created in the *unknown* state and stacks, as described by the type above, would always be created in the *empty* state.

Direct manipulation of objects defined by abstract data types is accomplished as follows. Firstly, the Paradox view mechanism is used to define one or more concrete syntaxes for the representation type. These must be defined in the REPRESENTATION of the class concerned, but may be made available to the outside world as part of the INTERFACE. The view definitions may refer to the interface of the class in order to incorporate a representation of the operations it supports. For the *program* type, the following simple view might be defined.

```
VIEW display(p: program)    = enclose( down( state(p)
                                              +
                                              text(p)
                                              +
                                              menu(operations(DEREF p))
                                        )
                                  )

       state(p: program)      = type name(DEREF p)

       menu(ops: operations) = enclose( down( flatten(ops, op name) ) )
```

In these definitions, the *enclose* operator takes an image as its operand and places an enclosing box around it. The operator *down* takes an ordered set of images and constructs a new image by placing each image in the set one below the other. *Flatten* takes a structured object and constructs an ordered set of images, of the first level of components in the structure, by applying the view function, specified as its second argument, to each in turn. It is assumed that programs have textual implementation descriptions and that *text* represents a suitable view for such a representation. *Op name* is a standard textual view of an operation and *type name* is a standard textual view of a type. *Operations* is a function associated with objects of type class and returns a list of the objects which represent the operations supported by their class.

An instance of a program may now be created and displayed by the use of the *show* operation. This takes an object and a reference to a view and produces a corresponding image on a display device. Subsequent images of the same object may be displayed as the result of applying the operations supported by its class. Some examples of the images which might be defined by the preceding view descriptions are shown below.

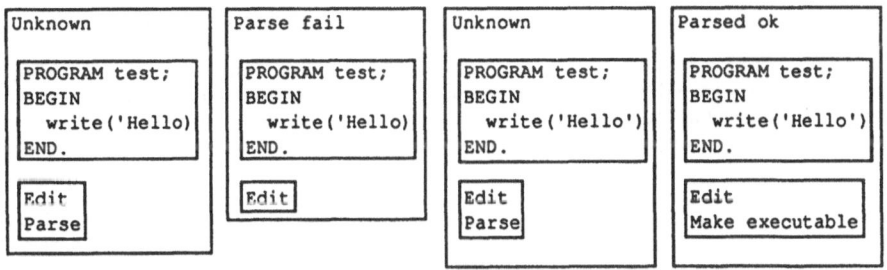

Whenever *show* is used to generate an image, the individual components of the image are associated automatically with the objects of which they are projections, e.g. in the images above the names of the operations on programs would be associated with the objects which represent the operations. If a user points at any component of an image, e.g. by using a mouse, the object associated with it is added to a queue of objects which can be accessed by a read operation.

The only exception to this is where an object is described by a class type. In this case, no object association is made, i.e. users can look at the representations of objects defined by abstract data types but they may not touch them. Of course any images generated during the application of the operations of a class will be images of its representation type and then the preceding rule will not apply. In this way users are allowed to traverse a hierarchy of objects through the application of operations which may reveal different levels of detail as they become appropriate.

Operations pointed at by the user may be read and executed to provide direct manipulation of program objects. The available set of operations will change automatically to reflect the current states of the objects concerned. With a few simple extensions, this mechanism provides the basis for strongly typed user interfaces to objects described in terms of sets of abstract states.

4.2. Using Abstract States to Describe a Programming Environment

Using the modified class constructor defined earlier, the type program can now be described as follows.

```
TYPE
  program = CLASS
              INTERFACE
                FUNCTION edit(program): unknown
                FUNCTION parse(unknown): parsed
                FUNCTION make executable(parsed ok): executable
                FUNCTION run(executable): executable
              STATES
                unknown      = (parse, edit)
                parse fail = (edit)
                parsed ok  = (edit, make executable)
                executable = (edit, run)
                parsed       = UNION (parsed ok, parse fail)
              REPRESENTATION
                ...
            END
```

A simple refinement to the program type which has proved to be very useful in practice, is to provide an explicit initialisation operation to make every new program a null program in the language in which it is described. If programs are represented textually, the empty string of characters is rarely a valid program. By initialising the representation to the minimal sequence of characters necessary to represent a syntactically correct program, useful visual clues as to the nature of the object being manipulated are provided when concrete views are presented during the evaluation of the edit operation.

From a teaching point of view, this is also consistent with encouraging students to develop and test their programs incrementally using the parse, make executable and run operations at frequent intervals to check that they have not strayed from their external specification, i.e. programs are not created as linear strings, starting at the beginning and finishing at the end, but by a planned series of refinements.

So far, the notion of program discussed in this paper is independent of the way in which programs are represented. The language in which a program is defined is just one of the attributes of its representation of which the current definition is independent. The program type may therefore be parametrised by a language definition to allow programs defined in different languages to be manipulated via a consistent set of operations.

What is the type of a language? Clearly, it is desirable to abstract away from the detail inherent in the classical set theoretic definition of a language. Such detail is relevant to the definition of the implementation of operations on languages but not to the use of those operations as part of the program development process. Languages are therefore defined by 6-tuples consisting of the types of the *source* and *code* representations for programs defined in a language and four functions representing an *editor* and a *parser* for the source representation, a *translator* to translate from the source to the code representation and an *interpreter* to execute the code representation. A type constructor function for languages defined in this way is shown below.

```
FUNCTION new language (source: type,
                       code  : type,
                       e     : ANY editor,
                       p     : ANY parser,
                       t     : ANY translator,
                       i     : ANY interpreter
                       ) = language
WHERE language =
  IF ( editor     = FUNCTION (source): source  )
     AND
     ( parser     = FUNCTION (source): Boolean )
     AND
     ( translator = FUNCTION (source): code    )
     AND
     ( interpreter = FUNCTION (code): void      )
  THEN
    CLASS
      INTERFACE
        FUNCTION edit (language): unknown
        FUNCTION parse (unknown): parsed
        FUNCTION translate (parsed ok): executable
        FUNCTION run (executable): void
      STATES
        unknown     = (parse, edit)
        parse fail  = (edit)
        parse ok    = (edit, translate)
        executable  = (edit, run)
        parsed      = UNION (parsed ok, parse fail)
      REPRESENTATION
        unknown     = source
        parse fail  = source
        parsed ok   = source
        executable  = RECORD source, code END
        edit        = FUNCTION (l: language): unknown =
                         IF type of (l) IS executable
                         THEN unknown (e (l.source))
                         ELSE unknown (e (l))
        parse       = FUNCTION (u: unknown): parsed =
                         IF p (u) THEN parsed ok (u)
                         ELSE parse fail (u)
        translate   = FUNCTION (s: parsed ok): executable =
                         executable (s, translate (s))
        run         = FUNCTION (e: executable): void = i (e)
    END
  ELSE error
```

Given this definition of *language*, the concept of a program type parametrised by a language can be represented as follows.

```
TYPE program =
     CLASS (l: language)
        INTERFACE
          FUNCTION edit (program): unknown
          FUNCTION parse (unknown): parsed
          FUNCTION make executable (parsed ok): executable
          FUNCTION run (executable): executable
        STATES
```

```
unknown       = (parse, edit)
parse fail = (edit)
parsed ok  = (edit, make executable)
executable = (edit, run)
parsed     = UNION (parsed ok, parse fail)
  REPRESENTATION
unknown    = l.unknown
parse fail = l.parse fail
parsed ok  = l.parsed ok
executable = l.executable
FUNCTION edit(p: program): l.unknown = l.edit(p)
FUNCTION parse(p: unknown): l.parsed  = l.parse(p)
FUNCTION make executable(p: l.parsed ok) = l.translate(p)
FUNCTION run(p: executable): executable = (l.run(p); p)
END
```

The next stage in the design of the environment is to provide a frame work for organising a number of programs. In a programming laboratory, students need to group together the different programs associated with different exercises and also different versions of the same program. Therefore, some kind of hierarchical program store is required. A possible representation of the type *context* ,which was chosen to fulfil this need, is shown below.

```
TYPE context            = LIST OF entry

     entry              = RECORD entry name, entry definition END

     entry definition   = UNION program definition, context END

     program definition = UNION
                            program(pascal), program(hope) ...
                          END
```

Instances of objects of type context are presented to users in a form based concrete syntax which concentrates the user's attention on one list of entries at a time. Another reason a form-based representation was chosen was that it can be manipulated relatively easily by using a mouse, or by commands issued directly from a keyboard. This representation hides the details of the values of entries. However, these may be displayed during the evaluation of the available operations.

CONTEXT Exercise one			
EXPLORE ⬆ ⬇ Insert Delete			
OBJECT TYPE	**NAME**	**STATE**	**OPERATIONS**
Program (Hope)	Prototype	Executable	Edit, Run
⇒ Program (Pascal) ⇒	Production 1 ⇒	Executable⇒	Edit, Run
Program (Pascal)	Production 2	Parsed ok	Edit, Make Exec
Program (Pascal)	Production 3	Parse fail	Edit
Context	Experiments		Explore

The above image also shows the concrete representations of the operations associated with the context class, which was constructed to hide the representation type described previously. On the second line of the form are the two arrows which represent the entry selection operations and these are followed by the legends representing the names of the operations which allow entries to be inserted or removed at the currently selected entry position. The *explore* operation shown against the only entry of type context represents the operation which allows the user to inspect the details of a nested context.

```
TYPE context =
      CLASS
         INTERFACE
            PROCEDURE up
            PROCEDURE down
            PROCEDURE insert
            PROCEDURE delete
            PROCEDURE explore
         STATES
            empty      = (insert)
            not empty = (insert, up, down, delete, explore)
         REPRESENTATION ...
      END
```

The next step in the development of the programming environment was to augment the *entry definition* type associated with contexts to include objects of type *system*. A system is a composition of modules and sub-systems of the sort used to represent more complex pieces of software than can conveniently be expressed as single programs. Therefore, a system can be defined in much the same way as a context, both from an abstract and a concrete point of view. It will support operations for inserting and deleting new modules or sub-systems and for exploring the structure of any selected sub-system. In addition, it will have similar characteristics to objects of type program in that it will support operations such as *parse, make executable* and *run*. Its state set will be a superset of that defined for programs.

```
TYPE system =
      CLASS
         INTERFACE
            FUNCTION insert(system): unknown
            FUNCTION delete(system): empty or unknown
            FUNCTION explore(system): system
            FUNCTION parse(unknown): parsed
            FUNCTION makeexec(parsed ok): executable
            FUNCTION run(executable): executable
         STATES
            empty             = (insert)
            unknown           = (insert, delete, explore, parse)
            parse fail        = (insert, delete, explore)
            parsed ok         = (insert, delete, explore, makeexec)
            executable        = (insert, delete, explore, run)
            empty or unknown = UNION empty, unknown END
            parsed            = UNION (parsed ok, parse fail)
         REPRESENTATION...
      END
```

The module types supported in a system may be constructed in much the same way as program types and may also be parametrised by languages. The languages which describe modules will usually have source and a code representations in common with the languages used to describe programs, but the parsers will generally be different. The mechanism used to resolve references between modules and to construct an executable representation of a whole system is beyond the scope of this paper. However, it is appropriate to point out that in the scheme implemented, a *definition-before-use* ordering was enforced on the entries in a system and that the interface to a sub-system was formed by concatenation of the interfaces of its components.

The users interact with system objects through a form based concrete representation similar to that used for contexts. They may explore and modify the hierarchical structure of a system and update its components by application of the operations applicable to them, e.g. by parsing and editing modules or programs. Whenever the state of any component of a system is changed, the state of the system as a whole must be updated accordingly, e.g. if a parse operation places any component into a *parse fail* state, then the system of which it is a component must also be placed in a *parse fail* state. This process must be repeated for all affected systems until the outermost system is reached. The following definition of the parse function illustrates how this is achieved in terms of a simplified system representation type.

```
TYPE system    = LIST OF component
     component = UNION program(...), module(...), ..., system END

FUNCTION parse(s: system): parsed = p(s)
   WHERE
     FUNCTION p(rest: system): parsed =
       IF is nil(rest) THEN parsed ok(s)
       ELSE
       IF type of(DEREF head(rest)) IS unknown THEN
       BEGIN
         (DEREF head(rest)):=parse(DEREF head(rest));
         IF type of(DEREF head(rest)) IS parsed ok
         THEN p(tail(rest))
         ELSE parse fail(s)
       END
       ELSE p(tail(rest))
```

If the edit operations supported for objects of type module can distinguish the updating of a module interface from the updating of its implementation, it is possible to minimise the amount of re-parsing and re-translation needed to restore an executable system to an *executable* state after a change is made. The parse operation for systems defined above already supports this possibility as it only re-parses entries which are in an *unknown* state, i.e. those entries already in a *parse ok* state would not be re-parsed.

4.3. Adding New Object Types to the Environment

If it becomes necessary to enhance the functionality of objects described by Paradox types, two options are available. Firstly, the set of operations associated with any class types may be augmented. Secondly, the set of types included in any unions may be extended provided that existing dependencies on their orderings are maintained. In addition, it is sometimes feasible to define coercion functions which will transform existing objects of some type into new objects of some derived type. In order to allow new types of object to be made available within the programming environment, it would be sufficient to extend the union type which defines context *entry definitions*. However, in order to allow users to add their own object types, without being given access to the full power of the Paradox type domain, a different approach was taken.

A new type called *user type* was created and included in the *entry definition* type for contexts. Instances of *user type* represent pro-formers for abstract data type definitions with operations defined by objects of type *program*. The user must provide programs to describe the initialisation and finalisation of the objects being defined, and a number of sets of programs to represent its abstract states. When a *user type* object is defined in this way, it may be referred to when the *insert* operation is used to add a new object to a context. The information stored in a context to represent user defined objects includes a reference to the object which must be created by the initialisation program, and an indication of the current state of the object. A standard interface to this information allows the programs which represent the operations associated with the user defined type to maintain the state information in accordance with the required semantics. From a user interface viewpoint, context entries described by user defined types are manipulated in the same way as objects described by system defined types.

This mechanism formalises the concept of a *suite of programs* in a fashion which even permits the utility of abstract data types to be conveyed to hardened COBOL programmers! An example of its use might be the definition of a simple document formatting system. For this application, programs would be written to create new *documents*, to allow *documents* to be edited, to perform the required formatting operations, and perhaps to produce statistics derived from their contents.

4.4. Final Implementation of the Programming Environment

Some of the details of the design of the programming environment have been simplified in the preceding sections in order to keep this paper to a reasonable length. In addition to those items which have already been mentioned, the following differences exist between the system as it has been described and that which was implemented. The result type of the *parse* operation associated with a *language* was not Boolean. The type used in practice allows information about the nature of a parsing failure to be made available to other operations supported by the same language, e.g. the *edit* operation can use this information to indicate the position and nature of the fault.

An extra state was also associated with both programs and systems to allow for failures during execution of the *run* operation. As a result of the *make executable* operation, all programs and systems are initially placed in an *executable ok* state to demonstrate that they have not yet failed. The program or system then remains in this state until it is edited or the execution of a run operation reports a failure. In the latter case it is placed in an *execution failed* state to indicate that it is not "bullet proof". The run operation may still be applied, but the *executable ok* state can only be restored by modifying the program or system concerned. A *run result* is also made available so that the *edit* operation can indicate the position and nature of an execution failure in much the same way as was described for parsing failures.

5. CONCLUSIONS

An extension to the concept of abstract data type has been described which permits the natural expression of the concept of object state as part of the description of object type. The type domain of the Paradox environment has been extended to support this facility and it has been used to design and implement the organisational aspects of a program development environment for use in an undergraduate programming laboratory. As Paradox already provides integrated mechanisms for specifying abstract syntax, concrete syntax and semantics, the extension also provides a way of integrating the design of the functionality of a class of objects with the design of the user interface to objects in the class.

The programming environment has been used by classes of 100 or more students since October 1987. The students have responded well to the system and the teaching staff involved have been provided with improved mechanisms for keeping track of student progress compared to the file based system used previously.

As the interface to the system has formalised the program development process, it is much easier to assess the *way* in which students develop programs rather than merely the results they achieve. Further work is being undertaken on recording and analysing histories of program states to provided high level feed back to tutors on student progress and to attempt to detect common problems so that they can be rectified at an early stage.

ACKNOWLEDGEMENTS

The author would like to acknowledge the efforts of Chris Tan, Alan Florence, Chris Harrison and Bulent Ozcan, who have all contributed to the development of the Paradox teaching environment. Also Brian Rich, Dave Blakeman and John Twigg of ISTEL limited and ISTEL's support for related research, which provided a source of ideas and problems, during the period in which the work reported here was carried out.

REFERENCES

1. Atkinson, M.P., Bailey, P.J., Chisholm, K.J., Cockshott, W.P. & Morrison, R. "An Approach to Persistent Programming". *The Computer Journal* 26, 4 , November 1983, pp. 360 - 365.

2. Bouch, G., "Software Engineering with Ada". Computing and Information Sciences Series, Benjamin/Cummings Publishing Company, 1983, pp. 202 - 205.

3. Bourne, S.R., "The UNIX System", International Computer Science Series, Addison-Wesley, 1982.

4. Brinch Hansen, P. "Distributed Processes: A Concurrent Programming Concept". In *Concurrent Programming*, ed. Gehani, N. & McGettrick, A.D. Addison-Wesley, 1988, pp. 216 - 233.

5. Campbell, R.H. & Haberman, A.N. "The Specification of Process Synchronisation by Path Expressions". Lecture Notes in Computer Science 16, Springer-Verlag, New York, 1974, pp. 89-102.

6. Goldberg, A. & Robinson, D. "SmallTalk-80: The Language and its Implementation". Addison-Wesley, 1983.

7. Martin, J.J., "Data Types and Data Structures". Series in Computer Science, ed. Hoare, C.A.R., Prentice-Hall International, 1986, pp. 59 - 60.

8. Milner, R., "A Calculus of Communicating Systems". In *Lecture Notes in Computer Science*, 92, Springer-Verlag, 1980.

9. Powell, M.S., "Strongly Typed User Interfaces in an Abstract Data Store". *Software Practice & Experience*, Vol 17, No 4, 1987.

10. Powell, M.S., "An Input/Output Primitive for Object Orientated Systems". *Information & Software Technology*, Vol 30, No 1, 1988.

11. Powell, M.S., "Incremental Compilation, Partial Evaluation and Persistence". *Proc. of the 2nd International Workshop on Persistent Object Systems*, Universities of Glasgow and St. Andrews, PPRR-44, August 1987.

12. Tye, S.T., "A Prototype Abstract Data Store". PhD Thesis, University of Manchester, 1985, Computation Department, UMIST.

Exploiting the Potential of Persistent Object Stores

David Stemple
Computer and Information Science Department
University of Massachusetts at Amherst

ABSTRACT

The full potential of persistent object stores will not be reached by implementing massive database management systems that interpret schemas in order to carry out their tasks. Nor will the compiler technology of current programming languages, in which the compilers fully and inflexibly determine the implementations of the base constructs of the languages they compile, be able to deliver the required performance when faced with high level specifications of database systems. What is needed is a more robust implementation architecture along the lines proposed by the EXODUS project at the University of Wisconsin. Techniques for hand-generating fast implementations of strategic functions combined and integrated with generative techniques along the lines of "fourth generation" languages should be developed in order to deliver the promise of persistent object stores, i. e., avoidance of the impedance mismatch and straightforward management of complex persistent structures. This paper outlines some of the possibilities for features in an "open compilation" approach to implementing database management systems using a persistent object store. One of the salient features of this approach is starting with a formal specification language and using the formality of the language to help the implementers build efficient and correct implementations.

1   INTRODUCTION

Generating efficient programs from high level specifications is a difficult task for experienced programmers, and is currently beyond the capabilities of programming language compiler technology. When the system specified is a database system, characterized by a large amount of persistent data and many programs sharing the data, some degree of efficiency can be achieved by limiting the structures and operations that can be used with persistent data and taking a largely interpretive approach to data manipulation. This is the approach of most current database management systems. Limits on the structures and operations allow certain specifications, such as moderately complex queries on stereotyped information structures for bulk data, to be effectively optimized. However, these limits produce a lack of uniformity in the means of specifying the dynamic properties of a database system: nonpersistent information is manipulated in a "host language" often in a style quite distinct from the style used to manipulate the persistent data. The result of this approach to database technology has been to make the specifications of complex applications using persistent data, such as design, graphics and artificial intelligent systems, more complex than they need to be. The approach has also made it difficult to produce efficient implementations for these systems since the optimization techniques do not always work on data whose natural structure and use does not conform to the structures chosen for persistent data.

Many have recognized the desirability of treating persistent and non-persistent data in a uniform manner and some have proposed languages that address the issue [1]. The uniform treatment (in the system specification) of the persistent data of database systems and the nonpersistent data typical of programming languages involves both specification and implementation issues. First, it requires a uniform means of specification that combines the set-orientation and data independence of database management systems with the type definition and abstraction capabilities of modern programming languages. Second, uniform specifications of database systems will require sophisticated methods of generating implementations if a high level of efficiency is to be achieved. Clearly a robust persistent object store could be used to simplify the implementation problems engendered by taking a uniform stance at the specification level.

Mapping from a high level specification language into an efficient implementation on persistent store is a difficult task. It is possible that the formal theory of a good specification language can be used to simplify this task. We believe that such a formal database theory must be one that supports mechanical reasoning about complex systems, especially about their dynamic properties. We have developed a formal specification language, ADABTPL, whose theory is a version of Boyer-Moore computational logic. [6] The ADABTPL theory supports mechanical reasoning and has been used to build a verifier for proving that transactions obey integrity constraints. [23] While other languages and their supporting theories may be as good, we will use ADABTPL as the specification language in the rest of this paper.

Techniques such as those used in database management systems for assigning data structures to objects and optimizing access to the structures will have to be combined with compilation methods used in code generation for very high level programming langages. In order to be effective on system specifications that treat persistent and non-persistent data uniformly, compilation will have to operate over a wider range of implementation choices and be more interactive than is usual in current programming language compilers. It will not be sufficient to employ programming language oriented approaches in which the only mechanism for assigning different implementation choices to operations is to program different versions of the operations and bind calls to the different versions. Traditional compilation techniques cannot easily handle the synthesis of efficient implementations for high level queries and updates of information aggregates such as sets. A systematic treatment of query optimization and transaction implementation over a robust set of implementation choices will require hybrid generative techniques buttressed by theoretical support.

In the remainder of this paper we will outline an architecture for developing database systems that addresses some of the features that we think will be required to make persistent object stores reach their potential. We follow a discussion of the architecture with a review of some of the diverse roots of our approach.

2 PROPOSED ARCHITECTURE

The database system development architecture being proposed has basically three levels starting with a semantic level in which the structure of the elements of the world to be modelled are specified in some semantic model, such as the Entity-Relationship Model. We will not deal with this level beyond providing for its support at the second level, the ADABTPL language level. The capability of formally capturing the substance of a large range of semantic data models was one of the design criteria for ADABTPL. The third level is the implementation of the specified system in a language that provides access to atomic persistent data, such as C with a persistent object server. The method of generating implementations from ADABTPL specifications is the focus of this paper. Generating an implementation involves the interaction of the system designer with advisor programs and includes assigning storage structures to specified information aggregates as in the ANSI concept of *internal schemas*, as well as assigning implementations for crucial functions used in the specification of both schema and transactions. These assignments are used by generators to produce the low level code for the specified system. Throughout the implementation design phase feedback on the current assignments are produced by advisor programs.

The development of a database system (an application rather than a database management system) proceeds in stages. In each stage feedback, iteration and refinement occur. The top level semantic level is prepared using whatever tools are available to support the semantic model. This level is mapped into an ADABTPL specification which is refined by adding whatever forms of constraints and update details are not provided by the semantic model. Transactions are tested for consistency with the schema's constraints and suggestions are given for their improvement. The database specifier changes incorrect transactions (or constraints) based on the feedback. When the specifier is satisfied (for the time being) that the specifications in ADABTPL are complete enough for implementation efforts to begin, the database implementer (like the specifier probably a team) starts by choosing parts of the specified database to be the stored base. This is analysed by the system in order to validate its ability to supply unstored parts by view materialization methods. In case the stored part is insufficient, feedback on corrections is provided to the implementer. When a sufficient base is determined, data structures are chosen for database components, and programs for important functions in transactions, queries and/or constraints are either chosen from a library or written in terms of the chosen data structures. Generators of implementations for transactions and queries that use these choices are now used to compile the transactions and queries of the database system. Screen formats and output style must also be designed and given to generators for production of the interface code. If a new programming language is to be utilized, then generators for programs in it as well as its interfaces must be generated.

2.1 Choices and Feedback

As just described, the design of an implementation meeting the ADABTPL specification of a system will comprise a series of choices and consultations with advisor programs. The advisor programs will validate, evaluate and suggest choices of structures and function implementations. The following steps will be taken while designing an implementation once an initial specification has been developed:

- Choose the part of the specified database that will be stored, the rest to be treated as views.

- Assign data structures to parts of the stored database.

- Assign programs to certain functions.

- Assign screen formats to transactions and predefined queries.

- Define interfaces between programming languages and transactions.

- Pose alternate forms of parts of the specification to be tested for equivalence.

- Retract certain choices and make new choices and assignments.

During the process of making implementation choices the system will provide the designer feedback including the following:

- Validation of the adequacy of a choice for the stored base, including the functions that define the view data.

- In case a chosen base is insufficient, delineation of the missing parts.

- Options for storing different parts of the database, using heuristics and information contained in the integrity constraints.

- Validation of equivalence of alternate specifications or analysis of differences.

- Translations of transactions into implementation language using current assignments of structures and programs.

The choices made by a designer will be kept in a design audit trail that will provide input to transaction and query implementation generators. The generators will use the choices to produce implementations in a lower level system. The lower level system could be a database management system, or a programming language system that provides support for transactions over persistent storage. In order to use a particular implementation system with our architecture, the system will have to be described in ADABTPL terms, during which default implementations will be chosen for implementing those parts of an ADABTPL specification for which a designer makes no implementation choice.

2.2   Key Architectural Features

We will now discuss the key features of the proposed architecture. The features which we will highlight are those most likely, in our opinion, to be aided by the kind of mechanical reasoning we have developed in the ADABTPL system. We will not dwell on the implementation of screen interfaces or of costing advisors, or other facilities that will be needed, but for which our kind of theoretical analysis may be of little advantage over traditional approaches.

In ADABTPL specifications, the database may contain redundancies in order to simplify the specification of transactions and integrity (or due to their origination in a schema integration activity). This can lead to inefficiencies if the database specification is taken as a direct representation of the physical database. The system designer can choose to have only parts of the specified database maintained in persistent storage. Using our architecture, a designer will work with advisor programs that help choose a nonredundant base for the physical data (if that is desired). The effect of this is to make certain parts of the database be views rather than base data. The choice will have to be validated as to its ability to support the complete, specified database.

This approach to redundancy in the specified database not only leaves the determination of what is a view and what is not a view to decisions made independently of the semantic specification of the database, but also facilitates storing "non-normalized" forms of the data in cases where efficiency favors such decisions. The "anomalies" supposed to result from such an approach are ameliorated by the automated handling of the complexities of updating combined with the cost-savings due to avoided processing (for example, avoiding excessive joins by storing the join of two static relations that are accessed frequently and always joined when accessed). [1] This is in contrast to relational normalization design techniques in which the normalized design is used both as the semantic and physical base of the system. The benefits of separating the semantic specification from the physical design in this manner will be determined by the resulting efficiency of physical designs that are attainable without prohibitive effort on the part of the designer.

One technique that a designer will be able to use in designing an implementation is to pose alternate specifications for constraints and functions and have them validated as equivalent to the original forms. This will allow the use of different though equivalent specifications as starting points for implementation designs. The reason that this is useful is that it is often easier to work from one form of a specification than from another

---

[1] The ADABTPL system would ensure that the join was lossless, or not allow it as a valid implementation choice.

in generating implementations. (This is unfortunate but true due to the necessarily incomplete nature of mechanical reasoning about complex systems.)

A major goal of our architecture is to provide an effective means of implementing databases using physical structures that are significantly different from the structures used in their specifications. This goal of "data independence", one of the early promises of database management systems, is notably lacking in hierarchical and network systems, partially because of their lack of set-oriented manipulation interfaces. It is also lacking in relational systems that force the relational model on the physical structure. It is interesting to read in Stonebraker's *Readings in Database Systems* [31] that IBM had a project to build a relational frontend for IMS. The motivation for such a product includes serving the tremendous customer base of IMS as well as the possibility of achieving high levels of efficiency underneath a relational interface. The project was abandoned, according to Stonebraker, due to "semantic difficulties in building an SQL to DL/1 translator." Database management systems have not yet attained true data independence wherein a specification of comparable abstraction to that of the relational model can be implemented in any of a large range of supporting data structures.

Our approach requires a formal understanding of data structure options and their means of supporting the high level semantics. To achieve the formality required for effective data independence, we can exploit an idea first articulated by Date and Hopewell [11] and used to some degree in the data description and translation work started by Senko [22] and which culminated in the EXPRESS system. [26] More recently, Batory has developed similar ideas and used them in part of his database implementation effort. [3] The basic idea is to capture the semantics of a data structure as a function or query on another form of the information. For example, a hierarchical structure for storing a parent and a child relation together could be defined using the almost relational query/function:

```
factor(join(Parent, Child, Parent.Id=Child.ParentId),
            Attributes(Parent))
```

This gives the operations, joining on the Parent key and factoring the Parent attributes, that need to be performed on the Parent and Child views to produce the hierarchical data structure. This form of data structure specification is the opposite of the normal approach to view definition, in which the view is defined as a function on stored data, but under the right conditions can be used for the view materialization needed in query execution. It can be used more directly, though also with care, for updates specified using the higher level view. Its major feature is that it provides a formalism needed to reason about data structures that is the same as that supporting the ADABTPL reasoning used to validate transactions and to produce other feedback to system designers. We intend to develop a technology for transforming ADABTPL specifications using this approach, which we call the *data algebra approach*. This method of specifying the map from logical to physical structures can be used in conjunction with generative, rule-based techniques, as exemplified by Prietula and Dickson's prescription. [19] A particular challenge will be the accommodation of object-oriented implementations that use internal forms of unique identifiers. We are reasonably sanguine about the prospects for dealing with this problem, since data translation work has dealt extensively with pointers and we are dealing with much better structured systems due to the use of integrity constraints in the highest level of system definition. This approach is close to methods used in the EXODUS query optimizer generator which uses a rule-based approach to generating the query optimizer itself. [13]

While the proposed architecture could use as the implementation system a database management system that includes schemas, a query system and programming language interface, the full potential of the approach will only be attained by using a lower level implementation system. It is not clear at this point what facilities a low level system should contain, but the current frenzy of activity in persistent object stores should produce viable alternatives for experiments.

A method for designing tailored database system implementations would not achieve its full potential if it did not address the fact that a system specification is never static and a physical design must change as either its specification or its performance requirements change. [33,27] Two aspects of change that must be accommodated in database systems are the generation of new implementations for parts of the specification and the translation of existing data into new forms. The proposed architecture facilitates both these activities. The generation of new implementations is facilitated by the semi-automatic nature of the implementation and the fact that it is driven and controlled by formal specifications. The data algebra approach can be used to generate data translation programs by virtue of the consistent grounding of specifications in executable semantics. To specify a transformation is to write source code for a translator. In order to make the translator efficient, the same design process used to generate an efficient database implementation must be used. While our data algebra approach will have much of the power of the EXPRESS system, it is hoped that our problem is simpler by virtue of only dealing with data whose formal semantics are known. We are not starting with internal forms of data generated by programs with no concrete semantics, as was the case for most uses of the EXPRESS system.

One kind of optimization that should be investigated is compiling the results of computations that search large extents of static data. This is an expanded version of what is called "constant folding" in programming language compilers and was one of the features of previous work by the author.[28] It involves precomputing at "compile-time" the result of searching or processing a part of the database that is declared to be constant (at least over some stretch of time). This allows specifications that contain the search specification to remain unchanged, while the code that implements them contains the results of the search rather than the search code. This represents a kind of "on-the-fly view materialization" strategy. Declarations that certain parts of the database are constant would need to be verified by checking time stamps or some other method before executing code compiled using the declarations. The method for doing this would be similar to that used in DB2 for verifying that the assumptions made in optimizing SQL queries are still valid whenever the compiled version of a query is executed. Failure to verify the assumptions (or declarations) can cause an automatic recompilation or an exception to be raised, whichever is desirable.

The kind of reasoning that has been implemented in the ADABTPL constraint maintenance system can be profitably combined with techniques such as the extended constant folding described above to achieve many kinds of optimization including semantic query optimization. For example, this approach can be applied to optimizing rule-based systems in which rules are held in the database as first class objects, a feature of ADABTPL. The rules could be declared constant and the rule searching code, a part of the application in the ADABTPL system, could be optimized using ADABTPL reasoning at compile-time to determine what rules could possibly be activated after each transaction execution. Only the possibly activated rule set would be searched after a transaction, and these searches themselves could be compiled and optimized using techniques currently under development for treating unification and rule processing as database functions specifiable in ADABTPL. This would provide a method for transforming prototype rule-based systems into production code without reprogramming.

The problems of distributing a database, an important issue in any modern database management architecture, must be addressed. It is not clear to us at this point how distribution choices should be integrated with the choices we have discussed so far. We see basically three possibilities:

- Distribution is a separable layer that can be addressed more or less independently of other implementation issues. (This seems unlikely to us, but should be examined carefully because it represents an ideal decomposition.)

- Distribution choices can be treated like other data structuring choices using the data algebra approach.

- Distribution choices and methods of handling them are inseparably connected to the underlying implementation system and must to be dealt with in an ad hoc fashion.

The maintenance of libraries of implementation idioms, in which generic specification fragments are related to physical designs that have proven to be useful choices, will be required in order to make the architecture more useful. The forms that these libraries should take and how and when they should be accessed will need to be determined. It will be a significant challenge for the system to produce generic forms of particular choices that a user has decided are worth remembering. We expect that the ADABTPL approach to higher order functions and theory can provide leverage toward solving this problem, though we also expect generalization to require user input in most cases.

3 ROOTS OF THE APPROACH

The earliest expression we have found of a declarative formal description of a mapping between different levels of data in a database context is that of Date and Hopewell, [11] in which they use relational calculus to express the mapping. One of the major early contributions to the effort of systematizing the high to low level mapping was that of Senko and his co-workers, in their seminal work on the Data Independent Access Method. [22] This work introduced a powerful way of thinking about multiple levels of data structures and the mapping between them. It influenced probably the most sophisticated work on data translation, the EXPRESS system. [25,26,14] This effort showed the feasibility of general purpose transformers that could be generated from declarative specifications of data structure source and targets, even when working with the chaotic data semantics of the time. There has been much work in automatic restructuring of databases since the EXPRESS system, e. g., [?,24], but little attention has been paid to exploiting any of this work in helping designers specify the mapping from high level specifications to efficient implementations in a low level system. The best work in this area appears to be that of Batory [3]. Batory has developed a transformation model that may be an effective basis for efficient development of implementations of higher level database specifications, a possibility that he is pursuing in the Genesis project. [4] His work is close to the data algebra approach.

The other roots of the proposed architecture lie in early expressions of the advisability of using abstract data types and "objects" in the specification and implementation of database systems. [5,16,35,2] Recent work in this area abounds, over twenty-five systems currently being built [34], though it has for the most part an ad hoc theoretical basis or limited use of generative techniques beyond programming language compilers. We believe that the object-oriented database work will suffer the difficulties of the Codasyl approach unless it is given the proper formal basis (a problem we have started addressing [30]) and supplied with the sophisticated techniques needed to achieve true data independence, the major problem addressed by the proposed architecture.

A notable exception to most of the object-oriented database implementation work, at least in the generation architecture, is the EXODUS project at the University of Wisconsin. [7,8,13] Another effort that is also very innovative is the Napier project at the Universities of Glasgow and Saint Andrews. [17]

While not explicitly object-oriented, our early work in the generation of database system implementations foreshadowed some of the newer techniques implemented and proposed. [28,29] In this work we developed techniques for compiling Codasyl schemas into what were essentially the managers for record types handled as objects. Each record had its own operations since they could be quite different based on the Codasyl sets in which they were automatic members. Though it is not clear how much of this work is useful when truly high level schemas, ADABTPL versus Codasyl, are involved, we believe that several of the techniques, e. g., precompiling database searches through constant areas, could be effective.

The EXODUS approach is by far the closest to that outlined in this paper. EXODUS departs from the static, interpretive DBMS architecture and represents an attempt to build a modular and modifiable framework in which many high level models can be implemented on many different styles of implementations. This motivation is identical to ours. The EXODUS developers are taking a "DBMS Generator" approach, and like ours one that combines many techniques in the mapping from high level specifications to low level implementations.

The EXODUS Storage Object Manager is the low level, most stable part of EXODUS. It includes file objects, concurrency control, and primitive version control support. On top of this manager are generic access method code and "operator methods" written in E, the EXODUS extended C. [20] This level can be extended by database implementers who are implementing a particular application or generic support for a data model. In this they can make use of a type manager with facilities for specifying class "hierarchies" and a file catalog. In addition to these components, EXODUS includes lock manager and recovery protocol stubs that allow implementers to implement concurrency control algorithms for new access methods, one of the difficult parts of DBMS system development. Experimentation is underway with generating user front ends, and a query optimizer generator has been implemented.

The EXODUS query optimizer generator, in essence a generator generator, is one of the most sophisticated parts of the architecture and represents the wave of the future in our opinion. (See also the description of another generator generator by Cleaveland [10] for an example of successful use of this technology.) A number of researchers are looking into rule-based generation of optimized query implementations, including using semantics in the process. The ADABTPL approach to mechanical reasoning represents an instance of sophisticated rule-based reasoning and allows the natural inclusion of a system's semantics in any transformation task, such as query optimization. The use of rule-based transformation in implementing transactions and access methods should be investigated in addition to the work on queries.

A major difference between the EXODUS and ADABTPL approaches is the attention spent on the low level aspects of the problem by the EXODUS group and the attention paid to the high level problems by the ADABTPL group. While the Wisconsin researchers built an object manager and query optimizer generator to support a wide range of data models, the ADABTPL researchers built a theoretical framework to bridge semantic and data models and implemented a mechanical reasoning apparatus for reasoning about systems specified using this framework. The ADABTPL work was done in anticipation of using a target implementation system along the lines of the EXODUS architecture. We believe that effective use of such an architecture requires powerful mechanical design tools and that only a robust theoretical basis and mechanical reasoning capabilities will make it possible to implement these tools. We have built the theory, implemented the basic mechanical reasoning, and defined the specification language that we believe are needed to support the development paradigm implicit in such systems as EXODUS.

While implementation of semantic models is clearly related to the method discussed in this paper, e. g., DAPLEX, Taxis, IRIS, [9,18,15] the work done to date has been quite limited in the underlying choices of data structures and the means of making or extending the choices. The ADABTPL architecture offers a new means of implementing semantic data models by providing a formal specification language to use as a target language into which the the semantic level can be compiled. This not only gives the semantic data model a formal expression, it also provides a platform on which an effective implementation can be built.

The generation of set implementations involved in the architecture described here is superficially similar to work done in the SETL context [12,21], but it differs in several fundamental ways. These include the ADABTPL reliance on sophisticated type definition facilities that incorporate constraints as well as the use of (higher order) Boyer-Moore computational logic. Another important difference is our emphasis on secondary storage and massive data instances rather than on primary storage and relatively small instances. In any case, the SETL experience needs to be studied for its relevance even if its lessons need considerable translating in order to use them in the database context.

POSTGRES represents one of the many attempts to extend the relational model, the arguments for which have been widely disseminated. [32] Though extending relational systems has large commercial value and a tremendous amount of experience and creative ability is being brought to bear on the problem, the fundamental difficulties of an interpretive architecture underlying nonuniform specification of systems with limited formality and expressiveness remain. While POSTGRES or some other system extending the relational model may turn out to be the surviving technology for implementing database systems, fundamentally more formal, more expressive specification languages and innovative shifts of development paradigms should be investigated.

4 SUMMARY

We have outlined a database system architecture for producing implementations from formal specifications. Some of the salient features of the architecture are

- use of an interactive, generative approach to database system implementation partially based on transforming formal specifications

- the type system and functional logic basis of the ADABTPL specification language

- the extended Boyer-Moore style of reasoning and its exploitation in the database system implementation process

- the data algebra approach to mapping from information specifications to data structures.

We believe that an architecture such as that proposed here, the lower levels of which are similar to the EXODUS approach, is essential to delivering the full promise of persistent object stores. We believe that fully formal specifications and robust mechanical reasoning capabilities are required to achieve acceptable efficiency in systems involving large amounts of complex persistent objects. Without sufficient formal support, object-oriented database systems will go the way of Codasyl systems: their complexity will be unmanageable and render them unusable across a large segment of potential application areas.

References

[1] M. P. Atkinson and O. P. Buneman. Types and Persistence in Database Programming Languages. *ACM Computing Surveys*, 19(2):105-190, June 1987.

[2] J. Baroody and D. J. DeWitt. An Object-Oriented Approach to Database System Implementation. *ACM Transactions on Database Systems*, 6(4):576-601, 1981.

[3] D. S. Batory. Modelling the Storage Architecture of Commercial Database Systems. *ACM Transactions on Database Systems*, 10(4):463-528, December 1985.

[4] D. S. Batory, J. R. Barnett, J. F. Garza, K. P. Smith, K. Tsukuda, B. C. Twichell, and T. Wise. *Genesis: A Reconfigurable Database Management System*. Technical Report, Department of Computer Science, University of Texas at Austin, March 1986. TR-86-07.

[5] R. Bayer. 1974. Personal Communication.

[6] R. S. Boyer and J. S. Moore. *A Computational Logic*. Academic Press, New York, 1979.

[7] M. Carey, D, J, DeWitt, J. E. Richardson, and E. J. Shekita. Object and File Management in the EXODUS Extensible Database Management System. In *Proceedings of the Twelfth International Conference on Very Large Databases*, Kyoto, Japan, pages 91-100, 1986.

[8] M. Carey, D. J. DeWitt, D. Frank, G. Graefe, M. Muralikrishna, J. E. Richardson, and E. J. Shekita. The Architecture of the EXODUS Extensible DBMS. In *Proceedings of the First International Conference on Object-Oriented Databases*, Pacific Grove, California, pages 52-65, 1986.

[9] A. Chan, S. Danberg, S. Fox, W. K. Lin, A. Nori, and D. Ries. Storage and Access Structures to Support a Semantic Data Model. In *Proceedings of the Eighth International Conference on Very Large Databases*, Mexico City, Mexico, pages 122-130, 1982.

[10] J. C. Cleaveland. Building an Application Generator. *IEEE Software*, 5(4):25-33, July 1988.

[11] C. J. Date and P. Hopewell. File Definition and Logical Data Independence. In *Proceedings of the ACM-SIGFIDET Workshop on Data Description, Access and Control*, San Diego, California, pages 117-138, 1971.

[12] R. B. K. Dewar, A. Grand, S. Liu, J. T. Schwartz, and E. Schonberg. Program by Refinement, as Exemplified by the SETL Representation Sublanguage. *ACM Transactions on Programming Languages and Systems*, 1(1):27-49, 1979.

[13] G. Graefe and D. J. DeWitt. The EXODUS Optimizer Generator. In *Proceedings of the ACM-SIGMOD International Conference on Management of Data*, San Francisco, California, pages 160-171, 1987.

[14] B. C. Housel and N. C. Shu. A High-level Data Manipulation Labguage for Hierarchical Data Structures. *ACM SIGPLAN Notices*, 8(2):155-169, 1976.

[15] P. Lyngbaek and V. Vianu. Mapping a Semantic Model to the Relational Model. In *Proceedings of the ACM-SIGMOD International Conference on Management of Data*, San Francisco, California, pages 132-142, 1987.

[16] N. Minsky. Another Look at Data Bases. *ACM FDT*, 6(4):9-17, 1976.

[17] R. Morrison, A. L. Brown, R. Carrick, R. C. Connor, and A. Dearle. *The Napier Reference Manual*. University of St. Andrews, 1988.

[Navathe-Fry-76 S. B. Navathe and J. P. Fry. Restructuring for Large Databases: Three Levels of Abstraction. *ACM Transactions on Database Systems*, 1(2):138-158, June 1976.

[18] B. Nixon, L. Chung, D. Lauzon, A. Borgiba, J. Mylopoulos, and M. Stanley. Implementation of a Compiler for a Semantic Data Model: Exierence with Taxis. In *Proceedings of the ACM-SIGMOD International Conference on Management of Data*, San Francisco, California, pages 118-131, 1987.

[19] M. Prietula and G. Dickson. Flexible Interfaces and the Support of Physical Database Design Reasoning. In *Proceedings of the First International Conference on Expert Database Systems*, Charleston, South Carolina, pages 329-342, 1986.

[20] J. E. Richardson and M. J. Carey. Programming Constructs for Database System Implementation in EXODUS. In *Proceedings of the ACM-SIGMOD International Conference on Management of Data*, San Francisco, California, pages 208-219, 1987.

[21] E. Schonberg, J. T. Schwartz, and M. Sharir. An Automatic Technique for Selection of Data Representations in SETL Programs. *ACM Transactions on Programming Languages and Systems*, 3(2):126-143, 1981.

[22] M. E. Senko, E. B. Altman, M. M. Astrahan, and P. L. Fehder. Data Structures and Accessing in Data Base Systems. *IBM Systems Journal*, 12:30-93, 1973.

[23] T. Sheard and D. Stemple. Automatic Verification of Database Transaction Safety. To appear in *ACM Transactions on Database Systems*.

[24] B. Shneiderman and G. Thomas. An Architecture for Automatic Relational Database System Conversion. *ACM Transactions on Database Systems*, 7(2):235-257, June 1982.

[25] N. C. Shu, B. C. Housel, and V. Y. Lum. CONVERT: A High Levek Translation Definition Language for Data Conversion. *Communications of the ACM*, 18(10):557-579, October 1975.

[26] N. C. Shu, B. C. Housel, R. W. Taylor, S. P. Ghosh, and V. Y. Lum. EXPRESS: A Data EXtraction Processing and REStructuring System. *ACM Transactions on Database Systems*, 2(2):134-174, June 1977.

[27] A. H. Skarra and S. B. Zdonik. The Management of Changing Types in an Object-Oriented Database. In *Proceedings of the First International Conference on Object-Oriented Databases*, Pacific Grove, California, pages 483-495, 1986.

[28] D. Stemple. A Database Management Facility for Automatic Generation of Database Managers. *ACM Transactions on Database Systems*, 1(1):79-94, March 1976.

[29] *A Database Management Facility and Architecture for the Realization of Data Independence*. PHD thesis, University of Massachusetts at Amherst, Department of Computer and Information Science, 1977.

[30] D. Stemple, A. Socorro, and T. Sheard. Formalizing Objects for Databases using AD-ABTPL. In *Proceedings of the Second International Workshop on Object-Oriented Database Systems*, Bad-Muenster am Stein-Ebernburg, Germany, pages 110-128, 1988.

[31] M. Stonebraker. *Readings in Database Systems*. Morgan Kaufmann, 1988.

[32] M. Stonebraker and L. Rowe. The Design of POSTGRES. In *Proceedings of the ACM-SIGMOD International Conference on Management of Data*, Washington, D. C., pages 340-355, 1986.

[33] R. W. Taylor and D. Stemple. On the Development of Database Editions. In *Database Management*, J. W. Klimbie and K. L. Koffeman, editors, pages 263-269, North-Holland, 1974.

[34] S. M. Thatte. Report on the Object-Oriented Database Workshop: Implementation Aspects. In *Addendum to the Object-Oriented Programming Systems, Languages and Applications Conference*, Orlando, Florida, pages 73-87, 1987.

[35] H. Weber. A Software Engineering View of Data Base Systems, In *Proceedings of the Fourth International Conference on Very Large Databases*, West Berlin, Germany, 1978.

Browsing, Grazing and
Nibbling Persistent Data Structures

A. Dearle, Q. Cutts and G. Kirby
University of St Andrews

ABSTRACT

Here we describe a browser that provides a two and a half dimensional viewing mechanism for persistent data structures. The browser is an adaptive program which learns about its environment; this knowledge is stored in the persistent object store. It achieves this by making use of a compiler that is a dynamically callable data object in the environment. Other novel features of the design of the browser include the use of an event–driven software architecture in which all applications are programmed in a passive object-oriented style.

1. INTRODUCTION

The requirement to examine data structures often arises in computer applications. This requirement may be satisfied by a tool known as a browser. Such a tool, the PS-algol object browser, is discussed in [4]. It has proved useful for traversing the data structures found in persistent object stores, often permitting insight to be gained into the behaviour of complex and highly dynamic systems. It has also been of great value in debugging data structures such as the program graphs of the intermediate language, PAIL [3].

In this paper, after an initial discussion of the PS-algol object browser, a new object browser is described. In addition to the functionality of the former, the latter is capable of displaying the topology of complex data graphs. Like the PS-algol browser, the new one is an adaptive program that learns about its environment incrementally. It does this by dynamically creating programs, compiling them and linking them into the running program. The browser also utilises an event–driven software architecture [2]; this architecture and the browser's interaction with it are described fully below.

2. THE PS-ALGOL OBJECT BROWSER

The PS-algol object browser may be used to traverse arbitrary graphs. When the browser encounters an object, it interrogates its rule base to see if it has a procedure capable of displaying that kind of object. The interrogation of the rule base involves matching on type using structural equivalence. If the browser finds such a procedure, it is applied to the object supplied as a parameter. If, however, the browser does not find a rule for the object, it must produce one. This is achieved by automatically generating the source of a browsing procedure for that type of object. The source is then compiled using a compiler that is a first class data object in the environment. The resultant procedure, keyed by the type of the object, may then be added to the rule base. Finally, the procedure is applied as described above and the browsing continues.

The procedures produced by the PS-algol object browser all present the user with a menu that permits the fields of objects to be interrogated. Primitive objects, such as integers, are displayed using procedures written at browser construction time. For example, if an object of the class:

structure *x*(int *a* ; string *b* ; pntr *c*)

is encountered, the menu shown in Figure 1 will be displayed on the user's screen.

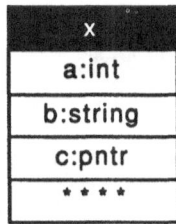

Figure 1: A menu for a structure type.

The structure of the menu indicates to the user the shape of the encountered object. The fields of the menu, namely "a:int","b:string" and "c:pntr", are all light-buttons. When "clicked" with the mouse, the value associated with the corresponding field of the structure is displayed. In the case of the pointer field, *c*, the menu is replaced on the screen by another which displays the object referred to by field *c* of the original object. This process may be visualised by a stack of menus being placed on the screen, with only the topmost menu being visible at any time. The last light-button (marked "****") permits the user to return to the object that was displayed immediately before the current one, or in the case of the first object to finish browsing. This operation is akin to popping the stack of menus.

Such a menu may be produced by the (slightly simplified) segment of PS-algol code shown in Example 1, which may be stored in the persistent store and used by any program. The procedure takes a pointer to an instance of a structure of some class as a parameter; this class is statically unspecified. In practice, the browser will ensure that this procedure is always supplied with a pointer to the structure class declared in the first line of the procedure. The first line of the procedure (after **begin**) merely serves to declare the relevant type, in the local context. The procedure constructs two vectors, one of strings and one of procedures. These are supplied to the procedure *menu* which generates a procedure that will place a menu on the screen at the co-ordinates specified when it is called. The procedure returned by 'menu' is finally called in the third to last line of the example, after checking that the pointer passed to the procedure is of the expected class.

```
let traversex = proc( pntr p )
begin
        structure x( int a ; string b ; pntr c )          ! Declare the structure class
                                                           ! which this procedure
displays.
        let return = proc() ; {}                           ! An empty procedure

        let strings = @1 of string [  "a:int",             ! Declare a vector of strings
                                      "b:string",          ! with lower bound 1
                                      "c:pntr" ,            ! for the menu entries.
                                      "****" ]

        ! Next declare a vector of procedures - the menu actions.
        let procs = @1 of proc() [  proc() ; write p( a ),  ! Display the integer a.
                                    proc() ; write p( b ),  ! Display the string b.
                                    proc() ; Trav( p( c ) ) ,  ! Browse the object c
                                    return ]                ! Return - do nothing.

        let this.menu = menu( "x",            ! The title.
                              strings,        ! The entries - a vector of strings
                              procs )         ! The actions - a vector of procedures.

        if p is x
        then this.menu( 20,20 )               ! Display menu at source position 20,20.
        else Error()                          ! Take some error action.
end
```

Example 1: A procedure to display objects of class x.

3. EXPERIENCE WITH THE PS-ALGOL OBJECT BROWSER

The PS-algol browser was originally designed to aid the debugging of abstract program graphs. Since then it has proved an indispensable tool for navigating around the persistent object graph. However, it does have one major drawback, namely the limitation of only displaying one object at a time. The PS-algol object browser may, therefore, be considered to give a one dimensional view of two dimensional data structures. This has the additional undesirable consequence that, using the browser, it is impossible to discern the difference between the data structures shown in Figure 2. When viewed by the PS-algol object browser, both these data structures will cause a potentially infinite list of menus of the form shown in Figure 3 to be placed on the screen.

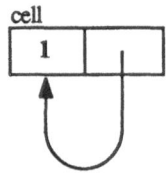

cell

Figure 2(a): A data structures.

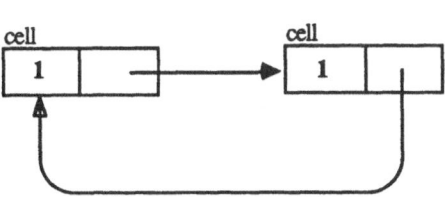

Figure 2(b): Another data structure.

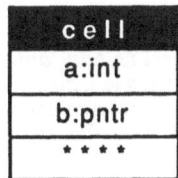

Figure 3: The menu for the data structure in Figure 2.

A more desirable situation would be to present the user with diagrams similar to the ones shown in Figures 2 showing the topology of the graphs being browsed, whilst still retaining the ability to "click" on fields to discover the values associated with them. A new browser, which is the subject of this paper, has been constructed which satisfies these requirements. Before describing this browser, we first describe the event–driven software architecture which the browser uses heavily.

4.   AN EVENT–DRIVEN SOFTWARE ARCHITECTURE

The Event-Driven Software Architecture [2] provides the applications programmer with a number of tools useful for programming applications for a bitmapped workstation. From a user's (as opposed to a programmer's) point of view the most obvious of these is the window manager. The *window manager* provides typical window services to the applications programmer. Another module, the *interactive window manager*, provides users with a menu-based interface to these services.

The architecture also provides applications programmers with an event-driven scheduling mechanism. This allows applications to be programmed in a passive style, each application being suspended until being re-awakened by some external event. The event distribution mechanism is described below.

4.1.   Notifiers

The notifier concept is fundamental to the design of the architecture. A notifier can be thought of as an event distribution procedure. An event, which may be a mouse button selection, mouse movement or key depression, is passed to a notifier, which then determines whether the thread of control should be passed to any one of a number of registered applications.

In most systems, programs are written as active objects. Specifically, they read input by continually polling the keyboard and mouse until an event is received. In a notifier system, however, applications are passive, in that they are called by the notifier when an event occurs which concerns them. If all applications are written in this style, they will never be trapped in busy loops. As all applications are input-driven, a radically different style of programming is required. It should be noted that some applications are not well suited to this paradigm – for example, procedures that get some input, process it, and return a result.

Any application wishing to run in the system must first register with a notifier by passing it two procedures. These two procedures constitute a notification. The first, called *examineEvent*, determines whether an event is relevant to the application; the second, called *processEvent*, is the action required when such an event occurs. A notifier will pass the thread of control to the second procedure if an event is deemed important to the application by the first procedure. When a notification is submitted to a notifier, a third procedure is returned which, when called, will remove the notification from the notifier.

A notifier is comprised of two procedures: an *addNotification* procedure that allows new notifications to be registered with a notifier, and a *distributeEvent* procedure which takes an event as a parameter. The *distributeEvent* procedure permits events to be passed into a notifier. Since the *distributeEvent* procedure of a notifier and the *processEvent* procedure of a notification both have the same type, notifiers may be arranged into a notification hierarchy.

4.1.1. Events

An external event can currently take two forms:

     1.   **structure** mouse(**cint** X.pos, Y.pos ; **c*cbool** the.buttons)

which is the structure returned by the PS–algol *locator* function, and,

     2.   **structure** Chars(**string** chars)

which is used to encapsulate keyboard events.

Instances of the structure class "mouse" are used to encapsulate events relating to mouse movement. The fields of this structure class permit the position of the mouse and the state of the buttons to be obtained. The second structure class "chars" is used to encapsulate keyboard events. This class is provided so that keyboard events may be injected into the PS-algol infinite union **pntr.**

4.2. The event monitor

The event monitor is the only active application in the architecture and provides events to the top-level notifier of the notification hierarchy. An event monitor is a simple loop which gathers all events and passes them to the *distributeEvent* procedure of the notifier at the top level of the notification tree. The procedure that generates an event monitor takes two parameters: the first is a procedure which returns a boolean value, determining whether the event monitor should terminate, and the second is the *distributeEvent* procedure of the top-level notifier.

Once a top-level notifier has been initialised, and some applications have been registered with it, the event monitor passes any input to it using its *distributeEvent* procedure. Subsequently, any registered applications, when called, may add extra elements to the list within the notifier, or remove themselves from it.

4.3. The window manager

The window manager is responsible for controlling a collection of overlapping windows. When the window manager is initialised, a package of procedures is returned which create and manipulate windows within the system. An interactive window manager is also available, which provides a convenient user interface to the window system.

In the system, a window manager is an instance of a structure containing procedures to create windows, delete them, manipulate them within the window manager display area (*e.g.* move them around, bring them to the front or the back), and resize them. The window manager also allows windows to be iconised, opened (de-iconised), and made current.

Unlike most window managers, the window manager does not manage a physical device but a window. This allows window managers to be created inside windows being managed by another window manager. In order to instantiate this sequence, a function is provided to create a window for a physical device. Although this feature sounds rather esoteric, we will show its utility in the construction of the browser.

When the window creation procedure is called, an instance of a window is returned. The window structure contains procedures that allow the manipulation of: the size of the window, its title, the application associated with the window, the style and position of the icon associated with the window, the cursor associated with it, and the graphical contents of the window.

Windows contain a default application — an empty procedure — when they are created; this procedure may be changed later. The system has a notion of a current window, which will normally take all character input, and only the application therein will be active. The current window is the only one whose application has an entry in the notifier; when another window is made current, the previous entry is removed from the notifier, and the new application registered. This prevents the notifier's internal list of notifications from becoming too long.

4.4. The interactive window manager

The interactive window manager provides an interface to the procedures made available by the window manager package. For manipulating windows when partially obscured, a background menu is provided. This contains the following options :

Delete	removes the window clicked on, and its associated application.
Move	moves the window around until another click occurs.
Push/Pop	brings a window to the front if it is not there already; if it is, then it is put to the back.
Quit	quits the interactive window manager.

4.5. The tile manager

The architecture also provides a tile manager which may be used to manage windows. A tile manager has similar functionality to a window manager, the difference between them being that tiles, unlike windows, may not overlap. The panel items briefly discussed below all make use of tile managers to manage the graphical resources they use.

4.6. Panel items

A number of panel items such as light-buttons, choices, sliders, menus, etc. are available as predefined applications. In the browser, we will only make use of light-buttons and sliders. A light-button associates an area of a window with a procedure. When a light-button is selected, the user receives visual feedback: the button is highlighted, and the associated procedure is executed. Sliders also associate an area of a window with a procedure. However, they permit real values to be chosen from within a specified continuous range.

4.7. Menus

The architecture provides a procedure that generates pop-up menus. However, like the procedure supplied by the PS-algol system, this menu only remains on the screen whilst one of the procedures registered with it is active. In the browser, a menu is required that will stay on the screen indefinitely. This kind of menu may be constructed using windows and light-buttons.

5. A 2½D OBJECT BROWSER

Let us assume that the browser is called with a pointer to the data structure shown in Figure 2. Initially, two objects are displayed to the user: a panning tool and a menu representing the first object in the data structure.

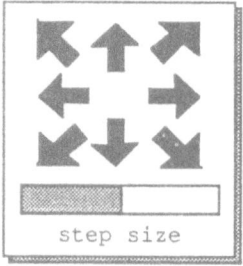

Figure 4: The panning tool.

5.1. The panning tool

Using the browser, the user's screen represents a view onto a conceptually infinite surface. Visual representations of objects are placed on this surface by the browser. The panning tool, common to many applications of this kind, permits users to move the view port around the surface. The panning tool may be considered to be attached to the viewport since it does not itself move when the view changes. The panning tool permits the view to be panned in one of eight directions. A slider is provided in the panning box controlling the distance traveled across the surface each time one of the arrows is clicked.

5.2. The first menu

The other object on the screen immediately after calling the browser is a representation of the object passed to the browser as a parameter. In the case of the data structure shown in Figure 2(b), the menu will look like the one shown in Figure 5.

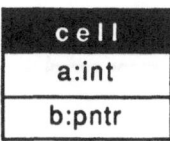

Figure 5: First menu for the data structure shown in Figure 2(b).

Unlike the menus provided by the first PS-algol object browser, this menu will remain on the screen until explicitly deleted. Like the panning tool, this menu has the functionality of a window and may be pushed and popped, moved, and deleted. These functions are provided by the interactive window manager initiated by the browser. The title bar of the menu also provides access to these functions via the first, second, and third mouse buttons, respectively.

The other fields of the menu are implemented by light-buttons. If the field marked "b:pntr" is clicked, a new menu will appear on the screen showing the object referred to by field b of the object. This change is shown in Figure 6.

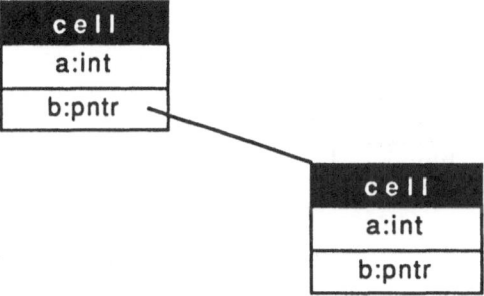

Figure 6: Two menus being displayed showing object references.

5.3. Object placement

At this point in the design of the browser, a problem was encountered, namely where should new objects be placed on the screen. This problem was solved with reference to that paragon of good interface design – MacDraw [4]. In MacDraw, when an object is selected, like so,

it is possible to duplicate it. By default, this causes a copy of the object to be placed to the right and down from the original object like so:

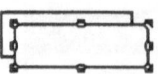

If, however, the duplicated object is moved to another position and another duplication performed, the next object will be placed relative to the new object in the same position as the second object was placed relative to the first.

This object placement strategy is used for displaying objects in the browser. The user may at any time move objects to any position he or she chooses; alternatively if the screen becomes too cluttered, objects may be removed from the screen.

5.4.   Discovering relationships

Another design decision that emerged was how the browser should actually behave. Consider the graph for the data structure in Figure 2(b), shown partially displayed in Figure 6 and in its final form in Figure 7. The dilemma concerns whether or not to show relationships between objects already on the screen and new objects. In the case of this example, whether to draw a line showing the relationship between the second object and the first when the second is object is displayed.

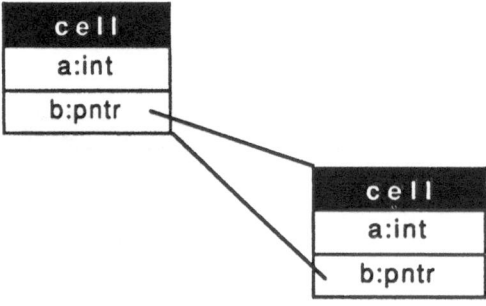

Figure 7: Two menus being displayed showing all object references.

The decision made in the browser was to allow relationships only to be displayed by discovery. The browser does not display object references unless the user has clicked the field that makes the reference. As a consequence of this decision, the user may easily see where he or she has been already.

5.5.   Universes

The need to provide separate universes was recognised early in the design of the browser. Consider a universe populated by three objects called "Graham", "Quintin" and "Al".

Suppose we want to look at all the objects referenced by "Graham", "Quintin" and "Al", respectively. Viewing all these objects at the same level of visual abstraction may lead to confusion, with the user unable to discern which objects are associated with which. Such a situation is likely to arise if the user's screen is too cluttered. This situation may be viewed as shown in Figure 8.

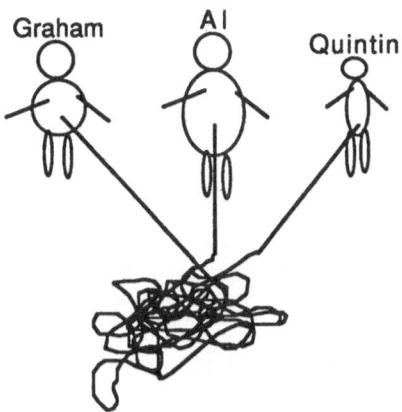

Figure 8: Shared internal references.

A more desirable situation would be for the data structures referenced by each of the objects to be displayed in a new, logically separate universe. Figure 9 shows such a separation, and here it is clear which objects are referenced by "Graham","Quintin" and "Al" respectively. Presenting objects in separate universes makes it easier to compare data structures and provides the user with the ability to logically partition the view space in any way he or she chooses.

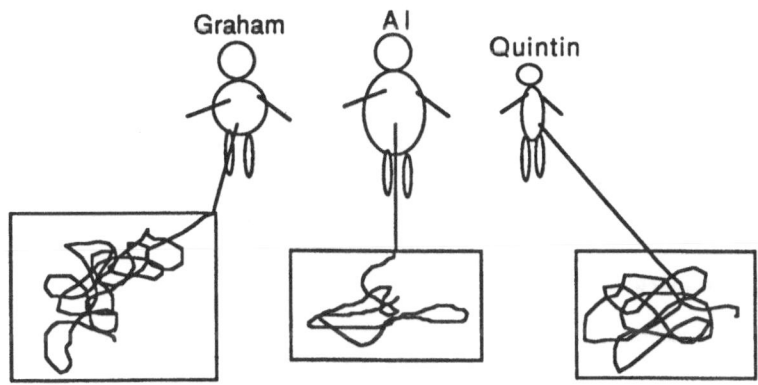

Figure 9: Internal references in separate universes.

In the $2\frac{1}{2}$D object browser, each universe is represented by a window. Like the whole display, this window may be thought of as a viewport onto an infinite surface on which objects are placed. Objects displayed in this new universe may, of course, open up yet more new universes. Figure 10 shows a snapshot of the browser just after a new universe has been opened onto the original data structure shown in Figure 2(b).

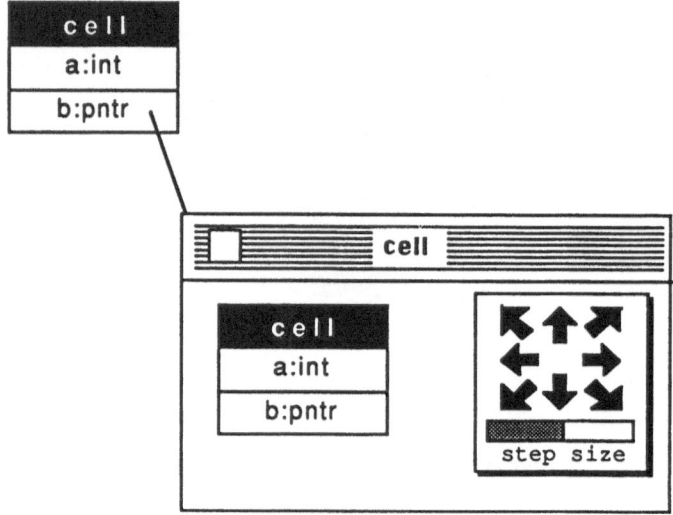

Figure 10: Separate universes in separate windows.

The light-buttons in the menus permit three choices to be made with the three mouse buttons (on the Sun workstations being used to develop the current version). They correspond to: viewing the object referenced by the field in the same universe, viewing it in a new universe and deleting it.

6. CONSTRUCTION OF THE BROWSER

The browser is entirely implemented in PS-algol. It may be considered to be implemented in three pieces: the man-machine interface, the transient visual object manager and the adaptive persistent knowledge base. Each of these parts is orthogonal to the others and will be dealt with separately.

6.1. The man-machine interface

All of the man–machine interface is provided using the event-driven software architecture (EDSA). Most of the components are "off the shelf", that is they are provided by the architecture as predefined applications. The only exceptions to these are the menus and the panning tool. The menus are implemented as windows containing a tile manager which manages the menu entries. This permits menus to be implemented which may overlap, be moved around, pushed and popped etc.

Although the window manager provided by EDSA manages windows and permits line drawing on windows, it does not support the infinite plane concept described earlier. Therefore, a data structure must be maintained by the browser to manage the positions of on-screen objects and the relationships between them.

6.2. The visual object manager

The visual object manager (VOM) is responsible for maintaining information on: the position of all objects on the screen; the known interdependences between objects on the screen; the relationship between screen objects and objects from the data structure being traversed. Notice that this problem is very similar to the problems encountered in constructing a Persistent Object Management System [5].

The objects managed by VOM are arbitrary pointers and windows. It is not obvious how these objects may be sorted, so they are stored unsorted. This means that all the searches for objects are linear. This does not represent a problem since the number of objects in a universe should never be too large. VOM therefore maintains a list of the following structures:

> **structure** keeper(**pntr** object, window, refersTo, referredToBy)

> where

> *object* is a pointer to the data structure object being represented on screen
> *window* is a window (menu) on screen representing the object ·
> *refersTo* is a list of windows referred to by this window
> *referredToBy* is a list of windows that refer to this one

The VOM provides a number of functions that maintain and operate on this data structure. These include:

> *WinOnScreen* which returns the window associated with an object,
> *ObjOnScreen* which returns an object associated with a window,
> *addObject* which provides the manager with information about a new object,
> *removeObject* which removes an object from the manager, and
> *ObjectIsReferenced* which returns true if one object refers to another.

6.3. The adaptive knowledge base

The $2\frac{1}{2}$D object manager, like the PS-algol object browser, is an adaptive program [7]. That is, it learns about the object universes in which it operates. The reason for this approach is that in most programming and database systems, there are a potentially infinite number of types which may occur in the system. This represents a problem when writing a program to browse over them. In general, one cannot write a static program to anticipate all of the types that may occur without resorting to some magic or a second level of interpretation. Generally, object-oriented programming languages avoid this problem by resorting to a combination of conventions and dynamic typing. For example, one solution to this problem would be for every instance of a class to have a print method. This is not a safe solution to the problem since a print method may be overwritten by a method which performs a completely different function.

The browser maintains and uses a table which is used to store the procedures that display particular classes. This table contains procedures, each of which is capable of displaying a different type of object. A representation of this type is used to index the table. Whenever a suitable display procedure cannot be found by the browser, a procedure is called to generate the necessary compiled code. Since the class of any object may be discovered, it is easy (but not trivial!) to synthesize a procedure to display an object of that class. Such a procedure was shown in Example 1. This procedure may be compiled using the callable compiler provided by

PS-algol, and the resulting code entered into the table for future use. This stage is a combination of dynamic linking and memoising.

In a conventional programming system, the scheme described would be very expensive. The traversal program would have to recreate the traversal procedures in every invocation. In a persistent programming language, the table may reside in the persistent store and therefore any changes made to the table will exist as long as they are accessible. This has the effect that the browser **never** has to recompile traversal procedures. The program in effect *learns* about new data structures. It does so in a lazy manner, as it only learns how to display the classes that it is actually required to display.

6.4. Overall construction

The three parts of the browser, described above, are largely orthogonal to each other. The interface between the programs stored in the knowledge base and the man-machine interface procedures may be entirely encapsulated in a single procedure — the menu procedure. The menu procedure, which is passed as a parameter to the object display functions, must be dynamically bound to a particular window manager.

An instance of the VOM must be created for every new universe which is placed on the screen, including the first one. This knowledge is transient and is discarded when a universe is removed from the screen. On the other hand, the procedures stored in the knowledge base are stored in the persistent store and will be kept indefinitely.

7. CONCLUSIONS & FUTURE PLANS

Database systems are notoriously hard to manage. Part of this difficulty stems from the lack of good tools to manage them. Persistent data stores commonly contain complex data structures which cannot be described adequately using textual notations. Tools that permit these complex data structures to be viewed graphically are seen as being a viable alternative. A graphical view of a complex data structure may be used to assist managers of data to visualise the effect of change upon that structure.

Similarly, tools are required to allow data managers to change complex data structures. Writing code to make changes is error prone and expensive. It also requires a high degree of training on the part of the manager. As described in this paper, the browser does not provide any facilities for altering data structures. However this browser is merely a prototype, and it is easy to see how the strategy described in this paper could be extended to permit what might loosely be described as "data structure engineering". We expect to start experiments on this in the near future, constructing programs to change data structures directed by user gesture. This may be achieved using the callable compiler in a manner similar to techniques used in the browser. The data structures required to do this are already maintained by the $2\frac{1}{2}$D object browser.

Software engineering environments also suffer from a preponderance of textual interface tools [6]. In a persistent environment, such as that being constructed to support the language Napier [8], the browser is expected to be one mechanism with which a user may navigate a universe of potentially useful code. With a browser, the user may position him(her)self in an environment containing code to be reused. The provision of the first class compiler will permit the user to construct and compile new code which is bound to the code discovered in the database.

ACKNOWLEDGEMENTS

We would like to thank Fred Brown who co-designed the PS-algol object browser, the inspiration for this new browser; Tony Davie for his motivating comments that led us to start work on this browser; Richard Connor for his part in designing the notifier hierarchy and finally to Ron Morrison for his suggestions on, amongst other things, universes.

REFERENCES

1. Cockshott P. & Brown A.L. "CPOMS – The Persistent Object Management System in C", PPRR-13, Universities of St Andrews and Glasgow, Scotland, 1985.

2. Cutts Q. & Kirby G. "An Event–driven Software Architecture", PPRR-48, Universities of St Andrews and Glasgow, Scotland, 1987.

3. Dearle A. "A Persistent Architecture Intermediate Language", PPRR-35, Universities of Glasgow and St Andrews, Scotland, 1987.

4. Dearle A. & Brown A.L. "Safe Browsing in a Strongly Typed Persistent Environment", *The Computer Journal*, 31,6 December 1988, pp. 540-544.

5. *Inside Macintosh*. Apple Computer Inc. Addison Wesley, (1986).

6. Marlin C.D. "Language-specific editors for block-structured programming languages", *The Australian Computer Journal*, 18,2, May 1986, pp.46-54.

7. Morrison R., Dearle A. and Marlin C.D. "Adaptive Data Stores", Australian Joint Artificial Intelligence Conference – Proc. AI'88 Adelaide, Australia, November 1988, pp 135-145.

8. Morrison, R., Brown, A.L.,Connor, R.C. & Dearle, A. "The Napier88 Reference Manual", PPRR-77, Universities of Glasgow and St Andrews, Scotland, 1989.

Part II

Persistent Programming Languages

Persistent System Architectures

Malcolm Atkinson and Ronald Morrison
University of Glasgow   University of St. Andrews
Scotland   Scotland

ABSTRACT

Persistent Programming Languages are defined as those languages which allow any of their values to have lives of any duration. The first ten years of research into those languages are reviewed. The motivation for such languages has increased. There are significant technological developments pertinent to their implementation. To obtain their benefits requires a radical revision of the architecture of computer systems, and a major commitment to the paradigm. A suggested architecture is proposed, and this paper takes the unusual step of proposing an experiment, which will require considerable resource, to develop and evaluate this new system architecture.

1. INTRODUCTION

It is now ten years since a group in Scotland began the implementation of a persistent programming language. This paper reviews the progress in those ten years, and then suggests the next major step in persistent programming research. The review concludes that persistent programming languages have the capability of supporting applications programs and many components currently thought of as system components. The next step will demonstrate the value of persistent languages as a foundation for system software. It will also realise the target of 'seamless' computing which that research began to explore ten years ago, and provide efficient implementation of this class of languages. Such a seamless system is expected to yield very large productivity improvements for the implementers of large application systems and for the implementers of application building tools such as the successors to 4GLs. This paper indicates the structure on which such a system will be based.

The motivation for and form of our new architecture, and a major motivation for persistent programming languages is an evolution in our view of the total computation system. This is shown diagrammatically in Figure 1.

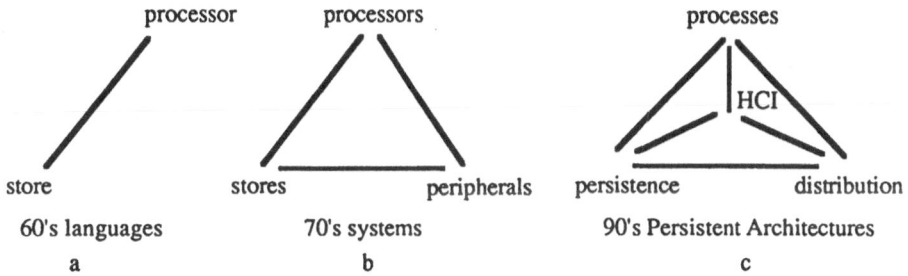

processor	processors	processes
store	stores peripherals	persistence distribution
60's languages	70's systems	90's Persistent Architectures
a	b	c

Figure 1: Views of computation

The view in early languages - such as Algol - 60 is epitomised by the structure shown in 1a. The store and processor were the foci of interest. Other languages had a very limited view of peripherals, but even in the 70's most languages formally embodied only part of the computational system - for example, Ada depends on the definition of a suitable library and conventions.

The operating systems of the 70's, often designed in the late 60's and still structurally the same today (e.g. UNIX™), are based on a view of computation corresponding to figure 1b. Proprietary operating systems are typically more closely based on this view, treating various stores (e.g. RAM and discs) in one functional group, and peripherals in another. This leads to a complex interdependent mess of subviews visible to programmers, for example, backing store is abstracted away in virtual memory and pipes, visible as a store for random access methods, and as a peripheral for serial access methods. But they all interfere with one another when you need transactions.

We perceive and support a trend to view the total computation more abstractly, for example the design of all aspects of the system is (or should be) influenced by the requirement to communicate effectively with humans about its state and actions. In such abstractions, functionality is grouped differently. For example, some aspects of peripherals are now grouped with the previous store functions to achieve persistence (e.g. tapes for recovery), some aspects of peripherals (e.g. communications links) and backing stores have been hidden within distribution, while other aspects of peripherals (e.g. screens and keyboards) have been gathered within the abstraction of HCI. Stores also provide the state for processes.

This trend to abstraction (for most programmers) and the regrouping of functions makes it appropriate to revise the architecture on which the system is based.

We reconsider the major issues in persistent programming from this perspective. Section 2 presents the motivation for persistent systems, and section 3 the general model envisaged for persistent systems. In section 4 we offer a definition of persistent programming languages, and show that they are a subset of database programming languages. We are concerned that some people have used the word "persistent" in a weakened sense, where it is not available to all data types. In section 5 a brief history of persistent programming is given, as a summary of progress and as access to the body of literature. The interaction between programming language research and database research is of continuing importance.

The recognition of persistence as an orthogonal property of languages (section 6) leads to a discussion as to why all languages do not have persistence or persistent dialects. First the issue of comprehendability is addressed and we show that a persistent programming language is intrinsically simpler than the separate language and database system it replaces. The fundamental issues concerning performance are considered and it is argued that if we can make operating systems perform adequately, then we can also build persistent languages of adequate performance.

The radical changes in the way we now view the *total* computational system lead to a different way of dividing up functions and make it appropriate for most application programmers to program with a more abstract model of the *whole* computational process. These ideas (introduced in sections 2 and 3) are amplified in the closing sections of this paper. A suggested architecture for supporting such a mode of applications programming is presented, and, we argue, its efficacy should be tested by properly designed experiments.

2. MOTIVATION FOR PERSISTENT PROGRAMMING

The initial motivation for building persistent languages arose from the difficulties of storing and restoring data structures arising in CAD/CAM research. (See start of figure 3)   Contorted mappings were needed to store program data structures represented as arrays, references and records onto database structures. Similarly, database structures are not simple to map to program data structures. These contorted mappings had a number of costs:

i)   they introduced concepts extraneous to the required computation or data, obscuring code and confusing programmers;

ii)   they did not precisely preserve information and were not subject to type checking, consequently they were a source of errors;

iii)   it was difficult to *incrementally* translate in both directions and consequently more data than necessary was loaded and unloaded per program run;

iv)   there were large computational overheads performing the translations; and

v)   concurrent use of the data was more difficult to provide (partly as a consequence of iii).

These contorted mappings have their origins in the limitations of computer technology at that time. Arrangements for using a computer as a store (e.g. databases) were divorced from arrangements for using it as a symbol manipulator (e.g. programming languages). Constructs which are useful for organising information in a store are relevant to the computation. Similarly, operations and constructs needed in the calculation are pertinent to operations on the store. Design criteria applicable in one context are applicable in the other (e.g. modularity is needed in both).

The loss of adequate typing (ii above) arises in two ways. The transformation from the types in the programming language, to the types in the storage form, and the inverse mapping, are not checked to establish that one is the exact inverse of the other. There are higher level types, not made explicit in the mapping or stored data, and so their conventions may be lost. (The present search for standard data interchange formats, e.g. EDIF, STEP, etc. considers description of specific conventions - higher level types?) For example, in an early system a matrix was stored as a Codasyl set of row records, each row record owned a Codasyl set which held records corresponding to the elements of the matrix.   Although this complex Codasyl structure represented an array, this was not apparent from the data description, and each programmer had to know the transformations in detail. Persistent languages eliminate the first source of loss, and reduce the second problem.   This problem of depending on unspecified conventions is further addressed by data models implemented in persistent languages, but there always remains some structures that programmers may not make explicit.

Persistent programming languages were created to solve the problems enumerated above. They eliminate discontinuities in the computational model, and economise on design and implementation effort by utilising the same concepts and constructs throughout the total computational system. They attempt to give equal importance to the computer as a 'filing cabinet' (databases) and the computer as a 'symbol manipulator' (programming). In any given application it is possible that data or algorithm will dominate, but it is inappropriate for a data centred or algorithm dominated view to be built into a language which is the foundation technology of implementation for a wide range of applications.   In long lived systems, the emphasis may gradually move from a data centred view to an algorithm dominated regime (or vice versa), so that an implementation technology biased to one or the other may eventually prove a handicap

3.   PERSISTENT PROGRAMMING LANGUAGES

Persistence is a property of data values which allows them to endure for an arbitrary time. For example, heap technology is introduced into programming languages, to extend the persistence of data from the activation period of a block to the execution time of a program. This is still not full persistence since there is an upper bound (the execution time) to the longevity of data. It is as important that brief lifetimes (transience) should be included in persistence otherwise a programmer has difficulty with intermediate results.

We identify three principles which direct the provision of persistence [16]:

i) *persistence independence:* the persistence of a data object is independent of how the program manipulates that data object, and conversely, a fragment of program is expressed independently of the persistence of the data it manipulates;

ii) *persistent data type orthogonality:* consistent with the general programming language design principle of data type completeness, all data objects, whatever their type, should be allowed the full range of persistence;

iii) *orthogonal persistence management:* the choice of how to provide and identify persistence is orthogonal to the choice of type system, computational model and control structures of the language.

Compliance with these principles is a requirement for a programming language to be recognised as a Persistent Programming Language. Note that persistence independence implies that the language may not require the programmer to explicitly request movement of values between long term and short term storage. Implementations of persistence must achieve a consistent semantics for data, irrespective of its duration, for example, sharing of mutable structures must be preserved. Similarly, implementations must ensure that the presence of persistence does not weaken type checking.

4. PERSISTENT ARCHITECTURE OVERVIEW

As a result of the regrouping derived from new views of computation (e.g. to organise naming there is just one mechanism, rather than one in file directories, one in program libraries, one for commands, one in programs. Storing files, storing program modules, storing data, currently supported by DBMS, will all be supported by the same storage mechanism) a new architecture for the total system is proposed. An overview is presented diagrammatically as figure 2.

Applications

X11	OOPLs	OODBMS	DBMS	CASE	Filing System	4GL$^+$

Logical Persistent Languages

Physical Control
Tuning & Diagnostic
System for Experts

Persistent Implementation Language

	processors	Persistent Store Support - Large Address Space, Object addressing, Stable (transactional) store	Data transfer Mechanisms

Figure 2: A new architecture for persistence

The lowest level provides mechanisms out of which physical persistent may be efficiently built - e.g. very large address spaces giving object addressing, large physical memories, reliable memories, locking mechanisms, data transfer mechanisms, and instruction execution. We may see this as a development of Massive Memory Architectures [85].

The next level provides the run time support for Persistent Abstract Machines (PAMs) one per LPL required at the level above [47]. These PAMs take care of provision of storage of objects of any size and provision of their type system, their protection regimes, their concurrency regimes and their transaction primitives. The logical persistent languages protect the programmer from physical and storage aspects of the system. They will typically be very high level strongly typed languages, such as those being developed (Napier, Galileo, Machiavelli) and will include appropriate support for bulk and index types.

To cope with failures, to monitor engineering performance, and to deal with physical re-mappings, there will be an interface for experts to access the internal state of these PAMs. It is carefully 'roofed-in' to prevent the direct use of this information in the upper layers.

Application support systems are then built in terms of the LPLs as we describe later in this paper. We believe this brings economies and assists in achieving consistent semantics. These are used, optionally, in conjunction with an LPL to build application systems.

5. HISTORY OF PERSISTENT PROGRAMMING

A recent survey [23] presents an overview of the treatment of persistence in DBPLs, here we summarise the history of persistent programming languages and show the related DBPL landmarks in figure 1, the notes explaining figure 1 appear in figure 2.

Year	PPLs	Relational DBPLs	Other DBPLs
1974	Need recognised[1]	Pascal/R[2] & Aldat[3] under construction	
1977	Design Automation Data Requirements[4]	Pascal/R[2] paper	
1978	Need for persistence identified[5]		
1979	Attempts at persistent Pascal & persistent Algol 68 Nepal designed[6] S-algol[7] implemented	Astral[8], Rigel[9] Theseus[10] proposals	
1980	PS-algol version 1[11] implemented		Taxis[12] SDM[13]
1981	Building Persistent[14] Object managers	Plain definition[15] published	Daplex[16]
1982	Shrines[17] Transitive closure problem[18]		

Year	PPLs	Relational DBPLs	Other DBPLs
1983	PS-algol version 2[19] Galileo[21] EFDM[23] RAQUEL[24] Persistent Ada proposed[26]	Modula/R[20] built Adarel[22] proposed	Adaplex[25]
1984	PS-algol version 3[27] Amber[28]		
1985	Napier[29] design begins Appin 1 Workshop[30] CPS-algol[32]		Poly[31]
1986	PS-algol version 4[33] Persistent Architecture proposed[36]	DBPL[34] RAPP[35]	
1987	Appin 2 workshop[37] Roscoff workshop[38] Methodologies developed[40]		Quest[39]
1988	Napier version 1 implemented[41] DPS-algol[43]		Oberon[42] Modula-3[44]
1989	Persistent Systems track HICSS[44] Newcastle NSW Workshop[46] Oregon Workshop[47]		

History of Persistent Programming and DBPL landmarks

Figure 3

These notes are sometimes abbreviated to citation of relevant papers. Dates used are mostly those of papers on the work which obviously lags by up to 2 years behind the actual work.

1)   [Atkinson 74 a,b, 75, 77] [6, 7, 8, 9] all these mappings to text, relations or Codasyl model proved unsatisfactory.
2)   [Schmidt 77] [87].
3)   [Merrett 77] [72].
4)   [Atkinson & Wiseman 77] [10].
5)   [Atkinson 78] [11].
6)   [Atkinson et al. 82] [13] This language proposal proved too complicated, it proposed: inheritance, block structure, explicit name spaces, nested transactions, concurrency, objects and orthogonal persistence.
7)   [Cole & Morrison 82] [45].
8)   [Amble et al. 79] [4].
9)   [Rowe & Shoens 79] [86].
10)   [Shapiro 79] [88].
11)   [Atkinson et al. 81] [12] Orthogonal persistence for all the existing types in PS-algol.
12)   [Mylopoulos et al. 80] [78] Primarily a design aid in its early form.
13)   [Hammer & McLeod 81] [57].

14) [Atkinson *et al.* 83a, 83b, Cockshott 83, 87, 88a, 89, Brown & Cockshott 85, Brown 87, 89] [14, 15, 41, 42, 43, 44, 30,28, 29] A succession of versions .
15) [Wasserman *et al.* 81] [98].
16) [Shipman 81] [89].
17) Implementation of a POMS: shadow paging via VAX VMS memory mapping by Paul McLellan & Ken Chisholm - unpublished.
18) The transitive closure problem was identified at a workshop in UEA [Atkinson *et al.* 84] [17].
19) Added first class persistent procedures [Atkinson & Morrison 85a] [18].
20) [Koch *et al.* 83] [64].
21) [Albano *et al.* 83, 85] [2, 3].
22) [Horowitz & Kemper 83] [59].
23) An experimental version of Daplex, built using PS-algol [Kulkarni 83, Kulkarni & Atkinson 84, 86] [66, 67, 68].
24) An experiment with building relational databases and HCI using PS-algol [Hepp 83] [58].
25) [Smith *et al.* 83] [90].
26) [Hall 83] [56].
27) Addition of rectangular image types and other facilities to permit HCI programming [Morrison *et al.* 86a, b][73, 74].
28) [Cardelli 85] [36].
29) An intended successor to PS-algol [Atkinson & Morrison 85b] [19].
30) The first international workshop on Persistent Object Systems, held at Appin, Scotland [Atkinson *et al.* 85, 88b] [20, 25].
31) [Matthews 85] [71].
32) First experiment with concurrent persistent languages [Krablin 85] [65].
33) Added to PS-algol: events, exceptions, and the callable compiler [Philbrow *et al.* 89] [83].
34) [Matthes & Schmidt 89] [70].
35) [Hughes & Connolly] [60].
36) [Atkinson *et al.* 86] [21].
37) Second international workshop on Persistent Object Systems (see note 30), [Carrick & Cooper 87] [40].
38) 1st International Workshop on database database programming languages, Roscoff, Brittany, France [Bancilhon & Buneman 88] [27].
39) [Cardelli 88] [37].
40) Methodologies for organising persistent programs [Cooper *et al.* 87, Dearle & Brown 88] [51, 54].
41) An implementation of Napier88 revised from the original (see note 28) [Dearle 88, Morrison *et al.* 89c] [53, 77].
42) [Wirth 88] [99].
43) A design and prototype implementation for a distributed and concurrent persistent language [Wai 88] [97].
44) [Cardelli et al. 88] [38].
45) Proceedings of the 22nd Hawaii International Conference on System Sciences.
46) Proceedings of the third International workshop on Persistent Object Systems, Newcastle, NSW, Australia, January 1989
47) International Workshop on DBPLs, Oregon, June 1989 (follows from Roscoff, see note 37) [Hull & Su 89] [61].

Figures 1 & 2 are presented for two reasons:

    i)   for the new research student in PPLs or DBPLs, to use as a guide when reading into the subject; and,

    ii) to show that there is a considerable body of research into persistent languages which already interacts strongly with the DBPL and general programming language research.

5.1 Persistent Programming: where database and programming language research interact.

As an example of this latter interaction consider the search for effective bulk data types in persistent languages. Bulk data arises because long-lived applications have the time to accumulate large volumes of data which requires organisational models. Buneman and Ohori [32, 33, 79] have explored the integration of relation types with inheritance and record types, using a semantics similar to that developed by Cardelli [35] for multiple inheritance, and first exhibited in Amber [36]. This work by Ohori and Buneman was initiated in the early design discussions for Napier, as the relational type proposed for Napier generated a complex interaction of types [19]. It has led to a proposal for a language, Machiavelli, with extensional polymorphism [34] which they claim exhibits all the properties of object oriented systems, and is superior to Amber in avoiding loss of type information, when an extensionally polymorphic procedure is used. Similarly work on persistence for functional languages [5] is the basis for potentially large scale data structures with optimised access [92, 93]. That method of organising bulk data derives from notations present in Miranda [94] and Orwell [95] and has similarities with FQL [31]. Other approaches to bulk data potentially include facilities for the programmer to define the appropriate type, if sufficiently rich type systems can be defined [39]. In object oriented systems the extent of classes are often the only bulk type. In O_2 [26, 69] there is an explicit set construct, as well as these extents. Leibnitz [63] provides both sets, and sequences with various forms of ordering. There are difficulties in arranging to optimise expressions involving these bulk types, in the context of languages which have objects or are data type complete [100]. The elaboration of this example is not meant as a survey of current work on bulk objects [61] in PPLs, but rather to illustrate the following aspects of persistent programming languages (and to some extent DBPLs) consequent on persistence being an orthogonal property of data:

i)   that it benefits from research into programming languages;

ii)   that, potentially, once persistence is a well developed concept, with good supporting implementation methods, it can be composed with any (nearly any?) good programming language design to yield a persistent programming language; and

iii) that it is the concern of PPL designers to face both the issues of programming languages and of databases and to synthesise designs that effectively address both domains.

These last two aspects are now considered further.

6. PERSISTENCE AS A SEPARATE DIMENSION

'Dimension' is used here, to indicate a property that can vary independently of the other properties of a programming language. We argue that the investigation of persistence is independent of the investigation of other aspects of the language, such as computational model, control structures, type systems etc.

But, if this is the case, why aren't there a plethora of persistent programming languages to match all the non-persistent ones?

To answer this we first consider the questions:

i)   is persistence absent since, when it is combined with an arbitrary programming language, it is intrinsically difficult to understand? and,

ii)   is persistence absent because it is intrinsically too difficult to implement?

iii) are the same effects (and possibly some others) achieved in a different manner?

The first question is the most fundamental, since the understandability of a language (primarily for the programmers who use it, but also for those who implement it) is the most important property of any language. This question is a question about the nature of those programmers. To build a particular application they either have to:

a) understand language X and database (filing system) Y and the interface XY between them, or

b) understand language X', where X' is X with persistence added.

We contend that the latter option is intrinsically easier for application programmers. If the data representation and operations of X and Y differ (if they don't the system reduces to X') then the representation of the same information will differ in X and Y. The programmer then has to organise the translations and movements of data between X and Y. In the case of X' neither these explicit translations nor the explicit organisation of movement are necessary. At present, in both systems, the programmer still has to assist with the organisation of concurrency, transactions, recovery, etc. In both systems problems of scale, distribution, name organisation, etc. may also arise. It is unlikely that separation of the support system into two components will help with any of these additional requirements, indeed, in general, such separation means that each has to be considered twice when using X and Y, but only once when using X'. (Even when using X' they may still be intrinsically difficult factors to specify and implement.) In reality, much of the present implementation of these factors in present day application programming depends on the use of a third support component, an operating system Z, which we discuss shortly (sections 8 & 9).

The two options may be summarised by the following diagrams:

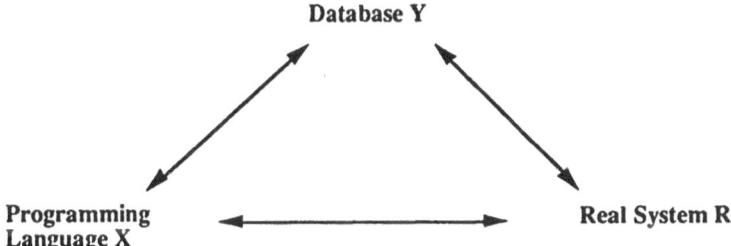

USING A COMPOSITION OF LANGUAGE AND DATABASE

USING A PERSISTENT PROGRAMMING LANGUAGE

These diagrams emphasise the simplification achieved by PPLs. In the former, the applications system builder (attempting to model, administer or control a real system R) is concerned with maintaining three mappings: XY, YR and XR. In the latter, the applications systems builder (undertaking the same task) has to maintain correctly only one mapping X'R. This should be intellectually easier. Not only is the number of mappings reduced, but the possibility of inconsistency errors, where XY followed by YR is a different mapping (for some information) from the direct mapping XR, is eliminated. In general, the mappings have to operate in both directions. A consequence, in the former system, is that mapping X to Y followed by Y to X may not be information preserving. The avoidance of translation and, potentially, the support of type checking throughout the data's lifetime, eliminates this class of errors from the persistent programming system.

Philosophically, we can argue that if there was a case for two support components X and Y, they would evolve to be similar. Both are required to support models of the same set of real systems {R}. Eventually, any feature or concept which assists in building the mapping XR, will prove useful in YR and vice versa. Consequently they will both eventually be based on the same concepts, and there would be no logical benefit in keeping them separate.

The use of X' is neutral about the precedence of data and program. In contrast most combinations of X & Y give a data centred view. Design and decisions regarding the data precede the work on programs, and it is often difficult for the programmer to influence the model created in database Y as a result of insight developed while programming the application. In other cases, where Y is a filing system (which carries very little semantics about the data it stores) the programming decisions dominate. In a persistent system X', program and data have equal precedence and may be designed incrementally, in either order. Practice, disciplines, and methodologies may then choose any pattern of design, specification and construction that is appropriate to the application, without constraint from the implementation technology, X'.

These arguments imply that the addition of persistence to a programming language leads to an intrinsically simpler system to understand, for building a complete application system.

We therefore consider whether the difficulty of their construction and support is an impediment to their widespread use.

7. THE COST OF PERSISTENT SYSTEMS

The question, "Is persistence absent because persistence is too hard to implement?" is interpreted here as a question regarding the cost of engineering to support a persistent programming language. We can review the support of a PPL as requiring three components:

A) a mechanism for translating the constructs in the language into appropriate data structures, including the representation of procedures (e.g. code generation);

B) a mechanism for interpreting (called 'executing', 'evaluating etc.') those data structures; and

C) a mechanism for managing (creating, storing over a lifetime, etc) those data structures.

Mechanisms A and B for PPLs are not intrinsically different from the same mechanisms for other languages, see for example Dearle 1988 [53]. Mechanism C, however, is the focus of much attention, and with the present state of widely available technology raises difficulties. It is, therefore, discussed in more detail.

Mechanism C can be divided into three subcomponents:

C1   The provision of sequences of bytes of *stable storage* in which to store the values that represent the information;

C2   The provision of addressing mechanisms for identifying the sequences of bytes of storage; and,

C3   The provision of stores and interfaces which make those byte sequences and addresses consistently available to mechanisms A and B.

When stated in this form, these may be recognised as components of a typical operating system. For example, the segments of Multics [80] provide such sequences of bytes, and are addressed by segment numbers, and made accessible through an address faulting and paging mechanism. Why then isn't C trivially provided by copying the operating system technology? The reasons commonly put forward are two fold:

i) The populations of byte sequences have different properties from those in operating systems; and

ii) the stability requirements are more severe.

7.1 Properties of Chunks

These differences may arise because the operating system offers the programmer facilities to manage physical mappings whereas, the PPL presents logical mappings. The differences are considered in turn. We will call the byte sequences 'chunks' [15], though they are sometimes called 'objects', as well as 'segments' in the literature. Crucial properties of the load imposed on component C are then:

P_1 the total number of chunks created in the lifetime of the system, which determines the required size of an address based on issuing each with a sequence number;

P_2 the peak population, which determines the required size of an identifier which can only address those extant;

P_3 the peak 'active' population of chunks, which determines the required size of an address (used as an optimisation) to access 'active' chunks;

P_4 the average number of bytes of data excluding addresses per chunk;

P_5 the average number of copies of addresses per chunk, which determines the cost of increasing the size of a representation for addresses;

P_6 the maximum number of bytes plus addresses required for a chunk, which places constraints on the automatic transfer mechanisms and within-chunk addressing;

P_7 the distribution of chunk sizes, which would be of interest if we already knew and had utilised properties P1 to P6;

P_8 the access patterns to, and within, chunks, which is relevant for designing C3;

P_9 the update patterns to, and within, chunks, which is relevant to designing stable stores (e.g. space for after images), locking mechanisms, etc.

These properties have not yet been measured for any persistent system under a 'normal' application system load. When obtained they should be compared with typical values of the equivalent properties measured and available for the segment populations of operating systems. Either set of values may represent intrinsic properties of application system loads, or artifacts of our present immature application building methods and supporting systems. There is clearly a need to compile such statistics, even if they represent a transient in our engineering techniques, before we can argue rationally that persistent systems require different support technology. Until that argument is made, and the relevant support technology explored, the argument of whether support for persistence is intrinsically more costly, cannot be concluded. Meanwhile, some of the partial arguments can be reviewed. Before doing so, the stability requirements are also enumerated.

7.2 Stability requirements

An idealised provision of stable store would ensure that any data given to the care of that system be preserved indefinitely with a certainty that it will not be lost or changed accidentally. Such an absolute guarantee of data integrity is prohibitively expensive, and, in the limit, physically unrealisable e.g. the next event may destroy the store in which it is written, therefore, it must be written elsewhere immediately - which defies relativistic constraints - and the duration 'indefinitely' exceeds the life of the universe. Obviously, stability must be quantified, to indicate how much the consumer will pay to get what reliability. Again the variation in stability required can be compared with operating systems.

In some applications, such as banking, the organisation is prepared to pay for duplication of transactional data in the autotellers, a "warm" system duplicating the actions of the active central system, and a standby system holding duplicates of archives and the transaction log. The operating system for the combined machines (whether written by operating system writers or by a systems team supporting the application) is expected to preserve every transaction that has completed. But the stability is not absolute, customer's key depressions may be wasted, the whole of the data may be lost if a nuclear weapon strikes the city where the bank has its headquarters, etc. After such an event, the state of the data may not be recoverable. In the middle ground, most users expect that the operating system of the 'service' machine they use will at least restore the state of all 'permanent' files up to their state at the last archive (e.g. yesterday evening). At the other extreme, most users of a personal machine are aware - through painful experience - that floppy-discs and hard-discs sometimes become unreadable, and that when that happens they will lose everything they haven't explicitly copied to another disc. Nevertheless, they often go for months without backing-up files that are quite important to them, because they aren't prepared to invest the necessary effort to make frequent archival copies of active files.

In the same sense, when supporting persistent systems, we may find such a range of stability requirements. It is difficult to parameterise these, but the following are suggestions:

S1) What percentage of the data is required to automatically survive a failure of any or all of the equipment at a single site (configuration)?

S2) What percentage of the data is required to be restorable to a previous state after a software accident?

S3) What percentage of the data must be protected from deliberate attempts to misuse it?

S4) If data is restored, how recent a state is required?

S5) What processing overhead is acceptable to achieve stability?

S6) What equipment overhead is acceptable to achieve stability, e.g. should the RAM be built of battery backed CMOS with 100% additional bits for error correction?

S7) How quickly must the data be restored?

S8) How quickly must an error be detected, e.g. in the execution of erroneous software, in order that data it changed may be retrieved?

S9) When the accident is of human origin, how is the part of the data to be restored identified, and how are subsequent dependent changes dealt with?

Most, if not all, of these parameters can have the same range of values in the operating system's requirements. Similar correspondence can be established between operating systems and most other aspects of a persistent language e.g. protection, accounting for and limiting resource use, etc. This leads to consideration of the relationship between operating systems and persistent programming languages.

8. OPERATING SYSTEMS and PERSISTENT PROGRAMMING LANGUAGES

If the diagrams in section 6 are redrawn to show the operating system Z we get the following:

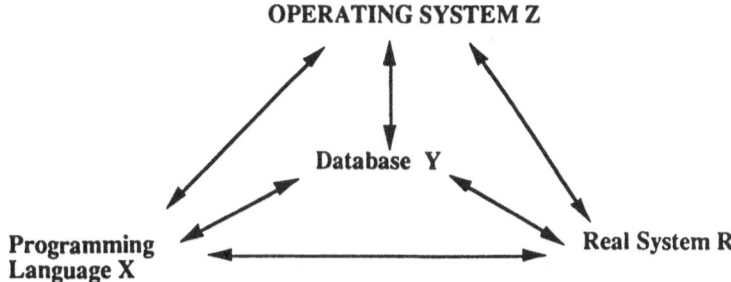

Using a composition of language, database and operating system

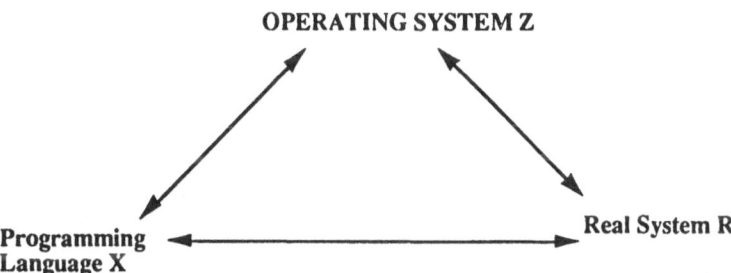

Using a persistent programming language and operating system

The relationships between Z and the other components are not all data and representation mappings as in the earlier diagrams. Z provides functions which enable X, Y & X' to operate, e.g. the ability to execute a machine instruction, to do a disc transfer, or to wait 5 seconds etc. There is a mapping of data across ZY and ZX', as the operating system may make (usually minor) changes to the bytes (e.g. adding framing data) when storing data on behalf of Y and X'. The interface ZR is typically active if R includes people, who then stimulate and communicate with the other components via the operating system.

Again we note that the additional support component introduces complexity. The applications programmer has to understand and use the operating system, while understanding and using the other components X &Y or X'. The interaction between Z and these components may not be easy to understand. For example, if some data is stored directly in Z's files, and other data stored via Y (or X'), then if the rollback facilities of Y (or X') are used to restore an earlier state, the programmer or user will be responsible for explicitly restoring those files to the corresponding state.

Again we therefore propose a simpler system:

persistent
programming X"      Real System R
language

Using a Complete Persistent Programming Language

In this system the functions of the operating system have been subsumed into the new persistent programming language X". The advantage is a seamless world for the applications programmer, where there is one coherent model of computation, not just calculation, covering everything necessary for application programming, in a single consistent framework. The conceptual advantage to the application's programmer is obvious, and there are many more application programmers than systems programmers.

There is a philosophical argument as to why it is likely to be both desirable and feasible. An operating system provides an abstract (higher level) machine,

F_1) Independent of the supporting hardware, e.g. that machine has process creation operations, file operations, character stream I/O operations, etc; Some of the principal functions of this abstract machine are:

F_2) To organise the concurrent execution of processes;

F_3) To provide and manage storage;

F_4) To provide a filing system, including stable storage, naming of long term data, protection, security,and incremental update;

F_5) To provide incremental delayed binding mechanisms, e.g. to bind a program, identified by a file name, to a process, then to bind data, identified by some other file names, to that executing process; and

F_6) To provide a control language enabling users to organise their computations.

But it is also the task of a programming language to provide an abstract (higher level) machine, with a semantics independent of the supporting hardware. If it were persistent then that programming language would also need to provide functions F_2 to F_5 consistently defined in F_1. If that language, as is now likely, also had an interactive (immediate execution) mode of operation, then it could also service F_6, otherwise an interpreter written in the language would service F_6.

Therefore, there is very considerable overlap in the functions of an operating system and a persistent programming language. Furthermore, they are trying to support the same people, manipulating similar data, with similar algorithms, tackling similar applications. Therefore, we would expect the requirements, loads, data properties, etc to be the same. The major difference being the expectation of seamlessness for the persistent programming approach.

If the operating system and the persistent programming language implement the same functions for loads described by the same parameters it is redundant effort to implement both, and it generates unnecessary complexity for programmers. Often the two implementations will conflict and interfere deleteriously.

The subsumption of operating system functions into the language cannot be complete. Certain physical controls, for example, will need to be handled separately as shown in Figure 1. However, all the logical functions of an operating system, as listed above, could be incorporated.

The above argument is only sustainable if we accept a closed world hypothesis, i.e. that entire systems are implemented in isolation within this persistent system. Elsewhere we discuss ways of relaxing that hypothesis.

9. PERSISTENT SYSTEMS IMPLEMENT OPERATING SYSTEMS

Section 8 established that there is a large overlap between the functions provided by an operating system and a PPL. The work of implementing the run-time system of a PPL (we call this run-time system a "persistent system") may be potentially redundant duplication of the effort in writing an operating system. When they are implemented separately they will conflict (e.g. for physical memory space) and present a more complex support system for applications programming.

How should we proceed to implement X" to avoid such duplication? We conclude that the persistent system should be built directly on the hardware of the host machine. The operating system should then be built by writing code in X". This does not differ fundamentally from the approach which justified the design of Oberon [99]. It differs significantly in detail, as it is intended that the functions of X" are much higher level, for example, they abstract over the store hardware, so physical store mapping is no longer a consideration for the operating system writer. Similarly, processes and concurrency may be supported in the PPL [76], so that any residual operating system functions are likely to be relatively trivial to implement. We illustrated the implementation of such a residual function, the filing system [22] in an envisaged PPL. The PPL, X", would already provide the storage, and concurrent access to arbitrary data structures, and persistent name management. The implementation of a typical, UNIX™ -like filing system then requires very little code. PPLs also require incremental binding mechanisms which meet requirements F_5 [24].

The early implementations of PPLs did not attempt to cover the fundamental functions of an operating system. The implementations, e.g. versions of PS-algol, Amber, Poly, Galileo, etc. fall short of this approach. In each case they are implemented **on top of** an operating system (invariably UNIX™), and lose much in potential efficiency by duplication and interface traversal costs. They also fall short in another respect. These languages have depended on the surrounding operating system for many functions, e.g. process creation, and have not provided such functionality themselves. Therefore, they are incomplete and, even if implemented properly, would not provide sufficient primitive functions from which to provide or implement the operating system functions F_2 to F_6. It may be also argued, that the example languages cited have not been targeted at the system writing process, and hence have too many high level constructs, whereas a balance towards efficiency oriented constructs [99] would be more appropriate. This is a moot point, but is separate from the discussion here, since we consider the persistent programming language to be based on any appropriate language design with orthogonal persistence. The inclusion of polymorphic processes within the value space of Napier [75, 76, 77] is a significant step towards providing sufficient primitive functions.

Another group of experiments concern the design of appropriate computer architectures to support persistent systems [43, 85, 84]. In principle, these experiments, which explore new architectures, would build their own operating system and persistent languages. Consequently, they might explore the structure outlined above. However, so far they have not been able to do this, as building the experimental hardware, and getting a minimal system operational has consumed the available effort. Perhaps the project most advanced (in this sense) is the implementation of Leibnitz on the Monads machine [63]. Many of the experiments also seek to build hardware which will support the targets of modern operating systems better. For example, to have much larger address spaces, to deal with distribution, to allow smaller units of protection and store to be economically supported, etc. Such goals will benefit systems where persistence is the lowest complete system supported, as the goals and loads that motivate those changes in operating systems also apply to persistent languages, as explained above.

The arguments given above (sections 7 and 8) suggest that the functions and load on a persistent system and an operating system are sufficiently similar, that we should experiment with new relationships between them.

An operating system and any PPL will only have the same functionality if they have the same target. Each operating system designer has in mind a particular universe of applications {R} (see section 5). Similarly each language designer has a target universe {R}. Only when these two are the same will the two systems require similar functionality. For both languages and operating systems the initial universe of application is usually simple and well defined, though the definition may not be made explicit. Subsequently, partly via the misunderstandings of users, and partly via inconsistent enhancement, the definition often becomes blurred.

The operating system will not then totally disappear. Some of its kernel's implementation technology will be relocated, after a check that it is essential and appropriate, or reimplemented, in the run time system of the PPL. These primitives will be presented within the PPL, so they may be used by all programmers. The rest of the operating system contains either useful or essential superstructure. That superstructure would then be implemented in the PPL using those primitives. Experience with operating system design would then be utilised, in the specification, design and implementation of modules and procedures providing that superstructure from persistent libraries.

This new architecture has some similarities to research into lightweight operating systems where the rest of an operating system has then been implemented on top of the lightweight system.

10. PERSISTENT SUPPORTING DATABASE SYSTEMS

It was argued [58] that the persistent language should provide all the central functions (concurrency, transactions, stable store, recovery) of any DBMS for any data model. Subsequently, it has been shown that it is relatively straightforward to implement various data models using a persistent language which has the following features:

        i)   delayed incremental binding;
        ii) an extensible type system; and
        iii) reflection facilities such as a callable compiler.

Examples of such demonstrations are given in [51, 52, 68, 49, 1]. Experiments demonstrate the ease with which a persistent language may be used to implement an object oriented DBMS [48, 83].

When considered alone, the method of implementing DBMS via persistent programming languages is justified because:

    i)   it amortises the cost over many DBMS of providing the data model independent (perhaps 90% of code) operations (e.g. recovery, locking and concurrency etc.) , by these operations being implemented in the language, which is then used to implement many DBMS;

    ii)   it has been reported that operational prototypes of a new data model with reasonable interfaces have been implemented in as little as one month [50];

    iii)   the DBMS is then portable, since the implementer of the persistent programming language provides the same abstract machine via each implementation; and

89

iv) quite high level data structures, naming systems, transaction mechanisms and concurrency arrangements will become common to more than one DBMS, thus facilitating interworking and comparison.

If the superstructure of the operating system were also built using a PPL (section 9), then it will have common underlying behaviours and structures and hence more compatible semantics with the persistent programming language, and with the DBMSs implemented in it. Therefore, we may expect interworking between the DBMSs and operating system to be made easier.

If persistent programming languages perform as expected, new application systems would be implemented in them. The various DBMS and operating systems would still be useful for two reasons:

i) to accommodate invested effort (e.g. implemented systems, existing skills); and

ii) to behave as libraries of related functions of established utility (abstract data types) for use in the construction of new applications.

The hypothesis that efficient DBMS can be built using a good quality PPL as foundation should be tested for production work. It is based on the argument that suitable optimisations may be written within the language, for example, repeated binding is avoided by calling the compiler, and optimisations, such as transformation of expressions may be performed when preparing the parameters for such a call of the compiler. Data structures, such as indexes can be built using the PPL, or built into the PPL. Foundation work on the utilisation of reflection in encoding updates has been done by Stemple & Sheard [91].

In the interim we see two advantages to using PPLs to implement DBMSs based on various data models:

i) it is sufficiently easy to produce a reasonable prototype, that data models can be readily evaluated to verify their claims that they aid in system design and construction; and

ii) the lower cost of implementing the data model, and the improved ease of interworking, may modify system design and construction behaviour, as people may now prefer to build one application using two data models, each suited to different parts of the application.

This whole area is ripe for further research and experimentation, as better quality PPLs become available. It is especially important to measure the factors identified in earlier sections.

11. CONCLUSIONS

The persistent programming paradigm has been presented as a strong contender for greater exploration, development and use. The arguments for its use in application programming have been presented before, but they are brought together in this paper and made explicit.

The growth in persistent language research and its implementation is shown to be significant over the past ten years. In particular, there are now 9 persistent programming languages in use or under development, as shown in the following table:

Persistent Programming Languages

Language	Status
PS-algol	several implementations in use.
Napier	first implementation complete.
Leibnitz	first implementation nearly complete.
χ	being implemented [62].
E	being implemented.
Galileo	implemented and in use.
Poly	implemented.
Amber	implemented.
Persistent Prolog	being implemented [46, 55].

Exploration of the addition of orthogonal persistence to a variety of other languages is recommended. To aid those who might wish to do this, we discuss the systems which support this. In most cases they now present, at some level, an abstract stable store which could be used to support a variety of languages. There are several attempts to build hardware well adapted to this purpose.

The relationship between existing persistent systems and operating systems is shown to be unsatisfactory. In particular, they represent duplicated implementation effort, and often conflict in their use of machine resource. More seriously, the combination presents an unnecessarily complex environment to applications programmers.

We identify the potential of persistent programming to be considerable. The preliminary research has been done, and the time is now ripe for major research and development projects which will bring it to much wider production use in various ways. The maximum gain will only be realised if we are prepared to totally restructure our computing systems.

The exploration of the potential for high performance persistent systems requires that a new hardware and software architecture be built and evaluated. Such an architecture would be similar to that shown in Figure 2. In particular, it would have an appropriate hardware support for a large scale object store. This hardware may be a modern conventional machine, or some specialised architecture designed to support such systems. Separate projects are required to determine whether such specialisation is worthwhile. The persistent system and PPL would be derived from present PPLs and their implementations, but considerable redesign, development and high performance optimisation is required to make a valid PAM, and foundation for application packages. These packages all need implementing to a high standard. Only at that point, can a typical large scale application begin implementation. When that is operational the engineering measurements can begin. Such an experiment is long term, perhaps 10 years, and involves significant investment, which will include a substantial proportion of routine development work.

Such high cost experiments are essential if we are to explore the potential of different architectures. The persistent archiecture proposed is now ready for such an experiment.

ACKNOWLEDGEMENTS

This work was supported by grants from Alvey Initiative and the British Science and Engineering Research Council and by collaboration with STC Technology Ltd., at both the Universities of St.

Andrews and Glasgow. GIP Altaïr have also contributed to the work at Glasgow. A grant from the British Royal Society towards travel to Australia, helped to provide the time to look at persistence more generally, and the opportunity to discuss it with enthusiasts in the field.

REFERENCES

1.   Abderrahmane, D. Thesis in preparation, University of Glasgow, Department of Computing Science, 1990.

2.   Albano, A., Cardelli, L. & Orsini, R. "Galileo: A strongly type interactive conceptual language", Tech. Rep. Internal Technical Document Services, A.T. & T. Bell Laboratories, Murray Hill, New Jersey, U.S.A., 1983.

3.   Albano, A., Cardelli, L. & Orsini, R. "Galileo: A strongly typed, interactive conceptual language", *ACM Trans. Database Syst.*, 10, 2 (June 1985), 230-260.

4.   Amble, T., Bratbergsengen, K. & Risnes, O. "Astral: A structured and unified approach to database design and manipulation", in *Proceedings of the Database Architecture Conference,* Venice, Italy, (June 1979).

5.   Argo, G., Fairbairn, J., Hughes, R.J.M., Launchbury E.J. & Trinder, P.W. "Implementing Functional Databases", in *Proceedings of the International Workshop on Database Programming Languages,* Roscoff, France, September 1987, 87-103.

6.   Atkinson, M.P. "PIXIN: a network modelling language", IFIP Congress 1974, North Holland, 1974, 296-300.

7.   Atkinson, M.P. "A survey of current research topics in data-structures for CAD", in *Programming Techniques for CAD*, (ed. M.P. Sabin), NCC publications 1974, 203-218 and 297-316.

8.   Atkinson, M.P. *"Network Modelling"*, Ph.D. Thesis, Cambridge University (1975).

9.   Atkinson, M.P. "IDL: A Machine-independent Data Language", *Software Practice & Experience,* 7, 1977, 671-684.

10.   Atkinson, M.P. & Wiseman, N.E. "Data management requirements for large scale design and production", *ACM SIGDA* 7, 1, March 1977, 2-16.

11.   Atkinson, M.P. "Programming Languages and Databases", *Proceedings of the 4th International Conference on Very Large Data Bases,* Berlin, (Ed. S.B.Yao), IEEE, September, 78, 408-419.

12.   Atkinson, M.P., Chisholm, K.J. & Cockshott, W.P. "PS-algol: An Algol with a Persistent Heap", *ACM SIGPLAN Notices*, 17, 7, July 1981, 24-31.

13.   Atkinson, M.P., Chisholm, K.J. & Cockshott, W.P. "Nepal - the New Edinburgh Persistent Algorithmic Language", in *Database,* Pergammon Infotech State of the Art Report, Series 9, 8, January 1982, 299-318.

14.   Atkinson, M.P., Chisholm, K.J. & Cockshott, W.P. "Algorithms for a Persistent Heap", *Software Practice and Experience*, 13, 3, March 1983, 259-272.

15.   Atkinson, M.P., Chisholm, K.J. & Cockshott, W.P. "CMS - A chunk management system", *Software Practice and Experience*, 13, 3, March 1983, 273-285.

16. Atkinson, M.P., Bailey, P., Chisholm, K.J., Cockshott, W.P. & Morrison, R. "An approach to persistent programming", *The Computer Journal,* Nov 1983, 26, 4, 360-365.

17. Atkinson, M.P., Bailey, P., Cockshott, W. P., Chisholm, K.J. and Morrison, R. "Progress with persistent programming" in *Databases - Role and Structure* (Eds. Stocker, P.M. Gray, P.M.D. and Atkinson, M.P.) Cambridge University Press, Cambridge, England 1984, 245-310.

18. Atkinson, M.P. & Morrison, R. "Procedures as persistent data objects", *ACM TOPLAS ,* 7, 4, Oct. 1985, 539-559, .

19. Atkinson, M.P. & Morrison, R. "Types, bindings and parameters in a persistent environment", *Proceedings of Data Types and Persistence Workshop*, Appin, August 1985, 1-24.

20. Atkinson, M.P., Buneman, O.P. and Morrison, R. (Eds.) *Proceedings of the Persistence and Data Types Workshop,* Appin August 1985, Persistent Programming Research Report 16, Universities of St. Andrews & Glasgow, Scotland.

21. Atkinson, M.P., Morrison, R. & Pratten G.D. "Designing a Persistent Information Space Architecture", *Proceedings of Information Processing 1986*, Dublin, September 1986, (ed. H.J. Kugler), 115-119, N. Holland Press.

22. Atkinson, M.P. & Morrison, R. "Polymorphic Names and Iterations", in *Proceedings of the International Workshop on Database Programming Languages*, Roscoff, France. (eds. Buneman & Bancilhon) September 1987, 206-223.

23. Atkinson, M.P. & Buneman, O.P. "Types and persistence in database programming languages", *ACM Surveys*, 19, 2, June 1987, 106-190.

24. Atkinson, M.P., Buneman, O.P. & Morrison, R. "Binding and Type-Checking in Database Programming Languages", *Computer Journal,* 31, 2, March 1988, 99-109.

25. Atkinson, M.P., Buneman, O.P. & Morrison, R. *Data Types and Persistence,* Springer Verlag, Berlin, 1988.

26. Bancilhon, F., Barbedette, G., Bensaken, V., Debbel, C., Gamerman, S., Léclude, C., Pfeffer, P., Richard, P. & Velez, F. The design and implementation of O_2, an object-oriented database system. In *Proceedings of Advances in Object Oriented Database Systems II Workshop*, Bad Munster, West Germany, Springer Verlag, September 1988, 1-22.

27. Bancilhon, F. & Buneman, O.P. (eds.) *"The Proceedings of the International Workshop on Database Programming Languages",* Roscoff, MIT Press, 1988.

28. Brown, A.L. "A distributed stable store", in *Proceedings of the Second International Workshop on Persistent Object Stores,* Appin, Scotland, August 1987, 461-468.

29. Brown, A.L. "Persistent Object Stores", Ph.D. Thesis, University of St. Andrews, Scotland, 1989.

30. Brown, A.L. & Cockshott, W.P. "CPOMS - A revised version of the Persistent Object Management System in C", PPRR-13-85, Universities of St. Andrews & Glasgow, Scotland, 1985.

31.   Buneman, O.P., Frankel, R.E. & Nikhil, R.   "An implementation technique for database query languages", *ACM Trans. Database Syst.* 7, 2, June 1982, 164-186.

32.   Buneman, O.P. "Data types for Database Programming", in *Data Types and Persistence* (Atkinson, M.P., Buneman, O.P. & Morrison, R. eds.), Springer-Verlag, Berlin, 1988, 91-100.

33.   Buneman, O.P. & Ohori, A.   "A domain theoretic approach to higher order relations", in *ICDT 86: International Conference on Database Theory* (Rome), Springer-Verlag, Berlin, 1987.

34.   Buneman, O.P., Ohori, A. & Breazu-Tannan, V.   "Database Programming in Machiavelli - a Polymorphic Language with Static Type Inference", in Proceedings of the ACM SIGMOID Conference, Portland, Oregon, U.S.A., May 1988, 46-57.

35.   Cardelli, L.   "A semantics of multiple inheritance", in *Proceedings of the Sophia-Anapolis Workshop,* Springer-Verlag, Berlin, 1984, 51-67.

36.   Cardelli, L.   *Amber,* Tech. Rep. A.T. 7 T. Bell Labs., Murray Hill, N.J., U.S.A., 1985.

37.   Cardelli, L. "Quest" in *Proceedings 1st European Conference on Extending Database Technology,* Springer-Verlag, Berlin, LNCS 303, 1988.

38.   Cardelli, L., Donahue, J., Jordan, M.J., Kalsow, W. & Nelson, G.   *Modula-3 Report,* Olivetti Research Centre, Palo Alto, Ca, U.S.A. 1988.

39.   Cardelli, L. & Mitchell, J. "OOPSLA '88 Tutorial: Semantic Methods for Object-Oriented Languages", September 1988.

40.   Carrick R. & Cooper, R.L.   *"The Proceedings of the Second International Workshop on Persistent Object Systems",*   PPRR-44-87, Universities of St. Andrews & Glasgow, Scotland, 1987.

41.   Cockshott, W.P. Orthogonal Persistence, Ph.D. Thesis, University of Edinburgh, 1983.

42.   Cockshott, W.P. "Persistent programming and secure data storage", *Information and Software Technology,* 29, June 1987, 249-256.

43.   Cockshott, W.P. "Addressing Mechanisms and Persistent Programming" in *Data Types and Persistence* (Atkinson, M.P., Buneman, O.P. & Morrison, R. Eds.), Springer-Verlag, Berlin, 1988, 235-252.

44.   Cockshott, W.P. "Design of POMP - Persistence Object Management coProcessor", in *Proceedings of the Third International Workshop on Persistent Object Systems,* (ed. J. Rosenberg), January 1989, 51-64.

45.   Cole, A.J. & Morrison, R. *An Introduction to Programming with S-algol,* Cambridge University Press, Cambridge, England, 1982.

46.   Colomb, R.M. "Issues in the Implementation of Persistent Prolog", in *Proceedings of the Third International Workshop on Persistent Object Systems,* Newcastle, N.S.W., Australia, January 1989, 67-79.

47. Connor, R., Brown, A., Carrick, R., Dearle, A. & Morrison, R.   "The Persistent Abstract Machine", in *Proceedings of the Third International Workshop on Persistent Object Systems,* Newcastle, N.S.W., Australia, January 1989, 80-95.

48. Cooper, R.L.   "The Implementation of an Object-Oriented Language in PS-algol", in *Proceedings of the Third International Workshop on Persistent Object Systems,* Newcastle, N.S.W., Australia, January 1989.

49. Cooper, R.L.   "On the Utilisation of Persistent Programming Environments", Ph.D. thesis, University of Glasgow, Department of Computing Science, 1989.

50. Cooper, R. L. & Atkinson, M.P.   "Requirements Modelling in a Persistent Object Store", in *Proceedings of the 2nd International Workshop on Persistent Object Stores,* Appin, Scotland, August 1987.

51. Cooper, R.L., Atkinson, M.P., Dearle, A. & Abderrahmane, D.   "Constructing Database Systems in a Persistent Environment", in *Proceedings of the Thirteenth International Conference on Very Large Databases,* Brighton, September 1987, 117-125.

52. Cooper, R.L. & Atkinson, M.P.   "A Requirements Modelling Tool Built in PS-algol", *Persistent Programming Research Report 54,* Universities of Glasgow and St. Andrews, 1987.

53. Dearle, A.   "On the Construction of Persistent Programming Environments", Ph.D. Thesis, University of St. Andrews, Scotland, 1988.

54. Dearle, A. & Brown, A.L.   "Safe Browsing in a Strongly Typed Persistent Environment", *Computer Journal,* 31, 2, March 1988, 540-544.

55. Gray, P.M.D., Moffat, D.S. & Du Boulay, J.B.H.   "Persistent Prolog: A Searching Storage Manager for Prolog", in *Proceedings of the First International Persistent Object Systems Workshop*, August 1985, PPRR 16, Universities of Glasgow and St. Andrews, 353-368.

56. Hall, P.A.V.   "Adding database management to Ada", *SIGPLAN Notice (ACM)* 13, 3, April 1983, 13-17.

57. Hammer, M. & McLeod, D.   "Database description with SDM: A semantic database model", *ACM Trans. Database Systems,* 6, 3 September 81, 351-386.

58. Hepp, P.E.   "A DBS Architecture Supporting Coexisting Query Languages and Data Models", Ph.D. Thesis, University of Edinburgh, Scotland, 1983.

59. Horowitz, E. & Kemper, A. *AdaRel: A relational extension of Ada,* Tech. Rep. TR-83-218, Department of Computing Science, University of Southern California, Los Angeles, California, U.S.A, 1983.

60. Hughes, J.G. & Connolly, M.   "A Portable Implementation of a Modular Multiprocessing Database Programming Language", *Software Practice & Experience*, 17, 8, August 1987, 533-546.

61. Hull, R. & Su, J. "On Bulk Type Constructors and Manipulation Primitives: A Framework for Analysing Expressive Power and Complexity", in Database Programming Languages 2nd International Workshop, (eds. Hull, R., Morrison, R., & Stemple, D.) Morgan Kaufman, 1989, 396-410.

62. Hurst, A.J. & Sajeev, A.S.M. "A capability based language for persistent programming: Implementation issues", in *Proceedings of the Third International Workshop on Persistent Object Systems,* Newcastle, N.S.W., Australia, (ed. Rosenberg, J.), January 1989, 186-201.

63. Keedy, J.L. & Rosenberg, J. "Uniform support for collections of objects in a persistent environment", in *Proceedings of the 22nd Hawaii International Conference on System Sciences* (ed. B. D. Schriver), Jan 1989, II, 26-35.

64. Koch, J., Mall, M., Putfarken, P., Reimer, M., Schmidt, J.W. & Zehnder, C.A. *Modula/R report - Lilith version,* Tech. Rep. Institute für Informatik, Eidgenossische Technische Hochschule, Zurich, 1983.

65. Krablin, G.L. "Building flexible multilevel transactions in a distributed persistent environment", in *Proceedings of the Persistent and Datatypes Workshop,* Appin, Scotland, August 1985, 86-117.

66. Kulkarni, K.G. Evaluation of Functional Data Models for Database Design and Use, Ph.D. Thesis, University of Edinburgh, Scotland, 1983.

67. Kulkarni, K.G. & Atkinson, M.P. "Experimenting with the Functional Data Model", in *Databases - Role and Structure,* Cambridge University Press, Cambridge, England, 1984.

68. Kulkarni, K.G. & Atkinson, M.P. "EFDM : Extended Functional Data Model", *Computer Journal,* 29, 1, 1986, 38-45.

69. Lécluse, C., Richard, P. & Velez, F. "O_2, an Object-Oriented Data Model", in *Proceedings of the ACM-SIGMOID Conference,* Chicago, June 1988.

70. Matthes, F. & Schmidt, J.W. "The Type System in DBPL", in *Proceedings of the 2nd International Workshop on Database Programming Languages,* Portland, Oregon, June 1989, 219-225.

71. Matthews, D.C.J. *Poly Manual,* Tech. Rep. 63, Computer Laboratory, University of Cambridge, Cambridge, England, 1985.

72. Merrett, T.H. "Relations as programming language elements", *Inf. Process. Lett.,* 6, 1 February 1977, 29-33.

73. Morrison R., Dearle, A., Brown, A. & Atkinson M.P. "An integrated graphics programming environment", *Computer Graphics Forum,* 5, 2, June 1986, 147-157.

74. Morrison, R., Brown, A.L., Bailey, P.J., Davie, A.J.T. & Dearle, A. "A persistent graphics facility for the ICL PERQ", *Software Practice and Experience,* 14, 3, 1986, 351-367.

75. Morrison, R., Brown, A., Carrick, R., Connor, R., Dearle, A., & Atkinson, M.P. "The type system of Napier", in *Proceedings of the Third International Workshop on Persistent Object Systems,* Newcastle, N.S.W., Australia, January 1989, 253-270.

76. Morrison, R., Brown, A.L., Carrick, R., Barter, C.J., Hurst, A.J., Connor, R., Dearle, A. & Livesey, M.J. "Language design issues in supporting process-oriented computation in persistent environments", in *Proceedings of the 22nd Hawaii International Conference on System Sciences* (ed. B.D. Schriver), January 1989, II, 736-744.

77.   Morrison, R., Brown, A.L., Connor, R. & Dearle, A.   The Napier 88 reference manual, PPRR 77, University of St.Andrews, Scotland, 1989.

78.   Mylopoulos, J., Bernstein, P.A. & Wong, H.K.T. "A language facility for designing database intensive applications", *ACM Trans. Database Syst.,* 5, 2, June 1980, 185-207.

79.   Ohori, A. "Orderings and types in databases", in *Proceedings of the Roscoff Workshop on Database Programming Languages,* Altaïr, France, September 1987, 149-163.

80.   Organick, E.I. *The MULTICS System,* MIT Press, Boston, Mass., U.S.A. 1972.

81.   Philbrow, P. "The mongoose benchmark", internal note, November 1988.

82.   Philbrow, P. & Atkinson, M.P. "Exception Handling in a Persistent Programming Language, *Computer Journal,* in press.

83.   Philbrow, P. & Harper, D.J. & Atkinson, M.P. "An object oriented programming methodology in PS-algol", in *Proceedings of the 2nd Workshop on Database Programming Languages*, Portland, Oregon, U.S.A., June 1989, 313-330.

84.   Pose, R.D. "Capability based, tightly coupled multiprocessor hardware to support a Persistent Global Virtual Memory", in *Proceedings of the 22nd Hawaii International Conference on System Sciences* (ed. B.D. Schriver), Vol. II, 36-45.

85.   Rosenberg, J., Koch, D.M. & Keedy, J.L. "A massive memory supercomputer", in *Proceedings of the 22nd Hawaii International Conference on System Sciences* (ed B.D. Schriver), (January 1989), I, 338-345.

86.   Rowe, L. & Shoens, K. "Data abstraction, views, and updates in Rigel", in *Proceedings of ACM SIGMOD International Conference on Management of Data,* Boston, Mass., U.S.A. May 79, ACM, New York, 71-81.

87.   Schmidt, J.W. "Some high level language constructs for data of type relation", *ACM Trans. on Database Syst.* 2, 3, September 1977, 247-261.

88.   Shapiro, J.E. "THESEUS - A Programming Language for Relational Databases", *ACM Trans. Database Syst.,* 4, 4, December 1979 493-517.

89.   Shipman, D.W. "The functional data model and the date language DAPLEX", *ACM Trans. Database Syst.,* 6, 1, March 1981, 140-173.

90.   Smith, J.M., Fox, S. & Landers, T. *Adaplex: Rationale and reference manual,* 2nd Computer Corporation of America, Cambridge, Mass., U.S.A., 1983.

91.   Stemple, D. & Sheard, T. To be presented EDBT 2, Venice, March 1990.

92.   Trinder, P.W. & Wadler, P.L. "List comprehensions and the relational calculus", in *Proceedings of the Glasgow Workshop on Functional Programming,* (eds. Hall, C.V. *et al.*) University of Glasgow, 1989, 187-202.

93.   Trinder, P.W. "A Functional Database", D. Phil. thesis, University of Oxford, 1989.

94.   Turner, D.A. *Miranda System Manual,* Research Software Ltd., Canterbury, England, 1987.

97

95. Wadler, P.L. *An introduction to Orwell,* Oxford University Handbook, December 1985.

96. Wadler, P.L. "List Comprehensions", Chapter 7 of *The Implementation of Functional Programming Languages,* Peyton-Jones, S.L., Prentice Hall, 1987.

97. Wai, F. Distributed Concurrent Persistent Languages: an Experimental Design and Implementation, Ph.D. Thesis, University of Glasgow, Scotland, 1988.

98. Wasserman, A.I., Shurtz, D.D., Kersten, M.L., van Reit, R.P. & van de Dippe, M.D. "Revised report on the programming language PLAIN", *ACM SIGPLAN Notices,* (1981).

99 Wirth, N. "The Programming Language Oberon", *Software: Practice and Experience,* 18, 7, July 1988, 671-690.

100. Zdonik, S.B. "Query Optimization in Object-Oriented Databases", in *Proceedings of the 22nd Hawaii International Conference on System Sciences* (ed. Schriver, B.), January 1989, II, 19-25.

Issues in the Implementation of a Persistent Prolog

Robert M. Colomb
CSIRO Division of Information Technology

ABSTRACT

Persistence in Prolog is both a problem and an opportunity. A problem because Prolog is at bottom a static language. Therefore an opportunity in that there is no impediment of existing language and implementation structures to be cleared away: a persistent Prolog can be developed *de novo*. This paper reports consistent and efficient implementations of dynamic procedures, which make use of a bitmapped index enabling the persistent store to have great flexibility in how it stores data. The bitmapped index can be processed at high speed using inexpensive specialized hardware. The resulting bitmap representation of sets of clauses can be used to implement a logically sound scheme for concurrency control which uses an optimistic strategy and has a fine granularity. Finally it is argued that Prolog is a completely dynamically typed language, probably fundamentally so, but several approaches to static typing are noted.

1. INTRODUCTION

Persistence in Prolog is both a problem and an opportunity.

Persistence is a problem because Prolog is at bottom a static language. There are only two kinds of objects in Prolog: the *clause* and the *variable*. The clause is built up out of *terms* which are constructed from *functions, constants,* and variables. A term is indistinguishable from a clause, so the clause is a hierarchical structure of things of the same kind. Clauses constitute both program and data. Conceptually, a clause is an axiom in logic, and a goal is a theorem to be proved. The Prolog interpreter is a theorem prover (for the Horn clause subset of first order predicate logic). The set of clauses is conceptually static, therefore trivially persistent.

A variable, on the other hand, is conceptually of very limited persistence. A variable is single assignment. Its scope is a single clause, and it persists only for the time its clause is active. A variable cannot be shared between two programs. A virtual memory system is thus adequate for storage of variable bindings.

Practically, the need for a dynamic clause store has been long recognized, and there has long been available in particular implementations the facility to update the clause store, using predicates usually called *assert* (add a clause to the program) and *retract* (remove a clause from a program). These facilities have been treated with suspicion by the logic programming community e.g. [14], and have been implemented in many different ways, with many pecularities. It is only recently that a sound semantics for clause base updates has been developed, described below.

There is therefore an opportunity for developing a persistent Prolog *de novo*.

Most Prologs have a dynamic clause base which persists only for the duration of execution of the program. Gray, Moffat and du Boulay [13] describe a primitive persistent clause store. One of the few widely available implementations with an integral persistent clause store is NU-Prolog [26]. It supports simultaneous read and writeusing the *transaction* mechanism described below. That system and a number of others have a loose coupling with a relational database manager [3, 15, 21].

Atkinson and Morrison [1] put forward a set of requirements for persistent environments, which reduce to:
    Rights to persistence independent of data type
    Data types should be described in abstract data type form
    The persistent data store should be concurrently accessible.
Objects can be bound to type either statically or dynamically: static where possible, dynamic where necessary.

Prolog has no static typing (which in itself can be a problem: the issue is discussed below), so that a persistent Prolog needs only a coherent shareable data store. The remainder of the paper considers first the dynamic clause store, then the issue of sharing data, then typing in Prolog. A conclusion section completes the paper.

2. DYNAMIC CLAUSE BASES

2.1 Semantics

A collection of clauses with the same principal functor, analogous to a relation in a database system, is called a *procedure* in Prolog. The problem of making procedures *dynamic* (able to be altered) has two aspects: semantic and implementational. The problem comes from the fact that Prolog has an inference engine as well as a program text. The inference engine attempts to satisfy a goal by successively unifying with each of the clauses in the corresponding procedure. Several clauses may unify. A clause unifying with the goal may have subgoals in its body, which the inference engine will attempt to satisfy before proceeding with the original goal. In the course of executing a subgoal, the procedure corresponding to the original goal may be altered. The semantic question is *what effect does the change have on the sequence of clauses responding to the original goal.*

Lindholm and O'Keefe [18] analyse the semantics of implementations of dynamic procedures. They describe a *logical view*, where the sequence of responding clauses is fixed at the time a goal is first encountered, an *immediate update view*, where changes occur immediately and are available to goals in progress (regarded as inefficient) and any other view as *implementational* (regarded as generally incoherent). The logical view has a *database semantics* in that parallel goals have the same respondents. They present an efficient implementation of the logical view based on a system of time stamps.

A similar analysis is presented in [10], which presents an efficient implementation of the logical view based on bitmap representations of the set of clauses responding to a goal. This approach is based ultimately on the work of [4,5], where a Prolog system consists of an amalgamation of the language and a metalanguage. A program in this scheme consists of a sequence of commands in the metalanguage, some of which are calls to the inference engine to compute a goal with respect to a *theory* (particular state of the set of clauses in the procedure) which will remain fixed for the duration of the goal. Other commands in the metalanguage permit the manipulation of theories by adding and deleting clauses.

2.2 Implementation

The critical implementational question, deriving also from the inference engine, is *how to identify the set of clauses responding to a goal*. Unification has much in common with a partial match search of a table, the naive approach to which is to perform a linear search of the table. This works well for small tables, but breaks down for large tables, *even if they are held entirely in real memory*. It is much more of a problem if the procedure may be held in secondary storage or is otherwise slow of access.

Most Prologs perform a linear search. Some implementations based on the Warren Abstract Machine such as Quintus Prolog or NU-Prolog use a hash- table index on the first argument of a clause (*first argument indexing*), which is comparable to the use of a primary key in a database and is not effective in partial match. There have been a number of approaches to clause indexing or filtering, described and analysed in [9]. The most promising are based on bitmap indexes, described and compared in [11]. NU- Prolog uses an indexing scheme based on bitmap indexes for database procedures, but uses a standard Warren Abstract Machine implementation otherwise. The WAM implementation uses multiple indexes for static procedures, but no indexing at all for dynamic procedures not stored in the database.

2.3 The Bitmap Index

A dynamic procedure can be considered as a table. In general terms, a table is a set of records, each of which has a number of attributes, each with a value. A bitmap index is a derived from a collection of predicates on the set of records. An example of a predicate is "the set of records whose *surname* attribute has a value beginning with the letter *C*". The set of records satisfying a predicate is represented in bitmap form, similarly to the representation of sets in Pascal. A *bitmap* is an array of bits, one per record. The bit corresponding to a record satisfying the predicate has the value *one*, while a record not satisfying the predicate has *zero* in its corresponding bit position.

A bitmap is a compact representation of a set: a table with 4096 records needs 512 bytes to represent a set. It turns out that in many cases a table can be adequately represented with a small enough collection of (quite abstract) predicates that the space taken up by the bitmaps is very much less that that taken up by the table. A compression of 10-1 can be expected. The techniques are described much more fully in [11]. A bitmap index can be therefore a quite compressed representation of a table.

Bitmap indexing is relevant to implementation of a persistent dynamic Prolog procedure in a number of ways.

First, its compressed size means that there is a range of table sizes (up to a few tens of thousands of records) for which the table must be held in secondary store but the index may be held in real memory. The partial match searches are performed on the index, so can be performed much faster [9]. This range of table size is insufficient for database problems, but is suitable for knowledge bases important in applications typically programmed in Prolog, for example language grammars or rule bases.

Even where the index must itself be held on secondary store, for up to about 100,000 records a linear search of the compressed index is a viable approach [8, 16]. For very large tables, the index becomes unwieldy in its simple form, but there are a number of more elaborate methods of processing the index which give excellent results [16]. The two level method of superimposed code indexing is described in [16] and as applied to NU-Prolog in [25].

Secondly, searches of the index can be expressed as a series of logical combination of predicates, so computed as a sequence of boolean operations on bitmaps. This simple computation lends itself to hardware implementation. An existing inexpensive device developed in collaboration with the author performs a logical operation on two 4096-bit bitmaps at a rate of 100 million bits per second, and a design has been prototyped of a VLSI version which is expected to be able to be able to perform a boolean operation on two 64k-bit bitmaps at a rate of nearly one trillion bits per second. (A 10 mips workstation can perform this operation at about 50 million bits per second.) This special hardware is applicable to the smaller more complex tables typically needed for applications programmed in Prolog.

Finally, objects important to the Prolog inference engine, such as the set of clauses responding to a goal, can be represented with bitmaps. This is the basis of the logical semantics of dynamic procedures described in [10], and will be used below.

There are a number of issues in the integration of a logic programming language with a persistent data store. Bocca and Bailey [3] examine the practical problems in the integration of a logic programming language (LPL) with a relational database (RDB):
    Tuple at a time (LPL) versus set at a time (RDB)
    Data type inconsistencies
    Order of evaluation (not defined in RDB)
    Garbage collection (in the LPL)
    Code in the RDB, making partial match filters difficult

The tuple at a time/ set at a time problem and order of evaluation problems both disappear if the persistent data store is fully integrated with Prolog. The clause indexing techniques noted above solve the problem of code in the RDB. The data type problem is discussed in a following section. Garbage collection is outstanding and will be considered below.

2.4   Garbage Collection

Prolog has two data stores, corresponding to its two classes of objects. Variable bindings and control information are held in (several) stack areas, while procedures are stored in a heap (which may be persistent). It is possible to collect garbage from the stacks [3, 24], but since the stacks are cut back when a goal fails to unify, the benefits of garbage collection of the stacks is limited, and few generally available implementations do it. The heap, on the other hand, requires garbage collection, particularly if it is persistent.

Garbage collection is the recovery of store no longer referenced. The techniques needed for identification of no longer referenced store depend greatly on the methods used for referencing store. Most implementations of Prolog rely heavily on pointers. In particular, the clauses in a procedure are usually linked in a chain. A number of approaches have been adopted to chain-linked procedures, e.g. [3, 6, 17]. The last implementation, for example, permits reclamation of retracted clauses by scanning of a local stack, which is linear in the number of retracted clauses and the size of the local stack.

Pointer-based implementations of data structures are difficult to implement in a persistent data store, since they severely constrain the ability of the store manager to move data around [7]. The bitmap- based implementation described in [10] uses pointers only in the stack area, and includes a set- based garbage collection scheme for the heap. A sketch of the algorithm will illustrate some of the power of the bitmap.

We wish to find the bitmap R of all clauses to be removed. If we know the bitmap D of all clauses which have been deleted and the bitmap A of all clauses which are alternatives in active goals, we can compute R simply by

$R := D \text{ } \textit{difference} \text{ } A$

When a clause is retracted, all the corresponding index predicate bitmaps are set to *zero* in the corresponding position. D is derived from the bitmap index as the set of clauses which fail all the index predicates, which can be computed by *or*-ing together all the index bitmaps, then negating the result.

When a goal is encountered on an indexed procedure, the set of clauses responding is computed by the indexing process, and the resulting bitmap is held on the stack. The bitmap A can therefore be computed by *or*-ing together all these bitmaps.

If the bitmaps can fit into content- addressable memory, D is computed in constant time, while A is linear in the size of the stack. The final computation of R is constant time, as well.

Once the set R of clauses to be removed is computed, the space to be recovered is entirely decoupled from the active program, and can be recovered by means appropriate to the storage mechanisms. The space recovered in the index can be re-used in place, in the same way that operating systems allocate disk blocks from a bitmap of free blocks. The active bitmaps need not be altered at all.

2.5 Summary of Dynamic Procedures

We have shown that dynamic procedures can be implemented in Prolog in a semantically defensible way, and that they can be efficiently implemented using a bit-mapped indexing approach which can in many cases be executed using inexpensive content- addressable memory. The resulting bitmap- based system for representing sets of clauses is shown to be very powerful, leading by way of example to a simpler and more easily computed garbage collection scheme, which is adapted to a persistent store.

3. CONCURRENT ACCESS TO A DYNAMIC CLAUSE BASE

The previous section has provided a persistent dynamic clause base for a single user, but with a database semantics providing a sound basis for concurrency. As with dynamic procedures, Prolog has some specific problems with concurrency which derive from its inference engine. These problems and approaches to their solution will be considered in this section.

The problem of a transaction in Prolog is summarized in [19]. A transaction consists of a series of store updates which are treated as atomic. The transaction is executed over a period of time, and for that time the state of the store must be constant except for changes made under control of the transaction. The store must therefore prevent other users from making changes in the resources needed for a transaction. We first consider the single- process transaction, then the problems of concurrency control.

3.1 All Solutions Approach

Naish *et. al.* [20] consider the special problems of concurrent dynamic procedure updates in Prolog. As noted above, procedures in Prolog can have several solutions. To preserve Prolog as a logic programming language, it is essential that dynamic procedures have a logical semantics. They define a transaction as analogous to an *all solutions* predicate. The *all solutions* predicate is a second- order logic extension to Prolog which computes all solutions to a goal, storing them typically in a list so that they can be further processed. The logical semantics for dynamic procedures described in the previous section ensures that the solutions computed by a dynamic procedure are independent of any changes made to the procedure during its execution.

In their scheme, a transaction is computed by a specially annotated goal, called a *transaction goal*. Each alternative for the goal may contain *asserts* and/or *retracts* . It is possible that more than one alternative will succeed, so that it is important that the duration of the transaction be for the entire evaluation of the goal. The approach is that all solutions to a transaction goal are computed, the set of clauses asserted and retracted collected over all the solutions succeeding, and the updates applied at the completion of the last solution, first retracts then asserts.

Note that there is no provision for update. (Very few implementations of dynamic procedures permit update.) This will simplify the resource locking problem, and is in conformance with [22], who argues for functional (i.e. update- free) databases. He claims they give superior crash recovery control, and better concurrency control. For example, a query is never either delayed or the cause of a delay.

3.2 Proposed Implementation Using Bitmaps

Bitmaps can give a simple implementation of this update strategy. For purposes of argument, we will consider that there is a single procedure. This involves no loss of generality, since it is possible to replace for example the two procedures

    p(a,b,c).

    q(d,e).
    q(X,a).

with the single procedure

    proc(p(a,b,c)).
    proc(q(d,e)).
    proc(q(X,a)).

At the start of the execution of the transaction goal, we will designate by T (for *theory*, following [4]), the set of clauses in the procedure at that time. No changes made to the procedure or its indexes will have any effect on the execution of the goal unless T is updated. During the course of execution of the goal, two bitmaps will be accumulated: A, the set of clauses asserted by the goal, and R, the set of clauses retracted by the goal. We can allow the goal to build the asserted clauses in the store and the index so long as T is not altered. When the transaction goal completes, then T can be updated

    $T := T$ *difference* R *or* A

The actual application of the update is thus done very rapidly.

We can designate the bitmap T as the *current theory*, and keep it as a permanent adjunct to the index, restricting any searches to the current theory simply by *and*-ing T with the bitmap produced as a result of the search.

3.3 Concurrency Control

Penney and Stein [23] describe two basic strategies for control of transactions: optimistic and pessimistic. Optimistic means allowing transactions to proceed until a conflict occurs, then aborting one of the conflicting transactions. This is useful in low-contention environments. Pessimistic means not allowing a transaction to start if there is a possibility of conflict: useful in high- contention environments. They claim that the larger the granularity of structures considered, the more likely there is to be contention. They describe a mixed approach. Following their analysis, an optimistic strategy seems suitable for the present case.

We assume that a sequence of concurrent transactions are initiated at times $t_1, t_2, \ldots$ These times are recorded. When transaction i is started, the (consistent) state of the dynamic procedure is recorded in the theory T_i, and that the updates generated by the transaction are recorded in the bitmaps R_i and A_i. Since the dynamic procedure is consistent at the start of a transaction and the update is performed atomically, all transactions can accept the current theory

$$T_i := T \text{ at time } t_i$$

During execution of transaction i, we will record in the bitmap S_i, the set of clauses which succeed, and will record in a table Q_i the queries made on the dynamic procedure.

When a transaction completes and is ready to commit, the optimistic concurrency control strategy requires checking all transactions which completed during its execution to determine whether any resources used by the transaction have been altered. It suffices to consider a single completed transaction. We will designate the set of clauses retracted by the completed transaction by R_c, and the set asserted by A_c. The present transaction is independent of the completed transaction if

- none of the clauses retracted by the completed transaction are clauses succeeding in the present transaction,

and if

- none of the clauses asserted by the completed transaction unify with any query generated by the present transaction on the dynamic procedure.

In symbols

(1) R_c *intersect* S_i is *null*

(2) No clause in the set represented by A_c unifies with any clause in Q_i

Condition (1) is a simple computation, while condition (2) depends on the number of clauses asserted by the completed transaction and the number of queries in the present transaction. One would expect both sets to be small, with the number of queries somewhat greater. If the number of queries is large, then the queries could be added to the dynamic procedure and the bitmap indexing, possibly hardware supported, used to speed the process.

If the present transaction fails to be independent of any of the transactions having completed during its execution, it must be aborted and retried. Assuming that no side effects are produced by the transaction goal other than *assert* and *retract*, it is simply necessary to restart the transaction goal using the backtracking mechanisms of Prolog. Note that the granularity of the resource locking is very fine.

The mechanism is immune to deadlock since the concurrency strategy is optimistic, and can be protected against starvation by for example aborting all transactions in process if the present transaction is aborted too many times in succession.

As described, the strategy assumes that transactions are not nested. It should be possible to extend the approach to nested transactions without a great deal of difficulty.

The proposed strategy for concurrent access to dynamic procedures preserves the logical soundness of Prolog, is easily implementable, and has a sound concurrency control strategy with a fine granularity which should result in an efficient implementation.

4. TYPES

Prolog implementations do not generally have provision for static typing. One exception in common use is *Turbo-Prolog* [26], which has a type structure similar to Pascal, but is considered unsatisfactory by the logic programming community.

Persistent environments go beyond classical static typing, however. For example, Atkinson and Morrison [2] describe the type system of Napier and a system for secure manipulation of a persistent data store using the name space. The data store has a combination of static and dynamic type binding, and the compiler is used to maintain the relationship between text string and name. This compiler "magic" is commonly used in Prolog to build clauses from input text. It is an important programming technique in the language.

A good implementation of Prolog is essentially a dynamically typed language. Recall that there are two kinds of objects, the clause and the variable. (A clause is a structured object, which may contain variables.) "Pure" Prolog executes by a sequence of unifications of goal clauses with procedure clause heads. The only computations performed by unification are comparison between atomic objects and variable binding. The equivalent of a type mismatch occurs for example if one of the clauses has a keying error resulting in an incorrect structure (e.g. insufficient arguments). The response of the inference engine is to fail unification, a normal occurrence. This can lead to strange behaviour, and the error may be difficult to identify, but at least the program does not execute with incorrect data.

Besides unification, a Prolog program will usually execute a number of *evaluable predicates*, which either perform computations such as arithmetic which are outside the capability of unification or perform extra-logical operations as side effects, such as *assert*. Atomic objects in Prolog are generally tagged with a type. Evaluable predicates relying on type will generally check the type of an atom at run time, and will either generate an error message or fail.

This dynamic typing is in fact polymorphic. Unification performs the minimal checking of structure, while evaluable predicates which can apply to different kinds of objects will select the correct operation at run time based on the object's tag.

Abstract data types are not generally provided in Prolog implementations, but they can be easily implemented by the use of name scoping, as in [19].

That said, still the need is often expressed for at least a modicum of static typing.

Goguen and Meseguer [12] present a full abstract data type design for Prolog built on equality using many-sorted logic as a theoretical base. The structure presented allows polymorphic typing to be represented fairly simply by specifying a minimal set of functionally specified operations required for the procedure to work. This approach is a major modification to Prolog.

Kluzniak [17] defines a *type* in Prolog as a subset of the powerset of the Herbrand Universe. It is possible in some circumstances to compute the type (or a superset) corresponding to a prolog procedure. The circumstances investigated are all for ground prolog, so the scheme has a very restricted application.

Zobel [28] defines a *syntactic type* for Prolog, which is an expression with which any solution to a goal invoking a procedure must unify. A procedure is given to derive type expressions from general prolog programs, with an application to detecting errors (e.g. if a type cannot be derived, no goal can succeed). The type expressions are polymorphic in that types can unify. A procedure will succeed for any goal whose type expression unifies with the type expression for the procedure. The research reported is promising, but does not provide a sufficient solution to be the basis of a practical implementation.

Neither the many sorted logic approach nor the syntactic type approach is entirely satisfactory.

It would appear that approaches based on assigning types to variables are not very practical, since a variable may be bound to any structure, resulting in a large number of possible types in a program.

An approach based on syntactic typing, either declared by the programmer or computed, is somewhat more promising. The compiler would attempt to unify each goal with the type expression of the corresponding procedure, reporting a syntax error if it fails. Difficulties arise from two sources. First, there is no difference between data and program in Prolog, so that any change to a procedure is in effect changing the program code. This makes it possible to circumvent any static typing scheme. Second, the structure of arguments to a procedure may be complex and variable. Consider the extreme case where the argument is a list containing a sequence of tokens input to a theorem proving system. The ideal type would ensure that the sequence were a well formed formula. Static typing is therefore very difficult. There seems to be no way to get around the necessity for dynamic typing.

The best approach in the short run is probably to improve the error detection facilities, perhaps by allowing the programmer to provide annotations, while the long term approach is probably to generate programs from higher level specifications which can be proved consistent.

5. CONCLUSIONS

This paper has shown that the main elements for a persistent Prolog are now available. A consistent semantics for dynamic procedures now exists, and can be implemented in a way that allows great freedom to the store manager yet also allows efficient execution. The implementation relies on a compressed bitmap index which can be processed using inexpensive fast hardware. It also naturally results in a simple representation of set of clauses. This representation can be used to implement a logically sound strategy for concurrency control which uses an optimistic strategy and has a very fine grain of resource locking. The implementation is expected to be quite efficient. Finally, it is argued that Prolog is presently a dynamically typed language, and despite a number of efforts at static typing, probably fundamentally so.

All the elements for development of a persistent Prolog now exist.

REFERENCES

1.   Atkinson, M.P. and Morrison, R. "Types, Bindings and Parameters in a Persistent Environment", *Persistence and Data Types,* Papers for the Appin Workshop August, 1985, Persistent Programming Research Report 16, University of Glasgow/ University of St. Andrews, Scotland, pp 1-24.

2.   Atkinson, M.P. and Morrison, R. "Polymorphic Names, Types, Constancy and Magic in a Type Secure Persistent Object Store" *Persistent Object Systems: Their Design, Implementation and Use,* Papers for the Appin Workshop August, 1987, Persistent Programming Research Report 44, University of Glasgow/ University of St. Andrews, Scotland, pp 1-12.

107

3. Bocca J. and Bailey, P. "Logic Languages and Relational DBMSs- The Point of Convergence" *Persistent Object Systems: Their Design, Implementation and Use,* Papers for the Appin Workshop August, 1987, Persistent Programming Research Report 44, University of Glasgow/ University of St. Andrews, Scotland, pp 346-362.

4. Bowen, K.A. and Kowalski, R.A. "Amalgamating Language and Metalanguage in Logic Programming", in Clark, K.L., and Tarnlund, S-A, *Logic Programming,* Academic Press, 1982, pp 153-172.

5. Bowen, K.A. and Weinberg, T. "A Meta-level Extension of Prolog", *1985 Symposium on Logic Programming,* Boston, IEEE Computer Society, pp. 48-53.

6. Clocksin, W.F. "Implementation Techniques for Prolog Databases", *Software: Practice and Experience,* vol. 17, no. 7, 1985, pp 669-675.

7. Cockshott W.P. "Addressing Mechanisms and Persistent Programming" *Persistence and Data Types,* Papers for the Appin Workshop August, 1985, Persistent Programming Research Report 16, University of Glasgow/ University of St. Andrews, Scotland, pp 369-389.

8. Colomb, R.M. "Use of Superimposed Code Words for Partial Match Data Retrieval", *Australian Computer Journal,* Vol. 17, No. 4, 1985, pp 181-188.

9. Colomb, R.M. and Jayasooriah, "A Clause Indexing System for Prolog Based on Superimposed Coding", *Australian Computer Journal,* vol. 18, no. 1, 1986, pp 18-25.

10. Colomb, R.M. "Assert, Retract and External Processes in Prolog" *Software: Practice and Experience* Vol 18 No 3, 1988 pp 205-220.

11. Colomb, R.M. "Enhanced Unification in Prolog Through Clause Indexing" *Journal of Logic Programming* (to appear).

12. Gougen, J.A. and Meseguer, J. "Equality, Modules and Generics for Logic Programming", *Journal of Logic Programming* vol. 1, no. 2, 1984, pp 179-210.

13. Gray, P.M.D., Moffat, D.S. and du Boulay, J.B.H. "Persistent Prolog: A secondary Storage Manager for Prolog" Papers for the Appin Workshop August, 1985, Persistent Programming Research Report 16, University of Glasgow/ University of St. Andrews, Scotland, pp 353-368.

14. Hogger, C.J. *An Introduction to Logic Programming,* Academic Press, 1984.

15. Ioannidis, Y.E., Chen, J., Freidman, M.A. and Tsangaris, M.M. "BERMUDA - An Architectural Perspecitve on Interfacing Prolog to a Database Machine" *Proceedings of the Second International Conference on Expert Database Systems,* George Mason University, Virginia USA, 1988, pp 91-105.

16. Kent, A. *File Access Methods Based on Descriptors and Superimposed Coding Techniques* PhD Thesis, Department of Computer Science, Royal Melbourne Institute of Technology, Australia, 1988.

17. Kluzniak, F. "Type Synthesis for Ground Prolog" *Fourth International Conference on Logic Programming,* University of Melbourne, Australia, MIT Press, 1987, pp 788- 816.

18. Lindholm, T. and O'Keefe R.A. "Efficient Implementation of a Defensible Semantics for Dynamic Prolog Code", *Fourth International Conference on Logic Programming*, University of Melbourne, Australia, MIT Press, 1987.

19. Moffat, D.S. "Modular commitment in Persistent Prolog" *Persistent Object Systems: Their Design, Implementation and Use,* Papers for the Appin Workshop August, 1987, Persistent Programming Research Report 44, University of Glasgow/ University of St. Andrews, Scotland, pp 68-77.

20. Naish, L., Thom, J., and Ramamohanarao, K. "Concurrent Database Updates in Prolog" *Fourth International Conference on Logic Programming*, University of Melbourne, Australia, MIT Press, 1987, pp 178-195.

21. Napheys, B. and Herkimer, D. "A Look at Loosely-Coupled Prolog Database Systems" *Proceedings of the Second International Conference on Expert Database Systems*, George Mason University, Virginia USA, 1988, pp 107-115.

22. Nikhil, R.S. "Functional Databases, Functional Languages" *Persistence and Data Types,* Papers for the Appin Workshop August, 1985, Persistent Programming Research Report 16, University of Glasgow/ University of St. Andrews, Scotland, pp 309-330.

23. Penney, D.J. and Stein, J. "Is the Disk Half Full or Half Empty?" *Persistent Object Systems: Their Design, Implementation and Use,* Papers for the Appin Workshop August, 1987, Persistent Programming Research Report 44, University of Glasgow/ University of St. Andrews, Scotland, pp 337-345.

24. Pittomvils, E., Bruynooghe, M., and Willems, Y.D. "Towards a Real-Time Garbage Collector for Prolog", *1985 Symposium on Logic Programming*, Boston, IEEE Computer Society, pp. 185-198.

25. Ramamohanarao, K., and Shepherd, J. "A Superimposed Codeword Indexing Scheme for Very Large Prolog Data Bases", *Third International Conference on Logic Programming,* 1986, Imperial College of Science and Technology, London, UK.

26. Thom, J. and Zobel, J. *NU-Prolog Reference Manual* Technical Report 86/10, Department of Computer Science, University of Melbourne, Australia, 1986.

27. Townsend, C. *Introduction to Turbo Prolog* , Sybex, 1986.

28. Zobel, J. "Derivation of Polymorphic Types for Prolog Programs" *Fourth International Conference on Logic Programming*, University of Melbourne, Australia, MIT Press, 1987, pp 817- 838.

A Capability Based Language for Persistent Programming: Implementation Issues

A. J. Hurst and A. S. M. Sajeev
Monash University

ABSTRACT

The Department of Computer Science at Monash University has designed and built a multiprocessor capability based computer system. One of the major tasks now being addressed is the question of language support for this system. It has always been the intention that besides being able to execute the more conventional programming languages, the architecture would be used to provide a persistent programming environment. To this end, a persistent capability based language has been designed.

In this paper, we present some of the novel features and details of the language, and show how it can exploit the capability architecture. The main feature of the architecture is that it provides a data space in which objects can have an existence outside the environment in which they were created (in other words, the basic persistent programming model). This is in addition to the normal data space of conventional programming languages, which can be regarded as a workspace, or transient data space.

The capability language provides an additional data type, called CAP, that denotes a set of values corresponding to capabilities at the architectural level. Variables of type CAP serve as a handle to the manipulation of persistent objects. Additional language constructs provide mechanisms for easily making transient copies of persistent objects and vice versa. Operations on persistent objects can be performed either directly, or by first making a transient copy of it, manipulating the transient object, and then copying it into the persistent object. Such mechanisms are required if we are to have control over the atomicity of persistent object manipulations, in order to preserve the persistent space integrity over system crashes.

However, it is not intended that the language be implemented only upon capability architectures. If such persistent languages are to be used with any seriousness, it is important that they be capable of implementation upon conventional architectures as well, albeit with perhaps lower levels of performance.

As a further issue, we discuss how the capability based language can be implemented upon a conventional architecture, by showing how key features of the language map into constructs that can be (and have been) implemented on an abstract machine, for which an interpreter based persistent system has already been constructed.

1. INTRODUCTION

Persistent programming is a style of programming in which the lifetime, or *persistence*, of a program object is an orthogonal attribute of the object. That is, programs may create and access objects whose lifetimes may extend beyond the lifetime of the program, independently of the nature or structure of the object. Persistence is not a new attribute – programs have employed *files* as instances of persistent objects from the earliest programming systems – what is new is the ability to add this attribute to all program objects.

Persistent programming languages have been proposed [4, 15]. In this paper, we discuss χ [17], a persistent programming language that differs from previous persistent languages in that it is targeted specifically for a capability based architecture. Capability architectures [8, 12, 14] are architectures with the property that addressing of objects is done with a system-generated address, that is guaranteed to be unique, and thus uniquely determines the object. Because of this property, object attributes may be attached to the system-generated address, called a *capability*, and this has profound implications for the security of object access within the system.

Capability architectures are relevant to persistent programming, because they provide unique lifetime names for objects. There is thus no constraint that addresses used within a program must ultimately be relinquished by the program. Once the address to an object is 'given up', it follows that the object itself is thereby made inaccessible, and cannot outlive the program.

However, we make the claim that χ can be implemented on non-capability style architectures, with similar performance to other persistent languages. The basic principle underlying this is that we maintain some form of 'long term address', distinct from the addresses used by the program, and maintained by the system. We describe here the characteristics of the language that are designed to exploit capability architectures, how these characteristics relate to implementation upon one particular capability architecture, and then sketch how the language may be implemented on other styles of architectures.

2. NOVEL FEATURES OF THE LANGUAGE

2.1. Store Model

Because all data objects in χ are first class, and enjoy the same rights and privileges, it is important that the persistent attribute be added in a way that does not conflict with or affect these rights. Thus, the basic mechanisms of data manipulation should be largely transparent to the lifetimes of the data.

Since the programmer needs control over the lifetimes of objects, χ offers a mechanism to provide this choice. We regard all objects as inherently persistent, and are contained in persistent environments in a unified persistent store. A language mechanism (described later) allows the programmer to specify the creation and deletion of such persistent environments explicitly. Operations exist to copy and manipulate objects between these persistent environments.

Hence the programmer is able to create data structures of arbitrary complexity and lifetime, which are independent of the lifetimes of the processes that create and maintain them. This we call the *pure persistence model* of programming.

However, it is not always efficient or convenient to use persistent objects for all computations, simply because of the extra overhead in specifying the persistence attribute. Hence χ distinguishes one persistent environment, known as the *workspace*. References to objects in the workspace do not need to specify the persistence attribute, and for this reason, the workspace may be regarded as an environment that models the conventional store of non-persistent programming languages. The workspace is used as the environment for containing many of the objects relevant to the current progress of computation, such as activation records, process control blocks, heaps, etc., as well as those objects regarded by the programmer as transient. Nevertheless, it is important to note that objects in the workspace should still be regarded as persistent objects.

Note that because the workspace is used to store objects that are relatively ephemeral, we shall sometimes regard it as the *transient store*, in contrast to the *persistent store* used for longer term objects. This distinction is a subtle one, as it is really only relevant when the underlying architecture is unable to guarantee the integrity of the workspace. This point is taken up later.

The rationale for providing the distinguished workspace as an implicit, rather than explicit, persistent object is threefold. The decision to consider objects as transient, by default, coupled with the ease with each transient copies of persistent objects and persistent copies of transient objects can be created make the language pragmatic in the following sense:

Efficiency A persistent object in the system is accessed by a capability. A capability, in order to be unique over the whole address space, is likely to occupy considerable space. (For instance, in the Monash Multiprocessor system, a capability is 128 bits long.) It is not economic to have every object as a persistent object. (To access an 8 bit character object, one then needs to use a 128 bit capability!) This forces each program to decide separately on its temporary objects, collect them together and keep them as a single persistent object. Even those programs which do not need to store any thing permanently must explicitly create at least one persistent object to manage its transient objects. The assumption that all objects by default are transient, saves the programmer from being bothered about the short-life of such objects. Neither are they forced to create explicitly persistent objects when they do not really need them.

Transaction Model The ability to make easily a transient copy of a persistent object and manipulate it preserves the original object from accidental losses due to hardware/software faults.

Portability The default transient objects are equivalent to the objects in programming languages run on conventional architectures. In other words, the space for such objects models the conventional programming space provided by them. This relation allows for easier implementation on non-capability style architectures, as outlined later.

2.2. Easy Handling Of Objects of Arbitrary Structure

Conventional programming languages allow arbitrary structuring of data using pointer variables. But the whole data object does not have a name of its own. In a persistent programming environment, facilities are to be provided for long term storage of data in their original structure. This becomes easier if there is a way to address the object as a whole when needed. χ provides this by defining objects as separate from variables, by considering variables as owners of objects and providing two assignment statements.

All variables initially own NIL. A copy assignment, v := e will evaluate the right hand side expression e, create a new object, store the value of the expression in the new object and make the variable v the owner of the object. If e is a variable, the copy assignment will make v own a newly created copy of the object owned by e; the object may be a linked structure, and the new object will be a copy of the whole structure. On the other hand, a share assignment v1 <- v2 (where v1 and v2 are variables) will make v1 share the ownership of the object of v2. In [16], it is shown how these concepts simplify the handling of objects with any arbitrary structure.

2.3. Persistent Objects and Capability Variables

χ, by default, regards all objects as transient. That is, their lifetimes do not extend beyond that of the environment in which they were created. On the other hand, persistent objects are those whose lifetimes do extend beyond the lifetime of the program. They are accessed using *capabilities*. Capabilities are unique unforgeable keys to objects, and define a set of access rights to the objects. In χ, variables of type CAP own capabilities. Capability assignments have semantics similar to other assignments. A share assignment involving two capability variables makes both variables own the same capability. A copy assignment involving two capability variables derives a new capability for the LHS variable to own. The derived capability has access to the same object as the RHS capability's object, but with a set of rights no greater than those of the original rights.

A copy assignment with a variable of arbitrary type on the LHS and a CAP type variable on the RHS creates a transient copy of the persistent object (whose capability is owned by the RHS variable) for the LHS variable to own. A copy assignment with a CAP type variable on LHS and an arbitrary type variable on RHS copies the LHS object into the persistent object represented by the RHS capability. If the capability is NIL, a new object is created.

A THRU construct provides for direct manipulation of object in the persistent space itself. The syntax is THRU v : t <- c : *statements* END THRU. The changes made to the persistent object whose capability is owned by c, through the variable v (called the *thru-variable*) will be reflected in the persistent object. The type of v must be compatible with that of the persistent object. (See next section.) A new persistent object is created if c owns NIL.

There is one restriction in using THRU:

> Inside a THRU block, a share assignment cannot have a variable declared outside the block on one side and a variable declared inside the block on the other side.

This restriction prevents the same area from being shared by two or more persistent objects. This is needed for the following reason. In a capability based system, persistent objects are mutually independent objects accessed using capabilities. They cannot share common areas. This does not exclude one object storing a capability in another object and giving indirect access. Let us explain it with an example. Suppose a user has a capability with read/write privileges to a persistent object P, and a read capability to another object Q. Since the user has a read capability to Q, it can create a link from P to a part of Q. Once this link is established, that part of Q has become a part of the object P as well. Now, since the user has a read/write capability to P, it is possible to write into that part. So, in effect, the user is writing into a part of object Q, even though, a write privilege to that object was not held. A capability based protection mechanism will normally result in a run time error when such a write occurs. This is a *surprise* to the user, since the attempt to write is made using a capability with write privilege (that of object P). χ, adhering to the *Law of Least Astonishment* [9], avoids this situation by imposing the above restriction.

2.4. Types

The language is strongly typed. The type of an object is the type of the variable which owned the object when it was created. The type of a persistent object is the type of the variable which owned the transient copy of the object from which the persistent object is created, or the type of the thru-variable which owned the persistent object when it was created (the latter, in case of direct access).

A variable v can own an object p (ie., variable v's type is compatible with object p's type) if

1. p is the same or a copy of an existing object q such that:
   either the variable v's type-name and object q's type-name are the same and variable v's type-structure and object q's type structure are same,
   or variable v's type is anonymous and has the same or a subordinate structure with respect to that of object q.

2. p is an object which resulted from the evaluation of an expression whose type is the same as that of variable v.

2.5. Processes, Operations and Procedures

χ's parallel programming features are based on the client/server model. A process can provide operations to be invoked by other processes. Processes communicate by invoking operations. Operations can be invoked by either SEND or CALL. If an operation is invoked by SEND, the invoker process continues with its execution [3]. On the other hand, a CALL invocation blocks the invoker till the call returns. Processes can be dynamically instantiated. Operations can be instantiated from procedures by providing the environment arguments. Processes, their instances, procedures and operations are all objects which can be made persistent if needed.

The process body is divided into three units [18].

1. The (mandatory) functional unit,
2. the (optional) synchronization unit,
3. the (optional) scheduling unit.

The functional unit describes the *resource* implemented by the process in terms of the data structures and operations applicable to it.

If the process acts as a server, then the synchronization unit would specify the conditions under which invocations to operations are accepted for execution.

The scheduling unit describes the priority relationship among the operation invocations.

The synchronization is specified using ACCEPT statements whose semantics is similar to the SELECT-WHEN-ACCEPT statements of Ada[1] [1].

The syntax is:

```
ACCEPT  guard :  OpName ;  statements
{ OR  guard :  OpName ;  statements }
END ACCEPT
```

where *guard* is a boolean expression, and *OpName* is an operation variable which is assigned an operation body in the functional part. The *statements* in the ACCEPT-syntax are statements related to the synchronization (for instance, to change the values of the guard). The control waits at an ACCEPT-statement till there is an invocation for an

---

[1] Ada is a trade mark of the U.S. Government, Ada Joint Program Office

operation corresponding to a true guard. Then that operation is executed followed by the synchronization statements. If there are more than one qualified operation, the choice is made non-deterministically.

The scheduling is specified using PREFER and PICK statements. The syntax of PREFER statement is:

```
PREFER  SchedGuard :  OpSet ;  statements
{ THEN  SchedGuard :  OpSet ;  statements }
END PREFER
```

where *OpSet* is a collection of *OpNames* separated by commas.

The PREFER statement lists the operations in order of decreasing preference. The first *OpSet* in the list with a true guard will be preferred to all the *OpSets* which come after it. Preference in this context means the following. If any of the operations in that set is eligible to be accepted by the synchronization unit, and there are invocations to at least one such operation, then it must be scheduled first. Otherwise, preference is given to another *OpSet* which comes after it and satisfies the above conditions. If all the guards are false then all *acceptable* operation invocations are scheduled. The ACCEPT statement can accept any one of them at random.

The syntax of PICK statement is similar to that of PREFER (obtained by replacing PREFER with PICK), but the semantics is different. The PICK statement expresses the priority relationship among the operations. *Priority* means the following. If there is an invocation for a higher priority operation, then all low priority operation-invocations will be kept pending till the high priority operation is executed. The PICK statement lists the operations in the order of decreasing priority. Invocations to the first *OpSet* with a true guard will be scheduled and invocations to no other *OpSets* in the same PICK statement will be scheduled, irrespective of whether the former are *acceptable* or not. Invocations to all *OpSets* get equal priority if no guard holds.

The scheduling statements which follow an *OpSet* are executed whenever an invocation to an operation in that *OpSet* is accepted for execution. These statements can be used to change the priority relationship. The statements in the scheduling unit have read-only access to variables of the sequential unit and the input parameters of the invocations. The scheduling unit can also declare variables for its own use.

A special variable, #p is available to the scheduling unit which gives the number of pending invocations for the specified operation p at any time.

One important thing to be pointed out is that the guard in the scheduling unit can be either a boolean expression or an arithmetic expression. If it is an arithmetic expression, then the invocations (among the many possible invocations of the same *OpSet*) which yield the least value of the arithmetic expression are scheduled.

Reference [18] gives examples and formal definitions of these constructs.

Procedure-parameter-passing-paradigm is used as a universal way of transferring objects between processes, or from operations to callers. This avoids the need of extra export/import statements, separate definition/description areas for processes, and is similar to the modularization mechanism available in PS-algol [5]. The process heading (which is similar to a procedure heading) shows the input (import) and output (export) parameters.

3. EXPLOITING THE CAPABILITY ARCHITECTURE

We explain briefly what the architecture provides and how that can be made use of in implementing the constructs of the language.

3.1. Description of the Capability Architecture

The multiprocessor system of Anderson, Pose and Wallace [2] organizes the memory available as a single virtual address space. Objects can be created in that space. For each object created, the system returns a 128 bit password capability. While creating the object, users specify the size of the object. (A data object can be viewed as a consecutive block of memory.) They also specify the right that the capability produced should have to the object. Object size can be changed.

An object is not dependent on others. That means that the same area cannot be part of two objects at the same time. Of course, an object can hold a capability to another object and thus effectively point to it. New capabilities can be derived from the original master capability.

3.1.1. Accessing an object   The logical address space for a process is divided into 32 windows of 512k words each. A persistent object must be loaded into one of the windows before accessing it. That means a process can manipulate at most 32 different objects at a time. To access an object, a kernel routine is called giving the capability and the window number on to which the object is to be loaded.

Changes made to a persistent object (loaded into a window) are visible by any process who has loaded the same persistent object into one of its windows.

A process object can be instantiated to create an instance, called a state object. It can be suspended or killed. Process instances (ie., state objects), like any other object, are persistent with capabilities provided.

A primitive message passing mechanism is available which processes can use to send and receive messages. The sender process keeps the message in a message block in the sender's logical address space and invokes the send kernel call with the capability of the receiver process and the address of the area of the message. The size of the message block is determined by the system. The call copies the message into the receiver's message buffer.

Similarly a receive kernel call copies a message (if any) in the message buffer to the process's logical address space. There is also a wait call which will suspend the process till a message arrives.

The multiprocessor also has an extensive "money based economic system", which is not described here. (See [2].)

3.2. Implementation of the Language on the Multiprocessor Architecture

In this section we shall discuss the implementation schema of important aspects of the language in the multiprocessor system.

3.2.1. Type Compatibility Checking   Type compatibility checking is mostly done at compile time. Run time type checking is needed only at the points where a persistent object is first accessed. There are three situations where this occurs.

 1. A variable can own a transient copy of a persistent object only if the variable's type is compatible with the persistent object's type.

2. A transient object owned by a variable can be copied into an existing persistent object, only if the transient object's type matches with the persistent object's type.

3. A persistent object can be accessed directly only if the type of the thru-variable matches the type of the persistent object.

As a result, run time type checking is needed in the transient to persistent and vice versa copy statements, as well as on entry to a THRU statement. All other statements are type-checked at compile time.

To provide for run time type checking, every persistent object must store its type information. We store this as a string encoding the structure. The header of every persistent object has a pointer to such a string (see Table 1). The code generated for accessing a persistent object (loading it into a window of the process) involves a call to a type checker where the type checker is supplied with the encoded type string of the variable involved. Type compatibility is determined by matching the supplied string with the type-string stored in the persistent object (taking into account that the string supplied can represent a sub-structure of the object's type).

Since run time type checking is needed only rarely, we believe that pattern matching for type checking would not affect the system behaviour adversely. Note that it is to be done only at the *entry point* of a direct access of the persistent object, or while making transient copy of a persistent object, or a persistent copy of a transient object.

3.2.2. Copying Objects Copying objects as a whole is a rule rather than an exception in χ. An algorithm for creating such copies, taking into account the possibility of cycles, is given in Knuth [11].

Even though at the language level objects are separate from variables, it is not necessary to implement them that way for simple types. Instead of creating an object, storing the value inside it and storing the address of the object in the variable, for simple types, the value itself can be stored in the location reserved for variable. Therefore, both the copy assignments and share assignments of simple types copy the value inside the RHS variable into the LHS variable. For compound types, the variable stores the address of the object. A share assignment involving compound objects is translated into copying the address in the RHS variable to the LHS variable. A copy assignment, on the other hand, will invoke the copy procedure for creating a new copy of the RHS variable's object.

3.2.3. Space for Transient Objects A single persistent object is reserved to allocate space for all transient objects. (Note that, from the architecture's point of view, an object is a contiguous section of memory locations.) Naturally, the capability of this space is not available to the user. A process when instantiated loads this object into a predefined window, the window-number being the same in all processes. This removes the need of adjusting the addresses of transient objects. (See Section 3.2.8.) Whenever a process terminates, it invokes a garbage collection process, which runs in parallel to regain the space used by the transient objects of the terminating process.

Note that processes are free to create objects within the transient space, and pass them as share parameters or results to other processes. Since such objects are subject to reclamation, some form of management (such as reference counting) is required. On the Monash Multiprocessor system, such management is provided through derived capabilities. A derived capability can give access to a *view* or *window* of a larger object (such as the transient object). These views restrict the accessible areas to an arbitrary (contiguous) part of the original object [13]. This is helpful when the When the object is garbage collected, the derived capability is revoked, thus outlawing subsequent attempts to access the object. It is the programmer's responsibility to make such objects persistent if they are required beyond the lifetime of the creating process.

3.2.4. The Persistent Space

The persistent management routines are used when a persistent object is accessed or created directly in the persistent space, in a transient to persistent copy, or in a persistent to transient copy. A persistent object in its first location stores a header with the information shown in Table 1:

Item	Type	Description
type_info	pointer	Points to type description as a string
startp	pointer	Points to the actual data
freep	pointer	Points to the free space

Table 1

3.2.5. Persistent to Transient Copy

An assignment v := c (v of any type, c of type CAP) results in a call to a *p_to_t_copy* routine. The capability with c and the type information of v are supplied as parameters. The routine creates a copy of the persistent object represented by the capability in the space for transient objects and returns the address of that transient object. (Note that if the variable is of simple type, no object creation takes place; the value and not the address is returned, which in any case goes into the location for the variable.) It results in a run time error if the capability is NIL, if the capability does not have a read right, or if the type information supplied is not compatible with the type information stored in the header of the persistent object.

3.2.6. Transient to Persistent Copy

An assignment c := v results in a call to a *t_to_p_copy* routine. The input parameters are the capability with c , the rights and the type information of v and the address of the object owned by v. The routine checks whether c is NIL. If it is NIL, it invokes a kernel call to create a new object with the rights specified (the default is all possible rights). The new object thus created is loaded into a window and the header is initialized including the type information. The object owned by v is copied into the new object. This is done by the same copy algorithm. The only change needed is to initialize the area for memory-allocation so that allocation routines will allocate memory from the new persistent object. After copying, the allocation area is reinitialized to the original one. The new capability is returned. If the capability is not NIL, then the routine loads the existing persistent object into a window, checks for type compatibility and copies, as in the previous case, the object owned by the variable v.

3.2.7. Accessing in the Persistent Space

A persistent object is accessed without copying by using a THRU statement. At the entrance of the statement (ie., THRU v : t <- c :), an *alias_p_object* routine is called. The capability owned by c, the rights and the type information represented by t are given as input parameters. If c owns NIL, a kernel call is made to create a new object whose capability should have the rights specified. The created object is loaded into a window and the header information is filled in. All spaces needed for the objects created by the thru-variable or local variables inside the THRU block will be allocated from the free space in the persistent object. This, plus the restriction imposed at the language level (see Section 2.3), will avoid pointers from a persistent object into an area inside another persistent object. This is necessary, since persistent objects cannot share common areas nor can one persistent object depend on another (except by owning capabilities).

3.2.8. Loading Objects into a Window A persistent object can be accessed only if it is loaded into a window of the process. We maintain a window counter, to indicate the next free window to load an object. If an object is loaded into the nth window, the system address for its first location is $(n-1)*2^k$ (where k is log_2 of the size of a window).

With the current processors used in the implementation of the multiprocessor system, an address is 24 bits, of which the most significant 5 bits represent the window number (starting from 0) and the next 19 bits represent the offset. In these systems, k is therefore 19. Later style processors to be used will have 32 bit addresses, organized as 5 bit window numbers and 27 bit offsets.

All pointers created within an object have an address corresponding to the current window. When the same object is loaded into another window, the addresses in the objects become meaningless since their most significant bits refer to the original window.

One way of solving this problem is to insist that an object is always loaded into the window with the same number as the one in which it was created. This becomes infeasible when two (or more) objects have to be accessed simultaneously where both were originally created (at different times or by different processes) in the same window.

Another solution would be to traverse through the object adjusting all the addresses to correspond to the current window, as a part of the loading procedure. This scheme has two weaknesses:

1. Not all parts of the object may be actually accessed, in which case, adjusting all the addresses would be unnecessary.

2. Consider the case where two processes are accessing the object directly (using THRU construct). By definition, the changes made by one process will be immediately visible to the other process. If process A adds a new node to a list, effectively stores an address in an existing node. The address stored would have the window number of the window in which process A has loaded the object. This is the address-value seen by process B. But this address is meaningless to process B if the same object is in another window of B.

This leads us to the next possible (and plausible) solution. Adjust the address only when it (the address) is used. (The address adjustment consist of replacing the most significant 5 bits with the current window number.) This scheme is similar to the address translation in the POMS system [6] where a PID is translated to a heap address, when it is detected.

3.2.9. Process Management A process object can be instantiated by the kernel call giving a capability to the process object. The kernel routine creates an instance called *a state object* and returns its capability. Immediately after instantiation, the process is sent a message which consists of:
1. capability of the instance
2. capability of the sender (if there are share parameters)
3. parameter addresses (the addresses may be values in the case of simple types)

The instantiator waits for a reply, if there are shared parameters. The instantiated process, after receiving the message executes the functional initialization of the process, upon completion of which it sends a message to its instantiator with the new addresses (values) of the shared parameters.

As mentioned, for a compound type, the address is passed. The address is relevant only with respect to the current process' logical address space. Therefore, when passing it to another process it must be translated to a capability + offset form. The receiving process can then load the same object (whose capability it receives) into one of its windows and access the argument from the offset.

Since the transient object is loaded into the same window in all processes, the address need only be the offset. (Note that, situations where offsets have to be passed for persistent objects have been carefully avoided in the language design. This would have been the case, if the restriction in the THRU statement was not imposed.)

3.2.10. Operation invocations An operation which is invoked may belong to the same process or another process. In the former case, it is equivalent to a procedure call in a traditional programming language. In the latter case, interprocess communication is involved. Since operation objects can be dynamically assigned to operation type variables, it is not possible to determine at compile time whether an invocation is local or external. The location for an operation type variable has a flag to indicate whether the operation body is external or internal. This flag is set when the variable is assigned an operation object, either by passing it as parameter in a process instantiation or through an assignment statement. If the operation is external, the location would also store the capability to the external process. If the operation is internal, only the address to which transfer of control must be made is stored.

At the time of an operation invocation, if the flag is set to external, a message is sent to the process whose capability is available, along with the parameters. If the flag is set to internal, then the translation is similar to a procedure invocation in traditional programming languages.

4. IMPLEMENTATION ON CONVENTIONAL ARCHITECTURES

We have discussed how the persistent store model of χ provides a workspace for the storage of transient objects, and we have argued that this provides portability across architectures. One of the major influences upon the adoption of a language for use in general purpose programming is its availability upon a range of architectures. Whilst we make no claims for the future of χ as a general purpose language, we felt that it was important that χ should be easily implementable upon a conventional architecture. This lead to the suggestion of a distinguished workspace, which, although philosophically regarded as persistent, can be practically regarded as transient on architectures that cannot provide primary memory as a long term resource.

On the Monash Multiprocessor implementation, the workspace is represented as a persistent object, and has no distinguished treatment. It can survive system crashes, logouts, and other events that normally cause loss of ownership of primary memory resources. On a conventional architecture, the workspace will be modelled by primary memory, and is therefore subject to such vagaries.

χ is designed to make this fundamentally different behaviour of the underlying architecture as transparent as possible to the programmer. This is of course, rather difficult, as a system crash and loss of primary memory is seldom transparent to the computer user!

The solution is to relax the performance constraint for conventional architectures. We insist that all explicitly persistent objects are maintained across loss of primary memory, and this in turn leads to extra overheads in their use. However, objects in the workspace can be handled in a conventional way, and do not have guaranteed persitence. Relaxing the persistence requirement for the workspace is not transparent, but confines the loss of data to that created since the last copy from persistent store. This is equivalent to a *transaction based model* of programming, for which techniques of implementation are well understood. Thus the difference between the Multiprocessor implementation and a conventional implementation is that no loss of data ever occurs in the first, and only loss of data since the last transaction commit occurs in the second.

The PAIL (Persistent Architecture Intermediate Language) system is one which can be interpreted by conventional machines. We explain the implementation of our language in PAIL running in the POMS (Persistent Object Management System) environment [6].

A few comments on the inter-relationship between PAIL and POMS may be appropriate here. PAIL is an intermediate language used as a target for compiler code generation. Appropriate back-ends then translate PAIL code into executable code. For systems with no machine language backends, and for portability purposes, an abstract machine code is provided, called *PS-code*. PS-code can be generated from PAIL code by means of a portable code generator. An interpreter for PS-code (written in C) then provides for the execution of programs translated via this process. This interpreter includes calls to a set of library routines that form the POMS sub-system, which handle the management of persistent objects.

4.1. Representation of Capabilities

In the POMS environment, capabilities could be represented by the system supplied PIDs (Persistent Identifiers). PIDs are unique 32 bit words generated by the system. Unlike in a capability architecture, where it is possible to have different capabilities with different rights for the same object, here we can have only one PID for one object. From the PID, it is possible to access the object in persistent store.

Objects in transient store are identified by their address. This address is just the conventional, linear homogeneous memory address, and is referred to in the POMS environment as a *local name*.

There is one important difference between PIDs and capabilities; objects identified by PIDs cannot be altered. This property lies at the very heart of the PS-algol system. When an object is stored in the persistent store, it may be referenced by its PID. This PID may be passed around the system, and stored in all sorts of places and objects. It may be essential to the behaviour of those objects that the referenced object does not change; this is a *persistent binding*. This behaviour is different from that required by the χ language, and so we cannot model capabilities directly by PIDs.

Recall that the semantics of a copy assignment between two capability variables creates a 'derived' capability for the LHS variable from the capability owned by the RHS variable. However, both capabilities denote the *same* object.

Persistent objects in χ are denoted by capability variables, and are capable of being altered by assignment. The mechanism that corresponds most closely to this model in PS-algol is the table data structure, wherein objects are identified by a key, and the result of looking up an object key is a (potentially persistent) pointer. The important point here is that the value of the table entry may be altered by an enter operation, and the binding between the table key and table entry is updated, but the object previously referenced by the entry is not altered.

Consider the following example. Suppose v1 and v2 are two capability variables, and v2 currently owns a capability which we shall represent as c2. Then we shall model the semantics of the variable v2 by representing it as a PS-algol string variable with value "c2". The persistent store is then modelled with a database whose keys are these string 'capabilities'. The share assignment v1 <- v2 creates a new 'capability' c1 from the capability c2 (possibly altering some encoding of rights), and sets the entry in the table to be the same object referenced by the original capability. The net effect is equivalent to the PS-algol expression v1 := s.enter(make.cap(v2),s.lookup(v2)), where make.cap is a procedure that takes a 'string capability', and returns a 'derived string capability', and **s.enter** and **s.lookup** are the PS-algol standard string table enter and lookup primitives respectively.

Thus we can model capabilities within χ by table keys within PS-algol. Note that such keys are generated by the system, and not by the user (thus preserving the access semantics of capabilities).

4.2. Persistent to Transient (and vice versa) copying

This is fairly straight forward in the POMS system. Persistent to transient copying occurs when a persistent identifier is dereferenced. The object is located in persistent space (called a *database*), space is allocated in transient store, and the object is copied into this space. System tables identifying the mappings between persistent identifiers and local names are updated; the persistent identifier is then altered to the local name, and execution proceeds.

Transient to persistent copying occurs upon a **commit** operation, and is programmed explicitly. All transient objects reachable from any opened database structure are copied to persistent store, with new persistent identifiers being allocated as necessary. Note that *all* objects are copied; the operation is not selective.

In χ, both directions of copying are selective. However, since we model capabilities by entries within a table, selective copying is possible just by referencing and updating table entries. For example, a **v := c** statement (causing a persistent to transient copy) is equivalent to an **open.database** call, where the database being opened is that containing the object **c**, and a subsequent reference to the database table entry corresponding to **c**.

Note that it is not known whether the database is opened for writing or just for reading. A simple strategy might be to always assume that the database is opened for writing, but this might be unduly restrictive, as the database is then locked against other users. Other strategies might be to require the compiler to determine whether there are any (potential) assignments to **c**, or to require the programmer to specify whether **c** is a 'constant' (open database for reading), or a 'variable' (open database for writing). This latter choice would require alteration to the language. Further work is required to determine the best strategy.

A **c := v** statement is equivalent to a table **enter** operation, followed by a **commit** call to actually update the persistent store. Because POMS copies all reachable objects, the commit will also update other 'capability' variables. However, since we are assuming that each assignment to a persistent variable causes an immediate effect upon the database, the only new objects to be entered into the database will be that created by the **c := v** statement.

After committing the object, items in the heap (which may now be part of the database) are still available if local variables have pointers to them.

4.3. The Implementation of the THRU Statement

The THRU statement makes sure that whatever is done on the object is visible immediately to other viewers who use the same capability.

This will create a problem in POMS because a capability may have already be mapped (and copied) from the persistent store to some other transient store in another process. POMS gets around this problem by adopting a single-writer-multiple-reader synchronization policy. In POMS, any change to a (database) object is visible to others only when the database is "committed". Moreover, when an object is accessed in the write mode, it automatically becomes inaccessible to others till the writer "closes" it.

We can therefore model the χ semantics by requiring that a THRU statement will open (and thereby lock) a database containing the 'capability' which is the subject of the THRU statement.

This results in a performance deterioration of the THRU statement execution. This happens since the object will be locked, so that another process trying to look into it will be delayed until the first process has come to the end of its THRU.[2]

4.4. Implementation of Interprocess Communication

POMS does not have a concept of processes. Hence the abstract machine must be extended to take care of processes, and interprocess communication through remote operation calls. The PAIL structures can be extended as follows (using the notation of [7]).

4.4.1. Process Definition
A process definition requires identification of its parameters, its body, and its symbol table (used to define the types of the parameters).

```
structure process.defn(pntr ps.params, ps.body.entry, ps.symb.table)
```

The components of this structure are:

ps.params is a cons list of symbol table entries for the process parameters.

ps.body.entry is a pointer to the following structure:

```
        structure process.body(pntr func.part, synch.part, sched.part) where
```
    func.part is a pointer to the tree of the functional part of the process.
    synch.part is a pointer to the tree of the synchronization part of the process.
    sched.part is a pointer to the tree of the scheduling part of the process.
  ps.symb.table is the symbol table for the parameters.

When a process is instantiated the the parameters in ps.params list are substituted and func.part tree of the process.body structure is executed. When that terminates, any share parameters are substituted back. After that, the synch.part tree is executed. Each process maintains a queue for invocations of its operations. During the execution of the synch.part, this queue is checked for operation invocations as explained in next section. A process terminates when its *synch.part* terminates.

4.4.2. Accept Statement
Each branch of an ACCEPT statement is translated into PAIL as an accept.choice structure:

```
    structure accept.choice(pntr choice.exp, op.name, action.exp)
```

The components of this structure are:

choice.exp is a pointer to the code for the boolean condition

op.name is a pointer to the symbol table entry for the operation name

action.exp is a pointer to the tree of statements

All the branches of an ACCEPT statement are kept in a list of cons structures. To execute an ACCEPT statement, the choice.exps of those op.names in the statement for which pending invocations exist in the queue are evaluated. The invocations corresponding to the TRUE choice.exps form the list of acceptable invocations. Any operation in this list can be accepted subject to scheduling constraints. So, the sched.part is evaluated on the

---

[2] This may have serious repercussions. For instance, suppose two processes are communicating with each other by using a persistent object as a semaphore. By the definition of the language, two or more processes can do this without either of them exiting from a THRU. But the above implementation scheme may take the processes to deadlock.

list. If the `sched.part` chooses one of the invocations in the list, then control transfers to the corresponding operation body At the end of the operation body execution, the synchronization statments pointed by the `action.exp` tree is executed to complete the execution of the `ACCEPT` statement. If the invocation queue is empty, or none of the `choice.exps` evaluate to TRUE, or the `sched.part` did not choose any of the *op.names* then the process gets blocked at the *ACCEPT* statement. It is woken up when a new entry is added to the queue, where upon the `ACCEPT` statement execution proceeds as before.

4.4.3. PICK statement   A PICK statement may appear in the scheduling unit. Its guards can be boolean or arithmetic expressions. Each branch of the PICK statement is translated to a `pick.choice` structure:

    `structure pick.choice(pntr choice.exp, op.list, choice.action)`

The components of this structure are:

`choice.exp` is a pointer to the tree for the pick-selector expression

`op.list` is a pointer to cons list of symbol table entries of the operation names

`choice.action` is a pointer to the tree for the pick-action

All the branches of a PICK statement are kept as a list of cons structures.

Given a list of acceptable invocations, the PICK and PREFER statements of `sched.part` are evaluated to choose one operation from it. In a PICK statement the `choice.exps` are evaluated in the order of occurrence. If the invocation corresponding to the first TRUE `choice.exp` is present in the list of *invocation queue*, then all invocations corresponding to subsequent `choice.exp` are removed from the acceptable list. If that invocation is present also in the acceptable list, then it is scheduled and the `choice.action` corresponding to that `choice.exp` is executed. Otherwise, the pruned acceptable list is passed on to the next PREFER/PICK statement.

4.4.4. PREFER statement   The PAIL code is similar to that for the PICK statement. But, the interpretation is different. The `choice.exps` are evaluated in the order of occurrence. If the invocation corresponding to the first TRUE `choice.exp` appears in the list of acceptable invocation then that invocation is scheduled and the corresponding *choice.exp* also is executed. Otherwise the acceptable list is passed on to the next PREFER/PICK statement.

In short, the difference between the interpretation of PICK and PREFER statement can be explained as follows: A PICK statement stops evaluation at the first TRUE `choice.exp` whose corresponding `op.name` is in the invocation queue, whereas the PREFER statement stops evaluation at the first TRUE `choice.exp` whose corresponding `op.name` is in the *acceptable list*; the *acceptable list* is a subset of the invocation queue.

If evaluating all PICK/PREFER statements does not result in scheduling any invocation, then one of the invocations remaining in the acceptable list is chosen at random for scheduling. (Note that the PICK statement evaluation removes from the acceptable list, invocations that must not be scheduled.)

4.5.   Implementation of copy and share statements

Since χ has two types of assignments, we need one more structure other than the `assign.op` structure provided by the PAIL architecture:

    `structure share.op(pntr lhs.exp, rhs.exp)`

The components of this structure are:

`lhs.exp` is a pointer to the code representing an address (of the LHS variable)
`rhs.exp` is a pointer to the code representing an address (of the RHS variable)

The interpretation of `share.op` is quite straightforward. `rhs.exp` must result in an l-value. The value at that address is stored at the location resulting from the evaluation of `lhs.exp`.

4.6. IFs and DOs

An IF statement of χ can be translated using the `if.op` structure. The casualty is the non-determinacy. In χ's IF, if more than one guard is true, any of the guard can be chosen non-deterministically. Since, programs are not allowed to assume the order in which the guards are evaluated and chosen, allowing determinacy at the implementation level will not affect the correctness of programs.

A DO statement can be translated into an if-statement within a while statement, where the looping condition is the disjunction of all the guards.

5. CURRENT STATUS OF THE IMPLEMENTATION

The user interface of the multiprocessor system is at present in a rudimentary stage. This has led us to do the compilation process as much as possible on a more "user friendly" system, and use the multiprocessor only to execute the generated code. Accordingly, the prototype implementation consists of two parts. One part does the lexical, syntax and semantic analyses and generates the intermediate code. The intermediate code is a variation of the PAIL code described in the last section. (Generating PAIL code, instead of some form of assembly code, should make the system easily portable to other architectures.) All of this is done in a Unix[3] environment. The intermediate code is then sent to the multiprocessor where it is interpreted.

The PAIL code in its original form is a structure of different types of nodes linked via pointers. Transferring such a code from machine to machine is cumbersome. This is overcome by modifying the PAIL structures and making them *textual*. The PAIL code is written to an array, where array indices are used instead of pointers. An element of the array is a union (in the sense of the language C) of all possible PAIL structures, along with header information to store its own index and the structure's type-code. The next free index is incremented each time a node is added to the code array.

The prototype development uses the language C and the *yacc* [10] compiler compiler. Persistent programming features and most of the conventional parts are currently operational. Implementation of parallel processing and polymorphism is progressing.

6. CONCLUSIONS

We have outlined the facilities of a language designed for persistent programming in a capability style architecture. We have also shown how the language might be implemented on more conventional architectures, by building upon existing intermediate architectures designed to support other forms of persistent languages. This approach requires relatively few alterations to the intermediate language.

---

[3] Unix is a trade mark of the Bell Laboratories

REFERENCES

1. American National Standard Institute, Inc., "The Programming Language Ada Reference Manual", ANSI/MIL-STD-1815A-1983, *Lecture Notes in Computer Science*, 155, Springer-Verlag, New York, (1983).

2. Anderson, M.S., Pose, R.D. and Wallace, C.S. "A Password Capability System", *The Computer Journal*, 29, 1, (1986), 1-8.

3. Andrews, G.R., "Synchronizing Resources", *ACM Transactions on Programming Languages and Systems*, 3, 4, October 1981, pp. 405-430.

4. Atkinson, M.P., Chisholm, K.J. and Cockshott, W.P. "PS-algol: An Algol with a Persistent Heap", *ACM SIGPLAN Notices*, 17, 7, July 1981, pp. 24-31.

5. Atkinson, M.P. and Morrison, R. "Procedures as persistent data objects", *ACM Transactions on Programming Languages and Systems*, 7, 4, October 1985, pp. 539-559.

6. Cockshot, W.P., Atkinson, M.P., Chisholm, K.J., Bailey, P.J. and Morrison, R. "Persistent object management system", *Software Practice & Experience*, 14, 1, January 1984, pp. 49-71.

7. Dearle, A. "A Persistent Architecture Intermediate Language", Universities of Glasgow and St. Andrews, PPRR 35, June 1987.

8. Fabry, R.S. "Capability Based Addressing", *Communications of the ACM*, 17, 1, July 1974, pp. 403-412.

9. Horowitz, E. "Fundamentals of Programming Languages", Springer-Verlag, 1983.

10. Johnson, S.C. "YACC: Yet Another Compiler Compiler", Bell Laboratories, New Jersey, 1978.

11. Knuth, D.E. "Fundamental Algorithms, The Art of Computer Programming", vol. 1, Addison-Wesley, Reading, Massachusetts, 1968.

12. Myers, G.J. and Buckingham, B.R.S. "A Hardware Implementation of Capability Based Addressing", *Computer Architecture News*, 8, 6, October 1980, pp. 12-24.

13. Pose, R.D. "Hardware to Support a Persistent Global Virtual Memory", *Proc. of the 22nd Hawaii International Conference on System Sciences*, 1989.

14. Rosenberg, J. and Abramson, D. "MONADS-PC – A Capability Based Workstation to Support Software Engineering", *Proc. of the 18th Hawaii International Conference on System Sciences*, 1985.

15. Rosenberg, J. and Keedy, L. "Data Engineering with Sets and Sequences", Proc. of the 1988 Australian Software Engineering Conference, Canberra, 1988, pp. 79-100.

16. Sajeev, A.S.M. and Olszewski, J. " Manipulation of Data Structures without Pointers", *Information Processing Letters*, 26, 3, November 1987, pp. 135-143.

17. Sajeev, A.S.M. "Language Constructs for Persistent Object Based Programming", *Proc. of the 7th IEEE Phoenix Conference on Computers and Communications*, Scottsdale, Arizona, March 1988.

18. Sajeev, A.S.M. "Separation of Functional, Synchronizing, and Scheduling Aspects of Processes", *Proc. of the 10th Australian Computer Science Conference*, Geelong, Victoria, February 1987, pp. 161-172.

Distributed PS-algol

Francis Wai
University of Glasgow

ABSTRACT

Fundamental to the concept of persistence is locality transparency whereby a programmer needs not be aware of the locality of data. It is argued that the locality transparency principle can be generalized in the context of a distributed environment. The implication is that syntax and semantics in the manipulation of remote data is the same as for local data. Distributed programming is then no more difficult than conventional persistent programming. But because of the locality transparency principle, many advantages offered in a distributed environment become inaccessible.

This paper presents a language design which on one hand supports persistent programming while on the other supports the kind of coding that requires the whereabout of data to be discovered; a language concept *locality* is introduced for such purposes. Other features of the language are presented: lightweight processes that may be made to run on a processor different from the one it is defined, a remote procedure call mechanism that supports call-by-value parameter passing semantics, dynamic typechecking with a hint of polymorphism of separately compiled communicating processes, and semaphores with syntactic support for common usages.

1. INTRODUCTION

Fundamental to the concept of persistence is locality transparency whereby a programmer needs not be aware of the locality of data; it may be in RAM or on disks depending on the computation history and its movement between different storage media is never explicitly controlled by the programmer. Since a programmer is not distracted by the whereabouts, structural representation and type of data, it results in more compact and concise code.

It was observed that the locality transparency principle of persistence can be generalized in a natural way in a distributed environment. The motivation being that movement of data over a network can be abstracted away in much the same way as data is over the I/O bus. In this way, the domain of locality of data in a persistent programming environment can naturally be extended to include remote devices as well. We believe many aspects of distributed programming can be supported within the existing framework of persistent programming without requiring changes. The manipulation of remote objects is both syntactically and semantically the same as if they were local objects. Distributed programming is no more difficult than conventional persistent programming.

There are many advantages offered in a distributed environment. For instance, data may be duplicated for easy access and resilience; resources such as printers and processors may be utilized to maximize throughput. However, because of locality transparency, there is no way to tell whether an object is local to the computation or remote. The objective of this paper is a language design which on one hand supports the locality transparency of persistent data while on the other hand allows coding of the kind that requires the whereabouts of data to be discovered.

The principal features of the language are distribution and concurrency. The two features are designed in such a way so that the overall semantics is straightforward and coherent. For example, processes may communicate over a network and the semantics of parameter passing is that expected in local communication. The novel features include:

- *Concurrency* is admitted through lightweight processes which are computational tasks that share the same address space; they may be created and run on separate processors.

- *Distribution* is achieved by providing a universal address space [9] that spans across the network.

- *Locality* a language concept to facilitate specific coding of distributed algorithm to give, for example, higher performance computations when necessary. The language still allows programs to be written according to the principle of locality transparency.

- *Remote Procedure Call* is a synchronous communication means whereby processes interact with one another using messages. The remote procedure call mechanism supports a call-by-value (as opposed to call-by-copy semantics) semantics of parameter passing. On the other hand, processes may also interact with one another through global environments which may be on remote stores.

- *Mutex* provides a store-based mechanism for process synchronization. Synchronized access to shared, remote environments based on *mutexes* is possible.

- *Non-determinism* and *separate compilation* of communicating programs are supported in the language. The latter is characterized by the signature matching algorithm so that changes in one software component has minimal impact on those wishing to communicate with it using publicized interface thus reducing the amount of re-compilation necessary.

The language is a descendant of PS-algol [2]; persistence, higher order functions and other features of PS-algol are retained. A significant portion of what is described here has been implemented. The system is implemented on Sun workstations running Unix™ 4.2 connected over a network where Internet Protocol is supported.

2.   DISTRIBUTED PS-algol

The design of the language is influenced by the desire to retain the programming style and application domain of PS-algol. A PS-algol program is a legal program in Distributed PS-algol (or DPS for short). The converse is not true. Many of the new features are more general than when first conceived mainly because of the design approach that permeates in PS-algol viz. simplicity, and simplicity through generality. For instance, a communication port can be shared, though in a controlled fashion, by more than one process. A server process may thus delegate its functions to other processes in a such a way that client processes are not aware of it.

In the language description below, whenever a term with an unusual meaning is introduced a different font such as this is used.

2.1. Entry

Processes can affect one another either by modifying global variables or by message passing. Message passing is the more general mechanism of the two in a distributed environment since no assumption of common stores is made. It is envisaged that message passing is a bootstrapping means for merging stores. Messages can be exchanged through ports which can be addressed from any process anywhere over a network. Similar approaches based on the idea of communication ports in process communication can be found in DP [3], CSP [5], Ada [1] etc. The approach taken here represents yet another one although it is rather close to that in Ada. The difference being that a communication port is a value and can be shared.

An entry is a bi-directional communication port. It is where a process receives messages and replies are sent. An entry is an object and can be constructed, for example:

    let anEntry := entry(-> int); 3

anEntry here denotes a communication port which, when a null message is received and accepted, returns an integer 3. We explained how a message is accepted later.

Entry variables and constants can be declared whenever and wherever they are needed just like any other values in the language, but the entry literals may only appear in the scope of the **process** construct (2.2). This is because an entry must belong to a process; but it can be shared by a group of processes in scope.

There is no limit as to the number of entries a process can associate with. An entry may take on different values. For example,

    anEntry := entry(-> int); 103

When a null message is now received at *anEntry* and accepted, the value returned is then 103. As in the case of procedures, such assignments are possible only if the types of the expressions on the left- and right-hand sides of the assignment match.

An entry resembles a procedure; it has a procedure-like header and an executable body. Like procedures, entries are first class values so that they can be shared. The primary reason for introducing entries is because procedures are abstraction over either statements or expressions and entries are for synchronous communication. They serve different purposes. Processes communicate using entries and are synchronized until the executions of the entries have been completed. This contrasts with procedure calls where callers are not synchronized.

2.2. Process Templates and Start

Concurrency is introduced by means of lightweight processes [4, 7]. Lightweight processes are computation units that share the same set of resources such as the heap and the i/o streams. However, a lightweight process is considered to be an independent activity in carrying out a specific task. A lightweight process can be introduced based on a process template. A process template is a passive object. Such an arrangement permits a number of identical but distinct processes to operate in parallel. In this way, concurrency can be introduced when and where it is needed.

The following is an example of a process template that once started runs forever. This is achieved by keep spawning itself.

```
let forever := process
                begin
                end
forever := process
            begin
              let x = start forever
            end
let y = start forever
```

The first declaration of *forever* serves as a reference for the following assignment as well as the recursion. The second declaration starts the chain of processes.

A process template may reference data in an outer environment. This allows a very efficient and neat way of communicating data among concurrent processes which may or may not be sharing the same address space. On the other hand, data local to a process template cannot be shared. This allows a process to have overall control of its resources.

Process creation is dynamic. The number of lightweight processes that can be made to run is not statically determinable. As such the language does not impose an upper bound on the number of lightweight processes that can be created. The actual upper bound is determined by the availability of memory which is a runtime property.

It is possible to start a process running on a remote machine, for example:

```
start forever as Forever at Fiji
```

The second expression in a **start** expression is taken to be the symbolic name of the lightweight process created. The name is used for binding with separately compiled programs. The lightweight process created is registered with this symbolic name at the locality *Fiji*. By default, it is taken to be the local one. A registration is required if the process is to receive messages from processes outwith the address space it is executing. In the absence of the second (and therefore the third) expression, no registration will take place and the process created can only communicate with other processes in the same address space. In any case, the lightweight process is made to run wherever it happens to be; it could be in the local address space or on a remote machine. If for any reason a registration cannot succeed e.g. name clashes or machine failure, a system event is generated.

The result of a **start** expression has type known as process handle. The type matching rule for process handles is unusual and is based on a notion of inclusion. This can be illustrated as follows:

```
let p1 := p2
```

If *p1* is of some process handle type then *p2* must also be of some process handle type. In addition, the signature (which is a list of entries) of *p2* must be a superset of that of *p1*. The idea is that an assignment of process handles such as the one above is allowed if and only if there is an enrichment of the signature concerned so that the new process handle can perform all that was expected of the previous value.

A DPS program consists of at least a top-level process which is made to run implicitly. All lightweight processes are children of it. A PS-algol program would simply be run as a single top-level process. A DPS program terminates when all processes have terminated. But the termination of parent and child processes is not conditional on one another. A number of separate DPS programs may interact as explained below.

The result of a **start** expression is a process handle. Process handles are immutable. They are used in denoting the target process in process communication.

2.3.   Communication

In order to facilitate process communication, the language supports a remote procedure call (RPC) mechanism. Such a mechanism allows processes to interact with one another wherever they happen to be. The use of the mechanism is not restricted to processes that are compiled together. They can be separately compiled and this could happen on remote machines. However, from a programmer's point of view, it makes no difference in communicating with a local or a remote process. In either case, the syntax is the same. The only notable differences are slower responses and possible machine or network failures in communication over a network.

An RPC is a synchronous activity. Processes which initiate RPCs are always suspended. They are resumed when some processes indicate a willingness to serve calls and the execution of entry bodies have terminated. There is no guarantee that suspended processes will ever be resumed since the entries they are calling may be ignored i.e. messages are received but never accepted or the execution of an entry body may go into an infinite loop. However, if there is machine or network failures or premature process terminations, system events are raised and the suspended processes concerned are resumed in order to handle them.

2.3.1.   Remote Procedure Call

An RPC is initiated as in a procedure call except in addition a process has to be specified. For example,

> let hisName = nameServer@exchange(myName)

where *nameServer* denotes a server process which has an entry known as *exchange*. It is convenient to call that process the server of the RPC and the executing process the client. The fact that the server may be a remote process is of no concern to the programmers. This is the basis for syntactic uniformity. Such syntactic uniformity is a convenience in distributed systems where the locality of a communicant may either vary over a period of time or simply be immaterial. We described later how process handles to remote processes can be introduced into the environment.

The semantics of parameter passing is call-by-value; the same as in procedure calls. Call-by-value is different from call-by-copy. In the latter case objects are always copied. Consequently, objects are considered to be bound to the locations where they were created. This is considered a hindrance in distributed programming with a conventional language. The main reason is that the propagation of side-effects, which is fundamental in conventional programming, has to be the responsibility of the programmers. Primarily we wanted a programming style that is consistent with persistent programming. This was achieved in PS-algol in which the store semantics enables a blackboard view (– many processes or blocks of code determined by the scope rules may see a part of the store/blackboard simultaneously) over different types of physical storage. This blackboard view of the underlying object stores is extended in the language. Of course, even on a multi-processor machine the simultaneity is not realizable due to bus contention and store arbiters. In a distributed system the approximation to simultaneity is less achievable.

2.3.2. Accept

The occurrence of an RPC is in part initiated by a client and in part by the willingness shown by a server. A server expresses its willingness to communicate by accepting calls from its entries. It is possible to specify more than one entry of interest; they are separated by the parallel bar "‖":

accept exchange ‖ others otherwise S

All the entry expressions are evaluated in parallel. An entry is said to be eligible for selection if it has a message. If there is more than one eligible entry, a non-deterministic choice will be made. The longest waiting message of the chosen entry is then selected. If a choice cannot be made and there is no **otherwise** part, the current process is suspended until a message for any one of its entries has arrived when the evaluation of the **accept** clause is repeated. If a choice cannot be made and there is an **otherwise** part, it is executed and the process continues.

2.4. Concurrency Control and Scheduling

The organization of the persistent store, which underlies the language, is perceived to be in the form of a graph whose nodes are collections of local and remote data. Although data are guaranteed to be transactionally secured or stabilized in a persistent store, accesses to nodes require coordination to guarantee atomic changes. Primitive concurrency control is supported in the language. Our approach is oriented towards optimism. We do not wish to impose a strict access regime so that the degree of concurrency attainable may not be uniform. It is allowed to vary according to the nature of applications.

2.4.1. Mutex and Lock

A simple data type and a construct are introduced to facilitate concurrency control. It is intended that concurrency control is achieved based on conventions and it is the responsibility of the programmers to observe the conventions they chose. However, because of higher order functions and persistence, it is believed that methods of accessing data can be packaged and users only need to know about publicized interfaces.

The new data type is **mutex** and the only value of this type is the literal **mutex**.

let x := mutex

In the declaration above, x is introduced as an object of type **mutex**. As with other values in the language, mutex objects are first class. Mutexes are usually used in order to gain access to protected resources. The language provides a construct for such purposes:

> lock x, y do S

The evaluation of the right-most clause *S* in a **lock** statement is conditional upon the seizure of all the mutexes specified. The evaluation of the mutexes follows a left to right order of evaluation. The executing process is suspended if any one of the mutexes cannot be seized. In this case, all the mutexes acquired hitherto are released. Subsequently, the release of any one of these mutexes triggers the re-evaluation of the **lock** clause. Upon completion of the right-most clause, all the mutexes are released. Any abnormal exit during the evaluation of the right-most clause, such as exceptions, will cause the release of all mutexes acquired.

Here is a simple example of how a block of code is guaranteed to be executed atomically:

```
structure atomic(proc(proc()) doIt)
let atomicCreate = proc(-> pntr)               ! creates an instance of atomic
              begin
              let m = mutex
              atomic(proc(proc() criticalRegion); lock m do criticalRegion())
                                             ! procedure doIt
       end
```

If mutexes are always acquired in the same order (when in different nested **lock** clauses), the **lock** clause is useful in avoiding deadlocks. Note that a mutex may appear more than once in a **lock** clause but the effect is the same as if it appears once; no deadlock will result. Note also that the following two programs are not equivalent.

> lock m1, m2 do S

and

> lock m1 do
> lock m2 do S

The first program guarantees that *m1* and *m2* are seized simultaneously whereas the second does not. In the second program, if *m2* cannot be seized, *m1* is not released.

The familiar P and V operations that are usually associated with semaphores are not supported explicitly. Instead they are built into the semantics of the **lock** construct. They are not supported in the language because their uses are often subject to abuses. Specifically, the two operations can be used in isolation, a process can force its way into a protected resource by executing a V operation. Moreover, their erroneous uses can affect the proper working of other processes e.g. a matching pair of P and V operations are applied onto different mutex objects. The provision of the **lock** construct is intended to eliminate these problems. This is ensured in that 1) the P and V operations are always used in pairs and 2) a pair of these operations always acts on the same mutex object.

2.4.2. Condition, Wait and Signal

The set of base types in the language is enriched with the data type **cond**. The only value of this type is the literal **cond**. An object of this type can be introduced into the environment as in:

> **let x = cond**

A cond object is intended to be used to signal events e.g. changes of state of some resource. In addition to equality, there are two operators for cond objects viz. **wait** and **signal**.

The execution of a **wait** clause may cause the suspension of the executing process if no signal has been received by any one of the cond objects in the list. When this happens, all the acquired mutexes, if any, of the inner most block are released. The process will only be resumed after a signal is sent to the appropriate cond object and all the released mutexes have been re-acquired.

The execution of a **signal** clause may cause the resumption of one or more suspended processes in the near future; there is no processor switch. A process suspended due to a **wait** has higher priority in acquiring mutexes it may have released. A **signal** is remembered if no process can be resumed immediately.

Because we have shared store semantics and access to remote entries, it would be possible to define a procedure "cond" which had in its block a mutex and a list of processes which yielded a pair of entries, signal and wait. This would have nearly the same semantics – the difference being that the release of other mutexes and the higher priority restart would not apply. These differences combined with the programmer convenience justify the introduction of **cond** as a primitive type in DPS.

2.4.3. Stop and Kill

Two operators are included to cause termination of some process. These are **stop** and **kill** and they are useful in discarding useless processes.

stop causes the executing process to terminate. **kill** causes the termination of a specific process such as *p* in **kill** p. If the process has already terminated, it has no effect.

If there are outstanding messages when a process is terminated, an exception is propagated to each of the client processes concerned. Similarly, RPC communication with terminated processes will cause an exception to be propagated to the communicating processes.

2.5. Locality

The main motivation behind the design of the language is to hide away distribution as much as possible. This is achieved in the language by supporting uniform access to both local and remote data. The same syntactic constructs can then be used on both local and remote data. For instance, it is possible to start a process running on a remote machine using the same construct to spawn a local process as in:

> **let** remoteProcess = **start** remoteProcessTemplate

where *remoteProcessTemplate* denotes a process template on a remote machine.

The lack of a notion of locality leads to a programming style in which distributed programming can be no more difficult than programming in conventional languages. This is certainly desirable as programmers are not distracted by distribution. As it has been mentioned in the introduction that it is not strictly desirable to hide distribution away altogether. We want to introduce a notion of *locality* into the language so that, when necessary, the locality of resources can be discovered. Thus programmers need not know the whereabouts of data unless they wish to program an explicit version of resilience and resource utilization. An illustrative example is given in Section 3.

Two new base types are introduced. These are **loca** and **node**. They belong to the generic type **locality**. A node is a space where lightweight processes may be started. A loca denotes a collection of nodes and other locas. It is the intention that a loca mimics a machine or a network representing a distinctive set of resources such as persistent stores, processors or devices. There are a number of primordial loca values defined in the language. From time-to-time, new primordial loca values may be created or changed without logical impact on existing programs or data. From time to time, we expect new loca to appear as machines are inserted (by means outside the scope of a programming language). Although this may have no impact on the semantics of programs, mechanisms must exist to a) allow such new locas to be discovered, and b) for nodes to be withdrawn.

The notion of locality is a relative one so that loca values that are not referenced and are not primordial (i.e. is in a 1 to 1 relationship with a loca) cease to exist. Consequently, nodes belonging to discarded loca values may become unreachable.

A loca value can be constructed or discovered as in:

> let ChristmasIsland = **newlocality**
> let Fiji = **locality** E

Both *ChristmasIsland* and *Fiji* denote localities but the latter represents one where the object denoted by *E* resides.

A hierarchical structure of localities can be composed. For example,

> **add** Atlantis **to** MythicalIslands

would make the locality *Atlantis* reachable from *MythicalIslands*. In addition to those language defined loca values, there are two distinct points in the hierarchical structure viz. **universe** which refers to the root and **here** which refers to the locality of the executing process.

As an example, **locality** 4 returns **here**. In general, immutable values always exhibit the same characteristic irrespective of their origins.

Three relational infix operators are defined for loca values. These are:

[equality]	$l_1 = l_2$
[in]	l_1 **in** l_2
[within]	l_1 **within** l_2

Two loca values are said to be equal if and only if their denotations are the same. A loca is said to be **in** another if and only if the former is a member of the collection of the latter. A loca is said to be **within** another if and only if there exists a sequence of loca values $l_i, l_j, ..., l_n$ such that l_1 **in** l_i & l_i **in** l_j & ... & ... l_n **in** l_2.

As an example, for any l of the generic type **locality**, l **within universe** always returns **true**.

As for loca values, a node value can be created: **newnode [in E]** or discovered: **node E**. A node is always created in some locality; the default is **here**. A node can be in one or more localities at the same time. We assume that the operation **newnode** either follows some external action introducing a machine/address space or that action in some way happens at the same time. Node operations refer to actions external to the language and are part of its relationship with its environment whereas loca operations are defined and implemented within the language. **newnode** may also declare a new loca which then matches the space correspond to the node.

The only relational operator defined for node values is equality. Two nodes are said to be equal if and only if their denotations are the same. Furthermore, a node value may appear as the left expression in **in** and **within**, the two relational operators for loca values.

2.6. Transcopy and Assign

Two store-to-store operations are supported for the atomic physical transfer of data between localities.

> **transcopy** myCV **to** aCompany

The **transcopy** operation transfers a copy of whatever is denoted by *myCV* to the locality denoted by *aCompany*. The amount of data transferred is determined by the type of the expression to be copied.

1) Values of the base types are immutable. Some of them are transferred as if they were declared in the remote stores. These include integer, real, boolean, picture, pixel, and string. For loca and node, only pointers to them are copied. For mutex and cond, suspended processes are not copied.

2) Process handles are transferred as immutable values. Copies resulting from such transfers are handles to processes on remote machines. The referrend processes and their entries are not copied.

3) Images are rectangular matrix of pixels and they are transferred in their entirety.

4) Vectors are always transferred with their top-levels installed in the remote stores. For example, transfer of a vector of integer, *int, could result in a vector of integers installed whereas transfer of a vector of vector of integer, **int, could result in a vector of *int installed.

5) Procedures, entries and process templates are copied in such a way so that their environments remain at the original site and are sharable.

6) Structures are copied in a similar fashion to vectors.

The rules above are meant to avoid phantom copying. In particular, there is no danger of copying an entire persistent store without programmers being aware of it.

Copying of data structures several levels deep can be achieved by copying individual levels. The **transcopy** operation preserves the properties of the objects copied. The effects of the same sequence of operations when applied to copies and their originals should be identical. However, it is the responsibility of the programmers not to destroy circularity and sharing during the copying process.

The term **transcopy** suggests a notion of atomicity and is distinguishable from the graphic construct **copy** which is for graphical manipulation. The **transcopy** operation fails if for any reason a copy cannot be installed in the locality indicated. In this case, an exception is raised. If the destination is a loca no assumption can be made as to which node has the copy installed.

There is a complementary operation to **transcopy**.

> **assign** myCopy **to** originalCopy

The semantics of the construct is straightforward; it resets the value of the second clause to the value denoted by the first clause. The effect of **assign** is the same as **transcopy**; only the top level of an object is copied. If for any reason the operation fails, an exception is raised. The effect of such assignment takes place in the locality of the value of the second clause.

2.7. Miscellaneous

In the context of communication, processes are either clients or servers. It is not suggested that a process cannot be both but only one at a time. In order that clients can communicate with servers, binding and typechecking must be resolved. Our approach to these matters is a static one but augmented with runtime support. The language does not specify any order of compilation of clients and servers. They can be compiled whenever and wherever it is deemed necessary. The rationale for this is because we do not have, nor do we think it is appropriate to have, the facilities outwith the system to maintain information on types, names and locations of clients and servers on a distributed system.

Process communication is always initiated with the stipulation of a process handle to a server. A handle to a separately compiled process can be introduced into the environment as in:

> **for** NameServer = "Name Server" **at** vanuata
> **with** exchange = **entry(string -> string) do** S

A process with the symbolic name *"Name Server"* is to be found in the locality *vanuata*. If found, the signature of this process is matched against that specified. Type matching of signatures is based on a notion of inclusion. The signature obtained is required to be a powerset of the one specified. This allows servers to evolve independently between program executions without affecting existing clients unnecessarily. If type matching succeeds, the identifier denotes the process handle to the server. Exceptions are raised if the process cannot be found or the type matching fails.

The scope of the identifier is basically confined to the clause following the terminal **do**. However, the process it denotes can be passed out to a global environment by assignments.

Once a handle to a process is installed, communication with it does not require further binding and typechecking. Thus the runtime overhead of binding and typechecking is constant independent of the frequency of RPCs. This is achieved since the required typechecking and binding are already performed at compile time for the majority of code (i.e. after the **do** above) and the remaining delayed check occurs once at installation time.

3. EXAMPLES

The two programs below together realize distributed free-hand drawing. The objective here is to permit whatever drawn on a screen of a machine to appear immediately on a screen of another machine connected over a network. The two programs share the same free-hand drawing package which is stored in a persistent store. In addition to setting up the screen into quadrants, the package provides a set of paint brushes and supports pop-up menu. The display uses two of the quadrants; one for local drawing and the other for displaying remote images. The main body of the package looks something like:

```
...
while true do begin
    moose := locator()
    if moose(the.buttons)(the.button) do begin
        let x = moose(X.pos)
        let y = moose(Y.pos)
        if x < bum.r then if y >= bum.b do controls(x, y) else
        if inBrushSet() then change.brush() else
        if inLocalDisplay() do ror brush onto limit paper at x, y
        end
    copy their(the.paper) onto rpaper
    end
...
```

The two programs are:

```
let root = open.database("demos", "friend", "read")
...
let make = s.lookup("sketch pad", root)(content)
structure paper.box(#pixel)
let their.paper := image 1 by 1 of off
let my.paper := image 1 by 1 of off
let their = paper.box(their.paper)
let mine = paper(my.paper)
let sketch = make(their, mine, ...)
my.paper := mine(the.paper)

let p = process
        with
          init = entry(#pixel -> #pixel)
        begin
        let init = entry(#pixel theirPaper -> #pixel)
          begin
          their(the.paper) := theirPaper
          my.paper
          end
        accept init
        end
    let aP = start p as "server"
```

```
        sketch()
```

and

```
        let root = open.database("demos", "friend", "read")
        ...        ! same as above
        my.paper := mine(the.paper)
        let x = process
                begin
                sketch()
                end
        let y = start x

        for p = "server" at vanuata with init = entry(#pixel -> #pixel) do
                their(the.paper) := p@init(my.paper)
```

Instances of the structure class *paper.box*, *their* and *mine*, are used to convey pointers to display areas between the programs and the package. The package is retrieved from a persistent store and is initialized with *their* and *mine* as two of the parameters. After the initialization, *mine* contains a pointer to the local drawing quadrant. One of the programs then initiates a communication with the other passing to it the pointer and the other responses by replying with the counterpart which is made synonymous with the expression *their(the.paper)*. The objective is accomplished simply by the clause *copy their(the.paper)* onto *rpaper*. Note that copy is the usual graphic construct in the language.

The following two programs illustrate one use of the *locality* facilities in the language:

```
        let p = process
                with
                epl = entry(**int),
                ep2 = entry(string -> string)
                begin
                let epl = entry(**int x)
                  for i = lwb(x) to upb(x) do
                      for j = lwb(x(i)) to upb(x(i)) do x(i, j) := x(i, j) + i + j
                let ep2 = entry(string s -> string); s ++ "n"
                while true do accept epl || ep2
                end
```

Here the assignments in the entry *epl* are the subject of concern. Assuming it is called by a remote process, the evaluation of the expression on the right and the actual assignment in the inner most part of the for-loop causes six messages to be exchanged. The total number of messages required for the entire operation is therefore six times the total number of elements in the vector. Further, each assignment is carried out as an atomic operation. A failure will invalidate previous assignments. The situation can be alleviated as follows:

```
        let p = process
                with
                epl = entry(**int),
                ep2 = entry(string -> string)
                begin
                let epl = entry(**int x)
                  begin
                  let y := vector 1:: 1 of vector 1:: 1 of 0
```

```
if locality x = here
  then y := x
  else begin
    y := transcopy x
    for i = lwb(y) to upb(y) do y(i) := transcopy x(i)
    end
  for i = lwb(y) to upb(y) do
    for j = lwb(y(i)) to upb(y(i)) do y(i, j) := y(i, j) + i + j
  if locality x ~= here do assign y to x
  end
let ep2 = entry(string s -> string); s ++ "'n"
while true do accept ep1 ‖ ep2
end
```

The body of ep1 is slightly modified here. The locality of the parameter is discovered. If it originated from a remote address space, a copy of it is installed locally. Upon completion of the assignments, the copy is transferred back to where it originates. Except in abnormal circumstances, a copy of a reasonable size vector can be sent in a single message. Thus the entire operation requires six or more messages but the number is an order of magnitude less than the total number of elements in the vector.

4. CONCLUSIONS

The process model is designed to take advantage of distribution; the separation of process declarations and their execution gives rise to the possibility of starting a process on any *locality*.

Coordinated accesses to shared resources may be achieved using semaphores. The choice of semaphores as the store-based synchronization primitive is to avoid imposing a single locking regime. Syntactic support is introduced to discourage mistakes in the use of semaphores. For instance, a block may be associated with a list of semaphores so that they are all claimed before it is entered, their claiming cannot cause deadlock, and however the block is left (by end of block, exceptions or machine events) none of them is retained inadvertently.

Remote procedure calls provide synchronous transfer of computation. The calling process is halted immediately, and if the called process accepted the call and returned a result, it is resumed. This is a reasonable compromise between feasible implementation and achieving identical semantics for remote and local procedure calls. The semantics of parameter passing was made consistent in both cases. We have statistics [8] to show that the mechanism is efficient and at least as good as other RPC mechanisms [6]. One factor which contributes towards efficiency is that typechecking is factored out by signature matching prior to a communication. Signature matching is performed dynamically and once only so that typechecking every message sent and received is avoided. Static signature matching is not acceptable for two reasons: 1) to avoid using a distributed database to keep type information which suggests global coordination contradicting our desire of utilizing only local evolving information about behaviour of neighbouring processors; 2) to facilitate bindings to be delayed so that software components may evolve independently.

The language concept of *locality* is an attempt to present programmers with the advantages of distribution in a manner coherent with the programming paradigms advocated in PS-algol. Together with the programming constructs **transcopy** and

assign, they provide programmers the tools to write code to assure data integrity, efficiency, recovery etc. Although *locality* allows us to present to the programmers the underlying network in a consistent manner, the present model represents our understanding of the matter at an initial stage. A deficiency of this model is that it falls short of arranging new locality values to be introduced without stepping outside of the language. A better notation or semantics may be developed once the benefits and deficiencies have been discovered.

ACKNOWLEDGEMENTS

We had a useful discussion with Prof. Chris Barter on many aspects of the language design. Prof. Ron Morrison provided stimuli throughout this work. The research benefits from the financial support of the following: SERC, Alvey and ICL/STC.

References

1. America National Standards Institute, Inc. "The Programming Language Ada Reference Manual ANSI/MIL-STD-1815A-1983". *Lecture Notes in Computer Science* 155, 1983.

2. Atkinson, M.P., Chisholm K.J. & Cockshott W. P. "PS-algol: An Algol with a Persistent Heap". *ACM SIGPLAN Notices* 17(7):24-31, 1981.

3. Brinch Hansen, P. "Distributed Processes: A Concurrent Programming Concept ". *CACM* 21(11);934-941, 1978.

4. Doeppner, T. "Towards a Workstation Operating System". *Proc. of the 19th Hawaii International Conference on System Sciences*, 1986.

5. Hoare, C.A.R. "Communicating Sequential Processes". *CACM* 21(8):306-317, 1978.

6. Larus, J.R. "On the Performance of Courier Remote Procedure Call under 4.1c bsd". UCB/CSD 82/123 University of California at Berkeley, 1983.

7. Rovner, P., Levin, R. & Wick, J. "On Extending Modula-2 For Building Large, Integrated Systems". DEC SRC Research Report, Palo Alto, CA 94301, 1985.

8. Wai, F. "Distributed Concurrent Persistent Languages: An Experimental Design and Implementation". PhD Thesis, Department of Computing Science, University of Glasgow, 1988.

9. Wai, F. "Transparent Network Addressing". Submitted to *Software Practice & Experience*, 1989.

The Implementation of an Object-Oriented Language in PS-algol.

Richard Cooper

University of Glasgow

ABSTRACT

The implementation of Object-oriented languages and databases has lead to new problems in the design of compilers, interpreters and programming support environments. We believe that persistent programming languages like PS-algol provide facilities which greatly simplify these problems. To illustrate this we decided to produce a minimal object-oriented programming language and implement it in PS-algol. The language includes typical object-oriented notions such as inheritance, encapsulation and message passing, but omits such orthogonal and well understood concepts as program structuring constructs and expressions. The implementation took about two weeks, including the design of the syntax. This work is part of an overall project to provide a general framework within which to describe the semantics and implementation of Semantic Data Models, Object-oriented Languages, Persistent Programming Languages, Object-oriented databases and Requirements Modelling Languages.

1. INTRODUCTION

During the last few years, the fall in the cost of high-performance hardware has shifted the emphasis in Computer Science towards the creation of software systems which are easier for people to use and moved the burden of flexibility onto the computer. One example of this trend is the development of Object-oriented languages (OOPLs), in which programming is eased by the closer correspondence of program elements with the real-world objects being modelled [15].

The elements of an Object-oriented language are typically:

- **object identity** - to every real-world object there corresponds one element of the program, the object may change state but the "containing structure" never changes;

- **classification of objects** - objects are grouped together into sets of objects, variously called types or classes, all members of a set being behaviourally similar;

- **inheritance** - one type can be defined as being the sub-type of another - the semantics of the sub-typing relationship varies from system to system, but one common approach is that objects of a sub-type inherit all the properties of the super-type;

- **encapsulation** - instead of manipulating the state of an object by directly by changing static properties of the object, the only interaction of the program with the object is by making calls to procedures which constitute the operations or methods provided for that type of object.

With such languages, a reasonable claim can be made that the program more realistically mirrors behaviour in the real world. Therefore, programming is simplified and the production of software made less expensive. A similar claim has been made for Persistent Programming

Languages (PPLs) [1], which exhibit rather different features, but which address many of the same issues. PPL's have developed from an understanding of issues which do in practice cause delays in program development. These issues include: the desirability of data-type completeness, so that a programmer doesn't have to be constantly aware of exceptions in the language; the problems of having to access a variety of software (editors, graphics packages, DBMS's, etc) all of which come with their own "languages"; and the effect on the program of making data outlive the program. If the long-lived data is handled in the same way as transient data, whatever its type, then programming is simplified by removing the requirements for additional components such as file managers.

The implementation of an OOPL is clearly a different proposition from providing an applicative or even a functional language. A lot of organising work is being done for the programmer by the language environment. This cannot be without cost to those providing that environment. Organising methods, inheritance and encapsulation in a software environment which gives the programmer as little help as writing C under UNIX, for instance, is a daunting prospect. The compiler and run-time support system must be pieced together with the semantic detail of the supporting software being lost in the programming detail.

In this paper, we show how implementing an OOPL in a PPL can alleviate these problems. First of all, however, it may be of some value to compare the two notions. In both kinds of language, we find that the elements manipulated are typed objects. All objects exist only as instances of some type, and may not be used as if they belonged to some other type, except in as much as they inherit some behaviour from some super-type. OOPL's do not directly address the problem of persistence, but it has been shown that they can be extended to do so [12]. On the other hand, PPL's do not necessarily provide inheritance mechanisms, although this paper will show that these are simple to implement within a PPL.

The crucial difference between PPL's and OOPL's lies in the support for dynamic aspects of the software system in these languages. In an OOPL, these are tied to the objects of the system, whereas in a PPL, data and program co-exist as elements with equal rights. What emerges from this comparison is that the methods of Smalltalk [6], for instance, can be programmed in PS-algol, with its first-class procedures - although the converse is difficult to imagine. In this paper, methods of building the significant facilities of an OOPL into a small PS-algol program are described. The language, called MINOO (minimal Object-oriented language), has been designed to consciously omit as many as possible of the common and well understood programming language features. There are no computational constructs, expressions or arbitrary length names. There are just typed objects, inheritance, the description of operations and attributes, overloading and dynamic binding. All data access in could proceed via message passing, although it was decided also to provide direct access to the attributes, because this was felt to be useful.

The rest of the section will consist of: a description of the important aspects of the PPL, PS-algol; a description of MINOO; the ways in which the various components of MINOO were implemented in PS-algol; and conclusions about the suitability of PS-algol for the task and for programming languages of the future.

2. PS-ALGOL

PS-algol is a block-structured, strongly typed language with orthogonal persistence [13]. Every element defined in the language consists of a quadruple of attributes: name; type; value; and constancy. Of these, only the value may change and then only if the object has not been declared to be constant. The type system is simple, but rich enough to include types to represent graphical data [11] and to include procedures as first-class objects (the language is data-type complete) [2]. Thus numerical, textual and graphical data are all handled in the same way as each other and in the same way as "programs" (i.e. procedures). The provision of first-class procedures also means that the compiler can be made available as a library procedure.

Therefore, programs can, during its execution, construct other programs as strings and then compile and run them.

Although the language is strongly typed, with all objects being bound to a type at compile-time, a mechanism has been provided which allows a program to retain flexibility over the nature of such bindings - the extensible union type. To illustrate its value, consider the PS-algol command:

> **structure** *address*(**int** *house*; **string** *street, city*)

which introduces a new class of objects, named *address*, with one integer field and two string fields. The name *address* is introduced as a constructor for instances of the class, and so:

> **let** *CS* = *address*("17", "Lilybank Gdns", "Glasgow")

creates a new object which is in the class *address*. The type of this object is **pntr** and the data type completeness of PS-algol means that the fields of a structure may be of any type. In particular they may be procedures or may be of type **pntr**. This provides a powerful modelling tool since data structures of arbitrary complexity may be represented in PS-algol.

However, a further feature is that all objects created as instances of any of these class constructors are of the same type: **pntr**. This means that programs can be written which manipulate objects without knowing which class they are in. The binding of program to data can be deferred for as long as necessary. In our interpreter, for instance, the objects of a given type of our language are stored in a structure specific to that type. Much of the interpreter, however, can manipulate an object without concern for its type and, being written in PS-algol, is free to do so as all objects are stored as objects of PS-algol type, **pntr**.

One system-defined structure class is *table*, which is used extensively in MINOO to hold sets of objects. A PS-algol table is a set of **string, pntr** pairs of which the string is used as a key for the insertion and retrieval of complex objects pointed to by the **pntr**.

The provision of first-class procedure is of critical importance to this work and should be explained here. PS-algol is data-type complete. Objects of any type may be variables, the arguments or results of procedures or stored as the fields of structures. A procedure is introduced as in the following example:

```
let minproc := proc( int a, b -> int)
    begin
        let result := a
        if a>b do result := b
        result
    end
```

which introduces a procedure variable, *minproc*, of type proc(int, int -> int, whose body is the block following the specification. Following this, *minproc* may be redefined to be any other procedure which takes two integer arguments and returns an integer result. Furthermore, we can make this a part of a structure by the following:

```
strucure somethings( proc( int, int -> int ) minprocfield; ... )
let athing = somethings( minproc, .... )
```

and get it out again with

```
minproc := athing( minprocfield )
```

We will use this facility to manipulate procedures like static data items to handle the operations of our language.

Having first-class procedures has brought with the ability to provide the compiler as a system function. The consequence of this is that we can provide polymorphism in a strongly typed environment. This is achieved by merging together the algorithm to be implemented expressed as a set of strings and the structure of a data item, which may be produced as a string, into a string which contains a legal PS-algol procedure appropriate for that type of data. This can then be compiled, stored and run against the data. The PS-algol browser was the initial example of this technology [5].

The callable compiler and **pntr** type together provide significant control over the way in which program and data are bound together and the timing of that binding. We are suddenly free of the usual decision between leaving data untyped to allow a given piece of code to access more than one type of data and explicitly writing in all the types of code we expect to encounter. In PS-algol, the type of data being manipulated can be deferred by using the **pntr** type until type-specific operations are required. Alternatively, the range of types which can be handled by a procedure can be made unlimited by using the callable compiler.

In the context of this implementation, the important features are the **pntr** type, the provision of first-class procedures and the callable compiler. The **pntr** type will allow to re-use the same software to handle various types of object. The first-class procedures are used to implement operations. The callable compiler is used to automatically generate system-defined operations, such as create an object, and to hold user-defined operations. Note, however, that although we have made no use of the persistence of PS-algol, by doing so we could trivially transform our language into a persistent one.

To set the scene, let us imagine we have an address type above, which in the rather diminished world of MINOO, may look like

:A . h:i, s:s, c:s ;

which may be interpreted as "define type *A* to have an integer attribute, *h*, and two string attributes, *s* and *c*". When the interpreter sees this it will construct the PS-algol structure:

structure A(int A.h; string A.s; string A.c)

to hold instances of this type. It will then embed this structure in system generated operations which create and display instances of the structure, dereference attributes and set attribute values. These operations will be created as strings, passed to the callable compiler and returned as compiled PS-algol procedures of a fixed type to be described later. It will create an instance of a special PS-algol structure called *type*, which contains all the information about the type including tables of dynamic and static properties and instances of this type, which will be inserted as they are created. The system defined operations will be installed in the table of dynamic properties, while the three attributes are installed in the table of static properties.

Note that the table of instances has no notion of the structure of the instances. The instances will only be manipulated via the operations of the type, which have been generated to handle their own type of object and so no run-time type clash can occur. Even so, the instances of all types can be held in a common structure with a resulting simplification of code.

3. A MINIMAL OBJECT-ORIENTED LANGUAGE

Before discussing MINOO and its implementation, the nomenclature used will be defined, since the nomenclature in the literature is varied. The basic entities of the language are called **objects**. A **type** is the abstract description of a set of objects with common properties. An **attribute** is a passive property of a type. An **operation** is an active property of a type. An object may be referred to as an **instance** of a type.

Each object in the language is an instance of a particular type. A type consists of sets of (notionally private) attributes and (public) operations. The basic commands of the language permit the creation of types, the creation of instances, the assignment of values to objects and the execution of operations. The commands have been provided in the form of old-fashioned single-character named commands (":" for type creation, "I" for object instantiation, etc.) to ease the implementation. Commands are terminated by semi-colons and all layout characters are ignored. There is no benefit in analysing the syntactic quality of MINOO, as its only purpose is to demonstrate how the relevant semantics may be implemented in PS-algol.

3.1 Type creation

There are three base types, "s" string, "i" integer and "b" boolean. User-defined types can be added by type creation commands. The syntax of type creation allows the user to specify a name for the type, optionally the name of a supertype, a set of attributes and a set of operations. For example:

$$:A \quad :B$$
$$. \quad k{:}s, \ l, m{:} C$$
$$! \quad f(\ q{:} \ s \ ) \ !\$!p(N{=}\text{"k"}, \ V{=}q \ ); \qquad R; \qquad ;,$$
$$r(\ \text{-} \ C \ ) \ I \ z{:}C = \$!g(\ N = \text{"l"} \ ); \qquad Rz; \qquad ; \qquad ;$$

is explained as follows:

> ":" introduces a type definition;
> "A" is the name of the type (all names are single letter);
> ":B" means A is a sub-type of B (inherits all B's attributes and operations);
> "." introduces the new attributes ;
> "k:s" introduces an attribute of type s (a system-defined base type for strings), whose
>   name is k;
> ",l,m:C" introduce two more attributes l and m of user-defined type C;
> "!" introduces the new operations, defined on type A;
> "f(q:s)" is the signature of the first operation - its name is f , it takes in a string
>   parameter q and has no result;
> "!$!p(N = "k", V = q);" is the first command of the operation - it takes object $ (which
>   means "self" in MINOO) and applies the operation p, passing in actual
>   parameter values "k" and q, for formal parameters N and V. p is a system
>   defined attribute-setting operation (see Section 3.5) which, in this case, sets
>   attribute named k to value of q;
> "R;;" terminates the operation, returning nothing;
> "," means there are more operations;
> "r(- C)" is the signature of the second operation, which returns an instance of type C;
> "Iz:C = $!g(N = "l");" - this command creates z, an instance of type C, initialised to
>   the result of executing another system defined operation which returns the value
>   of the named attribute;
> "Rz;;" terminates the operation, returning the value of z;
> ";" - the last semi-colon finishes the type definition.

So operation f sets the value of the k attribute to the input parameter, while r returns the value of the l attribute.

Thus, a type definition consists of its name, an optional supertype, a list of typed attributes and a list of operations. The supertype may be omitted, in which case the supertype is e or "entity". An operation has a list of typed arguments of arbitrary length and one or no result types. The body of an operation consists of a sequence of commands separated by semi-colons and these are drawn from instantiation, assignment and operation invocation commands terminated by an operation return command.

3.2 Instantiation

Objects are introduced into the system by Instantiation commands, These require the specification of the object's name and type. The values of the attributes of the object may also be specified. For instance, in the command

   $I\ a{:}A\ =\ (k="abc",\ l{=}X);$

   "I" introduces the instantiation command;
   "a" is the new object identifier;
   ":A" introduces its type;
   "=" introduces attribute values - this could be omitted and default values for the
      attributes would be assumed;
   " k="abc" " this gives k a string literal value;
   " ,l =X" gives l the value of object X, which must be of type C, or one of C's sub-
      types, of course;
   " ; " ends the instantiation - note property m takes a default value.

The values of the attributes can be specified as expressions of arbitrary complexity as described below.

3.3 Assignment

Object assignment is performed by commands like

   $A\ a = b$ or $A\ a = c!f(\ q = "abc"\ )$

where the "A" introduces assignment and the right hand side of the assignment may be any expression of the type established for a, when it was instantiated.

3.4 Operation Application

The application of an operation of an object is introduced as in

   $!\ c!f(\ q = "xyz"\ )$

where c is the object name, f the operation name, q the name of a parameter and "xyz" its input value. At command level, the interpreter prints out the value of the result of applying the operator. Use of the "!" command indirectly within an operation itself is only valid for operations that do not return a result, although other operations can appear as part of an expression.

3.5 System Provided Operations

Each type needs to have four operations automatically defined on it. These are:

   "c":   create an instance - it takes in a set of attribute name, value pairs and returns the
         created object. It is only called by an "I" command.

"*s*": (show) print an object - it recursively traverses the properties of the object, printing any base-type information it can find. Thus the program:

```
: A. k:s;                    ! Create type A, with one string field, k.
: B. l:s, m:A;               ! Create type B, with string field, l and a
                             !      field m of type A.
I a:A = (k ="abc");          ! Create an A called a, field set to "abc".
I b:B = ( l = "def", m = a ); ! Create a B called b, with fields set to
                             !      "def" and a.
! b!s();                     ! Apply the show operation.
```

which will give ("def", ("abc"))

"*p*": put an attribute value - it takes a attribute name as parameter N, a string, and a value as parameter V, and sets the attribute's value appropriately, as in:

```
! a!p( N = "k", V = "ghi" );
! a!s();                     will give       ( "ghi" )
```

"*g*": retrieve a property value, given the attribute value -

```
! a!p( N = "k", V = b!g( N = "l" ) );
```

retrieves property l of b and sets property k of a to it. Note that handling these operations "p" and "g", which have a polymorphic parameter, V, in a strongly typed environment may be expected to give some problems.

3.6 Extra Redundant Syntax

Although the above is sufficient, some extra syntax was added to make the process of testing the interpreter tolerable.

The usual dot notation for attributes was added - thus

> *b.l*   could replace $b!g(N = "l")$

in the above example. The effect, however, is identical, but does mean that the attributes have been rendered public, which might be desirable anyway.

Similarly, a print command was added:

> **P** *a,b*;   is the same as ! *a*!*s*(); ! *b*!*s*();

A dump facility was added - thus

> **D**;

applies the "*s*" operation to everything in the symbol table.

Finally "?" quits the interpreter.

3.7   Expressions

Given the two notations, an expression handler was built which permits the free mixing of "."''s and "!"''s. Thus imagining type C, with an attribute y of type D, where D has an operation o which takes a string parameter p, then

$a!r().y!o(p="123")$

is an expression which takes a of type A, applies its r operation, returning something of type C. This has the y attribute dereferenced and the resulting object has its o operation applied. The type of the expression is the same as the type of operation o.

4. THE IMPLEMENTATION

The first point to be noted was that the interpreter was written without recourse to automatic compiler-generation tools. Secondly, it was decided to implement the language incrementally, starting with the base types and gradually adding the other features.

4.1 The Type Structure and Base Types

A simple PS-algol structure was created to hold types:

structure *type(*	**string** *tname;*	
	pntr *subtypes;*	! a table of subtypes
	pntr *supertype;*	! a single supertype
	pntr *properties;*	! a table of name -> type
	pntr *operations;*	! ditto
	pntr *class* *)*	! a table of instances

Two base structures, a table of types and the symbol table were set up at this point. Then a most general type, "e" was created to act as the bottom of the type hierarchy. This looks like:

> **let** *eType* = *type(* "e", *table(),* **nil**, *table(), table(), table()*)

and is unique in having **nil** in its super-type field.

The three base types were then set up. They required, first of all, PS-algol structures to hold their instances. These were:

> **structure** *stringBox(* **string** *stringVal*)
> **structure** *intBox(* **int** *intVal*)
> **structure** *boolBox(* **bool** *boolVal)*

Then the three type structures were created. For strings, the type looked like:

> **let** *sType* = *type(* "s", **nil**, *eType, table(), table(), table()*)

That is, there are no sub-types of a base-type, the super-type is *eType* and the three final fields all initially contain empty tables. The attributes table will remain empty, the operations table will have the four basic operations ("c", "s", "p" and "g") inserted and the *class* table will have strings inserted as they are created. After *sType* is created, a reference to it in the sub-types field of *eType* is made.

The basic operations for these base types are fairly trivial. The "c" operation creates a new instance of a *stringBox* structure, for instance. The "s" operation will unpackage a *stringBox* structure and print the contents. The "g" and "p" operations, on the other hand, do nothing as these base-type structures have no attributes to manipulate.

4.2 The Interpreter and Expression Evaluation

The basic operation of the interpreter consists of a single control loop which seeks command characters and then continues to interpret a command of that type. The commands it expects are:":", "I", "A", "!", "P", "D" and "?".

149

The commands "I", "A", "!" and "P" all involve calls to an evaluator for expressions as described in Section 7.4.1.7. Expressions can appear in two places in the language. Here, they are to be directly evaluated with their results being used immediately by the command. They can also, however, appear in operation definitions, in which case they are to be stored for later evaluation. Therefore, the expression evaluator comes in a double form. It may be called either to evaluate the expression or to return a piece of PS-algol code, which when executed will perform the evaluation. The evaluator can handle base-type literals or complex expressions. The latter result in look-ups to get attribute values or the execution of the operation code. This this double operation is illustrated with the expression

$$a!r().y!o(p="123")$$

already encountered.

In command mode, this finds the object a; finds its type; finds the r operation and applies it; it then finds the resulting type and calls the g operation, with input $N ="y"$; this results in another object whose type is found; operation o is then found and applied with p set to "123". The result of the whole operation is the result of the expression.

If the expression appears in the definition of an operation, the code illustrated in Figure 1 is created.

```
let typeA := s.lookup( "A", T )              ! Type A looked up when a
                                             !    was instantiated.
let parameters1 := table()                   ! The parameters for r
let parameters2 := table()                   ! The parameters for g, which
s.enter( "N", parameters2, stringBox( "y" )) !    was inferred from the dot.
let typeY := s.lookup( "Y", T )              ! The type of the y attribute.
let parameters3 := table()                   ! The parameters for o found
s.enter( "p", parameters3, stringBox( "123" )) !  explicitly.
let typeO := s.lookup( "O", T )              ! The type of the O operation.

stringBox( s.lookup( "o", typeO(operations) )( ocode )(
     T, ST, s.lookup( "g", typeY(operations) )( ocode )(
          T, ST, s.lookup( "r", typeA(operations) )( ocode )(
               T, ST, a, parameters1 ), parameters2 ),
                    parameters3 )( stringVal ))
```

Figure 1: Generated Code for Expression Evaluation.

That is, it sets up references to tables for the parameters to the three operations and then does look-ups for the operations and applies them. The applications are performed from the innermost outwards. That is the code for operation r of type A is applied to an empty parameter set (*parameters1*). Then the g operation of type Y is retrieved and applied with the parameter N set to "y" (*parameters2*). Finally, the o operation of type O is retrieved and applied to the result of this, with parameter p set to "123" (*parameters3*). The result is packaged into a *stringBox*.

4.3 Type Creation

This is part of the interpreter proceeds as follows:

   a) Create a new type structure, with the name in it and all other fields empty.

   b) Scan the input for a supertype. If there is one, put a reference to it in the relevant field, otherwise use the default, *etype*. At the same time, put a reference to the new type in the *subtypes* field of the supertype.

c) Read the attribute names and types and insert them into the *properties* table, using the attribute name as the key and the type as the value.

d) Automatically generate the "c", "s", "p" and "g" operations and insert them into the *operations* table - see next section.

e) Read and parse the operation specifications and create operations for insertion into the *operations* table.

f) Insert the type into the table of types and quit.

Steps (a) - (c) and (f) need no further elaboration, but the generation of the system and user-defined operations are complex tasks and will be described in the next two sections.

4.4   Automatic Generation of the System Operations

This technique will be described with respect to the type:

: $B.l{:}s, m{:}A.$

where A is some previously defined type. From this input, the five lexemes B, l, s, m and A are available, where s and A have been checked to be valid types.

These can be used to build an appropriate PS-algol structure for B, which is

structure *TypeB*(**string** *B.l*; **pntr** *B.m*; **pntr** *B.super, B.type*)

(where the last two fields point to inherited attributes of the object and the object's type) and around this are built the four procedures. It was decided to create a procedure type sufficient to cater for user-defined operations as well and this is

proc(**pntr** *theTypes, SymbolTable, self, params* -> **pntr**)

where the first two parameters are required to import the local MINOO environment into a procedure so that the procedure can be compiled independently. In order to store these operations in tables, they need to be packaged into PS-algol structures. The following was chosen for the purpose:

structure *operation*(**string** *oname*;
                           proc(**pntr, pntr, pntr, pntr** -> **pntr**) *ocode*;
                           pntr *arguments, resulttype*   )

in the which the four fields hold the name, the compiled code, a table of argument name, type pairs, and a pointer to the type of the operation's result.

The operation building technique is illustrated with respect to the "s" operation which prints out an instance, as shown in Figure 2. The purpose of this operation is to print out the attributes of an object separated by commas and surrounded in parentheses. If the attribute is complex, this in turn is printed in a further set of parentheses. Inherited attributes are also to be printed, preceded by a colon.

The operation receives a pointer to the object as its third parameter, *OBJECT*. the first and second parameters import the type and symbol tables from the current environment, while fourth parameter is a dummy since *s* does not take any parameters. Following some initialisation, including building in the structure for this type and the general purpose structures for types and operations, it finds the object's type. Then it starts the printing with a "(", before directly printing field *l*, which it can do as it is a base type. Printing the other field is more complicated. It must look up the field's type (*A* in this case) and then find the "s" operation for type A, which can then be called with the value of field m as its principle (third) parameter. The inherited information is printed out in the same way as for complex attributes. The "s" operation is found from the type's supertype and the structure containing the inherited attributes is passed to it for printing.

```
proc( pntr T, S, OBJECT, dummy -> pntr )
   begin
     structure B( string B.l; pntr B.m; pntr B.super, B.type )
     structure type( string tname, tstruct;
                     pntr subtypes, supertype, properties, operations, class )
     structure operation( string oname; proc( pntr, pntr, pntr, pntr -> pntr ) ocode;
                     pntr arguments, resultype )
     let thetype = OBJECT( B.type )
     let TT := nil;                                    ! The type of an attribute.
     let subshow := nil                                ! The s operation of TT.
     let dummyResult := nil                            ! Receives dummy result form
     write "( "                                        !    recursive calls.
     let commas := ""                                  ! Flag to omit comma before
     write commas                                      !    first field.
     commas := ", "                                    ! Print commas from now on.
     write "",OBJECT( B.l ),""
     write commas
     TT := s.lookup( "A", T )                          ! Lookup type A.
     subshow := s.lookup( "s", TT( operations ) )  ! Get A's s operation.
     dummyResult := subshow(ocode)( T, S, OBJECT( B.m ), nil )     ! Print attribute.
     let superT = thetype( supertype )
     if superT( tname ) ~= "e" do                      ! Print inherited data if there are
       begin                                           !   any, i.e. supertype is not "e".
         write ": "
         dummyResult := s.lookup( "s",superT( operations ) )(ocode )
                           (T, S, OBJECT( B.super ), nil )   ! Print inherited values.
       end
     write " )"
     nil                                               ! A dummy result.
   end
```

Figure 2: The Automatically Generated Operation s.

This procedure was built entirely by string manipulation with only the parts underlined being derived from the type information. This string is passed to the compiler and the resulting compiled code is put into an *operation* structure, with name "s", a blank table of arguments and a nil for result type. This structure is then inserted into the *operations* field of the type being created.

4.5 User-Defined Operations

The interpretation of user-defined operations will be illustrated for the r operation of type A given above. This results in the creation of the PS-algol procedure given in Figure 3. This procedure takes in the table of types, the symbol table, the object and a table of the input parameters. It starts of by defining all of the structures it needs including its own type structure. Certain dummy variables are declared, not all of which are used in the context of this particular procedure.

```
proc( pntr T, ST, OBJECT, PARAMS -> pntr )
   begin
      structure type( string tname, tstruct;
                        pntr subtypes, supertype, properties, operations, instances )
      structure operation( string oname; proc( pntr, pntr, pntr, pntr -> pntr ) ocode;
                        pntr arguments, resultype )
      structure plist( string pname; pntr pvalue, pnext )
      structure A( pntr A.l; pntr A.m; string A.k; pntr A.super, A.type )
      structure stringBox( string stringVal )
      structure intBox( int intVal )
      structure boolBox( bool boolVal )
      let vobject := nil;let initials := nil
      let parameters := nil;                       let dummy := nil
      let ztype := s.lookup( "C", T )
      let parameters1 := table()
      s.enter( "N", parameters1, stringBox( "1" ))
      let typeA := s.lookup( "A", T )
      let z := s.lookup( "g", typeA(operations) )( ocode )
                                ( T, ST, OBJECT, parameters1 )

         z
   end
```

Figure 3: A User Defined Operation in MINOO.

Then the command "I z:C = $!g(N= "1")" is transformed into code which does the following:

> look up the type of z as ztype - this is not used here but would have been used if the initialisation had involved creating an entirely new object rather than copying one;

> set up a table of actual parameter values, with one entry pairing N and "1";

> find operation "g" of type A and apply it to the current object, OBJECT - the result is z.

Lastly, the "Rz" command is compiled by placing a reference to z as the last line of the procedure -this has the effect of returning the pointer to the object z.

Thus a general purpose compilation of MINOO "methods" into PS-algol procedures has proved possible. The basic method of this compilation is to turn strings in MINOO into strings of PS-algol code, noting any objects which need to be looked up from the environment. Those look-ups are then inserted into the procedure before the code which uses them.

4.6   Polymorphic Operations

It has been noted above that the system operations deal polymorphically with attributes of any type. There is no trouble in providing "s" (as shown in Section 4.4) and "p" since the calling program will know the type of the object which it sends. In the case of "g" however, there is a problem since it returns an object of unknown type. This point may be illustrated by looking at the procedure for "g" of type A in Figure 4. Here the procedure picks up the property name from the parameter table and checks which of the three attributes of A it is is. If it does not find the attribute in the current type, it refers to the super-type to find it. Whichever it is, it dereferences the field value from the structure and in the case of the string attribute packages it up in order to return it as a structure. What also happens though, is that the type of the result is inserted into the slot for the result type of the operation. This means that the calling program can use this field to check the type of the result in the same way as is done for non-polymorphic procedures.

```
proc( pntr T, ST, OBJECT, PARAMS -> pntr )
  begin
    structure type( string tname, tstruct;
                    pntr subtypes, supertype, properties, operations, instances )
    structure operation( string oname; proc( pntr, pntr, pntr, pntr -> pntr ) ocode;
                         pntr arguments, resultype )
    structure plist( string pname; pntr pvalue, pnext )
    structure A( pntr A.l; pntr A.m; string A.k; pntr A.super, A.type )
    structure stringBox( string stringVal )
    structure intBox( int intVal )
    structure boolBox( bool boolVal )
    let propname = s.lookup( "N", PARAMS )( stringVal )
    let theT = s.lookup( "A", T )
    let theO = s.lookup( "g", theT( operations ) )
    case propname of
        "l":  { theO( resultype ) := s.lookup( "C", T ); OBJECT( A.l ) }
        "m":     { theO( resultype ) := s.lookup( "C", T ); OBJECT( A.m ) }
        "k":        {theO( resultype ) := s.lookup( "s", T );stringBox( OBJECT( A.k ) ) }
        default:
          begin
            let superGet =s.lookup( "g", theT(supertype)( operations ) )
            let temp =superGet( ocode )( T, S, OBJECT( A.super ), PARAMS )
            theO( resultype ) := superGet ( resultype )
            temp
          end
  end
end
```

Figure 4: The Polymorphic Automatically Generated Operation, g.

This is an instance of a generally applicable technique installed directly into this procedure by the system. However, it is a general technique which could be extended, by replacing the result type field of the operation structure with two fields, one for its expected type and another for the returned type, which would be a sub-type of the expected type. In the case of "g" the operation would expect to return an entity object, but would actually return some other type which it would report in the returned type field.

4.7 Object Instantiation

The instantiation command depends heavily on the system-generated "c" operations. The command passes to the appropriate "c", the type table and symbol table, the type of the new object and a list of attribute name, initial value pairs. The values are derived by calls to the expression evaluator. The "c" operation then does the following:

> an instance of the type structure is created with a pointer to its type;
> if the type has a super-type, the "c" function of that type is called and a pointer to the resulting object is put in the super field;
> the list of initial values is scanned and fields of the structure filled in as appropriate;
> the new object is returned.

The returned object is then put into the class of the type and into the symbol table, which completes the functions of the "I" command.

4.8 Assignment and Operation Execution

The "A" command finds an object to be assigned to and then calls the expression evaluator to provide the new value. Operation execution is also a very short piece of code, which gets an operation, builds a table of input parameter values and calls the operation. If the operation has a result, this is printed by a call to the appropriate "s" operation.

154

4.9   Inheritance

Inheritance is achieved by pointer links. The type structure has two-way links between sub- and supertype. The instances have links from sub- to super-type values. When an attribute for an object is requested by a call to the "g" operation, the operation passes the request up to the super-type if the attribute is not defined in this type. When an operation is requested, again the search for the operation starts at the current type and is passed up the inheritance tree.

4.10   Summary.

In this section, some of the detail of the implementation has been described. The diagram in Figure 5 shows the layout of the underlying data structures. The user-defined types are shown in rectangular boxes split into five parts (the base types appear in single boxes). The type hierarchy is shown as diagonal lines. The five compartments represent the name, the sub-types, the operations, the attributes and the instances. Instances are shown in rounded boxes, attributes in rectangular boxes with two compartments (the name and the type) and operations are shown as lozenges containing the name, the table of arguments and the result type. Using this simple structure, together with two system objects containing tables of all the types and all the instances, all of the object-oriented data has been represented.

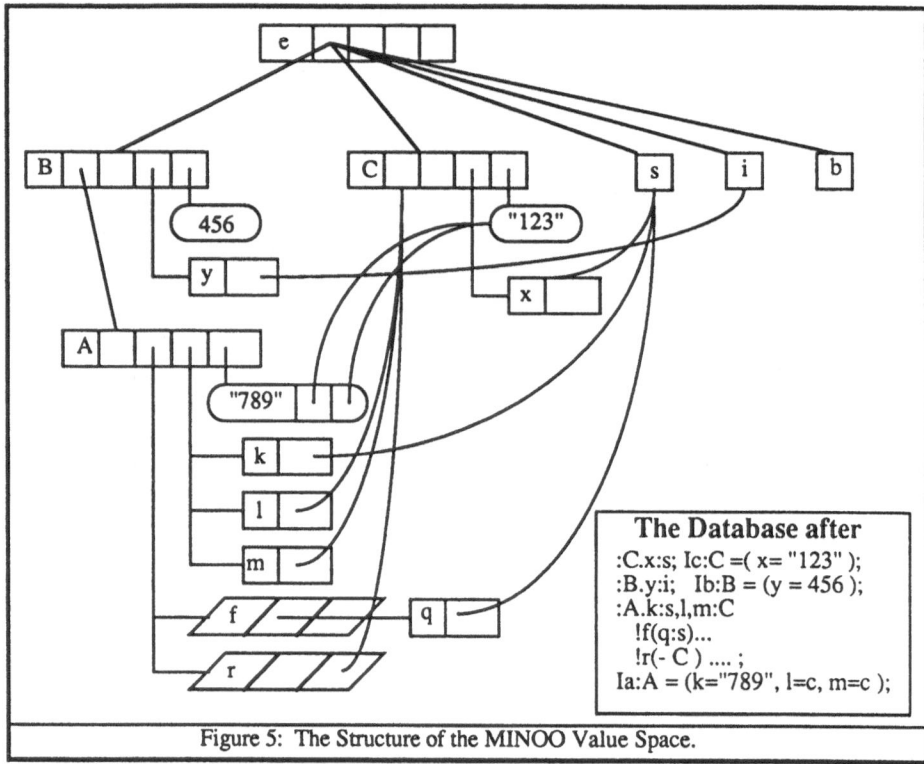

Figure 5: The Structure of the MINOO Value Space.

5   CONCLUSIONS

This paper has shown how an interpreter for a minimal Object-oriented Programming Language has been implemented in PS-algol.   The implementation has two main motivating forces. Firstly, we wish to evaluate PS-algol and to make suggestions for improvements, and secondly, we wish to evaluate high-level data modelling tools.

While avoiding some of the well-understood aspects of compiler construction, it demonstrates how implementations of the critical parts of a such a language can be achieved. Types and objects are represented by PS-algol structures. Inheritance is achieved by following pointer chains. Methods or operations are compiled into PS-algol procedures, which being first-class elements of the language may be manipulated freely and stored, retrieved and applied as required. Access to objects can be restricted to procedures stored as part of their associated type.

This work could proceed by developing the language to include further base types, multi-valued types, computational constructs and expressions, although it is believed that this would require no new technology. Experiments on the representation of types as objects in the system, on the other hand, may provide added simplicity in the resulting structure. More interestingly, multiple inheritance could be included as a method for investigating the semantic problems of inheriting from more than one super-type. Including parameterised or generic types is a significantly more difficult problem, but would permit experimentation with the various notions involved. The language could be given a sophisticated user interface, using the graphical tools described previously [4], and including software development tools like syntax-directed editors. Finally, the language could be made persistent. The implementation was never designed to include persistence, which was covered in other experiments. From these, it is known that adding persistence when implementing in PS-algol, is a very small task.

The constructs of PS-algol have been exercised and found to have been sufficiently robust enough to handle the demands of the implementation. The simplicity of the language is a great assistance in developing programs quickly. The power of the language structures and types, which manifest many of the important features of object-orientation (notably object identity and polymorphism), enabled a straightforward implementation of the interpreter. The ability to write general purpose procedures using the pntr type and the callable compiler simplifies the program, within the security of a strongly typed system and without the environment becoming full of type-ambiguous objects. However, we can see some problems with PS-algol, particularly with its type system and in the use of the callable compiler.

The type system has two principle weaknesses. Firstly, the types of base and complex objects are not well integrated. We can provide polymorphic procedures which range over any kind of structured object. It would be desirable to be able to range over all types, including string, int, etc. In the interpreter, we continually had to package and unpackage base-type objects and dealing with these exceptional conditions constitutes a significant part of the code. Secondly, in creating structures with pntr fields it would often be possible to specify the type of these fields and expect the compiler or run-time system to enforce the type. For instance, in the following structure for nodes of lists of string:

stringListNode(**string** *value*; **pntr** *next*)

it would be useful to force the *next* field to point to another *stringListNode* (or nil of course), but we cannot specify this in PS-algol. These problems point to the need for a much more powerful, uniform and high-level type system.

Having access to the compiler at run-time is one of the back-bones of our implementation. We can combine the algorithm and the type description into a string, compile that string and then apply the resulting procedure to the object. This is a very powerful technique, which effectively resolves the tension between the security of strong-typing and the expressive power of polymorphism. However, the way in which this is achieved in PS-algol is somewhat cumbersome.

Furthermore, in order to get any interaction or data sharing between the compiled operation and the environment from which it is called, one of two unsatisfactory methods must be used. Either shared data must be put into the Persistent Store and retrieved from there or, as is done here, the environment must be passed into the procedures as parameters. Every system- or user-created operation receives the type table and the symbol table as parameters, which means that it can traverse the environment with freedom as these are the two roots of all information. Neither of these techniques seems to be the natural way to model the the programmer's intention.

What is required to overcome both of these problems is some mechanism for saying compile algorithm A in the context of environment E, where A is parameterised. Quite what kind of parameterisation is useful here, whether by type or by data values seems a fruitful area for language design research. Clearly the language Napier [10] with its richer type system and environments goes a long way to satisfying all of our problems described here. We hope to redo our work in Napier and would expect to see considerable shortening and simplification of the code.

The main conclusion to be drawn from this experiment is that an implementation language like PS-algol greatly simplifies the task of implementing an Object-Oriented language. The components of such a language are naturally modelled in PS-algol and so the implementation is kept to a reasonable length (about 1200 lines of code for MINOO). For the implementation of real OOOPLs, such as Smalltalk [6] or Eiffel [9], having reduced the complexity of the task, it would also become possible to begin to tackle efficiency issues - for instance, by using the run-time compiler to tailor efficient code. Furthermore, compilers for dynamically typed languages such as Smalltalk can be written which extract statically inferrable types wherever they can and impose them with a resulting efficiency gain. Implementation in a language which simplifies the overall compiler construction task renders the task of doing this more tractable.

We see this work as a part of an attempt to provide a framework for the evaluation of higher-level data modelling tools, including Semantic Data Models, Requirements Models, Object-oriented Programming Languages and Object-oriented Databases. Work along this line has included implementations of Shipman's Functional Data Model [7], Greenspan's Requirements Modelling Language [3], an Entity-Relationship Modelling Tool [8] and the IFO data model [14]. As all of these can be implemented in a language like PS-algol, we can place them all within a common framework and start to move towards a more formal description of data models in general. From this, we can start to ensure that the process of data-modelling is well understood and that the tools provided are really appropriate.

ACKNOWLEDGEMENTS

This work was supported by the ESPRIT Project Number 834, COMANDOS. I would like to acknowledge the contributions to this work made by my colleagues on the Alvey PISA project and the ESPRIT Comandos project. In particular, Malcolm Atkinson has given much support and ideas for this and other projects; Al Dearle pioneered the use of the interactive compiler; David Harper has had many interesting discussions which influenced the work; and Kevin Waite furthered my understanding of Object-oriented programming. I would finally like to thank David McNally of St. Andrews University whose super-fast PS-algol compiler made the work even smoother than it otherwise would have been.

REFERENCES

1.   Atkinson, M.P. and Morrison, R., "An Approach to Persistent Programming", *The Computer Journal*, 26, 4, 360-365, 1983.

2.   Atkinson, M.P. and Morrison, R., "Procedures as Persistent Data Objects", *ACM TOPLAS*, 7, 4, 539-559, October 1985.

3. Cooper, R.L. and Atkinson, M.P., "Requirements Modelling in a Persistent Object Store", Proceedings of the 2nd Appin Workshop on Persistent Object Stores, *Persistent Programming Research Report* 44, Universities of Glasgow and St. Andrews, 1987.

4. Cooper, R.L., MacFarlane, D.K. and Ahmed, S., "User Interface Tools in PS-algol", *Persistent Programming Research Report 56*, Universities of Glasgow and St. Andrews, 1987.

5. Dearle, A. and Brown, A.L., "Safe Browsing in a Strongly Typed Persistent Environment",*The Computer Journal*, 1988.

6. Goldberg, A. and Robson, D., "Smalltalk-80: The language and its implementation", Addison-Wesley, Reading, Mass.

7. Kulkarni, K. and Atkinson, M.P., "EFDM: The Extended Functional Data Model", *Computer Journal*, 29, 1, 38-45, 1986.

8. McGonigall, S. "An Enity-Relationship Modelling Tool", Senior Honours Disertation, Univeristy of Glasgow, 1988

9. Meyer, B., "Object-oriented Software Construction", Prentice Hall International, 1988.

10. Morrison, R., Brown, A.L., Carrick, R., Connor R. and Dearle, A., "The Napier Reference Manual", Univeristy of St. Andrews, 1988.

11. Morrison, R., Dearle, A., Brown, A.L. and Atkinson, M.P., "An Integrated Graphics Programming Environment", *Computer Graphics Forum*, 5, 2, 147-157, June 1986.

12. Maier, D., Stein, J., Otis, A. and Purdy, D., "The Development of an Object-Oriented DBMS", *Proceedings of the ACM Conference on Object-Oriented Progarmming Systems*, Languages and Applications, 1986.

13. The PS-algol Reference Manual, Fourth Edition, *Persistent Programming Research Report* 12, Universities of Glasgow and St. Andrews, 1987.

14. Qin, Z. and Cooper, R.L., "An Implementation of the IFO Data Model", *Persistent Programming Research Report* , Universities of Glasgow and St. Andrews, 1989.

15. Stefik D. and Bobrow, D.G., "Object-Oriented Programming: Themes and Variations", *The AI Magazine*, 40-62, December, 1985.

Part III

Implementing Persistence

Aggregation, Persistence, and Identity in Worlds

Dennis G. Allard and David S. Wile

USC Information Sciences Institute

ABSTRACT

We have previously proposed an aggregation mechanism, called Worlds, for grouping information into conceptual units in an objectbase. This capability is neither object based nor relation based. Rather, it is concern based, consisting of an orthogonal cut through the objectbase of those aspects of objects and relations relevant to individual concerns, such as program sources, electronic mail, appointment calendars, etc. We draw an analogy with blueprints. Just as several blueprints are needed to characterize a house, several worlds are necessary to characterize a complex object. Worlds serve as units of persistence in our distributed environment where each workstation contains only a partial model of what is known about any given object. Object identity and integrity become issues in such a scheme. We opt for a weak notion of object identity based on keys or descriptions. Maintainence of contradictory information in different workstations about the same object is tolerated. Everything described is implemented, evolving, and in daily use.

1. OBJECT BASED COMPUTATION ENVIRONMENTS

We have implemented a computation environment called FSD, which stands for Formalized Software Development [2, 21]. FSD provides a specification language and computing environment, including database management, program development, and system prototyping. The specification language is AP5 [5, 6], a database programming language which replaces conventional data structures with a higher level *relation abstraction*. AP5 extends Common Lisp with an in-core database and incorporates first order logic formulas in constructs for stating invariants on the database, for querying and updating data, and for imperative and rule based control. Ephemeral relations used by programs *and* long lived database-like relations maintained by the user both reside in the database. Some of this information is persistent, some is not. A mechanism called Worlds [19] views the database as a collection of overlapping subdatabases and maintains data persistence. Tools built on AP5 and Worlds exist for program development, electronic mail processing, appointment scheduling, etc. Although we are programmers and our main activity involves research about programming, we use FSD to accomplish all of our computational needs. For this reason we refer to FSD as a computation environment rather than as merely a programming environment.

Past computing culture has employed the *file* as the fundamental organizational unit for large data aggregates. Files provide persistence of data, sharing and distribution of data, and organization of data. In object bases, all of these aspects of aggregates are still needed, but the representation of all data at all times in a parsed, uniform database does not blend well with files. In fact, there are no files in FSD. Worlds is the mechanism which is emerging as the primary tool for achieving these functions.

Global databases are designed for maintaining the persistence of information and for sharing that information. However, many programming environments, including FSD, have established private, local objectbases in workstations rather than relying on a monolithic global database. Persistence is then maintained by depositing subsets of the workstation data in a stable external store. Each workstation gives these subsets a localized meaning. We feel this is a much more natural model for persistence than those based on a global database in which everyone must agree on the "schema of things."

1.1. The Nature of Aggregates

Aggregates arise from a need for *focus, viewing, garbage identification, sharing, persistence, and hierarchy* [20]. If one considers the information needed to model a programmer's workstation environment, it is clear that aggregates arise from neither an object-centered view of the data, nor from a relation-centered view. In particular,

Appointments: first-name, last-name, works-on, work-extension,
     appointment-with
Mail: first-name, last-name, loginname, mail-drop, message-from, message-to
Programming: first-name, last-name, developed-by, maintained-by,
     work-extension, mail-drop, works-on
Documentation: first-name, last-name, author-of
Personal Appointments: first-name, last-name, home-address, home-phone

Figure 1-1: Relations involving Persons grouped by layers of concerns

the workstation will have *programs, appointments, people, mail, dates, documents, bibliography entries, biographic entries*, etc., and various relations between these objects. Consider the relationships in which an object of type *Person* might participate in such an environment: *first-name, last-name, loginname, works-on, home-address, home-phone, work-extension, message-from, appointment-with, developed-by, author-of, maintained-by, message-to, mail-drop*, etc. One would want to view aspects of Persons relevant to mail when reading mail, relevant to scheduling when looking at appointments, etc. Such a mixture of concerns prevents considering all the relationships involving a Person to be part of a single aggregate. Also, if a new relationship involving a Person is asserted does that mean all uses of the aggregate from before are invalid? Hence, the notion of aggregation based solely on object class is both inadequate and inextensible. Instead, the objects and relationships tend to naturally group into *layers of concerns*, as illustrated in Figure 1-1. *We conclude that aggregates must be able to represent sets of objects and subsets of the relationships involving the objects. These sets and subsets are not contained within single type or relation boundaries.*

1.2. Identifying Objects in Aggregates

Could we agree on a *universal* definition of the object Abraham Lincoln? Is this paper one of his "parts" because it mentions him? We think not. Rather, Worlds support individual models of objects, some of whose attributes we agree on in a shared environment. In the real world, the identity of an object is an agreement between two agents (people) that they are discussing the same thing. We believe this concept should be carried over into identifying objects in "the persistent store." This provides a perspective in which there is no sense of a global database of universally consistent aggregates. Rather, consistency of data is maintained with respect to *each* workstation's objectbase in which it is loaded, and only *when* it is loaded into that objectbase. Our approach is in contrast to systems which provide a 'strong' notion of object identity [7]. *We conclude that an aggregate must be able to identify the objects it contains descriptively, because there is no concept of a global object with its own identity over time.*

2. OBJECTBASE FRAMEWORK

We believe that our proposed aggregation mechanism will work with many of the data modelling languages currently under examination. But, since our experience is with FSD, we describe in this section those aspects of FSD's semantic data model [11] which we are assuming in this paper. Two distinguishing features of the system are of importance for aggregate usage:

- The database is a virtual memory database, with no a priori support for persistence.

- The database has mechanisms for monitoring and maintaining data integrity.

The particular mechanisms for maintaining integrity are not important, except for the fact that each database is a site for consistency maintenance applied to the data it contains. That is, databases have individual consistency constraints and can disagree with one other.

2.1. The AP5 Relation Abstraction

Intuitively, any data structure can be viewed as the representation of certain relations, where a relation is a set of tuples of objects. For example, a list may represent the type[1] *Reference* where Reference(x) $\equiv$ x is in the list, meaning that x is an object which models an item in a bibliography. A hashtable may represent the attribute *title*, where title(r,s) $\equiv$ r is a reference object which hashes to the string object s, meaning that s is the title of r. In AP5, our goal is to allow the programmer to forget about data structures and use the more abstract relation operations.

The operations on *transition relations* are those of *updating*, *testing*, and *generating*. A transition relation is one which may be explicitly updated in an *atomic transaction*.

---

[1]In AP5, the terms *type* and *attribute* mean unary relation and binary relation, respectively.

We declaratively associate a *representation* with a relation which indicates the data structures used to represent that relation and defines how to map the operations which are required of a relation onto operations on that data structure. A representation encapsulates the data structuring details of a relation, and is selected at declaration time from an extensible library. It is possible to redeclare a relation's representation for purposes of efficiency. Doing so will usually not require rewriting any AP5 code, just recompiling it.

In addition to transition relations, there are various kinds of *derived relations*. AP5 also has *consistency rules* which state invariants, in FOL, on the state of a workstation's database. An atomic transaction is guaranteed to preserve consistency. There are mechanisms for *repairing* violations so as to converge to a consistent state. Note, different workstations can have differing, even conflicting, sets of consistency rules. For example, one workstation's database might allow a Reference object to have no title while a different workstation required a title.

We recognize a distinction between *abstract objects* (objects which are creatable) and *values* (things like integers, atoms, strings). However, there is no *a priori* restriction as to which relations either kind of object can participate in. In other words, how an object is represented is orthogonal to its AP5 type. In the future, AP5 will distinguish between the notions of *modelling type* and *representation type*, and make this distinction more formal. In this paper, by type we mean modelling type.

Objects are classified in a type lattice. The structure of the data base is defined by this type lattice and by relations having those types as domains. The definitions of relations and various constraints on those relations is called a *domain model*, a notion akin to that of *schema* in database literature. Relations are strongly typed, i.e., their signatures are known. The details of which slots of relations form *keys* can be specified. Once a domain model exists, transactions *assert* and *retract* tuples of objects into and from the relations. We call tuples *relationships*. We say that a relationship is *in* or is *a member of* a relation. In this exposition we omit consideration of derived relations and composite objects. A composite object is one whose representation involves embedded abstract objects. Hence, an *object* may be considered to be an uninterpreted point which receives all its meaning by virtue of the relationships in which it resides.

3. DEFINING AGGREGATES VIA WORLDS

The defining characteristic for aggregation mentioned earlier is that aggregates must be able to represent partial relations and objects[2]. In section 3.1, we specify what we mean by *aggregate*, *World*, and *Worldspec*. Loosely, a world is a subdatabase, an aggregate is a set of objects and relationships belonging to a world, and a worldspec is a schema which constrains what is in a world. In section 3.2 we provide more detail about worldspecs.

3.1. Population

At an abstract level, an aggregate is simply a set of objects and a set of relationships

---

[2]Subsets of tuples in a relation and subsets of relationships involving an object, respectively.

in which the objects participate. We insist that all objects referenced by the relationships be in the set of objects. A question is how do we identify what objects and what relationships belong in an aggregate? That is, how do we *populate* an aggregate? The aggregate definer could provide a generator for the objects and the relationships, but this lacks any motivation for object and relationship membership in the aggregate, i.e., it does not necessarily correspond to any *conceptual layer* of the object base.

Alternatively, he could provide a set of objects, and we could define the aggregate containing all relationships between only those objects. In general this fails to discriminate adequately, for no partitioning of only the objects corresponds to the conceptual layers. Different aggregates can contain the same objects but have different relationships involving those objects. For example, a program module aggregate could include the *load-before* relationship between two program objects whereas a code analysis data aggregate could have the *calls-as-subroutine* relationship between the same two objects. In neither case should one aggregate get the relationship which is germane to the other just because the same objects are being related in *some* way in both.

Instead, the technique we have explored is to take the *closure* of a restricted set of relations over an initial set of seed objects. For example, a mail world could be specified by giving *Mailing events* as seed objects, restricted to the relations: *to, from, cc, date, body*, etc.

In essence, we call an aggregate so derived, a *world*, and the specification of the set of relations, a *world specification*. The most abstract version of the closure algorithm, stated in a quasi-formal language, is:

```
populate(seeds|set of object,S|world specification)
  local O|set of object, R|set of relationship;
  local function close(o)
    if o is in O then return;
    add o to O;
    ∀ r ∈ wrelationships(o,S) do add r to R;
    ∀ x ∈ wobjects(o,S) do close(x);
  end close;
  ∀ o ∈ seeds close(o);
  return <O,R>.
```

The pair $<O,R>$ constitutes the aggregate[3]. Notice that o is added to O before the closure is invoked recursively to allow for circular dependencies. Of course, the algorithm hinges on the definitions of *wrelationships* (all relationships involving o via relations in S) and *wobjects* (loosely, all objects related to o via relations in S). The latter is computed in terms of the former, so let us examine the former first. If the world specification is simply a set of relations, an adequate specification for *wrelationships* is simply to generate every relationship in the database and examine whether the relation associated with the relationship is a member of the world specification and whether the object o is in the relationship. Then *wobjects* is defined as the set of objects in the relationships computed by *wrelationships*, viz.,

---

[3]In our formalism, the aggregate is represented by a world instance which has associated with it the pair $<O,R>$, as well as the world specification from which this closure was derived.

```
wrelationships(o,S) =
  {r ∈ TheGlobalDatabase |
       o ∈ objects-of(r) and relation-of(r) ∈ S}
wobjects(o,S) =
  {x ∈ objects-of(r) | r ∈ wrelationships(o,S)}.
```

where *objects-of* a relationship is simply the set of objects in the relationship and
relation-of is the relation associated with the relationship.

We refine this specification by considering types to be somewhat more important
than simple unary relations. We use them to more finely filter relationships.
Consider two desired aggregates, *personal friends* and *business associates*. Suppose
that the world specifications for these two worlds are identical, except that one
contains the type *Friend* in lieu of *Person*. Assuming that the *office-of* relation is
part of the specification, our original closure algorithm would include in the *personal
friend* world any friend's office mates! By filtering out relationships involving
objects whose types are not in the specification, we eliminate such anomalies. This
involves redefining *wrelationships*:

```
wrelationships(o,S) =
  {r ∈ TheGlobalDatabase |
       o ∈ objects-of(r) and relation-of(r) ∈ S
       and ∀ x ∈ objects-of(r) wtype(x,S)}
```

where

```
wtype(o,S) ≡
      ∃ r ∈ TheGlobalDatabase |
         o ∈ objects-of(r) and relation-of(r) ∈ S
         and arity-of(relation-of(r)) = 1
```

where *arity-of* is the arity of a relation.

Furthermore, in order to avoid the unintentional inclusion of objects through *values*,
we can change the algorithm above so that it only closes over abstract objects. (We
later legitimize this further by allowing the world specification to contain *imported*
types, over which the algorithm never closes.)

This *specification* of the closure algorithm involving the generation of all
relationships in the entire objectbase, is unacceptably inefficient. Furthermore, the
closure algorithm is complicated by characteristics required by other uses of
aggregates, particularly objectbase persistence. Finally, in order to support
incremental population, the closure algorithm actually implemented is type directed
(more object-oriented) in its traversal of relationships.

3.2. World Specification

Additional constraints on aggregates are imposed by the uses for aggregates
mentioned earlier, viz, *focus, viewing, garbage identification, derivatives, hierarchy,
persistence* and *sharing*.

- They must have distinct interiors and exteriors when garbage
  identification within an aggregate is desirable;

- They must themselves be objects when derived and hierarchical
  relationships between aggregates are to be expressed.

- They must be able to identify descriptively the objects they contain, when the aggregate is used as the unit of persistence and sharing.

Although particular uses of aggregates may not require all such characteristics, world specifications are a compromise between features useful for each. This is a design decision which may be reversed if future experience reveals truly orthogonal dimensions in which differences exceed commonalities among the uses.

A worlds specification, worldspec for short, looks something like:

```
(DEFWORLDSPEC bibliography
  (:export Reference)
  (:internal
    (Reference
      (author @ !)
      (title @ !)))
  (:import <Person worldspec>
    (Person
      (last-name @ !)
      (first-name @ !))))).
```

More than one world can have the same worldspec. The worldspec is a schema which states that a library world contains References and Persons. References are internal to the world meaning that the world has the ability to create them (e.g., allocate their storage). Persons are imported meaning that the world must obtain them from another world, in this case a Person world. In the above worldspec, consider the pattern (author @ !). The @ means that that if an object of type Reference is in the world, then *author* tuples of which it is the first member are *maintained* by this world. This means that the range object must also be in the world and that no other world maintains those tuples[4]. The actual population algorithm is object-centered. Starting with objects in the world at @ slots in the spec, all objects at $ and ! slots must also be in the world. An object is in the world if it is either internal to it or imported to it. The ! means that the slot is a *key* for that type in that world. For example, the keys of a Reference are all of its authors and titles, in that an object of type Reference can be uniquely identified given its authors and titles. Keys can be used to locate objects when importing them. In some sense, imported objects are an extension of the notion of value in the object base, localized to the individual world.

World specifications are encapsulated, i.e., a world specification consists not only of types and their allowed relationships, as in the objectbase model, but also a classification as to which types and relations are *exported*. The semantics for exported types is that only objects in the world of those types can be imported by other worlds. Objectbases traditionally have a garbage identification problem, for it is assumed that any object and attribute is visible from any context. Encapsulation provides a handle on identifying garbage information via worlds. In the future we expect to limit visibility from outside a world to only exported types and relations, keeping other information hidden. Services based on the world would have access to the hidden information, via declarations which place them in the scope of the world's interior. This will allow this interior information to be changed more freely than if the entire schema were advertised to all users.

---

[4]The latest implementation of the system is permitting different worlds to maintain intersecting sets of tuples

Finally, a world contains information which allows an object's identity to be established in the world in a *descriptive* manner, rather than merely in a *prescriptive* (pointing) manner. This feature is included only for persistence and sharing, where reloading a world necessitates the ability to locate or create saved objects in the objectbase. Presently, we assume an object's type and a set of key attributes is enough to uniquely establish its identity with respect to a world. Keys need only be provided for imported and exported objects. All other objects can be generated at the discretion of the loading mechanism since they are guaranteed to be unique to the world itself. We discuss this more fully in Section 5.

The world specification only provides constraints that the schemata of the objectbase must satisfy. In particular, we have no way (yet) to use the description above to partially construct the full schema automatically. This construction is context sensitive, for these are not necessarily the only relations having as domains the types mentioned. For any given objectbase, the world specifications for the set of loaded worlds determines the full data base schema.

To summarize, at this point we have an aggregation mechanism for objectbases. We have a procedure for deciding what is in a world (instance), based on a world specification and on a set of seed objects associated with the world. At the boundary of the world are objects of types imported into the world specification. Both exported and imported types have associated key attributes (or n-ary relations) which determine their identity descriptively.

4. PERSISTENCE MAINTAINED THROUGH WORLDS

Persistence should be a property of particular clusters of information rather than entire object bases. We therefore allow users to make aggregates themselves persistent by explicitly "attaching" persistence to a world instance. Worlds are made persistent by saving the information they contain in a stable, external store. The object store is mutable and ephemeral, supports fine grain access via query, and maintains strong consistency, whereas the external store is stable and persistent, providing a "black box" for the information needed to represent a world. The operations provided are simply to *save* a world to the external store and *load* a world from the external store into an object base.

4.1. Consistency Issues

When a world is saved, it is saved as of a particular *world state*. Loading will attempt to make the world be in its most recent state, by default, but the user may request loading as of some prior state. If world W imports an object from world X, then saving W requires saving X, and loading W attempts to make X be in the state it was when W was saved.

Consistency issues arise when loading a world. If loading is merely being done in order to 'update' the enviroment, as when restoring data after a machine crash, then things are straight forward. But Worlds also permits loading into an enviroment which is not an ancestor of the saving environment. In this paper, we omit discussion of the consistency problem which such capability entails. Hence, we are restricting our discussion here to the relatively simple issue of using Worlds for persistency.

4.2. Distinguishing Features of Worlds

It is important for Worlds to operate at the AP5 relation abstraction level both in interfacing to the user and in maintaining persistent data. Since AP5 enables the user to produce efficient systems at the abstract level, world specifications retain the abstractions to enable a user to describe what data is to be kept by a world. Furthermore, the *save* operation actually represents the persistent data itself via the abstractions. This enables loading a world into different VMs where different implementations have been chosen for the same abstract relations. This can be common, so it is important to support.

Worlds is different from the persistency mechanisms in systems which provide DBMS extensions to a conventional language or embed persistency as a datatype [1, 16, 17, 18]. Worlds are orthogonal to AP5. Worlds do not have to impact on the runtime environment of AP5 at transaction time. There is no need for any kind of dereferencing or object id caching. Ap5 programs are compiled and operate independently of whether their data will be perserved in a world. Populating and saving are relegated to seperate moments in time. Hence, there is a tradeoff of increasing run time efficiency at the cost of decreased granularity of occurrances of committing and increased cost of time to perform commits.

Our work differs from efforts where the virtual memory is loaded with shared data from a central file server [15] due to the partial, layered nature of the information we store. We make no attempt to localize *all* information about an object in a single spot, but rather allow it to be additively composed from several sources, each containing information relevant to a single concern.

4.3. Aggregate Example

A simple analogy to a persistent aggregate is a **blueprint**, a construction aid for home building, sewer layout, power routing, etc. For those unfamiliar with blueprints, two extremely simplified examples are given in figure 4-1.

There ·are usually *plan* (overhead) and *elevation* (side) blueprints, giving area relationships and vertical relationships, respectively. Then there are detail blueprints of particular rooms, such as the kitchen, showing more of the same type of information in the plan and elevation blueprints, but in more detail. Orthogonal cuts also exist, such as wiring blueprints, landscape blueprints, and plumbing details. Furthermore these scale up to city block sized diagrams with alleys, sewage and drainage systems. Several points require emphasis:

- A blueprint is not simply a *view* of an object (a house, for example) but rather an aggregation of many related objects (rooms, walls) to show (graphically) their relationships from a *point of view* or for a particular purpose.

- Several blueprints are necessary to establish the relationships between the objects in a house. For example, the dimensions of a room are a combination of the *height* attribute from the elevation view and the *width* and *length* attributes from the plan view.

- The actual model of any object in the house varies considerably according

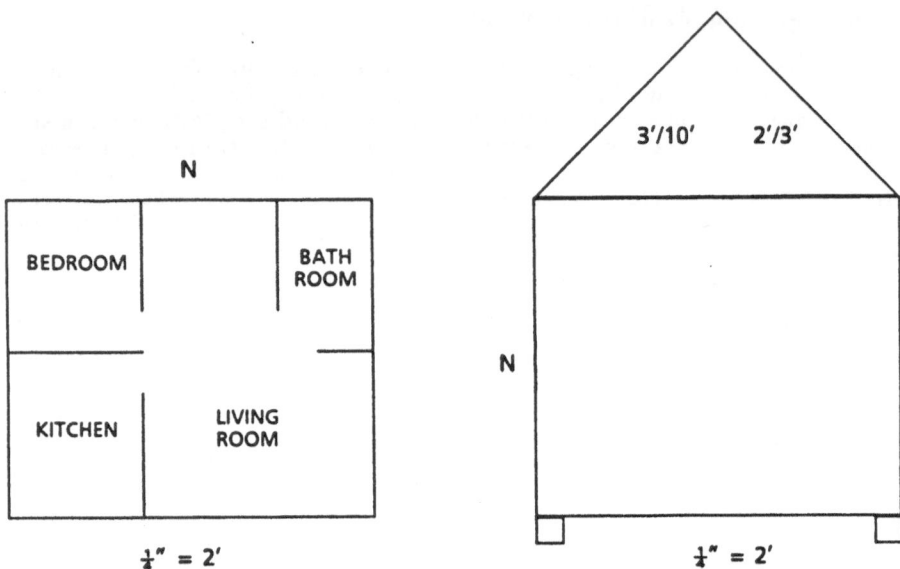

Figure 4-1: Plan and Elevation Blueprints

to which craftsman is reading which blueprints, and it is usually necessary for each workman to read more than one blueprint to form his model of the artifacts he creates.

- The identity of an object in a blueprint is not global. The object only needs to be described enough to uniquely identify it in the blueprints in which it participates.

These points carry over directly to objectbases in general. A (database) view of an object [3] is a fuzzier modelling concept than the aggregate we are proposing. It may be fair to characterize a world as a view of a set of objects, but its unique character arises from how it controls what is contained in the view and its use to maintain persistence.

If one were to attempt to create a global objectbase consistent with all aggregations used in the building trade (even for a particular house), there would be considerable chaos in arriving at agreement on exactly what objects are and what their properties are. Anyone who does not believe this need only examine the differences between insurance contracts for the interior of a house and the exterior, to see how difficult this task is. Just agreeing on the *definition* of the wall surfaces, built-in appliances, etc., is a major undertaking. Unilateral agreement of all craftsmen involved in the house construction would be equally unlikely, but more importantly, *unnecessary*.

5. OBJECT IDENTITY IN WORLDS

There is a hierarchy of object identity classes in computers. At a low level is the identifying of objects with virtual memory addresses or identifiers. At a higher level are sets of key attributes and attribute values which uniquely identify an object in some context. At a more general level are arbitrary descriptions involving a logical combination of various stored facts which uniquely identify an object. Finally, there is the *ex-machine* object which is being modelled by an object in the machine. We mention this last level because sometimes the machine object and *ex-machine* object coincide. For example, an object of type Person is often thought of as representing a person in the real world whereas an object of type mail is often considered to *be* the object of interest. There is a many to one mapping between lower levels and higher levels in this hierarchy.

A World is an entity which exists on no single machine, but is known to a community of machines, currently a network of workstations. Let W be a world. W provides a *partial model* of a set of objects. Loading W on machine M causes M to know those facts. When W is loaded M must determine which objects were already in M and which ones must be created. Loading W entails assuring the existence on M of objects which are modelled in W and the truth in M of the tuples which are modelled in W.

The notions of internal object and imported object enable maintaining object identity across different workstations. For a given object Z which is in world W, either Z is internal to W or imported to W from some other world X. Basically, W can create its internal objects when W is loaded on a workstation, M, and must look up its imported objects via key values which uniquely identify those objects in X. A current axiom on worlds is that an object must be internal in exactly one world, if it is in any world. We are considering dropping this requirement.

If W imports objects from X, W is said to be dependent on X, and X is said to be a precursor of W. Circular dependencies are not currently permitted.

Exporting an object is merely a granting of permission by a world that any other world may import that object. Let object Z be exported from W. Then it must have key attributes which uniquely identify it *with respect to* W. It is possible to export an object which was imported. It is possible that the 'same' object has different keys in different worlds. Let object Z be internal in W and not exported from W. Then all references to Z are known by W, and no mechanism for identifying Z from other worlds is necessary.

We can now identify an object with the world in which it is internal plus its key attribute values in that world. For example, a Reference object in the Bibliography world is identified in that world by it authors and title. In essence, Worlds provide the contexts in which objects have identity.

The worlds notion of identity permits certain novel objectbase features. It is possible to create *surrogate* imported objects instead of loading their containing world. For example, if the bibliography world needs the person H.Curry, it can choose to create a person object having his name, knowing that subsequent loading of a Person world which contains him can detect that he need not be recreated. The other side of the coin is that when loading an internal object of a world, a check is made to see if the loading machine already believes such an object exists. This is only necessary for exported objects and only possible for those internal objects which have keys specified, which all exported ones must.

Note that the FSD separation of specification from implementation is maintained in worlds. It is entirely possible to load a world into two different machines and obtain the same logical set of relationships over two different implementations of the involved relations and objects.

Each World assigns unique ids to all its objects. These are not guaranteed to remain fixed in value, but can be used under certain circumstances to improve robustness of world loading, to detect changes in key values and to aid in merging world saves.

5.1. Sharing

In FSD, sharing of data across workstations is accomplished via worlds and is based on the persistence mechanism. Copies of all shared data exist in each objectbase of the sharers. The most common use of shared worlds in our environment is a single-creator/maintainer, multiple-user world. This is true of small programming shops and university research environments where each individual is responsible for his piece of the system.

Sharing is loosely coupled, as in GEMSTONE [16], based on private informal arrangements of what to share and how to handle multiple updates. Presently, we tend to load all saved updates before making an update in order to discover inconsistencies in our own virtual memory rather than have others discover our effects in their virtual memories.

The save action is used for both *checkpointing*, providing a stable virtual store [4], and *committing* to the integrity of the aggregate in time. This can cause interference if an incomplete shared world is checkpointed and subsequently read as though it were committed.

6. RELATED WORK

The body of literature on views of data bases is extensive. To the extent that a view is simply some subset of the objects and relationships present in a database, a world is a kind of view, the one generated via our population algorithm. Of most interest in this area is the use of views to update the base information [13]. Of course, this is only problematical when the information in the view is *derived* from the base data. This is a harder problem than our use of worlds to save subsets of base data.

Recent work by Garlan, Kaiser, and members of the Gandalf project [8, 9, 12] deals with using views in software engineering environments. The focus of their work is on *synthesizing* the actual data from the several views of the data required by the different tools which access it. This too is a more difficult problem than we are attacking with worlds.

Another area of interest which may seem relevant is the *segmentation* of databases, usually involving cluster identification [10, 14]. These efforts emphasize the *efficiency* of the resulting database, rather than attempting to segment conceptual aggregates. In particular, these works tend to be very object-centered, keeping *all* information about an object in a single segment.

7. CHALLENGES

We are pleased with our experience to date using worlds to maintain persistence. Some challenges we are now confronting include providing objectbase analogs to file-based directories (including versioning), merging worldspecs, merging saved world instances, partially loading worlds, integrating world saving with an audit trail mechanism in FSD, and providing for tightly coupled sharing.

ACKNOWLEDGEMENTS[5]

We thank Bob Balzer, Don Cohen, Michael Fox, Rick Hull, Dennis McLeod, K. Narayanaswamy, and Surjatini Widjojo for many clarifying discussions.

REFERENCES

1. Malcom P. Atkinson and O. Peter Buneman. "Types and Persistence in Database Programming Languages". *ACM Computing Surveys, Vol 19, No 2* (June 1987), 201-260.

2. Robert M. Balzer. Living in The Next Generation of Operating System. Proceedings of the 10th World Computer Congress, Dublin, IFIP, September, 1986.

3. Chamberlin, D. D., J. N. Gray, and I. L. Traiger. Views, Authorization, and Locking in a Relational Database System. Proceedings of the National Computer Conference, AFIPS, June, 1975, pp. 425-430.

4. P. Cockshott. Stable Virtual Memory. Persistent object systems: their design, implementation and use, University of St. Andrews, Department of Computational Science, St. Andrews, Scotland, August, 1987, pp. 470-476.

5. Donald Cohen. Automatic compilation of logical specifications into efficient programs. AAAI86 Proceedings, AAAI, August, 1986.

6. Donald Cohen. Compiling Complex Database Transition Triggers. Proceedings of the 1989 ACM SIGMOD International Conference on the Management of Data, SIGMOD, June, 1989, pp. 225-234.

7. George P. Copeland and Setrag N. Khoshafian. Identity and Versions for Complex Objects. Persistent Object Systems: their design, implementation and use, University of St. Andrews, Department of Computational Science, St. Andrews, Scotland, August, 1987, pp. 407-428.

8. David B. Garlan. Views for Tools in Integrated Environments. Proceedings of the International Workshop on Advanced Programming Environments, June 1986.

---

[5]The research reported herein was funded by the Defense Advanced Research Projects Agency of the United States government, under contract number MDA903 81 C 0335.

9. A. N. Habermann, Charles Krueger, Benjamin Pierce, Barbara Staudt, John Wenn. Programming with views. Technical Report CMU-CS-87-177, Carnegie-Mellon University, January, 1988.

10. Mark Hornick and Stanley Zdonik. "A shared, segmented memory system for an object-oriented database". *ACM Transactions on Office Information Systems* (January 1987), 70-95.

11. Richard Hull and Roger King. "Semantic database modeling: survey, applications, and research issues". *ACM Computing Surveys 19*, 3 (September 1987), 201-260.

12. Gail E. Kaiser and David Garlan. Composing software systems from reusable building blocks. Twentieth Hawaii International Conference on System Sciences, Jan, 1987.

13. A. M. Keller. *Updating Relational Databases through View.* Ph.D. Th., Department of Computer Science, Stanford University, 1985.

14. D. Maier, J. Stein, A. Otis, A. Purdy. Development of an Object-Oriented DBMS. Technical Report CS/E-86-005, Oregon Graduate Center, April, 1986.

15. J. Eliot, B. Moss, S. Sinofsky. Managing persistent data with Mneme: issues and application of a reliable, shared object interface. University of Massachusetts, Amherst, 1988.

16. D. J. Penney, J. Stein, D. Maier. Is the disk half full or half empty? Persistent Object Systems: their design, implementation and use, University of St. Andrews, Department of Computational Science, St. Andrews, Scotland, August, 1987, pp. 382-406.

17. Harry H. Porter, III. Persistence in a Distributed Object Server. Persistent object systems: their design, implementation and use (in this volume), University of Newcastle, Australia, January, 1989.

18. Joel E. Richardson and Michael J. Carey. Implementing Persistence in E. Persistent object systems: their design, implementation and use (in this volume), University of Newcastle, Australia, January, 1989.

19. David S. Wile and Dennis G. Allard. Worlds: An Organizing Structure for Object-Bases. Proceedings of the ACM SIGSOFT/SIGPLAN Software Engineering Symposium on Practical Software Development Environments, Palo Alto, SIGSOFT/SIGPLAN, December, 1986, pp. 16-26.

20. David S. Wile and Dennis G. Allard. Worlds: Aggregates for Object Bases. Submitted to ACM Transactions on Programming Languages and Systems, July, 1988.

21. David S. Wile, Neil M. Goldman, and Dennis G. Allard. Maintaining Object Persistence in The Common Lisp Framework. Persistent Object Systems: their design, implementation and use, University of St. Andrews, Department of Computational Science, St. Andrews, Scotland, August, 1987, pp. 382-406.

Implementing Persistence in E

Joel E. Richardson
IBM Almaden Research Center

Michael J. Carey
University of Wisconsin—Madison

ABSTRACT

The E language is an extension of C++ providing, among other features, database types and persistent objects. The basis of persistence in E is a new storage class for variables, and physical I/O is based on a load/store model of the long-term storage layer. This paper describes in detail the implementation of the first E compiler and discusses our current research directions.

1. INTRODUCTION

The EXODUS Project at the University of Wisconsin has been exploring a toolkit approach to building and extending database systems [5, 7]. The first component of EXODUS to be designed and built was the EXODUS Storage Manager [6]. It provides basic management support for objects, files, and transactions. The E programming language [15, 16] was originally conceived, in part, as a vehicle for conveniently programming against this persistent store. E is the language in which database system code is written; that is, the abstract data types (e.g. time), access methods (e.g. grid files), and operator methods (e.g. hash join) are all written in E. E is also the target language for schema and query compilation; user-defined schema are translated into E types, and user queries into E procedures. In this way, E alleviates the impedance mismatch [10] between the database system and the application. Finally, the EXODUS Optimizer Generator [11, 12] allows the database implementor (DBI) to produce customized optimizers, given rules describing the query algebra. The first demonstration of a database system built with the EXODUS tools was given at SIGMOD-88. In the three weeks prior to the conference, we wrote a relational system (of course!) complete with indices and an optimizer. Most recently, the EXTRA data model and EXCESS query language have been designed [8], and this system is now being implemented with the EXODUS tools.

The design of E has evolved considerably from the early descriptions in [7]. The original intent was to design a language for writing database system code; the resulting language

This research was partially supported by the Defense Advanced Research Projects Agency under contract N00014-85-K-0788, by the National Science Foundation under grant IRI-8657323, by IBM through a Fellowship, by DEC through its Incentives for Excellence program, and by grants from the Microelectronics and Computer Technology Corporation (MCC) and GTE Laboratories.

[15, 16] is an extension of C++ [19] providing generic classes, iterators, and persistence. C++ provided a good starting point with its class structuring features and its expanding popularity as a systems programming language. Generic classes were added for their utility in defining database container types, such as sets and indices. Iterators were added as a useful programming construct in general, and as a mechanism for structuring database queries in particular. Persistence — the ability of a language object to survive from one program run to the next — was added because it is an essential attribute of database objects. In addition, by describing the database in terms of persistent variables, one may then manipulate the database in terms of natural expressions in the language. This paper describes the design and current implementation of persistence in E.

The remainder of the paper is organized as follows. Since E depends on the EXODUS Storage Manager to provide the basic persistent store, we begin Section 2 with a review of that interface. The remainder of the section introduces the E language by example, concentrating on those features related to persistence. Section 3 details the current prototype implementation of the E compiler. Finally, Section 4 concludes with a summary and a report on our current research.

2. REVIEW OF THE EXODUS STORAGE MANAGER AND E

2.1. The Storage Manager Interface

Of the components mentioned in the introduction, the EXODUS Storage Manager [6] is most important to the implementation of persistence. The Storage Manager provides *storage objects*, which are uninterpreted byte sequences of virtually any size. Whether an object is several bytes or several gigabytes, clients of the Storage Manager see a uniform interface. Each object is named by its object ID (OID), which is its physical address. Two basic operations, *read* and *release*, provide access to objects. The read call specifies an OID, an offset, and a length. These parameters name a byte sequence within the object which the Storage Manager reads into the buffer pool. The Storage Manager then returns a *user descriptor* to the client. This descriptor contains a pointer to the data in the buffer pool, and the client accesses the data by dereferencing through the pointer. When finished, the client returns the user descriptor to the Storage Manager in a release call. The release call also includes a flag indicating whether the client wrote the data or not.[1]

It is important to understand that data requested in a read call is *pinned* in the buffer pool until the client releases it. Pinning is a two-way contract: the Storage Manager guarantees that it will not move the data (e.g. page it out) while it is pinned, and the client promises not to access anything outside the pinned range. In addition, the client promises to release (unpin) the data in a "timely" fashion, because pinned data effectively reduces the size of the buffer pool.[2] In the subsequent discussions, pin and unpin are used interchangeably with

---

[1] Many details have been glossed over. For example, there are a number of other parameters in the read call, and releasing something "dirty" is actually a different call than releasing something "clean". However, this simplified model is sufficient for this paper.

[2] Actually, the EXODUS Storage Manager provides *buffer groups*. A buffer group is a set of pages requested by a transaction and managed with a specified page replacement policy. The idea is to avoid interference in the paging characteristics of different transactions. Thus, if a transaction leaves data pinned, the performance degradation is largely to itself.

read and release.

An example of a client's interaction with the Storage Manager is illustrated in Figure 1. A range of bytes containing a `struct S` is embedded at `offset` within the Storage Manager object having the given `oid`. The read call pins that range of bytes in the buffer pool. On return, the `ud` points to a user descriptor, whose first word contains a pointer to the pinned data. The statement after the read then multiplies the x field by 10. Finally, the data is released (unpinned). While the EXODUS Storage Manager is a powerful utility, it is necessary for the programmer to learn numerous procedural interfaces and to execute many steps in order to perform even simple tasks[3]; this complexity is one of the primary motivations for the E language.

The other important abstraction provided by the Storage Manager is the *file*. A file is a set of EXODUS objects ordered by OID. Files are disjoint; every EXODUS object resides in one and only one file. Operations include those to create or destroy an object within a file and to scan a file, returning each object's OID. The current implementation of E uses Storage Manager files and objects to realize the persistent store, although the basic approach could be adapted to other storage systems. An interesting result of this work will be an evaluation of the suitability of the current Storage Manager design for supporting a persistent language and insight into ways the design might be improved.

2.2. Review of E

As noted, E is an extension of C++ [19], which is itself an extension of C [13]. The essential concept in C++ is the *class*. A class defines a type, and its definition includes both the physical representation of any *instance* of the class as well as the operations that may be performed on an instance.[4] In C++ parlance, the former are called data members, and the latter, member functions (a.k.a. methods). Member functions are always applied to a specific instance; within the function, any (unqualified) reference to a data member of the class is bound to that instance. This binding is realized through an implicit parameter,

```
struct S { int x; float y; };
USERDESC * ud;

sm_read( oid, offset, sizeof(struct S), &ud );
((struct S *) *ud) -> x *= 10;
sm_release( ud, DIRTY );
```

Figure 1: Interacting with the EXODUS Storage Manager

---

[3]There are 23 interface routines to the Storage Manager, although only a few may be needed for a given application. Not shown in the above example are the (necessary) steps of initializing the Storage Manager, mounting a volume, and allocating buffer space via the buffer group mechanism [6].

[4]Unlike the abstraction mechanisms provided in CLU or Smalltalk, a C++ class does not necessarily hide the physical representation of instances. It is up to the designer of a class to declare explicitly which members (data and function) are private and which are public.

this, which is a pointer to the object on which the method was invoked. An unqualified reference to a member x of the class is equivalent to this->x.

The example in Figure 2 is a (nonsensical, but) complete C++ program which defines and uses a bounded stack of integers. Though not yet very interesting, it will serve as the basis

```
const STACK_MAX = 100;
class stack {
     int          stackTop;
     int          elems[ STACK_MAX ];
public:
     stack();
     void push( int );
     int pop();
     int empty();
}; /* class stack */

stack::stack() { stackTop = -1; }

void stack::push( int val ) {
     if( stackTop < STACK_MAX-1 )
       elems[ ++ stackTop ] = val;
     else
       printf("stack::push: Sorry, stack is full.");
}

int stack::pop() {
     if( stackTop >= 0 )
       return elems[ stackTop -- ];
     else
       printf("stack::pop: Sorry, stack is empty.");
}

int stack::empty() { return (stackTop == -1); }

stack S;

main() {
     while( ! S.empty() )
       printf("popped %d", S.pop() );

     for(int i = 1; i <= 10; i++)
       S.push(i);
}
```

Figure 2: The Stack Example

for future examples. The physical representation of a stack comprises an integer array holding the stack elements, and an integer index of the current top-of-stack. Because this representation is declared in the private section of the class definition, it is hidden from users of the class. Following the keyword `public` are declarations of the methods available to users of the class. The stack methods, of course, are those to push and pop elements, and to test if the stack is empty.[5] The bodies of the stack routines are elaborated following the class declaration. Consider the member function `push`. Note that, as mentioned, the references to `stackTop` and `elems` are equivalent to `this->stackTop` and `this->elems`, respectively. If the stack instance is not already full, the `push` routine increments the top-of-stack index and places the new element at that location.

In addition to the usual stack operations, notice that there is also an operation named `stack`. In general, a method whose name is the same as its class is called a *constructor*. Constructors are intended to initialize instances of a class and are called automatically whenever an instance is created, e.g. by coming into scope. Here, the constructor initializes the top-of-stack index to -1, indicating that the stack is empty.

Following the member function definitions, there is a declaration of a global stack instance, S. It is guaranteed that the stack constructor will be called for S by the time the main program runs; the mechanism to accomplish this initialization is described more fully in a later section. The main program itself does nothing particularly interesting in this example. It begins by popping all the elements, printing each value that it receives. Since the stack is initially empty, this loop does nothing. Then the integers 1 through 10 are pushed onto the stack, and the program exits. Clearly, running this program produces no output, nor will it

```
const STACK_MAX = 100;
dbclass stack {
    dbint        stackTop;
    dbint        elems[ STACK_MAX ];
public:

    /* as before... */

}; /* class stack */

/* all methods are as before... */

persistent stack S;

main() {
    /* as before... */
}
```

Figure 3: Making the Stack Persist

---

[5]Since the stack is bounded, in practice we would also include a method to test if the stack is full.

in any future run.

In order to introduce persistence into the language, E mirrors the existing C++ type system with constructors having the *db* (database) attribute. Let us informally define a db type to be:

(1)   one of the fundamental db types: dbshort, dbint, dblong, dbfloat, dbdouble, dbchar, and dbvoid.

(2)   a dbclass, dbstruct, or dbunion. Such classes may have data members only of other db types, but there are no restrictions on the argument or return types of member functions, i.e. they may accept or return non-db type values.

(3)   a pointer to a db type object.

(4)   an array of db type objects.

An object may be persistent *only* if it is of a db type. However, a db type object need not be persistent. Note that any type definable in C++ may be analogously defined as a db type. Furthermore, since persistence is orthogonal [3] over all db types, one can, if desired, program exclusively in db types and achieve the effect of strict orthogonality.[6]

Figure 3 shows (in boldface) the changes needed to convert the example of Figure 2 into an E program in which the stack is persistent. By changing the keyword `class` to `dbclass` and the type name `int` to `dbint`, and by giving `S` the storage class `persistent`, the effect of running the main program is altered as follows: The first time the program is run, no output is produced;   persistent stacks also are initialized to empty. However the ten integer values pushed at the end of the main program are preserved when the program exits. The next time the program is run, the first loop will pop these elements, and the user will see:

```
                   popped 10
                   popped 9
                     . . .
                   popped 1
```

Some explanatory notes are in order. First, changing `int` to `dbint` is not strictly necessary, since the compiler can (and does) infer this change within the context of the `dbclass`. Second, in this very simple example, the class, the persistent object, and the main program are all declared in one module. This is usually not the case, as one typically declares persistent objects in separate modules, and then links these with the various main

---

[6]An interesting "hack" is to define the following macros:
```
    #define      class        dbclass
    #define      struct       dbstruct
    #define      union        dbunion
    #define      int          dbint
    // etc...
```

programs that use them. This is a very brief introduction to the E language. For a full description, the reader is referred to [15]. (We note that several aspects of the language have been improved; the full description will appear shortly in [17].)

3. THE CURRENT IMPLEMENTATION OF E

In this section, we describe how db types and persistence have been implemented in the first version of the E compiler. We begin with a macro level description of the compiler's structure, showing how new functionality has been integrated with the phases of an existing C++ compiler. We then describe the phase involving db types and persistence, showing how declarations and expressions are processed.

3.1. Organization of the Compiler

The current E compiler is an extended version of the AT&T C++ compiler. We chose this as our starting point for several reasons, the main one being that we had access to the source code. We did not want to start from scratch because reimplementing the C++ subset of E was not our interest and yet would require a significant amount of time and effort. At the time we began work on E, there were only a few C++ compilers available; the AT&T compiler, in addition to being available, also had the advantage of being quite stable.

The AT&T C++ compiler (version 1.2.1) consists of a large shell script (CC) which spawns a number of processes, as illustrated in Figure 4. The original C++ source code is first processed by the standard C preprocessor, cpp. The result is then translated by the C++ front end, cfront, into C source code. This code is then compiled by the C compiler, cc, into binary form. Although not shown in the figure, cc itself comprises a series of processes: cpp (again!); ccom, which translates C into assembler code; as, the assembler; and ld, the link editor. If the result of the last step is an executable program, the compiler then performs an additional series of steps (enclosed in dashed box in Figure 4). A C++ program may declare an object of a class with a constructor. If the object is declared in the global scope, then the constructor for that object must be executed before the main program runs.

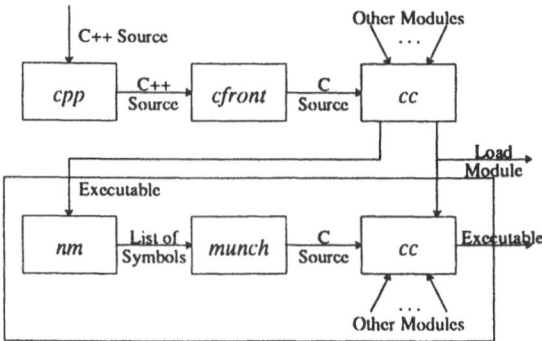

Figure 4: The Process Structure of CC

The extra steps in the dashed box are part of the mechanism that implements this feature.

The majority of the work in implementing E has involved extending the source code for cfront into an E-to-C translator called, appropriately, efront. The internal organization of efront is shown in Figure 5. Of the five phases shown, all but "db simplify" were part of the original C++ compiler. The parsing phase builds an abstract syntax tree of the source text. The parser consumes one external declaration at a time, e.g. one function definition or one global variable declaration. Only a few new keywords were added to this phase in order to handle constructs related to persistence. In addition, when this phase adds a type node to the syntax tree, where that node represents a fundamental db type (e.g. dbint) or a dbclass, a special flag is set in that node. In all other respects, it is like any other type node. This fact is important for the second phase, which handles most of the type checking. Slight changes were needed here to prevent, for example, assigning a db address to a non-db type pointer. Most other type checking is handled normally, and allows, for example, assigning a dbint to an int, or adding an int and a dbfloat. The simplification phase transforms C++ constructs into equivalent C constructs. This phase has been extended to also handle E generators and iterators. The new fourth phase, and the one which is the main concern of this paper, transforms constructs related to db types and persistence. Finally, the print phase walks the resulting C syntax tree, producing C source code.

The input to the db-simplification phase is thus a C syntax tree in which certain nodes are decorated. Any expression or object of a db type will point to a type node in which the "is db" flag has been set. Any object declared persistent will also have this storage class recorded as part of its symbol table entry. The code generation of this phase will therefore involve looking for decorated nodes in the syntax tree and applying tree transformations.

3.2. Transformations

This section details the transformations that are applied by the db simplification phase. It is the responsibility of this phase to locate the types, data declarations, and expressions that involve db types, and to transform them into equivalent C constructs. In particular, it is necessary to add the appropriate calls to the EXODUS Storage Manager so that persistent data is accessible to the program.

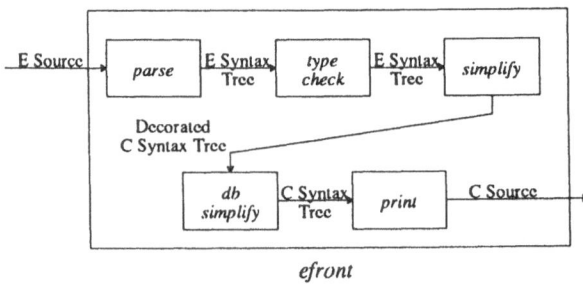

efront

Figure 5: Compilation Phases in Efront

3.2.1. Types

As described earlier, E provides a full complement of fundamental types having the "db" attribute. For the purposes of assignment, arithmetic expressions, and parameter passing, such types are equivalent to their non-db counterparts. A node in the abstract syntax tree that represents a fundamental db type is not changed by db-simplification. Such a node is simply printed by the print phase as its non-db dual.[7] For example, the declaration

```
dbint      x;
```

becomes

```
int   x;
```

A node representing a function type is processed by recursively transforming the function's return and argument types. If the function also has a function body, i.e. if it is a definition, then we apply the transformations described in Section 3.2.3. For now, we may simply observe that the following (pointless) function

```
dbvoid  fcn( dbfloat x,   dbint y ) {
    x = y;
}
```

is transformed[8] into:

```
char   fcn( x, y )
float x;
int    y;
{
      x = y;
}
```

A node representing a dbclass (or dbstruct or dbunion) is processed by recursively transforming the dbclass's data and function members. Although we do not show an example, it should be noted that, by the time db-simplify sees them, classes related to generators (i.e. generators and classes instantiated from generators) have already been transformed into an equivalent set of non-generator classes.

So far, the transformation of types is not very interesting. The one important translation occurs when a type node represents a pointer to some db type. Since a persistent object is stored in the EXODUS Storage Manager, the address of such an object must include its object ID (OID). And since every byte of the object is (potentially) addressable, its address must also include an offset. For example, if an object holds an array, a legal expression might return the address of the third element; this address has the same OID as the array, but with the offset incremented by the appropriate amount. This <OID,offset> pair is called a _DBREF, and in the C translation of every E program is a series of typedefs culminating in the following:

---

[7] The types "void" and "dbvoid" are printed as "char".

[8] For those more familiar with the AT&T cfront, names are still changed according to the usual rules. For the examples in this paper, such details are omitted where possible to avoid confusion.

```
struct _DBREF {
       OID            oid;
       int            offset;
};
```

Any type node representing a db pointer is transformed into `struct _DBREF`. So, for example, the declaration:

```
dbstruct  tree_node {
      tree_node * left;
      tree_node * right;
      dbint           data;
};
```

is printed as:

```
struct  tree_node {
      struct _DBREF left;
      struct _DBREF right;
      int           data;
};
```

For a method of a dbclass, `C`, the type of `this` is likewise transformed, since `this` has type `C*`.

3.2.2. Data Declarations

When the source code contains the declaration of some db type object, the correct transformation depends on the scope of the object and its storage class. Obviously, the most interesting case is the declaration of a persistent object. In E, an object which is declared persistent establishes a binding with a physical object at compile time. The name of the persistent variable is then the programmer's "handle" on the persistent object. The object is accessible to any program in which the variable's name is visible.

The general approach is illustrated in Figure 6. When the db-simplification phase sees the declaration of the (db) integer, x, it asks the EXODUS storage manager to create a 4-byte object. The OID of the new object is then introduced into the output in the form of a

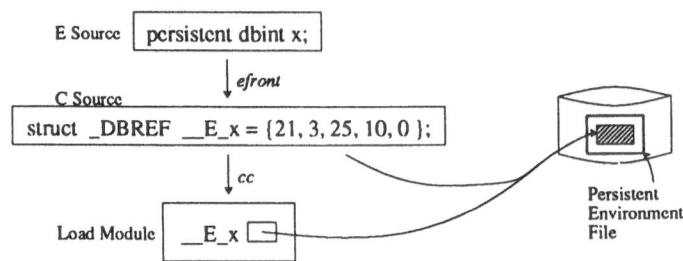

Figure 6: Compiling A Persistent Object Declaration

_DBREF structure with an initializing expression. This _DBREF variable is called the *companion* of x, and its initializer assigns the OID returned by the storage manager with an offset of 0.[9] Note that only the companion declaration appears in the C output.

Since all EXODUS storage objects must reside in some file, the compiler first asks the storage manager to create one file; all persistent objects declared in the source module are then created within this file. Thus, compiling an E source module which contains the declaration of one or more persistent objects yields both its C translation and a file in the storage manager containing the persistent objects. This file is called the *persistent environment* file, or simply, the .pe file, for the module.

If a db type object is declared external, db-simplification transforms this declaration into an external reference to the object's companion. For example,

```
        extern   dbint   x;
```
becomes
```
        extern struct _DBREF __E_x;
```
This allows functions in one module to access persistent objects declared in another via the usual C++ external reference mechanism. Conversely, it implies that if a module declares a *non*persistent db type object in the global scope, then a companion must be generated for that object as well. As usual, the companion must be initialized with the address of this object, which in this case is in main memory. Such addresses use a special OID indicating "in memory", and the actual address of the object is embedded in the offset. Thus, if the x mentioned above is simply declared in the global scope as:

```
        dbint   x;
```
then the translation is:
```
        int   x;
        struct _DBREF __E_x = { 0, 0, 0, -1, (int) &x };
```

The example of Figure 6 showed a persistent object declared in the global scope. Persistent objects may also be declared locally in a block. For example,

```
        int   counter() {
                persistent dbint x;
                return x++;
        }
```
In this case, although the object is persistent, its name is visible only within the block. Again, the object is created at compile time, and a companion is introduced into the local scope. Here, the companion is given the storage class static so that it need not be reinitialized every time the block is entered. The declaration in the above function becomes:

---

[9]The interpretation of the numbers composing the OID is not important for this discussion.

```
int   counter() {
        static struct _DBREF __E_x = { ... };
        /* return ... */
}
```

For nonpersistent db type objects declared local to a block, we do not need to do anything special. A local dbint, x, in the E source simply becomes a local int, x, in the C translation. This is because most expressions which use x, e.g. addition, *know* that x is not persistent;   a companion is not needed. In the case of an expression which takes the address of x, e.g. passing x by reference, a temporary companion is constructed, as described in the following section.

To be consistent with C++ semantics, a persistent object declared without an initializer will be initialized to all zero bytes. Thus, the above counter function will return 0 the first time it is called. A persistent object may also be declared with an initializer, as in Figure 7. In this example, the user has declared a persistent array of dbfloats, specifying the first 3 elements. In such cases, the compiler interprets the expressions (which must evaluate to constants) and sends the binary image of the object to the storage manager.

A more complicated initialization problem arises when the program declares a persistent object of some dbclass with a constructor. We will return to this problem shortly.

3.2.3. Expressions and Statements

Processing the declaration of persistent objects provides one part of the picture. Another part is the translation of expressions involving (possibly persistent) db type objects into regular C expressions which manipulate the objects. This section explains these steps in some detail. The set of expressions illustrated here is representative rather than exhaustive, and nonessential details have been omitted.

The current implementation employs a simple code generation technique. In a recursive descent of the expression tree, we look for nodes (subexpressions) whose type is marked "db." Such nodes are locally transformed into C expressions. If the node represents the *address* (Lval) of a db type object, then the translated expression will be of type _DBREF. If the node represents the *value* (Rval) of a db type object, then the translated expression

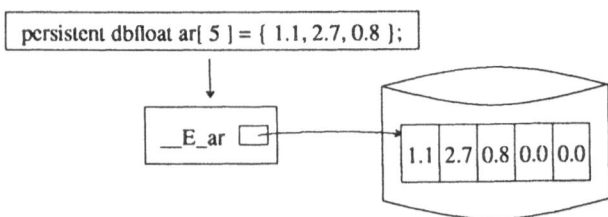

Figure 7: An Initialized Persistent Object

187

will produce that value at runtime.

One of the parameters to the recursive call specifies whether the Rval or the Lval of the expression is desired. For example, the simplest expression is the name of a variable, say, x. Suppose x is persistent and appears in the expression (x + y). Then we must transform the subexpression x into one which reads x, references it in the buffer pool, and (eventually) releases it. However, if x is instead part of the expression (&x), the correct action is simply to substitute the companion, __E_x, since all that is wanted here is the address of x.

The other parameter to the transformation procedure specifies whether the data will be written by the containing expression. Continuing with the previous example, in the expression, x + y, x is used but not changed. When we generate the read call for x, we must also generate the corresponding release call, which in this case should specify that x is clean. However, in the assignment, x = 1, x will definitely be written; the release call must specify that x is dirty.

In general, the release calls are not inserted into the local transformation, but are placed on a list kept by the compiler. At some point, often at the statement level, these calls are inserted. Release calls usually cannot be inserted locally because the result would be incorrect code. Consider again the expression x + y where x is a persistent dbint. In order to form the sum, the expression x must be transformed into an expression which pins x in the buffer pool, then produces x's value. The translated code looks something like[10] the following:

        (<read>, <deref expr>)

If the release call were inserted right after the read call, then the dereference would be illegal because the data has been unpinned. If the call were inserted after the dereference, then the comma expression would no longer produce the value of x as its result.

A third possibility is to introduce a local temporary and copy the bytes out of the buffer pool.

        (<read>, _tmp = <deref expr>, <release call>, _tmp)

The release call can be inserted as shown, with the temporary finally producing the correct value. This approach works, and in fact is necessary in several places. In general, however, the E code generator tries to take advantage of an important performance feature of the EXODUS storage manager: the resulting C program accesses the data directly in the buffer pool when possible, avoiding the additional copy operation.

Because the current code generator is an initial prototype implementation, the code it produces is not yet optimized. Local transformations usually result in more storage manager calls than are necessary, and, in fact, it is possible to pin data in the buffer pool redundantly. For example, in the assignment, x = x + y, x is simultaneously pinned for both occurrences. While the Storage Manager allows such redundant pinning of data

---

[10]In C, an expression, e, may comprise two expressions, e1 and e2, separated by a comma: e ::= e1 , e2. The expressions are evaluated left to right, and the type and value of e are those of e2 [13].

188

(since it supports sharing in general), clearly the performance of E programs will be significantly improved by eliminating such redundancies. These and other optimizations are the subject of current study and are not discussed further here.

3.2.3.1. Names

A simple name expression forms the basis of the code generator's recursive descent. Figure 8 shows the transformation of a name node. If the name is of a non-db type object, no action is taken.

As outlined in the previous section, if the node refers to a persistent or external object and the Lval is desired, then the name of the object's companion is substituted. The result is an expression yielding the address of the object. If the Rval is wanted, we substitute a call to the storage manager read routine, using the companion to obtain the OID and offset, and using the object's type to obtain the length. We also generate a release call (not shown here) whose mode (either dirty or clean) is determined by the second parameter to this invocation.

If the node refers to a nonpersistent db type object and the Rval is needed, no action is taken. Note that this meshes with the treatment of a nonpersistent object's declaration. That is, if we declare and use a nonpersistent dbint in a local scope, the translated code simply declares and uses an integer. Finally, the Lval of a nonpersistent, db type object is generated when needed by introducing a temporary _DBREF variable into the local scope and transforming the expression into one which first initializes the _DBREF and then produces its value as the result.[11]

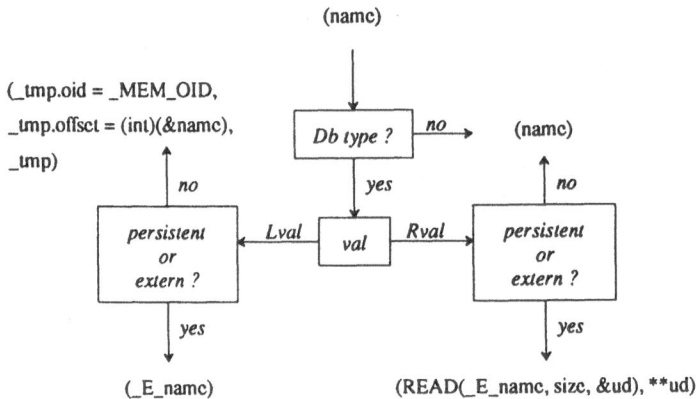

Figure 8: Transforming a Name Expression

---

[11]The alternative is to initialize, at the beginning of a block, a distinguished companion for each nonpersistent db type object declared in that block. This approach was deemed too expensive in general.

3.2.3.2. Dereferencing

The operators dot (.), arrow (->), and star (*) are simple to handle. Consider the pointer dereferencing operator, arrow, whose translation is shown in Figure 9. The expression on the left of the arrow results in a pointer to a structure, and the name on the right specifies a field in the structure. Translation of this node first transforms the expression on the left. Since we need the value of the pointer (not its address), we request the pointer's Rval, and since the expression only reads the pointer value, the release call (if generated) should specify "clean." In the figure, the expression resulting from this recursive descent is denoted by appending subscripts: $expr_{r,c}$ is the expression resulting from the transformation requesting "Rval" and "clean." If the result of transforming the pointer expression is not an expression of type _DBREF, then the pointer was not a db pointer, and no further action is taken. Otherwise, if the Lval of the expression is required, as in & (p->x), then we produce a new _DBREF in which the offset of the pointer expression is incremented by the offset of the field x in the structure. If the current expression's Rval is required, we first produce its Lval, and then use this _DBREF in a read call to the Storage Manager. The size of x's type determines the length parameter for the call. The other dereferencing operators, dot and star, are handled similarly.

One small optimization has been implemented for Lvalued expressions and is worth noting here. The illustration in Figure 9 shows that the result of the expression on the left side of the arrow is copied into a temporary _DBREF variable. In fact, if the result of the pointer expression is already held in a temporary, that variable is simply "promoted" to hold the Lvalue of the current expression, possibly with its offset incremented by the appropriate amount. In terms of the illustration, this step eliminates the copy: _tmp = ($expr_{r,c}$).

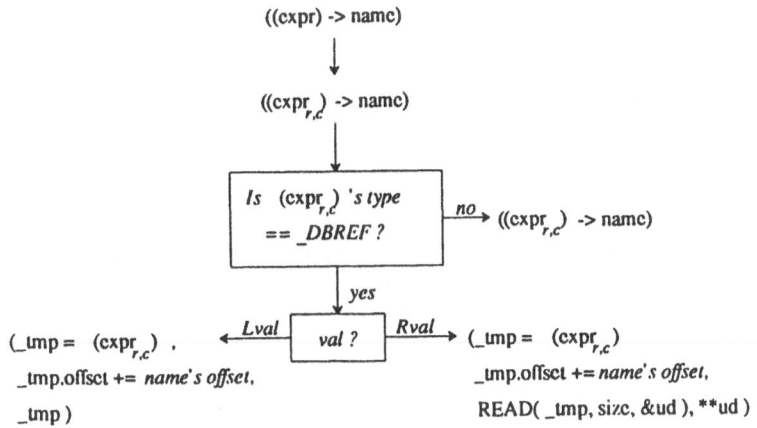

Figure 9: Transforming an Arrow Expression

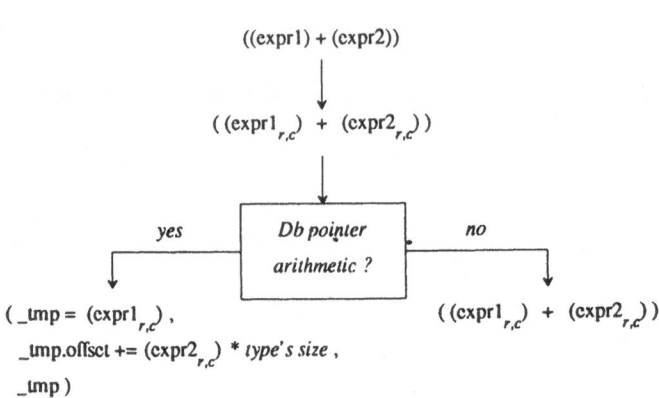

Figure 10: Transforming an Arithmetic Expression

3.2.3.3. Arithmetic Expressions

Processing arithmetic (and other) binary operators is particularly easy. As illustrated in Figure 10, we simply transform both operand expressions, specifying the Rval and "clean" in both cases. The only slight complication arises in handling pointer arithmetic. If, for example, after transforming the operands of plus (+), we discover that one of them resulted in a _DBREF value, then the expression represents arithmetic on a db type pointer. In a manner similar to the last section, we produce a new _DBREF expression in which the offset is incremented. This time, in accordance with C++ semantics, the increment is the product of the right operand times the size of the referenced type. Since pointers cannot be added, the operands in this example cannot both produce _DBREFs. However, two pointers *may* be subtracted, and the result is their integer difference divided by the size of the referenced type (as described in [13]). If those pointers are db pointers, the difference is formed by subtracting the offsets in the _DBREFs.

3.2.3.4. Assignment

As a final example, assignments are trivially handled as shown in Figure 11. To transform the left hand side of the assignment, note that we could request its Lval, and if this produces a _DBREF, we could then insert a read call to pin the destination of the assignment. We can achieve the same effect more simply, however, by requesting the Rval of the left hand side; the proper read and dereference are then added automatically at a lower level.

$$((\text{expr1}) = (\text{expr2}))$$

$$\downarrow$$

$$((\text{expr1}_{r,d}) = (\text{expr2}_{r,c}))$$

Figure 11: Transforming an Assignment Expression

As mentioned previously, here we must specify a dirty release for the left hand side, and a clean release for the right.

3.2.3.5. Statements

It was mentioned previously that the release call corresponding to a given read is usually not inserted into the local expression transformation. However, there are certain situations, particularly in transforming statements, where this insertion is necessary. Consider the return statement, and suppose a function f simply returns the value of x, a global persistent integer.

```
int f( ) { return x; }
```

Clearly, we must read x in order to return its value. It is in releasing x that we have a small problem. Obviously, we cannot release something before it is read. Without added complexity, we also cannot release it after the return, i.e. in the caller. Therefore, we have chosen to insert the release call within the return expression, and this requires the introduction of a temporary. The return statement thus looks something like:

```
return (read(x, &ud), _tmp = **ud, release(ud), _tmp);
```

Other statements containing expressions are treated similarly. For example, an if statement translates to:

```
if( _tmp = <transformed expr>, <release calls>, _tmp )
{ ... }
```

We should emphasize again that such temporaries are introduced only if necessary, i.e. if the expression pins data. Expressions involving only non-db types never suffer this overhead.

3.2.4. E Runtime Environment

Programs generated by E contain calls to the EXODUS Storage Manager. In our first implementation, E programs are actually linked with a copy of the Storage Manager. This is similar to PS-Algol, in which each program includes a copy of the CPOMS storage level [4, 9]. Efront itself also contains a copy of the Storage Manager, since it may need to create persistent objects at compile time. Any program that uses the Storage Manager must first call its initialization routines, specifying which database volume(s) must be mounted. Currently, E programs use only one volume, and its Unix file name is obtained from the environment variable, EVOLUME. Other parameters describing the runtime context are likewise given default values in the first implementation. For example, most Storage Manager calls also require a transaction id and a buffer group specifier (see footnotes 1 and 2). For now, programs run as a single transaction using a single buffer group.

A number of improvements will be made to this runtime environment in the near future. The Storage Manager, along with other support routines, will run as a server.[12] E programs will be dynamically loaded into the server, rather than each containing its own copy of the Storage Manager. The association between E programs and database volumes will be implicit because the programs themselves will be stored in the server. The EVOLUME

---

[12]In fact, a prototype of this server ran in the SIGMOD-88 EXODUS demonstration.

environment variable, currently the "weak link", will no longer be necessary. The programmer will control transactions via a `transaction` block in the E language, and will be able to associate different buffer groups with different parts of the code. We are currently investigating means by which the latter may be specified.

3.2.5. Supporting Other C++ Features

So far, we have described the general scheme that we have used for implementing persistence in E. We described our solutions to the problems of creating persistent objects, binding objects to program symbols, and generating code for expressions. This section discusses some further problems that are specific to extending the semantics of C++ to the world of persistent objects. Part of the solution depends on the new environment in which E programs will be compiled and run [18]. For this paper, we will describe certain of its features as needed.

3.2.5.1. Constructors & Destructors

Earlier, we outlined how the compiler processes the declaration of a persistent object for which an initializer has been specified. A more interesting problem arises when a persistent object is declared of a dbclass with a constructor. Consider again the stack class definition in Figures 2 and 3. The stack constructor initializes the top-of-stack index to -1, indicating that the stack is empty. By definition, a constructor is called when the object is created. Suppose, as in Figure 3, a program declares a persistent stack. Since the compiler creates the persistent object, it would appear that the compiler must also invoke the constructor. But how is this to be accomplished? The compiler, that is, efront, has only the abstract syntax tree for the program. Should we write an interpreter? In general, a constructor may call other functions arbitrarily; what if those functions are externally defined? In fact, unlike this example, it may well be that the constructor itself has not yet been defined but only declared.

In the first implementation of E, the problem is handled as follows. Observe that is it not strictly necessary to call the constructor at compile time. Rather, it is sufficient to ensure that the object is initialized before any program actually uses it, and that it is initialized only once. A very slight extension to an existing cfront mechanism provides a simple implementation satisfying these conditions. Before describing how constructors are called on persistent objects, then, we first review the mechanism used in cfront for initializing static objects.

Consider for the moment the non-db stack implementation in Figure 2, and suppose that the stack class and the stack S are defined in a module m separate from the main program. (The term "module" is used to emphasize that C++ programs are usually composed of separately compiled pieces.) Any program which includes m as one of its components must be sure to initialize S before the main program begins. In the general case, a given program comprises a set of modules, M, each of which contains a set, X_m, of objects needing initialization. The approach adopted in the AT&T C++ compiler involves first generating,

193

as part of the C translation, an initializer function, f_m, for each module in M.[13] This function simply calls the appropriate constructor for each object in X_m:

$$f_m \{$$
$$\quad constructor(\,x_{m_1},args_1\,);$$
$$\quad ...$$
$$\quad constructor(\,x_{m_n},args_n\,);$$
$$\}$$

In the case of the nonpersistent stack example, the initializer for module m would look something like[14]:

```
void _STI_m() {
     _stack_ctor( &S );
}
```

The first action of every C++ main program is to call the initializer function for every module in M. We shall omit the details of how these functions are bound to the calls made by the main program. The compilation steps enclosed in the dashed box in Figure 4 accomplish this binding.

Now, an E source module m contains, in addition to X_m, a set P_m of persistent objects, each of which is of a dbclass with a constructor. To implement the desired semantics, efront amends the initialization function, f_m, as follows:

$$f_m \{$$
$$\quad \text{persistent BOOL init = TRUE;}$$
$$\quad \text{if (init) \{}$$
$$\quad\quad \text{init = FALSE;}$$
$$\quad\quad constructor(\,p_{m_1},args_1\,);$$
$$\quad\quad ...$$
$$\quad\quad constructor(\,p_{m_n},args_n\,);$$
$$\quad \}$$
$$\quad constructor(\,x_{m_1},args_1\,);$$
$$\quad ...$$
$$\quad constructor(\,x_{m_n},args_n\,);$$
$$\}$$

When f_m is called for the first time, the persistent flag has the value TRUE. The flag is then cleared and constructors are invoked on the persistent objects in m. If the same program is run again, or even if another program containing m is run, these constructors will not be called again because the flag is itself persistent and shared by all programs that include m.

Once the basic E persistence mechanism was working, this solution was trivial to implement. Like most first solutions, though, it has several drawbacks. First, testing the persistent flag requires a read call to the storage manager. For a program consisting of n

[13]Obviously, modules for which X_m is empty do not need an initializer. We do not consider this case further.

[14]The actual name of the function is the name of the source file prepended with "_STI", for STatic Initializer.

modules, this implies a startup cost of as many as n disk reads.[15] Furthermore, a given module containing such a persistent flag will contribute one storage manager call to the startup cost of every run of every program in which it is ever used. Ideally, we would like to pay the initialization cost once, and thereafter incur no extra overhead.

Another shortcoming of this solution is that it does not extend to destructors. A destructor is the inverse of a constructor. Whenever an object of a class is destroyed, e.g. by going out of scope, the class's destructor (if it exists) is called first. A persistent object is destroyed by deleting the module containing its persistent handle (companion). If that object is of a dbclass with a destructor, we should, to be consistent, call that destructor. (The existing utility for module removal, *erm*, requires the user to specify explicitly all the object code modules required for calling the destructors.) The solution for constructors cannot be applied here because, while a flag can identify the *first* time the module is used, it cannot signal the *last*.

The above problems derive from a common source. While the first implementation of E maintains persistent *objects*, it does not maintain persistent *types*. That is, the current system does not maintain the association between a persistent object and its type, e.g. the code implementing its methods. The next implementation of E will operate in the context of the new environment to which we have alluded, and it will enforce the following rule: *The lifetime of every persistent object of type T must be subsumed by the lifetime of an implementation of T.* When a persistent object, x, of type T is declared, the environment will allow the compiler to identify which implementation of T is being used, and to bind x to that implementation. Note that this rule does not specify "the same" implementation of T over the lifetime of x. (We wish to allow a careful user to modify an implementation without necessarily invalidating existing objects.)

The above rule implies that the new environment will impose somewhat more structure on the way programs are built. Currently, for example, a source module includes (via #include) the header files containing the definitions of needed classes. Calls to member functions of such classes are typically left unbound until the application module and the class implementation modules are linked together. Under the new environment, source modules use *use* rather than include one another. Use is a semantically richer form of include. In particular, if several source modules all use a given source module, *m*, they *share* that module. Under #include, each would receive an independent, inline copy of *m*.

Returning to the problem of constructors, destructors, and persistent objects, the new environment will enable the compiler to verify that the declaration of a persistent object uses an implementation of the object's type (and not simply a declaration). The result is that the constructor for a persistent object will be called when the object is created, eliminating the need to test a persistent flag at startup time. Similarly, when we destroy a module containing persistent objects, we can then locate and call destructors automatically.

---

[15]However, given that a flag resides on the same page as other persistent objects in the module, at least some of these pages would presumably have been requested shortly anyway.

The details will be covered in [18].

3.2.5.2. Virtual Functions

The C++ mechanism which supports "true" object-oriented behavior — the late binding of code to a method invocation — is the *virtual* function. If a member function of a class is declared virtual, then the runtime calling sequence involves indirection through a dispatch table. In the AT&T C++ compiler, there is one such table for each class having virtual functions, and every object of the class contains a pointer to that table. Thus, the dispatch table is a kind of runtime type descriptor, and the embedded pointer plays the role of a type tag for each object. The amount of type information known to the compiler allows for a very fast implementation: A virtual function call adds at most one pointer dereference and one indexing operation to the cost of a normal procedure call.

When virtual functions are combined with persistence, the above implementation no longer suffices. Clearly, we cannot store the memory address of the dispatch table because that address is valid only for one program run. One approach is to make the dispatch table a persistent object. Then the addresses embedded in objects will be valid persistent addresses. This is the solution adopted in Vbase, for example [1, 2]. For E, however, this approach only pushes the problem back one step. The virtual functions themselves will be located at different addresses in different programs, and so the persistent dispatch table must be filled in when it is loaded. Furthermore, it leaves unresolved the addresses of other functions that may be called by the virtual functions. Since the actual dispatch table used in a given program is, in effect, specific to that program, there seems to be little benefit in making it persist.

For these reasons, we have implemented a different solution. For every dbclass C having virtual functions, the compiler generates a unique integer type tag, and every instance of C contains this tag. The dispatch tables are still main memory objects, and in addition, we introduce a global hash table (also a main memory object) for mapping type tags to dispatch table addresses. This table is initialized at program startup[16]; for each dbclass in the program having virtual functions, we enter its type tag and dispatch table address. The existing static initializer mechanism described in the previous section is used to initialize the hash table. Then, to call a virtual function at runtime, we hash on the type tag in the object to obtain the dispatch table address and proceed as before from there.

A problem that arises in this implementation is the management of type tags. Specifically, we must be able to distinguish the first use of a type from subsequent uses; in the former case, we must generate a new type tag, and in the latter, we must reuse the existing type tag. Obviously, name space management is a related issue, since types that happen to have the same name are not necessarily the same type. Once again, the current solution provides an initial implementation that will be improved in the next version. The compiler keeps a persistent table associating type names (character strings) with tags. Before generating a new tag for a type T, the compiler searches the table. If T's name is found, the associated tag is used. Otherwise, a persistent counter is incremented, generating a new tag, and a

---

[16]Unlike the (initial) constructor solution described above, this startup cost is negligible.

new entry is made in the table. Obviously, this solution disallows having two dbclasses with the same name (in different programs, of course), where both classes have virtual functions. The new environment for E will eliminate this minor restriction.

4. SUMMARY

4.1. Review

This paper has presented the design of the first implementation of persistence in the E compiler. We briefly reviewed E's place in the context of the EXODUS project and its client relationship with the EXODUS Storage Manager. We showed by example how one declares and manipulates persistent objects in E, emphasizing the ease with which one can convert a nonpersistent application into a persistent one.

The main body of the paper then described in detail the compiler's implementation. We began by showing at a macro level how we integrated E language extensions into an existing C++ compiler. We then described how the E compiler processes persistent object declarations, paying particular attention to how those objects are created and initialized. Next we described the current prototype code generator, which converts expressions involving persistent objects into equivalent expressions involving address calculations and calls to the Storage Manager. Finally, we described our current solutions to the special problems of handling constructors, destructors, and virtual functions in the context of persistence.

4.2. Relationship to Other Work

Like other persistent languages and object-oriented database systems, E reduces the impedance mismatch between the programming language and the persistent store (or database system). However, E is distinguished from other work in several ways. First, E is a direct extension of an existing systems level programming language, C++. All of the concepts and semantics of the base language have been preserved in the extension to persistence. The addition of db classes, for example, is really a minor syntactic extension. All of the concepts associated with C++ classes, e.g. constructors and virtual functions, are supported by E dbclasses. Also, the pointer manipulation facilities familiar to C and C++ programmers are preserved in the persistent world. A db pointer may be cast, incremented, etc. Another distinguishing feature of E is in its approach to physical I/O. By viewing the storage manager as a load/store machine, E departs from the persistent virtual memory model used in every other system of which we are aware. By scheduling loads and stores (pins and unpins), the E compiler realizes a number potential benefits. First, while object faulting implies loading the whole object, E pins only the portion of the object accessed by the program. When objects are small, the two methods are similar, but when objects are large, E should make significantly better use of available buffer space. This economy should be especially important in a multiuser environment. Secondly, the compile time scheduling of loads and stores provides the opportunity to apply optimizations. We expect to realize significant improvements in the performance of E programs in this way.

4.3. Status & Current Research

In addition to being a learning vehicle, the current compiler provides a demonstration of feasibility of the general approach to persistence taken in E. The db-simplification phase (and a number of supporting routines) were designed and added to the compiler during the Spring of 1988. The E compiler runs on a DEC VAXstation III under Unix 4.3, and was an integral part of a demonstration given at SIGMOD-88. At this point, the full cross product of dbclasses and persistence works correctly. Other features of E not covered in this paper, i.e. generators and iterators, also compile correctly. A test suite developed by a student over the summer has greatly aided in debugging the compiler (and in building our confidence in it).

The design of a new environment to support E program management is nearing completion. This environment will address several issues which we feel require better handling. These issues include a more integrated runtime environment, and the protection and control of source code. It will also allow a much more efficient implementation of constructors for persistent objects, as well as an equally efficient implementation of destructors.

The major research direction related to E is now in the optimization of E code. Optimizations will be applied to a number of areas. We seek to reduce drastically the the number of calls to the Storage Manager, both locally within an expression and globally within a procedure. The optimizations we seek are related to existing techniques such as the elimination of unnecessary loads and stores, global register allocation, and loop optimizations. However, because the "machine" for which E is targeted (i.e. the EXODUS Storage Manager) is quite different from a typical hardware machine (e.g. one with a fixed number of word-sized registers), optimizing E code is a research problem rather than a straightforward application of known techniques. For example, one potential new optimization is called "coalescing"; if several different pieces of the same object are pinned within the same or nearby regions of code, those separate requests could be combined into one request which pins a single spanning range of bytes. Whether coalescing is worthwhile depends both on the distance between the two ranges within the object and on the distance between the uses of those ranges within the program. Another important area for optimization will be processing arrays in a block-at-a-time fashion, rather than one element at a time. We are looking at techniques used in vectorizing compilers (e.g. [14]) for inspiration. After an appropriate set of optimizations have been chosen and implemented, we plan to investigate the performance of E code relative both to existing DBMSs and to systems that rely on object faulting.

ACKNOWLEDGEMENTS

While this paper has concentrated on the implementation of persistence in E, we should note that the other half of the implementation effort — generator classes and iterators — was the work of Dan Schuh. For that, and for his fearless journeys into the original source code, he has our deep gratitude. We would also like to thank the other members of the EXODUS project for their continued support.

198

REFERENCES

1. Andrews, T., and Harris, C., "Combining Language and Database Advances in an Object-Oriented Development Environment," *Proc. ACM OOPSLA Conf.*, Orlando, Florida, October, 1987.

2. Andrews, T., private communication, June, 1988.

3. Atkinson, M.P., Bailey, P.J., Chisholm, K.J., Cockshott, W.P., and Morrison, R., "An Approach to Persistent Programming," *Computer Journal*, 26(4), 1983.

4. Brown, A.L., and Cockshott, P., "The CPOMS Persistent Object Management System," Persistent Programming Research Report #13, 1985.

5. Carey, M., and DeWitt, D., "Extensible Database Systems," *Proc. Islamorada Workshop on Large Scale Knowledge Base and Reasoning Sys.*, Feb. 1986.

6. Carey, M., DeWitt, D., Richardson, J., and Shekita, E., "Object and File Management in the EXODUS Extensible Database System," *Proc. 12th VLDB Conf.*, Kyoto, Japan, Aug. 1986.

7. Carey, M.J., DeWitt, D.J., Frank, D., Graefe, G., Richardson, J.E., Shekita, E.J., and Muralikrishna, M., "The Architecture of the EXODUS Extensible DBMS," *Proc. 1st Int'l Workshop on Object-Oriented Database Sys.*, Pacific Grove, CA, Sept. 1986.

8. Carey, M., DeWitt, D., and Vandenberg, S., "A Data Model and Query Language for EXODUS," *Proc. ACM-SIGMOD Int'l Conf. on Management of Data*, Chicago, Ill., 1988.

9. Cockshott, W.P, Atkinson, M.P., Chisholm, K.J., Bailey, P.J., and Morrison, R., "Persistent Object Management System," *Software—Practice and Experience*, vol. 14, 1984.

10. Copeland, G., and Maier, D., "Making Smalltalk a Database System," *Proc. ACM-SIGMOD Int'l Conf. on Management of Data*, Boston, MA, 1984.

11. Graefe, G., and DeWitt, D., "The EXODUS Optimizer Generator," *Proc. ACM-SIGMOD Int'l Conf. on Management of Data*, San Francisco, 1987.

12. Graefe, G., "Rule-Based Query Optimization in Extensible Database Systems," Ph.D. Thesis, University of Wisconsin, Madison, August, 1987.

13. Kernighan, B., and Ritchie, D., *The C Programming Language*, Prentice-Hall, 1978.

14. Padua, D., Kuck, D., and Lawrie, D., "High-Speed Multiprocessors and Compilation Techniques," *IEEE Transactions on Computers*, C-29(9), September, 1980.

15. Richardson, J., and Carey, M., "Programming Constructs for Database System Implementation in EXODUS," *Proc. ACM-SIGMOD Int'l Conf. on Management of Data*, San Francisco, CA., 1987.

16. Richardson, J., Carey, M., DeWitt, D., and Schuh, D., "Persistence in EXODUS," *Proc. Workshop on Persistent Object Systems: Their Design, Implementation, and Use,* Appin, Scotland, 1987.

17. Richardson, J., Carey, M., and Schuh, D.T., "The Design of the E Programming Language," Computer Sciences Technical Report #824, University of Wisconsin—Madison, February, 1989.

18. Richardson, J., and Carey, M., "Environment Support for E," in preparation.

19. Stroustrup, B., *The C++ Programming Language*, Addison-Wesley, Reading, 1986.

Addressing in a Persistent Environment

P. A. Buhr
University of Waterloo

C. R. Zarnke
Waterloo Microsystems Inc.

ABSTRACT

An addressing scheme is proposed, called a structured addressing scheme, that will provide a consistent addressing structure for a persistent environment. A structured address is the internal analogue of a qualified name in a programming language (e.g. x.y.z) where each component of the address identifies a special kind of data item, called a memory, whose basic purpose is to hold/store possibly many objects. Memories are organized in a hierarchical fashion. Some memories correspond to physical storage media, but others exist for organizational reasons. Each component of a structured address is not defined by the hardware, but by the memory in which the object is contained. Hence, a component can be encoded by a memory (so it is not a direct displacement) to reduce the length of an address. The component can point indirectly to the next component or object in the memory, making it a handle. This indirection permits the object to be moved around within its memory for storage management reasons and yet still maintain a fixed address. Finally, the structured address has the advantage that it accommodates new memories easily.

1. INTRODUCTION

A **persistent environment** is a programming system in which users can create data items of any type that outlast the execution of the program that created them, and hence, persist until the user explicitly deletes them or an entity containing them. Persistent data has always existed in programming systems, normally in the form of files and databases. What characterizes a persistent environment is the way in which this persistent data is made accessible in a programming language and its execution-time environment. A persistent environment simplifies some of the difficult problems in existing systems and reshapes others so that they can be solved in a more consistent and coherent form. Work done in traditional systems is recast into a form that combines together ideas from programming languages, operating systems and databases to provide a powerful software development environment, with increased software reliability, more efficient program execution and more productive programming time. Several different approaches have been presented to achieve this goal [1, 2, 4, 10, 11, 12].

What is common across all these designs is that the processor(s) on which they execute deals only with addresses to one type of memory (usually volatile RAM), which has the basic property that it be able to respond at approximately the same speed as the processor (called **primary storage**). Persistent data must be contained in secondary storage (non-volatile disk, tape, etc.) because it is generally much larger than can be accommodated by primary storage and must persist even if power to the machine is interrupted. Secondary storage is implemented by a variety of physical media each having different addressing mechanisms. Not all items in secondary storage need to persist, but all persistent items must exist in secondary storage. The key point here is that the processor used to execute programs and manipulate the data within these programs, in general, cannot access any persistent data directly; however, this data is the most important data on a computer system.

This situation is reflected in the fact that most programming languages provide support for primary storage only. Access to persistent data is usually provided through a subsystem external to the programming language, such as a file system or database system (e.g. conventional files and directory structure). Because the definition of the persistent store is outside the programming language, the structures created are not directly usable in the programming language as are normal data structures. We believe that this dichotomy between persistent data, and volatile data should be mitigated as much as possible by presenting a uniform approach to manipulating data in a program [7, p. 49]. While the hardware is cast-in-stone to a large degree, the programming language can provide a uniform approach to addressing and accessing data.

To understand much of the mechanism we will be suggesting, it is necessary to understand the basic objectives of the system we are designing and building. First, we want to extend the notion of type safety to encompass all interactions within the system, and in particular, to interactions between a program and the persistent data it uses. Thus, it is necessary to retain the types of all persistent data so that appropriate type-checking can be done. Further, we plan to do type-checking statically. We believe that the best way of accomplishing this is to make all persistent data items definable in the programming language and to have a single programming language in the system.

Second, we want to adopt an object-oriented paradigm throughout the system. Most data will be contained in objects which define a particular set of operations that can be performed on the data. In other words, it is really objects which persist and not merely the data itself. This means it is necessary to make both data and code accessible when a persistent object is accessed. Further, objects are not normally copied in their entirety into the processes that access them. This is necessary to allow objects to be shared among processes. Thus, persistent objects must be independently accessible by multiple processes. Our mechanism for accomplishing this is to allow direct addressing of persistent objects and to make the object accessible through paging (called a segmented virtual memory scheme by Cockshott [6]). Database notions like transaction commital and nested transactions will be handled by write-through, shadow-paging and the programming language concurrency mechanism.

Third, we want to have an object which allows any type of data item to be defined and subsequently persist until explicitly removed. This will be accomplished with an instance of an ENVIR definition (see [4] for details), which is like a name space in other persistent systems, in that it relates names and type information with the objects created from them. One important difference between our ENVIR instances and name spaces is that the objects in an environment are operated on directly, whereas items in name spaces are essentially copied out of the name space, modified, and subsequently returned.

Since ENVIR's are objects, one environment can contain pointers to another. Thus, our name spaces can be structured like a traditional file hierarchy but this is accomplished through programming language mechanisms. Normal programming language qualification and scope rules allow referencing both up and down the hierarchy. Hurst discusses a similar scheme in [8], but he relies on a dynamic mechanism to bind names directly with objects in a name space context (this scheme is implemented in Napier [2]). We rely on normal programming language declarations in nested blocks to bind names to objects in the block context [5]. We believe our approach is more consistent with the way programming is done in a statically-typed programming language. Having multiple name spaces introduces problems of storing data items containing pointers, as these pointers may be relative to the name space in which the data structure was created. Hence, transferring or copying information from one name space to another may be non-trivial.

At the same time, we see a necessity for supporting file/database like objects. The facilities provided by traditional files and databases cannot be incorporated into name spaces without severe problems. Abstraction, sharability, storage management and access efficiency cannot be handled well if all of the data traditionally stored in files and databases is stored in the name spaces themselves.

Intimately tied in with addressing and accessing of data is storage management of the data. How data is allocated and whether it can be garbage collected affects the form of the address for the data. Storage management is one of the most difficult aspects of any system and this is even more so in a persistent environment where user-defined objects may persist along with system-defined ones. To accommodate storage management, the programming language allows type unsafe manipulation of pointers. This is necessary to allow system programmers to design and implement objects that require specialized types of storage management. Most users would never need to do this or even be allowed to do this; nevertheless, without this facility, all storage management operations must be written in another programming language, which would make the system multilingual.

What we shall describe in this paper is the underlying storage model we propose to use to allocate and manage persistent objects such as name spaces and file objects. The storage management of objects within the secondary storage will be definable in the programming language; however, this is an abstraction level that is invisible to the normal user. Then, by structuring this storage into a hierarchy, the addresses of the persistent data within the storage will follow directly.

2. ADDRESS SPACE

The unit which we will use as the building block for persistent storage is the address space. An **address space** is a series of contiguous bytes of storage, addressed consecutively from 0 to some maximum; such addresses will be called **uniform addresses**. These address spaces are analogous to address spaces that are created for executing programs, such as data and instruction address spaces. Address spaces are not accessible to a process until some explicit action is taken, either by the user or by the system. All address spaces are accessible in a uniform way as was the objective in Multics [9]. Finally, the physical storage media (disks, tapes, etc.) can be considered to be address spaces, too. In this case, a simple computation allows one to transform a uniform address into the corresponding address required by a physical device (e.g. track and cylinder).

3. MEMORY

A **memory** is an address space resulting from instantiation of the MEMORY construct that will be described later. In other words, a memory is an address space with some basic structure imposed on it by the programming language. A memory may contain many objects or only one. For example, a sequential file memory contains a single sequential file object which contains information about the records stored in the file memory. In traditional systems, a file is a memory; so too is a directory, which is simply a special kind of file which points to other files.

A memory has storage management as its primary function, whereas an object corresponds to an instance of a (class-like) definition made in the programming language. However, our memories are able to be defined in the programming language. Some memories will be quite simple (e.g. a sequential file memory) and some may be complex (e.g. disk memories), depending on the kind of storage management required.

3.1. Memory Hierarchy

A disk, and the files it contains, are both memories in our model; the file memory constitutes part of the disk memory. This is an example of a two-level hierarchy of memories. Such nesting exists in other situations, too:

1. A user may be assigned a **minidisk** that contains many files, where each minidisk is treated as a disk in its own right.

2. An operating system may be assigned a **partition**, where each partition is a portion of the disk used exclusively by a particular operating system (e.g. virtual machines).

Each of these cases is a memory hierarchy which consists of three levels instead of two. This can be generalized so that the memory hierarchy can consist of many levels. Some memories, such as those for disks, contain other memories; and some, such as those for files do not.

There does not need to be any correlation between memories and storage devices. Another organization that is permitted is to have a single memory that spans several disks (i.e. treat the several disks as a single memory for storage management purposes). Such a memory, or one corresponding to a single physical storage medium, will be called a **physical memory** and will constitute the root of a memory hierarchy; a system or network will normally contain several physical memories. A leaf memory in the hierarchy would be a memory such as that for a file, which it is not designed to accommodate other memories. Figure 1 shows an example memory hierarchy.

where a "group" is a submemory of the system memory and "usermem" is a submemory of a group. The system designer controls the structure of the memories that form the upper portions of the structure. Although a user will be able to create new memories by declaring files and similar objects, he/she may or may not be allowed to create memories which contain other memories (e.g. subdivide space into more minidisks) because of limitation imposed by the system designer.

Notice that the memory hierarchy does not have a large number of levels, and its organization is entirely independent of the organization of data that is contained within it.

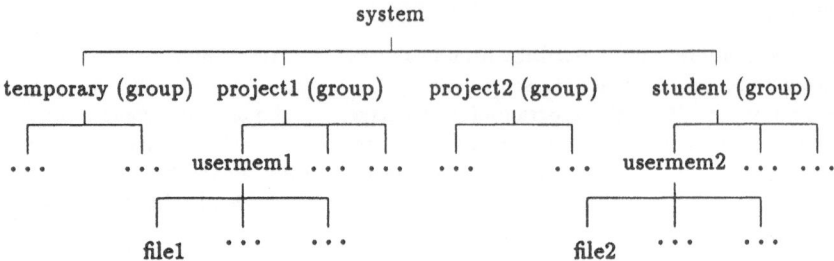

Figure 1: Memory Hierarchy

3.2.   Storage Management

An important capability of most memories, e.g. files, is that they can change size dynamically; that is, the maximum address that can be used to access data within the memory can be increased or reduced. This intrinsic property of an address space helps make storage management within the memory easier. However, it makes the storage management of the containing memory more complicated.

A memory in which repeated allocation and freeing is performed is vulnerable to fragmentation. Hence, these memories may need to use complex storage management algorithms to deal with this problem. Some form of compaction may be necessary to recover badly fragmented space; this, in turn, usually requires movement of the contained memories.

4.   OBJECTS

For this paper, an **object** is an entity in a memory which can be referred to from outside the memory. The kinds of objects that can be allocated in a particular memory will depend on the definition of the memory. One important kind of object is a file; another is a name space (i.e. an ENVIR instance). This discussion will focus on the simpler file as it illustrates the approach. Name spaces are defined in a very similar fashion, but internally are much more complicated objects than files.

A file is an object, namely, an instance of a polymorphic class definition made in the programming language. The class definition will contain control information, such as pointers to the first and last records contained in it, as well as defining the mechanism by which the individual data structures making up the object are organized and accessed. A file differs from an entity such as an integer because its instantiation causes the creation of a separate memory within which the instance of the file class is allocated; this memory also contains the storage for all the records in the file. We refer to this memory as the **file memory**.

A program begins execution having two or possibly three memories accessible: the program memory, the stack and the heap. Simple data items needed by the program are allocated on the stack or the heap. However, these memories cannot contain other memories (such as file memories); such objects are allocated in a memory that is able to accommodate them (such as a disk memory) and a pointer to them is used instead.

Each object in a memory has a unique "identifier" through which the object can be referred to from outside the memory. Thus, the identifier of an object within a memory

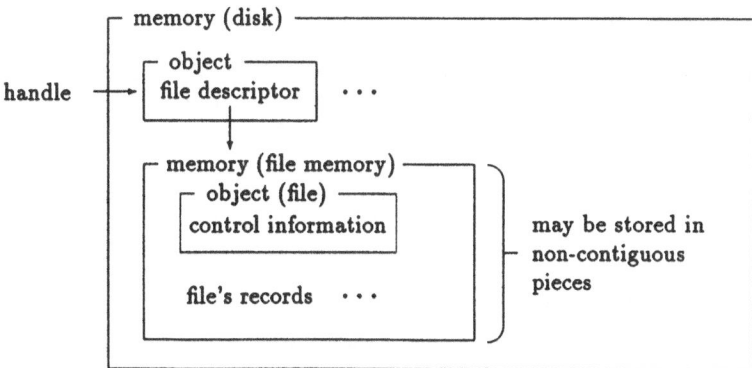

Figure 2: Memory Structure

must remain the same as long as the object exists. In some cases, this may require that the object identifier be a pointer to a pointer to the object; such an identifier is frequently called a **handle** and it allows objects within a memory to be moved around without affecting the identifiers to the object. This might be the case, for example, for a disk memory where files are reorganized occasionally to improve speed of access of information on the disk.

4.1. UNDERLYING OBJECTS

As stated, a file is contained in a memory which can expand and contract. The file memory is not necessarily stored as a contiguous area on the disk but as a series of extents (pieces) scattered throughout the disk memory. Pointers to these extents are contained in an object in the disk memory, usually called a **file descriptor**. We say that the file descriptor object **underlies** the file memory. Thus, a file consists of three levels:

1. the file object itself

2. the memory in which it is contained

3. an object underlying this memory (and hence underlying the original object)

The latter two are allocated in the next higher level memory (i.e. the disk). This structure is illustrated in Figure 2.

This is the model we use generally for all memories – each has an associated underlying object which is (usually) allocated in the next higher level memory in the memory hierarchy. In particular, there will be an object underlying the memory corresponding to a physical storage device; in the case of a disk memory, for example, this object interacts directly with the device hardware. This object is the disk drive and is not allocated in any memory.

4.2. Object Identifiers

An object has a unique identifier within the memory in which it is allocated, but this is clearly relative to that specific memory. To obtain a system-wide unique identifier for the object we need to specify, as well, the identifier of the memory in which it is allocated.

This is done by giving the identifier of the object underlying the memory. Similarly, the identifier of the underlying object will involve the identifier of the memory in which it is allocated, etc. Thus, we build up a system-wide identifier for an object by giving in order the sequence of identifiers of all underlying objects in which the object lies, plus the identifier of the desired object in its memory. Such a multi-component identifier is called an **object identifier**. It has one component for each level in the memory hierarchy containing the object. Hence, each memory in the memory hierarchy plays an active role in the formation of an object identifier. This identifier is the internal analogue of a qualified name in a programming language (e.g. x.y.z).

4.3. Dismountable and Distributed Memories

There is always a one-to-one correspondence between memories and underlying objects. This permits the identifier of the underlying object to be used as the unique means of identifying the corresponding memory.

For a physical memory, which includes dismountable and distributed memories, this structure is preserved. However, in this case, the underlying object exists in no memory and hence cannot be assigned an identifier relative to it. Instead, the object must be assigned an identifier that makes it unique within the system/network. This will be called its **memory identifier**. (The underlying object is the analogue of block zero of a disk, which contains the location of its root-level file directory.) This identifier is determined at the time the memory is created (initialized) and will probably include as part of its identifier the unique identifier for the system.

Each device, such as a disk drive, is controlled by a volatile object on the machine in which the device is installed. The object is volatile because it disappears when the machine is powered off. There is a network-wide table that relates the memory identifiers of all physical memories currently available on the network, to the volatile objects on which they are mounted.

When the system attempts to decode (dereference) an object identifier, it uses the memory identifier to find the volatile object (drive) on which the memory is currently located. Thus, from the memory identifier, the system infers the appropriate object to use to access the memory.

5. MAKING A MEMORY ACCESSIBLE

Because most memories are in secondary storage, they are not directly accessible by the hardware; hence, the objects within them are not accessible either. Conceptually, to make an object accessible, its containing memory is copied into primary storage. Clearly, copying the entire memory may not be possible if the size of the memory exceeds that of primary storage, or it may be inefficient even if primary storage is large enough and it makes sharing difficult. **Paging** offers a solution to this problem by allowing a partial copying, and it makes the copying invisible and under system control. From the user's standpoint, the object is accessed directly.

5.1. Representative

When a memory is made accessible by a program, the system will create an object in primary storage to keep track of the location of the partial copy (or set of pages). This object and the partial copy are analogous to an object and its overlying memory, except these are created in primary storage. In effect, we are creating a two level memory hierarchy in primary storage analogous to the memory hierarchy created in secondary storage. This primary storage analogue of the object underlying a memory we call a representative. It is an extension of the underlying object – the representative uses information in the underlying object to locate the memory, but it must also keep information about the copy in primary storage.

Besides holding data locating the copy of the memory, the representative also contains procedures defining how and when to make the memory accessible. The representative will operate in cooperation with the particular kind of storage management provided by the memory. It might bring all the pages into primary storage and hence simply perform swapping, or, it might perform prefetching and purge behind of pages so that there is a window of addressability that moves through the file as it is accessed. For a data base, the representative can keep certain areas of the primary index and data area constantly accessible and let other areas of the index and data be made accessible on a demand basis.

Only one representative for a particular memory is created, and it is used by all the accessors on that system. This property is essential because allowing duplicate copies (complete or partial) in primary storage is storage inefficient and causes consistency problems during concurrent access. To accomplish this requires that the system maintain information about which memories are being accessed and create a new representative only if one does not already exist; otherwise the existing representative is used.

We are currently trying to extend the role of the representative to deal with remote access to memories across a network. What is necessary is to have a representative created in the file server for the memory that is being accessed and a representative created on each machine that is accessing the memory. The representatives can then communicate with each other to manage paging/swapping and sharing/updating across the network.

6. FORMATION OF A MEMORY HIERARCHY ADDRESS

When an object is declared, both the instance and an address to refer to it are created. The address that is created may only have to be a simple identifier if it is only used within the memory in which the object is allocated. However, when a file is declared, the identifier that is returned for it must, in general, be able to be dereferenced in a memory other than the one it is immediately relative to. Therefore, the identifier of such an object must include a complete set of components from the root of the memory hierarchy to the newly allocated file. The following discusses the structure of the address and how it is constructed.

6.1. Component Value

Each component value of an object identifier may be the displacement from the beginning of the memory to the storage for the object. This value is determined at execution time when the object is allocated. The value returned from the allocation is the identifier of that object in the containing memory.

However, the value returned from allocation does not have to be the actual address of the item in the memory, it may be a handle. For example, a simple subscript value to an array of object pointers (to which handles point) might be returned. Thus, only this smaller amount of information, which is an encoded form of the location of the object, must be stored in the identifier. This is an important point, as it means that a component value need not depend on the size of the object's memory that it identifies.

Because a component may be encoded, it is necessary to decode the component after the memory to which it applies has been made accessible. Thus, each memory must contain a routine that transforms the component value into the address of the desired object within the memory. This routine would be called as part of dereferencing to actually locate an object in a memory.

7. MEMORY HIERARCHY ADDRESS RESOLUTION

An object identifier cannot be used by the processor to access an object as it uses normal addresses of entities in primary storage. In order to do this, the memory containing the object must first be made accessible. Making the memory that contains an object accessible involves dereferencing the object identifier, and making all of the lower level memories accessible, if necessary. Each successive component (except the last) of an object identifier is used to locate the object underlying a memory and to make it accessible (by paging or swapping). Then the next component is able to be used, since it is relative to the memory just made accessible.

Each component in the object identifier indicates an object in an overlying memory. Thus, in traversing the memory hierarchy, objects in several memories may have to be made accessible, and hence several representatives may have to be created, one for each object. It is the representative and the underlying object that make the overlying memory accessible to the processor.

The first step in resolving an object identifier is to locate the memory whose object identifier is given by the first component of the object identifier. The representative of all objects capable of holding physical memories are examined to locate the one holding the desired memory. This step may fail if no appropriate object can be found. Once found, the next component is decoded by passing it to the decode routine for this memory, which must be accessible because it is mounted. The decode routine returns the identifier of the object specified in the encoded component. This object underlies the next memory. The above process is repeated on the next component for the memory overlying the current object. However, this memory may or may not be accessible, and if not accessible, it must be made accessible to decode the next component.

Notice that the levels of the memory hierarchy nearest the root will normally remain active and hence they will already have representatives created. Thus, the first part of the object identifier will likely be able to be resolved quickly. Only for the later components of the object identifier will new representatives need to be created. All intermediate memories accessed must remain accessible until the access to the object is finished. This is because each memory is dependent on the one in which it is contained to be able to directly access its underlying object and to allow access to the blocks of the overlying memory.

7.1. Active Memory Tree

As has been mentioned already, only one representative is created for an object no matter how many accesses are made to it. To do this the system must have some way, during identifier resolution, of determining if a representative for an object already exists, and if it does then it uses the existing representative.

This is accomplished through the standard technique of maintaining a list (or tree) of the active memories in primary storage, called the **active memory tree**. The active memory tree is a hierarchy built in primary storage which contains the identifiers of all active objects. The structure of this tree corresponds to the structure of the memory hierarchy, but it is only the small subset of the memory hierarchy that is currently active. Each level in the tree represents a level in the memory hierarchy. At each level, there is a list of all the representatives for objects that are active. The size of the active memory tree is a function of the number of accessed objects.

The resolution of an object identifier may produce several entries in the active memory tree. Resolution yields the address of the representative of the last memory in the sequence.

8. PROGRAMMING LANGUAGE CONSTRUCTS

This section gives a simplified description of the programming language constructs that we intend to use to define the memories and objects described above (see [3] for a more detailed description).

8.1. MEMORY Construct

The **MEMORY** construct is a class-like construct defining a particular kind of memory. For example, a definition for a sequential file memory might look like:

```
FileDesc MEMORY SeqMemory(t : TYPE) FileDesc is the superclass for SeqMemory
    VAR RecordStart, RecordEnd : REF t

    PROC append(r : t) ... allocate & add a new record
    PROC rewrite ... destroy previous file contents & reinitialize
    PROC alloc(s : INT) RETURNS COMPONENT ... allocate storage for object
    PROC free(a : ADDRESS) ... free storage for object
    PROC decode(a : COMPONENT) RETURNS a : ADDRESS ... decode component
END MEMORY
```

Each kind of memory may provide different storage management primitives appropriate for the kind of object (or objects) to be allocated within it; for example, a disk memory would likely provide one kind of storage management for file memories and another for file descriptors.

Each memory must provide routines to allocate and free storage for objects created in the memory. This scheme can be further generalized by having the definition of an object specify which routines in the memory are used for its allocation and freeing. This allows specific allocation and freeing operation for different kinds of objects if each kind requires different storage management. As well, each memory must have a routine that decodes the object identifier components that are returned by the allocation routines. This routine can be designated by having a special name, such as **decode**.

Since a memory must do storage management, it must be able to manipulate and assign pointers as integers. Although this violates our objective of type safety, it appears to be a worthwhile sacrifice in order to be able to define memories in the programming language. Such violations are allowed only in memory definitions and these definitions will usually be written by system programmers and so type safety will not be ordinarily compromised.

8.2. Object Definition

The OBJECT construct is a class-like construct that defines a particular type of object. Because an object is allocated in a memory, the object definition must specify the type of memory to be created in. This is specified by making the object a subclass of the memory in which it is to be allocated. For example, a definition for a sequential file object might look like:

```
SeqMemory OBJECT SeqFile(t : TYPE) : SeqMemory(t)
                                    ALLOCATE alloc FREE free
    VAR FirstRecord, LastRecord, CurrRecord : REF t

    PROC read RETURNS REF t ... read a record
    PROC write(r : t) ... write a record
    ...
END MEMORY

VAR f : SeqFile(INT)
```

For the declaration of f, the compiler will generate the appropriate code to create an instance of the superclass SeqMemory and then a call to alloc to obtain storage for a SeqFile object and an object identifier component. When the block containing f is released, an appropriate call to free will be made.

The mechanism explained above, by which a memory and the object it contains is made accessible, makes the data items in them just ordinary variables which can be accessed and assigned to as usual. This is unlike traditional code for operating on files/databases which is written so that data from them is explicitly brought into primary storage. In this design, this distinction is largely blurred so that a programmer has a single uniform paradigm in which to work, that is, defining a memory or object is the same as defining a class. For example, updating a single variable in a traditional file involves explicitly reading in the block that contains the variable, changing it, and explicitly writing the block back to the file. In our case, only a simple assignment statement will modify any variable defined in the memory or object.

8.3. Object Underlying a Memory

The file descriptor contains the list of extents for the file memory and also routines that can be used to extend or reduce the size of the file memory and would look like:

```
OBJECT FileDesc
    VAR extents : [15] ExtentDescription

    PROC extend(size : INT) ...
    PROC reduce(size : INT) ...
END OBJECT
```

8.4. Representative

To make a SeqMemory accessible, a representative for its underlying object is created. This representative handles paging (or swapping) of the memory. The definition of the representative forms part of the definition of the underlying object so that its code can refer to the data items in the underlying object, as in:

```
OBJECT FileDesc
    ...
    REPRESENTATIVE no name, created by the system
        VAR ActivePages : [?] INT

        PROC PageFault(ADDRESS : INT) ...
        PROC PageOut(ADDRESS : INT)
    END REPRESENTATIVE
    ...
END OBJECT
```

The representative is created implicitly by the system on the first access to the memory and persists across all accessors. The system will call the routines in the representative when page faults occur or when pages must be paged out.

8.5. ENVIR

An ENVIR definition defines a new name space which allows types to be defined and any data items to be declared (see [4] for details). All types of definitions can be nested in an ENVIR definition which in turn could have further nested definitions, for example:

```
ENVIR eee    define an environment type
    CLASS ccc ...
    ENVIR fff ...
    VAR i : INT
    PROC p( ... ) ...
END ENVIR

VAR e : eee  create an environment
```

Like a class, it is possible to refer to data items in e from outside the ENVIR instance, for example:

```
e.i ← 2
e.p( ... )
```

What makes an environment instance different from a conventional block is that it can be used as a context for compilation and it can be dynamically changed, by adding or removing symbols from it, or by changing an existing symbol's definition. To accomplish this, an environment is made self defining by creating its own symbol table and retaining it along with the symbol tables of any nested definitions. As well, an environment has its own code area to store code derived from the definitions defined in its symbol table. Thus, there is a one-to-one relationship between an environment and its symbol table (unlike an instance of a class). Because of this relationship, we are able to assure that any change made to an environment symbol table will cause corresponding changes to the environment itself.

Because each environment has its own symbol table, it does not have to remain identical to its original defining type. Unlike a normal type which can have multiple instances, of which each one is identical in structure, each instance of an ENVIR definition can be extended independently, being described precisely by its symbol table. Hence, an environment is unique in that it provides a context for compilation (the symbol tables and its structure) and behaves like a data area. The data area, symbol table and code area allocated for an environment instance are created as separate memories. This mitigates much of the storage management problems associated with making dynamic additions and deletions of variable sized items within each.

Internally, storage management is aided by having the data area memory use handles to refer to items in the environment. Hence, it is possible to move items in the environment data area without affecting external addresses to these items. This allows garbage collection to be performed on the environment data area.

A complex ENVIR definition can be constructed that defines an environment for a user. It is constructed using the same basic building blocks as for a file, as in:

```
UserDataArea ENVIR User( ... )
    ...
UserDesc MEMORY UserDataArea( ... )
    ...
UserMiniDisk OBJECT UserDesc( ... )
    ...
MiniDisk MEMORY UserMiniDisk( ... )
    ...
```

Instantiation of the environment definition User, causes the implicit creation of the three memories to contain the information for that user's working environment. UserDataArea is the memory for the data area that contains storage for the simple variables that are declared in the environment. (Since the symbol table and code area are managed by the system, there is no explicit superclass for them; they are created implicitly.) UserDesc is the underlying object that maps the UserDataArea memory. UserMiniDisk is the memory that contains the blocks of storage for UserDataArea and the blocks of storage for any other memories allocated in environment User.

Entities declared in instances of environment User, that create a memory, must create it separately from the UserDataArea. This is because UserDataArea is not meant to contain other memories. It is meant to manage the storage for the environment which contains all the simple variables. The storage for objects such as files comes from the user's minidisk which also contains the environment data area, symbol table and code area.

When an object like SeqFile is declared in User instance, the compiler can determine that it cannot be allocated in UserDataArea from its definition and User's definition. The compiler then follows the superclass chain and discerns that a SeqFile can be allocated in UserMiniDisk, and hence creates a pointer to the SeqFile in UserDataArea and creates the file in UserMiniDisk. This is analogous to the situation of a procedure that allocates a local SeqFile. The SeqFile is not allocated on the stack with the procedure's local variables but instead is allocated in the memory in which the program executes, and points to the file from the stack. This mechanism allows the underlying memory for an object to be determined implicitly. If necessary, the underlying memory may be explicitly specified to allocate the object in a memory other than the users.

9. CODE SEGMENTS

Our language is block structured and allows separate compilation units at arbitrary levels in this structure.

```
OBJECT SeqFile ... COMPILABLE
   ...
   PROC read ... COMPILABLE
      ...
      PROC local ... COMPILABLE
      ...
   PROC write ...
   ...
```

Here each entity that has a COMPILABLE clause is eligible to be compiled separately, and components with no compilation clause are compiled as part of the node that contains them. In the above example, write is compiled as part of the compilation of SeqFile. As well, it is possible to define precisely the location of object code generated by the compilation of each compilation unit. By introducing a definitional-time declaration of a code area, called a **segment**, it is possible to have each compilation unit specify where its code will be placed, as in:

```
SEGMENT m, n    definitional-time declaration
OBJECT SeqFile ... COMPILABLE m   code is placed in segment m
   ...
   PROC read ... COMPILABLE n     code is placed in segment n
```

Object code is executed directly from segments; hence, it is not necessarily to link object code together to form the executable equivalent of a PROGRAM in Pascal.

The same scheme presented for managing data objects in memories is used for managing segments. A code image is the executable code produced by the compilation of a separate compilation unit of the programming language. A segment can contain several code images, just as disk memory can contain many objects (i.e. instances of definitions). Each code image will have an object identifier that can be used to refer to it.

9.1. Accessing Segments

Each segment is a memory, and hence must be made accessible before it can be accessed. This accessing will create a representative to page the segment that is accessed by the processor. A segment is made accessible when the context in which it is declared is entered. When an object is made accessible, the segment that contains the code to manipulate the memory must also be made accessible. Thus, the segment is made available as a result of the access to an object. To accomplish this, the object identifier of the code image is associated with the memory (as a field in the underlying object for the memory).

10. PROCESSOR ADDRESS SPACES

A **processor address space** is an address space that the processor makes use of in order to execute a program, such as the code segment, data address space, stack address space, etc. There are a fixed number of these (as defined by the processor). A memory address space may be larger than a processor address space in which case only a portion of the memory can be accessed directly.

The design presented here requires that the processor be capable of having several active address spaces. The idea of multiple active address spaces was developed in the Multics system. In the case of micro and mini computer systems, multiple active identifier spaces were introduced because the address space size on these systems severely restricted the amount of accessible memory. Hence, these systems were forced into multiple active address spaces not because of the desire to solve storage management problems but simply to be able to increase the amount of data that could be addressed.

Our system requires several address spaces to be directly accessible by the processor:

1. segment address space - memory for the code for the current object

2. stack address space - memory for the local variables of procedures and for parameters

3. heap address space - memory for the dynamically created objects

4. data address space - memory containing the current object

5. temporary data address space - memory for the objects that must be accessed temporarily, such as parameters in an inter-task call, or data moved from one memory into another memory

All the address spaces must be explicitly selectable in the identifier portion of an instruction. For example, the segment address space may be accessed explicitly because it may contain constants.

These five active address spaces will be accessed through five hardware registers on the processor. These hardware registers point to the representatives for the address space instead of to the actual data structure for a page table. This implies that the hardware is aware of the structure of a representative and not just of a page table.

10.1. Changing of Processor Address Spaces

During a procedure call, some or all of these address spaces may be changed. The conditions that cause each identifier space to change are situations such as the following:

1. The segment changes when a call is made to a routine in a different segment.

2. The stack and heap change during a call to a routine in another task.

3. The data area changes during a call to a routine contained in an object in another memory.

For example, the declaration:

```
VAR f : SeqFile(INT)
```

creates an object which creates a new memory. `SeqMemory` and `SeqFile` and all their routines will likely be compiled in one segment. Based on the definitions of `SeqFile` and `SeqMemory`, the compiler can determine which of the processor address spaces contain the various variables and routines that are used in the statements; and, if a variable or routine lies in another accessible address space that is not currently a processor address space, how this address space can be accessed.

10.2. Implications of Processor Address Spaces

During a call to a procedure, if a data item is passed by address as an argument or when a pointer is passed as an argument, it may be necessary to expand the address to identify the memory which it is relative to; one possible way of doing this is to pass the object identifier of the argument. However, constructing the complete object identifier dynamically, and dereferencing it in the called routine would be expensive. A simpler solution is to pass both the simple address of the data and the identifier of the representative of the object underlying the memory. This kind of variable or parameter is called a REPREF.

While it is conceivable to implement all such addresses using REPREFs, it is undesirable for routines that operate within the same memory. These can accept parameters by simple address which are known to be relative to the active memory.

Pointers to data internal to an object that are returned as results by public routines must be REPREFs, because the pointer is relative to an address space different from the caller's. If a simple REF is returned by the routine, it is the caller's code that constructs the REPREF using the object's representative pointer. If an actual REPREF pointer is returned, the REPREF is constructed by the callee's code.

When a REPREF is passed as an argument to a routine expecting a REF, a dynamic check is performed to assure that the REPREF is identifying the appropriate memory. If it is not the same, an exception is raised. This happens for:

```
OBJECT xxx
    PROC yyy( p : REF m )
        ...
    ...
VAR x : xxx
VAR y : REPREF m
x.p(y)
```

While y can point to data in different address spaces, it must point to x's when it is passed to a routine in x.

11. CONCLUSION

We believe this design provides a consistent approach for supporting access to secondary storage. It makes this storage available in the programming language in almost the same way as primary storage. Users can define its structure (within the constraints imposed by the system definitions), which objects appear in memory, how the storage in the memory is managed to contain these objects, and how the memory is made accessible to the processor. A memory interacts with the system in two ways: first, by interacting with the compiler and run-time system to allocate and free objects in a memory; secondly, by interacting with the addressing system through encoding and decoding of the component of an object identifier to a contained object.

Unlike traditional flat addressing schemes, the addressing system that results from this design specifies: a straight forward transformation for locating information, unique identifiers that can be reused if the memory that generated them can reused them, some amount of transportability through dismountable memories, and incorporation of devices as a direct consequence of the underlying-object/memory pairing. Finally, this design can be implemented, as there exists at least one processor, the Intel 386, with sufficient hardware capability to support multiple active address spaces.

REFERENCES

1. Albano, A., Cardelli, L., and Orsini, R. "Galileo: A Strongly-Typed, Interactive Conceptual Language". *ACM Trans. Database Syst.*, 10(2):230–260, June 1985.

2. Atkinson, M. P. and Morrison, R. "Types, Binding and Parameters in a Persistent Environment". In *Workshop on Persistent Object Systems: their design, implementation and use*, volume PPRR 16, pages 1–24, Appin, Scotland, Aug. 1985. Universities of Glasgow and St. Andrews, Scotland.

3. Buhr, P. A. and Zarnke, C. R. "A Design for Integration of Files into a Strongly Typed Programming Language". In *Proceedings IEEE Computer Society 1986 International Conference on Computer Languages*, pages 190–200, Miami, Florida, U.S.A, Oct. 1986.

4. Buhr, P. A. and Zarnke, C. R. "Persistence in an Environment for a Statically-Typed Programming Language". In *Workshop on Persistent Object Systems: their design, implementation and use*, volume PPRR 42, pages 317–336, Appin, Scotland, Aug. 1987. Universities of Glasgow and St. Andrews, Scotland.

5. Buhr, P. A. and Zarnke, C. R. "Nesting in an Object Oriented Language is NOT for the Birds". In Gjessing, S. and Nygaard, K., editors, *Proceedings of the European Conference on Object Oriented Programming*, volume 322, pages 128–145, Oslo, Norway, Aug. 1988. ECOOP'88, Springer-Verlag. Lecture Notes in Computer Science, Ed. by G. Goos and J. Hartmanis.

6. Cockshott, W. P. "Addressing Mechanisms and Persistent Programming". In *Workshop on Persistent Object Systems: their design, implementation and use*, volume PPRR 16, pages 369–389, Appin, Scotland, Aug. 1985. Universities of Glasgow and St. Andrews, Scotland.

7. Cockshott, W. P., Atkinson, M. P., and Chisholm, K. J. "Persistent Object Management System". *Software–Practice and Experience*, 14:49–71, 1984.

8. Hurst, A. J. "A Context Sensitive Addressing Model". Technical Report PPRR-27-87, University of Glasgow and St. Andrews, Scotland, 1987.

9. Organick, E. I. *The Multics System*. The MIT Press, Cambridge, Massachusetts, 1972.

10. Pitts, D. V. and P., D. "Object Memory and Storage Management in the Clouds Kernel". *Proc. of the 8th Int'l Conf. on Distributed Computing Systems*, pages 10–17, June 1988.

11. "Taxis'84: Selected Papers". Technical Report CSRG-160, University of Toronto, Toronto, Ontario, Canada, June 1984. Ed. by Brian Nixon.

12. Wileden, J., Wolf, A. L., Fisher, C. D., and Tarr, P. L. "PGRAPHITE: An Experiment in Persistent Typed Object Management". In *Proceedings of SIGSOFT'88: Third Symposium on Software Development Environments*, 1988. to appear.

Name-Based Mapping: Addressing Support for Persistent Objects

Edward F. Gehringer*
North Carolina State University

ABSTRACT

Systems supporting persistent objects need to address far more information than can fit in an ordinary virtual memory. The usual approach is to impose an additional level of indirection—an object name is mapped to an object number, which serves as part of a virtual address. The virtual address can then be translated in the normal manner. An attractive alternative is name-based mapping, where objects are referred to by *name* rather than by address. A set of registers and a cache can be used to translate names directly to physical addresses, bypassing the virtual-address middleman. This scheme effectively removes the limit on the size of a process's address space, since the number of possible names is essentially infinite. Name-based mapping has a number of other advantages. The cache, which cannot be modified by the programmer, is used to translate all addresses. It can therefore be used to enforce different protection domains within a single process. This permits software systems to be built out of larger but fewer processes, decreasing the overhead of managing large numbers of processes. In addition, name-based mapping removes the need for conventional static or dynamic linking. An architecture using name-based mapping can easily be adapted to support object-oriented languages efficiently. Unlike capability-based systems, name-based mapping requires only a special address-translation mechanism, rather than specially protected segments throughout memory. This paper presents the design and initial performance measurements based on simulation.

1. INTRODUCTION

Persistent object systems demand very large address spaces. First, they need to address stores that may be nearly as large as all of on-line storage. Additionally, they cannot afford to read in external object representations into an internal address space. One estimate is that 30% of the code in conventional programs is devoted to transferring information to or from files and databases [1]. Hence, the address space must not only be large, but also persistent. The same virtual address that refers to an object during an instantiation of one program must refer to the same object when it is accessed by another program [6].

A related problem is the difficulty of linearizing the addresses in a graph of processes and objects in such a way as to maintain protection and allow controlled sharing of objects [6], at the same time that some objects are being created or abandoned, while others are growing or shrinking. Much effort has been invested in this problem [21, 22, 25] but no solution has met with wide acceptance. This paper suggests that perhaps it is time to pursue a new approach: instead of placing each process into a single address space, let each object or module be an address space unto itself, with all intermodule communication by means of *names* rather than virtual addresses.

One obvious consequence of this approach is that each process acquires an object space which is essentially unlimited. Freed from the need to map each object to a distinct set of fixed-length virtual addresses, a process can simply make up a new name each time it creates a new object;

---

* This research was supported by the Office of Naval Research under contract N00014-88-K-0037.

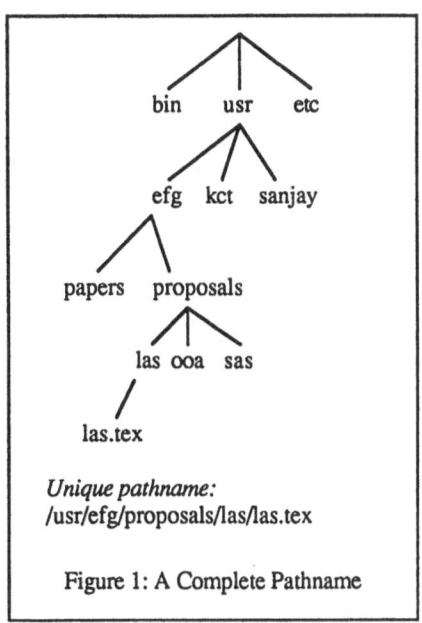

Unique pathname:
/usr/efg/proposals/las/las.tex

Figure 1: A Complete Pathname

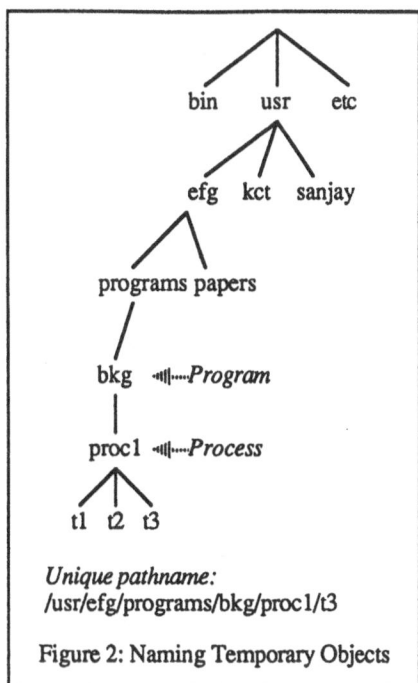

Unique pathname:
/usr/efg/programs/bkg/proc1/t3

Figure 2: Naming Temporary Objects

since names have no fixed maximum length, the process can never run out of them. Moreover, objects can be shared by name, and protected according to the rules of the underlying file system.

The next section of this paper gives an overview of the name-based mapping scheme. Section 3 identifies two fundamental differences between this proposal and previous methods of address mapping. The proposed scheme is described in detail in Section 4. Section 5 enumerates its advantages. Section 6 outlines the experiments that are being carried out to measure the performance of this scheme, and reports some preliminary results.

2. NAME-BASED MAPPING

Every method of addressing must allow a process to uniquely name each object it references. Virtual addressing achieves this goal by associating each object with a unique virtual address. It is important to note, however, that in any system with a tree-structured file system, each permanent object already *has* a unique name—its complete pathname from the root of the directory (Figure 1). The unique naming can easily be extended to temporary objects created while a process is running by assigning them sequential numbers within the process's own subdirectory (Figure 2), in the same way that a compiler names the temporary variables that it creates. It is also not difficult to extend the scheme to general list-structured directories by following the links from a filename back to the *oldest* parent of each directory (Figure 3).

In name-based mapping, operand references conceptually take the form

(object name, displacement)

instead of

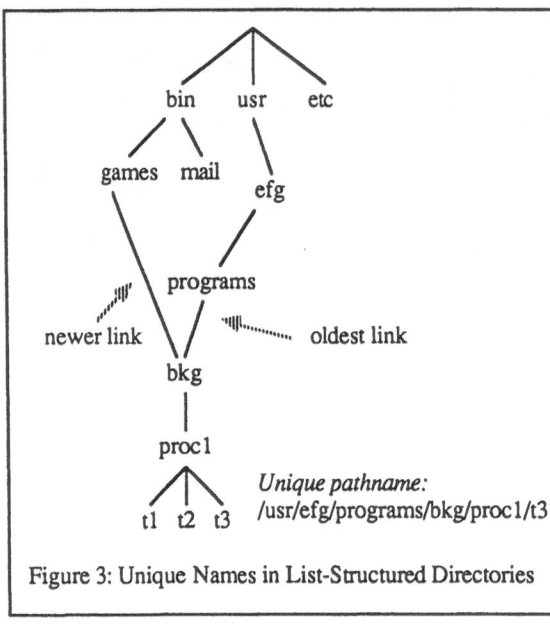

Unique pathname:
/usr/efg/programs/bkg/proc1/t3

Figure 3: Unique Names in List-Structured Directories

(page/segment number,
displacement)

Obviously, complete pathnames are too long to include in addresses in the instruction stream, but we can arrange the names used by a module into an array called the *local name table*, or LNT (Figure 4), and use indexes into the LNT in place of complete pathnames. (To save space, the LNT may hold relative pathnames instead of complete pathnames.) Each time an object is referenced, we (conceptually) hash the selected local name and look in a cache (similar to a translation lookaside buffer) to find where the object is located. The cache key is the hash of the object name.

Hashing during each operand reference would be prohibitively expensive, so the hash key is instead held in a *segment register*; the hash function is computed only when the segment register is loaded. (The segment register is loaded by a special instruction, which also causes the hash to be performed.) A program address therefore has the form

(segment register number, displacement)

The segment register contains a hash key which is searched for associatively in the cache, which then yields the physical address of the object. Figure 5 shows the complete addressing path for name-based mapping.

3. DIFFERENCES FROM OTHER ADDRESSING SYSTEMS

3.1. No Linear Address Space

The benefits of name-based mapping derive largely from two drawbacks it avoids: the need to linearize the address space, and the need to use clumsy data structures to achieve fine-grained protection. Other virtual-addressing schemes require each object to be assigned a distinct set of virtual addresses out of a linear range from 0 to 2^{n-1}. This is done to allow each object to be named unambiguously by the program. In one sense it is superfluous, because objects already have unique names—their directory pathnames. In another sense it is harmful, because a process can run out of ways to name new objects

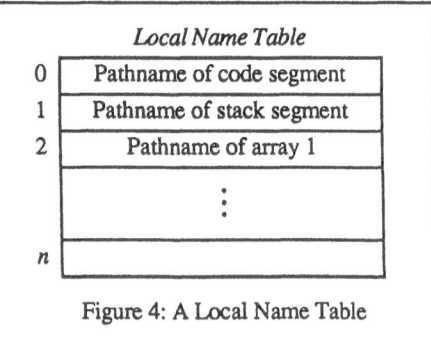

Figure 4: A Local Name Table

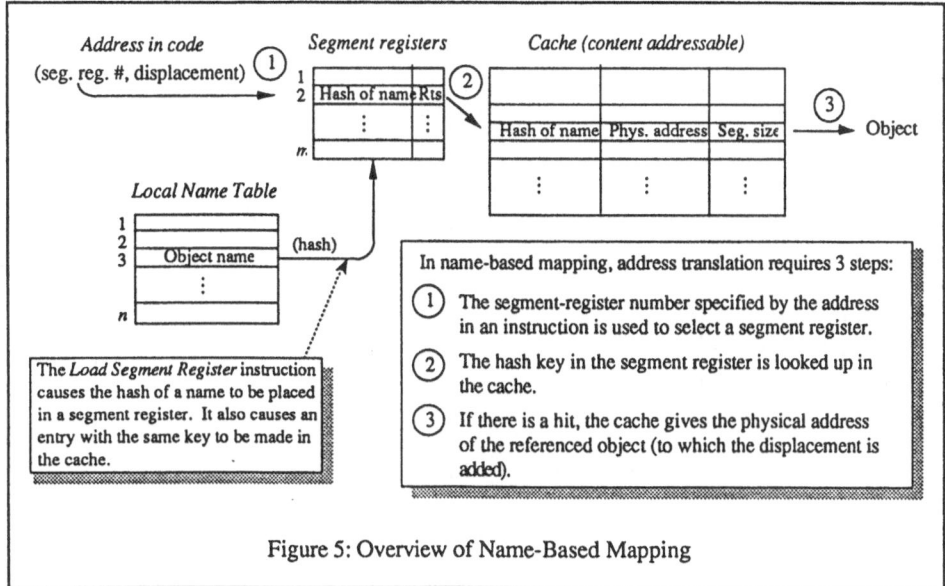

Figure 5: Overview of Name-Based Mapping

while there is still enough storage on-line to hold them.

Furthermore, the process of *linking* is essentially an artifact of the need to map a nonlinear name space onto a linear address space. Linking can be handled either statically or dynamically. Either is expensive. Large programs are composed of many modules. For efficient program maintenance, they must be able to be compiled separately, and not all modules are used each time the program is executed. Some, such as error-handling routines, are used only in unusual circumstances. Linking the whole program statically just before beginning execution is often a waste of time. Dynamic linking postpones linking until a module is first referenced [21]. External references are resolved, and a special linkage segment created. All nonlocal references must be made indirectly through entries in those linkage segments. To reduce the expense of indirection, Multics allowed linkage-segment entries to be loaded into segment registers, much like in name-based mapping. Depending on how many modules are linked dynamically, this strategy may cost more or less than static linking. By resolving references through a cache when they are actually made, name-based mapping removes the need for linking altogether.

A linear address space also inhibits the sharing of objects. Originally seen as a way to avoid the need for multiple copies of read-only data in memory, sharing is now most important as a means of facilitating concurrency. In either case, multiple processes must refer to the same object. In most systems, where each process has its own address space, it is impossible to guarantee that the processes will refer to the object via the same virtual address [18]. A de-facto standard solution adopted by capability-based systems of the 1970's, such as Hydra [30] and the CAP [20], as well as the Intel 432, was to employ a global *object table*, pointed to by *capabilities* held by individual processes (Figure 6). The object-table approach was embraced by object-oriented systems such as the bytecode implementation of Smalltalk-80 [9] and persistent object stores such as Objekt [10]. For small systems, this is a good solution, but for large systems, management of the object table became complex [3] and caused several extra memory references each time an object was created [22]. It is interesting to note that some object-oriented language implementations such as SOAR (Smalltalk on a RISC) [29] have reached the same conclusion.

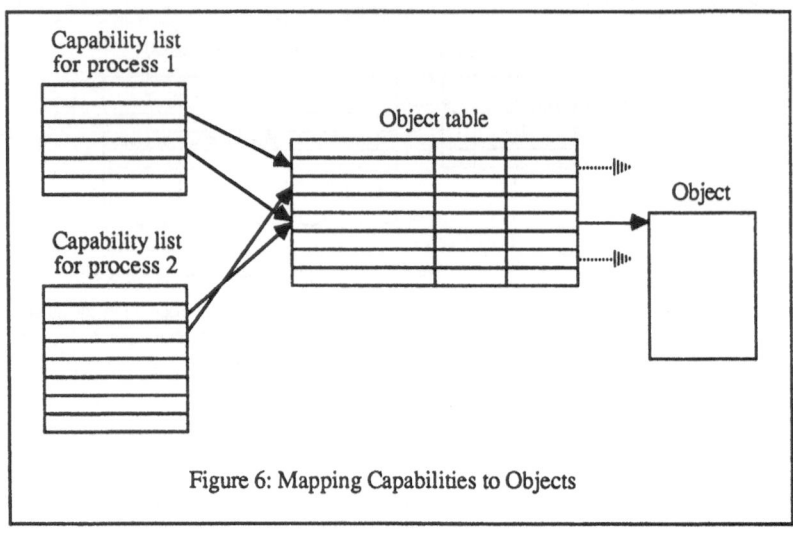

Figure 6: Mapping Capabilities to Objects

The alternative to giving each process its own address space is to assign processes distinct address ranges within a single systemwide address space. This facilitates persistence but complicates storage management in two ways. First, it forces the system to allocate address space in addition to allocating memory. Second, it makes it complicated to remove inaccessible objects, because all on-line memory must be garbage collected as a single unit. Since a global garbage collection would require a prohibitive amount of time, algorithms have been developed to garbage-collect virtual memory in pieces, one region of address space at a time [4]. To make such regional garbage-collection viable, the firmware must maintain tables of pointers that point outside their region. An implementation would be complex, and, to the author's knowledge, none has ever been attempted.

By contrast, name-based mapping simply avoids assigning virtual addresses. Figure 7 presents one way of visualizing the difference. Instead of mapping names to virtual addresses, which are in turn mapped to physical addresses, it avoids the virtual-address middleman and maps names directly to physical addresses. However, one could also view the addresses assigned by the compiler within a module as virtual addresses. Given that interpretation, we can say that name-based mapping associates a separate address space with each

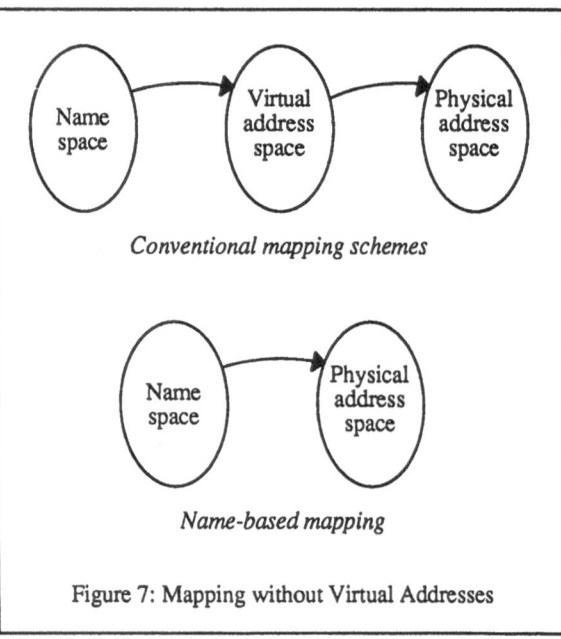

Conventional mapping schemes

Name-based mapping

Figure 7: Mapping without Virtual Addresses

module (or object) within a process, instead of with the process as a whole. In either case, there is no fixed limit to the number of virtual addresses available to a process.

3.2. Fine-Grained Protection without Protected Pointers

Large software systems often involve code written in more than one language. Multiple-language programs must be run, or otherwise libraries must be recoded in each new language. Multi-language code, however, requires the architecture to support intermodule protection.

If the goal is merely to run large programs written in a single language, then no special architectural features are needed; the compiler and linker can cooperate to assure that one module does not accidently or maliciously access data belonging to another. If multi-language or hand-modified object code is to be run, however, a protection problem arises. The architecture must police the boundaries between modules, guaranteeing that one module does not access (e.g., modify or copy) the private code or data of another. If the architecture does not do so, then modules that are suspicious of each other must run in separate processes, as is required, for example, in Unix. But creating and managing a process is more expensive than calling a procedure, so the efficiency of the system suffers [17]. A reliability problem arises as well, since different-language modules may inadvertently violate each other's assumptions. This ultimately increases the burden on the programmer, who may decide to rewrite code in a different language rather than deal with the problem of making two languages work together.

Over the years, several mechanisms have been proposed to provide intermodule protection based on capabilities. All four require protected pointers to be distributed throughout a process's address space. Special mechanisms must be added to the architecture to protect capabilities, and the presence of these mechanisms may present difficulties for the compiler writer who desires to generate efficient code [5].

By contrast, name-based mapping allows unprotected object names[1] to appear in executable code. A process may read or write them at will. A name must be presented to the file system the first time it is used; the file system is responsible for enforcing protection. This is at variance with the idea that capability protection is more secure because it is a ticket-oriented approach [24]; that is to say, the possession of a capability conveys the right to access an object.

The special mechanisms required by name-based mapping are relatively few: segment registers, a special kind of translation-lookaside buffer, and perhaps hardware support for rapid hash-function computation. A user process may read or write all of its memory in the usual fashion; its memory contains no protected pointers, and thus there is no need for separate data structures and special instructions to manipulate them.

4. IMPLEMENTING NAME-BASED MAPPING

In effect, name-based mapping gives each module or object its own private address space. All external procedure calls or object references must proceed through the cache. The cache is inaccessible to the programmer, and is therefore protected.

Hashing and collisions in the cache. Before an object can be referenced, a segment register must be loaded with its name. Actually, the Load Segment Register instruction causes a hash function of the name to be computed, and it is the hashed value that is loaded into the segment register. (Hardware support for hashing has previously been provided to aid address translation in several

---

[1]Although name-based mapping allows fine-grained protection, it does not require all objects to be small. An activation record, for example, can be a single object. So can a complicated data structure, such as an array of records, that is only manipulated by a single module. The dynamic protection of name-based mapping is only needed in places where sufficient checks cannot be made statically at compile time.

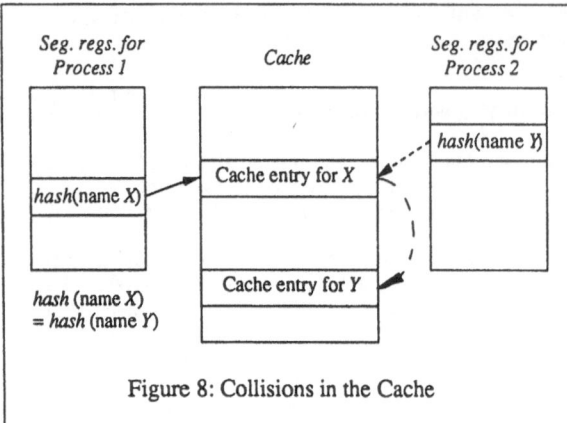

Figure 8: Collisions in the Cache

research and commercial systems [2, 11, 28].) When that segment register is named in an instruction, the cache is searched for its hash key, and if there is a cache hit, the physical address of the object is retrieved.

Our narrative has not yet considered what happens in case of a collision—when two names hash to the same key.[2] Clearly, there is no way to avoid this possibility, since the number of names is unlimited while the size of a hash key is finite. Note, however, that a collision can be detected when a segment register is loaded (Figure 8). When the hash key h of an object X is computed, it is looked up in the cache. If h is not found, there is no collision, and it can be inserted. If h is found, the physical address of X is compared with the physical address of the object already in the cache entry. If the two addresses are equal, an entry for X is already in the cache, and no action need be taken. If not, a collision has occurred, and X's name is rehashed according to a secondary hash function; the resulting key h' is then inserted in the cache (barring another collision). Ordinary hash-table management techniques can be used for deleting entries from the cache whenever their cache slots must be reused. The hashing scheme is reminiscent of the one used successfully on LOOM [15, 16], a software-only extension for providing Smalltalk-80 with a large (but not unlimited) object space.

Change of protection state. When an intermodule call occurs, the protection environment must change, as some objects belonging to the new module become accessible and the old module's objects become inaccessible. This requires segment registers to be saved and restored at intermodule procedure calls. This suggests incorporation of a register file with multiple register windows, similar to the one implemented on the RISC I [23].

In a register set with overlapping windows, some new registers become accessible and some old ones inaccessible each time a procedure call takes place. Since all objects must be referenced via segment registers, the only objects accessible to both caller and callee are those pointed to by the overlapping windows; it is here that parameters can be passed.

The RISC I used a rather large register set, with 138 (data) registers, of which 32 were accessible at a time. Name-based mapping should be able to get by with a much smaller ensemble of segment registers, for two reasons: For data registers, large windows are rarely needed; Huguet [13] found that a window of only 8 registers suffices for 93% of calls. Also, programs are likely to require fewer segment registers than data registers. A procedure's activation record can be treated as a single object, accessible via a single segment register. The same holds for a heap segment belonging to a single module, since the compiler can be trusted to produce code that manages it correctly. Only when an object is to be passed as an intermodule parameter does a protection issue arise; in this case, the object needs its own segment register.

In the way it uses segment registers, name-based mapping resembles the addressing structure of the Intel 432; a study of programs on this machine [5] suggests that few procedures would re-

---

[2]Two entries with the same key would be indistinguishable in the cache. This is *not* the same as when two entries with *different* keys happen to compete for occupancy of the same cache set or cache block. In that case, the older entry can simply be purged from the cache in favor of the newer entry.

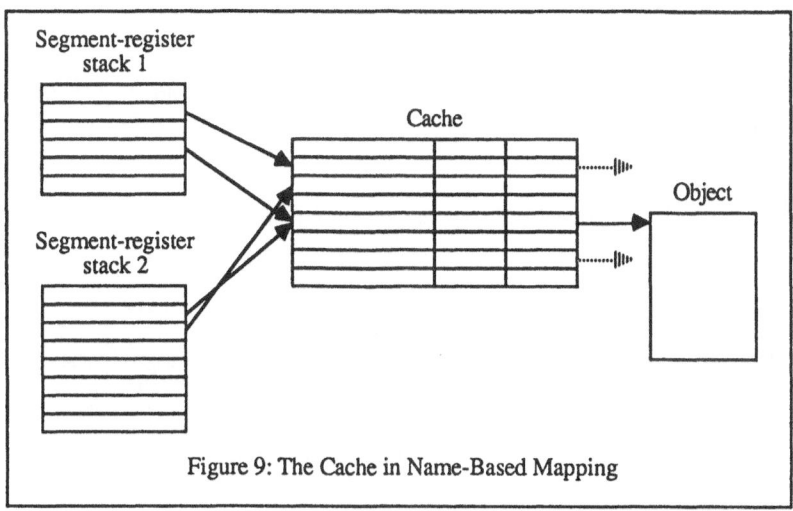

Figure 9: The Cache in Name-Based Mapping

quire a window with more than three segment registers. Huguet [12, 13] has developed a design for the efficient implementation of variable-size register windows, which could be profitably exploited for segment registers in name-based mapping.

Comparison with previous systems. Despite its comparatively modest memory-protection mechanisms, the name-based mapping scheme has much in common with capability-based addressing schemes. Capability-based systems give each process one or more capability lists; the capabilities are used to index into a global object table, which in turn points to objects (Figure 6). The name-based mapping scheme uses segment registers to point into a cache, which in turn points to objects (Figure 9). The name-based mapping scheme is also similar to address-extension mechanisms used on conventional microprocessors. The Intel 286, for example, uses a set of four segment registers, each associated with a cache register, that gives the physical address of the referenced object (Figure 10). However, only four entries, all associated with the current process, can be in the cache simultaneously. There is no register-window mechanism associated

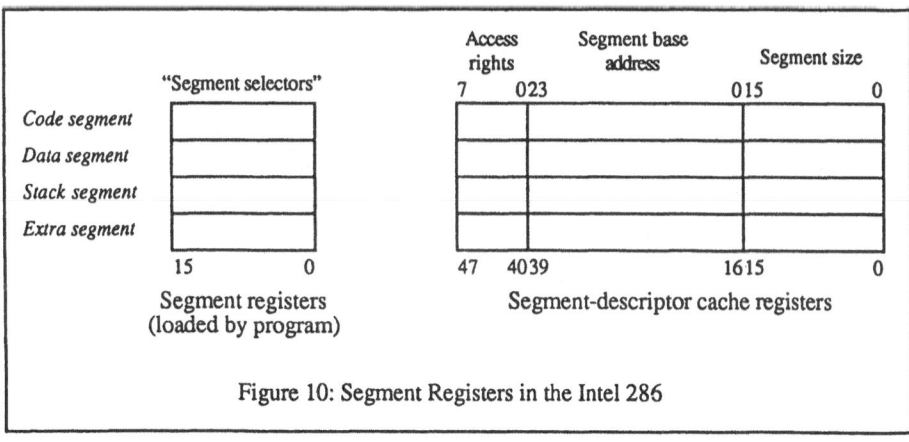

Figure 10: Segment Registers in the Intel 286

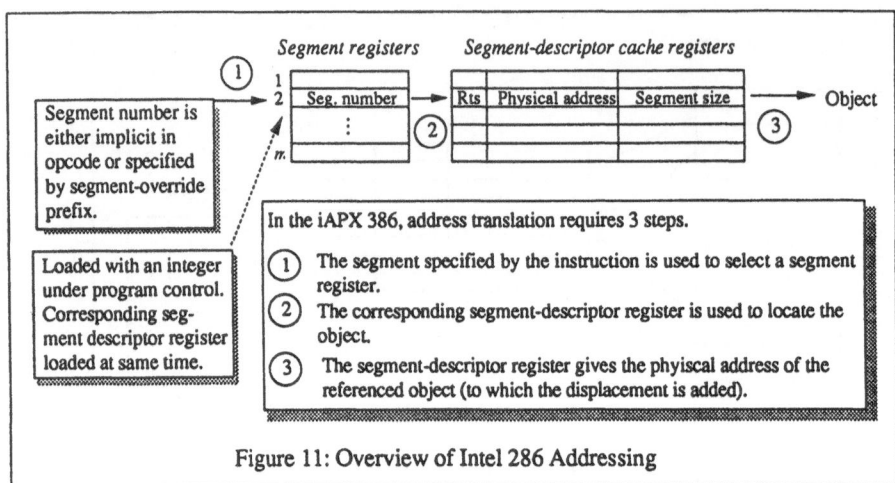

Figure 11: Overview of Intel 286 Addressing

with the segment registers, so they must be loaded and saved more frequently. Further, the 286 uses a Multics-like ring-based protection system, rather than the more general non-hierarchical scheme provided by name-based mapping.

To illustrate the similarity between name-based mapping and current addressing schemes, it is useful to compare it with address translation on the Intel 286 [8]. The Intel 286 addresses via a four-element segment-descriptor cache, while name-based mapping employs a larger, content-addressable cache. (Compare Figure 11 with Figure 5.)

In the listing below, the typeface indicates the system that the text refers to—Intel 286 in Roman, *name-based mapping* in italics.

Intel 286 addressing	Name-based mapping
1. The program executes an instruction to load a segment register with a segment "selector"—a segment number.	*1. The program executes an instruction to load a segment register with an entry from the local name table.*
2. The processor loads the segment number into the specified segment register.	*2. The processor loads the segment register with the hash of the object name.*
3. After the processor checks the access rights, it copies the corresponding segment descriptor from the segment table into the corresponding cache register.	*3. After the processor checks access rights (by directory lookup), it checks for collisions and copies the descriptor from the memory map into the cache (if the descriptor is not already in the cache).*
4. If there is a segment fault, it is detected and handled when the descriptor is copied.	*4. If there is an object fault, it is detected and handled when the descriptor is copied.*
5. On accesses to the segment, the cache register rather than the segment table is consulted to determine the object's physical address.	*5. On accesses to the object, the hashed name is looked up in the cache to determine the object's physical address.*

The two schemes have much in common, but the name-based mapping scheme requires hardware support for hashing, and clever organization of the memory map to allow rapid collision detection. It also incorporates a stack of segment registers and a larger cache, which would improve efficiency by loading cache entries less often. (The Intel 286 setup requires the Code Segment register and its corresponding cache entry to be loaded on each intermodule procedure call, for example.) The compiler is capable of managing the segment registers to optimize the number used. Through flow analysis, it knows when the contents of a segment register will be needed again, so it can make intelligent decisions on when to reload them. Algorithms can be developed to balance the cost of reloading a register that is already in use against the cost of allocating another register. (If more segment registers are used, the register set will overflow more frequently.)

5. ADVANTAGES OF NAME-BASED MAPPING

Name-based mapping yields a wide variety of benefits, in address-space size, intermodule protection, and efficient execution of object-oriented languages.

Support for persistent objects. Persistent object databases must give unique names to objects that survive the execution of a process, in order to access them in the future [27]. With name-based mapping, directory pathnames can serve as unique names. Considerable support is provided for making these names directly usable by a process, greatly reducing the overhead of mapping large numbers of names into a process's address space. It is straightforward to extend a directory hierarchy to a network, so a single address space can span a network, something that is very difficult to achieve with standard mapping schemes [6].

Flexible intermodule protection. The set of objects accessible to a process can change each time the process executes an intermodule procedure call. A process P with rights to call a procedure Q inherits all of Q's privileges when the call is performed. At the same time, process P can decide which of its objects to pass as arguments to Q, denying Q access rights to any of its other objects. This enables one process to do the work of several processes in an operating system such as Unix, which cannot very effectively enforce protection boundaries within a single process.

An essentially unlimited address space. With name-based addressing, a process can address as many objects as it can name. There is no fixed limit on the length of names, and hence the object space is limited only by the amount of on-line storage available on the system. There *is* a limit on the address space of an object or module: only a limited number of objects can be named by the fixed-length operand field of a Load Segment Register instruction, and an object cannot be accessed unless its name has been loaded into a segment register. But the operand field can be made large, say, 24 or 32 bits. With good modularization techniques, it is unlikely that any *module* of a program will ever approach this limit.

Support for procedure-based operating systems. Systems which provide separate processes to perform operating-system functions are called *process oriented*, while systems that provide those services by procedure calls are called *procedure oriented* [19]. Procedure-oriented systems are theoretically more efficient than process-oriented systems for several reasons [17], but they require hardware to provide flexible protection, such as that provided by name-based mapping. Procedure-oriented systems have fewer processes, so they incur fewer process switches (though more procedure calls). Process switches are inherently more expensive than procedure calls, due to the larger amount of state that needs to be saved. Procedure-oriented operating systems also make it easier to account accurately for CPU time and other resources consumed by user processes.

Facilitates incremental compilation. With name-based mapping, no object in a program holds the virtual or physical address of any other object. This makes it easy to recompile and relink portions of a program as they are changed. The benefits of incremental compilation, which have been available in Smalltalk and other object-oriented systems, become easy to add to any language.

Runs object-oriented languages efficiently. Name-based mapping is a natural for object-oriented languages. The performance of these languages depends on the ability to look up objects by name rapidly at run-time. Furthermore, the identity of a called method (procedure) can depend on the class (type) of its arguments as well as the method name. For this reason, object-oriented architectures have often included a *method cache* dedicated to mapping method names and argument classes to addresses [7, 14]. However, object-oriented systems have never exploited the possibilities of name-based mapping to obtain a large address space. Either they have been based on a limited physical address space, like the original Smalltalk-80 implementation [9], or have used virtual memory as an intermediary, mapping names first to virtual addresses, like SOAR [26, 29] and LOOM [15]. The cache in name-based addressing can be turned into a method-lookup cache simply by adding an argument-class field to each entry (Figure 12). Association would then be based on the (procedure name, argument class) pair. The author has previously explored the use of a method-lookup cache to provide intermodule protection [18].

6. INITIAL PERFORMANCE RESULTS

We have undertaken a simulation study of the performance of name-based mapping. The study involves programs in Smalltalk-80 and Ada. Different techniques are being employed to gather data from each language. In Smalltalk, the code for Kernel Methods classes has been modified to generate a trace of the methods that are called. This was done with relatively little effort, because the Smalltalk-80 system is malleable and self-documenting. Ada programs are being handled via source transformation: A grammar is fed to the *yacc* parser generator. The semantic routines of the resulting parser are written to add statements to perform measurements, such as to write a trace of the object names referenced or names of procedures called. The transformed program is then compiled and run, producing the trace.

The output from both languages is fed to a simulator. The simulator reads the trace, hashing names and entering them in the cache when a segment register is loaded, according to the name-based mapping scheme. An additive and multiplicative hashing scheme is used, and very few collisions are encountered. The collisions are resolved by rehashing; note that rehashing needs to be performed only when a segment register is loaded, not when a reference is made through the segment register.

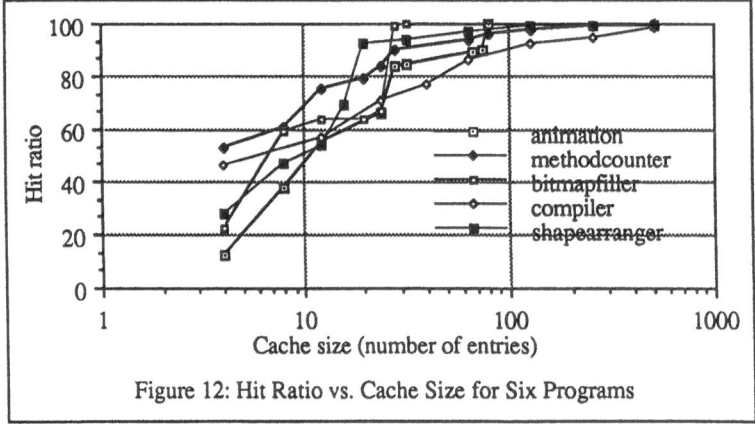

Figure 12: Hit Ratio vs. Cache Size for Six Programs

The cache hit ratio has been measured. At this writing, we have measured only Smalltalk-80 programs. The programs include the Smalltalk-80 compiler, an animation demo, a fractal-generating program, a pentominos game, and a utility called MethodCounter. None of them is truly a large application. The largest, the compiler, is less than 3000 lines of code. But note that it can be deceiving to measure a Smalltalk program's size in terms of lines of code, because all programs use the system's methods more heavily than programs in other languages use system routines. The system methods were included in our measurements. We are in the process of gathering a sample of larger Smalltalk programs.

The cache hit ratio was quite high in every case. A cache of 128 names was sufficient to give a hit ratio of 92% for each program (Figure 12). For the small programs (all except the compiler), the 128-entry hit ratio was at least 97.5%. To model the effect of multiple processes, a multiprogramming simulation was run for 1 million total name references with a time slice of 1000 references. The hit ratio (Figure 13) was similar to the uniprocess experiments. In fact, it exceeded the hit ratio for the compiler, as the smaller programs dominated the trace. It will be interesting to see if larger programs have such a high "locality of name reference," but the preliminary results are encouraging.

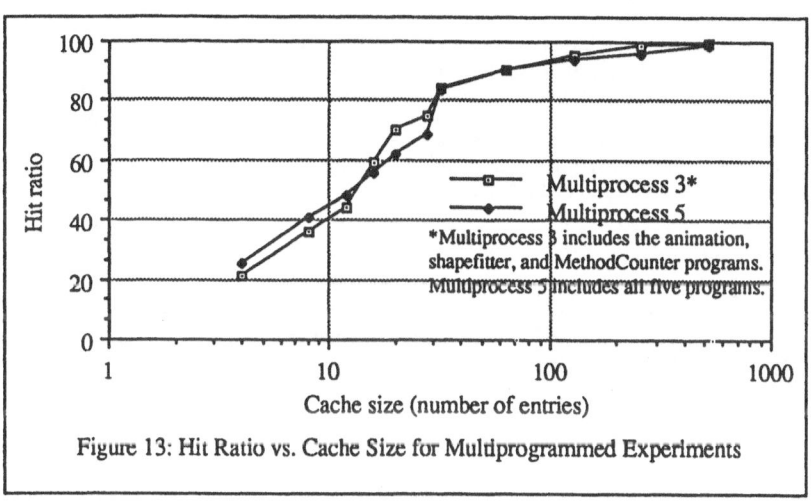

Figure 13: Hit Ratio vs. Cache Size for Multiprogrammed Experiments

7. FUTURE WORK

Larger programs. We are currently gathering a sample of Smalltalk programs drawn from industrial and academic environments. We have contacted several dozen sites and received commitments of programs from a large percentage of them. We have acquired a large sample of Ada programs from the Ada program repository at Sandia National Laboratories. The program transformer is currently being run on several dozen of these programs.

Address translation. When larger programs are run, the choice of a hash function will become more important. It must be easy to compute in hardware and it must minimize collisions in the cache. The size and format of a cache entry must be specified, and, since it will likely be larger than the caches in existing systems, its cost must be estimated. Another question is how to make effective use of the argument-class field in entries that do not point to methods in object-oriented languages. In a large cache, one cannot afford much unused space.

Memory management. This is the category that may well require the most investigation. One major issue is the design of the memory map. It may need to be searched to detect collisions every time a segment register is loaded with a hashed name that is already in the cache. To perform this search efficiently, the map needs to take advantage of the fact that objects with similar pathnames are likely to be stored close together in memory. It may also be possible to omit this search on some segment-register loads, such as when a segment register is loaded from another segment register that is already marked present.

Parameter passing. A side effect of name-based mapping is that all intermodule parameters must be passed by name. This is a potentially serious complication for modules that, in many languages, are able to communicate via pointers. One solution is to pass a table of pointers to a module the first time that the module is referenced. Subsequent references can then be made relative to those pointers. This is a viable approach for objects that are known when a module is first referenced. However, pointers to objects that are created or acquired later must still be passed by name. For this reason, our measurements will include a study of parameter-passing between modules.

8. SUMMARY

Name-based mapping is an alternative to conventional virtual-addressing mechanisms. If successful, name-based mapping promises to free persistent programs from the limitations of a fixed address space. It also offers a means of efficiently supporting intermodule protection at a fine-grained level without constraining data structures and without extra hardware beyond that required for address translation. To bring name-based mapping to fruition, the design must be further elaborated and studied empirically, and algorithms for address translation and memory management must be developed and refined.

ACKNOWLEDGMENTS

The Smalltalk program tracer was written by David Chinkes, from a prototype designed by Sam Adams and Eddy Yohon. Shrikant Rangnekar wrote the name-based mapping simulator and designed hashing algorithms for managing the cache.

REFERENCES

1. Atkinson, M. P., Bailey, P. J., Chisholm, K. J., Cockshott, P. W. and Morrison, R. "An approach to persistent programming." *Computer Journal*, 26,4, November 1983, pp. 360–365.

2. Abramson, A. "Hardware management of a large virtual memory." *Proceedings of the Fourth Australian Computer Science Conference*, Brisbane, May 11–13, 1981, pp. 1–13.

3. Almes, G. T. "Garbage collection in an object-oriented system." Ph.D. thesis, Department of Computer Science, Carnegie-Mellon University, June 1980. Available as technical report CMU-CS-80-128.

4. Bishop, P. B. "Computer systems with a very large address space and garbage collection." Ph.D. thesis, Laboratory for Computer Science, Massachusetts Institute of Technology, May 1977. Available as technical report TR-178, MIT Laboratory for Computer Science.

5. Colwell, R. P., Gehringer, E. F. and Jensen, E. D. "Performance effects of architectural complexity in the Intel 432." *ACM Transactions on Computer Systems*, 6,3, August 1988, pp. 296–339.

6.   Cockshott, W. P. "Persistent programming and secure data storage." *Information and Software Technology*, 29,5, June 1986, pp. 249–256.

7.   Dally, W. J. and Kajiya, J. T. "An object oriented architecture." *Proceedings of the 12th Annual International Symposium on Computer Architecture*, Boston, June 1985, pp. 154–161.

8.   Furht, B. and Milutinovic, V. "A survey of microprocessor architectures for memory management." *IEEE Computer*, 20,3, March 1987,pp. 48–67.

9.   Goldberg, A. and Robson, D. *Smalltalk 80: the Language and its Implementation.* Addison-Wesley, 1983.

10. Harland, D. M. and Beloff, B. "OBJEKT: a persistent object store with an integrated garbage collector." *ACM SIGPLAN Notices*, 22,4, April 1987, pp. 70–79.

11. Houdek, M. E. and Mitchell, G. R. "Translating a large virtual address." *IBM System/38 Technical Developments*, IBM General Systems Division, 1978, pp. 22–24. Also in *Electronics*, March 1979.

12. Huguet, M. "A C-oriented register set design." Master's thesis, Department of Computer Science, UCLA, June 1985. Available as Technical Report CSD-850019.

13. Huguet, M. and Lang, T. "A reduced register file for RISC architectures." *ACM Computer Architecture News*, 13,4, September 1985, pp. 22–31.

14. Ishikawa, Y. and Tokoro, M. "The design of an object oriented architecture." *Proceedings of the 11th Annual Symposium on Computer Architecture*, Ann Arbor, MI, June 1984, pp. 178–187.

15. Kaehler, T. "Virtual memory on a narrow machine for an object-oriented language." *OOPSLA '86: Object-Oriented Programming Systems, Languages, and Applications, Proceedings*, Portland, OR, September 29-October 2, 1986, *ACM SIGPLAN Notices*, 21,11, pp. 87–106.

16. Kaehler, T. and Krasner, G. "LOOM—large object-oriented memory for Smalltalk-80 systems." In G. Krasner, ed., *Smalltalk-80: Bits of History, Words of Advice*, Addison-Wesley, 1983, pp. 251–270.

17. Keedy, J. L. "A comparison of two process-structuring models." MONADS Report No. 4, Department of Computer Science, Monash University, 1979.

18. Nayak, S. and Gehringer, E. "Use of a method-lookup cache to support dynamic linking and information hiding." Technical report TR-88-17, Computer Studies Program, North Carolina State University, August 1987.

19. Needham, R. M. and Lauer, H. C. "On the duality of operating system structures." *ACM Operating Systems Review*, 13,2 , April 1979, pp. 3–19.

20. Needham, R. M. and Walker, R. D. H. *The Cambridge CAP Computer and its Operating System*, North-Holland, 1979.

21. Organick, E. I. *The Multics System: An Examination of its Structure.* MIT Press, 1972.

22. Organick, E. I. *A Programmer's view of the Intel 432.* McGraw-Hill, 1983.

232

23. Patterson, D. A. "Reduced instruction set computers." *Communications of the ACM*, 28,1, January 1985, pp. 8–21.

24. Peterson, J. L. and Silberschatz, A. *Operating System Concepts*, 2nd edition. Addison-Wesley, 1986.

25. Pollack, F. J., Cox, G. W., Hammerstrom, D. W., Kahn, K. C., Lai, K. K. and Rattner, J. R. "Supporting Ada memory management in the iAPX-432." *Proceedings of the Symposium on Architectural Support for Programming Languages and Operating Systems*, (SIGARCH/SIGPLAN), Palo Alto, CA, March 1-3, 1982, *ACM SIGPLAN Notices*, 17,4, pp. 117–131.

26. Samples, D., Ungar, D. and Hilfinger, P. "SOAR: Smalltalk without bytecodes." *OOPSLA '86: Object-Oriented Programming Systems, Languages and Applications, Proceedings*, September–October 1986, *ACM SIGPLAN Notices*, 21,11, pp. 107–118, .

27. Thatte, S. M. "Report on the object-oriented database workshop: implementation aspects." Technical report, Artificial Intelligence Laboratory, Texas Instruments, October 5, 1987.

28. Thakkar, S. S. and Knowles, A. E. "A high-performance memory management scheme." *IEEE Computer*, 19,5, May 1986, pp. 8–22.

29. Ungar, D. M. "The design and evaluation of a high performance Smalltalk system." Ph.D. thesis, Computer Science Division, University of California, Berkeley, March 1986. Also available from MIT Press, 1986.

30. Wulf, W. A., Levin, R. and Harbison, S. P. *Hydra/C.mmp: an Experimental Computer System*. McGraw-Hill, 1981.

Part IV

Object Stores

Generating and Manipulating Identifiers for Heterogeneous, Distributed Objects

Sandra Heiler and Barbara Blaustein
Xerox Advanced Information Technology

ABSTRACT

Systems that manipulate heterogeneous, distributed objects must provide origin- and location-transparent object identifiers. The problem is particularly difficult for systems that deal with "foreign" objects, i.e., objects that originate outside of the system or are manipulated by procedures that are external to the system. Such objects already have externally-assigned identifiers on which clients and application programs depend to access the objects. We describe an approach to providing system-processible identifiers for such objects that preserves the use of their externally-assigned identifiers.

We present a report of work in progress to provide a flexible identifier construction and manipulation mechanism for an Object Management System[1] that integrates heterogeneous software components and databases. In this system most objects are "foreign". The mechanism provides a uniform reference scheme for all objects, whether native or foreign, that makes transparent the objects' origins and locations, without requiring the overhead of "registering" each object with the system. In addition, we discuss some tradeoffs that will affect implementation of the mechanism.

1. INTRODUCTION

Object-oriented systems provide abstractions, such as "objects" and "messages" or "functions", that clients use to request work. The role of the system is to map requests expressed in these abstractions into invocations of procedures and concrete data structures that are passed as parameters among the procedures that implement the specified messages or functions. These data structures serve as *surrogates* for the objects that are referenced in the procedures that manipulate or produce them.

All types of objects, including explicitly created objects, derived objects, and objects that originate outside the system but are manipulated through it, need surrogates, or interpretable data structures, that can be passed as inputs or outputs among the procedures that actually manipulate the data of the objects. Moreover, the objects need some sort of "handles" by

---

[1]This work was sponsored in part by a tri-service project of the DoD under USAF contract F3615-87-C-1401.

which they can be referenced within the object-oriented system and which can be mapped to the structures that are processed by the manipulation procedures.

Object-oriented systems support the idea that objects have "identity" independent of their structure or behavior [3]. Usually such systems assign a unique, immutable object identifier (OID) to each object at creation to represent this identity. In most systems, the object's OID serves as its surrogate or as an appropriate handle that can be passed among the methods (procedures) that process the object.

Systems that must manipulate "foreign" objects, i.e., objects that originate in external systems or that are manipulated by external systems, usually assign each foreign object an OID, thus "registering" the object with the system. The OIDs allow these objects to be manipulated within the system. The system provides mappings between the system-assigned OIDs and the data structures or identifiers that represent or identify the objects in the external systems and which are passed as parameters between the object-oriented system and the external system

The problem with this approach is that the object-oriented system must generate and invoke the mappings between internal and external identifiers. These mappings may be difficult to generate, costly to maintain, and expensive to execute, especially if "foreign" objects make up the bulk of the data that the system must process.

In this paper, we describe the requirements of an Object Management System (OMS) that is designed specifically to integrate heterogeneous components. The goal of the system is to make the components interoperable, while preserving their autonomy, i.e., avoiding requiring any changes to the underlying databases and procedures. All objects produced or processed by the underlying databases, data servers, and applications are "foreign" to the OMS. In such a system, it is infeasible to pass OMS-assigned OIDs directly to the underlying systems or for client applications to refer to objects by their OMS-assigned OIDs..

The challenge of the OMS is to 1) preserve the use of the objects' external identifiers, 2) pass appropriate object surrogates among the underlying procedures, and 3) handle mis-matches between the client's reference to an object and the requirements of the underlying procedure that processes or produces it. Registering each "foreign" object and maintaining the mappings between its external identifier, its OMS-assigned OID, and the surrogate form required by the procedures that manipulate it is likely impractical if the number of objects is large. Generating and mapping to and from OMS-assigned OIDs is particularly wasteful if the underlying procedures can reference objects by the same external identifiers as users or client applications use to make their requests.

This paper provides a brief description of work in progress to provide a mechanism for assigning and manipulating object surrogates and identifiers in an OMS that integrates heterogeneous systems. The mechanism preserves externally-assigned identifiers for use by clients and application programs and provides a uniform scheme for accessing objects that makes transparent their origins and locations, without requiring that each object be registered with the OMS. In addition, it handles conversions from client-specified references to needed procedure arguments..

The ideas presented in this paper were influenced by ideas described in [2, 3]. Section 2 describes our OMS and the system requirements for identifier generation; Section 3 outlines our solution approach and defines characteristics of good solutions to the problem of constructing and manipulating OIDs; Section 4 identifies tradeoffs that will affect the implementation approach. Section 5 presents some conclusions.

2. THE PROBLEM

2.1. Context

The work described here was done as part of a project to develop an OMS for integrating existing and future databases and software tools for VLSI design and engineering environments. The system makes interoperable incompatible software tools and application programs and allows them to share data in repositories managed by disparate, autonomous data servers. The goal of the system is to make the components interoperable without requiring any modifications to the databases, the data servers, or the software tools themselves. The system must also be capable of accommodating objects sent to it from other OMSs.

The approach to providing interoperability is twofold: first we describe the heterogeneous components using terminology provided by a common data model; second we provide data access and procedure invocation services through the use of a common execution model. A schema captures the descriptions of all components, both data and procedures. The OMS then provides execution services using the information in the schema.

The model is FUGUE [1], an object-oriented, functional model that is based on three primitive types: *objects*, *functions*, and *types* and the concept of *function application*.

- **Objects** model the data in the underlying databases and the entities that are manipulated by the underlying applications, tools and servers.

- **Functions** are applied to objects to access their attributes, to perform operations on them, to trace relationships to other objects, or to test constraints on the objects.

- **Types** classify objects by the functions that can be applied to them. The type of an object determines this set of functions.

Types and functions are also modeled as objects. They have types, themselves, participate in type hierarchies, and have functions that can be applied to them to yield their attributes, perform operations on them, etc.

Objects and functions "bottom-out" in external data representations and programing language procedures. Both are developed independent of the model. The OMS has no control over the external representations and procedures. **Function application** consists of invoking these procedures, which are implemented in some programing language, and passing appropriate data structures that represent or reference the objects as input and output parameters. These external procedures manipulate the data representations associated with the objects and are, in fact, the *implementations* (or "bodies") of the functions. They are passed surrogates for the objects they process, i.e., expressions that can be interpreted by the recipient to identify the input or output parameters.

Data in underlying heterogeneous repositories are modeled as objects to which functions are applied to select and retrieve information, modify values, etc. Software tools, application programs, and data servers are modeled both as objects to be managed and manipulated and as functions to be applied to data objects. The procedures that comprise the software tools, application programs and data servers are modeled as the implementations of the functions.

The components of the OMS itself are modeled as objects, functions, and types that are implemented as pre-defined data structures and programing language procedures. The OMS provides built-in functions for describing data and procedures, creating and deriving new objects and functions, and invoking the function application mechanism.

There are no built-in OMS facilities for manipulating what are usually defined as base types, e.g., integers, reals, or strings. They are treated simply as objects like any others that are function arguments. They are passed to underlying systems that provide the function bodies exactly like other more complex objects. That is, adding two integers is performed in the same way as releasing a VLSI design, i.e., by invoking the procedure that implements the add function and passing surrogates for the integer objects to it, exactly like the system would invoke the procedure that implements the release function and pass a surrogate for the design object to it.

2.2. Handles, OIDs, and Data Representations

In object-oriented systems, objects (which are abstractions) are referenced by various forms of "handles" (expressions that evaluate to data structures) that may be, for example, character-string "names", queries that identify the objects by their attributes or relationships, and other function application requests (e.g., SQRT(4) is a handle for the integer 2). A handle may identify different objects at different times (e.g., the same query may yield a different object each time it is executed) or always refer to the same object.

In either case, the expression evaluates to a data structure that uniquely and permanently identifies the object, i.e., its OID. Each object has identity independent of any of its properties, structure or behavior; it is distinct from all other objects for all time. This identity is reflected in the object's OID, which is different from every other object's OID and is immutable.

OIDs serve multiple purposes in the OMS:

- They are used by clients to reference objects in requests for function application.

- They are passed to and from programing language procedures that implement functions that operate on or yield the object.

- They are used to store references to the object (so they can be passed to such procedures at a later time).

- They are input to type checking functions that support function application.

- They determine object identity, i.e., establish when two objects are "the same" object.

An OID is a fully-evaluated expression. Its value represents the object itself. The OID is the canonical form of the expression that represents the object, i.e., the form to which all handle expressions for a particular object evaluate. For example, "SQRT(4)", "SUCCESSOR(1)", etc., are all handles for an object whose OID is 2 (i.e., integer 2). The OID itself is also a handle for the object. In our model, we define object identity as OID identity. That is, two objects are "the same" object if they have identical OIDs.

Besides the data structures that serve as OIDs for them, some objects may have, in addition, a concrete "data representation", i.e., instance variables associated with the object. The data representation is an instance of a base type, e.g., integer or string, or a structure comprised of instances of base types. For example, an Employee object might have a tuple of strings (representing, for example, its name, address, department name) as its data representation; a Stack object might have an array of integers as its data representation.

The representation of an instance of a base type or a structure comprised solely of base types *is* the value of the object. Such objects are immutable and uniquely associated with the abstract object they represent. That is, integer 2 cannot be changed to be integer 3; instead, one changes references to integer 2 to references to integer 3. Therefore, representations of such types are usable as handles or OIDs for the abstractions they represent, so long as they meet the other requirements for OID use (such as supporting type checking, which we describe in Section 3.2).

For mutable types, however, the representation is a *related* object whose type is a base type or a structure comprised of instances of base types. A change to a mutable object must produce a different representation object because the representation object itself is immutable. Therefore, representations of instances of mutable types cannot be used as OIDs because the representation does not preserve the object's identity through changes. That is, the representation is not permanently associated with a unique object.

2.3. Requirements on the OID-Generation Mechanisms

Our OMS and other systems that deal with foreign objects must provide usable OIDs for both their own "native" objects, which include those that are created by the OMS or explicitly registered with it, and "foreign" objects that originate outside of the OMS, as well as base types like integer and string (if they are treated as objects). Each class of object has its own requirements on the OID generation mechanism as described below.

- Objects created by the OMS require only that the OMS generate unique, immutable identifiers, the equivalent of surrogates generated by DBMSs. "Type" and "function" objects are examples of OMS-native objects that require this form of OID generation. They are manipulated by the native procedures of the OMS so we are assured that the system-generated OIDs are compatible with the procedures that manipulate them. However, they need handles that are readily specified by clients and application programs.

- Instances of base types or "printable" objects include character- and bit-strings, integers, reals, etc. They can be thought of as having always existed , not requiring creation by either the OMS or an external system, so they cannot be assigned OIDs at creation. If they are to be treated as first-class objects, they need handles constructed from their values to allow clients and application programs to reference them.

- Objects created by external applications and servers include, for example, tuples in databases and records in existing files. In general, they are the objects in repositories that are managed (or populated) by procedures external to the OMS. Such objects usually have identifiers provided by the systems that created them that the organization can guarantee to be unique and immutable within the context of the creating system. For example, tuples in databases may be identified by keys or records in files may be identified by record numbers. These objects require handles constructed from their external identifiers to allow them to be referenced by clients and application programs.

- Foreign objects that are individually registered with the OMS (not just instances whose types were registered) can be given OMS-generated OIDs at registration. They require, however, that the OMS maintain the mapping between the OMS-assigned OID and the externally-assigned identifier that clients and applications will use to reference the object.

The OMS may be required to perform those mappings both to interpret requests to apply functions to the objects and to invoke the procedures of the foreign systems that implement those functions.

Registration is likely infeasible where the number of existing objects is large, particularly when each record, tuple, or even each field would have to be registered. The cost of such registration would include not only function calls to request registration, but generation of an OID and storage of the mappings between the OMS-assigned OIDs and the existing identifiers. In addition, the OMS would have to perform the mappings between client-specified forms to OMS-assigned OIDs and back to acceptable forms for processing of the objects by their source systems.

- Derived objects are objects that are constructed as the result of query expressions. They are members of sets (which have OIDs) where the members of the set are specified by an unevaluated expression, rather than by enumeration. That is, the surrogates or OIDs of the members are not necessarily materialized. Such objects are not explicitly "created" by the OMS at the time that the query expression is evaluated.

  Providing OIDs for virtual objects is traditionally a hard problem in database systems. For example, the sets that result from joins, projections or group-by operations need OIDs, yet we do not want specifically to manifest the member objects or to materialize their OIDs. Instead we want to manifest each virtual object one at a time, as the objects are needed for function application. That is, we want to materialize its OID on-the-fly, by binding the expression that defines the set of such objects to particular source objects and evaluating the result.

- Objects imported from other OMSs may have OIDs that overlap or conflict (in type information) with native objects. They may be received in either unevaluated or evaluated form, i.e., expression or OID form. The unevaluated form can only work when everything required for evaluation is sent along with the expression, e.g., the functions with appropriate implementations and interpretable handles for all other objects that are required for evaluation. The system needs to be able to construct OIDs in the recipient OMS from the handles (and ancillary information) passed from the sending OMS.

In general, objects created by the OMS need *generated* OIDs. Objects that are not specifically created by the OMS, either because they already exist or because they are created by external systems need *interpretable* OIDs. OID interpretation will vary from type to type, not only in the sources of the information needed to interpret the OIDs but in the method of interpretation as well.

The requirements on the OID interpretation and generation mechanisms are 1) that they be flexible enough to accommodate type-specific requirements; 2) that they provide a uniform interface that supports origin- and location-transparent references to objects; 3) that handles be constructable by clients, who may be human users or application programs; and 4) that they support mappings of object handles -- with and without evaluation -- to the formats required by the procedures that process the objects.

3. SOLUTION APPROACHES

This section describes our approach to the problem of providing OIDs for the various classes of objects described above. It addresses three aspects of the solution: specifying type-specific instructions for generating OIDs that meet the requirements defined above; supporting type checking; and detecting object identity or equivalence.

3.1   Generating/Constructing OIDs

We identify for each object type the form of OIDs for instances of that type and a function which generates or interprets those OIDs. An expression that binds this function to particular arguments constitutes a handle for a particular object. Evaluation of the expression produces the object's OID. The form of the resulting OID is determined by the function's signature. That is, the function definition specifies the *type* of the resulting object (which is an OID). This type must be a data structure, i.e., a subtype of a base type or structure of base types, e.g., a bit- or character-string. Section 4.5 describes the treatment of OIDs as objects.

The OID generation function is applied in response to a request to create or register an object or a request to manifest a derived object. Requests that reference un-registered foreign objects or derived objects identify the objects by handles specified as expressions in these functions. The expression is evaluated, i.e., the function is applied, only when the canonical or OID form is required. The purpose of the function is to describe to clients (both human and application programs) how to construct such OIDs.

The procedures that manipulate objects (i.e., the implementations of functions that apply to instances of the type) may place special restrictions on the form of handles they accept or produce. For example, an Ada procedure will require a different format for data structures than a C procedure. Various data servers that provide procedures will have even greater differences in the forms they accept. For each procedure, we provide a function that is applied automatically when the procedure is invoked to convert from the OMS OID form to the form required by the procedure and performs the reverse conversion on output.

Our approach applies to generating OIDs for all of the object classes described in Section 2.3. The approach provides a method of OID generation or construction that is uniform across all types, yet it supports type-specific OID structures. The OID actually consists of a pair <type identifier, identifier within type>.

In many systems, the handling of instances of the base types is a problem. Rather than treating them as first-class objects, the system provides special syntactic mechanisms that allow such objects to be referenced by their values, usually with some form of tag to specify the object's type. (Long strings require separate mechanisms to provide shorter forms, e.g., names, for convenient reference.) The approach requires the system to recognize these objects as instances of special types and treat them differently from the way other objects in the system are treated.

Another common approach to the handling of base types is to consider the first reference to such an object to be a request to "register" the object and get it a system-assigned OID. This approach has the disadvantage that it requires the system to recognize special forms that are not legal OIDs and to recognize the "first" reference in order to pass back a legal OID. In addition, it may require the system to maintain a record of OIDs for a (possibly) very large number of objects.

Our approach allows us to treat instances of base types or structures of base types as first class objects, like any other objects. Their OIDs can be constructed from their values. We construct their OIDs by coupling the type with the value of the object, since the object's value cannot change, e.g., integer_2 or real_2.0. The type is the type-specific part of the OID of the type object. The same approach can be used for any object which has an immutable value.

Similar functions, which couple the OID of the object's type with an external identifier that is guaranteed unique within the type and immutable, are used for constructing OIDs for various kinds of foreign objects. Note that there are no restrictions on the OID-constructor functions except those imposed by the semantics of OIDs. However, the approach, which is extremely flexible, raises important issues with respect to the ability to guarantee correctness of the results and to provide some level of homogeneity for the results. They are discussed in Section 4.

3.2. Type Checking

An important requirement of the OID generation or interpretation mechanism is that the results support type checking for function application. Note, however, that there is not a requirement to *determine* the object's type strictly from its OID. Rather, we must be able to determine whether the object is an instance of a specific type. Given a request to apply a function to argument objects, the OMS (or the compiler) needs to be able to determine whether the arguments, which are specified by their handles, match the types specified in the function signature.

In this context, the handle (with our without evaluation, depending on the degree to which compile-time type checking can be performed) is tested for membership in a specific type to determine whether the associated object is an instance of that type. Functions for type checking are, themselves, type-specific. This means that the OID generator/constructor function for the type only need be consistent with the membership test function for the type. The function signature determines which type-checking function is applied to the specified arguments.

Some functions are polymorphic, accepting as input instances of a variety of types. In this case, the type checking function is that of a union type, which ensures that the argument is an instance of any acceptable type. The consistency requirements between OID generation/constructor functions and type checking functions still holds. Union types and their type checking functions are in addition to these types. They simply request application of the type checking functions of their component types.

3.3. Object Identity and Equivalence

The final requirement on OIDs is related to object identity, i.e., determining when two objects are really "the same" object. We define object identity in our model as OID identity. This means that two objects can have identical representations but not be identical so long as they have different OIDs.

Objects can have multiple types. Furthermore, they can gain and lose types. Because we have allowed OID generation and type checking to be defined by type-specific functions, objects can have different OIDs in their different types (but they need not). For example, an object might be an instance of both types Employee and Student. The object might be identified by Social Security Number in both types, in which case SSN could serve as the OID or may be identified differently in each of its types, for example by Employee# in one type and StudentID in the other, in which case it would have different OIDs in each type.

The same rule applies even when the types of an object are in an IS_A relationship. For example, both Employee and Student may be subtypes of Person, whose instances might be identified by SSN or by a digitized compressed representation of a fingerprint. Types in an IS_A hierarchy can inherit the form (i.e., type) of their instances' OIDs and the function for constructing OIDs or they can supply their own.

Objects that have different OIDs in their different types (and possibly different representations as well) must be **coerced** to their other types to be interpretable as these types (i.e., to have functions of these types applied to them). Coercion functions must map the object's OID in one type to a legal OID for the other type. If the object has different representations in the different types, the representation must be mapped, as well. Coercion functions must provide mappings in both directions to allow the object to be interpreted as either type and for users of the object in one of its types to "see" modifications to the object that were made in others of its types.

The results of type coercions, then, can be different OIDs for a given object. We define the results as *equivalent* objects. We define this object equivalence as OID-equivalence as follows:

Suppose OIDx is the OID for object x of type X and OIDy is the OID for object y of type Y.

If   Coerce(OIDx, typeY) --> OIDy
then   object x is equivalent (has an equivalent OID) to object y.

That is, two objects are equivalent if one is the result of coercing the other to another of its types.

4. IMPLEMENTATION APPROACHES AND TRADEOFFS

This section describes the tradeoffs associated with various approaches to implementing facilities for OID generation or construction. They include tradeoffs among 1) the ability to provide a completely flexible mechanism to meet the requirements for accommodating both native and foreign objects; 2) the ability to guarantee correctness, i.e., uniqueness and immutability; and 3) the ability to provide adequate performance in the resulting system or at least to ensure that the mechanism does not imply insurmountable performance problems.

4.1. Flexibility vs Correctness

It is unlikely that we can both provide complete flexibility to the type definer for specifying expressions that evaluate to OIDs and also guarantee uniqueness and immutability of the results. However, we can provide some built-in facilities that may help in guaranteeing these qualities. First, we can guarantee these qualities for system-generated OIDs assigned to system-created objects. Second, we can provide built-in constructor functions that do not lose such qualities when applied to other OIDs for use by the type definer. For example, concatenation will preserve these qualities. Third, if functions are classified by mutability, we can detect the presence of mutable types in OID generation expressions and reject them.

In general, we cannot determine whether an arbitrary expression produces correct OIDs. It seems more important to trust the type definer in claims that a particular expression guarantees correctness (e.g., that database keys are unique and immutable) than to restrict the flexibility of the mechanism for specifying type-specific OIDs. This approach, which chooses to preserve the autonomy of the underlying systems and the type definer over the ability to control the results, is typical of all parts of the system we are defining.

4.2. How Important is Homogeneity for OIDs?

The need to store, search and manipulate OIDs implies that some degree of uniformity in size and structure might benefit performance. How important are such considerations as fixed length or structure? Can the system exploit such qualities among subsets of the OIDs it must deal with? Otherwise, does the generality of the function application mechanism obviate the need for such uniformity?

It is likely that the ability to apply type-specific procedures for storing, searching and manipulating OIDs will allow the system to cope with heterogeneity among OIDs while exploiting commonalities where they exist. The type determines the level of abstraction at which uniformity exists. For example, OIDs for objects of one type may be fixed length alphanumeric strings, whereas OIDs for objects of another type may be variable length but with a fixed structure that includes its length. OID manipulation functions for each of the types can be sensitive to the particular structures of the type.

Homogeneity among the constructed OIDs would allow the inclusion of more generic type membership test functions to be used by multiple types. Moreover, homogeneous OIDs for functions or types themselves might make it easier to implement the OMS or enhance its performance. We believe that the use of string names for OMS-native types such as types and functions will make it easier to use the system and will not raise difficult problems for the implementation.

4.3. Embedding Information in OIDs

In general, the more information that can be embedded in the object's OID, the better performance can be. The system has no need to apply what might be remotely executed functions to determine that information but can apply native functions to decompose the OID to get the same information. For example, object type and location are obvious choices for embedding because they are so often required by the OMS itself.

However, embedding information can cause problems with uniqueness and immutability because the embedded information may be invalidated by changes to the object. Typically, one might wish to embed location or type information for direct use by the OMS. However this information changes when an object is moved or its type is changed by coercion or new types are added.

Our objective is to determine whether it is ever "safe" to embed information in an OID. Obviously, constructed OIDs may contain information that is interpreted by external systems. The type definer makes this safe by guaranteeing that the information won't change. It is desirable to provide similar mechanisms for embedding information that can be interpreted by the OMS.

Two approaches to embedding information for the use of the OMS seem promising: 1) ensuring that the information is "safe" and 2) avoiding changes to the object. The first is accomplished by ensuring that if the information changes, the OID will remain constant and the the system that interprets the OID will not be misled. For example, we might interpret embedded location information not as "where the object is" but as "where the object was created", i.e., "where to look first for the object", i.e., as a hint, which is not invalidated by moving the object. The interpreter must ensure that this "location" either points to the object or to a path for locating the object.

One problem with this approach is that the information itself must not be invalidated by other system changes. For example, if the "location" information identifies a node and that node is subsequently removed from the configuration, the node pointer must continue to be correctly associated with the "location" of the object. In this case it might be better to embed an expression in the handle that always evaluates to an OID that can be correctly interpreted.

A second approach is to apply changes to equivalent objects and to maintain the equivalence relationship. Changes to object types may require such an approach. For example, if we identify an INTEGER object by an OID that concatenates type with value (integer_2), changing the type of the object to type REAL would mean that the OID was invalidated. Instead, we coerce the object to another of its types REAL, which produces an equivalent object with a similarly constructed OID (real_2.0).

Coercion and the handling of equivalent objects is not difficult where no updates can occur, as in the case of real and integer. Maintaining equivalence is more difficult for objects that can be updated because the updates must propagate to equivalent objects, which have their own representations. This means that the definition of the coercion function must, as well, modify update functions for both types to propagate to the equivalent object, in order to maintain the equivalence relationship.

4.4. Storing Unevaluated OID Expressions

Evaluating OID expressions requires function application, which implies planning and invoking procedures. Both may involve execution at a remote site and associated data movement. It may be advantageous to avoid such evaluation, storing the expression itself. Obviously, we need to store unevaluated handles that we want to yield results that are sensitive to the context in which they are evaluated. However, it is not clear when it is desirable to store unevaluated handles that always yield the same results (i.e., the same OID).

To determine this, two questions need to be answered:

(1) Is there assurance that the expression always yields the same result? That is, is later evaluation is guaranteed to yield precisely the same value as immediate evaluation or is the expression context-sensitive? Can we freeze the state of all needed data for later evaluation of the expression?

(2) Is there some saving to be gained by storing the unevaluated expression over storing its value? That is, is it likely that the expression will not need to be evaluated but can be used "as is" by the procedure that manipulates the object? or that evaluation will take place under more advantageous circumstances, e.g., when other operations would be executed at the remote site or the data would be available there? or that the unevaluated expression will require less space for storage than the evaluated form?

It is clear that unevaluated handle expressions must be stored as object references in cases where we want the evaluation to be context sensitive. The ability to store unevaluated expressions that always yield the same OID is available, then, at no cost. However, it will require further work to find the answers to the questions above to determine whether it is a good idea.

4.5. Bottoming-Out: Treating OIDs as Objects

The OMS ultimately "bottoms out" in OIDs, which are both instances of base types and objects that are processible by procedures provided by the OMS. In this sense, they can be considered to be "native" to the OMS. The goal is to provide means of identifying and manipulating them that are both consistent with the handling of other types and reasonably efficient to process.

Because OIDs are native to the OMS, we can restrict their structures so that we can recognize them as OIDs. However, because we allow them to be of different formats or structures, we must ensure that the OMS can detect their types by examining them, i.e., that functions that type-check OIDs apply to all OID forms. OIDs are simple data structures that can be mapped to the required data structures of the programming languages that implement the functions of the object's type. The OMS needs to know the types of these data structures in order to apply the functions that map them to and from the internally processible structures of the procedures.

5. CONCLUSIONS

Object management systems that must cope with "foreign" objects need a mechanism that allows them to generate OIDs from identifiers for these objects that were assigned by the external systems that created them. The system must not only accept requests in forms constructed from these external identifiers but must also map OIDs to the forms required for object handles by external procedures that process the objects. Registering every foreign object in order to get it a system-generated OID is impractical if the number of objects is large. Moreover, it is wasteful if the objects are to be manipulated by the systems that created them, which could process the external identifiers "as is".

The mechanism must allow the construction of type-specific OIDs. Yet, it should provide a degree of uniformity that allows origin- and location-transparent access to every object. It should accommodate all types of objects, including objects that are native to the OMS, such as Types and Functions, as well as instances of base types, which are treated differently from other objects in many systems.

The mechanism for OID generation or construction must be extremely flexible to accommodate the specific requirements of all object types. This requirement for flexibility severely limits the system's ability to guarantee the correctness of the resulting OIDs, i.e., that they are unique within the scope of the OMS and immutable . The system must rely on the type definer to guarantee the correctness of OIDs for instances of the type. By providing appropriate functions, the system can guarantee the correctness of OIDs for native types.

In our system we construct OIDs by coupling the type identifier with the type-specific identifier that is unique within the type. We use string names for the OIDs of type objects or function objects. This allows us to use externally-assigned identifiers as the type-specific part as long as they are guaranteed to be unique within the type and immutable.

The need to support type checking and and tests for object identity and equivalence imposes some restrictions on the flexibility of the OID construction mechanism. We require consistency within the type among functions for OID construction, type checking, and coercion.

The degree of flexibility that is needed requires that even the form of the OID be type-specific, e.g., that any data structure with the required properties be usable as an OID. However, to simplify the OMS, it is desirable to treat OIDs as system-managed data structures, i.e., as first class objects. This allows the OID construction and manipulation mechanisms, themselves, to be supported by the system in the same way as all other parts of the OMS.

There are tradeoffs between flexibility and performance. Performance may be improved by ensuring homogeneity among OIDs. Such levels of homogeneity can be provided for objects of different types. In addition, performance may be enhanced by allowing the storage and manipulation of unevaluated handle expressions. However, homogeneity cannot be enforced and the use of unevaluated expressions may not always be either beneficial or supportable. Our goal is to exploit situations where such approaches can enhance performance without mandating the existence of such situations.

REFERENCES

1.   Heiler S. and S. Zdonik, "FUGUE: A Model for Engineering Information Systems and Other Baroque Applications," *Proceedings of the 3rd International Conference on Data and Knowledge Bases*, Jerusalem, Israel, June, 1988.

2.   Kent W., "On Constructed and Generated Object Identifiers", to be published.

3.   Khoshafian S. and G. Copeland, "Object Identity," *Proceedings of the OOPSLA Conference*, Portland, OR, November, 1986.

The Evolution of the SSE Data Storage System into a Persistent Object System

S. L. Wright
Murdoch University

ABSTRACT

The SSE Data Storage System is a very flexible system for data storage designed to support the needs of scientists in data collection, reduction and analysis. This paper describes the DSS and how it can be viewed as a simple Persistent Object Store. Some suggestions for extensions to make it a true POS are presented together with some ideas for the design of a high-level language that integrates with the DSS to give a Persistent Programming Environment (PPE) .

1. BACKGROUND TO THE SCIENTIFIC SOFTWARE ENVIRONMENT

The ultimate aim of the Scientific Software Environment (SSE) project is to provide a complete problem solving environment that relatively computer-naive scientists can use to solve a wide variety of problems, thus improving the productivity of scientists. The initial work has concentrated on the provision of basic support facilities that relatively computer-aware scientists can use to simplify the coding of programs. The next phase will be to provide tools to help the production of software and the management of the software production process. Later phases will involve automation of the problem specification phase of problem solving.

2. THE DATA STORAGE SYSTEM

The Data Storage System (DSS) of the SSE was initially designed to store data in a convenient form and to avoid the packing and unpacking of data to and from files (which takes up a large portion of many programs). It provides mechanisms for organising hierarchies of data objects and provides access to these object from user-written programs.

2.1. Structure and Naming

A data object in the DSS is either primitive or structured. Primitive objects correspond to the elementary data types available in most languages (integers of various sizes,real,character) and some low-level types (byte, signed and unsigned words etc.). A structured data object consists of any combination of other primitive or structured objects (similar to the record structure of modern languages). Arrays of primitive and structured objects can also be constructed. Every data object can be referenced using its name constructed by combining the names along the path to the object separated by dots. Thus the overall organisation looks very similar to the file structuring of most operating systems (e.g. Unix) where primitive objects are at the leaves of the tree rather than files.

Note that the syntax for full object names is not determined by the DSS but by the SSE User Interface. Also the routine names and parameters used in this paper convey the semantics of the operations not the detailed syntactical form used by the SSE in order to avoid having to discuss other features of the SSE not directly relevant to this paper.

2.2.   Operators

Data objects stored in the DSS are totally dynamic and can be manipulated using operations such as:

    Create(parent_object_name, new_object_name, type, dimensionality)
    Delete(object_name)
    Extend(object_name, new_dimensionality)
    Read(object_name, program_variable)
    Write(object_name, data)
    Map(object_name, type, mode, virtual_address)
    UnMap(object_name)
    Reset_values(object_name)
    Move(object_name, new_parent, new_name)
    Copy(object_name, new_parent, new_name)

The DSS is a completely self describing system containing all information about the objects within it. This information is available via inquiry operations, e.g.

    Inquire_components(parent_object, list_of_component_objects)
    Inquire_dimensionality(object_name, dimensionality)
    Inquire_type(object_name, type)
    Inquire_values(object_name, values_available)
    Inquire_structure(object_name, ifstructured)
    Inquire_size(object_name, size)

2.3.   Access from High-level Languages - Use of Virtual Memory

The data objects stored in the DSS can be accessed and manipulated from programs written in high-level languages. As the data model for most languages is not powerful enough to deal with DSS data objects directly as language data structures it is normal to work at the level of primitives or arrays of primitives. Operations are available to read and write primitive data values to and from program variables but the most efficient way of handling this data is to map it directly into Virtual Memory. Thus in VMS Fortran :

```
    PROGRAM ZERO_ARRAY
    REAL R2(100000)
    ...
    CALL DSS_MAP(object_name, '_REAL', 'WRITE', VMAddress, SIZE, ...)
    CALL ZERO(%VAL(VMaddress), SIZE, ...)
    CALL DSS_UNMAP(object_name)
    CALL ZERO(R2,100000,...)
    ...
    END

    SUBROUTINE ZERO(R,SIZE,...)
    REAL R(SIZE)
    ...
    DO J = 1,SIZE
      R(J) = 0.0
    ENDDO
    ...
    END
```

The MAP call maps the REAL array from the specified data object into Virtual Memory which is then passed to subroutine ZERO. ZERO sees this as just a normal array, it does not matter if it is local to the program or not (both cases are shown in the example). Any modifications to the array made by the subroutine will appear in the data system when the data is un-mapped. This behaves very much like a persistent data store (with only the main program knowing if the data is local or external). The %VAL construct is just the VMS way of achieving this effect, similar methods can be used in other operating systems and languages.

It is possible to specify subsets of primitive data objects to be operated on so the whole object does not have to be manipulated by a program if it does not wish to.

3. 'TYPE' STRUCTURE OF THE DATA SYSTEM

Every object in the data system has a 'type'. Primitive objects have pre-specified type names (beginning with the _ character). The type for a structured object is an arbitrary character string (of up to 15 characters) chosen by the programmer when creating the object. As it is possible to change the structure and content of a structured data object at any time by inserting new components and/or deleting existing components the normal meaning of the word type as used in modern programming languages obviously cannot apply to data objects. As there is no mechanism for enforcing objects with the same type name to have the same structure it is purely a matter of convention established by application programs as to what they mean by a given type name. In order for the type names of data objects to be useful in the SSE, programmers are strongly advised to use the approach described in the following section.

3.1. Manipulating Data Objects as A.D.T.'s

A convention in the Data System is to define an object of a given type as consisting of a specified set of components of given types and dimensionalities. A program is entitled to add further components to an object for its own purposes but it cannot expect other programs that handle objects of this type to be able to manipulate these extra components. This view of types is 'enforced' by defining a set of routines to operate on a data object of a given type and a program is not 'allowed' to manipulate the defined components of a type by other means. What this means in practice is that there should be a minimum of two routines for a given type:

    Create_object(object_name, ...)

which creates the containing structure of the required type together with the defined components for that type and possibly some initial values for components. This is equivalent to the instantiation and initialisation of a variable of a specified type in a programming language. The 2nd routine is:

    Destroy_object(object_name, ...)

which disposes of an object of the given type by deleting the components and then the containing object. This is equivalent to leaving the context in which the object was instantiated (in a statically scoped language). In practice there will be a complete set of other operations for manipulation of data objects of this type.

This approach is similar to the implementation of Abstract Data Types in many languages, e.g. Modula-2:

```
DEFINITION MODULE Useful_Object;
TYPE object_type;
PROCEDURE Create_object(variable:object_type,...);
PROCEDURE Destroy_object(variable:object_type,...);
...
END Useful_Object .
```

Then in the IMPLEMENTATION MODULE the actual structure of the type and the actions of the procedures are elaborated.

If done properly this approach to data objects has all the advantages of a true ADT including the ability to completely hide the representation of an object and thus optimise use of an object in some way. A good example of this is the Sparse Matrix Package built on top of the Data System. Using this package a programmer can do all the necessary matrix operations without knowing how the matrix is actually stored in the Data System (e.g. as a list of the non-zero elements). This has the advantage of saving disk space without the programmer having to know the intricate details of any particular implementation of a sparse matrix.

3.2. Polymorphism

A programmer does not need to know the type of a primitive numeric object and arrange for the appropriate type of language variable to be used in order to manipulate the values. The programmer just asks the Data System to provide the data as the type required in the program and the Data System will perform any necessary conversions to and from the stored type to the required type. Any conversion errors in changing representations are signalled to the program. This is a simple kind of polymorphism in that a program can manipulate all the different numeric types using one programming language representation and one piece of code. Of course, as with all polymorphic procedures, care must be taken that the routine maintains the required semantics of the operations for all objects given to it.

4. IMPLEMENTATION

The Data System as outlined above is only one possible style of storing data objects that is possible in the SSE. It is implemented on top of other Packages as follows:

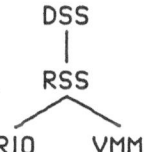

RSS (the Record Storage System) defines a data structure and method of storing and manipulating this structure on disk. It, in turn, is implemented using Packages in the Virtual Operating System layer of the SSE - RIO (Random-access I/O) and VMM (Virtual Memory Manager).

DSS just uses RSS to store its own particular form of data. RSS itself knows nothing about the content or meaning of what it is storing and can therefore be used as the storage mechanism for alternate types of system. This is the key to further development of the Data System into a Persistent Object Store and therefore the following discussion concentrates on the implementation of RSS. The implementation of DSS is very straight-forward and will only be discussed briefly as an example of using RSS.

4.1. RSS Implementation

The basic data structure manipulated by RSS is the **Record**. A record consists of three **domains**: RCD (record control domain), RSD (record static domain) and RDD (record dynamic domain). RSS attempts to keep the 3 components of a record together in the same physical block of the disk. However if the dynamic domain is too large to fit into a block with the other parts then it is stored separately in blocks set aside for this purpose (called Pure Data Blocks) The smallest unit of allocation of disk space is a group of 34 bytes (called a chip) . Every record in the RSS can be located by the unique address of its RCD, known as the Record ID (RID):

20 bits	4 bits
Block Offset	Chip Offset

RCD is a fixed length object that contains information about the other two domains and various fields for use by a Package using RSS for storing data:

Field	Size	Purpose
Parent RID	24 bits	RID of the parent of this record
Flags	8 bits	Flags used by RSS to indicate various states
Class/size	8 bits	Used by higher-level packages for storing information about their data organisation.
SDomSize	8 bits	Size of Static Domain
DDomSize	32 bits	Size of Dynamic Domain

RSD is a fixed length object which is used to store a small amount of data (< 256 bytes) that is static is size but not necessarily in value.

RDD is a variable length object which is used to store potentially large amounts of data (up to 2^{32} bytes) which can vary in size and content.

Ideally the RSS should be implemented as the basic storage mechanism in an Operating System and have access to disks at the physical block level. However the SSE is currently implemented on top of host operating systems and must therefore co-exist with an existing file system. To cope with this situation RSS introduces the concept of a partition. Each record must therefore be addressed using a Record Handle (RHD):

8 bits	24 bits
Partition ID	RID

On a host O.S, partitions are implemented as host files. In a stand alone environment they would act as a convenient way of segmenting disks into regions to help backup, shadowing and other tasks.

RSS Operations:

```
CreatePartition(host_name, initial_RCD, initial_handle)
DeletePartition(host_name)
CreateRecord(parent_handle, RCD, RHD)
DeleteRecord(RHD)
Adopt(parent_handle, RHD, new_parent_handle)
ReadRCD(RHD, program_variable)
ReadRSD(RHD, program_variable)
WriteRSD(RHD, data)
ExpandDDom(RHD, new_size)
ShrinkDDom(RHD, new_size)
MapDDom(RHD, length, offset, mode, virtual_address)
UnMapDDom(RHD)
ClearDDom(RHD)
```

4.2. DSS Implementation

DSS routines are implemented by defining 4 classes of record:

Class	Static Domain	Dynamic Domain
partition	-	name and RID of first object
structure	Type,Dimensions	list of RIDs pointing to components
component	No. of components	list of (name,RID) pairs
primitive	Type,Dimensions	data

DSS implements its operations (see section 2.2) by manipulating this data stored inside RSS using RSS operations. For example the data object:

```
struct  Position  OBJECT[2]
    struct  hms  RA
        _BYTE  Hours
        _BYTE  Minutes
        _REAL  Seconds
    end struct
    struct  hms  DEC
        ...
    end struct
    _REAL  Epoch
end struct
```

is implemented as follows (only the Static and Dynamic Domains are shown separated by a thick line) :

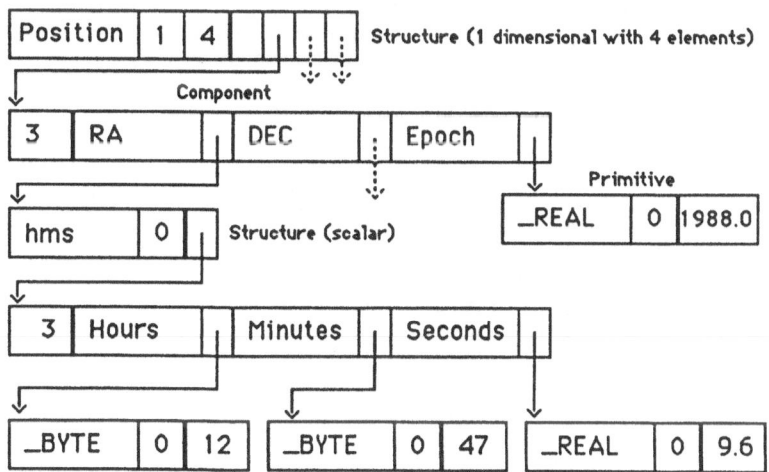

5. DATA SHARING AND OBJECT REFERENCES

The only relationship between records currently implemented in RSS is that each record knows the RID of its parent (the object containing the record). Packages on top of RSS can use this information to organise its own data, and also implement other relationships between data objects by adding further classes of records if desired. The main relationship between DSS objects is that an object can contain (own) other objects. This relationship gives rise to the hierarchy of Data System Objects and is achieved using the RSS parent relationship.

There are two other sorts of relationships which could be useful:

1) link - a transparent reference to another data object. This can be used to give the appearance that an object is contained in another object when, in fact, it is stored elsewhere. This enables sharing of data objects by creating a link to an object from within other objects.

2) Reference - a non-transparent reference to another data object. This can be thought of as a data object containing the name of another data object. The relationship can be followed to get access to the referenced object. This can be used to set up more general relationships between objects (graphs, rather than a hierarchy). A possible application here is in the implementation of HyperText systems (See e.g. [1]).

6. TBL PACKAGE

At about the time that a production version of DSS was being written (1983) . I wrote a package of routines for handling catalogue data on magnetic tape. Up to that time each different data catalogue had a different structure and set of routines for accessing it. A general purpose set of routines was implemented to access the tape on a record-by-record basis and to extract the field data. The basic parameters of the tape and the structure of the record were specified using a 'descriptor file' containing details of the offsets of the fields from the start of the record, etc.

This descriptor file is, of course, a simple data dictionary and the set of records on the tape can be considered to be a relational table. Modifying the lower levels of TBL to allow creation of and access to disk versions of the data and to allow random access was very easy. Routines implementing relational operators (project,select,join) were also implemented.

A natural extension would seem to be to use DSS to store data of this form leading to a package structure:

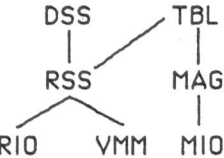

where MAG is the package used when accessing magnetic tapes and MIO is the SSE Virtual O.S. package for interfacing to magnetic tape drives.

However work on this integration has only started recently.

7. 'STRONG' TYPES AND STORAGE OF TYPE DESCRIPTIONS IN DSS

A relational table can be thought of as a 1D array of a fixed record structure. To support this concept it is convenient to introduce the notion of a 'strong' type (as opposed to the types introduced earlier which we should now call 'weak' types). A strong type (with name beginning with a ^ character) is an data object (of type _TYPE) stored in the DSS which is created using the routines:

    Create_Type(parent_type_name, type_name, ...
    Add_type_field(type_name, field_name, field_type, dimensionality, ...

Invocation of the first routine followed by multiple invocations of the second create the equivalent of a Pascal record type.

Note that every type has a parent type (whose components are included in the extended type) thus creating a type hierarchy. This allows a style of programming which has been discussed recently by Wirth [3]. The guidelines for programming with Data System Objects given in section 3.1 could now be type-checked using the interpretation that every object which has extra components added to it dynamically is an instance of a new extended type. Instances of objects extended from the same Base Type are then type compatible (with only the common components of the Base Type taking part in operations between extended objects).

An object of Strong Type is created in the usual way with Create:

    Create(parent_object,object_name,type,dimensionality)

the difference from creating an object of 'weak' type is that space can be set aside for the data as the exact form of the component data is known. Initially it is proposed that new components cannot be added to a strongly typed object, as the type hierarchy can be used to achieve the same effect in a much more rigorous way. Apart from this, no distinction is made between objects of 'strong' or 'weak' types. All of the Data System routines can be applied to both sorts of objects. It would seem useful to add three extra routines to enable record-by-record processing of strongly typed objects:

        ReadRec(object_name,variable_name)
        WriteRec(object_name,data)
        MapRec(object_name, mode, virtual_address)

If the storage layout on disk is the same as that used by a record variable in a programming language then data can be read or mapped directly into program record variables and accessed as such (which is considerably easier than getting and manipulating each component separately).

8. PERSISTENT PROGRAMMING ENVIRONMENT

Although the Data System provides persistent storage for program data in high-level languages in a relatively transparent way (only the top level of a program needs to set up the connection between permanently stored data and local storage in memory) it is very clumsy to have to deal with only primitive data types and existing languages cannot deal with the dynamic semantics of the data model used by the Data System. Thus in order to gain the full advantage of the Data System as a true Persistent Object Store a new language must be defined. A few properties of such a language are suggested in this section.

8.1. Existing SSE Environment

Currently the SSE Environment consists of a large number of application and utility programs which users can run to solve various problems. If a user wants to solve a new problem then a program must be written in a traditional (3rd generation) language, typically Fortran. These programs use the SSE Packages such as the Data System to help solve their problem. Users invoke application programs and interact with them using the SSE command language (SCL) whose major form is to invoke an application:

    program_name parameter1 = value, parameter2 = value

program parameters can be specified using keywords (as shown above) or positionally. SCL also has simple variables, control structures, macro facilities etc.. The proposal is to extend this language so that problems can be solved directly.

8.2. Constructs for a persistent programming environment

The major features that need to be added to SCL are the ability to define true procedures and the ability to declare and manipulate data objects. An important consideration is that the invocation of SCL procedures and external application programs should appear to be identical to a user. It is proposed that SCL should be an expression based language with dynamic typing but users can specify types at compile time, if appropriate, to enable some type-checking and more efficient code generation.

Procedures, types and variables are declared as follows:

    proc proc_name (type1 param1=default_value, type2 param2,...) = [statement_list]
    type type_name = struct (type1 field1=default_value, type2 field2,...)
    var variable_name = type_name (field1=initial_value,field2value,...)

A variable is transient unless the declaration is prefixed by the modifier **persist** in which case the external name of the object can be given if known at compile time, e.g.

    persist var local_variable_name < existing_external_variable_name
    persist var local_variable_name < new_external_variable_name = type(value)

or can be mapped at run-time:

    map local_variable_name, external_variable_name

Read-only objects can be prefixed by the modifier **const** and components of structures prefixed by the modifier **shared** are shared between instances of that structure (this can be used, for example, to define the equivalent of a SmallTalk Class).

All the usual operators between simple types should be available together with some special object manipulation operators such as the append operator, e.g.:

    x ++ (component_name = type(value))

which adds a new component to the data object x. This operator can also be used to extend array structures. The delete operator:

    x -- component_name

removes components (or array elements) from the object.

8.3. Storage of Procedural Code in the Data System - Objects

It is highly probable that this language would have to be compiled to an intermediate code which is then interpreted by a Virtual Machine. The implementation methods used by Icon [2] would seem to be a good model to work from as it has dynamic typing and variable size data structures.

Code produced by the compiler would, of course, be stored in the Data System and be operated upon in exactly the same way as all the other data objects. Therefore code could be stored as components in a data object enabling the implementation of Object-Oriented programming a la SmallTalk if this was desired.

9. CONCURRENCY, TRANSACTIONS AND VERSION CONTROL

The current version of the Data System allows a 1-writer,multiple reader form of concurrency. A programmer can explicity reserve and release a data object for modification using Lock and Unlock calls, or the system will automatically lock an object on the first attempt to access it in Write or Modify mode. A lock prevents other programs from accessing an object in Write or Modify mode but does allow access in Read mode. (The programmer can control whether an attempted write access is rejected with an error status, or whether the program waits for the lock to be released.) The actual data that the multiple readers get depends on how the system updates modified pages to the disk. As the current system is implemented on top of the VMS file system the granularity of the locking is at file level rather than the object level. This has not been observed to be too much of a problem, however the systems implemented have not used large-scale sharing of data objects between users, and this may be a problem for other types of applications using the Data System. A stand alone implementation should allow locking at the data object level.

Currently there is no concept of a transaction in the Data System. The time at which any alteration to a data object structure or value of a data object appears on the disk is totally dependent on how the Host O.S. does its updating, although the program can force consistency of virtual memory and disk versions of a data object. One possible approach to transactions (and also version control) is to use the link concept. When a program accesses an object in Write or Modify mode the system creates a skeleton of the object with links pointing to the original object. When a change is made the link is replaced by the modified copy (all other users see the original object, of course). On completion of a sequence of modifications (the transaction) the modifications could be integrated back into the original objects or, if version control is required, the time-ordered sequence of links to modified objects could be stored in another data object (version control structure).

REFERENCES

1.   Campbell, B. and Goodman, J.M. "HAM: A general purpose hypertext abstract machine". *CACM* , 31, 7, pp. 856-861.

2.   Griswold, R.E., Griswold, M.T. "The Implementation of the Icon Programming Language", Princeton University Press, 1986.

3.   Wirth, N. "Type Extensions". *ACM Trans. on Prog. Lang. and Systems*, 10, 2, pp. 204-214.

Persistence in a Distributed Object Server

Harry H. Porter, III
Portland State University

ABSTRACT

In the context of a large object store, we define *persistence* to require that objects be *shared* – both between sites and between different sessions at a single site – and *reliable* in the face of site and network failures. We are developing a fully distributed object server, called PORTLANDIA, that will function as the lowest level in the implementation of an object-oriented programming system. We begin by describing PORTLANDIA's model of persistence, as seen by users of the shared object space PORTLANDIA provides. Then, we describe the implementation of persistence in PORTLANDIA, giving emphasis to the details of object paging and the network protocol.

1. OUR DEFINITION OF PERSISTENCE

A straightforward definition of *persistent* objects is "those objects that are stored on disk and cached in RAM during user sessions." This definition is adequate for a single-user system, since (1) it captures the requirement that objects survive between user sessions and (2) it implies that objects survive across hardware failures. In the context of the distributed object server we are designing, we define persistence to require that objects are both *shared* and *reliable*. By shared, we mean that objects can be accessed from different sites as well as from different sessions at a single site. That is, objects are shared across time *and space*. By reliable, we mean that objects survive transparently across hardware and network failures.

Another definition of persistence is appropriate for strongly typed languages where programs may be executed against (or with respect to) a disk-based[1] object repository. In such systems, one program may create an object and place it in the repository (perhaps implicitly) for subsequent programs to access [e.g., 1, 2, 3, 4]. For these languages, we might define a persistent object as any program value that is stored along with enough type information to prevent type errors when subsequent programs access the object. This emphasis on type safety is inappropriate for the object server we are designing, since no notion of type exists at the server level.

2. PORTLANDIA: A DISTRIBUTED OBJECT SERVER

We are developing PORTLANDIA, a Persistent Object Repository for a Typed Language

---

[1] We use the terms "disk" and "RAM" as abbreviations for non-volatile and volatile storage.

Assuming a Non-server-based, Distributed Implementation Archictecture[2]. PORTLANDIA is a fully distributed object server that will function as the lowest level in the implementation of an object-oriented programming system [16]. A PORTLANDIA installation consists of a local area network connecting several sites (i.e., workstations), each running an instance of the server. Higher-level functionality, which is not discussed in this paper, will be implemented on top of the local server. Instances of the higher layers in the system will not communicate directly but, instead, will communicate indirectly by referencing objects in a shared, global object space.

The objects implemented by the PORTLANDIA server are essentially untyped records containing primitive values and references to other objects. There is no notion of types, inheritance, or behavior; these will be provided by the higher level in the design of the system. Thus, the object model provided by PORTLANDIA, as described so far, is very similar to the model provided by the Smalltalk heap manager to the Smalltalk interpreter.

There are two novel features in the PORTLANDIA design. (1) Objects are moved to the sites where they are used. In other object server approaches, messages are sent to the remote site containing the object where the messages are then executed. (2) The system is *symmetric* in the sense that objects are distributed evenly across all workstations. Every site functions as both an object repository and a processing site for user sessions. Conceptually there is no central server, although one implementation technique discussed below involves a central nameserver. This central server functions as an accelerator: it is not necessary to normal functioning of the system but reduces network traffic by eavesdropping on object movement to help sites quickly locate remotely stored objects.

The distributed object server also provides support for historical versions of objects. Most objects are *current* but objects can recreate their past states if their history was explicitly captured during earlier processing. Since historical objects can be used to communicate state from an earlier session to a later session and since one motivation of maintaining historical data is to provide reliability against user errors, PORTLANDIA's historical versioning mechanism also addresses the two issues of persistence: sharing and reliability. We will describe the historical versioning model after describing other aspects of the PORTLANDIA design on which historical versioning is dependent.

3. THE LANGUAGE-LEVEL MODEL OF PERSISTENCE

3.1. Local vs. Shared Objects

To support intersite sharing of objects, every object is either *local* or *shared*. This distinction is part of the object model provided by PORTLANDIA to higher levels in the system, not an implementation detail of the server. A shared object may be accessed from any site, while a local object is only reachable from a single site. When a reference is followed from one object to a second, shared object, the second object is first moved to the active site if it is not already there. Local objects may point to other local objects at the same site and to shared objects, but shared objects may only point to other shared objects. This constraint, which is enforced by the PORTLANDIA server, implies that one site can never possess a reference to another site's local objects.

---

[2] Portlandia, recently discovered by city elders, is the patron goddess of the object-oriented capital of the world.

The shared/local distinction is also used as the grain of inter-session sharing. A user may initiate a session at any site. The session initially has access to the same set of shared objects, regardless of site. Local objects are created during the session and are discarded when the session is gracefully terminated.

The distinction between local and shared objects is both visible from outside the server and exploited within the implementation of the server to enhance performance. Given the current capabilities of hardware, sharing and resilience of objects is essentially incompatible with CAE/CASE/CAD performance requirements [9]. Disk and network hits are so expensive that, to satisfy these requirements, the majority of references must be to objects that are already resident in local RAM. Our design places local objects in RAM to ensure fast access. When a shared object is accessed, it is transparently cached in a local object for at least the duration of a transaction and possibly much longer.

3.2. Transaction/Commit Protocol

The transaction/commit model is used for concurrency control. Each site executes a single thread of transactions and, within a transaction, access to shared objects objects is exclusive. Two-phase locking is used for concurrency control: once an object is referenced by one transaction, it is locked and any other sites that wish to access the object must wait. PORTLANDIA includes a lightweight process scheduler at each site, so accessing a shared object that is in use at another site will not stop all activity at a site. (There is also a *testAndLock* operation which will not block a process when a shared object is tied up. We expect most accesses to shared data to go through librarian objects [17] which will use the *testAndLock* operation so an application won't normally need to worry about blocking.)

When an object is first accessed, it is moved to the site performing the access and locked for the remainder of the transaction. Since objects remain at their present site after the transaction until they are needed at another site, commits can be completed without network communication. This scheme will work well in engineering applications, where objects are typically accessed repeatedly over several hours from only one site. Communication occurs frequently (i.e., transactions may be committed every few minutes) but relatively little data is actually transmitted upon each communication (i.e., one act of sharing might be a mail message or a bookkeeping notice between librarians).

3.3. Checkpointing for Reliability

Resilience at a single site is supported by periodically taking a checkpoint of memory. We suggest that the simplicity of checkpointing outweighs the additional reliability afforded by logging techniques. Because commits occur irregularly and some transactions may span several hours, the granule of sharing (the transaction) is inappropriate as the granule of reliability. Commit operations are executed according to the requirements of sharing and concurrency control by the user; checkpoints are executed more frequently to safeguard the work done during long transactions. For example, a background process might wake up every 30 minutes and execute a checkpoint operation.

3.4. Modifiable vs. Immutable Objects

One class of object – objects containing executable code – must be shared to a much greater degree than other objects. To efficiently support this sharing, a distinction is made between modifiable and immutable objects. Immutable objects may be shared easily by copying. Immutable objects may be made reliable more efficiently, since they need to be copied to disk only when created. Like the shared/local distinction, the modifiable/immutable distinction is part of the object model implemented by the server, not an implementation technique.

3.5. Historical Versions

Various versioning models have been proposed to support (1) versions across time, (2) versions across releases, (3) versions across representations, and/or (4) versions across configurations. At the server level, PORTLANDIA only supports versions across time since (2) through (4) are too application-dependent to merit low-level support. PORTLANDIA provides an operation, called *makeHistorical*, to capture the current state of an object. By default, object references refer to the current state of an object. The *getVersionOf* operation maps an a current object reference and a time into a historical version of that object.

When *makeHistorical* is invoked on an object, it captures the complete state of the object, including all reachable objects. The newly created historical versions are also made immutable. Thus, current objects may reference historical versions, but newer objects will never be reachable from older objects.

4. IMPLEMENTATION OF PERSISTENCE

4.1. Checkpointing and Atomicity

As part of the commit operation, a checkpoint is always made. Checkpoints may also be made between commits by explicitly invoking the *checkpoint* operation.

In its simplest form, a checkpoint consists of writing the entire RAM image to a disk. Writing contiguous words of memory to contiguous sectors on disk can be expected to drive the disk at its maximum transfer rate. Nevertheless, commits may occur frequently (for example, every 10 seconds) and checkpoints may require a couple of seconds to complete. Many computers are equipped with hardware to support virtual memory. While we do not intend to use any address translation mechanism, we can use the *dirty bits* in the page table hardware to tell which memory pages have been modified since the last checkpoint. We only need to write out the dirty pages.

It is entirely possible that a hardware failure will occur during the checkpoint process. A checkpoint that is incompletely written to disk is useless. One solution [7] is to allocate two identical regions of disk to contain checkpoint images and use each alternately. To determine whether a checkpoint is complete or not, we allocate two words in memory. One word is at the lowest usable address and the other word is at the highest. These words contain a sequence number and are normally identical. After making a checkpoint to disk, both words are incremented. During crash recovery, we examine both checkpoint images on disk. If the low and the high sequence word are equal, we can assume the checkpoint image was written without interruption. We can also use the sequence numbers in the checkpoint images to determine which image was written most recently. (Note that the pages containing the two sequence numbers will be marked dirty when the numbers are incremented.)

At first glance, the two techniques (dirty bits plus alternating copies) look incompatible. They can be made to work together with the following algorithm. Assume RAM consists of N pages and that we have allocated two disk regions of N blocks each, which we will call EVEN-REGION and ODD-REGION. (For simplicity, assume that RAM page size equals disk block size.) The i-th page will be checkpointed to either the i-th EVEN-REGION block or the i-th ODD-REGION block, but a complete checkpoint of N pages will be split between the two regions.

When we are ready to take a checkpoint, we first identify the dirty pages. If the i-th page is dirty, we write it out to either the i-th EVEN-REGION block or the i-th ODD-REGION block, whichever one does not contain the most recent copy of the i-th page. We can use an N-bit vector (called VALID-BLOCK-LIST) to remember which pages were most recently checkpointed to the EVEN-REGION and which were checkpointed to the ODD-REGION. If we also represent the dirty list as an N-bit vector, we can update the VALID-BLOCK-LIST with an exclusive-or operation. Let's update the VALID-BLOCK-LIST before we do any writing to disk. The VALID-BLOCK-LIST will then tell us where to write dirty pages. Let's also assume that the VALID-BLOCK-LIST resides within the first page of RAM.

After a crash, how do we recover a RAM image from the two regions? The first and last pages, which contain the sequence numbers, are always dirty and are both written at every checkpoint to the same region. First, we read both copies of these two pages to determine which pair represents the most recently written, complete checkpoint. Since the VALID-BLOCK-LIST resides in the first page, we now know where to find the rest of the checkpointed RAM.

4.2. Maintaining Consistency between Disk and RAM

Smalltalk-80 assumes that everything of interest will fit in main memory at once and that the checkpoint model is adequate. Unfortunately, this assumption is false and objects must be transferred to/from the disk between checkpoints. With checkpointing, the sticky issue is how to keep changes to disk-based objects in sync with RAM-based objects in the presence of a site crash. For example, assume that an object is transferred from disk to RAM, modified, and then written back to disk. Then the site crashes. During the recovery, we can easily restore the state of RAM, but we must also restore the state of the disk.

Recall how shadow pages are used to atomically update large numbers of disk pages [e.g., 12]. All disk pages containing valid data are initially reachable from a single root page. During a transaction, pages are never updated in place on the disk. Instead, a new page is allocated from a pool of unused disk pages and the modified data is written to that page. The root page, which is cached in RAM, is updated to point to the new page rather than the old page. Finally, at commit-time, the root page is written to disk atomically.

Our design uses exactly this scheme. In our case, the entire RAM image serves as the "root page". The algorithm for making checkpoints described above implements the atomicity of the update. The only detail remaining is the management of the free pool.

We maintain two free lists: the RECENTLY-FREED list and the TRULY-FREED list. Disk blocks in the RECENTLY-FREED list became free since the last checkpoint. Thus, they still contain data that must be recovered if the system crashes before the next checkpoint completes. Blocks in the TRULY-FREED list became free before the last checkpoint and can be overwritten when a new disk block is required.

When a disk-resident object is referenced, a disk block is read into a RAM buffer and all the objects on the page are copied into heap objects, with reformatting as necessary. The disk block is then added to the RECENTLY-FREED list. When objects are written out to disk, they are first copied into a buffer (with any necessary reformatting), a disk block is obtained from the TRULY-FREED list, and the data is written out to disk. The checkpoint operation consists of (1) writing out dirty RAM pages to the checkpoint area on disk (incrementing the two sequence numbers and updating the VALID-BLOCK-LIST as described above) and (2) moving all blocks in the RECENTLY-FREED list to the TRULY-FREED list.

How are the free lists represented? Each list is expected to be very long – perhaps too long to hold entirely in memory. We cannot use objects to represent each free list since the object manager might try to move objects to/from disk when we modify one of the lists, causing undesirable recursion.

Instead, we use *free-list-chain-blocks*. A free-list-chain-block contains the disk address of the next free-list-chain-block plus as many addresses of free disk blocks as will fit in the remaining space. The head block of each of the two free lists is always kept in RAM, and the remaining free-list-chain-blocks are on disk. Obviously, the free-list-chain-blocks are themselves in-use and, thus, are not free blocks. By keeping the head blocks of the two free lists in memory, the allocation and liberation of free blocks can usually be done quickly.

4.3. Object Identifiers

The object server uses two types of object identifiers, which we call *Persistent Object Identifiers* (POIDs) and *Object-Oriented Pointers* (OOPs). Every sharable object is assigned a POID when created and its POID never changes. POIDs are unique throughout all sites in a PORTLANDIA installation and are constructed by appending the site number at which the shared object was created to a sequentially incremented integer to insure uniqueness. We expect each site running PORTLANDIA to be assigned a 16 bit site number. POIDs are 64 bits long and consist of 2 flag bits, a site number, and a 46-bit unique integer field.

OOPs are not shared between sites and correspond exactly to Smalltalk-80 OOPs. Each RAM-resident object is assigned an OOP which is (essentially) a memory address. (Actually, OOPs are 32-bit pointers to object table entries.) When a shared object is read into RAM (either from disk or from the network) it is assigned an OOP. When an object is written out to disk or the network, its OOP will become collectable garbage. The user of PORTLANDIA is unaware of the distinction between OOPs and POIDs. He sees only one kind of reference.

4.4. Tracking Persistent Objects with the PERSISTENT-OBJECT-TABLE

Every shared object is present at exactly one site in the installation. (We'll relax this assumption when we discuss read-read sharing below.) If an object is present at the local site, it is either RAM-resident or disk-resident, but not both. When a disk block is read into RAM, all the objects it contains become RAM-resident and the disk block is added to the RECENTLY-FREED list.

To locate shared objects, we maintain an index called the PERSISTENT-OBJECT-TABLE. There is a single entry in this table for each locally-resident, shared object, whether disk- or RAM-resident. Each entry maps a POID into either a disk block address or an OOP. There are no entries for *foreign objects*, i.e., objects resident at other sites.

RAM-resident objects normally contain OOPs to other objects but may also contain POIDs. When a POID is dereferenced and the PERSISTENT-OBJECT-TABLE indicates that the desired object is already in RAM, the object is accessed immediately. As a side effect, the POID is replaced by the OOP to speed up future references.

When the PERSISTENT-OBJECT-TABLE indicates that the desired object is disk-resident, a disk block is first read in. The desired object and any other objects on that disk block are moved into the heap. It is certainly possible at this time to scan the newly read objects and translate any POIDs referring to RAM-resident objects into OOPs. However, we adopt the lazy approach by waiting until the POID is dereferenced.

4.5. Paging Objects to Disk

One goal of building a persistent object store is to completely hide the existence of volatile storage from the user. His model should be that all objects are stored on a reliable, non-volatile storage medium. As such, it is unacceptable for a system to fail – or even a transaction to abort – due to insufficient RAM[3]. What, then, do we do when the RAM heap fills up?

First, we use a variation of the generation scavenging algorithm [20, 21, 22] to collect local garbage, i.e., unreachable RAM-resident objects and their OOPs. In particular, we can collect local objects but all RAM-resident shared objects are always reachable through the PERSISTENT-OBJECT-TABLE. Also note that, since disk-based objects never contain OOPs (only POIDs), no disk I/O is required during garbage collection.

If the garbage collector fails to find enough free space, RAM-resident objects are *off-loaded* to the disk. (In theory, the objects could be off-loaded to either the disk or the network, but we only off-load objects to disk.) The first step in off-loading is to select some objects to be off-loaded. Obviously, shared objects that have not been used during the current transaction should be off-loaded before objects that have been used more recently. (To support locking objects during transactions there is, associated with each shared object, the number of the last transaction which accessed the object. We can use this in selecting objects for off-loading.)

If an object to be off-loaded contains OOPs, these must be chased and translated back to POIDs. Then, to off-load the object, we obtain a disk block from the TRULY-FREED list and write the object to disk. Finally, the RAM-resident object is mutated into a *tombstone*[4]. Any future references to the tombstone are trapped and the object will be brought back into RAM. Tombstones are very small (a flag word and a POID) and can be collected by the garbage collector if no RAM-resident objects reference them.

4.5.1. Object Clustering

Objects are often small (e.g., 100 bytes) and it is very inefficient to transfer a single object at a time. We cluster objects on disk and on network transfers using the same, simple rule. Given that object X is selected for off-loading (or requested by another site on the network), look at

---

[3] In fact, it is just such large transactions that we most wish to avoid aborting.

[4] Supporting the *becomes:* operation is one motivation for using an object table.

every RAM-resident object referenced by object X. Any such object that is also available for offloading is then added to the disk (resp., network) block until the block is full. Note that this clustering algorithm is dynamic in the sense that no static clustering relationships are required.

4.6. Off-loading Local Objects

The PERSISTENT-OBJECT-TABLE is, itself, stored in local objects. In general, we wish to allow for millions of objects to be present on disk at any one time. Thus, the PERSISTENT-OBJECT-TABLE will probably be too large to keep in memory and specific parts of the table must be paged to/from disk when accessed. This is an instance of a more general problem: what happens when, after offloading all shared objects, there is still insufficient space in the heap?

We must then select some local objects for off-loading to disk. The selected objects are assigned *pseudo-POIDs*, entered into the PERSISTENT-OBJECT-TABLE, and off-loaded to disk in exactly the same way shared objects are off-loaded. Since off-loaded local objects will never be garbage collected, we prefer to select the local objects to be off-loaded from the older generations.

Finally, to deal with a PERSISTENT-OBJECT-TABLE that is so large that it overflows onto disk, we need only to store the table's root in a RAM-resident object that is marked "not off-loadable". For efficiency, we may also mark other RAM-resident objects as "not off-loadable".

4.7. Network Protocol for Object Migration

Recall that, when a shared object is created, it is assigned a unique identifier (POID) which does not change during the object's existence and, thus, does not contain information about the object's location. Each site knows which shared objects are stored locally but has no information about where other objects are stored. When a site (call it S) references a non-local object (say object X, whose POID is 12345), the PORTLANDIA server at site S broadcasts a request to all other sites saying, "Whoever has object POID=12345, please send it to site S when you are done using it." This message is called the *initial-request*.

Ignoring failures (and efficiency) for a moment, the process at site S that needs some shared object X begins by queueing a request for X and suspending. A communication process will be awakened, dequeue the request, and broadcast it to other sites. In the normal case, the foreign site possessing the object (say site T) will reply directly to the requesting site by sending object X using a *here-it-is* message. The communication process at the requesting site receives X, enters it into the PERSISTENT-OBJECT-TABLE, and sends an *acknowledgment* message back to site T. The original process is then reawakened.

What if the object is tied up in a transaction at site T? In that case, site T makes a note to send X immediately after the next commit operation. Since the initial broadcast request may be lost (due to network failure, local site failure, or remote site failure), site S must rebroadcast the request periodically until the object is received. If, upon receiving the request, site T determines that the object is tied up in a transaction, site T will send back a message saying "I probably got your request; no need to rebroadcast frequently." (Of course, site T may promptly crash and forget the request, so site S will still need to rebroadcast the request every few minutes.)

To support persistence of objects in the face of network and site crashes, we need to consider everything that can go wrong in the scenario above. First, network message may be lost because (1) the target site is currently down or (2) the target site received the message but crashed before completing a checkpoint. (Error-checking codes ensure that all corrupted messages are treated as lost messages.) Second, messages can be duplicated. For example, the sending site can take a checkpoint, send a message, crash, come back up, and retransmit the same message.

The approach PORTLANDIA adopts is to make a checkpoint immediately before every message is sent. (Conceptually, at least. An optimization will be introduced below to reduce the required disk I/O.) Once site S determines its need for X, it makes a note of its outstanding request for object X, commits to this fact, and then broadcasts the *initial-request* message. After this commit, site S is committed to eventually receiving X and will repeat the *initial-request* message until it receives and commits X.

When site T decides that object X is to be sent to site S, site T marks object X as *in-transit* in its PERSISTENT-OBJECT-TABLE, commits this fact, and then send a *here-it-is* message containing the object's data to site S. Site T will then continue to respond to *initial-request* messages for X by re-sending the *here-it-is* message until site T receives an *acknowledgment* message.

When site S receives a *here-it-is* message for object X, it first checks to sees if it has an outstanding request for object X. If not, it simply sends an acknowledgment back to T. (If site S has no outstanding request for X, it should not receive X's data. S could have received object X long ago and subsequently transmitted it on to some third site. Receiving X's data again would create a duplicate copy of X in the network, which is strictly forbidden.) If site S has an outstanding request for X, it allocates a RAM-resident object to store X's data, enters X into its PERSISTENT-OBJECT-TABLE, eliminates its outstanding request for X, commits, and finally sends an *acknowledgment* back to site T. (The *acknowledgment* need not be immediate and will be piggy-backed onto a later message. This will be discussed below.)

When a site T receives an *acknowledgment* for X, it can free all storage associated with object X and forget that X ever resided there. Site T responds to spurious *acknowledgments* by ignoring them.

In summary, there are three types of messages (*initial-request*, *here-it-is*, and *acknowledgment*) and the server takes a checkpoint before sending every message[5]. The checkpoint ensures that, should there be a network and/or site failure, the message can always be resent. Conversely, all messages are idempotent in the sense that they can be repeated without significant impact. Figure 1 summarizes PORTLANDIA's basic object migration path.

4.7.1. Logging to Support Reliable Communication Efficiently

To avoid the cost of taking a full checkpoint before each message transmission, a

---

[5] So far, a fourth message (call it the *I-probably-got-your-request-but-can't-send-the-object-right-away* message) has been mentioned, but it affects only performance, not correctness.

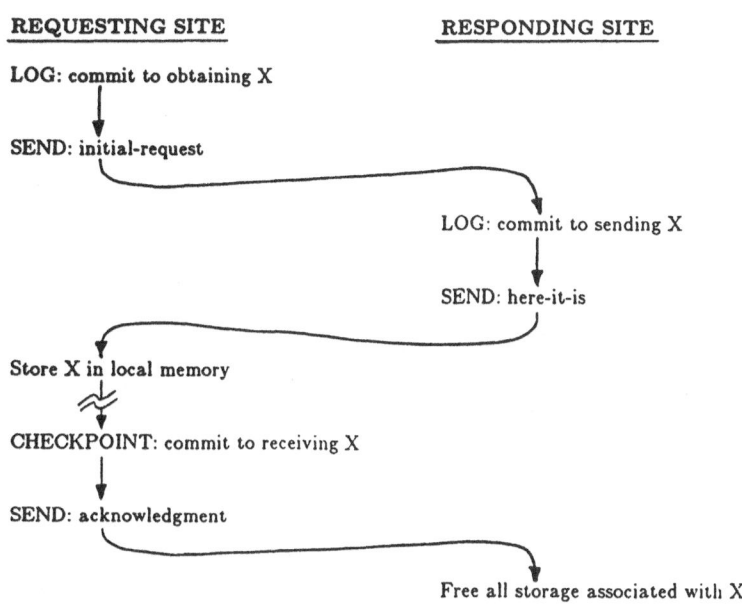

REQUESTING SITE   RESPONDING SITE

LOG: commit to obtaining X

SEND: initial-request

LOG: commit to sending X

SEND: here-it-is

Store X in local memory

CHECKPOINT: commit to receiving X

SEND: acknowledgment

Free all storage associated with X

Figure 1: Basic Network Protocol for Object Migration

COMMUNICATION-LOG is maintained on the disk. This log is kept in a fixed-sized area of the disk and is independent of the area containing the two checkpoint regions and the area containing blocks in the TRULY-FREED list, blocks in the RECENTLY-FREED list, and blocks containing disk-resident objects.

There are three types of records written to the COMMUNICATION-LOG corresponding to the three kinds of messages. The records are generally quite short and, to save disk space, several records are written in each disk block. Every time a new record is added to the log, it is added to the end of the log immediately (before any network communication) by overwriting the last block in the log. To support atomicity of log updates and resilience against uncompleted disk writes, two copies of the log are written in parallel using a sequence number scheme similar to the scheme described above for checkpointing RAM. The COMMUNICATION-LOG is emptied and begun anew at each checkpoint; if the allocated disk space is insufficient to hold the next record, a checkpoint will be forced. The COMMUNICATION-LOG is only read during crash recovery to update the recovering site's state to be consistent with the messages it sent since the last completed checkpoint.

The *initial-request* log record notes the fact that the recovering site had committed itself to receiving an object (e.g., X) before crashing. It contains little more than X's POID. If the log doesn't contain an *acknowledgment* record for the same object, the recovering site will then resume its effort to receive X by re-sending the *initial-request* message.

The *here-it-is* log record notes that the recovering site had committed itself to sending object X. This record contains the object's POID but need not contain the object's actual data. Why? Because the checkpoint of the recovering site's state still contains object X's data, as it was a the time of the last checkpoint. And we know that object X was not modified between the checkpoint and the crash, or else the site would have considered X to be in-use and would have delayed committing itself to sending X until after the next commit.

Finally, we avoid logging *acknowledgment* records altogether by delaying acknowledgment messages until directly after the next checkpoint. As *here-it-is* messages are received, a list of *pending-acknowledgment* records is accumulated. As the last step of checkpoint processing, we go through this list and send all pending *acknowledgment* messages. We do not expect object movement to be random. Instead, we expect objects to migrate in herds from a single site to another site all at once. By delaying *acknowledgments*, we can group many acknowledgments into a single network message, thereby reducing the per-object overhead of the *acknowledgment* messages.

4.7.2. An Optional Name Server to Eliminate Broadcast Messages

When requests for an object are broadcast, all sites are slowed down momentarily to process the message and check their PERSISTENT-OBJECT-TABLEs to see if they possess the desired object. To address this inefficiency, a *name server* can (optionally) be added to the network. A name server contains a mapping of POIDs to sites. A name server's mapping need not be entirely accurate: given a POID, the name server knows where the object *probably* is. When site S wants an object, instead of broadcasting a request to all sites, it sends the *initial-request* directly to name server. The name server then forwards the message to the most likely site. If the name server forwards the message to the wrong site, the request will be ignored and effectively lost. Thus, retransmissions of the *initial-request* should be broadcast to all sites. (The name server just ignores these broadcasts.) To keep its mapping up to date, the name server "snoops" on the network. Whenever the name server sees a *here-it-is* message, it updates its mapping.

4.8. Supporting Multiple Readers

One shortcoming of the design presented so far is that multiple readers of an object are not allowed to proceed in parallel. Any distributed system worth its salt should accommodate multiple readers. Previously, we implied that an object was at exactly one site at a time (ignoring "in-transit" objects). Such a normal object is called a *writable* object since whoever has it can modify it. To support reading, we allow a *writable* object to divide into two identical *readable* objects. For example, consider an object residing at site S. Site T needs to read the object, so it broadcasts a *read-request* message which is just like the *initial-request* message discussed above, except that site S responds by transforming the writable object into two readable objects and sending one of the readable objects to site T. If another site U also wants to read the object, either site S or site T can further divide the object. Now there are three readable versions of the object throughout the network.

What happens when site V wants to write an object that has been transformed into multiple readable versions? Site V broadcasts an *initial-request* message causing everybody to send their readable versions to site V, where they are merged back into a single writable object. Since some sites could be temporarily down, how do we know when we have collected all outstanding readable copies? Associated with each object copy is a *strength*. Objects are given a strength of 1.0 when they are created. Whenever an object is replicated to create two readable copies, the original strength is split between the two new objects. Whenever readable objects are coalesced back together, we add their strengths back together. Writable objects are then defined as those objects with a strength of 1.0.

5. RELATED RESEARCH

There have been a number of projects to integrate various object-oriented ideas into complete, working systems. In Servio Logic's Gemstone database system, for example, messages are sent to a central object server where they are executed [11, 12, 15]. Gemstone is a variant of the Smalltalk interpreter, modified to support large object spaces, resilience in the presence of a server crash, and indexing and associative retrieval of set objects.

D. Decouchant, who is building a distributed memory manager for Smalltalk [8], uses proxy objects and moves an object from one site to another by swapping the object with its proxy. Two other groups [5, 14] maintain local proxies for remote objects and forward messages to remote sites. Both groups are concerned with distributing objects in the context of Smalltalk. Their implementations are written solely above the virtual machine interface and do not attempt to replace existing, local object management. [13] also discuss extensions to the Smalltalk model to support sharing and persistence.

Other relevant work in the area of distribution, concurrency control, and/or persistent object storage certainly includes [7, 6, 10, 18, 19, 23, 24].

6. SUMMARY

In the context of PORTLANDIA, the distributed object server we are currently designing, *persistence* is defined as *sharing* plus *reliability*. The concept of sharing objects in general seems to subsume both sharing objects across sites and sharing objects across sessions. We discussed how sharing and reliability are provided in the object model implemented by the server. Objects are either local or shared and shared objects are shared using a transaction/commit protocol. Reliability is achieved using a checkpoint model of periodically saving local state (both local and shared objects) and is done independently of transaction committing. Then, with a scary lack of detail or rigor, we outlined a few ideas on how we plan to implement these features in the PORTLANDIA system.

REFERENCES

2. Andrews, T., and Harris, C., "Combining Language and Database Advances in an Object-Oriented Development Environment," *OOPSLA-87 proceedings*, p. 430-440, Orlando, Florida, 1987.

2. Atkinson, M.P., Morrison, R. and Pratten, G.D., "A Persistent Information Space Architecture," Persistent Programming Research Report 21, Universities of Glasgow and St. Andrews, 1986.

3. Atkinson, M.P. and Morrison, R., "Types, Bindings and Parameters in a Persistent Environment," *Proceedings on the Appin Workshop on Data Types and Persistence*, Universities of Glasgow and St. Andrews, Persistent Programming Research Report 16, August 1985.

4. Bancilhon, F., Barbedette, G., Benzaken, V., Delobel, C., Gamerman, S., LéCluse, C., Pfeffer, C.P., Richard, P. and Velez, F., "The Design and Implementation of O$_2$, an Object-Oriented Database System," *Proc. of the Second Intl. Workshop on Object-Oriented Database Systems (ooDBS-II)*, Bad Münster am Stein/Ebernburg, 27-30 September 1988.

5. Bennett, J.K., "The Design and Implementation of a Distributed Smalltalk," *OOPSLA Conference Proceedings*, Orlando, FL, p. 318-330, 1987.

6. Caplinger, M., "An Information System Based on Distributed Objects," *OOPSLA Conference Proceedings*, Orlando, FL, p. 126-137, 1987.

7. Cockshot, W.P., Atkinson, M.P., Chisholm, K.J., Bailey, P.J. and Morrison, R., "A Persistent Object Management System," *Software-Practice and Experience*, vol. 14, p. 49-71, 1984.

8. Decouchant, D., "The Design of a Distributed Object Manager for the Smalltalk-80 System," *OOPSLA Conference Proceedings*, Portland, OR, p. 444-452, 1986.

9. Ecklund, E. and Ecklund, D., "CAD Performance Requirements for Persistent Object Systems," *Proceedings of a Workshop on Persistent Object Systems*, Appin Scotland, 1987.

10. Liskov, B., "Distributed Programming in Argus," *CACM* 31(3), p. 300-312, March 1988.

11. Maier, D., Stein, J., Otis, A. and Purdy, A., "Development of an Object-Oriented DBMS," *OOPSLA Conference Proceedings*, Portland, OR, p. 472-482, 1986.

12. Maier, D. and Stein, J., "Development and Implementation of an Object-Oriented DBMS," in *Research Directions in Object-Oriented Programming* (eds. Bruce Shriver and Peter Wegner), MIT Press, 1987.

13. Merrow, T. and Laursen, J., "A Pragmatic System for Shared, Persistent Objects," *OOPSLA Conference Proceedings*, Orlando, FL, p. 103-110, 1987.

14. McCullough, P., "Transparent Forwarding: First Steps," *OOPSLA Conference Proceedings*, Orlando, FL, p. 331-330, 1987.

15. Penney, J., Stein, J. and Maier, D., "Is the Disk Half Full or Half Empty?: Combining Optimistic and Pessimistic Concurrency Control Mechanisms in a Shared, Persistent Object Base," *Proceedings of a Workshop on Persistent Object Systems*, Appin Scotland, p. 337-345, 1987.

16. Porter, H., Ecklund, E., Ecklund, D., Anderson, T.L. and Schneider, B., "A Distributed Object Server," *Proc. of the Second Intl. Workshop on Object-Oriented Database Systems*

(ooDBS-II), Bad Münster am Stein/Ebernburg, 27-30 September 1988.

17. Porter, H., Ecklund, E., Ecklund, D., Anderson, T.L. and Schneider, B., "A Distributed Smalltalk Object Model," Technical Report, Computer Research Laboratories, Tektronix, Inc., 1988.

18. Skarra, A., Zdonik, S. and Reiss, S., "An Object-Server for an Object-Oriented Database System," *Intl. Conf. on Object-Oriented Database Systems*, Pacific Grove, CA, 1986.

19. Spector, A.Z., "Performing Remote Operations Efficiently on a Local Computer Network," *CACM* 25(4), p. 246-260, April 1982.

20. Ungar, D., "Generation Scavenging: A Non-disruptive High Performance Storage Reclamation Algorithm," *Proceedings of the Software Engineering Symposium on Practical Software Development*, Pittsburgh, PA, 23-25 April 1984.

21. Ungar, D.M., *The Design and Evaluation of a High Performance Smalltalk System*, Ph.D. Dissertation, UC Berkeley, available from MIT Press, 1986.

22. Ungar, D. and Jackson, F., "Tenuring Policies for Generation-Based Storage Reclamation," *OOPSLA Conference Proceedings*, Orlando, Florida, 25-30 September 1988.

23. Weiss, S., Rotzell, K., Rhyne, T. and Goldfein, A., "DOSS: A Storage System for Design Data," *2nd Design Automation Conference*, June, 1986

24. Wiebe, D., "A Distributed Repository for Immutable, Persistent Objects," *OOPSLA Conference Proceedings*, Portland, OR, p. 453-465, 1986.

A Simple Object Storage System

Marc Shapiro, Laurence Mosseri

Institut National de la Recherche en Informatique et Automatique
Rocquencourt, France

ABSTRACT

We describe the Object Storage System (OSS) of the distributed object oriented operating system SOS. Our experience suggests that it is possible to cleanly integrate an efficient object storage system in an existing object-oriented language, with out special language constructs. The two key elements in our system are: separating the stored objects from their containers (which are objects too); and a generalized pointer type, which allows to efficiently refer to an object, within its container, in a location-independent manner.

1. INTRODUCTION

We present some features of the object storage service (OSS) for the SOS operating system [4]. SOS is a research program to build a distributed operating system, where all interfaces and communication is based on small-grained objects. Many elementary objects may execute together in a *context* or address space (similar to a Unix process with lightweight tasks); they communicate via invocation, i.e. plain (type-checked) procedure calls. Related elementary objects, executing in different contexts may be grouped to form a single distributed object or *group*. Objets in a group have mutual communication privileges.

To gain access to a remote service, a client object must first acquire a *proxy* [5] for the service: a local interface object for the group implementing the service. The proxy is *migrated* at the time of need (e.g. at first access) into the client's context. An object may be arbitrarily complex.

A storage server for the OSS is a particular context which is backed up on a long-term storage device. An elementary object is made persistent simply by migrating it to a storage server.

In the sequel of this paper, we explain the main features of objects, contexts, groups, and migration as they pertain to the storage of complex objects. We will show that in a rich object-oriented environment, it is possible to implement a simple, automatic, efficient, fully type-checked object storage facility. No special language or compiler features are needed, nor are complex OS mechanisms. All that is needed are: generic (parameterized) types, inheritance, and a conceptual separation between the stored objects and the storage containers. We conclude with considerations on the suitability of our current prototype, written in in C++ [6] and guested on top of a vanilla Unix, and planned extensions.

273

2. SOS OBJECTS

In this section, we will describe the normal programmer's new of SOS objects. The next section will describe them from the point of view of the OSS.

An object is an instance of a C++ *class* [6]. An object which must be khown to SOS is be of a class derived (i.e. inheriting) from class sosObject.[1] The base sosObject uses no data but defines the interface to a few virtual procedures which allow the SOS to invoke it, as we will see shortly.

The programmer of a derived class X may freely extend sosObject with arbitrary data, methods, and interface. The system may call those methods declared in the sosObject interface, which should be redefined by X. Users of class X may create and destroy instances, and may invoked their methods, as allowed by the X interface.

In C++, instantiation of an object runs a programmer-defined *constructor*. Consider instanciating class Y, which derives from X, which itself derives from sosObject. The constructor for class sosObject is first executed, then X's constructor, and finally Y's.[2]

Accordingly, when an SOS object is created, a constructor for *sosObject* is first called, which implements all the mechanism for interfacing with SOS, e.g. allocating an entry for it the object descriptor table. Thus, inheritence is enough to implement transparent interfacing with the operating system.

The object descriptor carries such information as a unique object ID (a 64 bit-number), group membership information, and references to *pre-requisite* objects, this object's required environment.

When an object is migrated, the system copies the data to the target context, and calls a special constructor to *re-initialize* the instance. But, just before this last step, the system checks for the presence of the pre-requisites; if not present it (recursively) migrates the latter. One of any object's prerequisites is its *code* object, which carries compiled methods for its class. The code object reinitialization constructor performs type-checking[3] and dynamic linking.

Note that a reinitialization constructor does not have to worry about copying the data or fixing pointers; that is taken care of by the generic OSS mechanisms we will describe now.

3. OSS MECHANISMS

In many object-oriented systems, I/O is performed by recursively calling encode/decode procedures [2] for each base class and each component object, with some mechanism to resolve forward and circular references. See for instance the description of the I/O facility

---

[1]sosObject is not a universal root: classes which need not to be known to the OS at run-time don't have to derive from sosObject. In the sequel we will refer to such non-SOS objects as "plain objects".

[2]When the instance is destroyed, the destructor procedures are called in the opposite order: first Y's, then X's, and finally sosObject's.

[3]Type-checking is not perfectly safe, as the type information is hashed into a 32-bit value.

for the OOPS C++ class library [1]. For large objects, this is potentially inefficient, and is a bad use of paged virtual memory. For small objects, it inefficient to do I/O and disk allocation on a per-object basis as this mechanism implies. In all cases, encode translates an internal, structured representation to a flat, ASCII-like representation; this process is expensive and most often overkill.

In SOS instead, the OSS handles the generic aspects of object I/O, i.e. copying data and resolving references, in the OSS. Data is transferred in raw form without encode/decode. On output, there is no overhead. On input, the re-initialization constructor is called, which needs to perform only class-specific data transformation. (For instance, the re-initialization constructor of code objects calls the dynamic linker and type-checker.)

Container objects are separate from thier content objects. The pointers that are part of the data in a container are lazy-evaluated.

3.1.   Object Containers

An object is a typed, programmer-defined abstraction, manipulated via a specific procedural interface. Internally, such an object takes up space in memory or on disk. For the system, this space is interpreted as untyped data (e.g. an array of pages) with a specific I/O semantics (e.g. paged to some file on disk). To capture this duality we introduce the concept of a *container*.[4] A container is an sosObject which manages memory and has an input/output interface. The memory it manages may contain one or many objects, which may be sosObjects, or plain objects, or primitive data types: integers, characters, etc.

A container is migrated as a whole. On input, all the memory it manages is mapped[5] into the target context. The reinitialization constructor of the container fixes the pointers it contains, as described in the next section.

Since memory may be allocated and released dynamically, a container is not necessarily a contiguous block of memory: indeed it is typically created in memory as a collection of small contiguous blocks (which we call segments), each containing a single object or datum. Segments may be added to (resp. removed from) an existing container by a declaration procedure. This adds it to (resp. removes it from) the linked list of pointers, described in the next section.

On output the memory is written out in raw form, without any transformation. We simply arrange to coalesce the blocks into a single, contiguous file.

3.2.   Pointers

Objects may be arbitrarily complex, and contain pointers to other data. On output, such pointers must be followed to write all the data. On input the pointers must be converted to contain valid addresses in the target context (as it may not be possible, or desirable, to allocate the pointed data at the same address as before).

---

[4]Previously referred to as a "storage objet" or simply a "file".
[5]In our prototype it is actually copied, as virtual memory is under the control of Unix.

Standard C++ pointers are indistinguishible at run-time from ordinary data without extra information, and therefore cannot be used for pointer-following and translation. A alternative is to use Object Identifiers, which are location-independent. This is not reasonable however, for two reasons. First, there are a lot of pointers, and it would be prohibitively expensive to go through a system call to resolve the OID, each time a "pointer" is dereferenced. Second, to replace pointers entirely with of OIDs would impose an awkward, unnatural, error-prone programming style.

Therefore we define a new data type ref (for "reference"). A ref is a structure associating: a real C++ pointer to the datum; the OID of the container for that datum; a key within that container (usually an offset); and a link field (all the ref's of a given container are linked together in a list).

When a container is output, its ref list is examined to find all the segments attached to it; each of them is written in raw form, if it has been modified since the last output.

On input, the container is read (mapped) into memory, and every pointer field of each of its ref from its list is reset to nil.

Its correct value of a ref is lazy-evaluated. The first time the ref is dereferenced, its pointer field is found to be nil. This causes the referenced container's input method to be invoked, which will read its data into memory if necessary. Then, using the key field, the datum's new address is computed and stored in the pointer field. The datum is now adressable directly via the pointer field.[6]

Fortunately, ref's may replace ordinary pointers with very little effort, because C++ allows to define *coercion* operations. Whenever the compiler expects a pointer and sees a ref instead, the coercion operation is generated. The coercion operator executes precisely the dereferencing procedure described in the last paragraph.

There is one small last difficulty: a pointer refers to an object of a particular type. If suffics to make ref a generic type parameterized by the type of the pointed object. Generic type do not exist in the current versions of C++, but they can be faked using macros.

4. GLOBAL VIEW

In this section, we will show the relations between complex objects and containers.

We will use the example of a "Document", a tree consisting of a root node (the description of the Document itself); interior nodes (Chapter, Section, and Paragraph objects), and leaves, which are portions of Text.

Such an Document is created by a Document Editor application. One or more objects are allocated per segment, connected together via ref's. The segments are attached to one or more containers, by threading the contained ref's of each container on a linked list. Finally the containers (and consequently, the contained objects) are made permanent by exporting them to a storage server.

---

[6]In effect this is a software emulation of the segmentation hardware of, for instance, Multics [3].

Let us suppose (arbitrarily) that the root objects of all documents are stored in a single container R, and individual "chapter" objects in separate containers.

Now suppose we start a fresh editor and wish to access some existing document. The editor must first find the ref of the root object Root1 for that document (e.g. by asking a name server), which we will call RR1 ("ref to Root1"). Then the editor will ask to instantiate Root1, de-referencing RR1: the root container R will be read into memory, and all the ref's it contains will be reset. Then the pre-requisites for Root1 will be loaded, including the Code object for class "Root of Document". The re-initialization constructor for Code will dynamically link it, and will check that the data is of the type expected by the editor (in this case, "Root of Document"). Finally, the re-initialization constructor for the Root1 is invoked, which in this case is a no-op.

Now suppose that Root1 contains ref's for the individual chapters. The pointer field of these have been reset to nil when container R was input. If we try to access Chapter 1, its ref will be de-referenced, which reads in its container, and dynamically links and type-checks its code. If we now access Section 1 of Chapter 1, we de-reference its ref, in the Chapter 1 data. Since the container is already in memory, it needs not to be read again. However the code for Sections is loaded, linked, and type-checked, and the pointer portion of the ref is set to its correct value. If we access Section 1 again, we will use that value directly.

When we subsequently access Section 2 of Chapter 1, both its container and its code are in memory. All that needs to be done is fix the value of its pointer field. And similarly for the other Sections of Chapter 1, and for Paragraphs within Sections, etc.

The editor may also access another document without additional overhead, since the "Root" container and code is already in memory.

REFERENCES

1. Keith Gorlen. OOPS, a C++ object-oriented program support class library. In *USENIX C++ Workshop*, Santa Fe (New Mexico), November 1987.

2. M. Herlihy and B. Liskov. A value transmission method for abstract data types. *ACM Transactions on Programming Languages and Systems*, 4(4):527–551, October 1982.

3. E.I. Organick. *The Multics system: an examination of its structure*. MIT Press, Cambridge, Mass. (USA), 1972.

4. Marc Shapiro. SOS: a distributed object-oriented operating system. In *2nd ACM SIGOPS European Workshop, on "Making Distributed Systems Work"*, Amsterdam (the Netherlands), September 1986. (Position paper).

5. Marc Shapiro. Structure and encapsulation in distributed systems: the Proxy Principle. In *Proc. 6th Intl. Conf. on Distributed Computing Systems*, pages 198–204, IEEE, Cambridge, Mass. (USA), May 1986.

6. Bjarne Stroustrup. *The C++ Programming Language*. Addison Wesley, 1985.

Part V

Measurement of Persistent Systems

Monitoring Execution of PS-algol Programs

Charles Zdzislaw Loboz
Department of Computer Science
Australian National University

Abstract

Monitoring program execution produces huge amounts of data. The various methods for reducing monitoring overhead are proposed and their performance for a sample of small programs given. For the sample programs the size of the trace files was reduced from tens of megabytes to tens of kilobytes by using basic blocks, monitored program locality and looping, general compression algorithms.

1. INTRODUCTION

The analysis of a program execution inherently involves the problem of *monitoring* a program execution. This problem, although not being an end in itself, is a key factor of obtaing good raw data about program behaviour. In fact, a number of paper exists which focuses mostly on the problem of monitoring - [3, 8, 10, 13, 14, 20, 26, 27, 28] to enumerate only a few. At the same time it seems impossible to find papers analysing in details the problem of reducing the monitoring overhead and presenting solutions to the obstacles encountered while trying to monitor program execution.

The main problems in this area are concisely summarized in [7]:

> existing facilities are difficult to use and the results are frequently misleading. Major shortcomings include inadequate or incomplete resolution, inability to relate measurement data to the source program and excessive overhead.

The commonly recognized problem of monitoring is the overhead. Alexander and Wortmann [2] note that `the time to interpret a program and analyse the data produced was, on average, two orders of magnitude greater than the time required to simply execute the program'.

1.1. Frequency analysis and sequence analysis

Monitoring of a program execution may be divided into two types - frequency monitoring and sequence monitoring. Frequency monitoring consists of counting the number of times given occurence took place (like execution of a given instruction). Sequence monitoring attempts to analyse also in which order things had happened during program execution. This classification, although not mentioned in papers found, seems natural from the point of view of what is monitored and how it is instrumented.

Most of the papers report the frequency monitoring [4, 30], only some papers attempt to measure some sequence-of-execution characteristics on the language level [5, 6]. More papers deal with a sequence of execution characteristics in some form on the machine level [2, 21, 16, 17]. The reason for using mostly frequency analysis seems to be the artifact problem. To analyse frequencies it is enough to set aside some memory for counters and install counters in critical points of the run-time system, which usually requires only several kilobytes of memory and about 1--2 % of program time - [18].

Analysis of sequence of events requires plenty of computer resources to produce the information, store it and analyse. With computers executing several millions of instructions per second the tracing an execution of a short program can produce several hundreds of megabytes - hardly a practical file size to work with, as it may not fit into any available output device! Kobayashi [17] mentions that programs in his sample frequently executed more than 5mln instructions - and because a magnetic tape can store only that much he was forced to use sampling.

While such overhead may acceptable for a (very) casual use, it precludes full analysis of program execution on a routine basis. It can be hardly expected that a user of a language will accept such a slow-down factor.

2. REDUCING THE MONITORING OVERHEAD

The approach used by authors of papers which report monitoring real-life programs varies - some are using frequency measurements , some avoid the overhead problem using short sample programs or small data sets. The high cost of a sequence analysis is clearly perceived by many authors but usually the problem of reducing it is omitted. On the other hand the papers proposing (or even applying) some overhead-reduction methods do not report any numbers on savings received.

To reduce the measurement artifact the simplest solution is to limit the list of activities we want to measure - [3]. The artifact is thus reduced but, as Coutant et al. [7] point out , this is equivalent to making some a priori assumptions about program behaviour, which is dangerous, especially in the case of high-level languages. The oldest paper known to the author, addressing this problem, is that by Knuth and Stevenson [15]. The authors are trying to find optimal points in a program source code to place software probes in order to measure statement frequencies.

Some papers are addressing a software-engineering problem, but such, that can be easily adapted to our needs. In software testing the problem is formulated as follows: while testing a program, in which points the software probes should be automatically inserted to obtain (after program execution) an information how much program code - and which program code - was not executed. Such information is then used to examine thoroughness of a test.

In [25] and [24] the Kirchoff's law is used to formulate a system of edge-flow equations of a program graph and probes inserted into each edge to find out if every path path of a program was executed. Probert [24] proposes usage of even smaller number of probes for `well-delimited programs'. To simplify and shorten his derivation a bit - in goto-less programs one path being taken is equivalent to the other path not being taken - so it is enough to insert a probe into one path and deduce the rest while postprocessing data. If only two way branches are allowed $2n$ probes are needed, but using Probert's method - only $n+2$ (where n is a number of branches in the program).

3. INSTRUMENTATION OF THE PS-ALGOL SYSTEM

This paper presents the instrumentation used and overhead savings obtained while monitoring some sample programs written in the PS-algol language. The PS-algol language belongs to the Algol family of languages [23]. Its associated virtual machine is described in [22] and the intermediate semantic program representation called he PAIL tree in [9].

The PS-algol system with PAIL operates in the following way:
1. the source program is translated into its PAIL tree representation
2. the code generator produces from the PAIL tree the PS-machine code
3. the code is run on an virtual machine interpreter

Thus the program execution can be seen as a walk through its PAIL tree.

To monitor program execution modifications were made in the code generator and in the interpreter. The code generator, while entering or leaving the PAIL tree node inserts into the PS-machine code a pseudoinstruction with this node number. At the same time the node description, containing the node type and other information, is written to a separate file (static-info).

The run-time code interpreter recognizes node-enter and node-leave pseudoinstructions and upon encountering them writes node numbers to the trace file. The information that must be dynamically processed is thus reduced to PAIL-tree node numbers, as the information about the node contents is kept in the static-info file.

After the test program is run the trace file contains the PAIL-tree node numbers in order of their processing. The analysing program reads node numbers from the trace file and the nodes' description from the static-info file. In this way the walk through the PAIL tree may be fully reconstructed. Also, such an instrumentation enables us to trace program execution on 3 levels: virtual machine level, PAIL tree level and even the source code level (the source program can be reconstructed from its PAIL tree form).

4. TESTING AN OVERHEAD SIZE

To test the monitoring overhead 7 test programs were run on a monitored system:
- queens - finding one solution to 8 queens problem, Wirth's coding
- 8qn - finding one solution to 8 queens problem, straightforward coding
- acker - ackerman function, input parameters 3,4
- erat - Erathosthenes' sieve for primes in 1..10,000
- huff - finding Huffman encoding for a 1000 line PS-algol program
- knight - knight's tour on a chessboard size 5 by 5, Wirth's coding
- gauss - Gauss-Jordan method with partial pivoting for random array, n = 100

The monitoring overhead is summarized in Table 1. The trace file contains four bytes per each node traversal. Upon entering a node 3 bytes are generated: one for enter-node operation, two for a node number. Upon leaving a node one byte for leave-node operation is generated. The trace file size is over two hundred kilobytes even for such a short problem as finding one solution to 8 queens problem. Additionally, even so innocently looking program as knight's tour on a chessboard size 5 by 5 produced the trace file with 30 megabytes of information!

Table 1: Global overhead characteristic

program	queens	8qn	acker	erat	huff	knight	gauss
trace (kb)	219.5	1,053.2	1,350.2	909.0	24,355.3	29,624.9	47,050.7
nodes (k)	56.2	269.6	345.6	232.7	6,234.9	7,584.0	12,045.0
instrs (k)	29.7	134.3	151.5	191.6	3,749.1	3,469.6	14,521.3
ins/node	0.5	0.5	0.4	0.8	0.6	0.5	1.2

Slightly startling may look the low number of the PS-machine instructions executed per one PAIL-tree node traversed - usually half an instruction per node. There are several reasons for this: about half of the node traversals does not involve processing any PS-machine code, as they contain `administrational information'. Additionally, the PS-algol virtual machine is no RISC design - the instruction set consists of almost 256 instructions.

The test programs used here are short and simple - so we must be prepared that the `real world' programs will produce traces at least an order of magnitude longer - i.e. hundreds of megabytes. Such overhead is obviously unacceptable and significant reduction must be sought.

5. GOING FOR BASIC BLOCKS

The idea of using basic blocks (as defined in [1]) as a trace tool to reduce trace file size has obviously been around for a while in different forms. Kobayashi [17] mentions that to reduce the trace size only jump instructions in the machine code were traced. The same method is mentioned by Alexander and Wortmann [2]. Although this is not identical to the basic block trace it is very similar.

The basic preposition of the method is that if the first statement of the basic block is executed then all others must be executed, too. While tracing a program execution we can emit to the trace file only the identifiers of the basic blocks and the program flow can be reconstructed using them and a basic block information stored in the static file. It may be expected that, on average, one basic block contains more than one instruction (machine instruction, PAIL node or source statement) so the trace file size will be reduced.

In Figure 1 the source code for the main procedure of the *queens* program is shown with the beginning of basic blocks marked with block identifiers in curly brackets. The graph shows the control flow of this procedure.

Figure 1: The 'try' procedure from the queens program - basic blocks

```
let try := proc(int i -> bool);nullproc
try := proc(int i ->bool)
begin {1} let j :=0; let q := false
repeat begin {2} j:=j+1; q := false;
    if a(j) and {3}b(i+j){4} and {5}c(i-j){6} do
    begin {7}
        x(i) := j; a(j) := false
        b(i+j) := false;   c(i-j) := false
        if i<8 then begin {8}
            q := try(i+1){9}
            if ~q do begin {10}
                a(j):=true
                b(i+j):=true;
                c(i-j):=true
                end {11}
        end
        else {12} q := true {13}
    end {14}
end
while ~(q or {15} j=8) {16}
{17} q
end
```

The code generator was modified to insert into the PS-algol machine code basic block identifiers instead of the PAIL-node markers. The PAIL information and basic block information was written to the static-info file. The PS-machine interpreter was modified to write to the trace file only basic block identifiers (2 bytes per basic block).

The reduction of the trace file size obtained will obviously depend on the program characteristics - how many instructions (or PAIL nodes) per basic block it has and which basic blocks are most frequently executed. Additionally we may expect some savings in the run-time system, as less monitoring information has to be processed.

Table 2 shows that an execution of one basic block is equivalent to an execution of 6 to 8 PAIL tree nodes or 3 to 5 virtual machine instructions. This means that the reduction in trace size is more than 10 - as instead of four bytes per node we are using now two bytes per basic block. The *gauss* program characteristics is very different from that of the other programs - its basic block execution is equivalent to an execution of 32 PAIL nodes and the reduction in trace size is significantly higher.

Table 2: Basic block trace characteristic

name	queens	8qn	acker	erat	huff	knight	gauss
trace size (kb)	13.1	76.9	100.9	79.8	1,748.7	2,136.6	733.5
compression coeff.	16.7	13.7	13.4	11.4	13.9	13.9	64.1
blocks (k)	6.7	39.4	51.7	40.9	895.3	1,094.0	375.6
nodes / block	8.4	6.8	6.7	5.7	7.0	6.9	32.1
instructions / block	4.4	3.4	2.9	4.7	4.2	3.2	38.7

It is difficult to compare these results with others, as - despite an extensive search - no other such data was found. Taking into account, however, that one basic block is roughly equivalent to a sequence of instructions with a jump instruction of some kind appended, the results are similar to that of MacDougall [19] which reports for his Cobol sample 25% of machine level instructions being branches, Chevance [5] reports 22% of Cobol statements (dynamically) being GOTOs, Kobayashi [16] gives average instruction path length for Fortran programs running on an IBM System/370 as 6.7, for Cobol programs 4.3. Also, Haikala [12] reports on 7 to 10 instructions executed on average between transfer of control on B6700, Wiecek [30] 3.9 instructions on VAX-11 for compiler programs.

The reduction obtained by using the basic block trace is significant, but the sizes of the trace files for test programs are still high - for longer programs they are in order of megabytes. Keeping in mind that "real-world" programs may produce traces an order of magnitude longer we need to look for further possibilities of reducing the trace size.

6. COMPRESSING BLOCK TRACE

There are several possibilities of reducing the trace file size even more. They will be now examined one by one. They will be all applied to the block trace file. The block trace file contains identifiers of all executed basic blocks in order of execution. Each block identifier is two-bytes long.

6.1. Basic blocks paths

Looking at the program control flow we can notice, that the graph traversal may be described in terms of basic block *paths*. For basic blocks having only one successor in the graph we can emit to the trace file only the identifier of the first basic block, because the successor must be executed if the predecessor was. This rule may be applied recursively to obtain paths length greater than one. For example in the *queens*' procedure we have paths of basic blocks {1,2}, {8,9} and so on.

This method is cheap both in implementation and run-time overhead, as the paths of the basic blocks can be obtained during compilation. Thus the run-time system needs only one bit per each basic block processed to know if the block number should be written out to the trace file or not. Rather unfortunately it looks like the savings achieved while using this method are small (Table 3, row 'path') - on test programs the average compression ratio was 1.4 and for the *gauss* program there were virtually no savings! So, it is disputable if this approach is really worth using in view of the complication added to the compiler/code generator.

Similar method called by the authors "Linear Code Sequence And Jump" was used by Hennel et al. [14] while testing for correctnes a set of Fortran programs, but although its saving feature was mentioned, no numbers were reported on the size of the savings.

6.2. Loop reduction

It seems to be a common knowledge, that most of the program execution takes place in loops. This can be used to compress the trace size.

The run-time system keeps the identifiers of the last n blocks executed in a buffer before writing them to the trace file. If a repated sequence of such block identifiers is found in the buffer then we have a loop. Instead of writing out all the blocks, we can write only the repeat factor and the block identifiers of one loop. Using a circular buffer and limiting maximum looked-for loop length the encoding of this method may give reasonably small execution time. Note, that only the lowest level loops are detected by this method.

The method was tested with a maximum loop length being limited to 64 basic blocks. The reduction of the trace file size received while using this method ranges from 1.5 to 5 for our test programs (Table 3, row 'loop'). While analysing the trace in details it transpired that the main reason for this fairly small compression coefficient for most programs was the fact that loop repetition facctor was usually small and loop sequences were interspersed with some not-in-loop block identifiers.

The method was then modified, to keep in an additional buffer recently encountered loops and write to the trace file loop position in the buffer whenever possible. The compression ratio was at least doubled in comparison with the previous method. (Table 3, row 'loopb').

6.3. Stack compression

Another compression method tried is based on a loop detection algorithm as described by Kobayashi [17] (a similar algorithm was also used by Clark [6] to analyse locality of list references).

A stack of recently used basic block identifiers is implemented in the run-time system. When a basic block identifier processed by the run-time system resides on the stack, then its stack position is emitted, the block identifier in the stack is moved to the top of the stack. If the block identifier is not in the stack then it is put on the top and the block identifier emitted. If we have a loop then we have a long runs of identical stack distances. They may be compressed by emitting stack distance preceeded with the repeat factor.

The efficiency of this method depends on how localized the code is - if the probability of finding the block identifier in the stack is near 1.0 the compression coefficient should be near 2.0, assuming that the stack position can be encoded in one byte and block identifier in two bytes. Additionally, we can expect savings from not writing out the repeated sequences of stack distances.

The method was tested with the stack size 64. The compression coefficients (Table 3, row 'stack') were generally better than for any of the previous methods, reaching - for the *gauss* program - 32.1! It used twice as much CPU time as loops.

6.4. General compression algorithms

Two general compression methods: Huffman-based encoding and Lempel-Ziv adaptative compression algorithm were tried also on a block trace files. For the text files they are giving roughly similar results with compression coefficients ranging from 1.5 to 3.0.

Standard UNIX programs *compact* [11] and *compress* [29] were used. The performance of Huffman encoding was rather poor - compression coefficients ranged from 1.5 to 4.5 (Table 3, row 'Huffman'). Lempel-Ziv's performance was sensational (Table 3, row 'Lempel - Ziv') giving for longer files compression coefficients about 30! The main reason behind this succes story is the greedy string-parsing method which enables better encoding of randomly scattered patterns which are not exactly loops and short loops. It is worth noticing, that *any* Huffman-based algorithm cannot use less than one bit per block identifier on output, so for block traces the theoretical maximum compression obtained cannot be better than 16 - while the LZW method gives compression coefficients almost twice as good.

Table 3: Summary of the compression coefficients for different methods

program	queens	8qn	acker	erat	huff	knight	gauss
paths	1.4	1.3	1.4	1.0	1.4	1.4	1.0
loops	1.5	1.5	13.5	4.4	2.1	1.9	15.3
repeated loops	2.4	2.0	25.8	15.8	3.4	5.1	24.1
stack	3.2	4.8	2.4	14.1	4.6	4.2	32.1
Huffman	2.88	2.44	1.56	3.99	2.39	2.64	4.66
Lempel - Ziv	9.5	14.9	32.0	29.0	26.3	30.3	59.0

7. COMBINED METHODS

Some of the methods applied may be used together to obtain further reduction. For example we can apply LZW method to compress the output of any other method (except LZW and Huffmann). Table 4 gives the total compression coefficients received after applying LZW method to the original block trace and to the outputs of other methods.

Table 4: Compression coefficients for combined compression methods

name	queens	8qn	acker	erat	huff	knight	gauss
LZW(raw)	9.5	14.9	32.0	29.0	26.3	30.3	59.0
LZW(path)	8.6	13.8	31.3	28.8	23.9	27.2	59.3
LZW(path(raw))	11.9	17.9	44.7	29.8	32.9	36.8	59.4
LZW(loop)	5.0	8.2	4.1	5.3	7.1	8.3	5.5
LZW(loop(raw))	7.6	11.9	54.9	23.7	14.9	15.9	84.9
LZW(loopb)	5.2	9.4	5.0	5.8	10.6	10.2	11.5
LZW(loopb(raw))	12.3	19.1	129.8	91.9	35.7	52.3	277.4
LZW(stack)	4.2	5.7	25.4	4.0	9.4	13.0	3.8
LZW(stack(raw))	13.7	27.6	61.1	57.1	43.0	54.1	122.4

As expected, the compression coefficient of the LZW method is lower when applied to an output of any loop-reduction method than to the raw block trace file - because some regularities in the original file are lost after going through the loop compression. Additional factor is the size of the compressed file - the LZW algorithm works better on longer files.

For both loopb and stack methods the combined compression coefficient is better (for all programs) than the compression coefficient of the method or LZW algorithm.

8. DISCUSSION OF RESULTS RECEIVED

As it may be seen from the compression factors the size of the trace file may be reduced to quite manageable level - from tens of megabytes to tens of kilobytes. Although combination of many techniques is possible, to achieve siplicity of the design it may be better to use not more than 3 of them in cascade: basic block, stack compression method and LZW algorithm. Table 5 gives the sizes of trace files (in kilobytes) before and after applying each of them to the output of the previous one.

Table 5: Sizes of trace files (in kilobytes) before and after compression

program	queens	8qn	acker	erat	huff	knight	gauss
after node trace	219.5	1,053.2	1,350.2	909.0	24,355.3	29,624.9	47,050.7
after block trace	13.1	76.9	100.9	79.8	1,748.7	2,136.6	733.5
after stack cmpr	4.1	15.9	41.9	5.7	380.9	512.6	22.8
after LZW cmpr	1.0	2.8	1.7	1.4	40.7	39.5	6.0

No other paper was found to report any solution of this kind to the overhead problem therefore these results cannot be compared with others.

The above results should be by no means construed as a universal solution to the problem. The sample programs used in tests are small and the reduction in size seems to be heavily program-dependent. The problem how these techniques will work on large-scale program remains an open question.

If such a reduction will be possible for bigger programs it will open a possibility of using program execution tracing routinely.

REFERENCES

1. A.V. Aho and J.D. Ullman. *Principles of Compiler Design.* Addison-Wesley Publishing Company, Reading, Massachusetts, 1977.

2. W. G. Alexander and D. B. Wortman. Static and dynamic characteristics of XPL programs. *Computer,* 8(11):41-46, 1975.

3. J. Arthur and J. Ramamathan. Design of analysers for selective program analysis. *IEEE Transactions on Software Engineering,* SE-7(1):39-51, 1981.

4. D.Brailsford, E. Foxley, and K.Mander. Run-time profiling of Algol 68-r programs using DIDYMUS and SCAMP. *SIGPLAN Notices,* 12(6):35, 1977.

5. R.J. Chevance and T.Heidet. Static profile and dynamic behavior of Cobol programs. *SIGPLAN Notices,* 13(4):44-57, 1978.

6. D.W. Clark. Measurements of dynamic list structure use in Lisp. *IEEE Transactions on*

Software Engineering, SE-5(1):51-59, 1979.

7. G.A. Coutant, R.E. Griswold, and D. R. Hanson. Measuring the performance and behaviour of Icon programs. IEEE transactions on Software Engineering, SE-9:93-108, January 1983.

8. M. de Prycker. A performance analysis of the implementation of addressing methods in block-structured languages. *IEEE Transactions on Computers*, C-31(2):155-163, 1982.

9. A. Dearle A persistent architecture intermediate language. Persistent Programming Research Report 35, University of Glasgow, Department of Computing Science; University of St. Andrews, Department of Computational Science, Glasgow G12 8QQ, Scotland, St. Andrews, KY16 9SS, Scotland, 1987.

10. E. Foxley and D. Morgan. Monitoring the run-time activity of Algol 68-r programs. *Software - Practice and Experience*, 8:29-34, 1978.

11. R. G. Gallager. Variations on a theme of Huffman. *IEEE Transactions on Information Theory*. IT-24(6):668-674, November 78.

12. I. J. Haikala. More design data for stack architectures. Proc. of the 1982 Conf., 1982.

13. M. A. Hennel, D. Hedley, and M. Woodward. Quantyfying the test effectiveness of Algol-68 programs. *SIGPLAN Notices*, 12(6):36-41, 1977.

14. M. A. Hennel, M. R. Woodward, and D. Hedley. On program analysis. *Information Processing Letters*, 5(5):136-140, 1976.

15. D. E. Knuth and F. Stevenson. Optimal measurement points for program frequency counts. *BIT*, 14:313-322, 1973.

16. M. Kobayashi. Dynamic profile of instruction sequences for the IBM System/370. *IEEE Transactions on Computers*, C-32(9):859-861, 1983.

17. M. Kobayashi. Dynamic characteristics of loops. *IEEE Transactions on Computers*. C-33(2):125-132, 1984.

18. Z. Loboz. PS-algol machine monitoring. Persistent Programming Research Report 36, June 1987, University of Glasgow - University of St. Andrews, Scotland, UK.

19. M. H. MacDougall, Instruction-level program and processor modelling. *Computer*, July 1984.

20. S. Matwin and M. Missala. A simple, machine independent tool for obtaining rough measures of Pascal programs. *SIGPLAN Notices*, 11(8), 1976.

21. G. McDaniel. An analsysis of a MESA instruction set using dynamic instruction sequences. SIGPLAN Notices, 17(4), 1982.

22. PPRR-11. PS-algol abstract machine manual. Persistent Programming Research Report 11, 1985. University of Glasgow - University of St. Andrews, Scotland, UK.

23. PPRR-12. The PS-algol reference manual - fourth edition. Persistent Programming Research Report 12, University of Glasgow - University of St. Andrews, Scotland, UK.

24. R. L. Probert. Optimal insertion of software probes in well-delimited programs. *IEEE*

Transactions on Software Engineering, SE-8(1):34-42, 1981.

25. C. Ramamoorthy, K. Kim, and W. Chen. Optimal placement of software monitors aiding systematic testing. *IEEE transactions on Software Engineering*, SE-1:403-411, July 1975.

26. G. D. Ripley. Program Perspectives: A relational representation of measurement data. *IEEE Transactions on Software Engineering*, SE-3(4): 296-300, 1977.

27. G.D Ripley and R.E. Griswold. Tools for the measurement of SNOBOL4 programs. *SIGPLAN Notices*, 10(5), 1975.

28. R. Snodgrass. Monitoring in a software development environment: a relational approach. *SIGPLAN Notices*, 19(5):124-131, 1984.

29. T. A. Welch. A technique for high performance data compression. *IEEE Computer*, 17(6):8-20, June 1984.

30. C. A. Wiecek. A case study of VAX-11 instruction set usage for compiler construction. *SIGPLAN Notices*, 17(4):177-184, 1982.

Performance Evaluation in a Persistent Object System

Peter J Bailey
University of Glasgow

ABSTRACT

This paper describes some recent results of installing instrumentation into a PS-algol implementation. The results are presented in graphic form together with a discussion of their implications.

1.   INTRODUCTION

The object of the work described in this paper was to build instrumentation into parts of the PS-algol abstract machine [4]. By taking dynamic measurements of the abstract machine it was hoped to identify areas of improvements within the structure of the abstract machine and so gain some insight in to how to go about making it more efficient. To this end the abstract machine implementation was modified and two test cases run against it. An analysis of the data produced is given followed by observations and conclusions to be drawn from the data.

It should be noted that this paper describes only interim results. This research requires far more information to be obtained from a much wider range of test cases.

2.   INSTALLED INSTRUMENTATION

The implementation of PS-algol used for this research was release 4.8 and was running on a Sun 3/60 with 4Mb of memory and a local 327Mb disk. This machine was running under SunOS version 4.0.

The instrumentation added to the abstract machine covers two distinct areas of the PS-algol implementation:

- machine instructions;
- objects.

2.1.   Instruction Instrumentation

Initially it was intended to obtain results for three different aspects of the abstract machine instruction set, namely:

1.   instruction execution speed;
2.   the number of instructions executed between jumps;
3.   the number of instructions executed between PID (Persistent IDentifier) de-references [4].

Measurement of the abstract instruction execution speed, combined with the relative number individual instructions executed, was intended to identify hot spots within the abstract machine. The highest precision timers provided on the available hardware provide timings in microseconds. Unfortunately the resolution of these timers is 16.67 *milli*seconds [3]. It was found by experimentation that all the abstract machine instructions execute in less time than the resolution of these timers. It was therefore decided to forego such instruction timing.

In order to get an insight into the modularity of programs written in PS-algol, measurement of the number of instructions executed between jumps was made. Should the results show that there are a large number of instructions executed between jumps, then this would imply that the programs were monolithic in nature.

Measurement of the number of instructions executed between PID de-references provides information on the way in which the persistent store is used by the programmer. PID de-reference in this context means any pointer de-reference which requires access to the database in order to bring into volatile store the required object. There is also important information to be obtained by considering the temporal spacing of PID de-references. For example, an initial burst of PID de-referencing followed by a protracted absence, would imply that an initial working set of data had been extracted from the database, followed by activity working within that set., whereas temporally regularly spaced PID de-references might imply that at most a minimal working set had been created.

Other information that can be obtained from measuring the number of instructions executed between PID de-references is, how well the underlying POMS (Persistent Object Management System) [2] code is supporting database access. For example, if there are a large number of cases where PID de-references are separated by very few instructions, say between one and ten, then this may indicate that some pre-loading by the POMS code would significantly reduce the number of PID de-references.

2.2. Object Instrumentation

The instrumentation of objects within the PS-algol environment consists of two parts:

- measurement of the size and type of objects dynamically created;
- measurement of the size and type of objects brought in from the database.

By measuring the size and type of objects created during program execution, it was intended to discover whether there are any ways in which a different space allocation algorithm would be advantageous. For example, if it turned out that the average object size was close to that of a block, then allocation could be made in block size units aligned on block boundaries, thereby taking advantage of any underlying hardware/software support.

Measuring the size and type of objects brought in from the database is intended to give information concerning the use made of objects stored in the database. For example, if the results show that the most prevalent objects brought in are of a similar size, then this may have an impact on the persistent object storage regime.

3. TEST CASES

One problem in writing test cases for a system with which one has been closely involved in the design, is that it is extremely difficult not to produce code which takes advantage of specific implementation aspects of the system. It was therefore felt a requirement that the test cases be written by someone not involved in the original system design.

It was decided that a package of programs, written at Glasgow by S Blott and R Cooper [1], would provide a useful suite of test cases. This package of programs provides the user with a bibliographic database, with facilities for: initially bulk loading the database from a file containing bibliographic references; scanning a source paper replacing citations in the running text with consistently formated citations and finally producing a sorted list of citations; various browsing and editing features for manipulation of the stored citations. The suite of programs consists of approximately 6,713 lines of source code and 236 procedures contained within 36 source modules. The user interface to this package consists of multiple windows and menus, manipulated by a mouse, with textual input provided via a standard keyboard.

For each of the four sets of measurements taken, the package was run twice, once for bulk loading the database from a source file consisting of 320 discrete entries held over a total of 3,212 lines and once for application to a test paper consisting of 32 citations held in 435 lines of source text.

4. RESULTS AND OBSERVATIONS

The data described below was obtained by running a modified interpreter which sequentially dumped information into a standard UNIX file. These files contain streams of instruction counts or object types and sizes, depending upon the specific test. After running the test cases just over 18Mb of data was produced. This data was then analysed and condensed by use of a Mac II running S-algol. The data resulting from this analysis was then further refined into graphical form using various Macintosh applications.

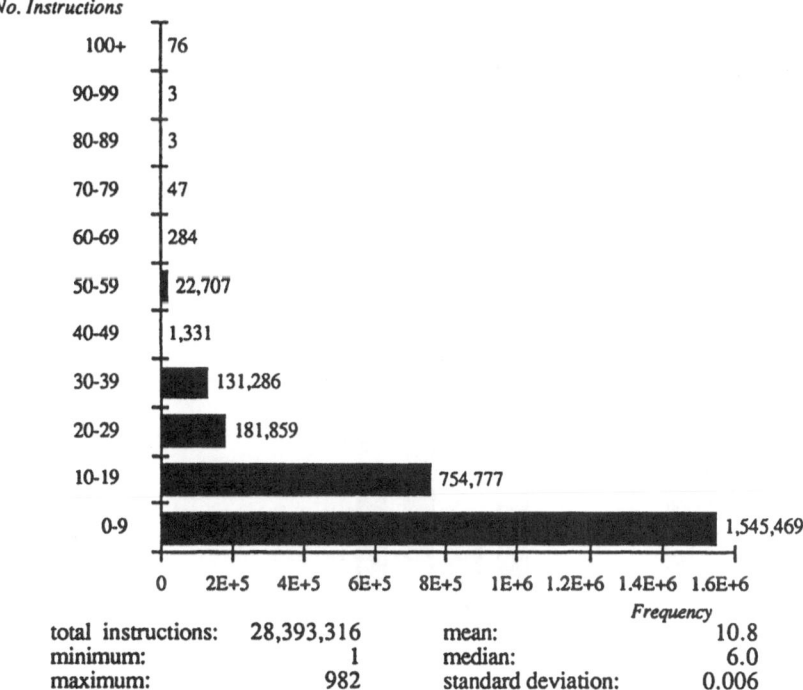

total instructions:	28,393,316	mean:	10.8
minimum:	1	median:	6.0
maximum:	982	standard deviation:	0.006

Figure 1: Instructions Between Jumps For Database Loading

The results obtained from bulk loading the database with respect to the number of instructions executed between jumps are given in figure 1. To simplify the presentation of the results, they are given in the form of a frequency diagram, followed by a table of calculated values. The x-axis indicates the range of instructions executed between jump instructions and the y-axis indicates the frequency of occurrence of a given range.

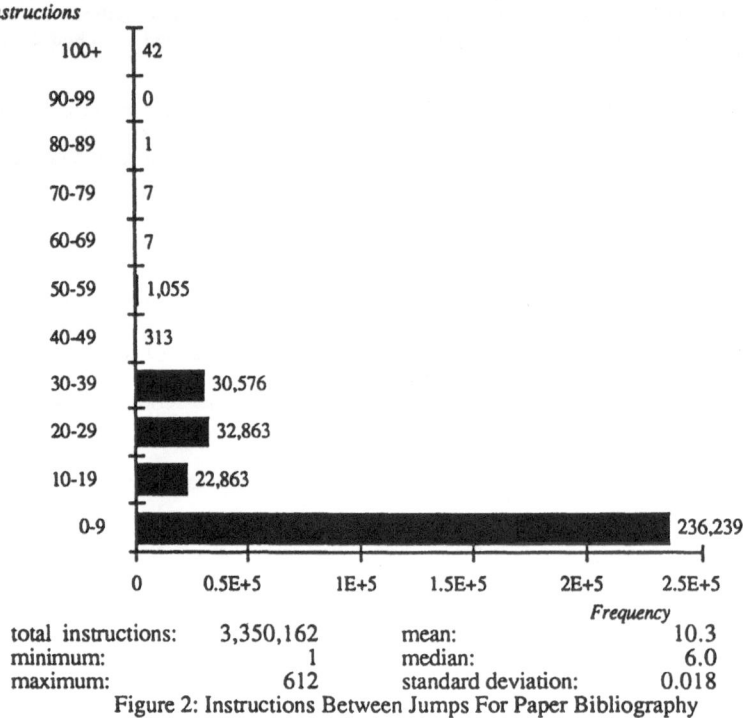

total instructions:	3,350,162	mean:	10.3
minimum:	1	median:	6.0
maximum:	612	standard deviation:	0.018

Figure 2: Instructions Between Jumps For Paper Bibliography

A similar set of figures were obtained by using the package to scan the sample paper. These are given in figure 2.

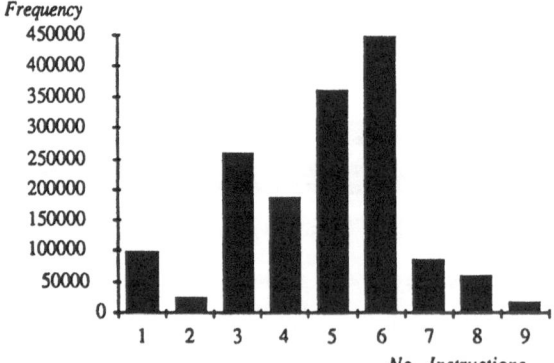

Figure 3: Instructions Between Jumps For Database Loading

It may seen by comparing both sets of results that there is a very close correlation between them. Perhaps the most important information to be gathered from these results are that jump instructions account for just under 10% of the total number of instructions executed.

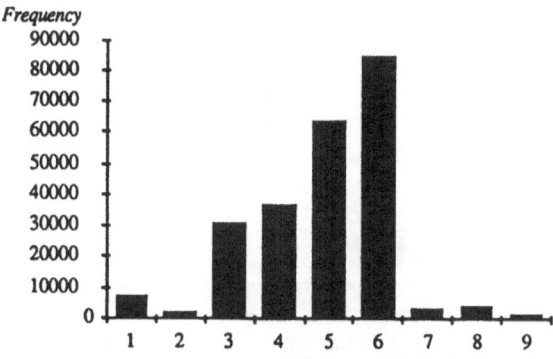

Figure 4: Instructions Between Jumps For Paper Bibliography

This immediately gives an upper bound to the possible increased efficiency through jump instruction optimisation.

A further expansion of the instruction counts in the range one to nine is given in figures 3 and 4. Inter jump counts of one (jumps to jumps) account for between 2.3% and 3.8% of all jump instructions executed. This clearly indicates what effect optimising them out would produce.

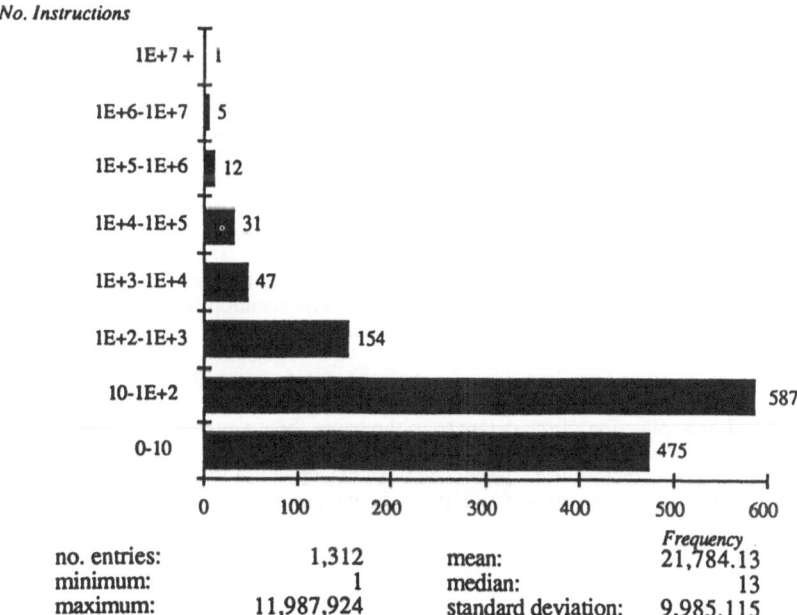

Figure 5: Instructions Between PID De-references For Database Loading

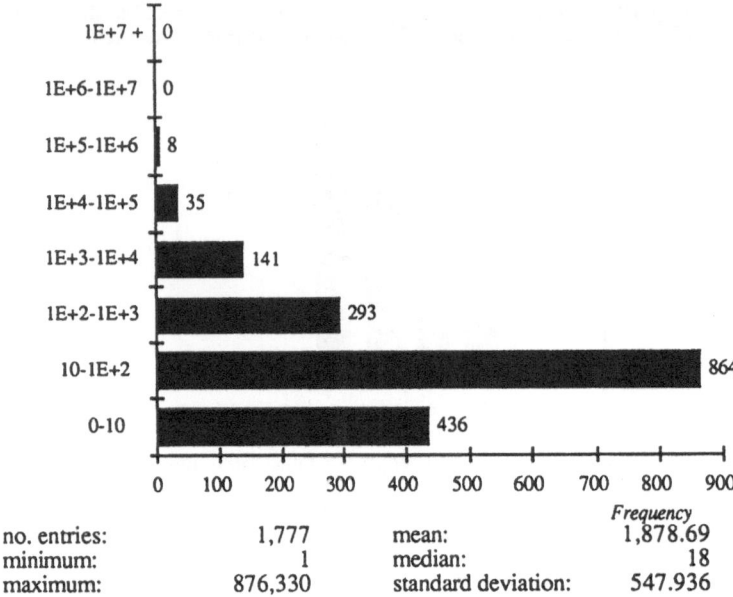

No. Instructions

1E+7 +	0
1E+6-1E+7	0
1E+5-1E+6	8
1E+4-1E+5	35
1E+3-1E+4	141
1E+2-1E+3	293
10-1E+2	864
0-10	436

Frequency

no. entries:	1,777	mean:	1,878.69
minimum:	1	median:	18
maximum:	876,330	standard deviation:	547.936

Figure 6: Instructions Between PID De-references For Paper

Results obtained for determining the number of instructions executed between PID de-references can be found in figures 5 and 6. It is quite clear from the calculation of standard deviation that the data is particularly badly skewed.

By analysing both the bulk loading data and the paper data in a temporal manner, it was observed that there was initially a flurry of activity from the database, followed by an extremely long period of zero database activity (11,987,924 instructions to be exact), followed by a short burst of database activity towards the end of program execution. This can be explained by the program initialising a working set from the database, using that working set during program execution and then creating a fresh working set for the program termination.

This is quite encouraging from an overall system point of view, in that it indicates that database accesses are clustered within distinct time periods during program execution. This will be useful when considering the scheduling of multiple concurrent PS-algol processes.

Another observation to be made from both sets of data is that there are a significant number of PID de-references which are separated by less than ten instructions. For database loading there were 475 or >36%. For application of the database to the paper there were 436 or >24% This implies that a strategy of *eager loading* should be investigated, by which is meant loading some or all of the objects which are themselves referenced by the object whose PID is currently being de-referenced. To get a more precise view of how this should be implemented will require more data gathering and analysis.

The data obtained by counting object sizes and types for both dynamically created objects and those brought in from non-volatile store, is presented at the end of the paper. It is portrayed in tabular form, with information given for each object type regarding the number of objects, minimum, maximum and total object sizes and the mean, median and standard deviation for these sizes. There is also presented, with each table, another set of values taken over the whole range of object types.

String

no. entries:	220,863
minimum:	2
maximum:	259
total size:	809,235
mean:	3.664
median:	3
standard deviation:	0.008

File

no. entries:	1
minimum:	132
maximum:	132
total size:	132
mean:	132
median:	132
standard deviation:	0

Structure

no. entries:	47,251
minimum:	3
maximum:	20
total size:	204,054
mean:	4.319
median:	4
standard deviation:	0.005

Vec.pntrs

no. entries:	118,271
minimum:	4
maximum:	103
total size:	509,684
mean:	4.309
median:	4
standard deviation:	0.008

Vec.procs

no. entries:	3
minimum:	13
maximum:	19
total size:	47
mean:	15.667
median:	15
standard deviation:	1.44

Vec.intbs

no. entries:	117,261
minimum:	4
maximum:	19,118
total size:	2,348,492
mean:	20.028
median:	20
standard deviation:	0.171

Frame

no. entries:	686,531
minimum:	12
maximum:	67
total size:	13,737,460
mean:	20.010
median:	19
standard deviation:	0.005

Code.vec

no. entries:	15
minimum:	5
maximum:	5
total size:	75
mean:	5
median:	5
standard deviation:	0

Imdesc

no. entries:	237922
minimum:	7
maximum:	7
total size:	1,665,454
mean:	7
median:	7
standard deviation:	0

Overall Results

No. entries:	1,428,118
Minimum:	2
Maximum:	19,118
Total Size:	19,274,633
Mean:	13.497
Median:	16
Standard Deviation:	0.016

Figure 7: Dynamic Object Creation For Database Loading

Figures 7 and 8 show the data derived from measuring the size and type of objects dynamically created while bulk loading the database and applying the database to the paper. All sizes are given in 32 bit words. The total number of objects at 1,428,118 and 202,338 indicate just how

String

no. entries:	7,691
minimum:	2
maximum:	52
total size:	38,838
mean:	5.05
median:	3
standard deviation:	0.071

File

no. entries:	2
minimum:	132
maximum:	132
total size:	264
mean:	132
median:	132
standard deviation:	0

Structure

no. entries:	2,454
minimum:	3
maximum:	17
total size:	11,070
mean:	4.511
median:	4
standard deviation:	0.026

Vec.pntrs

no. entries:	29,374
minimum:	4
maximum:	53
total size:	144,540
mean:	4.921
median:	4
standard deviation:	0.035

Vec.procs

no. entries:	2
minimum:	13
maximum:	19
total size:	32
mean:	16
median:	13.5
standard deviation:	2.121

Vec.intbs

no. entries:	29,111
minimum:	6
maximum:	2,007
total size:	479,027
mean:	16.455
median:	16
standard deviation:	0.130

Frame

no. entries:	76,182
minimum:	14
maximum:	48
total size:	1,646,436
mean:	21.612
median:	20
standard deviation:	0.021

Code.vec

no. entries:	915
minimum:	5
maximum:	5
total size:	4575
mean:	5
median:	5
standard deviation:	0

Imdesc

no. entries:	56,607
minimum:	7
maximum:	7
total size:	396,249
mean:	7
median:	7
standard deviation:	0

Overall Results

No. entries:	202,338
Minimum:	2
Maximum:	2,007
Total Size:	2,721,031
Mean:	13.448
Median:	16
Standard Deviation:	0.027

Figure 8: Dynamic Object Creation For Paper

hard the space allocation machinery is being utilised. Having between 37% and 48% of the objects created being frames, shows how much room there is for improvement in the area of redundant frame removal This in turn will have an impact on the number of garbage collections required.

String			Structure	
no. entries:	249		no. entries:	116
minimum:	2		minimum:	3
maximum:	67		maximum:	14
total size:	1,850		total size:	678
mean:	7.43		mean:	5.845
median:	4		median:	5
standard deviation:	0.569		standard deviation:	0.275

Vec.pntrs			Vec.procs	
no. entries:	328		no. entries:	43
minimum:	4		minimum:	5
maximum:	131		maximum:	27
total size:	5,426		total size:	481
mean:	16.543		mean:	11.186
median:	4		median:	9
standard deviation:	1.528		standard deviation:	0.955

Vec.intbs			Frame	
no. entries:	197		no. entries:	36
minimum:	4		minimum:	17
maximum:	7,807		maximum:	125
total size:	12,743		total size:	2,548
mean:	64.685		mean:	70.778
median:	20		median:	74.5
standard deviation:	39.41		standard deviation:	5.834

Code.vec			Imdesc	
no. entries:	157		no. entries:	191
minimum:	5		minimum:	7
maximum:	453		maximum:	7
total size:	9,636		total size:	1,337
mean:	61.376		mean:	7
median:	33		median:	7
standard deviation:	5.762		standard deviation:	0

Overall Results

No. entries:	1,317
Minimum:	2
Maximum:	7,807
Total Size:	34,699
Mean:	26.347
Median:	7
Standard Deviation:	5.989

Figure 9: Importation Of Objects For Database Loading

Figures 9 and 10 show the data derived from measuring the size and type of objects imported from non-volatile store into RAM, for both bulk loading the database and applying the database to the paper. From both sets of data it can be seen that the same types of object are the most prevalent, these being strings, structures, vectors of pointers and vectors of integers/booleans. The prevalence of the later may be explained by the fact that images are internally held in this PS-algol implementation as vectors of integers. With any user interface based on interaction via menus, there are bound to be a lot of images being manipulated.

String		**Structure**	
no. entries:	479	no. entries:	299
minimum:	2	minimum:	3
maximum:	45	maximum:	14
total size:	2,860	total size:	1,666
mean:	5.971	mean:	5.572
median:	3	median:	5
standard deviation:	0.311	standard deviation:	0.129
Vec.pntrs		**Vec.procs**	
no. entries:	342	no. entries:	34
minimum:	4	minimum:	5
maximum:	131	maximum:	27
total size:	5462	total size:	374
mean:	15.971	mean:	11
median:	4	median:	7.5
standard deviation:	1.348	standard deviation:	1.072
Vec.intbs		**Frame**	
no. entries:	196	no. entries:	31
minimum:	4	minimum:	21
maximum:	97	maximum:	123
total size:	4,719	total size:	2,164
mean:	24.077	mean:	69.806
median:	20	median:	76
standard deviation:	0.881	standard deviation:	6.072
Code.vec		**Imdesc**	
no. entries:	102	no. entries:	190
minimum:	5	minimum:	7
maximum:	453	maximum:	7
total size:	7,886	total size:	1,330
mean:	77.314	mean:	7
median:	51	median:	7
standard deviation:	7.736	standard deviation:	0

Overall Results

No. entries:	1,673
Minimum:	2
Maximum:	453
Total Size:	26,461
Mean:	15.816
Median:	5
Standard Deviation:	0.734

Figure 10: Importation Of Objects For Paper

It is interesting to find the mean and median values indicating the prevalence of such small objects. This implies that the algorithms dealing with the movement of objects from non-volatile store into RAM should be tuned for transference of small objects.

It is also important to notice that in all four sets of data involving object sizes and types, the mean and median sizes range from 13.4 to 26 and from 5 to 16 words respectively, yet the minimum size is 2 and the maximum sizes range from 453 to 19,118. This supports the theory that the algorithms dealing with object movement and creation should be optimised for handling small sized objects.

5. CONCLUSIONS

Conclusions based on such small amounts of data would inevitably be somewhat tenuous, however the data gathered may be used to target more specific areas for future measurement. Such areas would include:

1. further investigation into the importation of objects from non-volatile store, with a view to *eager loading* of objects;
2. further analysis of the storage algorithms for objects in non-volatile store, with a view to possibly using clustering techniques for holding associated data;
3. removal of redundant frame generation.

The reason for including the tables of data in this paper is so that they may be used by other persistent environment implementors. It should be emphasized that the data reported here is simply the start of a more detailed study of the internal workings of a persistent object system.

REFERENCES

1. Cooper, R. L., Atkinson, M. P. and Blott, S. M. "Using a Persistent Environment to Maintain a Bibliographic Database", Universities of Glasgow and St Andrews, PPRR-24, 1987.

2. Cockshott, W. P., Atkinson, M. P., Chisholm, K. J., Bailey, P. J. and Morrison, R. "POMS: a Persistent Object Management System", *Software Practice and Experience*, 14, 1, pp. 49-71, January 1984.

3. Getitimer "SunOS release 4.0 Manual 2", Sun Microsystems, 1988.

4. Persistent Programming Research Group "The PS-algol Abstract Machine Manual", Universities of Glasgow and St Andrews, PPRR11, 1985.

Part VI

Transactions and Persistence

Transactions on Persistent Objects

P. Brössler
Universität Bremen

B. Freisleben
Technische Hochschule Darmstadt

ABSTRACT

Persistent objects are a powerful modeling tool for the design and implementation of complex software systems. Scope, lifetime, and sharing are orthogonal concepts applicable to any type of object. In order to maintain the integrity of important objects and to improve the overall system reliability, the transaction mechanism can successfully be applied to a persistent object system. This paper discusses several alternatives for the realization of transactions in such an environment. It also presents new techniques for object-oriented concurrency control and recovery, based on the notion of *layered transactions*.

1. INTRODUCTION

A proper marriage between persistent programming [2] and the object model [13] promises to offer many benefits for future software development. The object model is a powerful tool for mastering the complexity of large software systems by decomposing them into information-hiding modules [22] and by providing rich abstraction mechanisms to aggregate, classify and inherit properties of objects for expressing structural relationships between them. Since all objects have the same architectural structure, consisting of a semantically appropriate operational interface which encapsulates the data, algorithms and other implementation details, objects allow the treatment of all software resources in a uniform manner. Persistent programming aims to provide a uniform method of accessing data structures, irrespective of their sizes and lifetimes and thus eliminates the conventional dichotomy between transient computational objects and permanent file or database objects. This not only avoids a very substantial number of duplicated mechanisms to access, protect and synchronize the two kinds of objects, but also does not force the programmer to flatten rich structures of computational objects before they can be made persistent. Thus, the programming effort is reduced, the code is simplified and the system performance is enhanced.

Although a symbiosis of the two programming paradigms seems to be highly desirable, the attractiveness of the combined approach is somewhat impaired due to the problems encountered when trying to make it a reality. When viewing each of the two individually, we find that many implementations of object oriented systems have suffered from severe performance penalties, because they failed to take advantage of the object properties in an efficient and straightforward manner. This was due to the lack of suitable programming languages support and serious inadequacies in conventional computer architectures, in particular in relation to the basic support necessary to store, address, protect and share objects [14]. On the other hand, the persistent programming approach to extend existing or invent new programming languages that provide automatic access to file systems, and more recently due to the need for sharing, to general-purpose or special-purpose databases [2, 4, 6] is subject to a number of similar problems. Interfacing programming languages to databases is a difficult task [3] which not only involves a great deal of design considerations to overcome the impedance mismatch [20] between the programming language data structures and the database data structures, but also is debatable in terms of flexibility and implementation efficiency.

We strongly believe that the successful production of a persistent object system requires an integrated approach in terms of both hardware and software, such that an object-oriented programming environment is coherently supported by dedicated architectural features. For example, the need for a database system as a persistent object repository can be entirely eliminated if all objects share a large virtual single-level storage. It has recently been pointed out [20, 27] that such a uniform memory abstraction in which primary memory acts as a cache of the whole secondary storage is ideally suited for implementing persistent object systems. However, several attempts have been made to support a uniform virtual memory in both research and commercial environments [11, 12, 19], but most of them proved to be unsatisfactory because the size of virtual addresses was insufficient to allow all objects to be addressed directly and because the lack of unambigous system-wide names created many problems in sharing objects [12]. In these systems persistent information is usually still held in files which may be mapped into the address space of a process by special mapping operations [31]. The feasibility of the uniform virtual memory approach has been successfully demonstrated within the MONADS project, which included the building of an entirely new computer system, the MONADS-PC [23], to provide all the architectural features essential to support object oriented and persistent programming with the LEIBNIZ programming language [8, 15].

The main focus of our research is the problem of maintaining the consistency of shared objects despite the possible concurrency of conflicting accesses and the presence of failures. This problem domain has up to now not been investigated in the context of the MONADS project, but it is of primary importance in a single-level storage environment since no sophisticated database management system can come to the rescue. Our solution consequently uses some of the concepts for consistency control from database systems to enable users in our programming environment to overlook all effects of multi-user mode as well as the possibility of certain classes of failure. It is based on a layered transaction model for executing operations on objects. We demonstrate its integration into our programming environment and show how it can be implemented within the single-level storage architecture.

2. THE NEED FOR TRANSACTIONS

The possibility of structuring various kinds of large software systems with persistent objects promises to produce better software in less time. However, as computer applications are rapidly expanding into many new areas, such as computer aided design systems, multi-media systems and expert systems, the demands on the functionality of such applications increase. Among these are the need for high degrees of reliability, availability and concurrency, raising the fundamental questions of how to preserve the consistency of shared objects and how to make them highly reliable in the presence of failures.

The transaction concept [10] has proven to be an easy to use mechanism to solve these problems in database systems by executing operations with the special properties of persistency, atomicity and serializability. Carrying over these properties to a persistent object environment is useful in several respects:

- The aim of *persistency* is to guarantee that object states survive the loss of volatile memory (due to power failure or crashes) and even the partial or complete loss of at least one permanent storage medium (e.g. disk head crash).
- The aim of *atomicity* is to guarantee that either a new object state is reached completely or no effect remains at all.
- The aim of *serializability* is to guarantee that any parallel execution of objects is equivalent to some serial order, so that users and programmers do not have to be aware of concurrency.

It is clear that these properties are certainly desirable in persistent object systems. Several question arise: What kind of transactions are appropriate for this environment? In which way should transactions be specified? And last but not least how and where should transactions be managed? In the following we will compare different answers to these questions.

3. TRANSACTIONS IN PERSISTENT OBJECT SYSTEMS

It is not surprising that some research groups, recognizing the benefits of transactions for sharing and fault tolerance, have chosen to use a general-purpose [4, 20] or special-purpose [2] database management system (DBMS) for implementing persistent objects. However, both approaches have some disadvantages.

The typing system in general DBMS's is quite puristic, consisting of a few basic types, a record constructor plus some form of collection, either relations or sequences. This usually means that the types in persistent programming languages do not match the types in database systems. So either the types of persistent objects have to be restricted or an expensive transformation between the two type systems is necessary. The reason to use a general DBMS as a base for persistent objects is the illusion which it gives of a transaction-oriented single level storage that allows for sharing and reliable permanent storing. But this can only be achieved in the face of serious problems of efficiency and parallelism [20]. As an example consider a DBMS with page locks and undo/redo logging of pages. If several objects are placed on one physical page no parallel activities on these different objects are possible. If one byte is changed in an object's representation, up to three pages (original, before image and after image page) have to be written to disk. Furthermore, a general DBMS cannot take any advantage of the semantic properties of objects. This means that nearly no update parallelism on objects is possible, because the DBMS is not able to distinguish compatible operations from incompatible ones.

By using a special-purpose DBMS most of these problems can be solved. The transaction mechanism can be specially tailored to the requirements of the persistent object structures and no overhead must be paid for features not useful in the persistent programming language. However, the tight connection between DBMS and programming language results in a low degree of flexibility if it is desired to use other languages in conjunction with the DBMS.

These disadvantages lead us to the view that using a database system does not provide enough flexibility and efficiency for general persistent objects. We propose an alternative approach for implementing fault tolerant persistent objects. It is based on transactions operating on a large virtual single-level storage on top of which a transaction mechanism for persistent objects is built.

4.   TRANSACTIONS ON OBJECTS

A transaction service for general persistent objects based on the object type itself offers many advantages:

- sophisticated concurrency control methods (few lock-waits)
- low concurrency control overhead (few lock-requests)
- low I/O overhead at time of commit
- flexible fault handling (high fault tolerance).

4.1.   Examples

The possible advantages can be illustrated by the following example: Suppose a banking system has to be designed. The most important object type clearly is account. There have to be operations to open and close accounts, to deposit and withdraw money, to set an overdraft limit, and others. The next object type is branch. Operations on this type are applied to a set of accounts of one branch, such as transfer money, sum of all accounts, find accounts based on some predicate, and so on.

Without considering any concrete implementation we can expect the following problems to occur when not exploiting object type specific properties: No parallel deposit or withdraw operations would be possible on two accounts that are stored on the same physical page. Each update of an account would have to be recorded on the disk by writing an entire page, even if only one integer number was changed.

As an example from the operating system area let us look at a print server and its clients. Clients may issue several print requests before commit. Nothing should actually be printed until the commit occurs. After the commit everything should be printed, even if the print server crashes. The order of jobs from one client must not be changed. Interleaved serving of print requests from different clients may be acceptable, for example if different print forms are to be used. What sort of problems do we have to expect when using transactions without exploiting type-specific properties? Print requests could for example be unnecessarily delayed if request blocks from different clients are stored on common pages. The concurrency control would also have to forbid interleaved service, since this would clearly violate serializability at the memory level. Our conclusion is that transaction management at such a memory level is not flexible enough.

4.2.   Using Semantic Knowledge

Many researchers have pointed out that the transaction model can be improved greatly by using semantic knowledge derived from object types [1, 20, 25, 28]. The proposals usually assume flat object types, such as counters, queues, or directories. They then show that a higher level of parallelism can be achieved by taking into account the commuting operations or the semantic ordering constraints. Increment operations on a counter do not conflict, they can be executed in any order as long as the new value is not returned. Insert/Remove/Fetch Operations on a directory commute as long as different entries are involved. There are a many more examples, but there are also many problems which have to be discussed:

- How do these kinds of transactions fit into object hierarchies?
- How can the compatibility between operations be determined and specified?
- Are there any theoretical limits to concurrency based on types?
- What are the relationships between such concepts and recovery or persistency?

4.3. Layered Transactions

We answer these questions by modifying Weikum's concept of *layered transactions* [30] for use in a persistent object environment. The basic idea is to regard the execution of an object operation as a transaction which in turn may be built up from other operations and therefore more basic transactions. At the lowest hierarchy level are virtual memory transactions with operations applied to virtual memory pages. A group of operations applied to one or more objects can be regarded as a transaction if it is classified as an independent new operation.

Layered transactions were originally proposed for multi-level database architectures with a fixed number of hierarchy levels, such as pages, records and relations. In contrast we apply the concept to an arbitrary hierarchy which is dynamically determined by each object's individual structural relationships. Layered transactions have advantages similar to nested transactions [17, 18] which have been identified as a suitable mechanism for reliable distributed computing. Both approaches are useful for decomposing transactions into smaller units, thereby providing increased fault tolerance: subtransactions may fail independently of their invoking transaction and of one another, so that alternate subtransactions could replace the failed ones in order to accomplish the successful completion of the whole transaction. In addition, parts of the same transaction may run concurrently while ensuring that their parallel execution is serializable.

However, there are some important differences between nested transactions and layered transactions. Locking protocols for nested transactions do not release any locks when a subtransaction is commited. Usually these locks are inherited by the parent transaction. In layered transactions all locks held by an operation that is executed as a (sub)transaction are released at the end of this operation. The caller of this operation retains a more abstract lock which is based on the type of the called operation. The early release of locks looks like a violation of serializability, but in fact it is based on the notion of *multi-level serializability* [29].

By relying on the underlying transaction mechanism (either more basic objects and/or the uniform virtual memory) it is possible to avoid introducing a new transaction hierarchy level for particular objects. There is an inherent tradeoff between more transaction levels with higher levels of parallelism or fewer transaction levels with lower overhead. The underlying assumption is that using more semantic knowledge increases the possible parallelism. Transaction management for specific objects (or types of objects) can be switched on or off without affecting the overall transaction properties. If the parallelism achieved by transactions on objects is insufficient then a further improvement is possible by executing some internal operations as transactions.

In some cases no parallelism can be gained by a new layer of transactions. A complex object as a pure structural aggregation of unshared subobjects without any new operations should rely on the transaction properties of its subobjects, since no improvement is possible. Another example is objects that have operations with pure read/write semantics and an implementation which does not create any *pseudo conflict* [30]. These occur when several objects happen to share underlying objects or memory pages.

Concurrency control using layered transactions is based on *abstract* locks associated with operations on an object. These are recorded in a conflict table to prevent the release of uncommited changes to an object. When checking whether a lock can be granted it is not necessary to consider any other object. Deadlocks have to be detected by a standard detection scheme and one of the transactions forming the cycle has to be aborted. In a general persistent object system deadlocks can involve several objects on different hierarchy layers, so system-wide deadlock detection is needed.

As in the nested transaction model persistency is only necessary for top-level operations. A commit of suboperations does not guarantee the new object state to survive crashes or other failures. For top-level commit two different strategies are possible: Relying on the persistency based on techniques on the virtual memory (e.g. cache/safe) or checkpointing plus operation logging. Since operation logging needs some mechanism to force the log to stable storage and suffers from an widely varying time for crash recovery, we favour the use of virtual memory for persistency in case of crashes. The virtual memory transaction mechanism is responsible for restoring the commited state of the main memory after a crash, so no redo for operations has to occur in this case. Disk failures such as head crashes occur very seldom compared to system crashes. Loss of commited data due to these failures can be prevented by using checkpoints and operation logs, because operation logging takes more time for recovery, but needs less memory. After the loss of permanent storage a global redo based on operations starting with the newest checkpoint has to take place.

In many applications a complete undo after a system crash may not be acceptable. While it may be acceptable to repeat a banking operation involving a few key strokes, the situation is quite different for so called *design transactions* [16], e.g. in a CAD system. After the restart of the system the last operation-consistent state should be available to the designer, so that the work can be continued without a significant loss of work. Atomicity still makes sense because partly executed operations may lead to invalid object states. This *operation persistency* must not have any implications on serializability. Flushed objects still have to be protected by (operational or virtual memory) locks. This also means that locks on these objects have to be made persistent too. In other words, if a transaction is to be restarted at some checkpoint instead of at the beginning, the complete transaction state has to be restored. Checkpoints are guaranteed to be *level-i consistent*, which means operation-consistent at some level i. Level 0 has the usual meaning of atomicity, either the whole transaction or nothing. Level 1 means that after a restart objects are set to the state after the last successful outermost operation, and so on. The definition of i may happen dynamically according to the objects themselves, thereby automatically enforcing persistency at certain points.

Abort operations are handled by aborting the transactions of all underlying operations, including the virtual memory transactions. There is a very strong relationship between type-specific concurrency control and recovery. The abort has to be possible without affecting any other transaction. Since basic locks are released early and have possibly been acquired by another transaction already, abort has to take place in form of inverses. If there is no inverse operation for some operation, then the abort has to happen in form of aborts of all underlying operations in reverse order. The situation may happen recursively and is earthed by the virtual memory transactions. Operations without a nonambigous inverse cannot be compatible to other operations with a conflict at a lower level.

4.4. Real Operations

There is another class of operations that cannot be undone. These are operations which have an irreversible external effect, such as handing over money at an automatic teller machine (ATM). Such "real" operations have to be deferred until top-level commit. They may be either compatible or incompatible with other operations, but there are two restrictions in terms of the implementation: 1) The changes that are applied to an object state by a real operation cannot be observed before top-level commit, even by following operations of the same top-level operation. 2) Real operations have to be idempotent, since their execution may be restarted in case of crashes during commit processing. Idempotent execution may for example be realized by checking first whether the operation has already taken place. In our ATM example the ATM itself could prevent the repeated execution of the same command.

5. THE PROGRAMMING ENVIRONMENT

In the following we describe the steps that are necessary to use object-oriented transactions. Objects consist of three parts:

1. a type specification based on a set of abstract operations (also called *class*)
2. one from possibly many implementations for this type
3. instance data, that is what distinguishes one object from all others

Object types are defined in the design phase of a system. Figure 1 shows as an example a rough specification in a dialect of the programming language LEIBNIZ [8].

The information for concurrency control and recovery is based on these abstract types, but should syntactically be separated from this definition, because it does not contribute to the semantics of these types. We introduce *transaction pragmas* for this purpose. Concurrency control and recovery information are based on the abstract specification of objects, but not part of it. The INVERSE clause is used to specify the inverse operation that can be used by the system to compensate an operation. The COMMUTES clause is used to advise the system with which other operations on the same object an operation is compatible. An example can be seen in figures 2 and 3.

```
OBJECT TYPES
  TYPE account
    open(IN name, address, type, INOUT pin).
    close.
    deposit(IN amount).
    withdraw(IN amount) RAISES rejected.
    balance(OUT amount).
    set_limit(IN amount).
  END account

  TYPE branch
    create(IN branch_name, location).
    transfer(IN from_account, to_account, amount) RAISES rejected.
    query(IN search_predicate, OUT {account}) RAISES search_failed.
    statistic.
    interest_calculation(IN rate).
  END branch
END OBJECT TYPES
```

Figure 1: Definition of a Simple Banking System

In order to simplify the task of type specification a default assumption is included: When no INVERSE clause is given, the operation does not change the object state. Note that there are operations without a unique inverse operation (such as the square function or a delete operation). NO INVERSE means that the object state cannot be recovered at this level, if necessary this has to be done in terms of underlying operations. As a consequence the possible concurrency is restricted in these situations. If an inverse operation exists in theory but is not part of the type definition it may be defined as part of transaction pragmas. In some cases the undo operation needs parameter values which are not derivable from the call parameters, but have to be retrieved using another operation. Without loss of generality we assume that exactly one such retrieve operation can be defined as a prerequisite for an undo operation. Such an artificial operation defined in the pragma part is not part of the object's interface but has to be provided in the implementation. In our example close and open on accounts are inverses, but as shown in figure 4 an extension is necessary.

Omitting the COMMUTES WITH clause prevents any parallelism on this object. This means that transactions executing this operation require exclusive access to the object. The clause COMMUTES WITH ALL allows unrestricted parallelism at this level. This does not mean uncoordinated, unserializable updates on the object. The reason is that there is always at least one underlying transaction level which guarantees serializability, e.g. transactions at the virtual memory level.

Whether two operations commute may depend

- solely on the two operations (example: counter increment and decrement)
- on parameter values (example: insert and remove on directories with named entries)

```
BEGIN TRANSACTION PRAGMAS
  TYPE account
    open
      INVERSE is close.
    close
      INVERSE is open.
    deposit(amount)
      INVERSE is withdraw(amount)
      COMMUTES WITH deposit, withdraw, set_limit.
    withdraw(amount)
      INVERSE is deposit(amount)
      COMMUTES WITH deposit.
    balance
      COMMUTES WITH balance, set_limit.
    set_limit
      COMMUTES WITH deposit, balance.
  END account
END TRANSACTION PRAGMAS
```

Figure 2: Pragmas for Concurrency Control and Recovery of Type account

- on object states (example: withdraw and deposit commute only if the balance before the deposit is higher than the amount to be withdrawn)

Accounts are also an example for nonsymmetric commutativity. Whereas the sequence withdraw and deposit may always be swapped, deposit and withdraw may or may not be. Another refinement of our example is necessary and is shown in figure 5.

This means that withdraw commutes with the set of all uncommited deposits as long as these are not necessary to allow the withdraw operation and with all withdraw operations as long as the balance is high enough. The general concept behind this technique is called the *Escrow Method* [21].

6. IMPLEMENTATION ISSUES

In this section we briefly sketch some important aspects of the implementation mechanisms that are needed for the concept of layered type-specific transactions on objects. The implementation mechanisms are threefold. First, there is a compilation process which takes transaction pragmas and produces specific run-time tables. Second, the procedure call mechanism offered by the architecture is extended to take care of concurrency control and recovery by using these tables. Third, the uniform virtual memory is extended to include basic transactions, including a very efficient crash recovery scheme.

What is the relationship between typed transactions on objects and virtual memory

```
BEGIN TRANSACTION PRAGMAS
   TYPE branch
     create
       NO INVERSE.
     transfer(a, b, amount)
       INVERSE transfer(b, a, amount)
       COMMUTES WITH transfer,
                      query(*, {acc}) WHERE (a,b NOT in {acc}).
     query(*, {acc})
       COMMUTES WITH query, statistic,
                      transfer(a,b,*) WHERE (a,b NOT IN {acc}).
     statistic
       COMMUTES WITH statistic, query.
     interest_calculation(rate)
       INVERSE interest_calculation(1/(1+rate)).
   END branch
END TRANSACTION PRAGMAS
```

Figure 3: Pragmas for Concurrency Control and Recovery of Type branch

transactions? The latter provide a full transaction support, including serializability, atomicity and persistency for all types of objects. The former allow higher levels of parallelism, more efficient recovery and more flexible faults handling. Transactions on objects have to be built upon a more basic transaction mechanism, which offers persistency, concurrency control, and recovery for access to instance variables (direct object representation). Both approaches have to be used together to achieve a satisfactory result.

```
   TYPE account
     open
       INVERSE is close.
     close
       INVERSE is create(n, a, t, p); deposit(am)
       DERIVED BY get_state(n, a, t, p, am).
     get_state(OUT name, address, type, pin, amount)
       COMMUTES WITH get_state, balance.
     ...
```

Figure 4: Additional Operation for an Inverse Operation

```
withdraw(amount)
  INVERSE is deposit(amount)
  COMMUTES WITH {deposit(v)} IF balance-SUM(v)+limit>=amount,
                 withdraw IF balance+limit>=amount
                 set_limit(am) IF am>=balance.
limit(OUT amount)
  COMMUTES WITH ALL EXCEPT set_limit.
```

Figure 5: Commutativity under certain Conditions

6.1. Compiler

The compiler computes a commutativity relationship, which is then used during run-time to determine the granting of locks. Constructing this relationship requires the concept of *closed schedules* [30]. A closed schedule consists of all executed but not yet commited operations plus all corresponding inverse operations. The idea is that undo operations are executed as normal operations and therefore are managed by the normal concurrency control method. To be able to undo operations without affecting any other (top-level) transaction, the lock mode of an operation is calculated based on the commuting properties of the operation and the associated inverse operation. This is how recovery influences concurrency control. If the inverse operation of a commutable operation is a simple write operation, then no high parallelism is achievable.

The implementation of object types may contain *exception handlers*. If an exception occurs which is not handled within the innermost object, then this exception is transformed into a transaction abort at this level. Then the same exception is raised one (calling) level above and so on. An exception handler may take specific actions (*forward error recovery*) or just abort and raise another exception (*backward error recovery*). No explicit restoring of persistent objects has to be done within exception handlers, since this is part of the general transaction mechanism.

6.2. Transactions in a Large Uniform Virtual Memory

Providing transactions by the operating system and the uniform virtual memory hardware looks very promising since it enables all system and application software to benefit from this service. A transaction management at this level allows the use of efficient page-oriented transaction mechanisms and at the same time allows most of it to be hidden from the user or programmer. The benefits of using a large virtual memory for persistency and recovery have recently been recognized [27], but an efficient implementation is only possible if a certain degree of architectural support is provided.

The interface to the virtual memory manager is extended by introducing three new (microcoded) machine instructions. These instructions are generated by the compiler according to the transaction pragmas or by the operating system interface when a user wishes to execute a program as a transaction explicitly.

Shadows are paged to a separate shadow paging area and originals are either un-modified or modified and commited. The normal paging strategy (e.g. LRU) forces pages from main memory to disk.

Virtual memory transactions should be used as a *base* of a general object-oriented transaction mechanism. This is similar to [27] with the important differences that there are no superfluous periodic flushes to disk in our approach and that low-level consistency is already provided by the virtual memory. Virtual memory transactions are supposed to be quite short, only ensuring so called *operation consistency*. The reason is that locks and recovery information on virtual memory pages are only held until the corresponding object operation finishes, then concurrency control and recovery are taken over by this level. In our banking example, operation consistency means that accounts are either updated by deposit or withdraw completely or not at all. This does not already imply atomicity and serializability for procedures like transfer, which rely on other objects.

As a consequence pages as the locking unit do not present any harm to high par-allelism. In fact it allows a much higher level of parallelism than critical sections, which have been proposed by Schwarz [24] to achieve operation consistency. The I/O overhead caused by virtual memory transactions must also be seen in a dif-ferent light when these transactions serve only as a base for object transactions. Persistency is unnecessary for low-level operations, it is only needed for the over-all commit of operations on objects or for checkpointed states. How this can be achieved will be discussed in the next section.

6.3. Implementation of Transactions on Objects

In the following we briefly discuss some of the implementation issues involved in realizing our approach. We focus on concurrency control, recovery and persistency. In the sequel each of these issues is discussed.

Locks for (high-level) operations on objects are recorded in a special *lock segment* associated with each object. When an operation is called it is determined if it has to be executed as a transaction. If this is the case the lock segment is used to check the compatibility of the requested lock according to the abstract lock table generated by the compiler. In addition, each top-level transaction has a *lock stack* associated with it in which all requested locks are stored. When the operation terminates the stack is used to release all affected locks, thus implementing a standard two-phase locking protocol.

Recovery for general operations is implemented by placing code for an appropriate inverse operation (as generated by the compiler) on a *recovery stack* associated with each top-level transaction. Since some inverses may depend on the result of an operation it is sometimes necessary to delay the completion of the recovery information until the result is available. If an operation commits, all inverses are simply removed from the stack. An abort is handled by executing the code of the inverse operations in reverse order as long as no exception routine for some operation has been specified or a checkpointed state is reached. The discovery of an exception routine switches to forward error recovery for performing appropriate actions to handle the abort of a particular operation.

To guarantee persistency all pages accessed by a transaction are recorded and at top-level commit they are written to the safe. A problem may arise if some of

- VMBTA to start a virtual memory transaction
- VMETA to commit a virtual memory transaction and
- VMRTA to abort a virtual memory transaction.

The transaction state of a process is recorded in its context (a special register) so that the virtual memory component can access this information at any time. At the virtual memory level we are dealing with read and write operations on pages. Any other units (such as segments in varying sizes) would complicate the virtual memory management unnecessarily. Executing a series of these operations as a transaction requires a concurrency control method for ensuring serializability and a recovery technique for guaranteeing atomicity and persistency.

We use locking as the concurrency control method. To do this efficiently, it is necessary that pages must be locked (in read or write mode) automatically when a page is accessed for the first time. The test whether a page lock is already granted has to be performed by the hardware, otherwise every memory access would be slowed down unacceptable. Locking at the page level is implemented with the help of hardware enhancements in the address translation unit by automatically locking a page in the appropriate mode when it is accessed for the first time. Further improvements are conceivable by using special locking hardware to make the granularity of the locking unit smaller than a page [5]. Special microcoded semaphores [9] are used in conjunction with operating system scheduling routines to synchronize concurrent page accesses efficiently. If a page lock cannot be granted because it is already in an incompatible mode (write mode) a lock exception occurs, which is then handled by the kernel. The kernel is not only responsible for the scheduling of processes waiting for page locks, but also for the detection of deadlocks.[1]

A strict two phase locking scheme is implemented by maintaining lists of locked pages per process and releasing all these locks at time of commit or abort [26]. This is done by the kernel which instructs the locking hardware to release all these locks as a result of VMETA or VMRTA.

Persistency and atomicity are realized by using an extended shadow paging strategy called *cache/safe* [7]. This strategy does not attempt to restore the permanent storage after a crash, as it is usually done. It restores the main memory to the last transaction-consistent state by using a *safe*. The safe is a sequential cyclic log on disk to which all commited pages are written. (Once non-volatile main memory becomes available at an acceptable price the safe can be omitted without changing other system components). Before a page is modified by a process for the first time, a shadow (copy) is taken. This can be supported by the same hardware enhancement as it is used for write locks. This means that when the address translation unit encounters the first attempt of a particular process to update a page, a write lock has to be obtained and a shadow page is created. These two functions are executed by the kernel. Updates take place on these shadows. A transaction can be aborted by simply discarding all shadows, usually without any I/O operation. The commit operation flushes all shadows that have been created by this transaction to the safe, makes the shadows to the new originals and discards the old originals. The cache/safe technique has the advantages that consecutively stored objects are not declustered, commit processing is fast because no random I/O is necessary and that transaction abort can usually be performed without any I/O.

In contrast to the original proposal we have modified the approach in such a way that neither the original pages, nor the shadows have to be fixed in main memory.

---

[1]This is done by using a standard cycle detection algorithm. Deadlocks are resolved by raising an exception which can then either be handled by the affected process or simply lead to an abort.

these pages have also been used by other active transactions, since this may result in writing not yet committed information to the safe. The problem is solved by retrieving the necessary information for the inverses of such affected operations from the appropriate recovery stacks and force them also to the safe. During crash recovery all inverses stored in the safe are checked and executed if necessary. Inverses of commited transactions are marked as obsolete. This solution leads to flushing more information to the safe than actually necessary and the amount of information increases as the number of pseudo conflicts increases. However, we accept this as the price to be paid for achieving a high degree of concurrency.

7. CONCLUSIONS

In this paper we have described an approach to solving the problem of maintaining the consistency of shared persistent objects despite the possible concurrency of conflicting accesses and the presence of failures. Our solution is based on a layered transaction mechanism for general operations on objects with the lowest layer being transactions operating on virtual memory pages of a large single-level storage architecture. We have demonstrated how the proposed transaction model can be used and implemented in our persistent object environment with the help of dedicated architectural support, such as locking hardware and extension to the operation call mechanism. Further research is needed to prove the viability of our concepts by relying on actual implementation experiences.

ACKNOWLEDGEMENTS

We would like to thank James Leslie Keedy, John Rosenberg, and Gerhard Weikum for many discussions about parts of this work.

REFERENCES

1. J. E. Allchin and M. S. McKendry. Synchronization and Recovery of Actions. In *Proc. of the 2nd ACM Symposium on Principles of Database Systems*, 1983.

2. M. Atkinson, P. Bailey, K. Chisholm, W. Cockshott, and R. Morrison. An Approach to Persistent Programming. *Computer Journal*, 26(4), 1983.

3. M. Atkinson and O. Buneman. Types and Persistence in Database Programming Languages. *ACM Computing Surveys*, 19(2):105–190, 1987.

4. M. Butler. An Approach to Persistent LISP Objects. In *Proc. of the IEEE COMPCON Conference*, pp. 324–329, 1986.

5. A. Chang and M. Mergen. 801 Storage: Architecture and Implementation. In *Proc. of the 11th ACM Symposium on Operating System Principles*, pp. 109–110, 1987.

6. W. Cockshott, M. Atkinson, K. Chisholm, P. Bailey, and R. Morrison. Persistent Object Management System. *Software – Practice and Experience*, 14:49–71, 1984.

7. K. Elhardt and R. Bayer. A Database Cache for High Performance and Fast Restart in Database Systems. *ACM Transactions on Database Systems*, 9(4), 1984.

8. M. Evered. *LEIBNIZ - A Language to Support Software Engineering*. PhD thesis, Technical University of Darmstadt, Dept. of Computer Science, 1985.

9. B. Freisleben. *Mechanisms for the Synchronization of Parallel Processes (in German)*, volume 133 of *Informatik Fachberichte*. Springer–Verlag, 1987.

10. J. Gray. The Transaction Concept: Virtues and Limitations. In *Proc. of the 7th Int. Conference on Very Large Databases*, pp. 144–154, 1981.

11. IBM. *IBM System/38 Technical Developments*. IBM General Systems Division, 1980.

12. INTEL. *Introduction to the iAPX432 Architecture*. INTEL Corporation, no. 17821-001 edition, 1981.

13. A. Jones. *The Object Model, a Conceptual Tool for Structuring Software*, volume 60 of *Lecture Notes in Computer Science*, pp. 7–16. Springer–Verlag, 1978.

14. J. Keedy and J. Rosenberg. *Architectural Support for the MONADS III Computer Design*, volume 57, pp. 71–86. Springer–Verlag, 1982.

15. J. Keedy and J. Rosenberg. Uniform Support for Collections of Objects in a Persistent Environment. In *Proc. of the 22nd Hawaii Int. Conference on System Sciences*, 1989.

16. W. Kim, R. Lorie, D. McNabb, and W. Plouffe. A Transaction Mechanism for Engineering Design Databases. In *Proc. of the 10th Int. Conference on Very Large Databases*, pp. 355–362, 1984.

17. J. E. B. Moss. An Introduction to Nested Transactions. Technical report, University of Massachusetts at Amherst, 1986.

18. E. T. Mueller, J. D. Moore, and G. Popek. A Nested Transaction Mechanism for LOCUS. In *Proc. of the ACM Symposium on Operating System Principles*, 1983.

19. R. Needham. The CAP Project – an Interim Evaluation. In *Proc. of the ACM Symposium on Operating System Principles*, pp. 17–22, 1977.

20. P. O'Brien, B. Bullis, and C. Shaffert. Persistent and Shared Objects in Trellis/Owl. In *Proc. of the IEEE Workshop on Object-Oriented Database Management Systems*, pp. 113–123, 1986.

21. P. E. O'Neil. The Escrow Transactional Method. *ACM Transactions on Database Systems*, 11(4), 1986.

22. D. L. Parnas. On the Criteria to be Used in Decomposing Systems into Modules. *Communications of the ACM*, 15(12):1053–1058, 1974.

23. J. Rosenberg and D. Abramson. MONADS-PC: A Capability Based Workstation to Support Software Engineering. In *Proc. of the 18th Hawaii Int. Conference on System Sciences*, 1985.

24. P. M. Schwarz. *Transaction on Typed Objects*. PhD thesis, Carnegie-Mellon University, 1984.

25. P. M. Schwarz and A. Z. Spector. Synchronizing Shared Abstract Data Types. *ACM Transactions on Computer Systems*, 2(3), 1984.

26. M. Stonebraker. Virtual Memory Transaction Management. *ACM Operating Systems Review*, 18(2):8–16, 1984.

27. S. Thatte. Persistent Memory: A Storage Architecture for Object-Oriented Database Systems. In *Proc. of the IEEE Workshop on Object-Oriented Database Management Systems*, pp. 148–159, 1986.

28. W. Weihl and B. Liskov. Implementation of Resilient, Atomic Data Types. *ACM Transactions on Programming Languages and Systems*, 7(2):244–269, 1985.

29. G. Weikum. A Theoretical Foundation of Multi-Level Concurrency Control. In *Proc. of the 5th ACM Symposium on Principles of Database Systems*, pp. 31–42, 1986.

30. G. Weikum. *Transaction Management in Multi-Layered Database Systems (in German)*. PhD thesis, Technical University of Darmstadt, Dept. of Computer Science, 1986.

31. M. Young, A. Tevanian, R. Rashid, D. Golub, J. Eppinger, J. Chew, W. Bolosky, D. Black, and R. Baron. The Duality of Memory and Communication in the Implementation of a Multiprocessor Operating System. *ACM Operating Systems Review*, pp. 63–76, 1987.

319

Commutativity-Based Locking for Nested Transactions

Alan FEKETE, University of Sydney

Nancy LYNCH, Massachusetts Institute of Technology

Michael MERRITT, AT&T Bell Laboratories

William WEIHL, Massachusetts Institute of Technology

ABSTRACT:

We introduce a new algorithm for concurrency control in nested transaction systems. The algorithm uses semantic information about an object (commutativity of operations) to obtain more concurrency than is available with Moss' locking algorithm which is currently used as the default in systems like Argus and Camelot. We define "dynamic atomicity", a local property of an object, and prove that dynamic atomicity of each object guarantees the correctness of the whole system. Objects implemented using the commutativity-based locking algorithm are dynamic atomic.

October 5, 1989[1]

[1] This research was done while the first author was at Massachusetts Institute of Technology. The work of the first and second authors was supported in part by the office of Naval Research under Contract N00014-85-K-0168, by the National Science Foundation under Grant CCR-8611442, and by the Defense Advanced Research Projects Agency (DARPA) under Contract N00014-83-K-0125. The work of the fourth author was supported in part by the National Science Foundation under Grant CCR-8716884, and by the Defense Advanced Research Projects Agency (DARPA) under Contract N00014-83-K-0125.

1   INTRODUCTION

The abstract notion of "atomic transaction" was originally developed to hide the effects of failures and concurrency in centralized database systems. Recently, a generalization to "nested transactions" has been advocated as a way to structure distributed systems in which information is maintained in persistent modifiable objects of abstract data types. Examples of systems using nested transactions are Argus [6] and Camelot [10]. In these systems "atomic" objects can be created, and operations on these objects will be serializable, and the state of the objects will survive failures of the nodes on which they reside. In both Argus and Camelot the default algorithm used for concurrency control is the locking protocol of Moss [9], but the implementor of an object has the option to write his or her own concurrency control and recovery routine. In this paper we introduce a general algorithm that uses semantic information (that is, the type of the object) to obtain more concurrency than is available with Moss' algorithm. Our algorithm is described in a very general form. Many detailed implementation choices can be made and the correctness of the resulting more specified implementation follows from the correctness of our general algorithm. Due to lack of space, all details of the correctness proof have been omitted from this proceedings, but they can be found in [3].

As is well known, errors can result if different concurrency control techniques are carelessly combined within a single system. We do more than prove our algorithm correct. We give a local condition called "dynamic atomicity" on an implementation of an object. We use our recently developed theory [7] to show that if each object in a system is dynamic atomic, then the whole system is serially correct. In [3] we show that our algorithm produces a dynamic atomic object, as does Moss' algorithm. Thus our algorithm can be used on a few concurrency bottlenecks in a system, while the simpler algorithm of Moss can be used elsewhere, without violating serial correctness.[2]

We have also used our theory elsewhere to present and prove correctness of several other kinds of transaction-processing algorithms, including timestamp-based algorithms for concurrency control and recovery [1] and algorithms for management of replicated data [4] and of orphan transactions [5].

2   THE INPUT/OUTPUT AUTOMATON MODEL

The following is a brief introduction to the formal model that we use to describe and reason about systems. This model is treated in detail in [8] and [7].

All components in our systems, transactions, objects and schedulers, will be modelled by *I/O automata*. An I/O automaton A has a set of *states*, some of which are designated as *initial states*. It has *actions*, divided into *input actions*, *output actions* and *internal*

---

[2]Our earlier paper [2] contains a direct proof of the serial correctness of systems where Moss' algorithm is used for every object.

actions. We refer to both input and output actions as *external actions.* We call the classification of actions the *action signature* of the automaton, and the classification with the internal actions omitted as the *external action signature.* We use the terms in(A), out(A), ext(A) to refer to the sets of input actions, output actions and external actions of the automaton A. An automaton has a transition relation, which is a set of triples of the form (s',π,s), where s' and s are states, and π is an action. This triple means that in state s', the automaton can atomically do action π and change to state s. An element of the transition relation is called a *step* of the automaton.[3]

The input actions model actions that are triggered by the environment of the automaton, while the output actions model the actions that are triggered by the automaton itself and are potentially observable by the environment, and internal actions model changes of state that are not directly detected by the environment.

Given a state s' and an action π, we say that π is *enabled* in s' if there is a state s for which (s',π,s) is a step. We require that each input action π be enabled in each state s', i.e. that an I/O automaton must be prepared to receive any input action at any time.

A *finite execution fragment* of A is a finite alternating sequence $s_0 \pi_1 s_1 \pi_2 \ldots \pi_n s_n$ of states and actions of A ending with a state, such that each triple (s',π,s) that occurs as a consecutive subsequence is a step of A. We also say in this case that $(s_0, \pi_1 \ldots \pi_n, s_n)$ is an *extended step* of A, and that (s_0, β, s_n) is a *move* of A where β is the subsequence of $\pi_1 \ldots \pi_n$ consisting of external actions of A. A *finite execution* is a finite execution fragment that begins with a start state of A.

From any execution, we can extract the *schedule*, which is the subsequence of the execution consisting of actions only. Because transitions to different states may have the same actions, different executions may have the same schedule. From any execution or schedule, we can extract the *behavior*, which is the subsequence consisting of the external actions of A. We write finbehs(A) for the set of all behaviors of finite executions of A.

We say that a finite schedule or behavior β *can leave* A *in state* s if there is some execution with schedule or behavior α and final state s. We say that an action π is *enabled after* a schedule or behavior α, if there exists a state s such that π is enabled in s and α can leave A in state s.

Since the same action may occur several times in an execution, schedule or behavior, we refer to a single occurrence of an action as an *event.*

We describe systems as consisting of interacting components, each of which is an I/O automaton. It is convenient and natural to view systems as I/O automata, also. Thus, we define a composition operation for I/O automata, to yield a new I/O automaton. A collection of I/O automata is said to be *strongly compatible* if any internal action of any one automaton is not an action of any other automaton in the collection, any output action of one is not an output action of any other, and no action is shared by infinitely

---

[3]Also, an I/O automaton has an equivalence relation on the set of output and internal actions. This is needed only to discuss fairness and will not be mentioned further in this paper.

many automata in the collection. A collection of strongly compatible automata may be composed to create a *system S*.

A state of the composed automaton is a tuple of states, one for each component automaton, and the start states are tuples consisting of start states of the components. An action of the composed automaton is an action of a subset of the component automata. It is an output of the system if it is an output for any component. It is an internal action of the system if it is an internal action of any component. During an action π of S, each of the components that has action π carries out the action, while the remainder stay in the same state. If β is a sequence of actions of a system with component A, then we denote by $\beta|A$ the subsequence of β containing all the actions of A. Clearly, if β is a finite behavior of the system then $\beta|A$ is a finite behavior of A.

Let A and B be automata with the same external actions. Then A is said to *implement* B if finbehs(A) $\subseteq$ finbehs(B). One way in which this notion can be used is the following. Suppose we can show that an automaton A is "correct", in the sense that its finite behaviors all satisfy some specified property. Then if another automaton B implements A, B is also correct.

3 SERIAL SYSTEMS AND CORRECTNESS

In this section of the paper we summarize the definitions for serial systems, which consist of transaction automata and serial object automata communicating with a serial scheduler automaton. More details can be found in [7].

Transaction automata represent code written by application programmers in a suitable programming language. Serial object automata serve as specifications for permissible behavior of data objects. They describe the responses the objects should make to arbitrary sequences of operation invocations, assuming that later invocations wait for responses to previous invocations. The serial scheduler handles the communication among the transactions and serial objects, and thereby controls the order in which the transactions can take steps. It ensures that no two sibling transactions are active concurrently — that is, it runs each set of sibling transactions serially. The serial scheduler is also responsible for deciding if a transaction commits or aborts. The serial scheduler can permit a transaction to abort only if its parent has requested its creation, but it has not actually been created. Thus, in a serial system, all sets of sibling transactions are run serially, and in such a way that no aborted transaction ever performs any steps.

A serial system would not be an interesting transaction-processing system to implement. It allows no concurrency among sibling transactions, and has only a very limited ability to cope with transaction failures. However, we are not proposing serial systems as interesting implementations; rather, we use them exclusively as specifications for correct behavior of other, more interesting systems.

We represent the pattern of transaction nesting, a *system type*, by a set T of transaction names, organized into a tree by the mapping *parent*, with T_0 as the root. In referring to this tree, we use traditional terminology, such as child, leaf, least common ancestor (lca), ancestor and descendant. (A transaction is its own ancestor and descendant.) The leaves of this tree are called *accesses*. The accesses are partitioned so that each element of the partition contains the accesses to a particular object. In addition, the system type specifies a set of *return values* for transactions. If T is a transaction name that is an access to the object name X, and v is a return value, we say that the pair (T,v) is an *operation* of X.

The tree structure can be thought of as a predefined naming scheme for all possible transactions that might ever be invoked. In any particular execution, however, only some of these transactions will actually take steps. We imagine that the tree structure is known in advance by all components of a system. The tree will, in general, be infinite and have infinite branching.

The classical transactions of concurrency control theory (without nesting) appear in our model as the children of a "mythical" transaction, T_0, the root of the transaction tree. Transaction T_0 models the environment in which the rest of the transaction system runs. It has actions that describe the invocation and return of the classical transactions. It is often natural to reason about T_0 in the same way as about all of the other transactions. The only transactions that actually access data are the leaves of the transaction tree, and thus they are distinguished as "accesses". (Note that leaves may exist at any level of the tree below the root.) The internal nodes of the tree model transactions whose function is to create and manage subtransactions, but not to access data directly.

A serial system of a given system type is the composition of a set of I/O automata. This set contains a transaction automaton for each non-access node of the transaction tree, a serial object automaton for each object name, and a serial scheduler. These automata are described below.

3.1 Transactions

A non-access transaction T is modelled as a *transaction automaton* A_T, an I/O automaton with the following external actions. (In addition, A_T may have arbitrary internal actions.)

Input:
CREATE(T)
REPORT_COMMIT(T',v), for T' a child of T, v a return value
REPORT_ABORT(T'), for T' a child of T
Output:
REQUEST_CREATE(T'), for T' a child of T
REQUEST_COMMIT(T,v), for v a return value

The CREATE input action "wakes up" the transaction. The REQUEST_CREATE output action is a request by T to create a particular child transaction.[4] The REPORT_COMMIT input action reports to T the successful completion of one of its children, and returns a value recording the results of that child's execution. The REPORT_ABORT input action reports to T the unsuccessful completion of one of its children, without returning any other information. The REQUEST_COMMIT action is an announcement by T that it has finished its work, and includes a value recording the results of that work.

We leave the executions of particular transaction automata largely unconstrained; the choice of which children to create and what value to return will depend on the particular implementation. For the purposes of the schedulers studied here, the transactions are "black boxes." Nevertheless, it is convenient to assume that behaviors of transaction automata obey certain syntactic constraints, for example that they do not request the creation of children before they have been created themselves and that they do not request to commit before receiving reports about all the children whose creation they requested. We therefore require that all transaction automata preserve *transaction well-formedness*, as defined formally in [7].

3.2   Serial Objects

Recall that transaction automata are associated with non-access transactions only, and that access transactions model abstract operations on shared data objects. We associate a single I/O automaton with each object name. The external actions for each object are just the CREATE and REQUEST_COMMIT actions for all the corresponding access transactions. Although we give these actions the same kinds of names as the actions of non-access transactions, it is helpful to think of the actions of access transactions in other terms also: a CREATE corresponds to an invocation of an operation on the object, while a REQUEST_COMMIT corresponds to a response by the object to an invocation. Thus, we model the serial specification of an object X (describing its activity in the absence of concurrency and failures) by a *serial object automaton* S_X with the following external actions. (In addition S_X may have arbitrary internal actions.)

Input:
CREATE(T), for T an access to X
Output:
REQUEST_COMMIT(T,v), for T an access to X, v a return value

As with transactions, while specific objects are left largely unconstrained, it is convenient to require that behaviors of serial objects satisfy certain syntactic conditions. Let α be a sequence of external actions of S_X. We say that α is *serial object well-formed* for X if it is a prefix of a sequence of the form CREATE(T_1) REQUEST_COMMIT(T_1,v_1)

---

[4]Note that there is no provision for T to pass information to its child in this request. In a programming language, T might be permitted to pass parameter values to a subtransaction. Although this may be a convenient descriptive aid, it is not necessary to include in it the underlying formal model. Instead, we consider transactions that have different input parameters to be different transactions.

CREATE(T_2) REQUEST_COMMIT(T_2,v_2) ..., where $T_i \neq T_j$ when $i \neq j$. We require that every serial object automaton preserve serial object well-formedness.[5]

3.3 Serial Scheduler

The third kind of component in a serial system is the serial scheduler. The transactions and serial objects have been specified to be any I/O automata whose actions and behavior satisfy simple restrictions. The serial scheduler, however, is a fully specified automaton, particular to each system type. It runs transactions according to a depth-first traversal of the transaction tree. The serial scheduler can choose nondeterministically to abort any transaction whose parent has requested its creation, as long as the transaction has not actually been created. Each child of T whose creation is requested must be either aborted or run to commitment with no siblings overlapping its execution, before T can commit. The result of a transaction can be reported to its parent at any time after the commit or abort has occurred.

The actions of the serial scheduler are as follows.

Input:
REQUEST_CREATE(T), for $T \neq T_0$
REQUEST_COMMIT(T,v) for T a transaction name, v a value
Output:
CREATE(T) for T a transaction name
COMMIT(T), for $T \neq T_0$
ABORT(T), for $T \neq T_0$
REPORT_COMMIT(T,v), for $T \neq T_0$, v a value
REPORT_ABORT(T), for $T \neq T_0$

The REQUEST_CREATE and REQUEST_COMMIT inputs are intended to be identified with the corresponding outputs of transaction and serial object automata, and correspondingly for the CREATE, REPORT_COMMIT and REPORT_ABORT output actions. The COMMIT and ABORT output actions mark the point in time where the decision on the fate of the transaction is irrevocable.

The details of the states and transition relation for the serial scheduler can be found in [7].

3.4 Serial Systems and Serial Behaviors

A *serial system* is the composition of a strongly compatible set of automata consisting of a transaction automaton A_T for each non-access transaction name T, a serial object

---

[5]This is formally defined in [7] and means that the object does not violate well-formedness unless its environment has done so first.

automaton S_X for each object name X, and the serial scheduler automaton for the given system type.

The discussion in the remainder of this paper assumes an arbitrary but fixed system type and serial system, with A_T as the non-access transaction automata, and S_X as the serial object automata. We use the term *serial behaviors* for the system's behaviors. We give the name *serial actions* to the external actions of the serial system. The COMMIT(T) and ABORT(T) actions are called *completion* actions for T.

We introduce some notation that will be useful later. Let T be any transaction name. If π is one of the serial actions CREATE(T), REQUEST_CREATE(T'), REPORT_COMMIT(T',v'), REPORT_ABORT(T'), or REQUEST_COMMIT(T,v), where T' is a child of T, then we define *transaction*(π) to be T. If π is any serial action, then we define *hightransaction*(π) to be transaction(π) if π is not a completion action, and to be T, if π is a completion action for a child of T. Also, if π is any serial action, we define *lowtransaction*(π) to be transaction(π) if π is not a completion action, and to be T, if π is a completion action for T. If π is a serial action of the form CREATE(T) or REQUEST_COMMIT(T,v), where T is an access to X, then we define *object*(π) to be X.

If β is a sequence[6] of actions, T a transaction name and X an object name, we define $\beta|T$ to be the subsequence of β consisting of those serial actions π such that transaction(π) = T, and we define $\beta|X$ to be the subsequence of β consisting of those serial actions π such that object(π) = X. We define *serial*(β) to be the subsequence of β consisting of serial actions.

If β is a sequence of actions and T is a transaction name, we say T is an *orphan* in β if there is an ABORT(U) action in β for some ancestor U of T.

3.5 Serial Correctness

We use the serial system to specify the correctness condition that we expect other, more efficient systems to satisfy. We say that a sequence β of actions is *serially correct* for transaction name T provided that there is some serial behavior γ such that $\beta|T = \gamma|T$. We will be interested primarily in showing, for particular systems of automata, representing data objects that use different methods of concurrency control and a controller that passes information between transactions and objects, that all finite behaviors are serially correct for T_0. As a sufficient condition, or as a stronger correctness condition of interest in its own right, we will show that all finite behaviors are serially correct for all non-orphan non-access transaction names. (Serial correctness for T_0 follows because the serial scheduler does not have an action ABORT(T_0).)

We believe serial correctness to be a natural notion of correctness that corresponds precisely to the intuition of how nested transaction systems ought to behave. Serial cor-

---

[6] We make these definitions for arbitrary sequences of actions, because we will use them later for behaviors of systems other than the serial system.

rectness for T is a condition that guarantees to implementors of T that their code will encounter only situations that can arise in serial executions. Correctness for T_0 is a special case that guarantees that the external world will encounter only situations that can arise in serial executions.

4 SIMPLE SYSTEMS AND THE SERIALIZABIL-ITY THEOREM

In this section we outline a general method for proving that a concurrency control algorithm guarantees serial correctness. This method is treated in more detail in [7], and is an extension to nested transaction systems of ideas presented in [11]. These ideas give formal structure to the simple intuition that a behavior of the system will be serially correct so long as there is a way to order the transactions so that when the operations of each object are arranged in that order, the result is legal for the serial specification of that object's type. For nested transaction systems, the corresponding result is Theorem 1. Later in this paper we will see that the essence of a nested transaction system using locking algorithms like Moss' is that the serialization order is defined by the order in which siblings complete.

It is desirable to state our Serializability Theorem in such a way that it can be used for proving correctness of many different kinds of transaction-processing systems, with radically different architectures. We therefore define a "simple system", which embodies the common features of most transaction-processing systems, independent of their concurrency control and recovery algorithms, and even of their division into modules to handle different aspects of transaction-processing.

Many complicated transaction-processing algorithms can be understood as implementations of the simple system. For example, we will see that a system containing separate objects that manage locks and a "controller" that passes information among transactions and objects can be represented in this way.

We first define an automaton called the *simple database*. There is a single simple database for each system type. The actions of the simple database are those of the composition of the serial scheduler with the serial objects:

Input:
REQUEST_CREATE(T), for $T \neq T_0$
REQUEST_COMMIT(T,v), for T a non-access transaction name, v a value
Output:
CREATE(T) for T a transaction name
COMMIT(T), for $T \neq T_0$
ABORT(T), for $T \neq T_0$
REPORT_COMMIT(T,v), for $T \neq T_0$, v a value
REPORT_ABORT(T), for $T \neq T_0$
REQUEST_COMMIT(T,v), for T an access transaction name, v a value

The simple database embodies those constraints that we would expect any reasonable transaction-processing system to satisfy. It does not allow CREATEs, ABORTs, or COMMITs without an appropriate preceding request, does not allow any transaction to have two creation or completion events, and does not report completion events that never happened. Also, it does not produce responses to accesses that were not invoked, nor does it produce multiple responses to accesses. On the other hand, the simple database allows almost any ordering of transactions, allows concurrent execution of sibling transactions, and allows arbitrary responses to accesses. The details can be found in [7]. We do not claim that the simple database produces only serially correct behaviors; rather, we use the simple database to model features common to more sophisticated systems that do ensure correctness.

A *simple system* is the composition of a strongly compatible set of automata consisting of a transaction automaton A_T for each non-access transaction name T, and the simple database automaton for the given system type. When the particular simple system is understood from context, we will use the term *simple behaviors* for the system's behaviors.

The Serializability Theorem is formulated in terms of simple behaviors; it provides a sufficient condition for a simple behavior to be serially correct for a particular transaction name T.

4.1   The Serializability Theorem

The type of transaction ordering needed for our theorem is more complicated than that used in the classical theory, because of the nesting involved here. Instead of just arbitrary total orderings on transactions, we will use partial orderings that only relate siblings in the transaction nesting tree. Formally, a *sibling order* R is an irreflexive partial order on transaction names such that $(T,T') \in R$ implies parent(T) = parent(T').

A sibling order R can be extended in two natural ways. First, R_{trans} is the binary relation on transaction names containing (T,T') exactly when there exist transaction names U and U' such that T and T' are descendants of U and U' respectively, and $(U,U') \in R$. Second, if β is any sequence of actions, then $R_{event}(\beta)$ is the binary relation on events in β containing (ϕ,π) exactly when ϕ and π are distinct serial events in β with lowtransactions T and T' respectively, where $(T,T') \in R_{trans}$. It is clear that R_{trans} and $R_{event}(\beta)$ are irreflexive partial orders.

In order to state the Serializability Theorem we must introduce some technical definitions. Motivation for these can be found in [7].

First, we define when one transaction is "visible" to another. This captures a conservative approximation to the conditions under which the activity of the first can influence the second. Let β be any sequence of actions. If T and T' are transaction names, we say that T' is *visible* to T in β if there is a COMMIT(U) action in β for every U in ancestors(T') – ancestors(T). Thus, every ancestor of T' up to (but not necessarily including) the least common ancestor of T and T' has committed in β. If β is any sequence of actions and T is a transaction name, then $visible(\beta,T)$ denotes the subsequence of β consisting of serial actions π with hightransaction(π) visible to T in β.

We define an "affects" relation. This captures basic dependencies between events. For a sequence β of actions, and events ϕ and π in β, we say that $(\phi,\pi) \in directly\text{-}affects(\beta)$ if at least one of the following is true: transaction(ϕ) = transaction(π) and ϕ precedes π in β,[7] ϕ = REQUEST_CREATE(T) and π = CREATE(T), ϕ = REQUEST_COMMIT(T,v) and π = COMMIT(T), ϕ = REQUEST_CREATE(T) and π = ABORT(T), ϕ = COMMIT(T) and π = REPORT_COMMIT(T,v), or ϕ = ABORT(T) and π = REPORT_ABORT(T). For a sequence β of actions, define the relation $affects(\beta)$ to be the transitive closure of the relation directly-affects(β).

The following technical property is needed for the proof of Theorem 1. Let β be a sequence of actions and T a transaction name. A sibling order R is *suitable* for β and T if the following conditions are met.

1. R orders all pairs of siblings T' and T" that are lowtransactions of actions in visible(β,T).

2. $R_{event}(\beta)$ and affects(β) are consistent partial orders on the events in visible(β,T).

We introduce some terms for describing sequences of operations. For any operation (T,v) of an object X, let $perform(T,v)$ denote the sequence of actions CREATE(T)REQUEST_COMMIT(T,v). This definition is extended to sequences of operations: if $\xi=\xi'(T,v)$ then perform(ξ) = perform(ξ')perform(T,v). A sequence ξ of operations of X is *serial object well-formed* if no two operations in ξ have the same transaction name. Thus if ξ is a serial object well-formed sequence of operations of X, then perform(ξ) is a serial object well-formed sequence of actions of X. We say that an operation (T,v) *occurs* in a sequence β of actions if a REQUEST_COMMIT(T,v) action occurs in β. Thus, any serial object well-formed sequence β of external actions of S_X is either perform(ξ) or perform(ξ)CREATE(T) for some access T, where ξ is a sequence consisting of the operations that occur in β.

Finally we can define the "view" of a transaction at an object, according to a sibling order in a behavior. This is the fundamental sequence of actions considered in the hypothesis of the Serializabilty Theorem. Suppose β is a finite simple behavior, T a transaction name, R a sibling order that is suitable for β and T, and X an object name. Let ξ be the sequence consisting of those operations occurring in β whose transaction components are accesses to X and that are visible to T in β, ordered according to R_{trans} on the transaction components. (The first condition in the definition of suitability implies that this ordering is uniquely determined.) Define $view(\beta,T,R,X)$ to be perform(ξ).

Theorem 1 *(Serializability Theorem[7])*
Let β be a finite simple behavior, T a transaction name such that T is not an orphan

---
[7]This includes accesses as well as non-accesses.

in β, and R a sibling order suitable for β and T. Suppose that for each object name X, view(β,T,R,X) ∈ finbehs(S_X). Then β is serially correct for T.

5   DYNAMIC ATOMICITY

In this section, we specialize the ideas summarized in the preceding section to the particular case of locking algorithms. Locking algorithms serialize transactions according to a particular sibling order, the order in which transactions complete. Also, locking algorithms can be described naturally using a particular decomposition into a "generic object" automaton for each object name that handles the concurrency control and recovery for that object, and a single "generic controller" automaton that handles communication among the other components. We define the completion order and the appropriate system decomposition in this section.

We then give a variant of the Serializability Theorem, specialized for algorithms using the completion order and based on the given system decomposition. We call this theorem the Dynamic Atomicity Theorem, because it is stated in terms of a property of generic objects called "dynamic atomicity", which we also define in this section.

5.1   Completion Order

A key property of locking algorithms is that they serialize transactions according to their completion (commit or abort) order. This order is determined dynamically. If β is a sequence of events, then we define *completion(β)* to be the binary relation on transaction names containing (T,T') exactly if T and T' are siblings and one of the following holds.

1. There are completion events for both T and T' in β, and a completion event for T precedes a completion event for T'.

2. There is a completion event for T in β, but there is no completion event for T' in β.

The following is not hard to verify.

Lemma 2 *Let β be a finite simple behavior and T a transaction name. Then completion(β) is suitable for β and T.*

5.2   Generic Systems

In this subsection, we give the system decomposition appropriate for describing locking algorithms. We will formulate such algorithms as "generic systems", which are composed of transaction automata, "generic object automata" and a "generic controller". The general structure of the system is the same as that for serial systems.

The object signature for a generic object contains more actions than that for serial objects. Unlike the serial object for X, the corresponding generic object is responsible for carrying out the concurrency control and recovery algorithms for X, for example by maintaining lock tables. In order to do this, the automaton requires information about the completion of some of the transactions, in particular, those that have visited that object. Thus, a generic object automaton has in its signature special INFORM_COMMIT and INFORM_ABORT input actions to inform it about the completion of (arbitrary) transactions.

5.2.1 Generic Object Automata

A *generic object automaton* G for an object name X of a given system type is an I/O automaton with the following external action signature.

Input:
CREATE(T), for T an access to X
INFORM_COMMIT_AT(X)OF(T), for T any transaction name
INFORM_ABORT_AT(X)OF(T), for T any transaction name
Output:
REQUEST_COMMIT(T,v), for T an access to X and v a value

In addition, G may have an arbitrary set of internal actions. G is required to preserve "generic object well-formedness", defined as follows. A sequence β of actions π in the external signature of G is said to be *generic object well-formed* for X provided that the following conditions hold.

1. There is at most one CREATE(T) event in β for any transaction T.

2. There is at most one REQUEST_COMMIT event in β for any transaction T.

3. If there is a REQUEST_COMMIT event for T in β, then there is a preceding CREATE(T) event in β.

4. There is no transaction T for which both an INFORM_COMMIT_AT(X)OF(T) event and an INFORM_ABORT_AT(X)OF(T) event occur.

5. If an INFORM_COMMIT_AT(X)OF(T) event occurs in β and T is an access to X, then there is a preceding REQUEST_COMMIT event for T.

5.2.2 Generic Controller

There is a single generic controller for each system type. It passes requests for the creation of subtransactions to the appropriate recipient, makes decisions about the commit or abort of transactions, passes reports about the completion of children back to their parents, and informs objects of the fate of transactions. Unlike the serial scheduler, it does not prevent sibling transactions from being active simultaneously, nor does it prevent the same transaction from being both created and aborted. Rather, it leaves the task of coping with concurrency and recovery to the generic objects.

The generic controller is a very nondeterministic automaton. It may delay passing requests or reports or making decisions for arbitrary lengths of time, and may decide at any time to abort a transaction whose creation has been requested (but that has not yet completed). Each specific implementation of a locking algorithm will make particular choices from among the many nondeterministic possibilities. For instance, Moss [9] devotes considerable effort to describing a particular distributed implementation of the controller that copes with node and communication failures yet still commits a subtransaction whenever possible. Our results apply *a fortiori* to all implementations of the generic controller obtained by restricting the nondeterminism.

The generic controller has the following action signature.

Input:
REQUEST_CREATE(T) for T a transaction name
REQUEST_COMMIT(T,v) for T a transaction name, v a value
Output:
CREATE(T) for T a transaction name
COMMIT(T), for $T \neq T_0$
ABORT(T), for $T \neq T_0$
REPORT_COMMIT(T,v), for $T \neq T_0$, v a value
REPORT_ABORT(T), for $T \neq T_0$
INFORM_COMMIT_AT(X)OF(T), for $T \neq T_0$
INFORM_ABORT_AT(X)OF(T), for $T \neq T_0$

All the actions except the INFORM actions play the same roles as in the serial scheduler. The INFORM_COMMIT and INFORM_ABORT actions pass information about the fate of transactions to the generic objects.

The transition relation for the generic controller is given in [3].

5.2.3 Generic Systems

A *generic system* of a given system type is the composition of a strongly compatible set of automata consisting of the transaction automaton A_T for each non-access transaction name T (this is the same automaton as in the serial system), a generic object automaton

G_X for each object name X, and the generic controller automaton for the system type.

The external actions of a generic system are called *generic actions*, and the executions, schedules and behaviors of a generic system are called *generic executions, generic schedules* and *generic behaviors*, respectively.

The following variant of the corollary to the Serializability Theorem applies to the special case where the sibling order is the completion order and the system is a generic system.

Proposition 3 *Let β be a finite generic behavior, T a transaction name that is not an orphan in β and R = completion(β). Suppose that for each object name X, view(serial(β),T,R,X) $\in$ finbehs(S_X). Then β is serially correct for T.*

5.3 Dynamic Atomicity

Now we define the "dynamic atomicity" property for a generic object automaton; roughly speaking, it says that the object satisfies the view condition using the completion order as the sibling order R. This restatement of the view condition as a property of a generic object is very convenient for decomposing correctness proofs for locking algorithms: the Serializability Theorem implies that if all the generic objects in a generic system are dynamic atomic, then the system guarantees serial correctness for all non-orphan transaction names. All that remains is to show that the generic objects that model the locking algorithms of interest are dynamic atomic.

This proof structure can be used to yield much stronger results than just the correctness of the locking algorithm in this paper. As long as each object is dynamic atomic, the whole system will guarantee that any finite behavior is serially correct for all non-orphan transaction names. Thus, we are free to use an arbitrary implementation for each object, independent of the choice of implementation for each other object, as long as dynamic atomicity is satisfied. For example, a simple algorithm such as Moss's can be used for most objects, while a more sophisticated algorithm permitting extra concurrency by using type-specific information can be used for objects that are "hot spots". (That is, objects that are very frequently accessed.) The idea of a condition on objects that guarantees serial correctness was introduced by Weihl [11] for systems without transaction nesting.

Let G be a generic object automaton for object name X. We say that G is *dynamic atomic* for a given system type if for all generic systems S of the given type in which G is associated with X, the following is true. Let β be a finite behavior of S, R = completion(β) and T a transaction name that is not an orphan in β. Then view(serial(β),T,R,X) $\in$ finbehs(S_X).

Theorem 4 *(Dynamic Atomicity Theorem)*
Let S be a generic system in which all generic objects are dynamic atomic. Let β be a finite behavior of S. Then β is serially correct for every non-orphan transaction name.

Proof: Immediate from Proposition 3 and the definition of dynamic atomicity. □

6 RESTRICTED TYPES OF SERIAL OBJECTS

The correctness of the algorithm in this paper depends on semantic information about the types of serial object automata used in the underlying serial system. In this section, we provide the appropriate definitions for these concepts.

We first define the important concept of "equieffectiveness" of two sequences of external actions of a serial object automaton. Roughly speaking, two sequences are "equieffective" if they can leave the automaton in states that are indistinguishable to the outside world. We then define the notion of "commutativity" required for our algorithm.

6.1 Equieffectiveness

Now we define "equieffectiveness" of finite sequences of external actions of a particular serial object automaton S_X. The definition says that the two sequences can leave S_X in states that cannot be distinguished by any environment in which S_X can appear. Formally, we express this indistinguishability by requiring that S_X can exhibit the same behaviors as continuations of the two given sequences.

Let X be an object name, and recall that S_X is a particular serial object automaton for X. Let β and β' be finite sequences of actions in $ext(S_X)$. Then β is *equieffective* to β' if for every sequence γ of actions in $ext(S_X)$ such that both $\beta\gamma$ and $\beta'\gamma$ are serial object well-formed, $\beta\gamma \in beh(S_X)$ if and only if $\beta'\gamma \in beh(S_X)$. Obviously, equieffectiveness is a symmetric relation, so that if β is equieffective to β' we often say that β and β' are *equieffective*. Also, any sequence that is not serial object well-formed is equieffective to all sequences. On the other hand, if β and β' serial object well-formed sequences and β is equieffective to β', then if β is in $beh(S_X)$, β' must also be in $beh(S_X)$.

A special case of equieffectiveness occurs when the final states of two finite executions are identical. The classical notion of serializability uses this special case, in requiring concurrent executions to leave the database in the same state as some serial execution of the same transactions. However, this property is probably too restrictive for reasoning about an implementation, in which details of the system state may be different following any concurrent execution than after a serial one. (Relations may be stored on different pages, or data structures such as B-trees may be configured differently.) Presumably, these details are irrelevent to the perceived future behavior of the database, which is an "abstraction" or "emergent property" of the implementation. The notion of equieffectiveness formalizes this indistinguishability of different implementation states.

6.2   Commutativity

We now define an appropriate notion of commutativity for operations of a particular serial object automaton.[8] Namely, we say that operations (T,v) and (T',v') *commute*, where T and T' are accesses to X, if for any sequence of operations ξ such that both perform(ξ(T,v)) and perform(ξ(T',v')) are serial object well-formed behaviors of S_X, then perform(ξ(T,v)(T',v')) and perform(ξ(T',v')(T,v)) are equieffective serial object well-formed behaviors of S_X.

Example: Consider an object S_X representing a bank account. The accesses to X are of the following kinds:

- balance?: The return value for this access gives the current balance.

  deposit_$a: This increases the balance by $a. The only return value is "OK".

- withdraw_$b: This reduces the balance by $b if the result will not be negative. In this case the return value is "OK". If the result of withdrawing would be to cause an overdraft, then the balance is left unchanged, and the return value is "FAIL".

For this object, it is clear that two serial object well-formed schedules that leave the same final balance in the account are equieffective, since the result of each access depends only on the current balance. We claim that if T and T' are accesses of kind deposit_$a and deposit_$b, then the operations (T,"OK") and (T',"OK") commute. To see this, suppose that perform(ξ(T,"OK")) and perform(ξ(T',"OK")) are serial object well-formed behaviors of S_X. This implies that ξ is serial object well-formed and contains no operation with first component T or T'. Therefore, β = perform(ξ(T,"OK")(T',"OK")) and β' = perform(ξ(T',"OK")(T,"OK")) are serial object well-formed. Also, since perform(ξ) is a behavior of S_X, so are β and β', since a deposit can always occur. Finally, the balance left after each of β and β' is $(x+b+b')$, where x is the balance after perform(ξ), so β and β' are equieffective.

Also, if T and T' are distinct accesses of the kind withdraw_$a and withdraw_$b respectively, then we claim that (T,"OK") and (T',"FAIL") commute. The reason is that if perform(ξ(T,"OK")) and perform(ξ(T',"FAIL")) are both serial object well-formed behaviors then we must have a $\leq$ x < b, where x is the balance after perform(ξ). Then both perform(ξ(T,"OK")(T',"FAIL")) and perform(ξ(T',"FAIL")(T,"OK")) are serial object well-formed behaviors of S_X that result in a balance of $(x - a), and so are equieffective.

On the other hand, if T and T' are distinct accesses of the kind withdraw_$a and withdraw_$b respectively, then (T,"OK") and (T',"OK") do not commute, since if perform(ξ) leaves a balance of $x, where max(a,b) $\leq$ x < a+b, then perform(ξ(T,"OK")) and perform(ξ(T',"OK")) can be serial object well-formed behaviors of S_X, but the sequence

---

[8]This definition is more complicated than that often used in the classical theory, because we deal with types whose accesses may be specified to be partial and nondeterministic, that is, the return value may be undefined or multiply-defined from a given state.

perform(ξ(T,"OK")(T',"OK")) is not a behavior, since after perform(ξ(T,"OK")) the balance left is \$(x - a), which is not sufficient to cover the withdrawal of \$b.

7 GENERAL COMMUTATIVITY-BASED LOCK-ING

In this section, we present our general commutativity-based locking algorithm. The algorithm is described as a generic system. The system type and the transaction automata are assumed to be fixed, and are the same as those of the given serial system. The generic controller automaton has already been defined. Thus, all that remains is to define the generic objects. We define the appropriate objects here, and show that they are dynamic atomic.

7.1 Locking Objects

For each object name X, we describe a generic object automaton L_X (a "locking object"). The object automaton uses the commutativity relation between operations to decide when to allow operations to be performed.

Automaton L_X has the usual signature of a generic object automaton for X. A state s of L_X has components s.created, s.commit-requested and s.intentions. Of these, created and commit-requested are sets of transactions, initially empty, and intentions is a function from transactions to sequences of operations of X, initially mapping every transaction to the empty sequence λ. When (T,v) is a member of s.intentions(U), we say that U *holds a* (T,v)-*lock*. Given a state s and a transaction name T we also define the sequence *total*(s,T) of operations by the recursive definition total(s,T_0) = s.intentions(T_0), total(s,T) = total(s,parent(T))s.intentions(T). Thus, total(s,T) is the sequence of operations obtained by concatenating the values of intentions along the chain from T_0 to T, in order.

The transition relation of L_X is given by all triples (s',π,s) satisfying the following preconditions and effects, given separately for each π. As a convention, any component of s not mentioned in the effect is the same in s as in s'.

CREATE(T), T an access to X
Effect:
s.created = s'.created $\cup$ T

INFORM_COMMIT_AT(X)OF(T), T $\neq T_0$
Effect:
s.intentions(T) = λ
s.intentions(parent(T)) = s'.intentions(parent(T))s'.intentions(T)

s.intentions(U) = s'.intentions(U) for U ≠ T, parent(T)

INFORM_ABORT_AT(X)OF(T), T ≠ T_0
Effect:
s.intentions(U) = λ, U ∈ descendants(T)
s.intentions(U) = s'.intentions(U), U ∉ descendants(T)

REQUEST_COMMIT(T,v), T an access to X
Precondition:
T ∈ s'.created − s'.commit-requested
(T,v) commutes with every (T',v') in s'.intentions(U), where U ∉ ancestors(T)
perform(total(s',T)(T,v)) ∈ finbehs(S_X)
Effect:
s.commit-requested = s'.commit-requested ∪ T
s.intentions(T) = s'.intentions(T)(T,v)
s.intentions(U) = s'.intentions(U) for U ≠ T

Thus, when an access transaction is created, it is simply added to the set created. When L_X is informed of a commit, it passes any locks held by the transaction to the parent, appending them at the end of the parent's intentions list. When L_X is informed of an abort, it discards all locks held by descendants of the transaction. A response containing return value v to an access T can be returned only if the access has been created but not yet responded to, every holder of a "conflicting" (that is, non-commuting) lock is an ancestor of T, and perform(T,v) can occur in a move of S_X from a state following the behavior perform(total(s',T)). When this response is given, T is added to commit-requested and the operation (T,v) is appended to intentions(T) to indicate that the (T,v)-lock was granted. It is easy to see that L_X is a generic object i.e, that L_X has the correct external signature and preserves generic object well-formedness.

In [3] we prove the following result.

Theorem 5 *L_X is dynamic atomic.*

An immediate consequence of Theorem 5 and the Dynamic Atomicity Theorem is that if S is a generic system in which each generic object is a locking object, then S is serially correct for all non-orphan transaction names.

7.2   Implementations

The locking object L_X is quite nondeterministic; implementations[9] of L_X can be designed that restrict the nondeterminism in various ways, and correctness of such algorithms follows immediately from the correctness of L_X, once the implementation relationship has been proved.[10]

As a trivial example, consider an algorithm expressed by a generic object that is just like L_X except that extra preconditions are placed on the REQUEST_COMMIT(T,v) action, say requiring that no lock at all is held by any non-ancestor of T. Every behavior of this generic object is necessarily a behavior of L_X, although the converse need not be true. That is, this object implements L_X and so is dynamic atomic.

For another example, note that our algorithm models both choosing a return value, and testing that no conflicting locks are held by non-ancestors of the access in question, as preconditions on the single REQUEST_COMMIT event for the access. Traditional database management systems have used an architecture in which a lock manager first determines whether an access is to proceed or be delayed, and only later is the response determined. In such an architecture, it is infeasible to use the return value in determining which activities conflict. We can model such an algorithm by an automaton in which the granting of locks by the lock manager is an internal event whose precondition tests for conflicting locks using a "conflict table" in which a lock for access T is recorded as conflicting with a lock for access T' whenever there are any return values v and v' such that (T,v) does not commute with (T',v'). Then we would have a REQUEST_COMMIT action whose preconditions include that the return value is appropriate and that a lock had previously been granted for the access. If we do this, we obtain an object that can be shown to be an implementation of L_X, and therefore its correctness follows from that of L_X.

Many slight variations on these algorithms can be considered, in which locks are obtained at different times, recorded in different ways, and tested for conflicts using different relations; so long as the resulting algorithm treats non-commuting operations as conflicting, it should not be hard to prove that these algorithms implement L_X, and so are correct. Such implementations could exhibit much less concurrency than L_X, because they use a coarser test for deciding when an access may proceed. In many cases the loss of potential concurrency might be justified by the simpler computations needed in each indivisible step.

Another aspect of our algorithm that one might wish to change in an implementation is the complicated data structure maintaining the "intentions", and the corresponding need to replay all the operations recorded there when determining the response to an access. In [3] we consider Moss' algorithm, which is able to summarize all these lists of operations in a stack of versions of the serial object, at the cost of reducing available concurrency by

---

[9]Recall that "implementation" has a formal definition. The implementation relation only relates external behaviors, but allows complete freedom in the choice of automaton states.

[10]In [3] we give some techniques that can be used to prove an implementation relationship between two automata.

using a conflict relation in which all updates exclude one another.

References

[1] J. Aspnes, A. Fekete, N. Lynch, M. Merritt, and W. Weihl. A theory of timestamp-based concurrency control for nested transactions. In *Proceedings of 14th International Conference on Very Large Data Bases*, pages 431–444, August 1988.

[2] A. Fekete, N. Lynch, M. Merritt, and W. Weihl. Nested transactions and read/write locking. In *6th ACM Symposium on Principles of Database Systems*, pages 97–111, San Diego, CA, March 1987. Expanded version available as Technical Memo MIT/LCS/TM-324, Laboratory for Computer Science, Massachusetts Institute Technology, Cambridge, MA, April 1987.

[3] A. Fekete, N. Lynch, M. Merritt, and W. Weihl. Commutativity-based locking for nested transactions. Technical Memo MIT/LCS/TM-370, Massachusetts Institute Technology, Laboratory for Computer Science, August 1988. A revised version will appear in JCSS.

[4] K. Goldman and N. Lynch. Nested transactions and quorum consensus. In *Proceedings of 6th ACM Symposium on Principles of Distributed Computation*, pages 27–41, August 1987. Expanded version is available as Technical Report MIT/LCS/TM-390, Laboratory for Computer Science, Massachusetts Institute Technology, Cambridge, MA, May 1987.

[5] M. Herlihy, N. Lynch, M. Merritt, and W. Weihl. On the correctness of orphan elimination algorithms. In *Proceedings of 17th IEEE Symposium on Fault-Tolerant Computing*, pages 8–13, 1987. Also, MIT/LCS/TM-329, MIT Laboratory for Computer Science, Cambridge, MA, May 1987. To appear in Journal of the ACM.

[6] B. Liskov. Distributed computing in argus. *Communications of ACM*, 31(3):300–312, March 1988.

[7] N. Lynch, M. Merritt, W. Weihl, and A. Fekete. A theory of atomic transactions. In *International Conference on Database Theory*, pages 41–71, Bruges, Belgium, September 1988. LNCS 326, Springer Verlag.

[8] N. Lynch and M. Tuttle. Hierarchical correctness proofs for distributed algorithms. In *Proceedings of 6th ACM Symposium on Principles of Distributed Computation*, pages 137–151, August 1987. Expanded version available as Technical Report MIT/LCS/TR-387, Laboratory for Computer Science, Massachusetts Institute Technology, Cambridge, MA., April 1987.

[9] J.E.B. Moss. *Nested Transactions: An Approach to Reliable Distributed Computing*. PhD thesis, Massachusetts Institute Technology, 1981. Technical Report MIT/LCS/TR-260, Laboratory for Computer Science, Massachusetts Institute Technology, April 1981. Also, published by MIT Press, March 1985.

[10] A. Spector and K. Swedlow. Guide to the camelot distributed transaction facility: Release 1, October 1987. Available from Carnegie Mellon University, Pittsburgh, PA.

[11] W.E. Weihl. *Specification and Implementation of Atomic Data Types*. PhD thesis, Massachusetts Institute Technology, 1984. Technical Report MIT/LCS/TR-314, Laboratory for Computer Science, Massachusetts Institute Technology, Cambridge, MA, March 1984.

Transaction Groups :
A Model for Controlling Cooperative Transactions

Mary F. Fernandez
Stanley B. Zdonik

Department of Computer Science
Brown University

ABSTRACT

Many interactive applications that are being developed for high-performance workstations involve several users in a collaborative activity. Modern database systems synchronize activities on shared data by ensuring that the results are serializable. Serializability is often too limiting a correctness criterion for cooperative work. Instead, we need a way of specifying correctness in an application-dependent way, such that the database system can monitor the evolving schedules and determine when an activity would violate an assumption being made by another concurrent activity. The storage manager must be capable of supporting interactions with many cooperative activities each of which is composed of multiple agents. This paper discusses how a distributed object server can support heterogenous sharing protocols without interference. We define active entities called *transaction groups* that are used to isolate the behavior of one set of cooperating agents from another.

1. INTRODUCTION

Automated design activities (e.g. CAE, CASE, CACW) share a number of characteristics. They are usually performed by a *design group* of two or more people collaborating on a design task. Design groups are naturally dynamic entities. Some groups may exist for long periods of time while others are created and disbanned frequently. Membership in these groups may also change depending on the stage of a design effort and the assignment of people to other projects. Inter-group connectiviity may vary depending on which groups use other groups' work. Automated design tools must support this dynamic behavior. It would be advantageous for design applications to use an underlying database that supports, instead of hinders, a model of cooperative work.

ObServer is an object-oriented database under development at Brown University which facilitates cooperative work by providing an extended set of locks and database operations. These locks and operations support cooperation between transactions by permitting them to share "work in progress" and by notifying cooperating transactions when shared objects are updated or when other transactions require use of a locked resource. In designing ObServer, it became apparent that cooperative behavior must be controlled. Allowing cooperation among a privileged set of transactions should not subject all transactions to the possibly non-serial behavior of the group, nor make them privy to a group's uncommited changes. We propose a new mechanism, the *transaction group*, for facilitating and controlling this cooperation.

Transaction groups are heirarchically organized in a tree with leaf tranactions representing design applications and internal nodes representing groups. The root of the transaction group tree is the permanent database shared by all transactions. The input and output protocols of transaction groups are defined. Some input protocols include how group members will cooperate; which locks will be granted to group members; and how objects shared by the group will be saved and recovered. Output protocols determine how a group interacts with its parent. These include how and when object changes are propogated to other groups (e.g. when should group changes become available to the world at large); which locks a group will request from its parent on behalf of its members; and how a group intends to communicate with its siblings. We also discuss extensions to the model that include strategies for caching of objects, access control of objects by groups and recovery protocols for groups.

2. OBSERVER

ObServer is a general purpose object database. A complete description of ObServer's functionality is found in [HZ87]. Briefly, ObServer provides secondary storage of arbitrarily large objects for database transactions and facilitates cooperation between these transactions. In designing and using ObServer, it became apparent that while ObServer provides primitives to factilitate cooperation, it does not provide any mechanisms to control this cooperation. To illustrate how ObServer supports cooperative transactions, we first describe ObServer's transaction model.

A characteristic of design environments is the need for communication between cooperating transactions. A common source of interaction is the sharing of objects. If a transaction locks an object, it has control over that object until it releases the lock. In a design environment, this behavior may be too restrictive. The transaction may need to lock the object but would like information regarding other transactions' requests to lock the object. For this reason, ObServer supports communicative locking of objects. Each lock is a *lock mode, communication mode* pair. The lock mode specifies whether the transaction intends to read or write the object. In addition to normal read and write locks, ObServer provides non-restrictive locks that permit reading while another transaction writes, writing while other transactions read and multiple writers of the same object. The communication mode specifies whether the transaction wants to be notified if another transaction needs the object or if another transaction has updated the object. This allows transactions to lock objects as needed but allows them to be notified of other transactions' use of an object. The six types of lock modes and eight communication modes are specified below.

Lock Modes

NULL	*Provided to allow communication mode only.*
NR-READ	*Non-Restrictive Read. Permits other transactions non-restrictive read and write access to object.*
R-READ	*Restrictive Read. Prohibits other transactions from writing object.*
M-WRITE	*Multiple Write. Allows multiple transactions write access to object.*
NR-WRITE	*Non-Restrictive Write. Prohibits other transactions from obtaining restrictive read or write locks but permits reading with NR-READ.*
R-WRITE	*Restrictive Write. Provides exclusive access to an object. Other transactions cannot read or write the object.*

Communication Modes

N-NOTIFY	*No notification, only lock modes are effective.*
U-NOTIFY	*Inform transaction when object has been updated.*
R-NOTIFY	*Inform lock holder if another transaction cannot acquire a read-type lock.*
W-NOTIFY	*Inform lock holder if another transaction cannot acquire a write-type lock.*
RW-NOTIFY	*Inform lock holder if another transaction cannot acquire a read or write lock.*
UR-NOTIFY	*Combination of U-NOTIFY and R-NOTIFY.*
UW-NOTIFY	*Combination of U-NOTIFY and W-NOTIFY.*
URW-NOTIFY	*Combination of U-NOTIFY and RW-NOTIFY.*

343

Because of the semantics of lock and communication modes, not all forty-eight possible combinations result in valid locks. Table 1 specifies valid lock mode, communication mode pairs. An example of a "cooperative lock" is NR-READ/Unotify. The lock mode gives a transaction read access to the object but permits other transactions to lock the object (non-restrictively) for writing. If another transaction does write the object, the transaction holding the Unotify lock is notified that the object has changed. The transaction may then read the new version of the object. Another example is R-WRITE/RWnotify. The transaction obtains exclusive use of the object but is notified if other transactions must wait to obtain a read or write lock. This enables a transaction to release an object on demand.

Lock Modes	Communication Modes							
	N	U	R	W	RW	UR	UW	UR
NULL	I	V	I	I	I	I	I	I
NR-READ	V	V	I	V	I	I	V	I
R-READ	V	I	I	V	I	I	I	I
M-WRITE	V	V	V	V	V	V	V	V
NR-WRITE	V	I	V	V	V	I	I	I
R-WRITE	V	I	V	V	V	I	I	I

V = valid; I = invalid

Table 1: Valid Lock and Communication Mode Combinations

ObServer also supports an extended set of object and transaction operations. In a traditional transaction model, changes to objects become visible in the public database when the transaction that made the changes commits. Should the transaction abort, none of the changes made remain in the database. Long lived, cooperative transactions may need to share object changes prior to commit as well as access objects modified by other active transactions. ObServer provides additional oprations for installing object changes prior to transaction commit. If a transaction holds a write-type lock on an object, it may make the current version of the object visible to all transactions by *registering* the object. The transaction continues to hold its write lock, but other transactions may access the new version. *Commiting* an object installs the new object in the database and releases the lock held on the object. Commiting an object individually does not imply that the transaction commits. It simply permits the transaction to modify an object, make the new object visible to other transactions and release its lock. To release the lock without modifying the object, the transaction can *abort* the object. When a transaction commits or aborts, all its locks are released and the modified objects are either installed or discarded. In this scheme a transaction is permitted to register objects and then abort. This means that another transaction may read the modified objects even if the transaction that made the modifications has aborted. Although these primitives permit non-serial behavior, they also facilitate sharing between active transactions.

The following example illustrates the use of ObServer locks and object operations between two cooperating transactions. Consider two transactions, T_1 and T_2, which correspond to two design applications. The applications are used by two people collaborating on the design of an airplane jet engine. T_1 is updating the engine fuselage (O_F) and T_2 is modifying the turbine (O_T). T_1 is also reading O_T and wants to be notified if the object is updated. T_1 requests a NR-READ/Unotify lock on O_T. When T_2 updates O_T to O_T'', T_1 is notified of the update. T_1 may then reread O_t from the server. (See Figure 1).

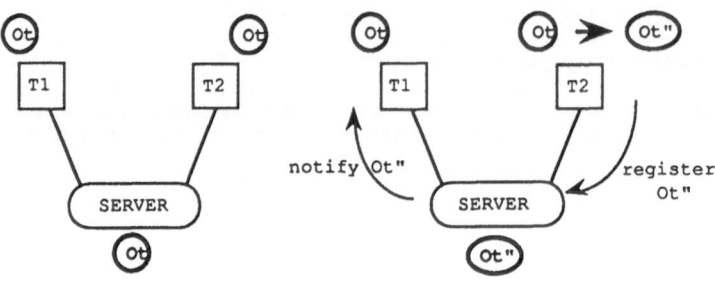

T1 has NRR/Unotify on Ot   T2 registers Ot"
T2 has NRW/Nnotify on Ot   T1 notified of update

Figure 1 : *Use of register and notify*

3. COOPERATION REVISITED

We now introduce a third transaction into our example and demonstrate how ObServer fails to insulate non-cooperating transactions from the effects of cooperating transactions. T_3 is a documentation monitor. The application executing T_3 rereads O_T whenever it is updated so that the engine turbine documentation may be updated to reflect design changes. T_3 holds a NULL/Unotify lock on O_T. When O_T is updated by T_2 , the server notifies both T_1 and T_3 that O_T has been updated. When T_1 and T_2 are making design changes, T_3 may be triggered to execute and could use an inconsistent or incomplete version of O_T (See Figure 2). T_1 and T_2 comprise a design group whose behavior should be isolated from other non-cooperating transactions.

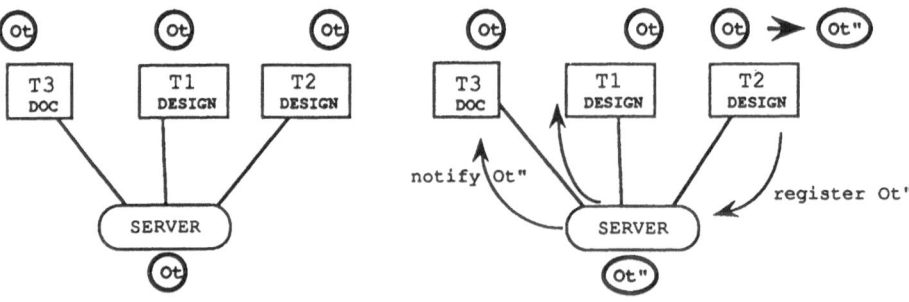

T3 & T1 have NRR/Unotify on Ot   T2 registers Ot"
T2 has NRW/Nnotify on Ot   Both T3 & T1 are notified of update

Figure 2 : *Notification of non-cooperating transaction (T3)*

345

ObServer fails to guarantee database consistency by not insulating non-cooperating transactions from the effects of cooperating transactions. In the previous example, T_1 and T_2 should be able to share in a non-serial manner, producing objects that may be incomplete or inconsistent. T_3 should not be privy to these changes until T_1 and T_2 agree that their objects are consistent. This failure is due, in part, to the fact that the database server is the locus for all transaction interaction. All inter-transaction communication is under the server's control. To solve this problem, we would like a mechanism that behaves much like a server (e.g. controls locking and communication, and caching of objects) but is the locus of sharing just for cooperating transactions.

4. RELATED WORK

The need for a transaction model that supports cooperative design activities was recognized during the development of complex, integrated CAD and CASE tools. Traditional databases supported a model of short-duration, serializable transactions. The application of this model to the long lived, interactive and distributed transactions of design tools was difficult. Thus the development of an extended transaction model to support both types of database transactions was needed. Proposed solutions have a number of similarities. All proposals assume that a separate area must exist for caching of shared objects. These areas can be permanent databases or temporary entities for storing object and lock information. This area can be considered the middle layer of a three-layer model consisting of public, group [KLA85,REH88] or semi-public [KIM84], and user or private databases. The public layer contains objects that may be accessed by any transaction. The group layer is restricted to a set of privileged users or transactions that are sharing objects. The user layer is accessible only by its owner. In both [KLA85] and [KOR87], transactions may only "belong" to one group or have access to one semi-public database. The structure of the database resembles a tree with the public database at the root, the semi-public databases as children of the root and the user transactions as children of the semi-public databases. [KIM84] permits transactions to "check out" objects from any other transaction thus producing a DAG of cooperating transactions. These approaches also recognize the need for an extended lock set to support the cooperative behavior of design transactions. In addition to the standard read and write locks, [LOR83] proposes a lock for writing and deleting an object and another for reading while others write. These locks are similar to ObServer's non-restrictive read and write locks.

Although the proposed models could support a multi-level heirarchy of group or semi-private databases, all maintain that a static three level model is adequate. They also assume that inter group cooperation is unnecessary and thus enforce serializability of the group transactions. They do not permit groups to share objects as member transactions do. In [KOR87], projects must abide by two-phase locking when requesting objects from the public database and in [KLA85], group transactions (GTs) are guaranteed to be serializable. This assumption limits the definition of group behavior. It should be possible to specify sharing protocols for groups as well as for transactions. The underlying database should thus support multiple levels of groups as well as heterogenous sharing protocols among the groups.

A characteristic of design activities not addressed by these approaches is communication. Cooperative behavior requires primitives for communication. Because the transactions cooperate by sharing objects, the mechanism for communicating should provide information on the use of the shared objects. For this reason, communicative locks are extremely useful. As a lock mode guarantees access to an object, a communication mode guarantees that the lock holder is notified of requests for the object. In this way, cooperation is inherently supported by the locking model. None of the previously mentioned approaches provide primitives for communicating about shared objects.

5. TRANSACTION GROUPS

We now define transaction groups and show how they can be used to control cooperative transactions. An object server can be accessed simultaneously by multiple transactions. Each server defines a protocol for how transactions can interact with the data that it manages. For example, it is often the case that a server defines a protocol that uses two-phased locking in order to guarantee serializable executions.

Our server can accept requests from transactions as well as from transaction groups. A transaction group is a process that is the locus of control for a set of cooperating transactions. The cooperating transactions interact with the transaction group and the transaction group interacts with the server on behalf of the cooperating transactions. A transaction group defines a protocol for its children, an *input protocol*, and participates in a protocol with its parent, an *output protocol*.

Transaction groups can interact with transactions or with other transaction groups. In this way, we can define arbitrary many levels of transaction groups to compose a transaction group tree. At each level, the transaction group must make the appropriate transformations between its input and output protocols such that its output protocol matches the input protocol of its parent.

First we consider input protocols. A transaction group accepts lock requests for objects from its members. These lock requests must match the locking protocol of the group. The locking protocol is defined by a *lock filter* which is the set of locks that the group may grant to its members. For example, in a completely cooperative group, the lock filter may include only those locks that have non-NULL communication modes. That is, all members must request locks that include notification information. A non-cooperative group might have a lock filter composed of only restrictive locks and no communication modes. Another protocol that may be defined is the *operation filter*. The operation filter is the set of permissible operations that a member may request from its group. In a cooperative group, intermediary object changes may be given to the group by registering the object. However, in a non-cooperative group, registering could violate serializability and would thus be omitted from the operation filter.

A transaction group's output protocols determine how the group interacts with its parent. If a group member requests an object for which the transaction group already holds a sufficiently strong lock, then the group can decide to grant the lock request and send a copy of the object to the requesting transaction. If the transaction group does not have the requested object or does not have a sufficiently strong lock, then it must request the object from its parent. Because the sharing protocols of a group and its parent group may differ, the group may have to transform the requested lock into a lock that is in the lock filter of its parent. The transaction group has a *lock translation table* that determines how this transformation should be made. Usually the lock is strengthened as a result of this transformation. For example, a transaction group may have cooperative input protocols, but wants to acquire objects for the group using restrictive locks. That is, the group's siblings may not access any objects used by the group non-restrictively since the group acquires restrictive locks. Thus a request for a NR-READ/Unotify lock by a group member would be translated into a RR/NULL lock request from the group's parent. The group acquires restrictive read rights and grants non-restrictive read/update notify rights. The lock transalation table must match the lock filter of the group's parent. That is, translated entries may not exist in the table that are not members of the parent's lock filter.

In addition to the lock translation table, each group has an output protocol that determines when objects used by the group may be returned to the group's parent. The *object propagation rule* specifies when a group may propogate changed objects to the parent. The rule may specify that objects are released only when all group members have committed or aborted. Thus the group guarantees that no further changes may be made to the objects by the group. The group may also return objects if the object is not being actively used by a member, or the group may register an object when notified by its parent that the object is needed. The operations used by the object propogation rule must match the operation filter of the group's parent. For example, if a group's parent has an operation filter that includes only *commit transaction* and *abort transaction*, the

TGengine	
Lock Filter	Permits restrictive read and write locks and update notification.
	{*NULL/Unotify, RR/NULL, RR/Wnotify,* *RW/NULL,*
	RW/Rnotify, RW/Wnotify, RW/RWnotify} Operation Filter
	commit transaction, abort transaction.

TGengine design	
Lock Filter	All locks. Operation
Filter	All transaction and object operations. Lock
Translation Table (member request, parent request) *(NULL,RR/NULL),*	
(MW,RW/NULL), (NRR,RR/NULL), *(RW,RW/NULL), (RR, RR/NULL)*	
Object Propogation Objects returned to parent when all members commit or abort. (e.g.	
when no group members exist).	

group may not propogate an object change by registering the object. To propogate the object, the transaction would have to commit itself which would require waiting for all its members to commit or abort.

Although we have only described two input protocols and two output protocols, many additional group protocols may be specified. These include rules for creating and destroying a group. A group could exist permanently or be destroyed when it has no members. Another input protocol specifies how a group handles a member abort. If a member aborts, the transaction group may initiate a rollback operation to a previously stable state of the group. Together these protocols determine the internal behavior of the group and its external interaction with its parent.

6. EXTENDED EXAMPLE USING NEW MODEL

We now apply the transaction group model to the design transactions described earlier. Two transaction groups are defined: TG_{engine} and TG_{engine_design}. TG_{engine} has two members, T_3 and $TG_{engine\ design}$. TG_{engine_design} also has two members, T_1 and T_2. The properties of each group are defined below.

Our previous example is reillustrated using the defined transaction groups. In Figure 3, T_1 requests a NRR/Unotify lock on O_T from its parent, $TG_{engine\ design}$. If the group already holds a sufficiently restrictive lock, T_1 is accommodated. If not, $TG_{engine\ design}$ must ask for an appropriate lock from its parent. Using the lock translation table of $TG_{engine\ design}$, a NRR/Unotify is converted to a RR/NULL. T_3 requests a NULL/Unotify on O_T from its parent, TG_{engine}.

In Figure 4, T_2 requests a NRW/RWnotify on O_T from its parent. Because TG_{engine_design} does not hold a sufficiently strong lock on O_T (it currently holds a RR/NULL), it must request a RW/NULL lock from its parent. When T_2 updates O_T and registers the updated object with TG_{engine_design}, only T_1 is notified of the update (Figure 5). The object propogation rule of TG_{engine_design} specifies that object changes are propogated from the group to its parent when all members have commited or aborted. In this way, intermediate versions of O_T are accessible only by group members and not visible to T_3 or to its siblings.

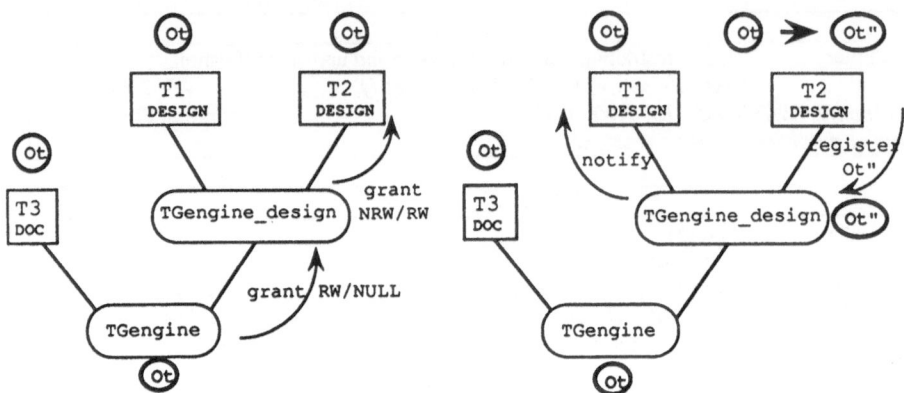

Figure 4 : TGengine_design requests
RW/NULL on Ot
T2 granted NRW/RWnotify on Ot

Figure 5 : T2 registers Ot"
T1 notified of update

After T_1 and T_2 commit, TG_{engine_design} also commits and the new version of O_T is propogated to the parent group TG_{engine} (Figure 6). At this time, T_3 is notified of the object update and may proceed in updating the associated documentation.

7. EXTENSIONS OF MODEL

In our discussion of transaction groups thus far, we have concentrated on their definition and logical structure. In a real database, transaction groups and their member transactions must exist in a distributed environement where minimization of network traffic is crucial to performance. Taking a final look at our example design environment, we consider the possibility that design transactions belonging to different groups execute at the same physical location, on the same machine. In Figure 7, note that T_1 and T_3 are executing on machine A, T_2 and TG_{engine_design} are executing on machine B and TG_{engine} is executing on machine C. Consider the case where $O_1"$ is a very large object. After T_2 has updated the object and

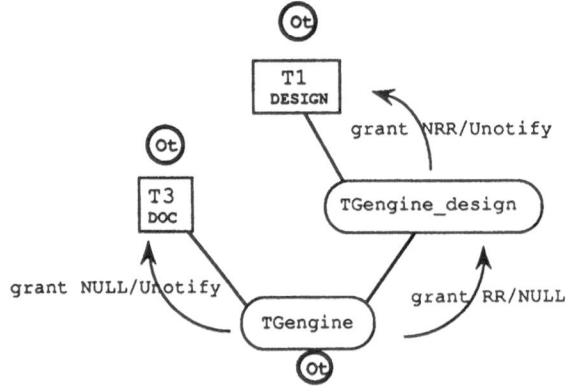

Figure 3 : TGengine_design requests RR/NULL on Ot
T1 granted NRR/Unotify on Ot
T3 granted NULL/Unotify on Ot

registered it with the group, T_1 reads the object. Machine A now has two versions of the object cached locally (O_t and O_t''). After TG_{engine_design} commits, T_3 will be notified of the update to O_t and will probably request the new version. However, the new version is already available locally. It would be more efficient if T_3 could be told (perhaps by its parent) how to access O_t'' locally so that it would not have to wait for the large object to be sent by the transaction group over the network.

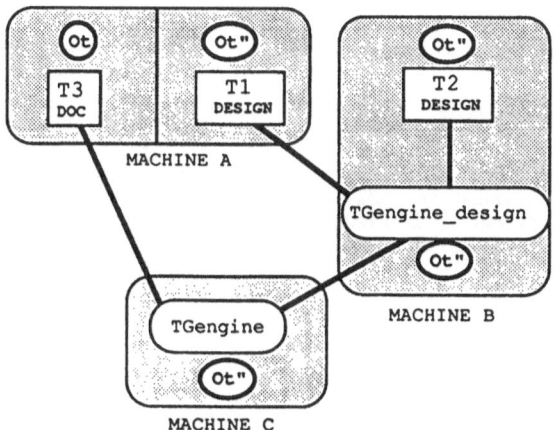

Figure 7 : Machine boundaries between groups
and their member transactions.

We are interested in determining how a transaction group can optimize movement of objects between its member transactions and pass on this information to its parent so that the parent may also move objects efficiently. We have already developed a model for a local cache manager that is responsible for caching objects at a workstation, for partitioning the caches so that transactions may only access objects it is permitted to use and for maintaining the transactions' access rights to these partitions. Since the transaction group has emerged as a mechanism for controlling the logical access to objects, it is a natural extension to have the transaction group also manage the physical location and movement of objects. This would require extending the protocol of a group to support distributed cache management.

The transaction group is a useful entity for isolating the effects of cooperating transactions and also for encapsulating their behavior. We would like to consider what types of additional protocols could be defined for transaction groups. Access control to objects could be defined easily as a transaction group protocol. This protocol could specify what types of objects may be accessed by the group, how they may be accessed, or how specific members may use group objects. This technique of specifying object access obviates having to attach an "access control list" to every object. Given sufficient right to change a group's protocol, the access rights for objects used by the group could be changed dynamically. The transaction group is also a good candidate for handling recovery for its member transactions. Because the model must work in a distributed network, issues of network partitioning and node failure must be considered. Since the transaction group is the "traffic cop" for all objects used by its members and thus knows where all copies of the objects are kept, it can be used to handle the checkpointing of group work, for performing recovery operations after a node failure and for guaranteeing that all copies of an object are equivalent.

8. CONCLUSIONS

Our original motivation was to design a model of transaction interaction that could support the cooperative behavior of design applications and the more restrictive behavior of traditional transactions in the same database. We developed a model that allows the specification of unique sharing protocols for each group and that permits groups to interact cooperatively. The model also supports the heirarchical nesting of groups to reflect the partitioning of projects in a design environment. In addition to sharing protocols, we recognized that transaction group protocols could include policies for managing the caching of large objects in a distributed environment and for controlling access to objects. Our future efforts include using the simple structure of transaction groups to develop more sophisticated techniques for distributed cache management and for determining how transaction group protocols can be specified and interpreted.

9. ACKNOWLEDGMENTS

The authors would like to thank Andrea Skarra, Cetin Ozbutin, and David Lyons for their comments. We would also like to express appreciation for support from IBM under contract No. 559716, by DEC under award No. DEC686, by ONR under contract N00014-88-K-0406, by DARPA under contract N00014-83-K-196, DARPA Order No. 4786, by Apple Computer, Inc., and by US West.

REFERENCES

1.   HORNICK, M. and ZDONIK, S. A Shared, Segmented Memory System for an Object-Oriented Database. *ACM Transactions on Office Information Systems,* Vol. 5, No. 1, Jan. 1987, pp. 70-95.

2.   KIM, W., et. al. A Transaction Mechanism for Engineering Design Databases. *Proc. of international Conference on VLDBs*, Singapore, 1984.

3.   KLAHOLD, P., et. al. A transaction model supporting complex applications in integrated information systems. *Proceedings of ACM SIGMOD,* 1985.

4.   KORTH, H.F., KIM, W., BANCIHON, F. On Long-Duration CAD Transactions. *Information Systems,* Vol 13., 1987.

5.   LORIE, R. and PLOUFFE, W. Complex Objects and Their Use in Design Transactions. In *Proc. Databases for Engineering Applications, Database Week 1983 (ACM)*, May 1983, pp. 115-121.

6.   REHM, S., et al. Support for Design Processes in a Structurally Object-Oriented Database System. In *Proc. of 2nd International Workshop on Object-Oriented Database Systems*, pp 80-96.

7.   SKARRA, A. and ZDONIK, S. An object server for an object-oriented database system. In *International Workshop on Object-Oriented Database Systems* (Pacific Grove, CA., Sept.) ACM, New York, 1986, pp. 196-204.

Part VII

Persistent Machines

The Persistent Abstract Machine

R.Connor, A.Brown, R.Carrick, A.Dearle, & R.Morrison

University of St Andrews.

ABSTRACT

The Persistent Abstract Machine is an integral part of a layered architecture model to support the Napier language. It interfaces cleanly with a persistent store, and allows persistence to be implemented without difficulty in a high-level language. The heap based storage mechanism of the Persistent Abstract Machine is designed to support the block retention nature of the Napier language. This allows the implementation of first class procedures and modules in programming languages with the minimum of effort. A primitive type system within the machine contains just enough information to allow machine instructions which behave differently according to the dynamic type of their operands. This type system, in conjunction with the block retention architecture, may be used to great effect to provide a fast implementation of polymorphic procedures, abstract data types, inheritance and bounded universal quantification.

1. INTRODUCTION

In recent years, research into persistent programming systems has led to the design of sophisticated database programming languages such as Galileo[1], PS-algol[15], and Napier[13]. These languages provide a wide range of abstraction facilities such as abstract data types, polymorphism and first class procedures that are integrated within a single persistent store. The development of these systems has required the design of a variety of new implementation techniques. For example, the development of the Napier system necessitated the design of reusable compiler componentry[9], an intermediate language[10], an abstract machine[5] and a persistent object store, all of which are integrated into a highly modular layered architecture[4]. Here we present the objectives and solutions which comprise the design of the Persistent Abstract Machine.

The Persistent Abstract Machine is primarily designed to support the Napier programming language. It is closely based on the PS-algol abstract machine[14], which in turn evolved from the S-algol abstract machine[3]. Due to the modularity of its design and implementation, it may be used to support any language with no more than the following features: persistence, polymorphism, subtype inheritance, first class procedures, abstract data types and block structure. Other features, such as object-oriented programming in the Smalltalk style[11] and lazy evaluation, may be modelled at a higher level using the same support mechanisms as first class procedures[2, 12]. This covers most algorithmic, object-oriented and applicative programming languages currently in use. The machine can thus be said to be multi-paradigm.

The Napier system is designed so that implementors wishing to use the abstract machine may compile to an intermediate level architecture, consisting of abstract syntax trees. A code generator is available to compile to the abstract machine level. This persistent architecture intermediate language, PAIL[10], supports all of the abstraction listed above, and is sufficiently high-level to ease the burden of compiler writing. Furthermore, it is possible to

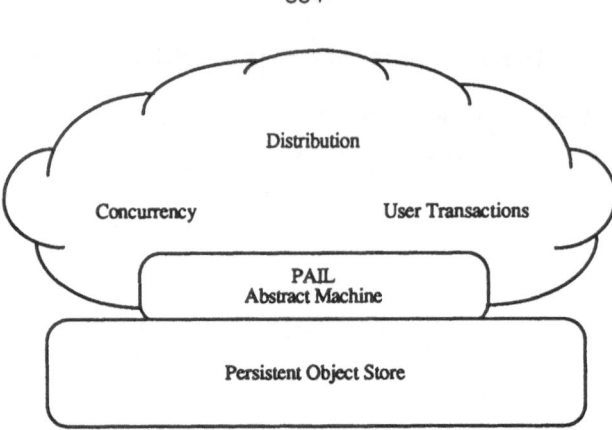

Figure 1: The Major Architecture Components

check at this level that correct (i.e. consistent) PAIL code has been generated, and so output from an untrusted compiler cannot cause a malfunction in the abstract machine. This assures that the persistent store may not be corrupted by the generation of illegal instruction sequences, removing the onus of segmentation protection from the store.

The design of the Persistent Abstract Machine is directly attributable to the Napier language. The major points fall into two sections:

1. The machine is an integral part of an entire layered architecture; in particular, it interfaces cleanly with the persistent store, and allows an elegant implementation of persistence in a high-level language. As another consequence of persistence, the machine exists in a single heap-based storage architecture. This architecture directly gives a method of implementing block retention, for almost no extra cost. This allows the implementation of first class procedures and modules in programming languages with the minimum of effort.

2. A primitive two-level type system within the machine contains enough information to allow machine instructions whose behaviour depends on the dynamic type of their operands. It has a fast and efficient integer encoding. In conjunction with the block retention architecture, the type system is used to great effect to provide a fast implementation of polymorphic procedures, abstract data types, and bounded universal quantification.

2. A HEAP BASED STORAGE ARCHITECTURE

One of the most notable features of the abstract machine is that it is built entirely upon a heap-based storage architecture. Although the machine was primarily designed to support a block-structured language, for which a stack implementation might be the obvious choice, the heap-based architecture was considered advantageous for the following reasons:

1. Only one storage mechanism is required, easing implementation and system evolution.

2. There is only one possible way of exhausting the store. In a persistent system this is an essential requirement, since applications should only run out of store when the persistent store is exhausted, and not merely when one of the storage mechanisms runs out. Although this

could be modelled in an environment with more than one storage mechanism, it would be expensive in terms of implementation and evolution.

3. The Napier language supports first-class procedures with free variables. To achieve the desired semantics, the locations of these variables may have to be preserved after their names are out of scope, which would not happen conveniently in a conventional stack-based system.

Stacks are still used conceptually, and each stack frame is modelled as an individual data object. Stack frames represent the piece of stack required to implement each block or procedure execution of the source language. The size of each frame can be determined statically, which leads to an efficient use of the available working space.

There is a trade-off with this implementation of stacks. As the stack frames are heap objects, the persistent heap has a right to treat them like any other object. This means that all addresses used in machine instructions must be two-part addresses, consisting of a frame address and an offset within the frame. Thus the abstract machine may not assume an absolute address for any stack location, with a consequent loss of speed. This is considered to be a relatively minor disadvantage when contrasted with the gains of such a flexible architecture.

The rest of this section describes the format used for all heap objects both used and created by the machine. In particular, the layout of a stack frame object is shown, and the procedure entry and exit mechanisms explained. An example is given of how these frames are used to model block retention.

2.1. Uniform Representation Of Heap Objects

The persistent heap upon which the abstract machine is built is designed to use a single object format, no matter the purpose of the object. All objects have the following format:

word 0	header
word 1	the size of the object in words
word 2..m	the pointer fields
word m+1..n	the scalar fields

where the header contains the following:

bits 8-31	the number of pointer fields in the object
bit 7	special purpose for use by abstract machine
bits 0-6	reserved for implementation experiments

This is very different from the PS-algol abstract machine, in which different types of object had information placed in their headers to allow the utility programs such as garbage collectors and object managers to discover the layout of the object. This coupled together the abstract machine, the compiler, the garbage collector, and the persistent object manager, making it impossible to change one without the others. The beauty of the new implementation is that the persistent store and its utility programs may be constructed completely independently from each other. This makes maintenance and change very much simpler, and allows for much freer experimentation with separate modules.

The format allows an object manager to know how to find the pointers in any object without requiring any knowledge about what the object may be used for. This allows it to follow store addresses at its own discretion. There are many reasons why this is desirable, not least that the store may now be responsible for its own garbage collection. It may, for example, be able to do this incrementally while there are no programs running. Other possibilities include distribution management, coherent object cacheing, and clustering.

This strict format calls for a small amount of extra work in the implementation and operation of the abstract machine, due to the constraint that all pointers in an object are contained in a contiguous block at the start of the object. This is not always a natural arrangement, and may cause some complication in the machine. The advantages of the arrangement, however, greatly outweigh the disadvantages.

2.2. Stack Frames

Stack frames, along with all other objects used by the machine, are thus restricted to the format described above. To achieve this, they are laid out as follows:

word 2	a pointer to the type descriptor for this frame, it includes a symbol table for this frame (TYPE)
word 3	the dynamic link (D LINK)
word 4	a pointer to the code vector for the frame's procedure (C VEC)
word 5	the static link for the frame's procedure (S LINK)
word 6	a pointer to the pail currently being executed (C PAIL)
word 7..1	the display for the frame's procedure (DISPLAY)
word l+1..m	the pointer stack
word m+1..n	the main stack
word n+1	the lexical level
word n+2	the return address for the frame's procedure (RA), an offset (in bytes) from the start of the procedure's code vector
word n+3	the saved offset (in words) of the LMSP from the LFB (MSP)

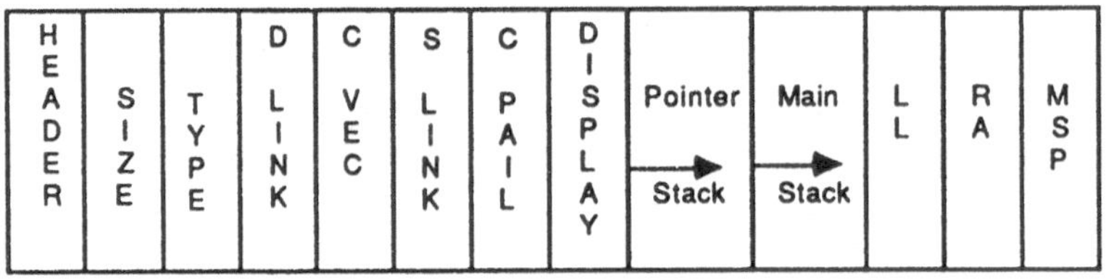

HEADER	SIZE	TYPE	DLINK	CVEC	SLINK	CPAIL	DISPLAY	Pointer Stack	Main Stack	LL	RA	MSP

Figure 2: Stack Frame Layout

Notice that the frame has a separate scalar (main) stack and pointer stack. This was a decision that was first made in the S-algol abstract machine, and continued into the PS-algol machine. Since a garbage collection could strike at any time in these machines, it was necessary to be able to find the pointer roots which were still required. The pointer stack naturally contains such pointers. Garbage collection using this format is the most efficient possible without resorting to a tagged architecture.

It is interesting that these separate stacks would in any case be enforced by the universal object format. This is because the object format itself is essentially designed by the same guiding principles as the previous machines' stack layouts.

2.3. Procedure Entry And Exit

Procedure entry consists of the following stages:

1. Load the closure
2. Evaluate the parameters
3. Apply the procedure

As a new context is entered, the code pointer and main stack top registers must first be saved. These are saved in the current frame, in the return address and main stack pointer locations. The pointer stack top does not need to be saved, as this may be calculated from the number of pointer fields in the frame's header on return.

The closure of the new procedure consists of the new static link and the new code vector. The locations of these items on the current pointer stack are known statically. A new object is created to act as the new procedure frame, the required size being found from the code vector. The local main stack pointer register is also set according to information found here.

The pointer stack may now be evaluated to the start of the new procedure's working stack. The new dynamic link is the old frame's address, the code vector and static link have already been accessed, and the PAIL pointer is found in the code vector. The old display is then copied to the new frame, and updated by pushing the new static link on top of it. The old lexical level is incremented and copied to the appropriate place.

The evaluated parameters may now be copied from the old stack frame to the top of the new stacks. The saved main stack pointer, and the number of pointers in the old frame, are adjusted to remove the parameters and the closure of the procedure being applied from the old frame's stacks. Now all that is necessary is to set the local frame base register to point to the new frame, and set the code pointer to the start of the abstract machine code in the current code vector, and the new procedure may start to execute.

The inclusion of both the dynamic link, which allows the dynamic call chain to be followed, and a pointer to the PAIL code from which the current code vector was generated, allows a great deal of debugging support, with a very small penalty in terms of execution speed.

2.4. The Block Retention Mechanism

The architecture described so far using individual stack frame objects and two-level addressing provides all the support necessary for a block retention scheme. This is required to support first class procedures which are allowed to have free variables, which may be shared between more than one procedure. Many languages have module constructs with essentially the same semantics. A simple example of this in Napier is:

```
let counter =
begin
        let a := 0

        proc( -> int )
        begin
                a := a + 1
                a
        end
end
```

358

The location "counter" is associated with the value of the following block, which is the procedure literal of type **proc(-> int)**. The code of this procedure first increments the location "a", and then returns "a" as the value of the block. The important point to notice is that the procedure literal value is in scope for longer than the free variable which it encapsulates.

In a traditional stack-based implementation of a block-structured language, the location used for the variable "a" would be free for re-use after the end of the block which contains the procedure. This does not work in this context, as the location may be subsequently used. Note too that it is the location itself, rather than a copy of its contained value, which is important. It is possible for two different procedures to use the same free variable, and so they must access the same location for the correct semantics to be preserved.

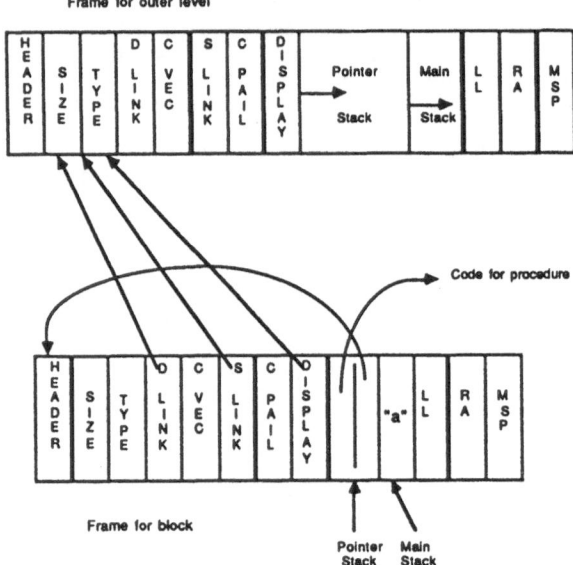

Figure 3: Just Before The Block Exit

The mechanism described above already performs block retention correctly with no further adjustment. When the main block is entered during execution, a new stack frame is created. The appropriate location in this frame is initialised with the integer value zero. A procedure is then pushed onto the pointer stack, consisting of the correct code vector and the environment, which points to the local frame. The situation is now as depicted in Figure 3.

The procedure value of this block is returned to the calling frame in the usual way. This consists of copying the procedure closure from the pointer stack of the block's frame onto the frame of the enclosing scope. The pointer stack of the block's frame is then retracted to remove the procedure value. This leads to the desired situation in Figure 4., where the variable "a" has been encapsulated in the value of the closure. The compiled code for the procedure contains the offset of "a" within the environment, and the location has been correctly preserved.

At compilation time when the code for the procedure is produced there is enough information to know the offset of the location "a" within its frame, and this is planted statically in the procedure's code. If the location is within an outer block, the address of the relevant frame can not be known. What is known, however, is the location within the environment frame which contains the address of the desired frame. This is one of the locations in the display, depending on the lexical level at which the free variable is to be found.

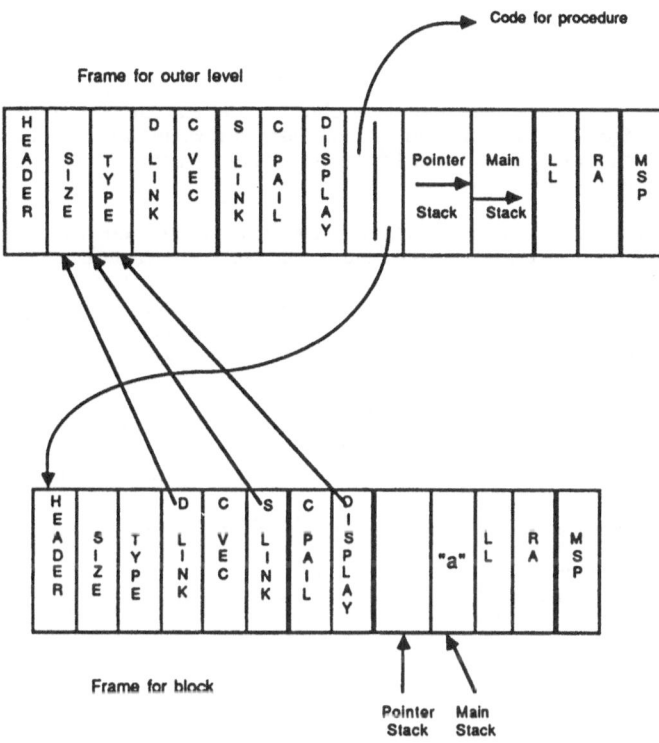

Figure 4: After The Block Exit

As frames are heap objects just like any other, and not distinguished by the object management system, frames which do not contain any encapsulated locations may be garbage collected in the usual way. This will not happen to frames which contain required locations, as they are pointed to by the encapsulating procedure.

A potential hazard of this system is that other values in the kept frame will also not be subject to garbage collection, as it is not known which of the values within a frame are required. In fact, a great deal of optimisation is possible here and it is unusual for objects which are not required to be kept.

3. A LOW-LEVEL TYPE SYSTEM

A major design decision was made to have non-uniform representation of different types of objects in the machine. Some systems, particularly those which support polymorphism and other type abstractions, have a uniform representation in which every object is wrapped in a pointer to a heap object[6]. This allows type abstraction to be implemented easily, but has a drawback in efficiency. The Napier system has a number of different representations for objects on the machine's stacks, including some which have part of their value on either stack. This causes problems with stack balancing and object addressing, solutions to which are presented below.

The abstract machine has its own type system, albeit a very low-level and unenforced system. It is a two-level system, one level describing object layout and the other including some semantic knowledge of the object. Most of the abstract machine instructions are typed, although no attempt is made to ensure that the operand is of the correct type ; the type acts in effect as a parameter to the instruction.

Many language constructs involve operations where the type of the operands is not known statically. As equality is defined over all types in Napier, but is defined differently according to the type of its operands, it is necessary to perform a dynamic type lookup wherever the operand type is not known statically. This happens in the case of variants, polymorphic quantified types, and witnesses to abstract data types. A further need occurs when statically unknown types are assigned into or dereferenced from other data objects, when it is necessary to find the dynamic type to calculate the correct size and addressing information.

Both levels of the type system are finite, and contain only a small number of different types. The first level of the type system contains information as to the location and size of the instruction's operand. The machine supports six different types of objects, which are:

Operand shape	Instruction prefix
single word, main stack	w
double word, main stack	dw
single word, pointer stack	p
double word, pointer stack	dp
one word on each stack	wp
two words on each stack	dwdp

The instructions which are typed in this manner are those instructions which need to know only the shape of the object upon which they operate. These are instructions such as stack load, assignment, duplicate, and retract. The machine operations need to know nothing about the semantic nature of the objects in these locations.

The other, slightly higher level, system is required when the operation does depend on the semantics of the operand. These are all the operations which involve comparison of two objects, in which case the shape of the object is not sufficient. The machine supports different types with the same object formats. An example of this is structures and strings: they both consist of a single pointer, but equality is defined by identity on structures and by character equality on strings. The types supported are:

High-level type(s)	Instruction suffix	Equality semantics
integer,boolean,		
pixel,file	.ib	word equality
real	.r	double word equality
string	.s	heap object equality
structure,vector,image,		
abstract data type	.p	identity (pointer equality)
procedure	.pr	identity (code and closure)
variant	.var	described later
polymorphic	.poly	described later

These are the seven different classes of equivalence defined by the abstract machine.

It would be possible to do a certain amount of static checking on abstract machine code to ensure that this type system is not broken, which could perhaps be useful if an untrusted compiler was producing abstract machine code. However, incorrect store instructions, such as addressing off the end of an object, could not be statically checked from abstract machine code. This is the main danger in allowing untrusted compilers to access the abstract machine at this level. As there is only one persistent store for all users, it is essential that untrusted machine code is not used.

3.1. Machine Type Representations

As these types are used dynamically by the abstract machine, it is necessary to represent them in the most speed-efficient manner possible, so that the machine may procure the required information in the shortest possible time. At various points during the running of the abstract machine, these dynamic type representations are interrogated for the following information:

> Total size of object
> Size of object on pointer stack
> Size of object on main stack

For this reason, integer representations for the types are chosen in such a way that this information may be calculated by fast arithmetic calculations from the representation. This is done by taking a binary representation of an integer, and splitting it into three fields:

> Most significant bits: Pointer stack size
> Middle bits: Further information
> Least significant bits: Main stack size

This means that the main stack size can be found by masking, and the pointer stack size can be found by shifting right. The total object size is calculated by adding these together. An alternative strategy would be to keep the total size, and calculate either the main or pointer stack size when required. However, the total size is required only for structure and vector creation, whereas the individual stack sizes are required for procedure application, which is expected to be the more common operation. The further information bits are needed to differentiate between objects of the same physical size with different semantics, like strings and other pointers.

There are no objects with more than two words on either stack, and only one further bit is necessary to differentiate between strings and the other single pointer types. This means that the types may be encoded in five bits thus:

Machine type	Binary representation	Decimal representation
Single word	00001	1
Double word	00010	2
Single pointer	01000	8
Double pointer	10000	16
String	01100	12
Variant	01001	9

3.2 Implementation Of Variants

Variants are language-level objects which have the semantics of a single labeled location which can be used, according to the label, to store an object of one of a number of different types. An example in Napier is:

rec type intList **is variant**(node : **structure**(hd : int ; tl : intList) ;
tip : null   )

This describes the type of a location which, if it is a list node will be of the described structure type, and if it is the end of the list will be of unit type. These are the semantics of variants as described in [7].

The information needed to represent a variant location in the Napier machine is: the value currently in the location; a representation of the label associated with the branch of the variant which the value is in; and a representation of the abstract machine type of the value. As the machine type is constant for each branch of the variant, it is possible to encode the branch label and the type in a single integer value. This is known as the variant tag. A variant may now be implemented by a compound object consisting of one pointer and one scalar word. The pointer represents the value, and the scalar word is the tag.

The value is represented in different ways depending on its type. If it is a single pointer type, that is structure, vector, string, or abstract data type, then the value itself is used as the pointer value. If it is any other type, then it is wrapped in a structure. The reason for this is that most values used in variant locations are expected to be single pointer types, and this non-general solution is an optimisation based on this. It is because of the different equality semantics that the object's machine type is required to be stored with the tag; projection requires only a test for the correct label representation, and if this does not fail then the type of the value is known statically.

The scalar tag consists of an integer which contains both the label and the type of the object. The labels are encoded in the first twenty-four bits of the word, and the type in the last eight bits. For each variant type, the type-checker allocates integers for each branch of the variant in a consistent manner, so that the label will match the same in other structurally equivalent types. Projection is done by integer equality, as the type will always match if the label does.

The equality tests are performed by first doing an integer equality on the tag. If this fails, then the equality fails immediately. If it succeeds, then the appropriate bits are read from the tag to get the machine type of the value. This is enough information to know how to find the value, and what equality test to do on it.

3.3. Implementation Of Type Abstraction

The support of language constructs which allow the manipulation of objects whose type is not known statically causes new problems with implementation. By static analysis, it is no longer possible to tell:

1. Which stack, and how many words, such an object needs.
2. Where to locate a field of a structure type object.
3. How to perform an equality operation on two such objects.

The Persistent Abstract Machine has polymorphic variants of all instructions whose operation depends upon which of the types is being manipulated. Stack balancing is performed by allocating two words to each stack whenever an object of statically unknown type is pushed onto a stack, thus making sure that there is enough room for it whatever its dynamic type is. This allows stack addressing to be performed statically even when the sizes of objects are non-uniform. If this strategy is used, then many instructions have polymorphic forms which do not need to know the dynamic type, as they simply operate on the relevant two words of each stack. This gives the idea that polymorphic object manipulation is a closed system, with the dynamic type only being needed when an object is entering or leaving the system.

For the operations which do need to know the dynamic type of the object, the information must be in a place where it may be dynamically found and interpreted. This is arranged by placing the machine type representation on the main stack of an artificially constructed frame on the static chain.

This is implementationally equivalent to either a quantified procedure being wrapped in a generating procedure, or an abstract use clause being wrapped in an extra block. The new outer level blocks have the necessary integer declarations - one for each type parameter. The compiler has enough information to know what or where the correct integer values are. It may be known statically, when a universally quantified procedure is specialised by a concrete type; its address is known if a quantified procedure is specialised by another parameter type; and it is information which is held as part of the structure of an abstract data type. The compiler now knows statically an address where the information necessary for the rest of the polymorphic machine instructions may be found.

For example, the polymorphic Napier procedure

```
let id = proc[ t ]( x : t -> t ) ; x
```

would be compiled as if it were

```
let id = proc( t : int -> proc( ? -> ? ) )
begin
        proc( x : ? -> ? ) ; x
end
```

where the question marks may stand for any type, and the value of the integer parameter depends on the type. As this information is planted by the compiler it may be done safely ; all the type checking is still done statically and safely.

When the quantified procedure is specialised, the compiler plants code to call this generator procedure.

id[int]

will be effectively compiled to

id(00001)

and so cause a call of the procedure, with the result being the value

proc(x : int -> int) ; x

and the machine type tag for integer planted in a known place in the static chain. When the compiler needs to know the machine type of an object for a polymorphic operation, it knows where it may be found.

For the implementation of abstract types, the same technique is used. The structure which contains the fields of an abstract type has extra fields which contain the concrete machine type corresponding to each witness type. This information can be planted on creation of the object. When an object of an abstract type is used, the compiler plants code to take this information out and place it in the outer block which is created.

3.4. Implementation Of Subtype Inheritance

The same implementation technique may be used to implement bounded universal quantification when subtype inheritance is used over structure types[8]. For example, in the procedure

    let noOfDoors = proc[c <: car](x : c -> int)
          x(doors)

    ! (this syntax means that the procedure is
    ! universally quantified over any subtype of car)

it is not known statically where the doors field will be found in the structure x. However, the information which is missing may be planted statically by the compiler in a suitable place, on the procedure call. A generator procedure will be created in the same way as for a universally quantified procedure, only the parameters to this procedure when it is called, at the time of specialisation, will be the offsets of each of the fields which belong to the known supertype over which the procedure is declared. So if

    type car is structure(doors : int ; fuel : string)

then the noOfDoors procedure will compile to something equivalent to

    let noOfDoors = proc(doorsOffset,fuelOffset : int -> proc(<: car -> int))
    begin
          proc(x <: car -> int) ; x(doors)
    end

where the compiler has enough information to know where to find the offset.

When the function is specialised, as in

    let fordDoors = noOfDoors[Ford]

the compiler plants the offsets necessary to access the fields "doors" and "fuel" in an object of type Ford.

4. CONCLUSIONS

The major aspects of the Persistent Abstract Machine design have been described. The abstract machine is an integral part of an entire layered architecture, which may be used from any level downwards by a user. It has been shown how the abstract machine interfaces cleanly with the persistent store, and allows persistence to be straightforwardly implemented in a high-level language .

The heap-based storage architecture of the machine supports a method of block retention for almost no extra cost. This allows the implementation of first class procedures and modules in programming languages with the minimum of effort.

A primitive type system contains just enough information to allow machine instructions which behave differently according to the dynamic type of the operands. This type system has a fast and efficient integer encoding.

Finally, this type system in conjunction with the block retention architecture may be used to great effect to provide a fast implementation of polymorphic procedures, abstract data types, and bounded universal quantification.

REFERENCES

1.   Albano, A., Cardelli, L. and Orsini, R. "Galileo: a strongly typed interactive conceptual language". *ACM Transactions on Database Systems* 10(2), 1985, pp. 230-260.

2.   Atkinson, M. and Morrison, R. "Procedures as Persistent Data Objects". *ACM TOPLAS* 7, 4, October 1985, pp. 539-559.

3.   Bailey, P., Maritz, P. and Morrison, R. "The S-algol Abstract Machine". University of St Andrews, CS-80-2, 1980.

4.   Brown, A. "A Distributed Stable Store", *Proc. of the 2nd International Workshop on Persistent Object Systems*, Universities of Glasgow and St Andrews, PPRR-44-87, August 1987, pp. 461-468.

5.   Brown, A., Carrick, R., Connor, R., Dearle, A. and Morrison, R. "The Persistent Abstract Machine". Universities of Glasgow and St Andrews, PPRR-59-88, 1988.

6.   Cardelli, L. "Compiling a Functional Language". *Proc. 1984 LISP and Functional Programming Conference*, Austin, Texas August 1984.

7.   Cardelli, L. "A Semantics of Multiple Inheritance". *Proc. International Symposium on the Semantics of Data Types*, Sophia-Antipolis, France, June 1984.

8.   Cardelli, L. and Wegner, P. "On understanding types, data abstraction and polymorphism". *ACM Computing Surveys*, 17, 4, December 1985, pp. 471-523.

9.   Dearle, A. "Constructing Compilers in a Persistent Environment". *Proc. of the 2nd International Workshop on Persistent Object Systems*, Universities of Glasgow and St Andrews, PPRR-44-87, August 1987, pp. 443-455.

10. Dearle, A. "A Persistent Architecture Intermediate Language". Universities of Glasgow and St Andrews, PPRR-35-87, 1987.

11. Goldberg, A. and Robson, D. "Smalltalk-80. The Language and its Implementation". Addison-Wesley, 1983.

12. McNally, D., Davie, A. and Dearle, A. "A Scheme for Compiling Lazy Functional Languages". University of St Andrews, Staple/StA/88/4, 1988.

13. Morrison, R., Brown, A., Connor, R. and Dearle, A. "The Napier88 Reference Manual". Universities of Glasgow and St Andrews, PPRR-77-89, 1989.

14. "PS-algol Abstract Machine Manual". Universities of Glasgow & St Andrews PPRR-11-85, 1985.

15. "PS-algol Reference Manual, 4th Edition". Universities of Glasgow and St Andrews PPRR-12-87, 1987.

Design of POMP - a Persistent Object Management Processor

W P Cockshott
University of Strathclyde

ABSTRACT

Pomp is a single board persistent object management processor designed to fit into a Sun Computer. When attached to a SUN Vme Bus computer it will allow that machine to create and manipulate a graph of persistent objects. These objects will exist over the lifetime of the hardware, and beyond that provided that other machines capable of reading the archive media exist.

Although the design is for a SUN computer, with minor modifications similar machines could be fitted to the buses of other computers.

1. OTHER RELATED WORK

POMP is similar to a number of other recent hardware experiments: the Linn Rekursiv [10], the IBM persistence coprocessor[9], the IBM 801 store[3], and a number of experimental machines built in Australia [1][11]. Like the IBM machine and the Rekursiv, POMP is designed to attach as a coprocessor to a host computer. Like the Rekursiv it is designed to attach to a SUN. Like the machine developed by Anderson [1] it uses a very large address space with 128 bit object identifiers. It differs from them in that it is optimised to allow efficient access to persistent objects from low level languages like C on the host machine. It does not demand the provision of new programming languages.

2. DESIGN OBJECTIVES

The POMP hardware with the assitance of its internal firmware has to ensure that data objects can be safely stored and recovered and that an individual object can be unambiguously identified over time. Its store has to be resilient under power failure and operating system crashes on the host computer. It has to prevent illicit access to data and ensure that data is only provided to programs on the host machine after the presentation of the appropriate authorisation.

The store provided by the POMP should correspond as far as possible to the Algol abstraction of an infinite store. This is obviously impossible in physical terms but this philosophy can be approached. If the store is so big that it can not be filled up in the lifetime of a single workstation, then from the point of view of that SUN computer the store is infinite. This has three implications:

1   The address space must be very large.
2   Garbage collection must be used to recover space
3   It must be possible to use cheap archival media

We want the POMP to support persistent programming languages executing on the SUN. For efficiency this implies that we can compile statements in persistent langauges directly into 68000 machine code on the SUN which can access the POMP without using any subroutine calls. This implies a hardware interfacing technique that allows the POMP to be accessed by programs running in user mode on the SUN and rules out an approach that would use operating system calls or procedure calls to access the persistent store. If this is achieved one can anticipate that POMP will allow access to databases considerably faster than a software DBMS in which accesses to data have to pass through some layers of software.

Since a computer is of limited use if it can not exchange information with other computers, some provision is necessary for collections of objects to be exported from and imported to the POMP. It is best if this can be done without the POMP having to perform any semantic interpretation of the data objects that are transfered. This is in accordance with the well understood principles of information hiding and division of responsibility.

The POMP object mechanism is such as to allow network software on the host to move objects about between different physical POMPs.

3. PERFORMANCE OBJECTIVES

3.1 Garbage collection

How fast should a POMP be able to create objects?

It depends upon what language you wish to run on it. Let us consider LISP and Prolog as two languages that manipulate objects that might be kept in the POMP. Edinburgh Prolog on the the SUN requires an object creation rate of a few hundred per second. Figures for LISP systems vary more widely. Gabriel [8] gives a peak CONS rate of 12k per second per MIP for Common Lisp. This figure applies to small programs that do not run out of heap so it disregards garbage collection. When garbage collection in a conventional LISP implementation is taken into account the effective object creation rate of LISP falls to about a third of this. If we compare POMP where the garbage collection runs concurrently with host program execution with a conventional Uniprocessor running LISP, we should be able to achieve a threefold increase in the CONS performance, taking us back to an effective rate of 12K per second per host mip.

LISP running on a 3 mip SUN would allow POMP 30 microseconds to recover space for a CONS cell and reallocate it. Given that POMP is using 128 bit identifiers this implies a CONS cell of 256 bits and a storage recovery rate of 1 megabyte per second.

An additional constraint upon the performance of the garbage collector is the requirement that no information about object identifiers be inadvertently included in new objects. This means that all fields of new objects must be cleared to zero on creation.

3.2 The size of PIDs

Persistent Identifiers [7] used on the POMP conform to the 7 layer model for persistent store as described in [8]. The PIDs have the format shown in Figure 1.

seg	ether address	time	passwd
16	48	32	32

FIGURE 1: the format of a PID

The PID is divided into 3 fields:
        An ethernet address of the host
        A 48 bit unique identifier
        A 32 bit password

The unique identifier must identify all objects that will be created on the machine. If a machine is in use for 10 years, 200 working days per year, 8 hours per working day it will be used for about 60,000,000 seconds. At about 12K objects per second this means 360,000,000,000 objects. This number could be encoded in 38 bits. If we allow for a 48 bit identifier then we are allowing for a 1000 fold improvement in object creation performance.

The password field is simple 32 random bits that are appended to make illicit generation of PIDs difficult. Given a system like this the objective is to minimise the possibility of a process being able to forge an identifier. If we kill any process that tries an non valid PID then the computational cost of finding a PID by exhaustive search becomes prohibitive.

3.3 Object Access Rates

How fast does a POMP need to access objects?

Edinburgh Prolog on a SUN 3 performs 15K object accesses per second (private communication from Edinburgh Prolog team). For CAD graphics Tektronix have stated a requirement for 100,000 object accesses per second [7], The distinct number of objects accessed will be lower. Each datum might represent a line and have 5 fields in it: (x1,y1)(x2,y2)plus a pointer to the next object. This means that graphics programs will demand one object to be identified per object drawn. Since a SUN 3 can only draw vectors at a rate of about 3k per second, this means the POMP would have to provide the SUN with only 3k objects per second in a CAD application.

A higher performance would be demanded by LISP. Gabriel gives figures of 50K object accesses per second per MIP in Common Lisp. On a 3 Mip SUN this implies 150K object accesses per second, or 6.6 microseconds per object. Is this feasible?

The code generated by the SUN C compiler to set up an object for access is:

```
                                                                     Clocks
    movl    _Win+0x4,a1      //a1 contains address of 10
                             //pidreg
    movl    a0@+,a1@+        //a0 points at a pid           9
    movl    a0@+,a1@+                                       9
    movl    a0@+,a1@+                                       9
    movl    a0@+,a1@+                                       9
L16:
aa: movl _Win+0x04,a0        // point at command reg        10
    movl a0@(0x10),d0        // get flag                    9
    andl    £-0x80000000,d0  // test valid bit              8
    jne L17                  9
    jra L16
L17:                                               // now do something to
                             // the object
```

The Motorola documentation for the 68020 gives this sequence as 82 clocks assuming that the flag was valid. On a 16Mhz machine this would take 5.1 microseconds. This is the time taken up by instructions executed on the 68020. Of these, only instruction "aa" allows time for the POMP to run in parallel to validate the PID and perform address translation. Following this the SUN must fetch a field (typically another PID) from the POMP which will take another 3 microseconds. This is a total of 8.1 microseconds or more than the 6.6 taken by common lisp. Given that other instructions must also be executed in a LISP interpreter it appears that the combination of SUN and POMP will always be slightly slower than Common Lisp on a SUN using an ordinary RAM heap. Most of this overhead arises from the greater length of PIDs as compared to ordinary addresses.

4. INTERFACES

4.1 Object access mechanisms and VME bus interface

For efficiency, one would like object access constructs in high level languages to compile down into single instructions or even to address modes on the target computer. This approach is possible if you build an entirely new processor with object addressing built in. The Rekursiv is an example of this. It is also feasible with certain microprocessors on the commercial market. The NS32000 series has sufficient status signals comming out of the CPU for a custom memory management chip to intercept certain of the addressing modes and convert them to use object addresssing[4].

On the Motorola processors used in the SUN, this approach is not possible, but there is an attractive alternative. The 68020 supports coprocessors and reserves part of its instructionset for these. Eight coprocessors are defined of which 2 have been reserved by Motorola. One possibility would be to add the POMP in as a standard Motorola coprocessor. Motorola define a series of interface registers and a protocol to be obeyed by attached coprocessors. This requires that additional hardware be directly connected to the CPU bus. This is not directly accessible on the SUN for meachanical reasons.

If you can not interface directly to the CPU bus, then the best alternative is the VME bus. It is no longer possible to use single instructions to access persistent objects, instead the coprocessor has to look like a set of memory mapped registers. This approach is a bit slower but has been found in other cases to be acceptable. For example the Weitek floating point chipset is often used as a memory mapped coprocessor.

Experience with compiling persistent programming languages leads us to believe that the best model is one that uses a set of PID registers to point at a group of persistent objects that are currently of interest. An optimising compiler can deduce useful PIDs to have in registers. Data is then accessed by an offset from one of these registers. POMP does this by having 8 window registers as shown in figure 2.

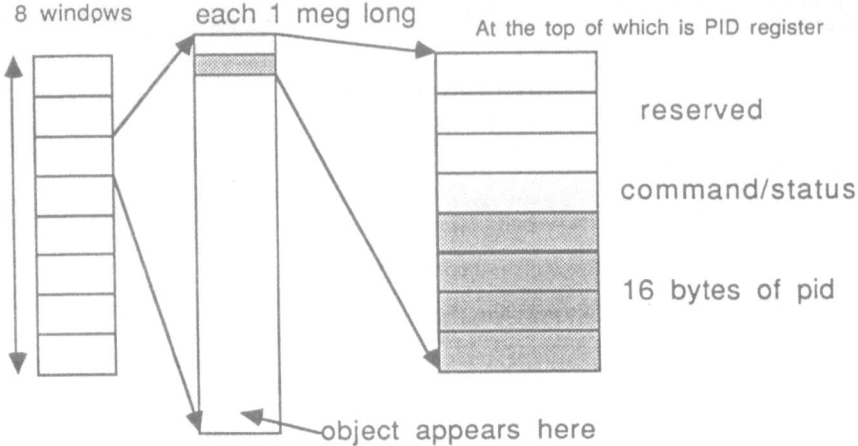

Figure 2: POMP window registers

The structure of a window can be defined in C as
struct RegComBlk{int pid[4],command,reserved[3];};
struct window{int ObjArea[262112]; struct RegComBlk RegArea;};

The idea is that you write a PID into the regarea and the object associated with it then appears in the objarea. The size of the object can be up to just less than a megabyte. The whole POMP occupies 8 megabytes of VME address space.

Each window has associated with it a command register. When this is written to by the VME bus master it accepts commands. When it is read by the bus master it yields status information. The commands allow new objects to be created, object sizes to be altered, and various operations that control the attributes of objects. When used as a status register it can signal when the object associated with a PID has become available, or pass back information about an object such as its size.

4.2 Other interfaces
The POMP has two other interfaces: the SCSI bus interface and an rs232 interface for diagnostic purposes. The SCSI bus is used to mount up to 7 disk controlers. The attached disk capacity could be as great as 14 drives. The internal architecture allows the addressing or 2 gigabytes of disk space. Optical disks can be obtained that interface to SCSI making this a suitable interface for archive purposes.

4.3 Software Requirements
A design objective is that the POMP can run on a SUN with minor alterations to the operating software. What is required is:

1. A device driver able to map the registers of POMP into the address space of a UNIX process and which will prevent other Unix processes accessing those registers for the duration. The driver must also be capable of fielding interrupts generated by POMP and telling POMP what interrupt vector to use.

2. Either a C program that directly uses the registers or a compiler capable of translating

languages like PS-algol or Prolog into sequences of instructions that use the window registers.

3. For multi user use, a modification to the operating system kernel to cause it to save the PID registers used by a process on context switch.

5. IMPLEMENTATION PHILOSOPHY

An object manager must maintain a persistent heap. It does so using physical devices with varying characteristics. The 4 device technologies available to the POMP are : CMOS static Ram, Dynamic Ram, Magnetic Disk, Optical Disk. Each of these technologies should be used for what it is good at.

Cmos Ram is fast and uses little power. With batteries attached it will store information for years. It is the ideal medium for persistent data storage. The disadvantage of it is its cost. In the future we may be able to use it for all our store. We can not afford that now.

Dynamic ram is almost as fast, but it is volatile. Its advantage is that it is cheaper than CMOS ram and it also packs much more densely onto boards. At present densities you can easily fit 50 megabytes onto a SUN VME board.

Magnetic disks are slow, but cheap and non volatile. They are suitable for holding the bulk of infrequently accessed data.

Optical disk drives are expensive and slower than magnetic ones, but the media is cheap and removable. Since they are write once, they are suitable for archives of objetcs that are unlikely to be needed in the future.

Although the characteristics of the devices differ, we want to hide these differences by a series of implementation layers. At the top level the SUN just sees persistent objects and does not know how they are stored.

The POMP has to have firmware and/or microcode to perform some of the tasks associated with object management. It is a good idea if the firmware itself can be structured into layers so that only the lowest layers know about the difference between types of media. If we can erase some of the differences in with circuitry even better. Figure 3 shows the implementation layers of the POMP.

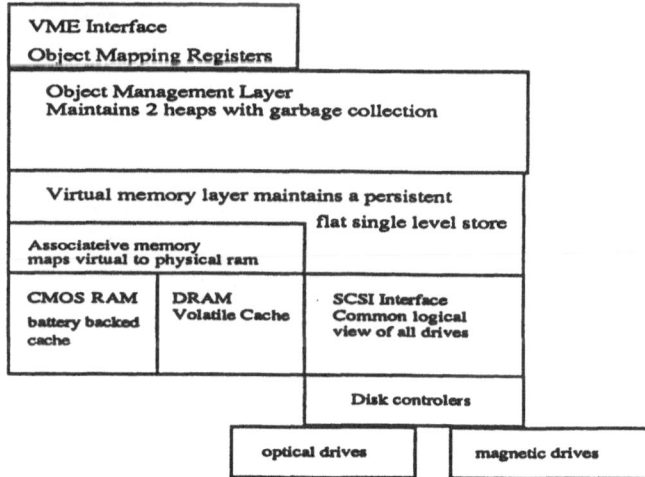

Figure 3 POMP Implementation layers

5.2 VME interface

The VME interface hardware has to provide 3 basic functions:

1. It must recognise when the board is being addressed and generate the appropriate VME address bus handshakes.
2. It must map window regiaters onto persistent objects residing on the POMP.
3. It must respond to commands to create objects etc.

These are 'intelligent' functions in that the actions to be taken may be quite complex. In order to provide this intellignce a microprogrammable interface is provided. The core of this is a 32bit 2901 style datapath provided by a pair of 16 bit wide 49c402 cpu chips. A set of 32 bit buffers provides paths allowing data to flow between 4 buses as shown in figure 4.

As can be seen there is an interface register file of 64 registers used for PID registers and memory mapping purposes.

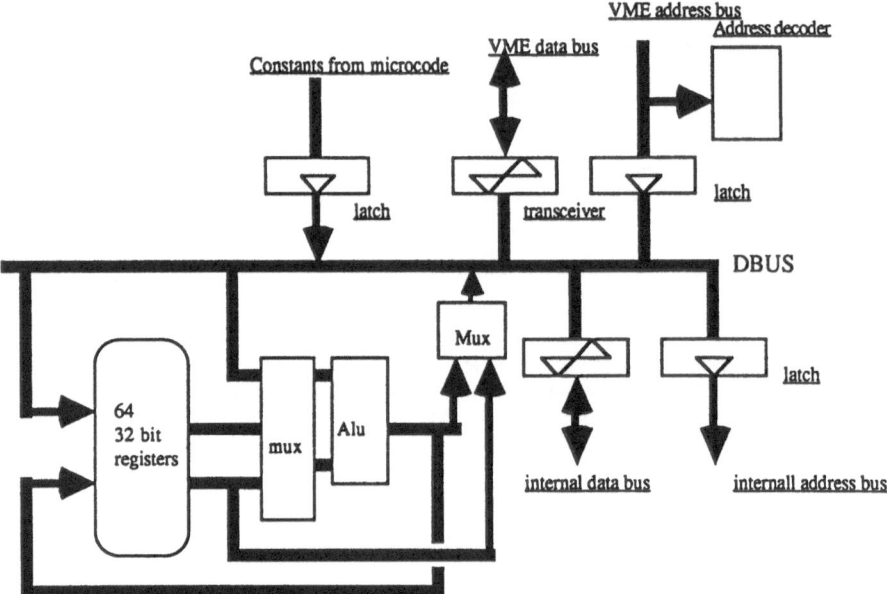

Figure 4 VME bus interface data path.

The 8 PID registers defined in the VME interface are implemented by using 32 out of the set of 64 registers in the bus interface. A further 8 registers are reserved as command/status. These are all accessible from the VME bus. Access is effected by triggering appropriate microcode routines. The address decode logic detects accesses to the window registers and provides a starting vector for the microcode. In the event of attempts to write to the PID registers or the command registers, the microcode gates the VME data-bus into the appropriate register. In the event of a read or write of a field of an object, the microcode computes the appropriate address within the internal address space of the POMP and then connects the internal and VME data buses to allow the SUN to perform a read or write to the internal ram of the POMP.

In order to speed the mapping between the two address spaces, each window register caches

373

the base address and size of the object it refers to. This is done using another 16 registers in the interface register file. When a field of a persistent object is accessed the sequence is:

1. temp:=POMP.address.bus:=VME.address.bus[19..0]+base.address

2. par
　　　connect POMP.databus to VME.databus
　　　error.flag := temp > limit

3. if not error.flag complete VME bus cycle
　else if VME.write then abandon cycle
　　　　else return a random number

Note that an attempt to address outside the bounds of an object has no affect on a write cycle and returns rubbish on a read cycle. Ideally we would like to abort the VME bus cycle in these circumstances, but this will cause the SUN operating system to panic so it is not practicable. The overhead for accessing a field of an object is only one microcode cycle since cycles 2 and 3 are overlapped with the memory access time. Given that the micro cycles are 80ns accessing objects is only slightly slower than accessing ordinary memory.

When a PID register is loaded, the interface microengine must determine where the object is in RAM. It does this by looking up a hashed table which maps PIDs to addresses. This will take an average of about 5 memory cycles of the internal memory or under 1 microsecond. In the event of a PID not being found in the hash table a signal is transmited to the object management layer of the hardware which handles the problem.

5.3 Object Management
Because of the layering built into the architechture the problem of persistence and the problem of object management are distinct. Persistence is supported by a stable virtual memory, object management by a concurrent garbage collection system. Objects are created by the microcoded processor repsonding to a request from the SUN to create a new object of a given size. The object's PID is returned in an interface register and the object created in an area of virtual memory called the Minor Heap.

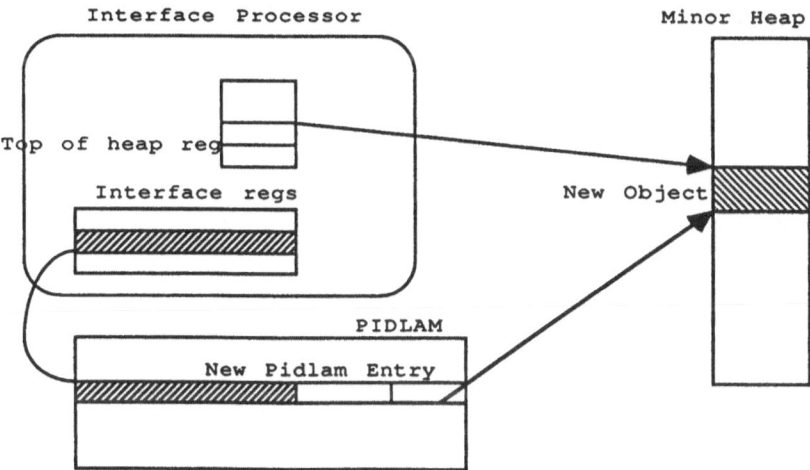

Figure 5: Creating a New Object

A spare register in the 49c402 interface processor points at the top of this heap. A new PID is created, the time and password field of the PID are generated by a real time clock chip and a hardware pseudo random number generator. The random number generator uses a chain code with additional noise bits fed in from the processor address lines. A new entry is made in the

PIDLAM [7] to point to the object.

Garbage collection is concurrent an runs on a second processor, a 68020. This runs a modified Baker garbage collector[2]. The original baker garbage collector used 2 semi-spaces and operated semi concurrently with the main program. It collected objects by copying objects from one space to the other in a breadth first traversal. The two major modifications we have made are to have the garbage collector really concurrent on a second processor and to improve its paging performance by maintaining two heaps.

The Minor heap is sufficiently small to fit into physical memory and resides in a locked down portion of virtual memory, whereas the Major heap is the size of the disk and is subject to paging. If the 49c402 fails to find a requested object in the PIDLAM of the Minor heap it can reauest the 68020 to fetch it from the major heap. Objects migrate between the two heaps in the way developed in PS-algol subsystems: objects in use by programs in the host reside in the Minor heap, inactive ones in the Major heap. However the object management software on the 68020 differs from a conventional PS-algol object manager in that both the major and minor heaps look to it like areas of virtual memory and transfers between them are acomplished by simple memory to memory block moves. These may initiate page faults which are handled by the 68020 paging software. The garbage collector on the 68020 can access the registers of the 49c492 allowing it to update the hidden base address and limit registers if an object is moved on the heap.

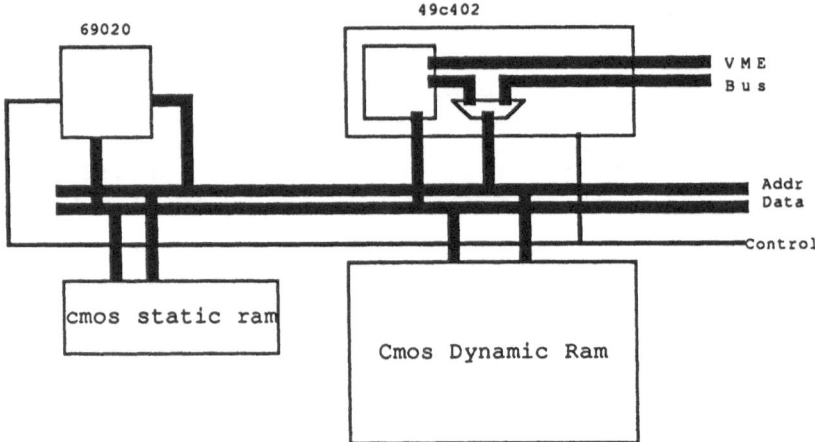

Figure 6: Overall internal Architecture of POMP

5.4 Virtual Memory Support

Since the amount of virtual memory is likely to be large, the use of page tables is uneconomic. If 2 gigabytes of disk were mounted in the virtual address space, then page tables would extend over several megabytes. Instead set associative cache technology is used to implement the virtual memory.

Memory is organised in banks: 5 banks of Cmos Static Ram each of 1 Megabyte and 3 banks of dynamic ram each of 16 megabytes. Associated with each bank of data ram there is a bank of Tag Ram. If we take the case of the dynamic rams, the tag rams associated with each bank are composed of 4096 by 8 bit words. The 32 bit internal address bus of the POMP is connected to these as follows:

Address bits	Go to
0 to 11	Drams
12 to 23	Address inputs of tag rams and to Drams

24 to 31   Data inputs of tag rams

The tag rams are used to store the high order bits of the virtual address of the page selected by lines 12 to 23 that is currently in this bank of memory.
A memory cycle proceeds as follows:
1. Row address strobe asserted to the DRAMS
       simultaneously the middle and high address presented to tag rams.
2. The tag rams compare the contents of their data word with the high
   address bits if they correspond a match signal is asserted.
   The ram address mux presents the column address to the DRAMS.
3. The DRAM controler asserts CAS. This is gated with the match signals
       so that only that bank which found a match will be enabled
4.   An acknowledge signal is asserted to complete the memory cycle.

There is no page translate overhead since the 'translation' occurs in parallel with the Row Address decode by the DRAM chaips. This process goes on in parallel in all banks. The bank that finds that it has the page responds. This is shown schematically in figure 7. Priority logic ensures that if more than 1 bank obtains a match, only one bank may respond to a read operation. If more than one bank obtains a match this indicates that 2 copies of a page are present in physical ram. Priority is given to the copy in CMOS ram.

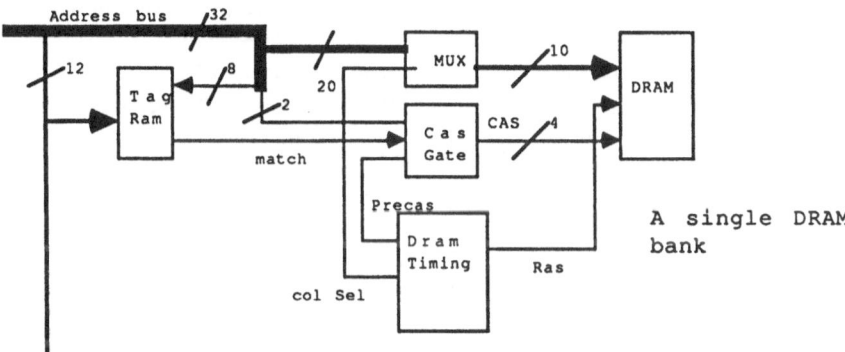

Figure 7 : Dram Control Logic

Persistence is ensured by only allowing writes to the battery backed CMOS ram. The DRAM is treated as a large read only disk cache. Writes are only permited to the DRAM by supervisor mode programs running on the 68020. Essentially this limits DRAM writes to the paging software. A policy is followed of taking a copy of any page that a user mode program (the garbage collector) tries to modify into battery backed ram before allowing the write to proceed. In consequence any write by a user program will be directed to an object in the minor heap which is loaded into battery backed ram. The garbage collector is provided with the abstraction of a very large nonvolatile store. Only the paging software needs to know about the difference between the different forms of memory. The hardware of the memory in conjunction with the paging policy provides the persistence.

6. Status of the Project
The POMP design has been completed. The initial development work was carried out at Memex Information Engines, Ediburgh. This company went into liquidation in early 1988. Alternative sources of funds are being sought to build a prototype at Strathclyde University.

References

1. Anderson, S and Wallace, C. S., "Support for persistent programming and Type Extension in a Capability based Multiprocesso," *Hawai International Conference on System Sciences 22*, vol. 22, Hawai, 1988.

2. Baker, H. G., "List processing in real time on a serial computer," *Communications of the ACM*, vol. 21, pp. 280-294, April 1978.

3. Chang, A and Mergen, M F, "801 Storage: Architecture and Programming," *Transactions on Computer Systems*, vol. 6(1), Feb 1988.

4. Cockshott, W P, Atkinson, M P, Chisholm, K J , Bailey, P, and Morrision, R, "POMS: A persistent object management system," *Software Practice and Experience*, vol. 14 (1), January 1984.

5. Cockshott, W P, "Building a microcomputer with associative virtual memory," *Persistent Programming Research Report*, vol. 20-85, Glasgow University Dept of Computer Science, Glasgow, 1985. Poppy

6. Cockshott, W P, "Persistent Programming and secure data storage," *Information and Software Technology*, vol. 29, pp. 249-256, Butterworth, June 1987.

7. Ecklund, Denise and Ecklund, Earl, "CAD Performance Requirements for Persistent Object Systems," *in Persistent Object Systems: their implementation and use*, vol. Persistent Programming Research Reports 44, Glasgow University Dept of Computer Science, Glasgow, August 1987.

8. Gabriel, R, *Performance and Evaluation of Lisp Systems*, MIT Press, 1985.

9. Georgiou, C J, Palmer, S L, and Rosenfield, P L, "An Experimental Coprocessor for Implementing Persistent Objects on an IBM 4381," *Second Intl Conf on Architectural Support for Programming Languages and Operating Systems*, IEEE, 1987.

10. Harland, David, *REKURSIV object oriented computer architecture*, Ellis Horwood, 1988.

11. Rosenberg, J and Keedy, J L, "Object Management and Addressing in the MONADS architecture," *in Persistent Object Systems: their implementation and use*, vol. Persistent Programming Research Reports 44, Glasgow University Dept of Computer Science, Glasgow, August 1987.

A Capability-Based Massive Memory Computer[1]

J. Rosenberg and D.M. Koch
University of Newcastle

J.L. Keedy
University of Bremen

ABSTRACT

Conventional supercomputers gain their speed from the use of complicated
and expensive multi-stage processor designs and/or the employment of a
large number of simple processors working in parallel. This paper
investigates another approach, based on using a massive main memory (in
the order of gigabytes). The paper discusses the advantages of this
approach in supporting database applications, VLSI applications and many
other applications working on large volumes of data. It is shown how the
architecture of the MONADS-PC system, a capability-based computer
developed in Australia by the authors, can be adapted to support such a
large memory. The architectural design of a new machine based on
MONADS-PC is given, with special emphasis on the addressing and
address translation issue.

1. INTRODUCTION

Computers which are capable of executing programs at very high speed, often known as
supercomputers, are in demand largely in scientific or mathematical environments.
Examples of such computations include weather forecasting, theoretical physics,
theoretical chemistry and combinatorics.

Such computers have normally achieved their exceptional performance not merely by the
use of very fast electronic circuitry but also by means of complicated and expensive
multi-stage processor designs (cf. the Cyber and Cray systems [1]). The basic problem
with this older style of supercomputers is their extremely high cost, deriving from their
specialised design, their ultra-fast components, and their relatively small market.

---

[1] Based on "A Massive Memory Supercomputer" by J. Rosenberg, D.M. Koch and J.L. Keedy which
appeared in *Proceedings of 22nd Annual Hawaii International Conference*, January 1989, pp. 338-345, ©
1989 IEEE.

Another approach to supercomputing has been the array processor (cf. ICL DAP [2] and STARAN [3, 4]), based on the use of many simple processors working in parallel on the elements of an array. The problems with such systems include their limited range of application and the difficulties in programming them for efficient use.

More recently considerable effort has been devoted to the idea of harnassing the power of many cheap modern microprocessors into a single system to serve as a supercomputer (cf. INMOS transputer systems [5] and the Wallace Multiprocessor [6, 7]). In this case there are synchronisation and control problems at the hardware level, and even more important, the programmer of such a computer faces the extremely difficult task of decomposing his problem into a parallel program. Parallel programs are notoriously hard to develop and the results are often very complex. The scientists and mathematicians who typically develop programs for supercomputers are usually unskilled in the esoteric arts of parallel programming, and are unlikely to want to sacrifice the extra time required for this task. Furthermore, many of the problems for which supercomputers are used are naturally sequential, and attempts to find algorithms which can take advantage of large numbers of parallel processors will in many cases be fruitless. (Attempts to automate this process, e.g. by the use of clever compilers, will in many cases be just as fruitless.)

Just as the cost of microprocessors has dramatically reduced with progress in VLSI technology, so also has the cost of main memory. This in principle opens up a quite different approach to the development of supercomputers: computers with a massive main memory rather than a large number of processors. It is perhaps less intuitively obvious that processing speed can be increased by increasing the size of memory than by increasing the number of processors. Nevertheless there are several factors which favour this view.

- At the theoretical computer science level support is derived from the *parallel computation thesis [8]*, which effectively equates memory space and computational speed, confirming the intuition of programmers that there is a memory space/processing time trade-off.

- At the more practical level, the equivalence of algorithmically computed functions and table look ups indicates that many sub-computations can actually be avoided if there is sufficient main memory to allow fast look up of values. This can apply equally to commercially relevant computations (e.g. tax calculation formula *vs* tax table) and to scientific/mathematical computations (e.g. square root algorithm *vs* table of square roots).

- However rapidly a processor can theoretically execute, its effective speed is limited by the availability in the main memory of the information which has to be processed. If data is unavailable the program's execution is halted until the disk access which makes it available is completed. Since the time taken to complete a disk access will typically cost of the order of 1,000,000 supercomputer instructions or more, a substantial improvement can be achieved by reducing the disk accesses through the provision of more main memory. (Many supercomputer problems require access to arrays which are very substantially larger than the available main memory typically configured onto supercomputers.)

For these reasons it is clear that in principle a computer configured with a massive amount of main memory but with a fairly conventional processor (in terms of speed) will, for the right kinds of program, perform extremely well and can claim to be called a supercomputer, at least in the same sense as a computer system designed to achieve its speed from the combined power of many microprocessors. In addition there are many other applications which would perform far better on a massive memory machine than on a conventional architecture, mainly because of their pattern of access to data. The following list gives a few examples cited by Garcia-Molina et al [9].

- The majority of database applications require only modest processing power but access vast quantities of data, often in an essentially random manner. The speed of execution of these programs is therefore largely governed by the time taken to retrieve data from secondary storage. This time could be eliminated if the database were held in main memory.

- VLSI design requires the manipulation of large quantities of data. Routing and layout algorithms typically access this data randomly and thus the execution of these algorithms on large designs can result in severe thrashing on conventional architectures.

- Artificial intelligence applications are well known for producing very large and complex temporary data structures, creating a substantial garbage collection problem in systems which have limited amounts of main memory. However, such time-consuming activity can be avoided if a massive main memory is available, by leaving the reclamation of all space until completion of the program.

These are but a few of many applications which would be well suited to execution on a massive memory machine. Other examples include problems in theoretical physics and mathematics which require the manipulation of very large matrices in an essentially random fashion. Many of these problems simply cannot be solved (in reasonable time) on a conventional computer.

In Garcia et al [10] a model is developed for program memory-reference behaviour. The effects of increasing the size of memory on program execution time is analysed by using a notional value called the *memory-bound factor* (MBF), which is the ratio of program execution time when half of a program's address-space fits in memory to the execution time when all of the address space fits into memory. Seven bench-mark programs are analysed using the model. The results showed that many applications achieve a dramatic reduction in execution time through the use of a large memory. For example, a program executing an algorithm to find the shortest paths between all pairs of nodes of a graph had an MBF in excess of 70, and a VLSI layout tool had an MBF of about 20. This gives us further confidence that a massive memory machine is an approach to supercomputing that is worth pursuing.

This paper reports on a project at the University of Newcastle which aims to construct such a massive memory computer (with an initial configuration of 4 gigabytes) to demonstrate the practicality of this approach to supercomputing. The computer, known as MONADS-MM will derive its effective speed from the use of massive amounts of main memory and consequently will have significant cost advantages over other kinds of supercomputer because:

(i) memory is cheaper than other kinds of computer component from which supercomputer power can be derived and is reducing rapidly in price;

(ii) the design of computers with large amounts of memory is relatively straightforward because of the regularity of the design, in contrast with supercomputers based on either complex processor designs or multiple microprocessors.

Of perhaps even more significance is the ease of writing programs for such computers. Sequential programs developed for earlier supercomputers can be used (subject to the availability of compilers), and new programs developed will be straightforward sequential programs. The parallel programming problems associated with using the multi-microprocessor alternative are avoided.

One of the first proposals for building supercomputers based on the idea of a massive main memory came from the ESP Project at Princeton [9], where the necessary theoretical studies were carried out to justify the development of such computers. At that time there was a basic electrical engineering problem in configuring massive amounts of main memory to a computer system and the main thrust of their research was to solve this problem. However, advances in the development of relatively cheap modern memory with substantially higher packing densities has now reduced this problem to a minimum. In the proposed machine there will be 32 memory cards each holding 128 megabytes, allowing for a total memory size of 4 gigabytes. This will be increased to 16 gigabytes when 4 megabit chips become available. More recently, the same group at Princeton have been continuing their research by using a custom-built VAX system configured with 128 megabytes of memory. However, they point out that this approach is limited because of the 32 bit address size [10].

It is this addressing problem which has led to the massive memory machine project at the University of Newcastle. The project has grown out of an earlier machine effort known as MONADS-PC [11]. This machine has already solved many of the addressing problems (for different reasons). In the next section these problems are discussed in more detail. Then follows a description of the MONADS-PC architecture and of the techniques used to adapt this structure for the massive memory machine.

2. ADDRESSING A MASSIVE MAIN MEMORY

For a program to take effective advantage of a massive memory it needs to be able to use large (virtual) addresses: a 34-bit address is the minimum needed to address the proposed sixteen gigabytes, for example. This is beyond the limit of conventional machine architectures, which typically have 32 bit virtual addresses (e.g. VAX) or less (half of which are often dedicated to addressing the operating system), and never have such large main memory addresses. Consequently, massive main memory machines pose a serious addressing problem for conventional architectures. We have found this view confirmed in questions to the chief architect of a new range of large UNIX-based computers at a recent conference; from his answers it was evident that arbitrary decisions would be made to lock down in the massive memory crucial operating system tables, system directories, etc. in an attempt to use the space available. However, such solutions are skirting around the edges of the problem and certainly do not resolve the addressing issues for the sorts of supercomputer problem mentioned above.

A further aspect of the same problem is the conventional approach to organising virtual memory page tables. Assuming four gigabytes of virtual addressing and a page size of 1 kilobyte, with each entry occupying four bytes, the result is a page table of 16 megabytes, which in itself is not serious, as it can be locked down in a massive memory, but given the conventional approach of using non-unique virtual addresses, each page table for each process must be so locked down, or some special alternative mechanism introduced to organise such page tables. Thus, while using a massive memory computer to process a single supercomputer application might not be impossible, the conventional organisation of page tables would mitigate strongly against more general purpose use of the computer for many processes.

Somewhat more serious is the poor performance which would be achieved by conventional system design in conjunction with a massive main memory. Processor speed is normally kept high by the use of an address translation look-aside buffer containing via a small fast memory the most recently used virtual page numbers and their corresponding physical page numbers. However, if the virtual addresses dynamically generated by programs are widely scattered, as is typically the case for supercomputer programs which access very large amounts of data, there would be many misses on the look-aside buffer, resulting in most memory references requiring a second memory reference to access the corresponding page table entry. If the size of the look-aside buffer is dramatically increased in an attempt to reduce this problem, with the usual non-unique addressing schemes the overhead of managing and flushing the buffer on process switches becomes serious.

A further problem derives from the fact that conventional system software (compilers and operating systems) has not been designed to take advantage of massive main memories. One of the fundamental aspects of any conventional operating system is a *file system*, which stores large amounts of data on disk and makes them available to programs in a small number of *buffers*. Programming languages are likewise organised to make permanent data sets and large data sets available via a file system. A little reflection confirms that file systems are in fact complex mechanisms designed, in part, to overcome the limitations of small addresses and small amounts of main memory in computer systems. In a massive memory system the file system technique of transferring information to buffers is clearly inappropriate. Attempting to overcome this problem by assigning a very large number of buffers to the file system would be inefficient and clumsy, because

(a) the memory would then be statically partitioned in an arbitrary way between the virtual memory manager and the file system (potentially very wastefully, because the optimum use of memory varies dynamically between the two)

(b) the file system would become a major main memory resource manager, duplicating the work of the virtual memory manager

(c) the information in file buffers is usually further transferred to the user program's own area for processing.

Thus it is evident that the efficient and convenient use of systems with a massive main memory is not simply a matter of scaling up conventional addressing techniques and using conventional software. These are the problems tackled in this project.

3. THE MONADS-PC SYSTEM

The starting point for the research is the previous architectural work of the MONADS Project, which has culminated in the development of the MONADS-PC system [11]. From the viewpoint of the massive memory machine project, the most relevant aspects of the MONADS-PC are its virtual memory structure and the software which supports this structure.

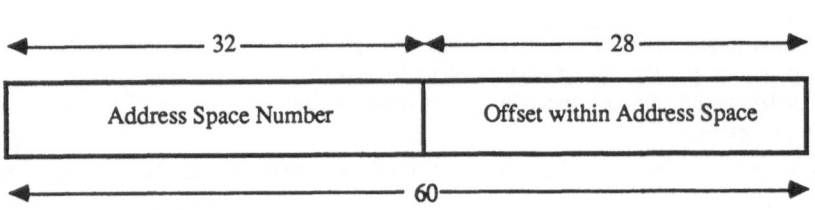

Figure 1: A MONADS-PC Virtual Address

Virtual addresses on the MONADS-PC are 60 bits in size. The address is divided into two parts, an address space number and an offset. This is illustrated in figure 1. An address space is used to hold a related group of segments (e.g. the code of a program, the data of a program or a process stack). When an address space is created it is allocated a unique number and this number is never re-used, even after the address space has been deleted. Address spaces are paged, with a page size of 4096 bytes. The 28 bit offset portion of a virtual address identifies a byte within the address space.

Each address space is divided into a number of logical segments. Segmentation and paging are treated orthogonally as independent concepts, and segment boundaries are not required to begin on page boundaries [12]. Programs never directly use virtual addresses; rather they address segments via segment lists. A segment list contains a number of capabilities for segments in an address space. The format of each segment list entry is shown in figure 2. Thus a segment list entry is effectively a capability for a window onto the address space. The entire structure is illustrated in figure 3.

Each process in the MONADS-PC system has a stack address space. This is used to hold linkage information on procedure calls, local data for procedures and for temporary storage during expression evaluation. The data on the stack is also held in segments and is addressed via segment lists.

The addressing environment of a process on MONADS is defined by the segment list entries of the segment lists which it can use. The valid segment lists for a process are made accessible via a table held at the base of the stack, in an area of memory not directly addressable by programs. The entries in this table are called *bases,* and can be viewed as capabilities for the segment lists. The base table is used to control access to both persistent and local data, including an implementation of block structure which is not dissimilar to that found in the Burroughs B6700 [13].

Address Space Number	Offset	Limit	Access Rights

Figure 2: A Segment List Entry

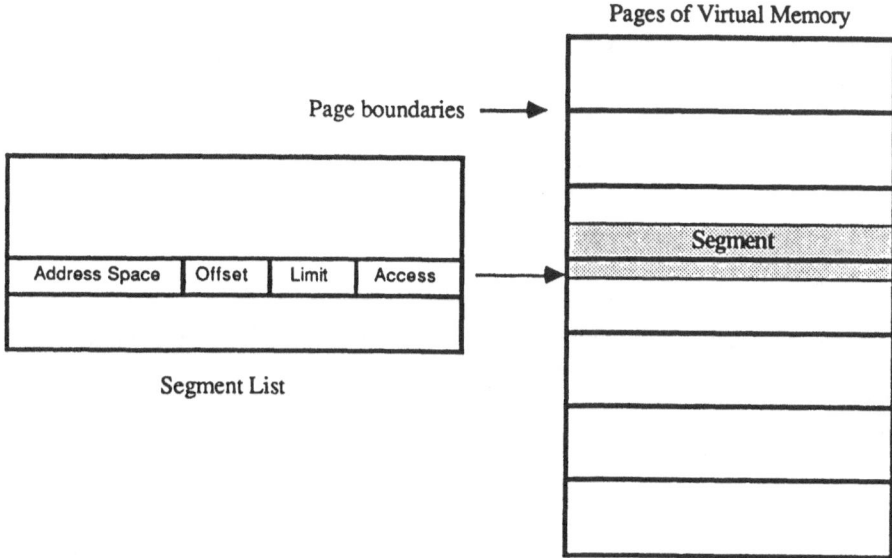

Figure 3: Segments Mapped onto Pages

Access to a byte in the virtual memory can therefore be achieved by specifying a base, segment list entry and an offset within the segment. Naturally, the bases and segment list entries are only modified by special system management instructions. Segments can themselves contain further segment lists and the structure can be nested to any level. This facility can be used to produce complex data structures (trees, linked lists, etc.) [14].

The MONADS-PC architecture supports up to 32 bases and (logically) 2^{32} segments per segment list. In order to reduce the size of addresses in instructions, and for efficiency reasons, 16 capability registers are available to a process. These have the same format as segment list entries and may be loaded from a segment list by a system management instruction. Thus machine instructions can address data by specifying a capability register and an offset (in the form of an index register and/or literal value).

The 60 bit virtual addresses are translated to 23 bit physical addresses by the address translation unit (ATU). The ATU contains a hash table with imbedded overflow. At all times the table contains an entry for every occupied physical page frame. The structure of each cell in the hash table is shown in figure 4. This table is used to access memory as follows. The page number portion of the virtual address (48 bits) is hashed to produce an address within the hash table. The key portion of the cell is compared to the page number; if it matches then the physical page number is extracted. Otherwise the link field is used to obtain the address of the next cell in the chain. This process continues until either a match is found or the end-of-chain is reached. The foreign bit indicates that a cell is part of a chain rather than being a primary entry point.

Virtual Page Key	Phys. Page #	F	E	R	M	C	Link Pointer

Where: F denotes cell is foreign
E denotes cell is end of overflow chain
R denotes page is read only
M is set by hardware when page is modified
C denotes page cannot be placed in cache

Figure 4: A Cell of the Address Translator Table

The process of chasing chains is controlled by a (hardware) state machine. In order to minimise chain length it is desirable that the hash table be sparsely occupied. The intended occupancy ratio of four to one requires, on average, 1.125 probes to translate an address. Thus the processor can view the ATU as a black box which, given a virtual address, either reads/writes the data or causes a page fault. This type of address translation scheme is further described in [15, 16]. The MONADS-PC system also has a conventional code and data cache to improve performance.

The MONADS-PC hardware was completed in 1985 and is fully tested and operational. Two prototypes exist currently and a third is under construction. It can be seen from the above description that the MONADS-PC approach solves the first of the problems, namely the efficient translation of large virtual addresses. Some scaling up is necessary to increase the size of the physical addresses and this is discussed in the next section.

The operating system of the MONADS-PC system, which is currently in an advanced state of development, has been designed to take advantage of the unusual features of the hardware. In particular it

- supports a software environment which views all major software resources (including programs, subroutine libraries, operating system modules, etc. *and files*) as information-hiding modules.
- organises the virtual memory page tables for virtual page number to disk address translation quite independently of the hardware address translation unit.
- supports a persistent virtual memory structure for modules, thus eliminating the need for a separate file system. All data are addressed directly in the virtual memory.

Of greatest significance for the proposed massive memory system are the elimination of separate file accesses via buffers and the independent organisation of page tables. In the case of a large data structure with pages held on contiguous blocks of disk, for example, the entire page table can consist of two words (a starting disk address and a count of blocks), thus eliminating the huge page tables required (because of the hardware design) in conventional virtual memory systems.

The second software contribution from the existing MONADS research is the object-oriented programming language LEIBNIZ, which has been designed to take advantage of the MONADS memory philosophy, and effectively directly provides powerful database facilities based on sets, sequences and tuples (equivalent to relational database facilities). In a massive main memory environment these facilities could be used directly in main memory, contributing both to simplified programming and to efficient execution [17, 18].

4. THE ARCHITECTURE OF THE MONADS-MM COMPUTER

MONADS-MM draws heavily on the experience gained and the architecture of previous MONADS machines. The design and implementation of a complete computer system is a major undertaking and thus we have attempted not to be innovative in all areas. Rather, the research effort is being concentrated on the massive memory, using conventional techniques, wherever possible, for the rest of the system.

Figure 5 shows a block diagram of the MONADS-MM computer. The design allows for up to eight processors. This is intended to allow the system to act as a conventional multi-processor machine. The provision of more than one CPU will also provide a higher degree of reliability and support graceful degradation in the case of a failure in a processor. The number 8 is chosen to utilise the available memory bandwidth without entering into the difficulties of implementing a large scale multiprocessor. In the initial configuration only one processor will be constructed. The inclusion of system-wide processor and memory buses allows for simple module replication and incremental system expansion. The major components of the system are described in the following sections.

4.1. Processor

The processor is basically a 32 bit computing engine. Although the general architecture has borrowed considerably from MONADS-PC, there are major differences. The MONADS-PC processor was a microcoded engine constructed using MSI TTL technology. The major reason for building our own processor was to provide support for the capability registers and large virtual addresses. The disadvantage of this approach was that a large volume of microcode had to be written for the usual arithmetic and floating-point operations. In addition we had to develop our own assembler and compilers.

In the massive memory machine we have taken a different approach. The processor is being based on an off-the-shelf RISC chip set. A final decision has not yet been made, but the most likely contender is the SPARC [19]. The major advantage of using a conventional processor chip is that the basic instruction set is provided. This eliminates much of the routine work involved in developing the system and opens the possibility of using existing compilers, possibly with some modification of the code generated.

The difficulty is that none of the commercially available chip sets supports addresses larger than 32 bits. Our solution is to build addressing hardware external to the processor. Two memory reference instructions will be generated for each access. The first instruction will output as its address the capability register number and will execute in minimum time. The second instruction will output the 32 bit offset relative to the capability register. The capability registers themselves will be held in high-speed RAM external to the processor chip and separate arithmetic units will be provided to perform the address calculations. Although the double-cycling will result in some performance degradation, this should be minimal since the number of memory references should be relatively low on a RISC system. In any case the resultant processor is certain to be faster than a microcoded system constructed using off-the-shelf technology.

386

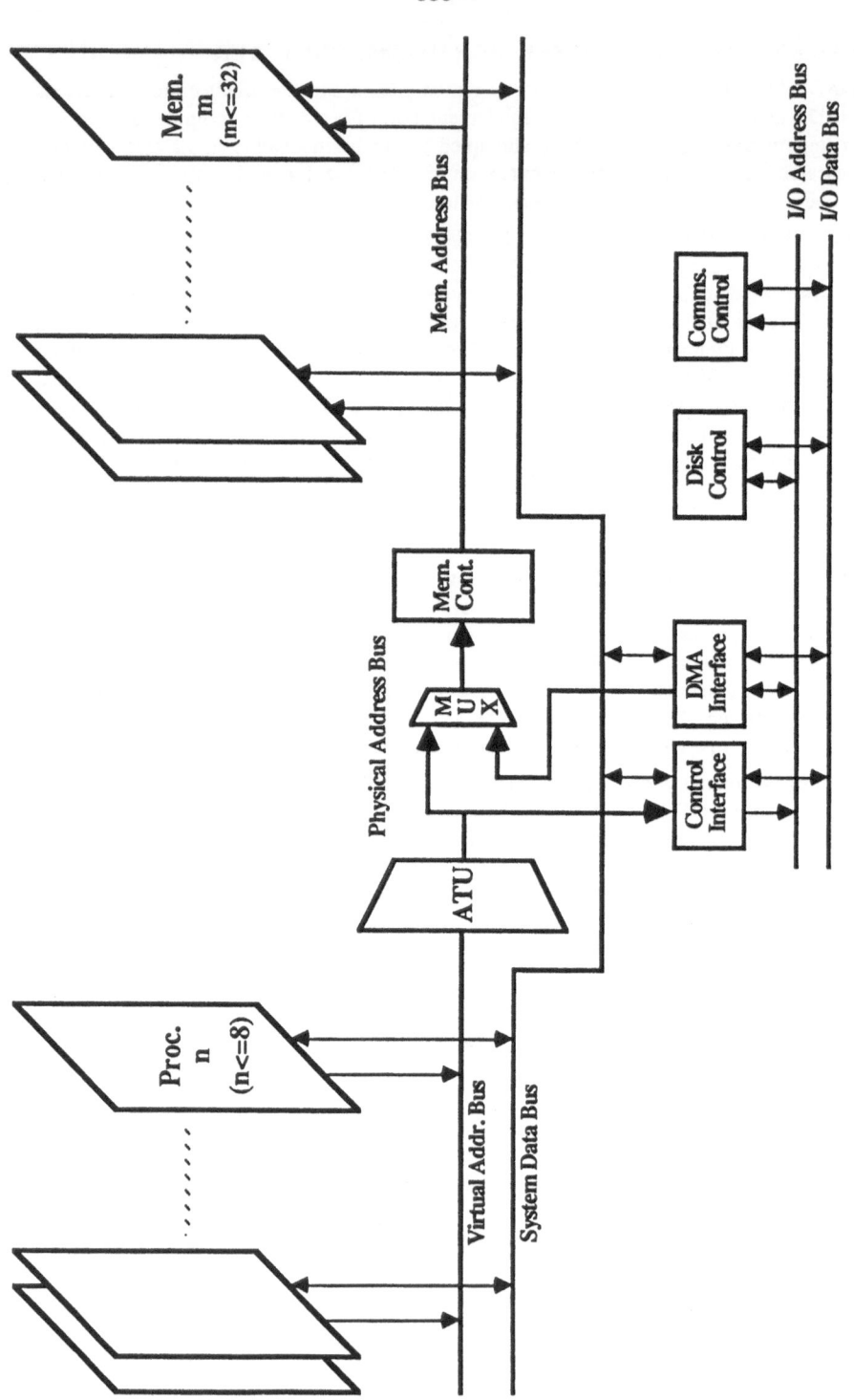

Figure 5: Block Diagram of the MONADS Massive Memory Computer

The virtual address size has been increased from 60 bits to 128 bits, consisting of a 96 bit address space number and a 32 bit offset. Thus the maximum size of an individual address space on MONADS-MM is 4 gigabytes. (This determines the maximum length of a logical segment, but many segments can be concurrently addressed via capabilities.) The increase in address space number size was not strictly necessary for the massive memory machine but has several architectural and management advantages and assists with the implementation of a network of MONADS machines [20, 21] utilising unique addresses throughout the network. It can be achieved without a substantial increase in complexity or cost.

The capability register structure is the same as MONADS-PC except that the relevant fields have been increased in size. Also there are 32 capability registers mapped as a sliding-window [22] to minimise saving and restoring registers on procedure calls. It is also expected that the first few entries in commonly used segment lists will be held in registers.

The target performance for the processor is an effective 5 million instructions per second. The object of the exercise is to gain dramatic throughput improvements via use of the massive main memory. A 5 MIP processor, while not exceptionally fast, will provide acceptable performance for this application. On the MONADS-PC the system management instructions are implemented in microcode since it is essential for overall system performance that these execute quickly. It is proposed that a small amount of dedicated high-speed RAM will provided for these and this will be entered by interpreting particular memory addresses as instructions. An on-board program-controllable cache will be provided to reduce memory traffic and improve performance.

4.2. Address Translation Unit

The address translation unit maps the very large virtual addresses to actual physical addresses. The address translation unit is designed using techniques similar to the MONADS-PC system, i.e. a hardware supported hash table. However, because the size of the hash table is directly proportional to the size of main memory, there are some difficulties.

Consider a page size of 4 kilobytes (as on MONADS-PC) and the proposed initial memory size of 4 gigabytes. This would imply a hash table with 2^{22} entries (assuming an occupancy ratio of four to one, which is required for reasonable efficiency) with each cell having approximately 141 bits. It is not feasible nor economical with current technology to build such a hash table using high-speed RAM. Two alternatives were considered. The first was to build a two level structure similar to that provided on the IBM System 38 [23] and the 801 [24]. This involves having a small fast associative memory associated with a hash table held in main memory. Although this technique is satisfactory in a conventional virtual memory, it was felt that the size of the memory and essentially random nature of accesses exhibited by many algorithms would result in poor performance.

The alternative approach adopted is to have two page sizes[2]. The two sizes supported are

---

[2] A scheme involving several page sizes was also considered, but was rejected due to the increase in complexity.

4 kilobytes and 64 megabytes[3]. An address space contains pages all of a single size and the size is encoded as part of the address space number. Thus objects are designated as either *small* or *large*. Small objects correspond to the objects supported in conventional systems, including for example, source and object programs, operating system tables, directories, process stacks and disk-based files. A 4 kilobyte page size has been found experimentally on the Monads-PC system to perform satisfactorily for this sized object. Large objects are those objects, such as sparse matrices, functions implemented as look-up tables, etc, which are especially appropriate for the massive memory. The choice of 64 megabytes as the page size for these objects is a convenient estimate based on the proposed memory size for the system (4 - 64 gigabytes), the size of the hash table required to support this memory and the average large object size, which it is anticipated will be in the order of hundreds of megabytes. All small objects and some large objects will have disk back-up, as in conventional virtual memory systems, but large objects will optionally have only a main memory copy which is created, used and deleted in the course of a single computation.

The main memory is effectively divided into 64 megabyte pages and some of these are further sub-divided into 4 kilobyte pages. The number of large pages which are sub-divided is a system configuration parameter and may be changed. It is envisaged that initially only one will be used, providing 64 megabytes of main memory for conventional purposes. With such a configuration the hash table will (assuming a 4 gigabyte main memory and an occupancy ratio of four to one) require 256 entries for large pages and 2^{16} entries for small pages. Such a hash table can easily be constructed using the same techniques as MONADS-PC. Since the page size is encoded in the address space number, which is part of the virtual address, a single hash table can be used for both large and small pages. The ATU can determine how many bits to match depending on the page size for the address space.

It should be noted that this structure does not prohibit the use of a different blocking factor for disk storage. Also, as was mentioned earlier, a large address space may be designated as temporary and may never be copied to disk.

Another difference between the ATU on MONADS-MM and MONADS-PC is that the address translation process will be pipelined to allow multiple concurrent translations to occur. This is essential given that the one ATU may be shared by several processors. (Since virtual addresses are unique system-wide, as in the MONADS-PC, the ATU does not need to be flushed on process switches.)

4.3. Memory Subsystem

Provision is made for multiple memory subsystems within one MONADS-MM system. Each memory subsystem provides for 32 memory array cards of 128 megabytes, providing an initial memory subsystem capacity of 4 gigabytes using 1 megabit memory devices. Zig-zag Inline Package (ZIP) devices will be used for the memory to maximise board density. The cards will be designed in such a way that 4 megabit devices may be used when economically feasible, yielding 16 gigabytes per subsystem. The boards are

---

[3] In fact the hardware is being designed in such a way that these sizes can be changed without major modification.

very simple and contain basically only the array and associated buffers.

One memory controller card is required per memory subsystem to provide access and refresh control to the memory array cards. The memory controller provides sufficient control to allow overlapped accesses to individual memory array cards, thus optimising memory subsystem throughput in a multiprocessor situation.

4.4. Input-Output Subsystem

The input-output system is separate from the memory subsystem. It utilises commercially available board level components in an industry standard bus[4]. Support will be provided for secondary storage devices, asynchronous terminal lines and an ethernet connection. The use of commercially available bus and board level components was a deliberate decision in order to reduce the amount of design effort required.

There are two purpose-built interfaces in the input-output subsystem. The first, the *control interface*, provides a path between processors and the input-output controllers. This interface is intelligent and able to perform complete input-output operations autonomously. The second purpose-built interface is the *DMA interface*. This provides a high-speed direct memory access channel between the input-output bus and the memory subsystem.

5. CONCLUSION

At the time of writing the MONADS-MM is in the process of being designed. The initial configuration will have one processor and 4 gigabytes of memory[5]. It is expected that the prototype will be operational by late 1989. By this time there will be a considerable body of test software available from the MONADS-PC system. We also intend to transport a number of mathematical applications which currently cannot be satisfactorily executed on a conventional architecture (a VAX 8550) due to a lack of memory, to the MONADS-MM system. The results of these experiments will be the subject of a future report.

ACKNOWLEDGEMENTS

This project was supported by the Australian Research Grants Committee (Grant Number A48716316) and the University of Newcastle Senate Research Committee (1988).

REFERENCES

1. Russell, R.M. "The CRAY-1 Computer System", *Comms. A.C.M.*, 21, 1, January 1978, pp. 63-72.

2. Gostick, R.W. "Software and Algorithms for the Distributed-Array Processors", *ICL Technical Journal*, 1, 2, May 1979, pp. 116-135.

---

[4] The bus to be used has not been finalised yet but it will either be VMEbus or a modified form of Multibus I, as was used on MONADS-PC.

[5] In view of the current upturn of memory prices, it may be necessary to delay the purchase of part of this memory.

3. Rudolph, J.A. "A Production Implementation of an Associative Array Processor: STARAN", *Proc. AFIPS FJCC,* 1972, pp. 229-241.

4. Batcher, K.E. "STARAN Parallel Processor System Hardware", *Proc. AFIPS NCC,* 1974, pp. 405-410.

5. INMOS "INMOS Transputer Data Handbook, INMOS, 1986.

6. Wallace, C.S. and Koch, D.M. "TTL-Compatible Multiport Bus", *Computer Systems Science and Engineering,* 1, 1, 1985, pp. 47-52.

7. Pose, R., Anderson, M. and Wallace, C.S. "Implementation of a Tightly-Coupled Multiprocessor", *Proc. 10th Australian Computer Science Conference,* Geelong, January 1987, pp. 330-340.

8. Goldschlager, L.M. "A Universal Interconnection Pattern for Parallel Computers", *J. A.C.M.,* 29, 1982, pp. 1073-1086.

9. Garcia-Molina, H., Lipton, R.J. and Valdes, J. "A Massive Memory Machine", *IEEE Transactions on Computers,* C-33, 5, May 1984, pp. 391-399.

10. Garcia-Molina, H., Park, A. and Rogers, L. "Performance Through Memory", *Proc. SIGMETRICS Conference,* May 1987, pp. 122-131.

11. Rosenberg, J. and Abramson, D.A. "MONADS-PC: A Capability Based Workstation to Support Software Engineering", *Proc. 18th Hawaii International Conference on System Sciences,* 1985, pp. 222-231.

12. Keedy, J.L. "Paging and Small Segments: A Memory Management Model", *Proceedings of the 8th. World Computer Congress, IFIP-80,* Melbourne, 1980, pp. 337-342.

13. Organick, E.I. "Computer Systems Organization, the B5700/6700 Series", Academic Press, New York, 1973.

14. Rosenberg, J. and Keedy, J.L. "Object Management and Addressing in the MONADS Architecture", *Proc. Workshop on Persistent Object Systems,* Appin, Scotland, 1987.

15. Abramson, D.A. "Hardware Management of a Large Virtual Memory", *Proc. 4th Australian Computer Science Conference,* Brisbane (Australian Computer Science Communications 3, 1, 1981, pp. 1-13).

16. Thakkar, S.S. and Knowles, A.E. "Virtual Address Translation Using Parallel Hashing Hardware", *Proceedings Supercomputing Systems Conference,* I.E.E.E., Florida 1985, pp. 697-705.

17. Keedy, J.L. and Evered, M.E. "Modularity in the Language LEIBNIZ", *Proceedings of the First Australian Software Engineering Conference,* Canberra, May 1986, pp 7-13.

18. Keedy, J.L. and Rosenberg, J. "Data Engineering with Sets and Sequences", *Proceedings of the 3rd. Australian Software Engineering Conference,* Canberra, May 1988, pp 79-100.

19. Cypress Semiconductor Corp. "CY7C600 RISC Family Users Guide", June 1988.

20. Abramson, D.A. and Keedy, J.L. "Implementing a Large Virtual Memory in a Distributed Computing System", *Proc. 18th Hawaii International Conference on*

System Sciences, 1985, pp. 515-522.

21. Broessler, P., Henskens, F., Keedy, J.L. and Rosenberg, J. "Addressing Objects in a Very Large Distributed System", *Proceedings of IFIP Conference on Distributed Systems*, Amsterdam, 1987.

22. Patterson D. "Reduced Instruction Set Computers", *Communications of the ACM*, January 1985, 28, 1, pp. 8-21.

23. Berstis, V., Truxal, C.D. and Ranweiler, J.G. "System/38 Addressing and Authorization", I.B.M. System/38 Technical Developments, pp 51-54, 1978.

24. Chang, A. and Mergen, M.F. "801 Storage: Architecture and Programming", *ACM Transactions on Computer Systems*, 6, 1, February 1988, pp. 28-50.

Support for Objects in the MONADS Architecture

James Leslie Keedy
Universität Bremen

John Rosenberg
University of Newcastle

ABSTRACT

The paper outlines those features of the MONADS computer architecture which support object-oriented programming. It begins by describing the MONADS view of objects and then shows how objects are efficiently supported in the system's large persistent uniform virtual memory. Direct architectural support for objects in stack and heap segments is discussed, and the idea of module capabilities and module call segments as a technique for efficiently invoking the operations of persistent major objects in a protected way is also described. Following a description of the underlying memory structure and its use of capability based addressing, the paper concludes with a short discussion of garbage collection, local area networks and a massive memory version of the hardware.

1. INTRODUCTION

The MONADS Project began in 1976 with the aims of developing improved software engineering techniques and stronger mechanisms for supporting protection and privacy of information. The early work was motivated in part by the information hiding technique and by capability based protection ideas. Out of this grew a concept which became known as the *MONADS architecture*. To demonstrate an efficient and realistic implementation of this, a series of computer hardware hardware projects were undertaken, culminating in the development of an entirely new computer system, the MONADS-PC [20]. This is a capability-based system with 60-bit virtual addresses, supporting a large persistent virtual memory which is segmented and paged in an unusual manner.

This has been complemented by the development of an operating system and a new programming language, LEIBNIZ. Together these provide a system suitable for object-oriented programming, with efficient support for temporary and persistent objects ranging from a few bytes to many megabytes in length.

In this paper we first discuss the nature of objects in the MONADS architecture, then describe in broad terms the main features of the architecture designed to provide efficient support for them.

2. OBJECTS IN THE MONADS SYSTEM

The MONADS view of objects has been strongly influenced by the information hiding technique [19], as applicable to the development of large software systems, and the data abstraction technique as supported by programming languages for the introduction of new types [4, 24, 17].

MONADS recognises a *class* of objects as a collection of objects which share a common interface specification. Such specifications are not directly recognised at the architectural level, but are the province of the LEIBNIZ language [5] and its supporting software environment. A class interface is formulated in information hiding terms, with the data, algorithms and other implementation details of objects encapsulated by procedural interfaces. The latter are of three kinds: *routines,* which change the state of an object, *enquiries,* which provide the caller with information about its state, and *naries,* which may operate on several objects of the same class.

A particular implementation for a class of objects is known as a *type manager.* Type managers and other code modules may be either separately compiled by the LEIBNIZ compiler or they may be embedded in the code of other modules.

This introduces a distinction between (separately compiled) *independent objects* and (embedded) *component objects,* which for efficiency and protection reasons are managed differently in the MONADS architecture. Architecturally recognised independent objects correspond to the separate major software resources in conventional software systems. However, in the MONADS systems all such objects have a single architectural structure, consisting of one or more interface procedures, possibly some internal procedures and optionally a group of persistent data segments (as well as temporary data needed during the execution of the code). *Programs* and *subroutine libraries* are simply modules with one or more interface procedures. *Files* are implemented as information hiding modules with persistent data segments, since the architecture makes no provision for free standing data segments [14]. The type managers of file modules use shared reenrant code. Other kinds of modules in conventional systems, e.g. *operating system modules,* can be implemented without difficulty using this same structure [8]. There is no provision for special kinds of module.

Independent objects are supported by various mechanisms which enforce information hiding and provide for protected but efficient inter-module communication. The component objects of modules, e.g. data abstractions, tuples, etc., are implemented at the compiler's discretion on a process stack or in a local or persistent heap. In the following sections we describe this architectural structure in more detail.

3. PROCESSES, STACKS AND STACK FRAMES

When a user is introduced to the system an *independent stack* is created; this persists in the virtual memory until he ceases to be a user. He may create further independent stacks to carry out multiple independent activities and he may also associate *subsidiary stacks* with an independent stack (similar in principle to Burroughs B6700 cactus stacks [18]) in order to execute concurrent computations.

Computations follow the procedure-oriented model [16], i.e. the services of independent objects are invoked as interface procedure calls, using the same stack and not causing a process switch.

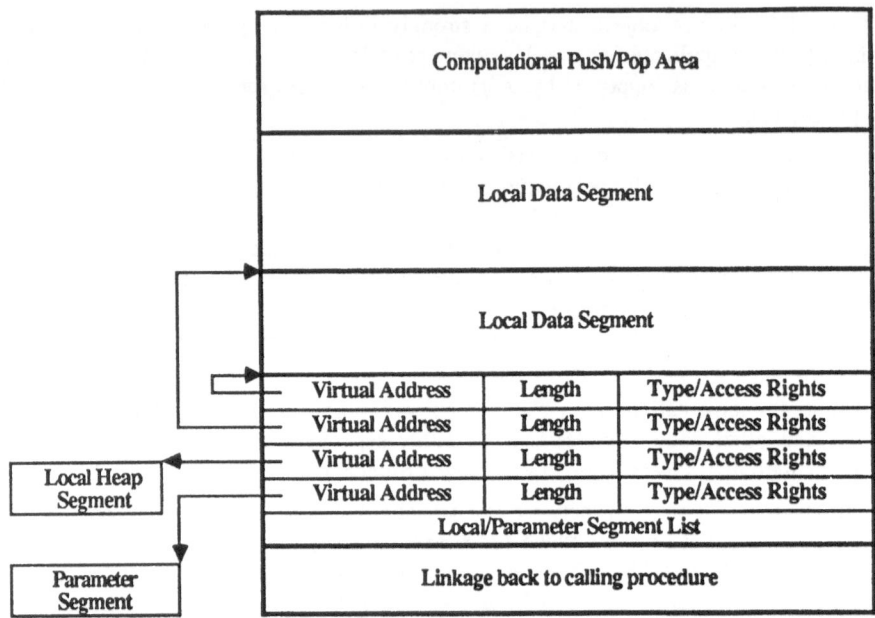

Figure 1: A Stack Frame

A stack frame consists basically of procedure linkage, a segment list, local data segments and a computational push/pop area. The segment list holds *segment capabilities*, containing the virtual address, length, type and access rights of the procedure's local segments and segments passed as parameters (Figure 1). The local data segments of a procedure may be located on the stack and/or in the module's local heap (see the next section). The computational area, which can be linked to the accumulator [9], provides temporary space for intermediate results needed in the evaluation of expressions, etc.

The architecture provides automatic support for lexical level addressing (up to 15 lexical levels). A snapshot of the stack would typically show that it consists of groups of stack frames associated with a history of inter-module calls, the individual stack frames representing procedure calls between and within modules (Figure 2).

The maximum size of a stack in the MONADS-PC is 256 megabytes, allowing ample scope for recursion and for long chains of inter-module calls.

4. LOCAL HEAPS

A *local heap*, also with a maximum size of 256 megabytes, is associated with the intersection of a process and a module. Segment capabilities on the stack serve as initial pointers into this heap. Within the heap are located segments which contain three major fields: a control section (containing type, length, garbage collection and similar information), a list of pointers and a segment content section (Figure 3).

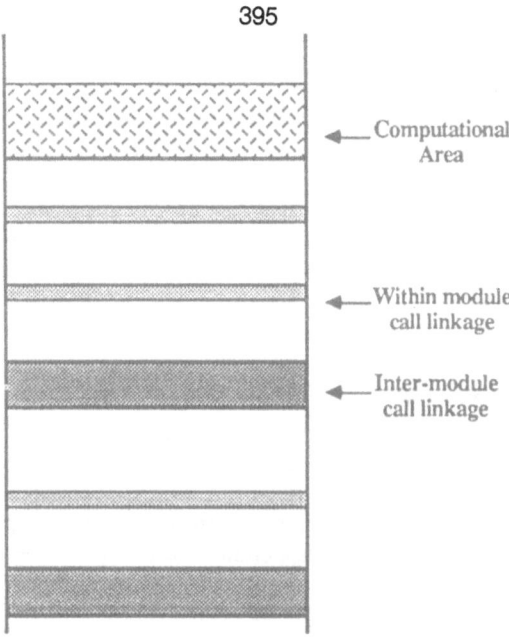

Figure 2: Stack Structure

Pointers in heap segments, unlike segment capabilities on the stack, are only one word long, since the length and type information for the referenced segment can be retrieved from the latter's control section. However, this difference is invisible at the machine instruction level, where pointers and segment capabilities are treated in a uniform manner, subject to the restriction that pointers to stack segments may not be stored in the heap.

The content section contains either normal data (as on the stack), or types of information of a sensitive nature, which modules may access only via special instructions (as defined in the type field of the control section). These special segments include *module call segments* and *module capability segments*. The purposes of these segments are explained in the following sections.

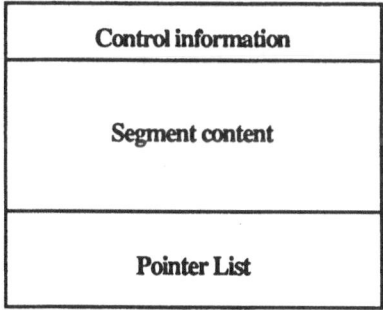

Figure 3: General Structure of a Heap Segment

5. MODULE CAPABILITIES AND DIRECTORIES

In order to link to another module and subsequently be permitted to call its interface procedures, a module must present a *module capability* for the target module. An *owner capability* is created for each newly created independent module and, subject to appropriate authorisations, copies of the capability may be distributed arbitrarily to other modules. A module capability has three major parts: a module identifier (which uniquely identifies the target module for the life-time of the system), some status bits (e.g. indicating ownership and the right to copy the capability) and a set of access rights (Figure 4). The latter indicates which of the interface procedures associated with the target module may be called by the presenter of the capability.

A directory in the MONADS system is effectively a list of symbolic names and associated module capabilities, together with a type manager which provides directory-like operations. Since a directory is a module like any other independent object, access to it is also via a module capability. Consequently a directory can contain capabilities for other directories; hence arbitrary networks of directories can be created. However, a mechanism exists to ensure that *owner* capabilities are always in tree structures, to avoid the problem of lost modules (since deletion of an owner capability results in deletion of the module).

Because module capabilities, being protected by the type/access rights information in segment capabilities and in the control section of heap segments, can be stored in any module, any module can serve as a directory, and consequently individual users or installations can easily develop their own directory software.

6. MODULE CALL SEGMENTS AND INTER-MODULE CALLS

A *module call segment* is created in a local heap when the owning module declares its intention to link to some other module. This involves presenting a module capability for the target module, which is used to set up information to allow the owning module subsequently to make a series of inter-module calls rapidly, by establishing addressing information required to effect these calls and allowing the system to make certain protection checks only once, rather than with each subsequent call. When a module call segment is set up, a new local heap is allocated for use by the target module when called via this module call segment.

The addressing information in a module call segment includes the address of a segment in the local heap of the target module, and whenever the target module is called this is made accessible to the module. This allows the target module to retain information between calls on behalf of the calling module, thus providing a straightforward way of implementing temporary data abstractions (Figure 5).

Module identifier	Status bits	Access Rights

Figure 4: A Module Capability

Normally a local heap is accessible only to its own module, but a segment capability for a local heap segment can be passed as a parameter to another module. The called module can then create new segments in the caller's heap and thus return values which are composed of complex structures (Figure 6).

An entire local heap is deallocated when the module call segment which contains its address is destroyed. This is safe because the rules do not allow pointers for segments in a local heap to exist elsewhere except on heaps and in stack frames which must already have been deallocated. However, this is a recursive process, with the local heaps for any module call segments contained in the heap being recursively deleted. Similarly all the modules whose owner capabilities are deleted with a heap, and any modules whose owner capabilities are in these modules, are also recursively deleted. To achieve these operations efficiently all the module call segments and all the module capability segments in a heap are linked into lists.

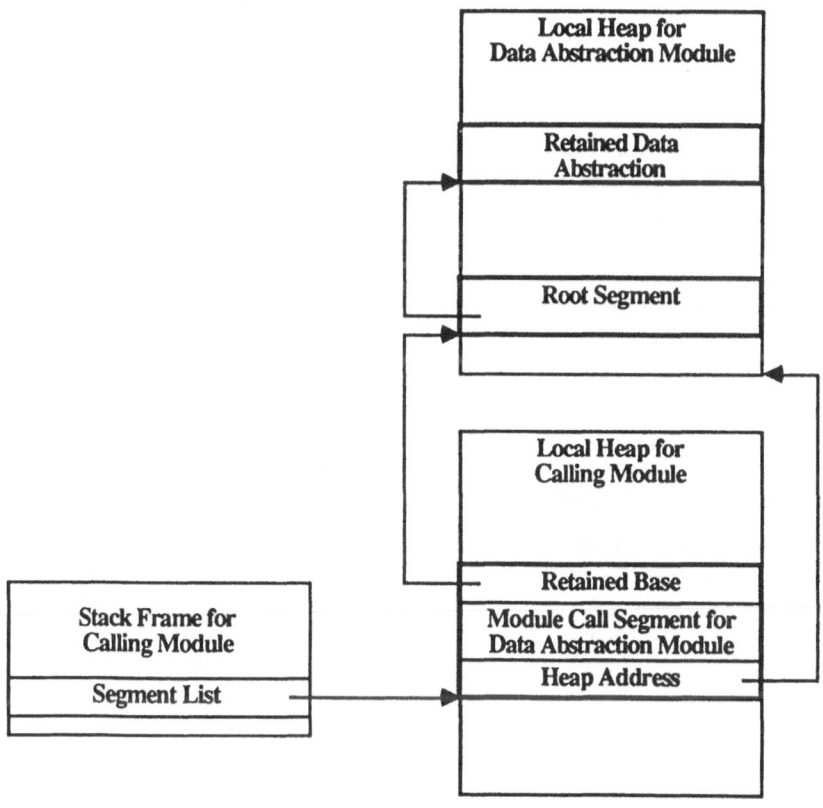

Figure 5: A Retained Temporary Data Abstraction

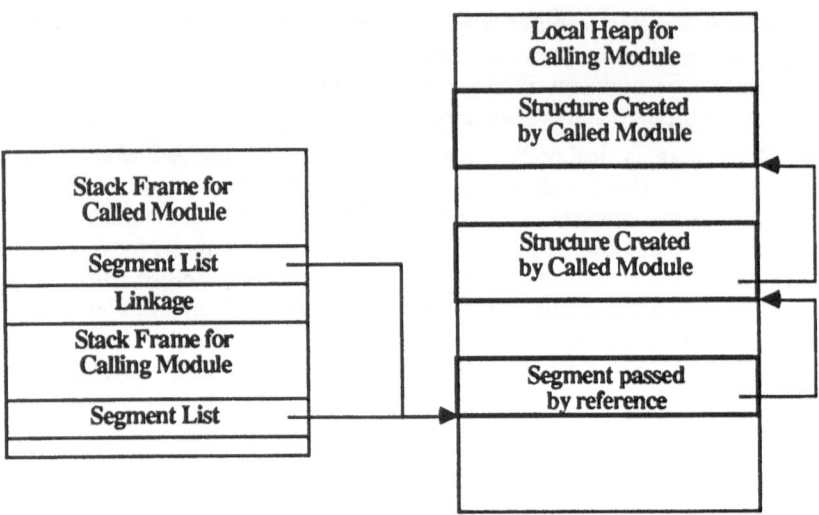

Figure 6: Returning a Complex Structure

7. SUPPORT FOR PERSISTENT MAJOR OBJECTS

Persistent independent objects, equivalent to files (and some operating system modules) in conventional systems, are integrated into the virtual memory of the MONADS system. But as indicated earlier, there are no free-standing data structures; persistent data structures, like temporary ones, are associated with a particular module. From other modules they can only be accessed indirectly via the interface procedures of the owning module's type manager.

To invoke the type manager's procedures for a particular persistent object a module capability must be presented, identifying the module instance, i.e. the object itself. From this the system is also able to locate its type manager (Figure 7). The access rights in the capability indicate which of the type manager's procedures may be called. The type manager does not have an independent right to access objects of its type.

The persistent information of an object is stored in a *file heap*, which also has a maximum size of 256 megabytes in the MONADS-PC System. Segments in this heap are organised in the same way as in local heap segments, with a control section, a list of pointers and a data section. The data section may contain normal data and module capabilities, but not module call segments. When a new object is created, its create procedure will *inter alia* create the root segment of the file heap, which will typically include a list of pointers to allow further segments to be created.

When a module call segment is created for an object, the address of the root segment in the file heap is stored into it, allowing its type manager on subsequent calls to address the segments in the heap.

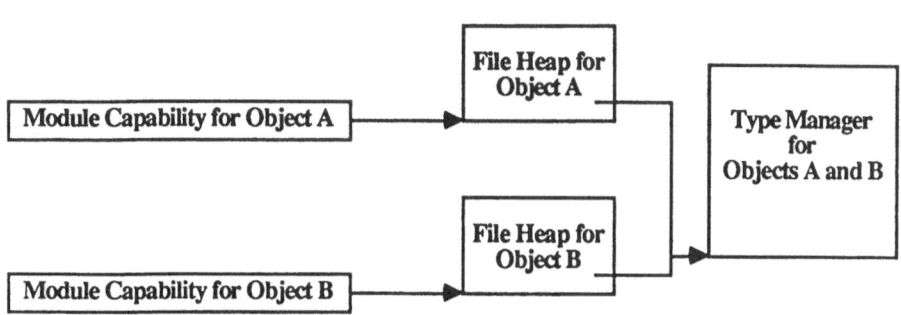

Figure 7: Locating a Type Manager from an Object Capability

The only pointers which may be stored in the segments of a file heap are the addresses of other segments in the same heap. (References to other persistent objects can be achieved by storing module capabilities.) However, pointers to the segments of a file heap may be stored in local heap segments of its file manager. (These are guaranteed to be deleted when the module call segment used to access the type manager is deallocated, i.e. in conventional terms - when the file is closed.)

8. NARY CALLS

A type manager may provide *nary procedures,* i.e. procedures which simultaneously operate on multiple objects of the same type (e.g. to compare, merge or copy them). In this case the caller sets up an *nary call segment,* which is a special kind of module call segment containing *inter alia* the addresses of the root segments in the file heaps of the appropriate objects for which module capabilities have been provided. The different objects can then be simultaneously addressed by the nary procedure.

9. TYPE MANAGERS AND OTHER CODE MODULES

Independent type managers and other code modules (e.g. programs and subroutine libraries) are initially created by a code manager module (e.g. a code generator or a static linker) as normal files, with individual interface and internal procedures and data segments being stored in separate linked lists. On completion of the compilation (or static linking operation) a set of special (but non-privileged) instructions are invoked which set up additional information and carry out certain checks before marking the object as an executable module.

Capabilities which view the module as a code manager file continue to exist and may be used, e.g. to access debugging information. However when the module is made executable a new capability is created with access rights which refer to the interface procedures of the new code rather than to the code manager procedures. Precautions are taken to ensure that a module is not modified while also being used as an executable module.

When a code module is being executed its procedures can only be addressed implicitly via procedure calls, but its associated data structures are made addressable to the code.

This not only allows constants to be addressed, but provides the opportunity to create and access variables associated with the type manager. Such variables might be used for example to count the number of invocations of the type manager's procedures (for statistical or accounting purposes) or to store general information about instances of the type (e.g. the "longest" object of a type for which "length" is an attribute). This has obvious applications in knowledge representation.

10. COMPONENT OBJECTS

In the MONADS system, as in the real world, major independent objects are usually composed of smaller component objects. The main emphasis in the design of the MONADS architecture has been to provide an efficient framework for implementing major independent objects, as this is the area in which conventional computer architectures are most deficient. Hence the introduction of module capabilities and module call segments as a means of providing an efficient dynamic linking scheme which is fully protected and permits efficient inter-module calling between all kinds of modules. Although these features of the architecture can also in principle be used to implement smaller component objects, the overheads in doing so (e.g. the management of a myriad of module capabilities and the creation of a myriad of module call segments) would not justify this except where tight protection is at stake. Consequently it is assumed that component objects within an independent module are normally handled by the compiler. The architecture has been so designed that compilation is not a privileged operation, and inter-module calling easily handles the various kinds of parameter passing used by different languages. Consequently a variety of different languages can be used to implement component objects.

The architecture does, however, provide a general framework to simplify the implementation of component objects. First, it provides a general segmented addressing scheme with efficient space allocation on the stack for static segments and a more general heap allocation scheme for more dynamic components. It also provides an efficient mechanism for calling internal procedures, with automatic lexical level management for block-structured languages. Interface procedures execute at lexical level zero, and internal routines corresponding to type managers for internal objects may also be efficiently called at lexical level zero.

As we have seen, the system directly supports a few crucial kinds of small objects, including module capabilities and module call segments; semaphores [13, 15, 12] are also supported. Other user defined components can take advantage of the protected but not restrictive pointer scheme which allows arbitrary networks of objects to be supported.

The preferred language for software development (for both system and applications software) on the MONADS Project is LEIBNIZ. This provides uniform support for both independent and component objects, hiding from the programmer the architectural differences in support for the two. Data abstraction, tuples (records) and information-hiding are merged into a single module concept which uniformly supports independent objects (with or without persistent data) and component objects [11]. Other features of the language are its very high level data structuring facilities (sets, bags, sequences and mappings) and its absence of files (which can be implemented externally as modules and internally via sets, sequences, etc.), its extensive use of pragmas to provide implementation efficiency and its support for concurrency.

11. THE VIRTUAL MEMORY AND ADDRESSING

Crucial to the efficiency of the above architecture is a suitable virtual memory and addressing structure. The MONADS architecture is supported in a large uniform persistent virtual memory which is paged and segmented and uses capability based addressing.

The MONADS-PC supports 60 bit virtual addresses which have a unique system-wide interpretation independent of the executing process. Consequently all objects can be handled uniformly without concern for the distinctions between computational memory and filestore which characterise conventional systems. This also avoids the many naming problems which are found both in conventional systems and in many capability based systems [6] and eliminates problems such as the non-uniqueness of addresses in address translation caches.

In order to avoid the page table/object table problems, the space management problems and the garbage collection problems which would arise if this huge virtual memory space were left unstructured, it is decomposed into 2^{32} *address spaces,* each with an addressing range of 2^{28} bytes. Separate address spaces are allocated for use as process stacks, local heaps and file heaps (including code modules). The 2^{32} address space numbers are not normally re-used and therefore provide a unique identification for their contents. Consequently the address space number of a file heap can be used in a module capability to identify persistent major objects and code modules. Similarly a stack address space number uniquely identifies a user throughout his period of accreditation in the system.

Pointers in heaps occupy a single 32 bit word. In file heaps there are no inter-address space pointers, so that only 28 bits are actually needed. In local heaps it is possible to store pointers to the code heap and one or, in the case of nary calls, several file heaps; the remaining four bits are used as an index into the list of heaps held in the module/nary call segment.

Segment capabilities on the stack may contain references to a variety of local heaps and file heaps (as a result of parameter passing) and consequently contain a full 60 bit virtual address.

To provide a uniform, efficient and simple addressing structure, segments are addressed by means of *capability registers.* The starting points for each kind of segment are known as *bases.* There are

- fifteen lexical level bases,
- one parameter base (which is used to set up parameters for a procedure about to be called),
- one retained base (to address the root segment in the local heap containing the information which a module retains between calls on behalf of its caller),
- one code base (to address data segments in the code heap), and
- fourteen file bases (of which at most one can be used except in nary calls).

Code is implicitly addressed via invisible capability registers, set up from information stored by the system when a file heap is converted to executable form.

Microcoded instructions exist to load a capability register

(a) from a base, leaving it pointing to a segment capability list on the stack or to a segment in the heap;

(b) from a capability in a segment capability list, in which case it points to a segment on the stack or in a heap;

(c) from a pointer in a heap segment, in which case it points to another heap segment, allowing its pointers and data to be addressed.

Cases (b) and (c) are handled by a single instruction which hides the different formats from the programmer/compiler.

Values in capability registers may be stored into heap segments or as parameters (using the special base), subject to the rules for storing pointers.

A capability register contains a full 60 bit virtual address, a 28 bit segment length, type information about the segment and various control and status bits to ensure that the rules are followed. Capability registers are implemented in fast memory, allowing rapid access to operands, which are normally addressed as a <capability register number, offset> pair, where the offset may be specified as a combination of a literal and an index register value. Scaling and bound checking are carried out in the obvious way.

A module can address sixteen capability registers, allowing operands to be encoded in a few bits, despite the size of virtual addresses. The contents of capability registers are invalidated on inter-module calls, although a shadow held on the stack allows them to be automatically reloaded (on demand) after the return. (The MONADS-PC also has several banks of capability registers to reduce the overheads of loading and unloading on inter-module calls and returns.)

The task of translating 60 bit virtual addresses into much smaller main memory addresses is achieved by means of an address translation unit which maps virtual pages into main memory page frame numbers. Each page is 4 kilobytes long, leaving 48 bit virtual page numbers. A central page table, implemented as a conventional linear list indexed by page number, would be inordinately inefficient. Instead a hash table (with embedded overflow) is implemented in very fast memory, producing for each virtual page number presented either the corresponding page frame number or a page fault indication. This hash table is proportional in length to the size of the main memory (with a loading factor of four to one to reduce the average chain length).

When a page fault occurs the page fault handler uses a different mechanism to locate the disk address of a missing page. It strips off the first 32 bits of the virtual page number, being the address space number of the faulting page. Encoded in this is also the unique volume number of the disk containing the address space. It is able to locate from this the page table for the address space, and hence the disk address of the missing page. It should be noted that the mapping from virtual page number to disk address does not involve data structures or mechanisms known to the hardware (unlike conventional schemes), leaving the software with complete freedom to define its own structures. Thus if the pages of a very large address space are placed in contiguous disk blocks on a large disk, its page map can be described in two words: a disk start address and a length field. But for smaller dynamic address spaces an indexing mechanism is used. In both cases the page map is actually located in the address space itself. Disks in the MONADS system in fact have completely self defining contents.

This scheme uses the fundamental model described in [7] to solve the problem of combining paging and segmentation without incurring high fragmentation overheads for small segments. However, the actual mapping technique is organised quite differently and is described in more detail in [1, 21].

12. DISCUSSION

Initial tests with the MONADS-PC indicate that it executes instructions at similar speeds to conventional systems using similar hardware technology. This is unusual for a capability based system which provides support for object-oriented programming. The main contributing reasons appear to be

- the elimination of a central object table [10];

- the separation of mechanisms for supporting major independent objects and the smaller component objects from which they are composed;

- the use of unique large virtual addresses to identify segments (avoiding the need to invalidate address translation caches on process switches or inter-module calls);

- the use of capability registers to ensure fast addressing in the main/virtual memory;

- the separation of the virtual to main memory address translation mechanism from that for translating virtual addresses to disk addresses.

Furthermore the elimination of a file system and of loader software is likely to result in the execution of far fewer instructions than in many conventional systems. However, proper comparative figures are not yet available.

One interesting aspect of the system design is its effect on the garbage collection problem. The potentially huge task of garbage collecting across the entire virtual memory has been eliminated by strict enforcement of the information hiding principle (ensuring that pointers may not be stored arbitrarily across the virtual memory) and by enforcing a simple ownership rule for major independent objects[1]. This mechanism appears to us to be simpler and more natural than other schemes which have been proposed to manage objects in a huge virtual memory [3].

Garbage collection is thus only a real issue for component objects in heaps. Garbage collection in local heaps is only undertaken at the specific request of the heap's owning module, and in most cases only becomes necessary when disk space becomes critical (unlike conventional systems, which may run out of addresses before running out of memory). However, in very many cases garbage collection will be entirely unnecessary in local heaps, since these are discarded as a complete unit when the caller of the owning module releases his module call segment. To simplify garbage collection in file heaps we have taken the decision that this is only undertaken when the object is inactive, i.e. there are no module call segments in existence for the object. This guarantees that all pointers are contained within the heap itself. These policies will be reviewed when we have more evidence of their effectiveness or otherwise.

---

[1] We dispute the point made by the designers of Hydra [23] that ownership is a policy rather than a mechanism, and is therefore architecturally inappropriate. It would be a simple matter to organise the operating system such that all owner capabilities are stored centrally, and are deleted when some other mechanism determines that the owned object is no longer referenced by other capabilities.

404

One test of an architecture's effectiveness is the ease with which it (and related software) can be applied in a homogeneous local area network. We are currently developing a small LAN of MONADS systems, based on the use of a shared virtual memory in which all addresses in the network are unique, as within a single MONADS system. In this way the normal unit of transfer between separate nodes is the virtual page. Each node detects its own page faults, and if possible resolves them locally. Otherwise it places a request on the network for the missing page. The only changes required to the software, apart from a network driver, are some small modifications to the process scheduler (for synchronisation reasons) and extensions to the page fault handler to request and transmit pages in the network and to synchronise their use [2]. All the higher level software, including directory management, command language interpreters, etc. can be left unmodified, since they are unaware of the virtual memory mechanism[2]. They are thus oblivious to actual configurations, including the location of disks and other peripherals (which are treated as modules in MONADS, accessed via module capabilities and module call segments).

Another interesting aspect of the architecture is its ability to make proper use, without software changes, of the massive amounts of main memory which are now being configured into new systems. This is because it has the virtual addressing capability to match huge main memories, and therefore will avoid the problems which conventional systems will experience in mapping small virtual addressing ranges to larger main memories. Furthermore its address translation technique is well suited the massive main memories. We are currently in the process of designing a new machine, to be known as MONADS-MM, which will have support for several gigabytes of main memory [22].

ACKNOWLEDGEMENTS

The MONADS Project is supported by grants from the Australian Research Grants Scheme, the Australian Telecommunications and Electronics Research Board and the Commonwealth Scientific and Industrial Research Organisation. Some of the ideas presented in this paper benefited greatly from discussions with Professor Ron Morrison of the University of St. Andrews.

REFERENCES

1. Abramson, D.A. "Hardware Management of a Large Virtual Memory", *Proc. 4th Australian Computer Science Conference,* Brisbane, 1981, pp. 1-13.

2. Abramson, D.A. and Keedy, J.L. "Implementing a Large Virtual Memory in a Distributed Computing System", *Proc. 18th Hawaii International Conference on System Sciences,* 1985, pp. 515-522.

3. Bishop, P. "Computer Systems with a Very Large Address Space and Garbage Collection", Ph.D. Thesis, MIT (MIT TCS TR-178), 1977.

4. Dahl, O.J., Myhrhaug, B. and Nygaard, K. "The Simula 67 Common Base Language", Norwegian Computer Centre, Oslo, 1968.

[2] For the sake of preserving unique addresses across networks the size of the address space number in virtual addresses will be increased to about 96 bits, allowing all processors ever to be built to generate unique virtual addresses which include processor number and disk number.

5. Evered, M. "LEIBNIZ - A Language to Support Software Engineering", Dr.Ing. Thesis, Faculty of Informatics, Technical University of Darmstadt, 1985.

6. Fabry, R.S. "Capability Based Addressing", *Comm. ACM*, 17, 7, 1974, pp. 403-412.

7. Keedy, J.L. "Paging and Small Segments: A Memory Management Model", *Proc. 8th World Computer Congress*, IFIP-80, Melbourne, 1980, pp. 337-342.

8. Keedy, J.L. "The MONADS View of Software Modules", *Proc. 9th Australian Computer Conference*, Hobart, 1982, pp. 560-574.

9. Keedy, J.L. "An Instruction Set for Evaluating Expressions", *IEEE Transactions on Computers*, C-32, 5, 1983, pp. 476-478.

10. Keedy, J.L. "An Implementation of Capabilities without a Central Mapping Table", *Proc. 17th Hawaii International Conference on System Sciences*, 1984, pp. 180-185.

11. Keedy, J.L. and Evered, M.E. "Modularity in the Language LEIBNIZ", *Proc. of the 1st Australian Software Engineering Conference*, Canberra, May 1986, pp. 7-13.

12. Keedy, J.L. and Freisleben, B. "On the Efficient Use of Semaphore Primitives", *Information Processing Letters*, 21, 4, October, 1985, pp 199-205.

13. Keedy, J.L., Ramamohanarao, K. and Rosenberg, J. "On Implementing Semaphores with Sets", *The Computer Journal*, 22, 2, 1979, pp. 146-150.

14. Keedy, J.L. and Richards, I. "A Software Engineering View of Files", *Australian Computer Journal*, 14, 2, 1982, pp. 56-61.

15. Keedy, J.L., Rosenberg, J. and Ramamohanarao, K. "On Synchronising Readers and Writers with Semaphores", *The Computer Journal*, 25,1, 1982, pp. 121-125.

16. Lauer, H.C. and Needham, R.M. "On the Duality of Operating System, Structures", *ACM Operating Systems Review*, 13, 2, 1979, pp. 3-19.

17. Liskov, B., Snyder, A., Atkinson, R. and Schaffert, C. "Abstraction Mechanisms in CLU", *Comm. ACM*, 20, 8, 1977, pp. 564-576.

18. Organick, E.I. "Computer Systems Organization, the B5700/6700 Series", Academic Press, New York, 1973.

19. Parnas, D.L. "On the Criteria to be Used in Decomposing Systems into Modules", *Comm. ACM*, 15, 12, 1972, pp. 1053-1058.

20. Rosenberg, J. and Abramson, D.A. "MONADS-PC: A Capability Based Workstation to Support Software Engineering", *Proc. 18th Hawaii International Conference on System Sciences*, 1985, pp. 222-231.

21. Rosenberg, J. and Keedy, J.L. "Software Management of a Large Virtual Memory", *Proc. 4th Australian Computer Science Conference*, Brisbane, 1981, pp. 173-181.

22. Rosenberg, J., Koch, D.M. and Keedy, J.L. "A Massive Memory Supercomputer" *Proc. of 22nd Hawaii International Conference on System Sciences*, 1989.

23. Wulf, W.A., Cohen, E., Corwin, W., Jones, A., Levin, R., Pierson, C., and Pollack, F. "HYDRA: The Kernel of a Multiprocessor Operating System", *Comm. ACM*, 17, 3, 1974, pp. 336-345.

24. Wulf, W.A., London, R. and Shaw, M. "An Introduction to the Construction and Verification of Alphard Programs", *IEEE Transactions on Software Engineering*, SE-2, 4, 1976, pp. 253-264.

Author Index